BIG DATA ANALYTICS

A Practical Guide for Managers

BIG DATA ANALYTICS

A Practical Guide for Managers

Kim H. Pries
Robert Dunnigan

CRC Press
Taylor & Francis Group
Boca Raton London New York

CRC Press is an imprint of the
Taylor & Francis Group, an **informa** business

AN AUERBACH BOOK

CRC Press
Taylor & Francis Group
6000 Broken Sound Parkway NW, Suite 300
Boca Raton, FL 33487-2742

First issued in paperback 2022

© 2015 by Taylor & Francis Group, LLC
CRC Press is an imprint of Taylor & Francis Group, an Informa business

No claim to original U.S. Government works

ISBN-13: 978-1-482-23451-0 (hbk)
ISBN-13: 978-1-03-234019-7 (pbk)
DOI: 10.1201/b18055

Library of Congress Cataloging-in-Publication Data

Pries, Kim H., 1955-
    Big data analytics : a practical guide for managers / Kim H. Pries and Robert Dunnigan.
        pages cm
    Includes bibliographical references and index.
    ISBN 978-1-4822-3451-0
    1. Management--Statistical methods. 2. Management--Data processing. 3. Big data. 4. Data mining. 5. Database management. I. Dunnigan, Robert. II. Title.

HD30.215.P75 2015
658'.0557--dc23   2014040184

Visit the Taylor & Francis Web site at
http://www.taylorandfrancis.com

and the CRC Press Web site at
http://www.crcpress.com

Contents

Preface

When we started this book, "big data" had not quite become a business buzzword. As we did our research, we realized the books we perused were either of the "Gee, whiz! Can you believe this?" class or incredibly abstruse. We felt the market needed explanation oriented toward managers who had to make potentially expensive decisions.

We would like managers and implementors to know where to start when they decide to pursue the big data option. As we indicate, the marketplace for big data is much like that for personal computing in the early 1980s—full of consultants, products with bizarre names, and tons of hyperbole. Luckily, in the 2010s, much of the software is open source and extremely powerful. Big data consultancies exist to translate this "free" software into useful tools for the enterprise. Hence, nothing is really free.

We also ensure our readers can understand both the benefits and the costs of big data in the marketplace, especially the dark side of data. By now, we think it is obvious that the US National Security Agency is an archetype for big data problem solving. Large-city police departments have their own statistical data tools and some of them ponder the usefulness of cell phone confiscation and investigation as well as the use of social media, which are public.

As we researched, we found ourselves surprised at the size of well-known marketers such as Google and Amazon. Both of these enterprises have purchased companies and have grown themselves organically. Facebook continues to purchase companies (e.g., Oculus, the supplier of a potentially game-changing virtual reality system) and has over 1 billion users. Algorithmic analysis of colossal volumes of data yields information; information allows vendors to tickle our buying reflexes before we even know our own patterns.

Previously, we thought Esri owned the geographical information systems market, but we found a variety of geographical information systems solutions—although the Esri product line is relatively mature and they serve large-city police departments across the United States. Database creators explore new ways of looking at and storing/retrieving data—methods going beyond the relational paradigm. New and old algorithmic methods called machine learning allow computers to sort and separate the useful data from the useless.

We have grown to appreciate the open-source statistical language R over the years. R has become the statistical *lingua franca* for big data. Some of the major statistical vendors advertise their functional partnerships with R. We use the tool ourselves to generate many of our figures. We suspect R is now the most powerful generally available statistical tool on the planet.

Let's move on and see what we can learn about big data!

MATLAB® is a registered trademark of The MathWorks, Inc. For product information, please contact:

The MathWorks, Inc.
3 Apple Hill Drive
Natick, MA 01760-2098 USA
Tel: 508 647 7000
Fax: 508-647-7001
E-mail: info@mathworks.com
Web: www.mathworks.com

Acknowledgments

Kim H. Pries would like to acknowledge Janise Pries, the love of his life, for her support and editing skills. In addition, Robert Dunnigan supplied verbiage, chapters, Six Sigma expertise, and big data professionalism. As always, John Wyzalek and the Taylor & Francis team are key players in the production and publication of technical works such as this one.

Robert Dunnigan thanks his wife, Flabia Dunnigan, and his son Robert III for their love and patience during the composition of this book. He would also like to thank Kim H. Pries for his depth of expertise in a broad array of technical subjects as well as his experience as an author. He skillfully navigated the process of proposing, developing, and finalizing what is a unique and practical offering in the field of big data literature. Robert would also like to thank his employer, The Kratos Group, for their interest and moral support during the writing of this book. Kratos is a remarkable company of which Robert is proud to be a part. Finally, thanks are due to Taylor & Francis for bringing this new perspective on big data to market.

Authors

Kim H. Pries has four college degrees: a bachelor of arts in history from the University of Texas at El Paso (UTEP), a bachelor of science in metallurgical engineering from UTEP, a master of science in engineering from UTEP, and a master of science in metallurgical engineering and materials science from Carnegie-Mellon University. In addition, he holds the following certifications:

- APICS
  - Certified Production and Inventory Manager (CPIM)
- American Society for Quality (ASQ)
  - Certified Reliability Engineer (CRE)
  - Certified Quality Engineer (CQE)
  - Certified Software Quality Engineer (CSQE)
  - Certified Six Sigma Black Belt (CSSBB)
  - Certified Manager of Quality/Operational Excellence (CMQ/OE)
  - Certified Quality Auditor (CQA)

Pries worked as a computer systems manager, a software engineer for an electrical utility, and a scientific programmer under a defense contract; for Stoneridge, Incorporated (SRI), he has worked as the following:

- Software manager
- Engineering services manager
- Reliability section manager
- Product integrity and reliability director

In addition to his other responsibilities, Pries has provided Six Sigma training for both UTEP and SRI, and cost reduction initiatives for SRI. Pries is also a founding faculty member of Practical Project Management. Additionally, in concert with Jon Quigley, Pries was a cofounder and principal with Value Transformation, LLC, a training, testing, cost improvement, and product development consultancy. Pries also holds Texas teacher certifications in:

- Mathematics (8–12)
- Mathematics (4–8)
- Technology education (6–12)
- Technology applications (EC–12)
- Physics (8–12)
- Generalist (4–8)
- English Language Arts and Reading (8–12)
- History (8–12)
- Computer Science (8–12)
- Science (8–12)
- Special education (EC–12)

He trained for Introduction to Engineering Design and Computer Science and Software Engineering with Project Lead the Way. He currently teaches biotechnology, computer science and software engineering, and introduction to engineering design at the beautiful Parkland High School in the Ysleta Independent School District of El Paso, Texas.

Pries authored or coauthored the following books:

- *Six Sigma for the Next Millennium: A CSSBB Guidebook* (Quality Press, 2005)
- *Six Sigma for the New Millennium: A CSSBB Guidebook,* Second Edition (Quality Press, 2009)
- *Project Management of Complex and Embedded Systems: Ensuring Product Integrity and Program Quality* (CRC Press, 2008), with Jon M. Quigley
- *Scrum Project Management* (CRC Press, 2010), with Jon M. Quigley
- *Testing Complex and Embedded Systems* (CRC Press, 2010), with Jon M. Quigley
- *Total Quality Management for Project Management* (CRC Press, 2012), with Jon M. Quigley
- *Reducing Process Costs with Lean, Six Sigma, and Value Engineering Techniques* (CRC Press, 2012), with Jon M. Quigley
- *A School Counselor's Guide to Ethics* (Counselor Connection Press, 2012), with Janise G. Pries
- *A School Counselor's Guide to Techniques* (Counselor Connection Press, 2012), with Janise G. Pries
- *A School Counselor's Guide to Group Counseling* (Counselor Connection Press, 2012), with Janise G. Pries

- *A School Counselor's Guide to Practicum* (Counselor Connection Press, 2013), with Janise G. Pries
- *A School Counselor's Guide to Counseling Theories* (Counselor Connection Press, 2013), with Janise G. Pries
- *A School Counselor's Guide to Assessment, Appraisal, Statistics, and Research* (Counselor Connection Press, 2013), with Janise G. Pries

Robert Dunnigan is a manager with The Kratos Group and is based in Dallas, Texas. He holds a bachelor of science in psychology and in sociology with an anthropology emphasis from North Dakota State University. He also holds a master of business administration from INSEAD, "the business school for the world," where he attended the Singapore campus.

As a Peace Corps volunteer, Robert served over 3 years in Honduras developing agribusiness opportunities. As a consultant, he later worked on the Afghanistan Small and Medium Enterprise Development project in Afghanistan, where he traveled the country with his Afghan colleagues and friends seeking opportunities to develop a manufacturing sector in the country.

Robert is an American Society for Quality certified Six Sigma Black Belt and a Scrum Alliance certified Scrum Master.

1

Introduction

SO WHAT IS BIG DATA?

As a manager, you are expected to operate as a factotum. You need to be an industrial/organizational psychologist, a logician, a bean counter, and a representative of your company to the outside world. In other words, you are somewhat of a generalist who can dive into specifics. The specific technologies you encounter are becoming more complex, yet the differences between them and their predecessors are becoming more nuanced.

You may have already guided your firm's transition to other new technologies. Think of the Internet. In the decade and a half before this book was written, Internet presence went from being optional to being mandatory for most businesses. In the past decade, Internet presence went from being unidirectional to conversational. Once, your firm could hang out its online shingle with either information about its physical location, hours, and offerings if it were a brick-and-mortar business or else your offerings and an automated payment system if it were an online business. Firms ranging from Barnes & Noble to your corner pizza chain bridged these worlds.

A new buzzword arrived: Web 2.0. Despite much hyperbolic rhetoric, this designation described the real phenomenon of a reciprocal online world. An disgruntled representative of your company responding by the archetypical Web 2.0 technology called social media could cause real damage to your firm. Two news stories involving Twitter broke as this introduction was in its final stages of refinement.

First, Brendan Eich, the new CEO of the software organization Mozilla (creator of the Firefox browser), stepped down after news surfaced indicating he had donated money in support of Proposition 8, an anti–gay marriage initiative in California, some 6 years before (in 2008). An uproar erupted—largely on Twitter—which led Mr. Eich to resign. Voices in

Mr. Eich's defense from across the political spectrum—including Andrew Sullivan, the respected conservative columnist who is himself gay and a proponent for gay marriage rights, and Conor Friedersdorf of *The Atlantic*, who was also an outspoken opponent of Proposition 8—did not save Mr. Eich's job. He was ousted.

The second Twitter story began with a tweeted complaint from a customer with the Twitter handle @ElleRafter. US Airways responded with the typical reaction of a company facing such a complaint in the public forum of Twitter. They invited @ElleRafter to provide more information, along with a link. Unlike the typical Twitter response, however, the US Airways tweet included a pornographic photo involving the use of a toy US Airways aircraft. This does not appear to have been a premeditated act by the US Airways representative involved—but it caused substantial humiliating press coverage for the company.

As the Internet spread and matured, it became a necessary forum for communication, as well as a dangerous tool whose potential for good or bad can pull in others by surprise or cause self-inflicted harm. Just as World War I generals were left to figure out how technology changed the field of battle, shifting the advantage from the offense to the defense, Internet technology left managers trying to cope with a new landscape filled with both promise and threats. Now, there is another new buzzword: big data.

So, what is big data? Is it a fad? Is it empty jargon? Is it just a new name for growing capacity of the same databases that have been a part of our lives for decades? Or, is it something qualitatively different? What are the promises of big data? From which direction should a manager anticipate threats?

The tendency of the media to hype new and barely understood phenomena makes it difficult to evaluate new technologies, along with the nature and extent of their significance. This book argues that big data is new and possesses strategic significance. The argument the authors make about big data is about how it builds on understandable developments in technology and is itself comprehensible. Although it is comprehensible, it is not easy to use and it can deliver misleading or incorrect results. However, these erroneous results are not often random. They result from certain statistical and data-related phenomena. Knowing these phenomena are real and understanding how they function enable you as a manager to become a better user of your big data system.

Like cell phones and e-mail, big data is a recent phenomenon that has emerged as a part of the panorama of our daily lives. When you shop online, catch up with friends on Facebook, conduct web searches, read articles referencing database searches, and receive unsolicited coupons, you interact with big data. Many readers, as participants in a store's loyalty program, possess a key fob featuring a bar code on one side and the logo of a favorite store on the other. One of the primary rationales of these programs, aside from decreasing your incentive to shop elsewhere, is to gather data on the company's most important customers. Every time you swipe your key fob or enter your phone number into the keypad of the credit card machine while you are checking out at the cash register, you are tying a piece of identifying data (who you are) with which items you purchased, how many items you purchased, what time of day you were shopping, and other data. From these, analysts can determine whether you shop by brand or buy whatever is on sale, whether you are purchasing different items from before (suggesting a life change), and whether you have stopped making your large purchases in the store and now only drop in for quick items such as milk or sugar. In the latter case, that is a sign you switched to another retailer for the bulk of your shopping and coupons or some other intervention may be in order. Stores have long collected customer data, long before the age of big data, but they now possess the ability to pull in a greater variety of data and conduct more powerful analyses of the data.

Big data influences us less obviously—it informs the obscure underpinnings of our society, such as manufacturing, transportation, and energy. Any industry developing enormous quantities of diverse data is ready for big data. In fact, these industries probably use big data already. The technological revolution occurring in data analytics enables more precise allocation of resources in our evolving economy—much as the revolution in navigational technology, from the superseded sextant to modern GPS devices, enabled ships to navigate open seas.

Big data is much like the Internet—it has drawbacks, but its net value is positive. The debate on big data, like political debate, tends toward misleading absolutes and false dichotomies. The truth, as in the case of political debates, almost never lies in those absolutes. Like a car, you do not start up a big data solution and let it motor along unguided—you drive it, you guide it, and you extract value from it.

Data itself is now an asset, one for companies to secure and hoard, much as the Federal Reserve Bank of New York stockpiles gold (though, for the sake of accuracy, the Federal Reserve only stores gold for countries other than the United States). Companies invest in systems to organize and extract value from their data, just as they would a piece of land or reserve of raw materials. Data are bought and sold. Some companies, including

IHS, Experian, and DataLogix, build entire businesses to collect, refine, and sell data. Companies in the business of data are diverse. IHS provides information about specific industries such as energy, whereas Experian and DataLogix provide personal information about individual consumers. These companies would not exist if the exchange of data was not lucrative. They would enjoy no profit motive if they could not use data to make more money than the cost of its generation, storage, and analysis.

One of your authors was a devotee of Borders, the book retailer (and still keeps his loyalty program card on display as a memorial to the company). After the liquidation of Borders, he received an e-mail message from William Lynch, the chief executive of Barnes & Noble (another favorite store), stating in part, "As part of Borders ceasing operations, we acquired some of its assets including Borders brand trademarks and their customer list. The subject matter of your DVD and other video purchases will be part of the transferred information… If you would like to opt-out, we will ensure all your data we receive from Borders is disposed of in a secure and confidential manner." The data that Borders accumulated were a real asset sold off after its bankruptcy.

Data analysis has even entered popular culture in the form of Michael Lewis's book *Moneyball*, as well as the eponymous movie. The story centers on Billy Beane, who used data to supplant intuition and turned the Oakland Athletics into a winning team. The relationship between data and decision making is, in fact, the key theme of this book.

GROWING INTEREST IN DECISION MAKING

Any business book of value must answer a simple, two-word question: "So what?" So, why does big data matter? The answer is the confluence of two factors. The first is that awareness of the limitations of human intuition, also known as "gut feel," has become obvious. The second is that big data technologies have reached the level of maturity necessary to make stunning computational feats affordable. Moreover, this computational ability is now visible to the general public. Facebook, Amazon.com, and search engines such as Bing, Yahoo!, and Google are prime examples. Even traditional "brick-and-mortar" stores match powerful websites with analytics that would have been unimaginable 20 years ago. Barnes & Noble, Wal-Mart, and Home Depot are excellent examples.

Many prominent actors in psychology, marketing, and behavioral finance have pointed out the flaws in human decision making. Psychologist Daniel Kahneman won the Nobel Memorial Prize in Economic Sciences in 2002 for his work on the systematic flaws in the way people weigh risk and reward in arriving at decisions. Building on Kahneman's work, a variety of scholars, including Dan Ariely, Ziv Carmon, and Cass Sunstein, demonstrated how hidden influencers and mental heuristics influence decision making. One of the authors had the pleasure of studying under Mr. Carmon at INSEAD and, during a class exercise, pointed out how much he preferred one ketchup sample to another—only to discover they came from the same bottle and were merely presented as being different. The difference between the two samples was nonexistent, but the difference with taste perceptions was quite real.

In fact, Mr. Ariely, Mr. Carmon, and their coauthors won the following 2008 Ig Nobel award:

MEDICINE PRIZE. Dan Ariely of Duke University (USA), Rebecca L. Waber of MIT (USA), Baba Shiv of Stanford University (USA), and Ziv Carmon of INSEAD (Singapore) for demonstrating that high-priced fake medicine is more effective than low-priced fake medicine.[1]

The website states, "The Ig Nobel Prizes honor achievements that first make people laugh, and then makes them think. The prizes are intended to celebrate the unusual, honor the imaginative—and spur people's interest in science, medicine, and technology."[2] It may be easy to laugh about this research, but just consider how powerful it is. Your perception of the medical effectiveness of what is in fact a useless placebo is influenced by how much you believe it costs.

The Atlantic ran an article in its December 2013 issue describing how big data changes hiring decisions. Although this phenomenon is not altogether understood, we have pilot studies, and yes, computers can often do a better job than people.[3] Hiring managers base their willingness to hire on a range of irrelevant factors in interviews. Consider some of these factors: firmness of handshake, physical appearance, projection of confidence, name, and similarities of hobbies with the person conducting the interview all influence employment decisions. Often, these extraneous factors have minimal relevance to the ability of someone to execute their job. It is little wonder that computers and data scientists have been able to improve companies' hiring practices by bringing in big data.

In 1960, a cognitive scientist by the name of Peter Cathcart Wason published a study in which participants were asked to hypothesize the pattern underlying a series of numbers: 2, 4, and 6. They then needed to test it by asking if another series of numbers fit the pattern. What is your hypothesis and how would you test it? What Wason uncovered is a tendency to seek confirmatory information. Participants tended to propose series that already fit the pattern of their assumptions, such as 8, 10, and 12. This is not a helpful approach to the problem, though. A more productive approach would be 12, 10, and 8 (descending order, separated by two), or 2, 3, and 4 (ascending order, separated by one). Irregular series such as 3, π, and 4, or 0, −1, and 4 would also be useful, as would anything that directly violates the pattern of the original set of numbers provided. The pattern sought in the study was any series of numbers in ascending order. Participants did a poor job of eliminating potential hypotheses by seeking out options that directly contradicted their original hunches, tending instead to confirm what they already believed. The title of this seminal study, "On the Failure to Eliminate Hypotheses in a Conceptual Task," highlights this intellectual bias.[4]

Wason's findings were pioneering work in this field, and in many ways Daniel Kahneman's work is a fruitful and ingenious offshoot thereof. As this is an introduction, we will not continue listing examples of cognitive biases, but they have been demonstrated many times in how we evaluate others, how we judge our own satisfaction, and how we estimate numbers. Big data not only addresses the arcane relationships between technical variables, but it also has a pragmatic role in saving costs, controlling risks, and preventing headaches for managers in a variety of roles. It does this in part by finding patterns where they exist rather than where our fallible reckoning finds the mere mirages of patterns.

WHAT THIS BOOK ADDRESSES

This book addresses a serious gap in the big data literature. During our research, we found popular books and articles that describe what big data is for a general audience. We also found technical books and articles for programmers, administrators, and other specialized roles. There is little discussion, however, facilitating the intelligent and inquisitive but non-technical reader to understand big data nuances.

Our goal is to enable you, the reader, to discuss big data at a profound level with your information technology (IT) department, the salespeople with whom you will interact in implementing a big data system, and the analysts who will develop and report results drawn from the myriad of data points in your organization. We want you to be able to ask intelligent and probing questions and to be able to make analysts defend their positions before you invest in projects by acting on their conclusions. After reading this book, you should be able to read the footnotes of a position paper and know the soundness of the methods used. When your IT department discusses a new project, you should be able to guide the discussions.

The discussion in this book ranges well beyond big data itself. The authors include examples from science, medicine, Six Sigma, statistics, and probability—with good reason. All of these disciplines are wrestling with similar issues. Big data involves the processing of a large number of variables to pull out nuggets of wisdom. This is using the conclusion to guide the formation of a hypothesis rather than testing the hypothesis to arrive at a conclusion. Some may consider this approach sloppy when applied to any particular scientific study, but the sheer number of studies, combined with a bias toward publishing only positive results, means that a statistically similar phenomenon is occurring in scientific journals. As science is a self-critical discipline, the lessons gleaned from its internal struggle to ensure meaningful results are applicable to your organizations, which need to pull accurate results from big data systems. The current discussion in the popular and business press on big data ignores nonbusiness fields and does so to the detriment of organizations trying to make effective use of big data tools.

The discussion in this book will provide you with an understanding of these conversations happening outside the world of big data. Louis Pasteur said, "In the fields of observation, chance favors only the prepared mind."[5] Some of the most profound conversations on topics of direct relevance to big data practitioners are happening *outside* of big data. Understanding these conversations will be of direct benefit to you as a manager.

THE CONVERSATION ABOUT BIG DATA

We mentioned the discussions around big data and how unhelpful they are. Some of the discussion is optimistic; some is pessimistic. We will start on the optimistic side.

Perhaps the most famous story about the capabilities of predictive analytics was a 2012 article in *The New York Times Magazine* about Target.[6]

Target sells nearly any category of product someone could need, but is not always first in customers' minds for all of those categories. Target sells clothing, groceries, toys, and myriad other items. However, someone may purchase clothing from Target, but go to Kroger for groceries and Toys R Us for toys. Any well-managed store will want to increase sales to its customers, and Target is no exception. It wants you to think of Target first for most categories of items.

When life changes, habits change. Target realized that people's purchasing habits change as families grow with the birth of children and are therefore malleable. Target wanted to discover which customers were pregnant around the time of the second trimester so as to initiate marketing to parents-to-be before their babies were born.

A birth is public record and therefore results in a blizzard of advertising. From a marketing aspect, a company is wise to beat that blizzard. Target saw a way to do so by using the data it accumulated.

As a Target statistician told the author of the article, "If you use a credit card or a coupon, or fill out a survey, or mail in a refund, or call the customer help line, or open an e-mail we've sent you or visit our Web site, we'll record it and link it to your Guest ID." The guest ID is the unique identifier used by Target. The statistician continued, "We want to know everything we can." The guest ID is not only linked to what you do within Target's walls, but also to a large volume of demographic and economic information about you.[6]

Target looked at how women's purchasing habits changed around the time they opened a baby registry, then generalized these purchasing habits back to women who may not have opened a baby registry. Purchases of unscented lotion, large quantities of cotton balls, and certain mineral supplements correlated well with second-trimester pregnancy. By matching this knowledge to promotions that had a high likelihood of effectiveness—again gleaned from Target's customer-specific data—the company could try to change these women's shopping habits at a time when their lives were in flux, during pregnancy.[6] The article propelled Target's data analytics prowess to fame and also generated uneasiness.

Target also did not communicate how tricky and resource-intensive such an analysis is. This may be an unfair criticism, as the article was directed at a general readership rather than at businesspeople who are considering the use of big data. However, a business reader of such stories should understand how nuanced, messy, convoluted, and maddening big data can be. The data used by a big data system to reach its conclusions often come with built-in biases and flaws. The statistics used do not provide a precise "yes" or "no" answer, but rather describe a level of confidence on a spectrum of likelihood. This does not make for exciting press, and it is therefore all but invisible in big data articles, except those in specialist sources.

There are many articles about big data and health, big data and marketing, big data and hiring, and so forth. These rarely cover the risks and rewards of data. The reality is that health data can be messy and inaccurate. Moreover, it is protected by a strict legal regimen, the Health Insurance Portability and Accountability Act of 1996 (IIIPAA), which restricts its flow. Marketing data are likewise difficult to link up. Data analytics in general, and now big data, have improved marketing efforts but are not a magic bullet. Some stores seldom track what their customers purchase, and those that do so do not trust each other with their databases. In any big data system, the nature of who can see what data needs to be considered, as well as how the data will be secured. It is very likely that your firm will own data only some employees or contractors can see. Making it easier to access this data is not always a good idea.

Later in this introduction, we will discuss data analytics applied to hiring and how poorly this can be reported. As a news consumer, your skepticism should kick in whenever you read about some amazing discovery uncovered by big data methods about how two dissimilar attributes are in fact linked. The reality is at best much more nuanced and at worst is a false relationship. These false relationships are pretty much inevitable, and we dedicate many pages to showing how data and statistics can lead the unwary user astray. Once you embrace this condition, you will probably never read news stories about big data without automatically critiquing them.

On the other side of the argument, perhaps the most astute critic of big data is Nassim Nicholas Taleb. In an opinion piece he wrote for the website of *Wired* magazine (drawn from his book, *Antifragile*), he states, "Modernity provides too many variables, but too little data per variable. So the spurious relationships grow much, much faster than real information... In other words: Big data may mean more information, but it also means more false information."[7]

Mr. Taleb may be pessimistic, but he raises valuable points. As a former trader with a formidable quantitative background, Taleb has made a name for himself with his astute critiques of faulty decision making. Taleb is a rarity, a public intellectual who is also an intellectual heavyweight. He is not partisan, developing devastating takedowns of sloppy argumentation with equal opportunity fervor. Taleb argues:

- The incentive to draw a conclusion may not align with what the data really show. With this, Taleb discusses the existence of medical studies that cannot be replicated. There are funding incentives to find significant relationships in studies and disincentives to publish studies that show no significant findings. The hallmark of a truly significant finding is that others can replicate the results in their own studies.
- There is not an absence of meaningful information in large data sets, it is simply that the information within is hidden within a larger quantity of noise. "Noise" is generally considered to be an unwelcome randomness that obscures a signal. As Taleb states, "I am not saying here that there is no information in big data. There is plenty of information. The problem—the central issue—is that the needle comes in an increasingly larger haystack."[7]
- One difficulty in drawing conclusions from big data is that although it is good for debunking false conclusions, it is not as strong in drawing valid conclusions. Stated differently, "If such studies cannot be used to confirm, they can be effectively used to debunk—to tell us what's wrong with a theory, not whether a theory is right."[7] If we are using the scientific method, it may take only one valid counterexample to topple a vulnerable theory.

This is an important article. In fact, the book that you now hold in your hands was conceived as a response. Taleb points out real flaws in how we use big data, but your authors argue we need not use big data this way. A manager who understands the promise and limits of big data can obtain improved results just by knowing the limits of data and statistics and then ensuring that any analysis includes measures to separate wheat from chaff.

Paradoxically, the flaws of big data originate from the unique strengths of big data systems. The first among these strengths is the ability to pull together large numbers of diverse variables and seek out relationships between them. This enables an organization to find relationships within its data that would have otherwise remained undiscovered. However, more variables and more tests must mean an increased chance for error. This book is intended to guide the user in understanding this.

A more widely recognized concept made famous by Taleb, not directed at big data but applicable just the same, is his concept of the "black swan".

The term, which he uses to describe an unforeseeable event, as opposed to just unforeseen, derives from the idea that if one conceives of the color white as being an intrinsic aspect of a swan, then finding a black swan is an unforeseeable experience that renders that expectation untenable. The Black Swan is a therefore a shock. The 1987 stock market crash and the terrorist attacks of September 11 are large-scale Black Swans, but smaller Black Swans happen to us in our personal lives and with our businesses.

Taleb is talented at bringing concepts into focus through the skillful use of examples. In this case, his example is of the comfortable turkey raised on a farm. He is fed, gets fat, projects ahead, and feels good about his life—until Thanksgiving.[8]

The field of predictive analytics is related to, and often very much a part of, big data. It has been quite powerful in boosting efficiency and controlling risk, and it is without doubt an indispensable technology for many firms. Even so, there is an uncomfortable truth. With little experience using data to understand a particular phenomenon (or perhaps without collection of the needed data), you will not be able to foresee it. Big data is both art and science, but it is not an all-seeing wellspring of wisdom and knowledge. It will not enable you to eliminate black swan events. It is up to the user of big data systems to understand the risks and limited data that act as a constraint on calculating probabilities for the phenomena being analyzed and to respect chance.

While Taleb's argument is among the most substantive critiques of big data, the general form of his criticism is familiar. Big data is not altogether dismissed, so the criticism is balanced. The flaw in most criticism of big data is not that it is polemic, or dishonest, or uninformed. It is none of these. It is that it is fatalistic. Big data has flaws and is thus overrated. What much of the critical big data literature fails to do is look at this technology as an enabling technology. A skilled user who understands the data itself, the tools analyzing it, and the statistical methods being used can extract tremendous value. The user who blindly expects big data systems to spit out meaningful data runs a very high risk of delivering potential disaster to his or her organization.

A further example is an article from the KDnuggets website entitled "Viewpoint: Why Your Company Should NOT Use 'big data'."[9] The article describes the difficulty of using data well and argues that the most gains can be obtained by using the data one's firm already possesses with wit. It also punctures some balloons involving the misuse of language, such as referring to Nate Silver's brilliant work as big data when in fact it is straightforward analysis. Your authors can attest to the importance of using a firm's data more effectively—we are experienced Six Sigma practitioners. We are accustomed to using data to enhance efficiency and quality and to reduce risk.

This article is still flawed. A more productive approach would be to look at where your organization is now, where it wants to go, and how big data may help it get there. Your organization may not be ready to implement big data now. It may need to focus on better using its existing data. To prepare for the future, it may need to take a more strategic approach to ensuring that the data it now generates is properly linked, so that a user's shopping history can be tied to the particular user. If your analysis leads you to conclude that big data is not a productive effort for your company, then you should heed that advice. Many firms do not need big data, and to attempt to implement this approach just to keep up with the pack would be wasteful. If your firm does see a realistic need for big data and has the resources and commitment to see it through, then the lack of an existing competence is not a valid reason to avoid developing one.

TECHNOLOGICAL CHANGE AS A DRIVER OF BIG DATA

We also discuss technology, including its evolution. The data sets generated every day by online retailers, search engines, investment firms, oil and gas companies, governments, and other organizations are so massive and convoluted, they require special handling. A standard database management system (DBMS) may not be robust enough to manage the sheer enormity of the data. Consider processing a petabyte (1000 TB, or 1 million of the hard drives on a medium- to high-end laptop) of data. Physically storing, processing, and locating all of this data presents significant obstacles. Amazon, Facebook, and other high-profile websites measure their storage in petabytes.

Some companies, like Google, developed their own tools, such as MapReduce, the Google File System, and BigTable, to manage colossal volumes of information. The open-source Apache Foundation oversees Hadoop (a data-intensive software framework), Hive (data warehouse on top of Hadoop), and HBase (nonrelational, distributed database) in order to provide the programming community with access to tools that can manipulate big data. Papers published by Google about its own techniques inspired the open-source distributed processing manager, Hadoop.

Another area for big data analysis is the use of geographical information systems (GIS). A typical example of GIS software would be the commercial product, ArcGIS, or the open-source product, Quantum GIS. Due to the complexity of map data, even an assessment at the municipality level would constitute a big data situation. When we are looking at the entire planet, we are analyzing big data. GIS is interesting not only because it involves raw numbers, but it also involves data representation and visualization, which must then relate to a map with a clear interpretation. Google Earth adds the extra complexity of zooming, decluttering, and overlaying, as well as choosing between political maps and satellite images. We now add the extra complexities of color, line, contrast, shape, and so on.

The need for low latency, another way of saying short lag time, between a request and the delivery of the results, drives the growth of another area of big data—in-memory database systems such as Oracle Endeca Information Discovery and SAP HANA. Though two very different beasts, both demonstrate the ability to use large-capacity random access memory (RAM) to find relationships within sizable and diverse sets of data.

THE CENTRAL QUESTION: SO WHAT?

As has been stated in this introduction, and as we will argue, big data is one of the most powerful tools created by man. It draws together information recorded in different source systems and different formats, then runs analyses at speeds and capacities the human mind cannot match. Big data is a true breakthrough, but being a breakthrough does not confer infallibility. Like any system, big data's limits cluster around particular themes. These themes are not straightforward weaknesses such as those found in poor engineering, but they are inseparable from big data's strengths. By understanding these limits, we can minimize and control them.

The specific examples of big data used so far are such that when we draw faulty conclusions, we suffer minor consequences. One of the authors had a bafflingly off-base category of movies recommended to him by Netflix and has received membership cards in the mail from the AARP despite being decades away from retirement, and has a spouse who was twice bombarded with baby formula coupons in the mail. The first time was soon before his son was born; the second time was brief and was triggered by erroneous conclusions drawn by some algorithm in an unknown computer.

False conclusions do not always come with small consequences though. Big data is moving into fraud detection, crime prevention, medicine, business strategy, forensic data, and numerous other areas of life where erroneous conclusions are more serious than unanticipated junk mail or strange recommendations from online retailers.

For example, big data is moving into the field of hiring and firing. The previously referenced article from *The Atlantic* discusses this in detail. Citing myriad findings about how poorly job interviews function in evaluating potential clients, the article discusses different means by which data are used to evaluate potential candidates and current employees.

One company discussed by the article is Evolv. On its website, Evolv—whose slogan is "Big Data for Workforce Optimization"—states its value proposition:

- **Faster, more accurate selection tools:** Evolv's platform enables recruiters to quickly identify the best hires from volumes of candidates based on your unique roles.
- **Higher Quality candidates:** Better candidate selection results in longer-tenured employees and lower attrition.
- **Post-hire engagement tools:** Easy to deploy employee engagement surveys keep tabs on what workplace practices are working for you, and which ones are not.[10]

To attain this, Evolv administers questionnaires to online applicants and then matches the results to those obtained from its data set of 347,000 hires that passed through the process. Who are the best-performing candidates? Who is most likely to stick around? *The Atlantic* states:

> The sheer number of observations that this approach makes possible allows Evolv to say with precision which attributes matter more to the success of retail-sales workers (decisiveness, spatial orientation, persuasiveness) or customer-service personnel at call centers (rapport-building). And the company can continually tweak its questions, or add new variables to its model, to seek out ever-stronger correlates of success in any given job.[3]

Big data has in many ways made hiring decisions more fair and effective, but it is still prudent to maintain skepticism. One of the most noted findings by Evolv is the role of an applicant's browser while filling in the job application in determining the success of the employee on the job.

According to Evolv, applicants who use aftermarket browsers such as Firefox and Chrome tend to be more successful than those applicants who use the browser that came with the operating system, such as Internet Explorer.

The article from *The Atlantic* adds some precision in describing Evolv's findings linking an applicant's web browser to job performance, stating, "the browser that applicants use to take the online test turns out to matter, especially for technical roles: some browsers are more functional than others, but it takes a measure of savvy and initiative to download them."[3] Other articles have made it sound like an applicant's browser was a silver bullet to determining how effective an employee would be:

> One of the most surprising findings is just how easy it can be to tell a good applicant from a bad one with Internet-based job applications. Evolv contends that the simple distinction of which Web browser an applicant is using when he or she sends in a job application can show who's going to be a star employee and who may not be.[11]

This finding raises two key points in using big data to draw conclusions. First, is this a meaningful result, a spurious correlation, or the misreading of data? Without digging into the data and the statistics, it is impossible to say. An online article in *The Economist* states, "This may simply be a coincidence, but Evolv's analysts reckon an applicants' willingness to go to the trouble of installing a new browser shows decisiveness, a valuable trait in a potential employee."[12] The relationship found by Evolv may be real and groundbreaking. It may also just be a statistical artifact of the kind we will be discussing in this book. Even if it is a real and statistically significant finding that stands up to experimental replication, it may be so minor as to be quasi-meaningless. Without knowing about the data sampled, the statistics used, and the strength of the relationship between the variables, the conclusion must be taken with a grain of salt. We will discuss in a later chapter how a statistically significant finding need not be practically significant. We must remember that statistical significance is a mathematical abstraction much like the mean, and it may not have profound human meaning.

The second issue raised by the finding relates to interpretation. *The Economist* was very responsible in pointing out the possibility of a coincidence, or what we are referring to in this book as a statistical artifact. *The Atlantic* deserves credit for pointing out that this finding (assuming it is legitimate) relates more to technical jobs.

However, remember a quoted passage in one of the articles, "Evolv contends that the simple distinction of which Web browser an applicant is using when he or she sends in a job application can show who's going to be a star employee and who may not be." Such statements should never be used in discussing big data results within your organization. What does "who's going to be a star employee" really mean? It grants too much certainty to a result that will at best be a tendency in the data rather than a set rule. The statement "and who may not be" is likewise meaningless, but in the other direction. It asserts nothing. In real life, many of those who use Firefox or Chrome will be poor hires. Even if there were a real relationship in the data, it would frankly be irresponsible for a hiring manager to place overriding importance on this attribute when there are many other attributes to consider. Language matters.

The points raised by the web browser example are not academic. The consequences for a competent and diligent job seeker who is just fine with Internet Explorer, or a firm who needs that job seeker, are not difficult to figure out and are certainly not minor. One of your authors keeps both Firefox and Internet Explorer open at the same time, as some pages work better on one or the other.

Another firm mentioned in *The Atlantic* is Gild. Gild evaluates programmers by analyzing their online profiles, including code they have written and its level of adoption, the way that they use language on LinkedIn and Twitter, their contributions to forums, and one rather odd criteria: whether they are fans of a particular Japanese manga site. The Gild representative interviewed in the article herself stated that there is no causal relationship between manga fandom and coding ability—just a correlation.

Firms such as Evolv and Gild, however, work for employers and not applicants. The results from their analyses should result in improved performance. It is the rule, and not the exceptions, that drives the adoption of big data in hiring decisions. One success story Evolv points out is the reduction of one firm's 3-month attrition rate by 30% through the application of big data. It is now helping this client monitor the growth of employees within the firm, based not only on the characteristics of the employees themselves but also on the environment in which they operate, such as who their trainers and managers were.

The case of Evolv is a good illustration of the nature of big data. Proper application of the technology increases efficiency, but a complex set of issues surrounds this application. Many of these issues relate to the potential of incorrect conclusions drawn from the data and the need to mitigate their effect. Yes, judgments can be baseless or unfair. What is the alternative? Think back to our discussion of the faultiness of human judgment.

When a big data system reveals a correlation, it is incumbent on the operator to explore that correlation in great detail rather than to take it superficially. When a correlation is discovered, it is tempting to create a *post hoc* explanation of why the variables in question are correlated. We glean a mathematically neat and seemingly coherent nugget. However, a false correlation dressed up nicely is nothing but fool's gold. It can change how the recipients of that nugget respond to reality, but it cannot change the underlying reality. As big data spreads its influence into more areas of our lives, the consequences of misinterpretation grow. This is why scientific investigation into the data is important.

Big data raises other issues your organization should consider. Maintaining data raises legal issues if it is compromised. Medical data is the most prominent of these, but any data with trade secrets or personal information such as credit card numbers fit in this category. Incorrect usage creates a risk to corporate reputations. Google's aggressive collection of customer data, sometimes intrusively, has tarnished that firm's reputation. Even worse, the data held can harm others. *The New Yorker* reports the case of Michael Seay, the father of a young lady whose life tragically ended at the age of 17, who received an OfficeMax flier in the mail addressed to "Mike Seay/Daughter Killed in Car Crash/Or Current Business."[13] This obviously created much pain for Mr. Seay, as it would for any parent.

Google Map's Street View has likewise been a curse for many, including a man urinating in his own backyard whose moment of imprudence coincided with Google's car driving past his house. That will be on the Internet forever. The *Wall Street Journal* carried an in-depth article describing databases of scanned license plates in both the public and private sector. These companies photograph and log license plates, using automatic readers, so a car can be tied to the location where it was photographed. Two private sector companies are listed: Digital Recognition Network, Inc. and MVTrac. A repossession firm mentioned in the article has vehicles that drive hundreds of miles each night logging license plates of parked cars. The majority of cars still driven in the United States are probably logged in these systems, one of which had 700 million scans.[14]

These developments may not impact your business directly, but as we will see in our later discussions of the advantages and disadvantages of big data, other technologies interacting with big data have the power to undermine your trade secrets or create a competitive environment where you can obtain useful analysis only at the expense of turning over your own data. It would be naïve to assume that those who see opportunity in gobbling up your company's information will not do so. In using big data, data ownership will be an issue. The question of who has a right to whose data still needs to be settled through legislation and in the courts. Not only will you need to know how to protect your own firm's data from external parties, you will need to understand how to responsibly and ethically protect the data you hold that belong to others.

The dangers should not scare users away from big data. Just as much of modern technology carries risk—think of the space program, aviation, and energy exploration—such risk delivers rich rewards when well used. Big data is one of the most valuable innovations of the twenty-first century. When properly used in a spirit of cooperative automation—where the operator guides the use and results—the promise of big data is immense.

OUR GOALS AS AUTHORS

An author should undertake the task of writing a book because he or she has something compelling to say. We know of many good books on big data, analytics, and decision making. What we have not seen is a book for the perplexed that partitions the phenomenon of big data into usable chunks.

In this introduction, we alluded to the discussion in the press about big data. For a businessperson, project manager, or quality professional who is faced with big data, it is difficult to jump into this discussion and understand what is being said and why. The world of business, like history, is regularly burned by business fads that appear, notch up prominent successful case studies, then fade out to leave a trail of less-publicized wreckage in their wake. We want to help you understand the fundamentals and set realistic expectations so that your experience is that of being a successful case study.

We want you as the reader to understand certain key points:

- Big data is comprehensible. It springs from well-known trends that you experience every day. These include the growth in computing power, data storage, and data creation, as well as new ideas for organizing information.

- You should become aware of key big data packages, which we list and discuss in detail. Each has its characteristics that are easy to remember. Once you understand these, you can ask better questions of external salespeople and your internal IT departments.
- Big data technologies enable the integration of capabilities previously not included in most business analytics. These include GIS and predictive analytics. New kinds of analysis are evolving.
- Data is not an oracle. It reflects the conditions under which it was created. There are biases and errors that creep into data. Even the best data cannot predict developments for which there is no precedent.
- Big data will open legal, logistical, and strategic challenges for your organization, even if you decide that big data is not right for your firm. Not only must a firm be aware of the value and security measures surrounding data that it holds, it must be aware of data that it gives up voluntarily and involuntarily to other parties. There are no black-and-white answers to guide you, as this is a developing field.
- Data analytics in big data still rely on established statistical tools. Some of these may be arcane, but there are common statistical tools that can apply a reasonability check to your results. Understanding analytics enables you to ask better questions of your data analysts and monitor the assumptions underlying the results upon which you take action.
- Your organization may already have the knowledge workers necessary to conduct analysis or even just sanity check results to ensure that they are accurate and yield results. Do you have a Six Sigma unit? Do you have actuaries? Do you have statisticians? If you do, then you have the knowledge base in-house to use your big data solution more effectively.

Now, on to our journey through this remarkable technology.

REFERENCES

1. Improbable Research. Winners of the Ig® Nobel Prize. Improbable Research. http://www.improbable.com/ig/winners/. Accessed April 16, 2014.
2. Improbable Research. About the Ig® Nobel Prizes. Improbable Research. http://www.improbable.com/ig/. Accessed April 16, 2014.
3. Peck, D. They're watching you at work. *The Atlantic*. December 2013.
4. Wason, P. On the failure to eliminate hypotheses in a conceptual task. *Quarterly Journal of Experimental Psychology*, 1960, 12(3): 129–140.

5. Louis Pasteur. Wikiquote. http://en.wikiquote.org/wiki/Louis_Pasteur. Accessed April 18, 2014.

6. Duhigg, C. How companies learn your secrets. *The New York Times*. February 16, 2012. http://www.nytimes.com/2012/02/19/magazine/shopping-habits.html?_r=0&pagewanted=all. Accessed April 19, 2014.

7. Taleb, N. (guest editorial, credited to Ogi Ogas in the byline) Beware the big errors of "big data." *Wired*. February 8, 2013. http://www.wired.com/2013/02/big-data-means-big-errors-people/. Accessed April 19, 2014.

8. Taleb, N. *Fooled by Randomness: The Hidden Role of Chance in Life and in the Markets*. New York: Thompson TEXERE, 2004.

9. Nevraumont, E. Viewpoint: Why your company should NOT use "Big Data." *KD Nuggets*. January 2014. http://www.kdnuggets.com/2014/01/viewpoint-why-your-company-should-not-use-big-data.html. Accessed April 19, 2014.

10. Evolv. Our expertise. Evolv company website. http://www.evolv.net/expertise/. Accessed April 19, 2014.

11. Javers, E. Inside the wacky world of weird data: What's getting crunched. *CNBC*. February 12, 2014. http://www.cnbc.com/id/101410448. Accessed April 18, 2014.

12. E.H. How might your choice of browser affect your job prospects? *The Economist*. April 10, 2013. http://www.economist.com/blogs/economist-explains/2013/04/economist-explains-how-browser-affects-job-prospects#sthash.iNblvZ6J.dpuf. Accessed April 19, 2014.

13. Merrick, A. A death in the database. *The New Yorker*. January 23, 2014. http://www.newyorker.com/online/blogs/currency/2014/01/ashley-seay-officemax-car-crash-death-in-the-database.html. Accessed April 17, 2014.

14. Angwin, J. and Valentino-DeVries, J. New tracking frontier: Your license plates. *The Wall Street Journal*. September 29, 2012. http://online.wsj.com/news/articles/SB10000872396390443995604578004723603576296. Accessed April 19, 2014.

2

The Mother of Invention's Triplets: Moore's Law, the Proliferation of Data, and Data Storage Technology

Is big data just hype? Is it really something new? If it is different, how is it different? If it brings a change, is it evolutionary or revolutionary change? While we wish we could present you with a clear-cut answer, we cannot. That argument has not been resolved as it will remain a matter of opinion.

Instead of presenting you with lofty scenarios of what big data may someday be able to do, we will show you how big data arose due to technological developments and the needs arising from more and more data. Seeing the changes that made big data a possibility—almost an inevitability really—will help you to sort out the knowledge from the hype. By using this bottom-up approach to explaining big data, we hope you will begin to see potential ways to use technology and vendor relationships that you already have to better use data that you already possess but do not use. The odds are that you will not want your first big data project to turn your facilities into something from a science fiction movie. Work is being done to make that a reality, but a lower-risk approach with a faster return is to simply pull together and use the data that you already have. In other words, we do not want to dazzle you. We want to help you make decisions *now*.

Big data is new in that its capabilities for processing data are unprecedented. By unprecedented, we do not refer merely to the quantity of data but also the variety of data. Big data technologies for crunching data in search of relationships between variables—both obvious and obscure— have developed alongside explosive growth in data storage capabilities. As data processing and storage capabilities demonstrate seemingly boundless growth, two other developments provide the data that fill that storage and provide the grist for the mills of modern processors.

Life used to be analog. We inhabited a world of records, letters, and copper phone lines. That world is disappearing. Sensors are becoming ubiquitous, from car engine computers to home burglar alarms to radio-frequency ID (RFID) tags. Computers metamorphosed into intermediaries for increasing quantities of transactions and interactions. LinkedIn and Facebook enable users to create public or semipublic personas; the Internet went from being an obscure medium for techies (informal term for profoundly involved, technologically aware users and creators) to being a global marketplace, and texting is now a quick way for friends to share tidbits of information. The background noise of modern life is data. Our data accumulate, they live, they are recorded and stored, and they are valuable in their own right.

In a sense, big data technologies are mature because we can comprehend them in terms of the technologies from which they developed, most of which have established histories. Computers became a possibility once Charles Babbage proposed the difference engine, an unrealized but logically fully developed mechanical computer, in 1822. Electronic computers came into their own in the twentieth century, with the code-breaking "bombes" (a bombe was a quasi-computer devoted to decryption solely) at Bletchley Park in Britain during World War II being concrete examples of how computers can shake the foundations of modern warfare. For all the awesome power of tanks, planes, and bombs, the great minds that cracked Axis codes—most famously the towering and tragic figure of Alan Turing—did something just as powerful. Deciphering those codes allowed them to penetrate the nervous system of the enemy's intelligence apparatus and know what it would do quickly enough to anticipate enemy actions and neutralize them.

Our current digital world can trace lineage back to this pioneering technology. To explore this development, let us start with the growth of processing power.

MOORE'S LAW

In 1965, Gordon Moore—who would go on 3 years later to cofound the company that would become Intel—published a paper titled, "Cramming More Components onto Integrated Circuits" in the journal *Electronics*. Though a mere four pages in length, the paper laid out the case for the now famous Moore's law. It is an intriguing read—after discussing advances in the manufacture of integrated circuits, Moore covers their advantages in terms of cost and reliability, the latter demonstrated by the inclusion of integrated circuits in NASA's Apollo space missions (it was Apollo 11 that landed Neil Armstrong and Buzz Aldrin on the moon). In his paper, Moore correctly foresees the use of this technology in successively increasing numbers of devices. Moore's law and the spread of the integrated circuit are a story of accelerated technological augmentation built on top of what had already been a whirlwind pace in the development of computer technology.[1]

This history of technological development leading up to Gordon Moore's paper is a compelling story on its own merits. The integrated circuit is a cluster of transistors manufactured together as a single unit. In fact, they are not *assembled* in any meaningful sense. The process of photolithography, or the use of light to print over a stencil of the circuit laid over a silicon wafer, means that transistors are etched together, emerging in a useful design as a single unit. The process is not entirely unlike using a stencil to paint writing on a wall, although the technology is clearly more demanding and precise. It means that there are no joins (e.g., solder joints) that can crack, and there are no moving parts to wear out. Moore was writing only 7 years after Jack Kilby of Texas Instruments had built the first working model of the integrated circuit—while most other employees of his firm were on vacation![2] Texas Instruments is still one of the leading manufacturers of integrated circuits, along with Intel.

Before the introduction of the integrated circuit, the transistor was the standard for data processing. The first patent for a working transistor (undemonstrated designs had received earlier patents) was patent number 2,524,035, awarded to John Bardeen and Walter Brattain of Bell Labs in 1950,[3] with patent number 2,569,347 being awarded to their colleague, William Shockley, the following year.[4] The transistor offered many improvements over its predecessor, the vacuum tube. It was easier to manufacture, more energy efficient, and more reliable. It did not generate as much heat and thus enjoyed a longer life. Still, it was a discrete device. Unlike the integrated circuit, in which millions of transistors can be a single array, transistors needed to be assembled before Jack Kilby's seemingly innocuous but world-altering insight. Individual transistor assembly generally meant the use of the older through-hole technology, where the leads to the discrete transistor went through the printed circuit board and were often wave-soldered.

Moore's argument in his paper, this artifact from the dawn of the integrated circuit, is nuanced and carefully argued. It is easy to forget this, decades later, when few commentators actually read it and the popular press reduces the concept to pithy sound bites about the increase in processing power versus time. What Moore composed was neither a lucky guess nor a bald assertion. It was an exquisite argument incorporating technology, economics, and perhaps most importantly, manufacturing ability. He famously argued that as more components are added to an integrated circuit of a given size, the cost per component decreases. In his words:

> For simple circuits, the cost per component is nearly inversely proportional to the number of components, the result of the equivalent piece of semiconductor in the equivalent package containing more components. But as components are added, decreased yields more than compensate for the increased complexity, tending to raise the cost per component.[1]

As of 1965, the number of components that could be included on an integrated circuit at the lowest price per component is 50. Moore foresaw the optimal number of components per circuit, from a cost per component point of view, being 1000 by 1970, with a cost per component that was 10% of the 1965 cost. By 1975, he saw the optimal number of components reaching 65,000. In other words, he perceives the cost of production declining as the technology secures itself in our culture.[1]

Before moving on to a technical discussion of the circuits, Moore stated, "The complexity for minimum component costs has increased at a rate of roughly a factor of two per year… there is no reason to believe [this rate of change] will not remain nearly constant for at least 10 years."[1] In fact, nearly 50 years after its formulation, Moore's law abides. Figure 2.1 is a powerful illustration.

Respected physicist Michio Kaku predicts the end of Moore's law, pointing out that the photolithography process used to manufacture integrated circuits relies on ultraviolet light with a wavelength that can be as small as 10 nm, or approximately 30 atoms across. Current manufacturing methods cannot be used to build transistors smaller than this. There is a more fundamental barrier lurking, however. Dr. Kaku lays out his argument thus:

> Transistors will be so small that quantum theory or atomic physics takes over and electrons leak out of the wires. For example, the thinnest layer inside your computer will be about five atoms across. At that point, according to the laws of physics, the quantum theory takes over. The Heisenberg

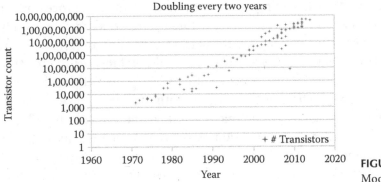

FIGURE 2.1
Moore's law.

uncertainty principle states that you cannot know both the position and velocity of any particle. This may sound counterintuitive, but at the atomic level you simply cannot know where the electron is, so it can never be confined precisely in an ultrathin wire or layer and it necessarily leaks out, causing the circuit to short-circuit.[5]

As pessimistic as Dr. Kaku's argument sounds, there is cause for optimism regarding sustained improvements in future computing power.

Notice that Dr. Kaku's argument is pointing out that the constraint on what can be accomplished is quantum theory, which is an elegant argument for the power of human ingenuity. Individual transistors within an integrated circuit are now so small that it is the physics of the individual atoms that make up the transistor that has become the constraining factor. The same ingenuity that brought us to this point will inevitably turn toward innovating in other forms—new approaches where the physics involved has not yet become a constraint.

The end of Moore's law, in other words, simply means the closing of one door to ever more powerful computers. It does not necessarily spell the end of other methods. In fact, one method is already well established, that being parallel computing.

PARALLEL COMPUTING, BETWEEN AND WITHIN MACHINES

The number of circuits running in a coordinated manner can be increased. This can be within a machine using multiple processors, multiple integrated circuits within a processor (known as a multicore processor), or a combination of these two approaches. These processors and cores simply divide the task of processing for the sake of speed and overall capacity, much as two people can make a cake faster if one prepares the frosting while the other prepares the cake. Another way to conduct parallel computing is between devices or components within a device, such as occurs with a mainframe computer. While parallel computing does nothing to promote the further miniaturization of individual components, an intelligently designed architecture will allow the continued miniaturization of the devices. These components shrink by moving the bulk of processing to one location while the output goes to another location. This sounds bizarre and confusing in the abstract, but you are familiar with it in the concrete.

When you run a web search on your cell phone, your phone is not querying its own indexes of web pages, and it is not running the algorithms that underpin the search. The phone and associated software conduct basic processing of your search, or query, and then pass these data to a server cluster located elsewhere. They then receive the output of that cluster's data processing and translate it back into a convenient layout that can be represented on your display. In this way, your phone can know how many copies of this book Amazon has in stock. This processing capability is how that small and unpretentious phone knows what song is playing in your favorite bar, the performance of your stock portfolio, how long your flight is delayed, and the driving directions to the Afghan restaurant in the northern part of Dallas, Texas, about which you have heard such enthusiastic reviews (most likely on the same phone!). One of the authors of this book has access to the following on his smartphone:

- Multiple e-mail services
- Up-to-the-minute readings from Doppler radar belonging to the National Oceanic and Atmospheric Administration
- A photographic representation of every outdoor spot on Earth
- Maps of all of North America and other places around the world
- Updates of the activities of most of his friends via social media
- Multiple ways of accessing music from online sources, both on a subscription and an ownership model
- Near instantaneous sharing of photos taken between his wife and him
- Multiple video streaming services

- The ability to identify a song by name and artist by holding the phone up to a speaker
- Images from traffic cameras lining the roads and intersections near where he lives
- The ability to purchase and immediately access books and music

All of these abilities are dependent on computing power located in servers of unknown location, accessed by his phone using an Internet connection. All of these services require huge amounts of computing power, relying on parallel computing. Parallel computing is ubiquitous both within computers and phones, and in the remote services that these devices access. It is this remote access that bypasses the limitations on what individual microprocessors inside individual computers and phones can accomplish.

When Fred, a Facebook user, visits his friend Anna's page, the "heavy lifting" processing necessary to deliver that page to Fred's computer occurs in a data center, which is where the system stores Anna's profile, and where the computing power exists to select only the correct information, subsequently returning it to Fred's computer. Likewise, when Anna sees Fred's new patio furniture in a Facebook post and decides to look for something similar on Amazon, the processing for the heavy lifting that delivers the results of her Amazon search back to her, and runs the payment transactions, takes place in a data center. A similar process is at play for web searches. None of this indexing of web pages or the search for specific terms buried in all of those indexed pages occurs on Fred's or Anna's computers. This is the heavy-duty work our devices outsource to data centers (Figure 2.2).

A single data center may very well be responsible for this processing for users all around the world at any given time, or it may be one of several data centers that each cater to a region. For this reason, data centers are large, warehouse-style buildings located near major sources of electrical power. They are often (but by no means exclusively) found in locations where natural cooling helps release the heat generated by all of the servers within. This is one reason so many data centers are located in the Pacific Northwest of the United States.

Data centers are not limited to Internet firms, however. To handle the deluge of data, the shipping giant UPS has two data centers, a 470,600 ft^2 facility in Mahwah, New Jersey, and a 172,000 ft^2 facility near Atlanta, Georgia, that hosts what UPS states is the largest IBM DB2 relational

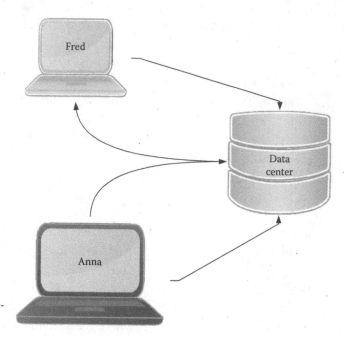

FIGURE 2.2
Data center interme-
diary to users.

database in the world. A football field (American football) is 57,600 ft², including end zones. These data centers could, between them, fully contain more than 11 such football fields. Between the two data centers, there is also enough air conditioning capacity to cool 3500 homes, along with 60 miles of underground conduit, 7000 backup batteries to maintain power until the generators can kick in during an outage, and 70,000 gallons of fuel to run their generators.[6] The UPS delivery person comes to your door and hands you a small computer with a touch screen upon which you sign using a stylus; these data centers are where those data go, with delivery date and time, along with your signature. In fact, if you order from Amazon you may even sign up to receive a text message when they deliver your package—yet another example of how a data point makes it back to your phone.

Google is famously opaque in providing information about its data centers, although it is opening up with photos of their interiors (it still remains close-mouthed on the size and statistics for its facilities). The Data Center Knowledge website lists what it believes to be 20 Google data centers in the United States and 17 overseas data centers.[7] Google lists only six US data centers and seven overseas data centers on its website. Its page lists data centers that did not make it to the Data Center Knowledge website, such as those in Finland (first phase completed in 2011, with a second phase estimated completion date of 2014), Singapore, and Chile.[8] What we see revealed, regardless of whose estimates we use, is that Google has a truly immense and global data center footprint. It must. As the dominant Internet search firm with other operations, among which are a web-based e-mail offering (Gmail), an online media store (Google Play), its own social media site (Google+), a video hosting service (YouTube), global satellite images (Google Earth), comprehensive mapping abilities (Google Maps), and the firm's bread and butter (Google AdSense). These services have worldwide reach and involve a tremendous amount of processing that the end user never sees.

Facebook is more transparent about its data centers, and they are truly gigantic. We would expect large data centers with a firm of "1.23 billion monthly active users as of December 31, 2013."[9] As this book is being written, the company currently operates a 333,400 ft² data center in Prineville, Oregon (and is building an identical facility next to it),[10] and a data center of approximately 300,000 ft² near Forest City, North Carolina.[11] The firm plans to construct a behemoth 1.4 million ft² facility, estimated to cost $1.5 billion, near Des Moines, Iowa.[12] There is also a 290,000 ft² facility in Sweden that is being finished.[13] The total square footage of all of Facebook's data centers, both constructed and planned, will be sufficient to fully contain over 46 football fields.

The spread of data centers has also given rise to one of the fast-rising buzzwords of the early twenty-first century: "the cloud." The cloud, cloud storage, and cloud computing all relate to movement of data storage and manipulation from one's own device—be it desktop, laptop, or mobile device—to a data center somewhere. Businesspeople are wise to be wary of buzzwords, but the cloud is a buzzword with substance behind it.

Processing is also establishing itself in the cloud as part of the software-as-a-service (SaaS) model. Salesforce.com provides serious, market-respected customer relationship management (CRM) to firms who access it through a website. Accounting packages, such as NetSuite and QuickBooks, have moved into the cloud. Though far from being a market changer, Google Docs has established a niche as a method for sharing and collaborating on documents in the cloud. These documents include spreadsheets, word processing, and presentations in a format similar to those of Microsoft Office. Microsoft is also offering cloud-based file sharing and collaboration through its SkyDrive service.

Moving from the public cloud (commercial applications that are used on a subscriber basis) to the private cloud (hosted solutions that are unique to a single customer), more and more companies are developing custom solutions that are hosted remotely in data centers. These solutions are created specifically for the company that initiated the project and are usually not shared with any other company.

We expect cloud computing to proliferate further. First of all, it provides companies a way to add capabilities while transferring the expenditures to operating expenses (OPEX) instead of capital expenses (CAPEX). Second, data centers generally offer a degree of protection and redundancy to data that is not possible when they are stored on a hard drive in the office. Third, data security in the cloud can be superb when it is in the right hands. With proper security, even the employees of the data center are physically unable to access any of the client's data. Private cloud solutions with no presence on the Internet are, as we discussed, only accessible to the intended client using a secure connection and can be very safe solutions that are, for all intents and purposes, part of the internal information technology (IT) solution. Finally, the cost of administering data on the cloud can be low since the staff administering the hardware are shared among customers of the hosting facility. If you need only a few minutes a week of work on your system, plus an occasional hardware upgrade, your firm does not need to pay full-time staff to handle that. You pay a fee for this benefit, along with the fees paid by other customers, to cover salaries and physical infrastructure.

Along with the growth of data centers is the continued growth in the computational capabilities achieved through the use of parallel computing within a single device. The history of parallel computing is inextricably intertwined with the history of computation itself. It is simply the strategy of breaking a problem up into smaller problems that are then distributed and processed concurrently. This concept will reappear as we delve into greater detail of how big data solutions function.

Multiple computers running side by side or the different components of a mainframe may handle parallel computing, but there is a simpler example of parallel computing that is running in most home and office computers and even on smart phones. This is the multicore processor.

A multicore processor is an integrated circuit that contains more than one central processing unit (CPU or core); it splits up processing tasks among these. In home use, the most common multicore processors are currently the dual-core and quad-core processors (the current Apple Macintosh Pro can run dual hexacores!), though some specialized processors may have more than 100 cores. The spread of multicore processors will be discussed in greater detail later in this chapter.

As we write this book, the Tianhe-2 supercomputer was unveiled in China, attaining 33.86 petaflops of processing power with a theoretical peak performance of 54.9 petaflops (a petaflop is 1015 flops, or FLoating-point Operations Per Second; the performance of a standard desktop computer is measured in gigaflops, one of which is equal to 0.000001 petaflop), toppling the Titan computer at Oak Ridge National Laboratory in the United States as the world's most powerful. Tianhe-2 accomplished this with 3,120,000 cores, based on 48,000 Xeon Phi chips and 32,000 Intel Ivy Bridge Xeon microprocessors spread across 16,000 nodes.[14] As impressive as this performance is, it is unlikely to stand as the record for long.

QUANTUM COMPUTING

One path that is beginning to gain traction around the physical limitations of Moore's law lies in the enigmatic field of quantum computing. A team of physicists from Purdue University in the United States and the University of New South Wales in Australia revealed the creation of a single-atom transistor of unprecedented precision in early 2012, which is viewed as a step toward full quantum computing.[15] In May of 2013, Google announced the opening of the Quantum Artificial Intelligence Lab at the Ames Research Center, a NASA facility located in Mountain View, California. The lab will host a D-Wave Two quantum computer.[16] The field of quantum computing is still fraught with uncertainty and controversy. Though this may affect your business in the future, for now you are safe to focus your energy on the standard silicon computing technology that currently dominates the market.

RECAP OF GROWTH IN COMPUTING POWER

Regardless of when and how it reaches the end of its useful life span, Moore's law has proven itself prescient and shaped expectations about the future of computing. An insightful article about Moore's law from June of 2003 (almost exactly 10 years before this passage was written) on CNet seems quaint now. In it, the author states

> A Dell Dimension released in 2000 with the 1 GHz Pentium III, 256 MB of memory, a 30 GB hard drive, a CD-RW drive and a DVD player cost $5,999. That's six times more expensive and about one-third as powerful as a midrange box Dell Computer released this week.

What we see in this quote is an example of the progress in performance produced in 3 years, from 2000 to 2003. At the time of this writing, you can purchase a Dell desktop in the $1000 price range with a 3.9 GHz processor with four cores (as opposed to the single core of the Pentium 3), 32 GB of memory, and a 1-TB hard drive. If the quotation above seems quaint now, how will the $1000 Dell of today appear to readers of this book 10 years from now?

STORAGE, STORAGE EVERYWHERE

Not only is computer processing power growing exponentially, but so is data storage. However, before exploring this field, it is important to understand the categories of data storage:

- Primary: This is mostly made up of what in modern computers is referred to as random access memory (RAM). Primary storage is the memory that holds the information that the computer is working on at a given time. Information in primary storage usually resides there for the short term, then disappears when the device is turned off. There are two types of primary data storage aside from the RAM:
  - Processor registers: This is information stored directly within the processor. This is the most easily accessible, and smallest, data storage within the computer.
  - Processor cache: This is the most heavily accessed information in the main memory of the RAM. Information is loaded into the cache to be more quickly accessed by the processor registers.
- Secondary: This is information stored on the computer that must be loaded into primary data storage for processing. The songs on your hard drive that you are not currently listening to and the Word files

you worked on a month ago are sitting in secondary storage. There are two categories of secondary storage:

- Internal storage: This is the storage that is part of the computer itself, such as the hard drive or the solid-state systems that are replacing mechanical hard drives.
- External storage: This includes flash drives (USB "thumb" drives and SD cards), external backup hard drives, CDs, and DVDs. Many well-known forms of obsolete external secondary data storage include floppy disks, tapes, and punch cards.

The boundaries between these different categories of data storage are not as neat as they appear. We currently see big data systems with "in memory" databases that have terabytes of RAM. This is not particularly efficient, but it is fast. Such systems blur the line between primary and secondary data storage.

We have a third category of data storage, referred to as tertiary storage, that involves the mechanical storage and retrieval of discs or tapes. An example of this approach would be the robotic retrieval system sometimes seen in science fiction movies (yes, such storage does exist). Tertiary storage falls beyond the scope of this book, as it is by definition difficult to access and use in a short interval. This method is generally used as backup storage for disaster recovery or as a way of delivering data that we would not access frequently enough to warrant being stored in secondary memory.

The most important aspect of data storage, for the purposes of this book, is the exponential growth in the long-term storage of data still in use. Hence, our focus will be on secondary storage. The explosive growth of computer processing power has a clear analogue in secondary data storage, with clear consequences for the development of big data.

The path from the punch cards of the Jacquard loom, an 1801 invention by Joseph Marie Jacquard, which used punch cards to command the loom to create the desired patterns in the cloth being woven, to the 64 GB SD card of today is a long and strange one. A brilliant article published in the *Proceedings of the IEEE* demonstrates the key developments in the evolution of data storage. The authors, Kazuo Goda and Masaru Kitsuregawa of the University of Tokyo, describe the development of computer data storage, not just how it developed, but why. The story of data storage does not begin with punch cards. After all, clay tablets date back much farther. However, clay tablets have never been used for electronic computation.

It is with the punched card and its supplantation by magnetic tape that Goda and Kitsuregawa begin their story.[17]

Magnetic tape was an improvement over the limited capacity of punched cards, but it was limited by the need to rewind and fast forward to locate key data (it was, after all, designed for the storage of audio). Those of us old enough to have purchased cassette tapes and rented VHS tapes, with their "Please be kind and rewind" stickers and penalties for failing to do so, can attest to this limitation. It is primarily for this reason that the invention of the disk was an improvement, as economics still did not work in favor of disks. Disks allowed random access of data rather than streaming in a series to the point of interest.

The data on a disk can be located easily in the order that it is needed simply by moving the read/write head, analogous to the stylus on a phonograph, to the needed sector of the disk. Those of us who still own vinyl records (usually purchased from the now obsolete record stores in a strip mall) also remember the trade-off between the portability of cassettes and the ease of navigating a record. The introduction of the compact disk (CD) resolved this trade-off, much as the hard drive would eventually do for internal secondary data storage. It took time, however, before the size of the disk ceased to be a liability.

Other drawbacks to the disk delayed its acceptance. One of these drawbacks was the higher storage capacity per dollar for tape after the early commercialization of the technology in the 1950s. It was not until we achieved more rapid increases in storage capacity per dollar for disks over tapes in the following decades that disks were able to take over their dominant role for secondary storage. Once the cost advantage of tapes declined, they were relegated to tertiary storage.[17]

The IBM 350 Disk File hard drive was the first magnetic disk to hit the market. It was first released in 1956 (but not patented until 1970) and was more than 68 ft^3 in size with 50 24-in. disks.[18] Its bulk belied its capacity. It could store only 3.75 MB (about the size of an MP3 audio file today) and was available for rent for $130 per megabyte per month, or $5850 per year ($50,100 adjusted to 2013 dollars).[17] The drive was a part of the IBM 305 RAMAC computer. The computer weighed over a ton, but was still cutting-edge technology in its day.[19] After all, it was the first to hit the market. Still, a comparison with what is on sale today illustrates the march of technology. The capacity of the 4-TB Seagate HDD ST4000DM000, with 4 3.5-in. disks of 1 TB each, is well over 1 million times greater[20] and carries a price of $145.00 on Amazon.com as we write this passage in late 2014.[21]

A further example highlights how the computer market has changed: Only 1000 RAMAC units were built before production ceased in 1961.[21] In 2012, the number of hard disk drive units shipped was 552 million. As impressive as that number is, it actually shows a decrease of 11.5% from 2011.[22]

IBM followed the 350 Disk File with a series of innovations in hard drive design. The IBM 1301, introduced in 1961, used multiple read/write heads, one to read each hard disk in the stack (remember, the hard drives under discussion feature multiple disks, or platters, arranged one above another in a stack), as opposed to the single head of the IBM 350, for which a second head was only introduced later.[23] This would be like placing a series of vinyl records one on top of another with a separate stylus for each record, enabling a user to select a song from any record in more or less the same time necessary to select a song from a single record. This design enabled capacity to increase without an adverse impact on access speed for files.

The growth of storage capacity as the physical size of the drives shrank necessarily meant that the density of storage on each disk increased. The density of the storage capacity for the 1301 was 13 times what it was for the 350.[24] One 1301 unit held 28 MB of information, available at a lease price of $2100 a month for one storage module or $3500 for two. The purchase price for the former was $115,500 and $185,500 for the latter.[25] An even more pronounced drop in cost accompanied this increase in storage density.

The first sealed hard drive was the IBM 3340, nicknamed the Winchester because of the two removable 30-MB modules during development phase (think 30–30 as in the Winchester .30–30 caliber lever action rifle). The disk platters and read/write heads were not accessible, simplifying loading and unloading of the disks. Production versions featured three different types of data modules, one with 35 MB of memory and two with 70 MB. Up to 32 of these modules could be connected.[26]

In 1980, Shugart Technology (now Seagate Technology) changed the hard drive market by releasing the much smaller 5-MB, 5.25-in. ST–506 hard disk drive for smaller computers, opening the market for more compact drives. The ST–506 is a direct ancestor to the smaller, more convenient hard drives found in desktops and laptops, including the 4-TB Seagate of today mentioned above.[26]

Goda and Kitsuregawa point out that, "In comparison with the IBM 350 of 1956, magnetic disks have achieved eight orders of magnitude higher area density and a million times larger drive capacity." The low costs and increased capacity of these smaller drives, thanks to such technological developments, made possible the rise of the redundant array of independent disks (RAID).[26]

The RAID is an important development, as some of the concepts will reappear in later discussions of big data. RAIDs resulted from the appearance of the physically small, low-cost hard disk drive along with the concept of "data striping" attended by redundant storage. This latter development originates from a 1978 patent awarded to Norman Ken Ouchi.[27] Striping is the splitting of data, storing it in "stripes" across separate disks. As the data are stored across disks, they can be accessed more quickly than data stored on one disk. If we think of a three-disk RAID, each disk can spin separately and be read with separate heads. Instead of being read sequentially, a large file can be read simultaneously by all three heads and then reassembled. Striping, however, requires redundancy. Striping without data redundancy means that the loss of a single disk will pull down all or most of the files that are striped onto that disk. Data redundancy, accompanied by striping, provides protection against the loss of whole disks or sectors. We will return to this concept during our discussion of the big data application Hadoop, which uses striping for fast processing and replicates each stripe three times by default (Figure 2.3).

The concept of the RAID is not monolithic. The user of a RAID can select the degree of striping and the degree of redundancy necessary to meet requirements. For a small business on a budget whose data are backed up elsewhere, no redundancy is necessary. For a firm that requires data on request, for whom a disk failure would be a serious disruption, redundancy is necessary and so disk failure on the RAID will cause a failover—a controlled transition—to another disk until the miscreant disk is replaced.

Whereas the RAID is an important step conceptually, in that it involves storing data across multiple disks, a further development, storage networking, has made it possible to cope with the increasing quantity of data. Goda and Kitsuregawa argue:

> As digital information matures, storage capacity has to keep pace too. However, it is almost impossible to expand administrative personnel at the same pace. The consequence is that the management burden per administrator is rapidly growing. Today, one primary concern of system owners is often how to manage large storage resources efficiently. Storage networking is a promising solution.[26]

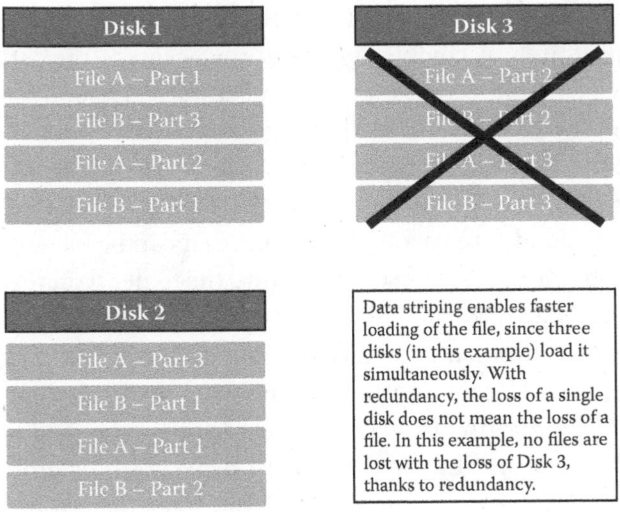

Disk 1
File A – Part 1
File B – Part 3
File A – Part 2
File B – Part 1

Disk 3
File A – Part 2
File B – Part 2
File A – Part 3
File B – Part 3

Disk 2
File A – Part 3
File B – Part 1
File A – Part 1
File B – Part 2

Data striping enables faster loading of the file, since three disks (in this example) load it simultaneously. With redundancy, the loss of a single disk does not mean the loss of a file. In this example, no files are lost with the loss of Disk 3, thanks to redundancy.

FIGURE 2.3
Simple model of data striping.

Storage networking generally relies on RAIDs as the underlying mechanism to store data. Traditionally, there have been the confusingly named storage area network (SAN) and network attached storage (NAS) technologies. The differences between these two modalities are not important for the purpose of this discussion, as they relate mainly to how the system is managed, how the storage is accessed (whether by fiber or by Internet protocols), and the intended quantity of data moved. What is important is that data storage physically remote from the computers that access it can now be accessed with nearly the same ease that we have with the computer's local hard drive.

Once data storage became a multidisk system accessed by multiple computers, it necessitated that data storage units themselves should be more active in processing how they store the data and share the data with the computers that access them. In other words, the storage is no longer simply a disk attached to a computer—in storage networking, the storage now *is* a computer. If two or more computers were accessing the same remote drive, yet controlling the read-write process as they do with their own hard drives, pandemonium would arise. The system would accidentally overwrite files and two users reading files at the same time would interfere with each other. Accessing data becomes one computer handing data back and forth with another computer.

We currently observe data storage transitioned to third parties. Whereas it is clearly easier to manage a single storage network within an organization, it is even easier and more cost-effective much of the time to outsource this storage entirely as complexity grows and access to the data is needed across large geographical distances. Cloud storage is one manifestation of the developments discussed in this overview of data storage.

Amazon and Apple offer cloud storage to those who purchase media files from them, as well as media purchased elsewhere. Services such as DropBox and Amazon Cloud provide off-site storage that can be blended nearly seamlessly—from the user's point of view—into the folder structure of one's own operating system. MediaFire provides storage in the cloud that also functions as a convenient way to transfer files too large to be sent as e-mail attachments. Carbonite and CrashPlan services automatically back up the data from individual computers, restoring the data to the personal or business user in the event of a hard drive crash or other loss of data. All of these services are similar in that they take data from a computer and store it in a data center, but they offer different services for different uses and varieties of users.

Whereas Amazon Cloud is useful for storing photos and media files for a consumer, Carbonite and CrashPlan protect the files of a computer through automatic backup, and we use them for business purposes (though family plans are available). To pull files from CrashPlan is not an easy or a fun task, but the value of its model becomes immediately apparent when a hard drive malfunctions. DropBox is effective for both business and personal use, and it is especially helpful in coordinating shared files between computers.

We also use the processing power of data storage servers to preserve our data, backing it up at intervals or concurrently creating multiple copies. This processing power has also found a new use with MapReduce, a technology developed by Google and made famous with the big data application known as Hadoop, to be covered in a later chapter. For now, it will suffice to say that this technology uses the processing power of the servers on which the data are striped to apply a divide–conquer–recombine algorithm. This algorithm allows us to access different data points in a single file at different points within the same file and then process them in parallel before sending the results to a central server that then recombines the results that it receives.

MapReduce is analogous to asking a group of 100 people to scan the indices of 100 books each to look for the earliest case of a particular concept mentioned in those volumes residing in a 10,000-volume special collection. Each person brings the earliest example he or she found, at which point you select the oldest example from those. By processing that many books in parallel, then refining the results, you could scan the entire collection of books in a single day. If a single person scanned the collection in a serial manner, the job would take much, much longer (in effect, we would add the time of all the scanners to get the linear result). The way that Hadoop functions is analogous—it can perform concurrently because the different servers in a Hadoop cluster can each process the data from their particular server before sending on the results for final integration using the MapReduce algorithm. This novel approach also demonstrates another development of big data, that processing and the storage are intimately related to big data solutions.

One clarification is in order: the inclusion of Amazon Cloud, DropBox, MediaFire, Carbonite, and CrashPlan is for illustrative purposes. For big data applications, other cloud data storage options are available from famous players such as Microsoft, Amazon, Google, and Rackspace.

GRIST FOR THE MILL: DATA USED AND UNUSED

Thus far in our discussion, we have focused on data storage and computing power with only a slight overview of sensors and computer mediation. This provides an important clue to the "Why here? Why now?" of big data. But something—data—needs to fill that storage. Unlike the processing and storage components of big data, the actual data collected and the sensors used to collect it vary wildly across industries.

At this stage in the evolution of big data, we see tremendous fermentation in the flow of ideas. Articles in news sources regularly appear demonstrating what big data can do, much of it counterintuitive. What we will likely see is that a percentage of these applications will succeed to varying degrees, whereas a certain percentage will fail. Big data does many things well. It detects regular patterns underlying a phenomenon, but it is blind in the face of meaningful, unexpected events (the "black swans" made famous by Nassim Nicholas Taleb). It finds statistical relationships between variables, but it requires a skilled data scientist to determine if the relationship is independent of the data or merely an artifact of the data. It can indicate what is happening but not always how to respond.

Much of the success or failure of a big data endeavor will hinge on the data itself. Some industries, such as insurance and financial services, swim in data and have learned how to harness its power. Other industries, such as marketing and agriculture, are coming into their own in applying data usage more effectively. The following discussion skims a few industries to demonstrate how ubiquitous data has become and covers some of its uses. This massive growth in data acquisition is what fills all the storage and consumes all the processing power we have discussed in this chapter. It is important to remember that most data possessed by a business is unused, with an estimate by IBM placing that unused data at 80%.[28]

In looking at your own organization, think of anything that tracks jobs, defects, customer feedback, items sold, geographies of customers and vendors, breakdowns in revenue or expenditure, global positioning system (GPS) location of users or equipment, gateways through which products pass (such as scanners and RFID tags), subscription data services, the sales funnel, breakage, fuel usage, exit and entry, and so on. Think of how you could store, combine, and analyze this data—this is the grist for the big data mills.

AGRICULTURE

Samuel Allen, the CEO of John Deere, has been quoted as saying the company's 8R line of tractors boasts more lines of code than the space shuttle.[29] Forget the hayseed stereotype all too often applied to farming (in fact, one of the authors developed his interest in how different components of a business interact by growing up in the farming industry). Agriculture is a sophisticated industry that has evolved into a key high-tech economic sector. Tractors and grain combines actuated much of the pioneering work in self-driving vehicles.

Precision farming, and more specifically variable-rate technology, relies on databases of field conditions. We can no longer assume that a field is homogeneous. Soils differ, nutrients differ, and water flows differ within the space of a few meters. Databases now interact with GPS technologies to vary the rate at which fertilizers and chemicals are applied as a tractor drives across the field. In other words, today's farming must account for small-scale differences within a field, using objective location metrics, and then act on those differences in the application of particular chemicals.

Monsanto, about whom we will discourse several times in this book, acquired the Climate Corporation, founded by former Google employees David Friedberg and Siraj Khaliq, for over $1 billion in 2013. The Climate

Corporation provides insurance that protects profits in the space not covered by federal crop insurance. This coverage is scaled by a particular farmer's productivity and covers rainfall over an unusually detailed 2.5 × 2.5 mile area, taking into account the soil's ability to cope with that weather.[30]

Monsanto also acquired Precision Planting—started by Gregg and Cindy Sauder in 1993 as a way to bring consistency to the planting of seeds—for $250 million in 2012. As an example of the data that its products are able to collect, consider the firm's 20/20 SeedSense monitor (slogan: "Quit planting with a blindfold on"). The monitor is a touch screen device installed inside the tractor, fed via a processor that in turn pulls in data from sensors on the planter. The advantages, according to the firm's website:

- Find hidden mechanical problems and correct them at planting
- Perfect planter performance by adjusting meters, vacuum pressure, transmissions, and speed
- Improve productivity by maximizing planter speed without compromising performance
- Measure and adjust downforce to eliminate costly root compaction and slotting[31]

An article in the *Peoria Journal Star* states

> Whether it's a planting system that adjusts the pressure used to plant seeds in the ground (the 20/20 Air Force sells for $5,000) or an iPad app the company developed earlier this year that provides soil type information, Precision Planting keeps developing new tools.
>
> Sauder said that gathering data is important, but it's just as important to make it easy to access that data. "Now we store data for the farmer on the cloud so that when he's in the field, the information streams in," he said.
>
> "We have 33 engineers on staff and have 45 patents directly involved with planting," said Sauder, who expects Monsanto to soon double the size of the Precision operation.[32]

Sensors and processors are now able to selectively remove product postharvest. In the processing plant of a business in which his family was involved, one of the authors has seen in action a machine that splits beans into separate streams, photographs them one at a time, and uses a jet of air to eject any undesired object before recombining the beans into a single stream for packing.

Agriculture is an industry that is comfortable with sensors and data from the markets and weather service. There is much room for big data to move to a more central role. We see developments on the insurance side as well as the production side. The data are there, and it is probable that shipping, storage, and marketing will become progressively more unified as well. It is not difficult to see how we could combine data captured from the air-blasting seed cleaner with per-acre yields and data about farming methods; for example, we could use this information with soils to calibrate farming methods that result in fewer defective beans.

The role of big data in agriculture, along with its advantages and drawbacks, will be covered further in our discussion of some of the consequences, positive and negative, of big data. Needless to say, agriculture is a technologically sophisticated industry.

AUTOMOTIVE

The role of computers and data points also plays a role closer to daily life for most of us in automobiles. Computers are essential to the functioning of cars. Computers control everything from antilock brakes to cruise control to the entertainment system. Even the functioning of the engine is controlled by computer:

> If a car's computer is down or does not work right, the car will not work (or at least it will not pass an emissions test). That is because now all major functions of an automobile are controlled, and monitored, by computers. If something goes wrong with the car, the computer will know and record a fault code long before a light comes on the dashboard (the automotive industry calls that a MIL, or Malfunction Indicator Light) alerting us that something is wrong.[33]

Since the 1996 model year, cars in the United States have been required to have a computer called the On-Board Diagnostics (OBD-II). That is the computer that records fault codes. During vehicle inspections, the diagnostic codes are pulled and analyzed from this computer using a plug that connects inside the car within 2 ft of the steering column. The system monitors performance and emissions, using largely standardized generic codes specified by the Society for Automotive Engineers, but with variations across car companies for the more specific, enhanced codes.

Event data recorders (EDRs) in automobiles function similarly to the "black box" used in aircraft, essentially to record the situation leading up to an accident. Trucking is a capital-intensive industry for which avoiding accidents is both the ethical (for safety reasons) and financially smart thing to do. Trucking firms can purchase an aftermarket system called the Eaton Vehicle On-Board Radar (VORAD) that both alerts drivers to hazards and records the details of an accident should one occur.[34]

Proactive measures using a tool such as VORAD include sending audio and visual alerts triggered by forward- and side-mounted radars, and measuring the status of different systems in the vehicle. In the event of an accident, somewhere between the final 2 and 10 minutes remain in system memory. These data include the movement of not only the truck but also the vehicles in its proximity. Specific data points collected include the distance in feet between the truck and other objects, the lateral distance between these objects and the main axis of the truck, the speed of these objects, the speed of the truck, the status of the brakes of the truck, the turn rate of the truck, the status of the system's alarms, the status of the side sensors, and the status of the turn signals.[34]

Eaton also offers a very different product to monitor the status of a truck. This product uses vibration sensors to monitor the drivetrain of a truck to motivate repairs before a problem becomes expensive.[35]

Several companies offer electronic alternatives to the government-mandated logbooks kept by over-the-road drivers. These may include GPS tracking and hours of activity, warning of violations, and highlighting of them.

GPS can be used for more than simply tracking truck drivers. The Mercedes Actros truck now comes with a feature—Predictive Power Control—that uses GPS to anticipate changes in the terrain ahead by matching the position of the truck with data about the road. This feature enables the truck to shift the transmission in addition to adjusting its speed and braking to maximize fuel efficiency. Mercedes estimates this system can gain a 3% savings in fuel used.[36] With a fleet of fuel-consuming trucks on the road, this seemingly unimportant single percentage point can accumulate savings.

A sharp-eyed reader will observe that our discussion of data in transportation does not quite fit with the concept of big data. There is much discussion of data points generated but not of data points analyzed. In fact, these data generally dissipate with the exception of data used in fleet management or cutting-edge applications such as the Actros truck. Is there in fact anyone analyzing these data and applying them? Indeed, it is occurring in the insurance industry.

The automobile insurer Progressive has the driver install a device called the Snapshot onto the OBD-II (remember...on-board diagnostics!) port of the car to monitor miles driven, hard braking incidents, and hours driven between midnight and 4:00 a.m. These data are then transmitted to Progressive.[37] This may not seem like much data, but a lot can be extracted from it. Here was some advice offered by Progressive for the 2013 holiday season:

> If you're looking for the best day to shop in the final days leading up to Christmas, Progressive found that December 22 should yield the least amount of congestion. The data also shows that Fridays are the worst day of the week to be on the road, while Sundays and Tuesdays are the best based on the number of driving trips taken. Progressive reviewed more than 9 billion miles of driving data from Snapshot®, its industry-leading usage-based insurance program, comparing time spent idling on December 10–31 (excluding Christmas) versus the same dates in April through November.
>
> "Because we collect billions of miles of driving data with Snapshot, we're always trying to find real-world applications of our analysis," said Dave Pratt, general manager of usage-based insurance for Progressive. "It doesn't get any more real than losing precious time sitting in traffic. You may spend less time idling if you run errands on a Tuesday versus Friday or Saturday."[38]

What Progressive practices is a basic form of what is called telematics. Telematics is the generation and recording of data about driving habits and is used to varying degrees in different countries. In the United States, telematics records how and when drivers drive, as we saw with Progressive. In Europe, the largest market worldwide for telematics-based insurance premiums, a GPS device also records *where* drivers drive. According to a 2013 white paper on the topic:

> Every second, a telematics device will produce a data record. This data record will include information such as date, time, speed, longitude, latitude, acceleration or deceleration (G-force), cumulative mileage and fuel consumption. Depending on the frequency and length of the trips, these data records or data sets can represent approximately 5 MB to 15 MB of data annually, per customer. With a customer base of 100,000 vehicles, this represents more than 1 terabyte of data per year![39]

Telematics is one example of the different strands of automotive data being collected into a large and powerful data set, used with sophistication by the insurance industry.

Data derived from telemetrics and the monitoring of data from the OBD-II computer, when matched to insurance claims and warranty repairs, help to pinpoint safety issues with vehicles or counterintuitive issues affecting vehicle reliability. One of the authors had an enlightening discussion with someone knowledgeable about automotive engineering regarding one American manufacturer's difficulties, which arose after creating a better suspension system in one of its vehicles (commonly used off-road). The new suspension had more problems than the old suspension, but it performed better than the old suspension. After a lengthy investigation (in the pre–big data age), the manufacturer discovered that by making drivers more comfortable on rough roads, the improved suspension also prevented them from understanding just how hard they were driving their vehicles. In other words, the new suspension performed so much better than the old suspension, the driver received less feedback from the vehicle. The improvement led to harder driving off-road, which in turn led to increased problems with the suspension. The investigation was costly and time-consuming. In the big data age and with the right kind of data, such an investigation takes place with much less effort and expense. Reliability analysts thrive on large quantities of data, as do marketers.

MARKETING IN THE PHYSICAL WORLD

A famous quotation attributed to retail pioneer John Wanamaker states, "Half the money I spend on advertising is wasted; the trouble is I don't know which half." A similar quotation, "I know half my advertising isn't working, I just don't know which half," originated with William Lever, one of the founders of Lever Brothers, which eventually merged with another firm to become household goods giant Unilever. Online advertising is an example of data generated in massive amounts on a constant basis to remove this uncertainty.

Gadgets that generate a constant stream of data surround you. A smartphone is, in fact, a small computer. Each time you turn it on or off, or visit a website with it, you are creating a data point. As this book was being written, controversy was raging about the National Security Agency (NSA) vacuuming up call detail records that indicate which phone numbers called which other numbers and for how long, as well as Internet metadata. According to documents released by the whistleblower Edward Snowden, the NSA and Britain's Government Communications Headquarters (GCHQ) intelligence service have worked out how to extract information about a cell phone user's political leanings and even sexual orientation by pulling cell phone data out of the phone with hacking apps such as Angry Birds.[40]

How could this be? Simple. The increasing capability of our daily gadgets means that we do more with them. Remember the 1 GHz processor, accompanied by 256 MB of RAM and 30-GB hard drive, of the Dell desktop computer in 2000? The iPhone 5 available as this is being written features a 1.3 GHz dual-core processor (64-bit) with 1 GB of RAM and either 16, 32 or 64 GB of secondary storage. One of the leading competitors for the iPhone, the Samsung Galaxy S4, features 16, 32 or 64 GB of secondary memory, the same as the iPhone 5, but features a 1.9 GHz quad-core processor with 2 GB of RAM. The secondary memory can also be expanded by up to 64 GB by inserting an SD card.

Either of these phones is more formidable than a desktop computer of 13 years ago. Both work their way into the center of their users' lives by making useful applications readily available free or for purchase and both are therefore geysers of user data. Remember the list of just those functions that require external servers for processing? Each of those functions sends back data to the same data warehouses that carry out that processing. Little bits of your life, powerful in the aggregate, are logged each time the computer is the intermediary in one of your interactions.

If you have heard songs you like but could not identify, there is an application ("app") for that. Shazam and SoundHound can be used to recognize songs; just play one of the apps and hold your phone in the direction of the speaker. Wikitude allows you to point your phone at a landmark, identify it, and look up information about it on Wikipedia. This "enhanced reality" program uses the phone's GPS and compass to determine what exactly the user is looking at. Links appear to hover over images of the landmarks that appear on the screen as they are being viewed through the device's camera.

Even the phone calls you make on your phone (it is easy to forget that this is what a telephone was originally designed to do!) now pass through servers. There was a time when human operators plugging in cables to jacks to create the circuit manually connected a phone call. Mechanical switches replaced manual intervention. Those days are long gone. Computers, more specifically racks of computers, are doing that job.

VOIP calls state as much in their name—VOIP stands for Voice Over Internet Protocol. Clearly, anything that passes through a computer probably leaves a data point. A phone call certainly does. Electronic switching generates data points, which can be accessed as call detail records. These document the time and length of a telephone call as well as whether it was outgoing or incoming and between which numbers the conversation was held. One of the ways that Skype calling and Vonage are able to improve on the pricing of traditional carriers on long-distance and overseas calling is that they are VOIP services. Both can be accessed at home or on a smartphone.

To better grasp the power of even basic data gathered from a cell phone, consider the fall from grace of *The New York Times* reporter Jayson Blair in 2003. His journalistic misconduct became obvious as errors in his stories accumulated over time, raising doubts as to whether he was even physically present in the places he referred to in his articles. *The New York Times* was able to confirm, using Blair's phone records, that he was in New York when he was supposedly writing from these remote locations, with both his company-issued cell phone and his office phone.

While it is obvious a landline phone gives away its user's location, the degree to which a cell phone can do so is unexpected by many people. In the wake of the Jayson Blair scandal, the online magazine *Slate* published an article explaining methods used to locate a cell phone. The two methods discussed were:

Tower location: This method can locate the user to within one or two square miles, and such data are stored indefinitely even though it does not appear on the user's bill.

GPS: Smartphones such as iPhones, BlackBerries, Windows phones, and Android phones have GPS capability. There is clear market demand for this feature, but it was also driven by the Federal Communications Commission (FCC) in the United States. requiring GPS to help first responders locate callers with "Enhanced 911".[41]

The *Slate* article goes on to illustrate this point with the case of the murderer of a girl—brought to justice in part by his erratic travel patterns around the time of the murder. The investigator knew his travel patterns because his cell phone records contained location data.[41] The police and forensic investigators may use data point information to remove dangerous individuals from where they can inflict harm on others.

During the writing of this book, Google acquired the electronic thermostat manufacturer Nest for $3.2 billion. How Google will use the data acquired through Nest devices is not certain, but now a thermostat can acquire information not unlike that already gathered about users of home alarm systems. Like many alarm systems, the Nest can be controlled through a smartphone. One analyst argues

> Companies that successfully automate, monitor and serve the connected home—not just in the domain of heating and cooling, but also in security, entertainment, lighting, and others—will have taken a giant step into an omniscience that can benefit consumers and utilities. Utilities can create tighter relationships with their retail customers by illuminating, in more detail than ever before, who they are, how they live, how they want to be talked to and how they spend.[42]

A thermostat is not a smartphone, but the Nest interfaces with smartphone apps. As anyone who has a home alarm system that interacts with a telephone can attest, the level of detail about when and how people enter and leave a home that comes through the phone is surprising. It would take little effort to reconstruct a person's hours (and whether that person worked away from home) using just that kind of data. With the Nest, it may be possible to obtain even more detailed information by looking at which rooms record what temperatures.

Furthermore, it is entirely possible to compare those who only heat certain rooms at a time with those who heat the whole house, or those who only heat the house while at home versus those who leave the heat on while away. As we will see later in this book, one firm is using Google Earth photos of houses with solar panels to extrapolate likely characteristics of the owners. Matching these data with occasions on which a person enters or departs will likely provide better marketing message targeting, such as grocery advertising about an hour before the individual arrives home or steak house coupons just as someone leaves for a weekly Friday outing.

Some retailers offer Wi-Fi hot spots for their customers, which makes the connection work much better while inside a structure that blocks cellular signals. It also gives away information about customers in the store, possibly even identifying who they are. One of the authors receives a personalized greeting on his phone and computer when logging onto the hot spots belonging to a frequented business. As we mentioned, most cell phones now also feature GPS capability. Businesses would prefer to offer personalized communications to customers who are near an outlet. In fact, this wish to personalize has reached the point of cliché in big data white papers and news reports. One company providing even more detailed information is Path Intelligence, through the use of its Footpath technology:

> [Footpath is] a revolutionary data product that clients pay for on a subscription basis. Behind the scenes, Path Intelligence gathers the information using locally installed devices combining hardware and patented software that discreetly and anonymously monitors the signals emitted by all mobile devices in a given space.[43]

Footpath is capable of triangulating some mobile devices, but it cannot identify any particular device outside of the context of how someone moves throughout the mall. Path Intelligence goes out of its way to point out that it cannot identify any individual person. In fact, because it cannot identify anyone, the company was unable to assist London police in locating the criminals who attacked malls during the 2011 riots. The website mentions that the firm only provides aggregated data, such as, "on average X% of people who visit Gap, also visit Starbucks," and it does not share any information with service providers.[44]

Path Intelligence clearly takes ethics seriously, as it stresses how it refuses to even log information that could be misused. Will others? There are legal issues with more detailed tracking, but it is likely that companies will push these boundaries in the coming years. With triangulation, the growth of facial recognition software, the ability to identify users through Wi-Fi hot spots, and the ability to pull information through apps, temptation awaits.

ONLINE MARKETING

Traditional advertising on television, in print, and by direct mail is targeted toward particular audiences. Advertisements for Xbox games will probably not appear in magazines dedicated to tying fishing flies or in *Reader's Digest*, but these ads will appear in gaming magazines. Glance through the advertisements in *American Scientist*, *GQ*, and *Cosmopolitan*. Tear them out and present them to a friend. Ask which advertisements go with which magazine. It is doubtful he or she will find the exercise of matching the ad with the magazine very difficult—demonstrating the relation of the journalistic content to the target audience.

One of the authors conducted a basic study as part of a small statistical project for a research methods class in college that touched upon a similar point. The study involved flipping through a sample of fashion magazines and a sample of science magazines, then counting the number of words in any advertising encountered, excluding disclaimers for medical advertisements. Unsurprisingly, advertisements in science magazines evince a much higher word count, intimating higher expectations of literacy on the part of their readership.

Advertising has traditionally been targeted at specific audiences to whatever extent seems possible. For all that, how does someone accurately target advertisements in a magazine such as *Wired*, which caters to techies, science fiction fans, and design enthusiasts? These audiences often overlap, but any single reader will find a certain percentage of the advertisements utterly irrelevant. How does one target advertisements to readers of *The Atlantic Monthly* or *The Economist*, which draw even more diverse audiences? This problem is addressed efficiently when advertising moves online and meets data.

Online advertising generates data points—using those data points helps the purchaser of such advertising better fathom the effectiveness of specific campaigns. In other words, what is the return per dollar spent on AdWords versus Facebook versus partnering with a complementary firm to print your QR codes (Figure 2.4) on their packaging? Which methods provide a higher number of visitors to your website per dollar? Do visitors who discover your site using one of these methods differ from visitors who use another? Now, an advertiser can develop an idea of which half

FIGURE 2.4
QR code for this book.

of the advertising budget is wasted (think of the legendary Wanamaker comment), then redirect that half to something more productive. Also note we could use A|B or multivariate testing to quantitatively define our benefits.

One example of marketing that generates profitable data points is the mass e-mail. Let us say that you go to your favorite Italian restaurant and sign up to receive its mailings. These mailings will usually contain images that are not embedded in the message itself. In other words, when you open the message, a photo of spaghetti will appear, but that image was never mailed to you. It sits on a server that could be anywhere. It was the address of that image that was mailed to you. When you open the message, a request is sent to download the photo of spaghetti. You see a well-designed advertisement, but in the process of opening that advertisement, you will send important information back to the restaurant, such as your e-mail address and the IP address of your computer.

The restaurant staff realizes how many advertisements they distributed and how many customers opened. Using the destination mail address, they know which particular customers opened the message. With the IP address, the restaurant also knows the geographic area where the recipient opened the message. In fact, it is probable that an individual working in advertising can watch a map and visualize the various locations of message viewing. These are data points that advertisers and their clients store and analyze, converting raw data to information.

A savvy business can put this information to good use and learn still more. For example, different advertisements may be sent to different customers. Which offer works better? Free garlic bread or an extra discount? Which subject lines for the e-mail message work best? It is possible to measure what percentage of those who open their e-mail message actually click on the coupon (also known as the "click-through rate"). Customer segmentation can be based on behavior (response to an advertisement) rather than simply on characteristics that may or may not be relevant (age, sex, residence, etc.). Capturing meaningful information provides more opportunities for the use of statistical analyses.

The approach we describe here is far from perfect. One author of this book has opened more than one loyalty program account with the same store, using different e-mail addresses, at different times. The coupons still flow to both addresses, but those received at one address are generally for a 15% discount while those sent to the other address are for 20%. These numbers are based on market segmentation of one form or another that the store defines, while they remain unaware that one customer is falling into more than one segment.

Imperfect as the method may be, though, the personalized approach is better than any other market segmentation strategy that advertisers used in the past. For example, after failing to take advantage of a special Father's Day offer e-mailed to him by another business, this same author subsequently received a message noting that a deal "sweetener" might change his mind (it did). The business was able to directly target customers who did not respond to previous messages aimed at them. Such skillful targeting would be impossible without a data-driven approach.

In fact, this is one of the primary reasons why e-mail programs such as Microsoft Outlook and web mail programs will not automatically display images embedded in e-mail messages. The programs enable the user to decide whether to view the images, thereby informing the advertiser that he or she read the message.

The analysis of user behavior extends beyond mass e-mail campaigns. In an interview with two of Netflix's staff members who are heavily involved with that firm's predictive algorithms, Vice President of Product Innovation Carlos Gomez-Uribe and Engineering Director Xavier Amatriain, *Wired* magazine pulled in several interesting insights into how they use customer watching and searching habits to inform program selections. These can be highly counterintuitive.[45]

For example, the method for anticipating viewing habits differs between the mail-order DVD rental side of the business and the streaming video side of the business (Netflix's business model offers separate subscriptions for the two different services). The importance of this difference is that Netflix estimates 75% of what a viewer watches is the result of what Netflix itself recommends based on what it knows of customers (a reinforcing loop). When a viewer must select a film and then wait for it to arrive, a bad selection cannot be instantaneously replaced with a better one. When a user streams videos, the investment is a few minutes. A bad movie can be stopped and then immediately replaced with a preferred movie. When the mail order rental model was Netflix's sole model, viewers had a strong incentive to rate movies in order to improve predictions. Viewers who stream videos tend to be less conscientious about rating movies. This difference has pushed Netflix into a much more behavior-based recommendation system as opposed to one relying on customers self-reporting.[45]

But Netflix is not merely basing its recommendation on the user alone. The algorithms that the firm uses compare viewing habits to those of others with similar viewing habits and extrapolates from what those others like to what you will probably like. What you report is less important than what you do, and what you do is aggregated and correlated with what others do. What others do, in turn, tells Netflix what you are more likely to do. This delivers results that are superior to those obtained by looking at how users report their own preferences. According to Mr. Gomez-Uribe, following up on a comment by Mr. Amatriain about customer ratings being more aspirational than reality-based, "A lot of people tell us they often watch foreign movies or documentaries. But in practice, that doesn't happen very much."[45]

These examples of data generated for the purpose of commerce do not do justice to this sophisticated and multilevel field. What they do, however, is provide yet another illustration of the degree to which data are generated steadily in day-to-day activities, and the degree to which those data enable others to shape how our world responds to us based on our own actions.

Facebook posts are data points. Web searches are data points. Google has become famous for the breadth of the data points it captures on its users and the duration for which it holds such data. Purchases made on Amazon can be revisited years after they occur, as can items saved on the user's "wish list." Retailers save products purchased while using a loyalty club card as data points.

Google has taken collection and analysis one step further. In learning about your daily life through those activities mediated by your phone and computer, it tries to predict what you will do next and serve relevant information. Google Now is a personal assistant application Google rolled out in mid-2012, using search and other history to offer up useful information without user inquiries.

Google Now uses the contents of the user's Gmail account, calendar, and web searches to provide answers to what it determines the user needs and when it is needed. If there are airline boarding passes in your Gmail account, Google Now will display them at the pertinent time. If you follow a particular sports team, that team's scores will be updated on your phone or tablet. Other information that Google Now provides, assuming that Google has this information about you, includes your appointments, stock prices, upcoming events, traffic situations, and, if traveling, sights to see.

Public reception regarding the use and abuse of data is mixed. Data are, after all, extremely powerful, particularly after sophisticated analyses, which can lead to customer concerns about privacy. Although technically impressive, Google Now also demonstrates the sheer quantity of information that Google collects and maintains about users. Jenna Wortham in the Bits Blog at *The New York Times* states

> The features that Google Now offers are mostly already available in some form or another, through third-party mobile apps and services. But it gets weird when Google starts to extend its reach into that territory, because Google already knows so much about us—things like who we e-mail and talk to the most, along with what we search for. When those smaller bits of data begin to get linked together in a more meaningful way, that knowledge can take on a larger, different context.[46]

The interest that marketers have in this technology is obvious. When a user of the Google Play store downloads an app, all of the functions of the phone the app accesses appear as a list for the viewer to read. Some apps make only scant use of the phone's data. Others pull in personal data, such as the user's contact list. Knowing what our friends like offers a view into what we ourselves may like.

On the other hand, firms who understand our preferences and operate openly in using our data to generate recommendations are offering us a valuable service. I think most of us have learned about music on Amazon, Pandora, or Spotify, music we would never have tried otherwise. Likewise, the recommendations on the Barnes & Noble website or Amazon point to authors we would have never discovered without the recommendation. As a business, the ability to provide recommendations a customer finds valuable increases the value that can be provided to the customer by increasing sales. Furthermore, once a customer begins to appreciate the service, it acts as one more contributor to customer loyalty.

ASSET RELIABILITY AND EFFICIENCY

Under the name of Predix, General Electric (GE) is applying some of the ideas underlying Google Now to gain efficiencies. The idea behind Predix is to use sensors within a machine, such as a jet engine, to anticipate when a problem is likely to arise or to locate a profitable efficiency. The information necessary to fix the problem is then sent to a device, such as a tablet, used by the technician who is to work on it.[47] Using a flexible interface, Predix helps the user overtake the problem, then provides all of the necessary context-specific information, and no more than what is necessary. GE is trying to squeeze out a 1% gain in efficiency. This sounds small, but "could mean something in the ballpark of $15 billion saved in jet fuel and other costs over just a handful of years."[48]

In science fiction movies, advanced functionality is the norm. However, the complexity of the Predix approach is staggering. The system needs to integrate diverse data:

- The behavior of the machine that indicates impending failure
- The magnitude of that behavior
- The tablet or other device being used by the technician
- The information the technician needs to resolve the problem
- The current status of problem resolution

With Predix, something radical is taking place. Data and computation become intermediaries between machine and mechanic—functioning as such because sensor technology can be comprehensively integrated with machinery.

GE sees its Predix system as offering value across industries and in a press release identifies two very different success stories,

> For St. Luke's Medical Center, which is using GE software to manage and analyze patient and equipment data, this means a 51-minute reduction in bed turnaround time and reduced patient wait times. Gol Airlines is using software to better track, analyze and adapt its flight routes and fuel consumption and predicts it will see $90 million in savings over the next five years.[49]

In fact, Predix solutions exist for oil and gas, aviation, rail transport, healthcare, power and water, and energy management.[50]

We covered package tracking earlier in this chapter. This ability, when matched to other data such as telemetry, boosts the efficiency of logistics. A package shipped using the US Postal Service has the option of being tracked for a small extra fee (one of the authors used the tracking number of his package to watch it wander to the wrong state for several days before arriving, due to the zip code being that of a previous address while the rest of the address was current). Courier services such as FedEx, DHL, and UPS also offer such tracking services, with that of UPS being used in our earlier example.

UPS has moved one step further and rolled out their On-Road Integrated Optimization and Navigation (ORION) system in late 2013 to minimize miles driven by its trucks. As a result, it expected to save 1.5 million gallons of fuel by the end of the year. The firm already saved 3 million gallons of fuel in a 2010–2012 pilot rollout. The company estimates it can save $50 million per year by shaving one mile from each driver's route. Aside from the cost savings, the program will also enable the company to better time deliveries for the roughly 6 million members of the UPS MyChoice program.[51]

Now, ORION uses 250 million address data points, map data, historical GPS data for similar routes, and package data, all being run on an algorithm, which is the equivalent of 1000 pages. The average route features 200,000 routing possibilities. Even though ORION does not yet incorporate up-to-date streaming data to provide insights into traffic conditions, weather, and other factors that could influence the route, it is already demonstrating the ability to improve the efficiency of drivers.[51]

We believe such systems will become more common and will incorporate further data points related to energy usage, the financial implications of current rates of breakdown, heat and humidity of the operating environment, and other factors that influence decisions made around timing of particular operations and maintenance, as well as which factors keep the machine running smoothly. In this way, data influence the best time to shut down the system for maintenance or which expenses related to maintaining the internal environment can be relaxed without reducing performance. Manufacturers could conduct better root-cause analysis of machine failures and logistics firms could better adjust for obstacles to ensure timely and reliable service.

PROCESS TRACKING AND AUTOMATION

In 1983, the US Patent Office awarded the patent for the first device to be named radio-frequency identification (RFID) to Charles Walton. RFID tags have become common enough that we do not even notice them. Have you ever had an item you just purchased set off a store's antitheft system guarding the doors? An improperly deactivated RFID tag caused the embarrassment that ensued. RFID tags can either be battery powered and detectable from several hundred meters or they may be powered by the presence of the reader's electromagnetic field, sending signals only as far as several feet.[52]

RFID tags are now used in logistics, manufacturing, and security. They track the path of items through warehouses and facilitate the billing of highway tolls. They are embedded into passports and ID security badges.

In north Texas, the North Texas Tollway Authority (NTTA) administers the tollways. Drivers who have an account with the NTTA receive a sticker containing an RFID chip, which they attach to their windshields. The NTTA strategically placed RFID readers on the on-ramps, off-ramps, and across the highways. Each time a car with one of these stickers passes below one of these readers, the car's presence creates a data point and the NTTA records the passage of the car, automatically deducting the toll.

In other words, the movement of a car creates a data point across a specific location. This triggers the withdrawal of funds from a customer account established with the NTTA, which creates another data point. When the system senses a particular account is deficient, it withdraws funds through the bank account or credit card of the vehicle owner, creating another data point. The withdrawal shows up on the driver's bank or credit card statement, creating another data point. The vehicle triggers the sensor once and precipitates a series of actions, each of which generates a data point. Hence, data feeds a system that keeps an extensive network of toll roads operating smoothly.

A different, but functionally similar, set of actions occurs with bar code readers, credit card swipers, motion detectors, and many thermometers and pressure gauges. We should understand the sensor, then, as a gateway between the sensed event or condition and the data system designed to track such events or conditions.

When we move directly into our discussion of big data, we will see that the data collected by sensors are frequently not recorded, and that recorded data are often unused. An organization may not record data for a variety of reasons:

- They already record too much data for the current storage systems to handle.
- They may use the sensors as a warning for the immediate presence of a particular event or threshold, with historical trends not viewed as important (think of the door dingers that were once common on the doors in stores, letting the staff know that a customer had just entered).
- Moving the data from temporary storage to permanent storage, such as from the laptop hard drive to the organization's servers, may not be a priority to management or staff.
- The organization may simply be unaware of the capabilities of the systems that it owns.

One of the strengths of big data systems occurs because we can integrate, analyze, and report on this sensor data and compare it to other data, thus allowing much insight into how processes are functioning. Both of the authors of this book are Six Sigma practitioners, and as such, understand the value of sufficient high-quality data in improving processes, whether as a means of increasing throughput or as a means of increasing quality.

The manner in which the NTTA uses data allows the efficient use of its toll roads. Regardless of whether a driver has a toll tag, there is no reason to stop at a tollbooth unless one is passing through the Dallas–Fort Worth Airport, where there are no toll booths. Those drivers with a toll tag enjoy a harmonious experience of driving without having to manually pay anything. Cameras identify those drivers without toll tags and photograph their license plates, after which they pay slightly more for using the road.

There is much to learn about using big data and sensors skillfully in other processes. A pull system, the most efficient system in Lean, can be automated using concepts similar to that used by the NTTA. We can streamline the layout of a warehouse or logistics network and we can scrutinize the security of a process in greater detail while minimizing bureaucratic roadblocks.

TOWARD A DEFINITION OF BIG DATA

Now we have a basic understanding of what big data is and from whence it arises. Let us try to define it.

One of the most common ways to describe big data is through the three Vs. These are volume, velocity, and variability. Sometimes we might include a fourth V, either variety or veracity. Let us take these apart and study them one at a time.

Big data processes large volumes of data by design; we measure the volumes in some cases reaching petabytes, but usually at several terabytes. A petabyte is 1 million GB, whereas a terabyte is 1000 GB. A gigabyte is greater than the amount stored on a standard CD. Facebook claims the largest Hadoop cluster in the world, weighing in at roughly 100 PB as of mid-2012.[53] As of late 2012, the Internet Archive, which strives to be a permanent record of Internet materials—whether text, audio, or visual—that would otherwise disappear in time, claimed to have approximately 10 PB of material on its servers.[54]

Two different but equally valid conceptions of velocity exist. One is the speed with which data arrive and the other is the speed with which we extract meaning. Let us study these separately. We can divide data into either streaming or static data. Algorithms using minimal human intervention are running rising amounts of trades of stocks, bonds, commodities, futures, and other investments. Algorithmic trading has even earned its place in the venue of the popular and thought-provoking series of TED talks.[55] Algorithmic trading relies on streaming data, so traders can understand movements in the market as they occur (and rely on static data to understand the consequences of analogous past events).[56]

Algorithmic trading is the use of computers to analyze relevant data points to gain advantage in terms of the velocity of data analyzed and the speed at which a trader can take action based on that analysis, often within microseconds (millionths of a second). Traders and their computers analyze the data almost as quickly as they emerge. An illustration closer to home of streaming data is the traction control on your car. As data from sensors feed the computer—providing insights into how the car interacts with the road—the car makes perspicacious real-time modifications. This establishes one way to think about velocity.

Static data includes the data that reside on the computer system of the department of motor vehicles in the state in which you have official residence (US drivers). We do not analyze static data when it materializes, but rather we store it as a resource in order to manage the comparatively slow process of tracking address changes and expiration dates. In your home, the archives of your taxes, projects, and family photos on your hard drive constitute static data. Yes, we update these data regularly, but we do not refresh them in real time.

As mentioned in the case of algorithmic trading, static data can inform how we use streaming data. In the field of predictive analytics, we find patterns by analyzing gargantuan quantities of static data to derive relationships from the data. We identify patterns and then seek for them in the new data that arrive—often streaming data—to anticipate problems or opportunities. An example of this usage is our discussion of sensors anticipating mechanical failures.

The other meaning of velocity relevant to big data is the need to expeditiously process these immense quantities of data, whether streaming or static. This requires a mix of flexibility and speed. When a web-based retailer offers suggestions for other products that may interest you, it will generally lose your sale if the software takes an unjustifiably long time to integrate your information and act. Whether you are at BN.com, Amazon.com, eBay, or Walmart.com, an e-commerce website will process data based on your activity and deliver you a response immediately. In these situations, the time and money relationship becomes apparent.

Also, antifraud measures used by credit card firms need high-speed processing and equally prompt action. We suggest criminals are unlikely to sit and wait for you to cancel your stolen cards before they use them. One of the authors was once fueling a rental car while traveling. The trip was outside of his usual travel routine, and the card was rejected at the pump. Frustrated, he started walking toward the gas station to complain about what appeared to be a malfunctioning card reader when his phone rang with an unfamiliar number. His credit card company already flagged this particular fill-up as suspicious and initiated a call to him. Responsiveness, too, is velocity. As we can see, the speed at which data are sought and integrated and the speed at which conclusions are drawn from them are interrelated in real-world applications. We could have swapped our examples for the two aspects of velocity without negatively affecting the applicability of those examples.

By design, the software upon which we build big data solutions incorporates data that are messy. Another word for this untidiness is variability. In some ways, this feature of big data is related to volume. The more data you have, the more likely it is there will be differences in format across sources.

It is expensive to normalize data, to make it neat. To do so requires the time of skilled knowledge workers and plenty of computer time and power. Think of how different systems may store customer names. A single customer may be entered differently by different sales contacts, becoming "John Doe," "J. Doe," "Doe, John," and "John Q. Doe", despite being the same person whose data are being collected multiple times by the same company. A standard database will not automatically lump these names together, so the data must be harmonized and very often vetted using other data sources, such as unique identifying numbers, to ensure that different people with similar names are not being confounded (confounding occurs when one value is indistinguishable from another value).

These large quantities of data are often not generated by the same systems. A big data solution will often pull together multiple data repositories, such as a firm's accounting package, its CRM software, its e-mail records, and its database of service calls. Organizations are beginning to understand the value of data that cannot be fit neatly into tables. Reports written in prose, quick e-mail messages, blizzards of tweets from angry or happy customers, and YouTube demonstrations are all valuable sources of data. All of these defy attempts to load them into standard database tables.

The three Vs illuminate big data and its characteristics, but they fall far short of a formal definition. The reason for the popularity of the three Vs is probably due in large part to this tendency of big data to elude a firm definition that encapsulates its diverse characteristics.

A 2011 paper by the McKinsey Global Institute describes big data thus:

> "Big data" refers to datasets whose size is beyond the ability of typical database software tools to capture, store, manage, and analyze. This definition is intentionally subjective and incorporates a moving definition of how big a dataset needs to be in order to be considered big data—i.e., we don't define big data in terms of being larger than a certain number of terabytes (thousands of gigabytes). We assume that, as technology advances over time, the size of datasets that qualify as big data will also increase. Also note that the definition can vary by sector, depending on what kinds of software tools are commonly available and what sizes of datasets are common in a particular industry. With those caveats, big data in many sectors today will range from a few dozen terabytes to multiple petabytes (thousands of terabytes).[57]

The authors of this definition understand the fuzzy boundaries dividing big data from other data storage and processing phenomena, but they take that subjectivity too far. While big data evolves, some characteristics of big data remain constant. That is what the three Vs capture. To be useful, a definition must confront both those aspects of big data that remain constant and those aspects that vary. Fuzziness is natural when trying to define a broad and complex phenomenon, but even so, this definition is fuzzy to the point of being nebulous.

IBM's definition is enlightening but limits itself to the nature of the data sources processed by big data systems:

> Every day, we create 2.5 quintillion bytes of data—so much that 90% of the data in the world today has been created in the last two years alone. This data comes from everywhere: sensors used to gather climate information, posts to social media sites, digital pictures and videos, purchase transaction records, and cell phone GPS signals to name a few. This data is big data.[25]

This approach is definition by example, but it does not discuss the tools used to make sense of big data and the characteristics captured by the three Vs. We find this unfortunate, as IBM is clearly an innovative firm operating on the cutting edge of these big data tools and will likely remain so for the near future.

Gartner builds on the three Vs and adds a "so what?" clause to the end of the definition: "Big data is high-volume, high-velocity and high-variety information assets that demand cost-effective, innovative forms of information processing for enhanced insight and decision making." This definition is definitely moving in the right direction, but it still does not provide a sense of big data and therefore needs further refinement.[58]

The introductory Hadoop course at Big Data University defines big data as "a term used to describe large collections of data (also known as data sets) that may be unstructured and grow so large and quickly that it is difficult to manage with regular database or statistics tools."[59] This interpretation conveys a real and concrete sense of big data.

Since we know big data is a difficult phenomenon to define, we proffer the following characterization:

> Big Data (n): (1) The proliferation of data, both structured and unstructured, as the result of exponential growth in the capabilities of computer processing power, data storage capacity, the use of computers to mediate transactions and social interactions, and the density of sensors, all at a decreasing cost. (2) The computer hardware and software infrastructure that has been created to quickly and accurately draw insights from large volumes of highly variable, and often unstructured, data appearing at a voluminous arrival rate. This is accomplished through methods including, but not limited to, distributed processing, in-memory data storage, job partitioning, parallel processing, and sparse array management.

We intend that this definition should address the data itself, as well as the hardware and software developed to cope with this data. Our take on the problem lacks some of the grace of the more succinct definitions, but we believe that ours provides a firm footing for further discussion. We intend it to provide rigor and stability as we explain more specifically how big data is the same and how it is different from what came before it.

PUTTING BIG DATA IN CONTEXT

The replacement of horse-drawn carriages by the automobile provides a convenient analogy to where big data currently stands in relation to older data analytics technologies. In fact, the automobile was once known as the "horseless carriage." As it evolved, it became clear that users required new approaches to steering, braking, and controlling acceleration. For a variety of reasons, the manufacturers maintained other aspects of the carriage, such as the physical size and the four wheels.

Early cars transformed recognizably from these carriages, but as cars began to outnumber horses, and as new ways of controlling the car were needed in the absence of the horse, the car evolved away from the general carriage appearance.

Many concepts from older paradigms of data management carry over to big data. The changes in most of these technologies are evolutionary rather than revolutionary; however, the organization of the systems and their use have changed in a much more disruptive manner. In our analogy, the big data car is becoming a distinct technology at this stage, but one can still comprehend its carriage lineage. Where our analogy breaks down is that we should not expect the carriage to become obsolete, regardless of how far the car and the carriage diverge technologically.

The most common exemplars of data for business, company data warehouses, accounting packages, and enterprise resource planning (ERP) systems function as the basis for business intelligence, and this business intelligence performs as expected: it reports key performance indicators programmed as the result of careful study followed by coding. This paradigm is too rigid for many of the jobs that data are now doing, but it is not going away in the near future—nor should it. The reason for the longevity of this approach is that it is extremely effective at performing its mission. It is reliable and repeatable and provides a single right answer to common questions.

Big data's strength is in looking for relationships among huge numbers of variables that may not map injectively to each other (injective mappings are one-to-one). Big data techniques process data more quickly than is possible in the traditional data warehouse. Moreover, the creation of a new big data system is significantly faster and less expensive than the creation of a new data warehouse. It is also easier to reconfigure after it has been created and much more immediate in delivering results. Since a big data system does not incorporate the rigid procedures found in an ERP system or accounting package, it is ill-suited to replace such systems.

Your big data system may well pull information from ERP and CRM software packages, but this should only be used in analytics or exploration for which this type of data is valuable. A big data system that pulls in your firm's financial information is well suited for identification of inefficiencies and fraud, but it is completely unsuited to ever becoming your accounting system of record. Where big data can help you with that data is to identify factors that are associated with waste, risk, or opportunity. If we consistently find a particular variable or relationship to be of great value, then we can add it to your ERP or CRM software as a new key performance indicator (KPI). In this way, big data can inform the use of your more traditional systems.

As big data can so easily integrate different formats, it can also erode silos within your organization. Big data systems that enable the discovery of different information are ideal for placing all of your information about a customer, product, or market in a single place where your managers, salespeople, or engineers can find a tremendous amount of diverse information without sinking time into searching different databases and piecing information together.

KEY CONCEPTS OF BIG DATA AND THEIR CONSEQUENCES

The capabilities enabled by big data invert the old methods of data analysis. We search colossal quantities of data and then find emergent explanations for relationships. There is tremendous value and risk to this approach. A team from IBM estimates that 80% of data generated are unstructured and unused. Unstructured data includes research papers, social media feeds, and web searches. These sources share little in common in terms of formatting. They require greater computing power to use in a data management system. These data now form the core from which we refine insight. Big data also grow at 15 times the rate at which structured, tabulated data grow. The inversion of the old methods enables the use of these data. Without the big data approach, it would be impractical to analyze these data and use them to develop insights for your organization.[28]

The IBM team argues that big data solutions are of greatest benefit under particular circumstances. It states (direct quote)

- Big data solutions are ideal for analyzing not only raw structured data, but also semistructured and unstructured data from a wide variety of sources.

- Big data solutions are ideal when all, or most, of the data needs to be analyzed versus a sample of the data; or a sampling of data isn't nearly as effective as a larger set of data from which to derive analysis.
- Big data solutions are ideal for iterative and exploratory analysis when business measures on data are not predetermined.[28]

The IBM authors repeat a point we made earlier in this chapter. Scrubbing data is expensive, but scrubbed data are valuable. If a company wishes to recall records of servicing previously conducted on a particular vehicle, a relational database makes much more sense than does a big data solution. Big data allows the vetting of data to see what exactly should be scrubbed and what would be a waste of resources to scrub.[28]

Before, when a firm wanted to integrate a new data source, it had to expend effort on putting data that could not be used in the original format into a standardized, computer-readable format even if most of that data turned out to be of no practical use. After all, it is only when it was analyzed that the useful and nonuseful could be distinguished and separated. Big data avoids this expense, and its flexibility functions well to drive decisions as to which data are worth cleansing and which data are not.

Big data is ideal for nuanced comparisons of distributions between populations or samples, for example:

- How do apartment dwellers differ from homeowners in the sports they watch and pay for?
- How do traffic patterns on our website differ for those who click through from different categories of news articles?
- Which policing methods are most effective in lowering property crime in our city?

Here are some examples of scenarios for predictive analytics:

- What are the purchasing patterns to indicate that a female customer is probably pregnant?
- What variables measured by the sensors inside this machine predict when it is at high risk of malfunctioning?
- How much more likely is a customer to default on the loan he holds with us if a new charge appears on his credit report?
- What factors indicate a high risk that a high-value customer may move to a competitor?

Sentiment analysis through the monitoring of unstructured and semis-tructured online posts yields these questions:

- How is sentiment toward our brand evolving in response to our cooperation with hurricane relief efforts?
- Is our proactive, Twitter-based approach to dealing with our recent recall helping control the damage from our recent public relations flub?

Complex combinatorial calculations where the optimal solution is effectively impossible to find might produce these questions:

- How could I better route our aircraft, taking into account travel patterns, weather, and the competition's current routing?
- What factors should play a role in my trading algorithm, and how should I weight them?

We advise a word of caution. Statistical errors are a small but real danger when analyzing the relationships between and among a small handful of variables. Under the old paradigm, this is how we might conduct such an analysis. It was necessary to posit a question to answer and to deliberately seek the data to answer the question.

We just argued, though, that one of the promising things about big data is that it turns this model on its head. The approach is promising in that relationships that would remain hidden before can now surface. It is in this promise that the danger of big data lurks. When we investigate the causes and relationships between dozens or more attributes, we will almost certainly develop some statistical errors. In fact, when we run comparisons of large numbers of variables, it is entirely possible that a majority of the relationships we discover will be erroneous.

Is this a reason to give up, to throw away big data as too imperfect a tool to be of use? No. It is a reason, though, to understand big data with sufficient depth that we can ask difficult questions of our in-house analysts and firms from which we purchase services relying on big data. As we will see in our chapters on data and on statistics, big data confronts many of the same issues with statistically significant, yet meaningless, results that have recently caused embarrassment to the scientific profession. Scientists are engaged in a vigorous and meaningful discussion of how to control this problem. The scientific method has survived embarrassing gaffes and brought us the moon landing, the eradication of smallpox, and unprecedented agricultural productivity. Big data, too, will survive.

SUMMARY

We have looked at the technological developments that, together, have made big data a possibility. These developments have been the simultaneous growth of processing power, data storage, and the data itself. As the ability to process data grew, along with the data that needed to be processed, we found new methods to handle diverse data types and messy data, often as the result of technologies created to bring order to the Internet. Big data is not an entirely new technology, but rather a novel application of these existing technological trends.

Most data collected by an organization remain unused. In our discussion, we saw how big data is not yet employed to its full potential. We witnessed how much data are truly being generated, some of which are recorded and some of which are not. We also examined how some industries are beginning to put big data approaches to work in examining these data. By taking such a look at one's own industry or organization, it is possible to discern the benefits of big data.

Finally, we stepped back and observed how big data inverts the old paradigm of "call and response" databases. With big data, it is more common to look for relationships and then explain them. This approach holds the promise of revealing novel and meaningful relationships that would otherwise remain undiscovered, but it also means that erroneous revelations are a near certainty.

REFERENCES

1. Moore, G. Cramming more components onto integrated circuits. *Electronics* 38(8): 1965. http://download.intel.com/museum/Moores_Law/Articles-Press_Releases/Gordon_Moore_1965_Article.pdf. Accessed June 21, 2013.
2. Texas Instruments. The chip that Jack built. Texas Instruments. http://www.ti.com/corp/docs/kilbyctr/jackbuilt.shtml. Accessed June 22, 2013.
3. Bardeen, J. and Brattain, W.H. Three-electrode circuit element utilizing semiconductive materials. Patent 2,524,035. Issued October 2, 1950. http://www.freepatentsonline.com/2524035.html. Accessed June 22, 2013.
4. Shockley, W. Circuit element utilizing semiconductive material. Patent 2,569,347. Issued September 25, 1951. http://www.freepatentsonline.com/2569347.html. Accessed June 22, 2013.
5. Kaku, M. *Physics of the Future*, pp. 37–41. New York: Doubleday, 2011.
6. UPS. Data centers fact sheet. UPS. http://www.pressroom.ups.com/Fact+Sheets/UPS+Data+Centers+Fact+Sheet. Accessed July 10, 2013.

7. Miller, R. Google data center FAQ. Data Center Knowledge. iNET Interactive. May 15, 2012. http://www.datacenterknowledge.com/archives/2012/05/15/google-data-center-faq/. Accessed July 12, 2013.

8. Google. Data center locations. Google. http://www.google.com/about/datacenters/inside/locations/index.html. Accessed July 12, 2013.

9. Newsroom. *Facebook*. https://newsroom.fb.com/Key-Facts. Accessed March 8, 2014.

10. Metz, C. Facebook lets you spy on its data centers. *Wired*. April 18, 2013. http://www.wired.com/wiredenterprise/2013/04/facebook-data-center-dashboard/?utm_source=Contextly&utm_medium=RelatedLinks&utm_campaign=Previous. Accessed July 12, 2013.

11. Miller, R. Inside Facebook's North Carolina data center. *Data Center Knowledge*. December 3, 2012. http://www.datacenterknowledge.com/inside-facebooks-north-carolina-data-center/. Accessed July 12, 2013.

12. Metz, C. Facebook catapults $1.5 billion data center into Iowa. *Wired*. April 22, 2013. http://www.wired.com/wiredenterprise/2013/04/facebook-iowa-data-center/. Accessed July 12, 2013.

13. Miller, R. Facebook goes global with data center in Sweden. *Data Center Knowledge*. October 27, 2011. http://www.datacenterknowledge.com/archives/2011/10/27/facebook-goes-global-with-data-center-in-sweden/. Accessed July 12, 2013.

14. Dongarra, J. Visit to the National University for Defense Technology Changsha, China. *Netlib*. http://www.netlib.org/utk/people/JackDongarra/PAPERS/tianhe-2-dongarra-report.pdf. Accessed June 23, 2013.

15. Metz, C. Physicists foretell quantum computer with single-atom transistor. *Wired*. February 20, 2012. http://www.wired.com/wiredenterprise/2012/02/sa-transistor/. Accessed June 23, 2013.

16. McMillan, R. Google, NASA open new lab to kick tires on quantum computer. *Wired*. May 16, 2013. http://www.wired.com/wiredenterprise/2013/05/google-dwave/. Accessed June 23, 2013.

17. Goda, K. and Kitsuregawa, M. The history of storage systems. *Proceedings of the IEEE*. 100, May 13, 2012. http://ieeexplore.ieee.org/stamp/stamp.jsp?tp=&arnumber=6182574. Accessed July 1, 2013.

18. History of IBM magnetic disk drives. *Wikipedia*. http://en.wikipedia.org/wiki/IBM_350#IBM_350. Accessed July 5, 2013.

19. The IBM 350 RAMAC disk file: Designated an international historic landmark by the American Society of Mechanical Engineers. *The American Society of Mechanical Engineers*. February 27, 1984. http://www.magneticdiskheritagecenter.org/MDHC/RAMACBrochure.pdf. Accessed July 5, 2013.

20. Desktop HDD Data Sheet. *Seagate Technology*. http://www.seagate.com/files/staticfiles/docs/pdf/datasheet/disc/desktop-hdd-data-sheet-ds1770-1-1212us.pdf. Accessed July 6, 2013.

21. Seagate Desktop HDD 4 TB SATA 6Gb/s NCQ 64MB Cache 3.5-Inch Internal Bare Drive ST4000DM000. Amazon.com. http://www.amazon.com/Seagate-Desktop-3-5-Inch-Internal-ST4000DM000/dp/B00B99JU4S/ref=sr_1_1?s=electronics&ie=UTF8&qid=1373165711&sr=1-1&keywords=hard+drive+ST4000DM000. Accessed July 6, 2013.

22. Coughlin Associates. Data storage consulting. http://www.tomcoughlin.com/. Accessed July 5, 2013.

23. Goda, K. and Kitsuregawa, M. IBM 1301 disk storage unit. IBM. 2012. http://www-03.ibm.com/ibm/history/exhibits/storage/storage_1301.html. Accessed July 5, 2013.

24. IBM 1301 disk storage unit. *Computer History Museum*. http://www.computerhistory.org/revolution/memory-storage/8/259/1041. Accessed July 5, 2013.

25. IBM. What is big data? IBM. http://www-01.ibm.com/software/data/bigdata/. Accessed June 26, 2013.

26. Goda, K. and Kitsuregawa, M. IBM 3340 direct access storage facility. *IBM*. 2012. http://www-03.ibm.com/ibm/history/exhibits/storage/storage_3340.html. Accessed July 5, 2013.

27. Ouchi, W.K. System for recovering data stored in failed memory unit. Patent 4,092,732. May 30, 1978. http://www.freepatentsonline.com/4092732.html. Accessed July 6, 2013.

28. Eaton, C., DeRoos, D., Deutch, T., Lapis, G., and Zikopoulos, P. *Understanding Big Data: Analytics for Enterprise Class Hadoop and Streaming Data*, p. 30. McGraw Hill, 2012.

29. Gruly, B. and Singh, S.D. Deere's big green profit machine. *Bloomberg Businessweek*. July 5, 2012. http://www.businessweek.com/articles/2012-07-05/deeres-big-green-profit-machine. Accessed June 17, 2013.

30. The Climate Corporation introduces total weather insurance. *AgriMarketing*. Climate Corporation news release. November 2, 2011. http://www.agrimarketing.com/s/70796. Accessed March 10, 2014.

31. 20/20 SeedSense. Precision planting web site. http://www.precisionplanting.com/Products/20-20-SeedSense/Performance.aspx. Accessed March 10, 2014.

32. Tarter, S. Bringing "smart iron" to ag tech. *Peoria Journal Star*. July 7, 2012. http://www.pjstar.com/x1052259649/Bringing-smart-iron-to-ag-tech. Accessed March 10, 2014.

33. Blickenstorfer, C.H. The computer in your car: What is OBD-II (OnBoard Diagnostics)? *Pen Computing*. http://www.pencomputing.com/frames/obd2.html. Accessed July 21, 2013.

34. Danaher, D., Ball, J., Buss, T., and Kittel, M. Operation of the Eaton VORAD collision warning system and analysis of the recorded data. June 14, 2012. Veritech Consulting Engineering, LLC. http://www.veritecheng.com/eaton-vorad-collision-warning-system/. Accessed July 21, 2013.

35. Diagnostic tools: Help eliminate truck vibration problems. http://www.eaton.com/Eaton/ProductsServices/Truck/DiagnosticTools/index.htm. Accessed July 21, 2013.

36. Webster, A. Mercedes truck uses GPS to predict what's ahead and shifts gears to save fuel. *The Verge*. May 21, 2012. http://www.theverge.com/2012/5/21/3034462/mercedes-actros-truck-gps-fuel-efficiency. Accessed July 21, 2013.

37. Progressive. How Snapshot works. http://www.progressive.com/auto/snapshot-how-it-works/. Accessed March 8, 2014.

38. Holiday drivers spend nearly a quarter of their time in the car idling: Progressive Insurance analyzes more than 9 billion miles of driving data to identify best and worst days for holiday errands. Progressive website. December 17, 2013. http://www.progressive.com/newsroom/article/2013/December/holiday-driving/. Accessed March 8, 2014.

39. Telematics: How big data is transforming the auto insurance industry. SAS white paper. 2013. http://www.sas.com/resources/whitepaper/wp_56343.pdf. Accessed March 8, 2014.

40. Satter, R. Report: Spies use smartphone apps to track people. Associated Press. January 27, 2014. http://bigstory.ap.org/article/report-spies-use-smartphone-apps-track-people. Accessed March 8, 2014.

41. Koerner, B. How do cell phones reveal your location? *Slate*. May 12, 2003. http://www.slate.com/articles/news_and_politics/explainer/2003/05/how_do_cell_phones_reveal_your_location.html. Accessed July 20, 2013.

42. Davis, C. Will Google and Nest make power companies more innovative? *Greentech Efficiency*. March 12, 2014. http://www.greentechmedia.com/articles/read/Will-Google-Plus-Nest-Make-Power-Companies-More-Innovative. Accessed March 17, 2014.

43. Path Intelligence website. About. http://www.pathintelligence.com/about/. Accessed March 12, 2014.

44. Path Intelligence website. Privacy. http://www.pathintelligence.com/technology/privacy/. Accessed March 12, 2014.

45. Vanderbilt, T. The science behind the Netflix algorithms that decide what you'll watch next. *Wired*. August 7, 2013. http://www.wired.com/underwire/2013/08/qq_netflix-algorithm/. Accessed March 16, 2014.

46. Wortham, J. Will Google's personal assistant be creepy or cool? Bits blog. *The New York Times*. June 28, 2012. http://bits.blogs.nytimes.com/2012/06/28/will-googles-personal-assistant-be-creepy-or-cool/. Accessed July 20, 2013.

47. General Electric. GE's new monitoring & analysis software suite maximizes business value with proven analytic capabilities and access to data in the cloud. General Electric. June 20, 2013. http://www.ge-ip.com/news/ge-s-new-monitoring-analysis-software-suite-maximizes-business-value-with-proven-analytic-capabilities-and-access-to-data-in-the-cloud/n3099. Accessed July 6, 2013.

48. Vanhemert, K. GE's radical software helps jet engines fix themselves. *Wired*. October 10, 2013. http://www.wired.com/design/2013/10/three-design-trends-ges-using-to-make-software-for-jet-engines-and-wind-turbines/. Accessed March 8, 2014.

49. General Electric. GE launches 14 new industrial Internet predictivity technologies to improve outcomes for aviation, oil & gas, transportation, healthcare and energy. GE Press Release. October 9, 2013. http://www.genewscenter.com/Press-Releases/GE-Launches-14-New-Industrial-Internet-Predictivity-Technologies-to-Improve-Outcomes-For-Aviation-O-430f.aspx. Accessed March 16, 2014.

50. GE. Productivity products fact sheet. http://files.gereports.com/wp-content/uploads/2013/10/24_PRODUCTS-_FACT_SHEET.pdf. Accessed March 16, 2014.

51. Konrad, A. Meet ORION, software that will save UPS millions by improving drivers' routes. *Forbes*. November 1, 2013. http://www.forbes.com/sites/alexkonrad/2013/11/01/meet-orion-software-that-will-save-ups-millions-by-improving-drivers-routes/. Accessed March 16, 2014.

52. Wikipedia. Radio-frequency identification. Wikipedia. http://en.wikipedia.org/wiki/RFID. Accessed March 17, 2014.

53. Ryan, A. Under the hood: Hadoop distributed filesystem reliability with Namenode and Avatarnode. June 13, 2012. https://www.facebook.com/notes/facebook-engineering/under-the-hood-hadoop-distributed-filesystem-reliability-with-namenode-and-avata/10150888759153920. Accessed June 17, 2013.

54. Internet Archive Blogs. 10,000,000,000,000,000 bytes archived! October 26, 2012. http://blog.archive.org/2012/10/26/10000000000000000-bytes-archived/. Accessed October 4, 2014.

55. Slavin, K. How algorithms shape our world. *TED*. http://www.ted.com/talks/kevin_slavin_how_algorithms_shape_our_world.html. Accessed June 26, 2013.

56. Petabox 4. http://archive.org/web/petabox.php. Accessed March 12, 2014.

57. Manyika, J., Chui, M., Brown, B., Bughin, J., Dobbs, R., Roxburgh, C., and Hung Byers, A. Big data: The next frontier for innovation, competition, and productivity. McKinsey Global Institute. May 2011. http://www.mckinsey.com/insights/business_technology/big_data_the_next_frontier_for_innovation. Accessed March 12, 2014.

58. Gartner. Big Data. IT Glossary. http://www.gartner.com/it-glossary/big-data/. Accessed March 12, 2014.

59. Chaudhri, A. What is Hadoop? Big Data University. Online course downloaded from www.bigdatauniversity.com. Accessed July 12, 2013.

3

Hadoop

Hadoop is the primary standard for distributed computing for at least two reasons: (1) it has the power and the tools to manage distributed nodes and clusters, and (2) it is free from the Apache Foundation. MapReduce and Hadoop Distributed File System (HDFS) are the two different parts of Hadoop. Apache lists the following projects as related to Hadoop:[1]

- Ambari: A web-based tool for provisioning, managing, and monitoring Apache Hadoop clusters, which includes support for HDFS, Hadoop MapReduce, Hive, HCatalog, HBase, ZooKeeper, Oozie, Pig, and Sqoop
- Avro: A data serialization system
- Cassandra: A scalable multimaster database with no single points of failure and excellent performance
- Chukwa: A data collection system for managing large distributed systems
- HBase: A scalable, distributed database that supports structured data storage for large tables
- Hive: A data warehouse infrastructure that provides data summarization and ad hoc querying
- Mahout: A scalable machine learning and data mining library
- Pig: A high-level dataflow language and execution framework for parallel computation
- ZooKeeper: A high-performance coordination service for distributed applications

Advantages:

- We can distribute data and computation.
- Tasks become independent; hence, the tasks are independent.

- We can more easily handle partial failure (entire nodes can fail and restart).
- We avoid crawling panics from failure and tolerant synchronous distributed systems.
- We can use hypothetical implementation to work around "laggards."
- It has a simple programming model—the end-user programmer must only write MapReduce tasks.
- The system has relatively flat scalability (adding more subsystems results in real improvements).

The name Hadoop has gained ubiquity since Doug Cutting affixed the name of his son's toy elephant to the application he created. Hadoop is based on two now-famous papers published by researchers at Google, "Bigtable: A Distributed Storage System for Structured Data"[2] and "MapReduce: Simplified Data Processing on Large Clusters."[3] While the specific application of the concepts underlying these papers will be discussed later in this chapter, it is important to note that the product is an open-system application using the Google-tested ideas to power Internet firms as well to drive enterprises managing large quantities of data internally. Of course, a substantial array of support businesses have arisen to provide enterprises with the technical knowledge needed to install Hadoop expeditiously and to provide a meaningful set or subset of useful support tools.

The Apache Software Foundation, a nonprofit organization of developers, supports Hadoop along with other products. Because Hadoop is open source, there are many firms that contribute to its development, including Yahoo!, IBM, and Facebook. In fact, Facebook's Hadoop cluster, with 30 PB in storage (as of 2011),[4] is believed to be the world's largest data farm (a metaphor for huge arrays of clusters).

What is this Hadoop, how does it work, and why has it spread faster than clever cat photos on Facebook? Let us start with why it has spread. It has spread because it is the right solution to the data needs of the modern organization. In an earlier discussion, we covered how the spread of sensors and the growth of computers as mediators of relationships and transactions have fueled the growth of data. We also touched on "the three *V*'s": volume, velocity, and variety. Much as there are fish that thrive in the depths of the ocean, where common sense would tell us that life is impossible, Hadoop thrives on resolving data issues that have confounded the genius of programmers since the dawn of computation. We would like to note that distributed computing existed before Hadoop; for example, a well-known example of early-in-the-game ray tracing (seen by one of us) by the long-since defunct Apollo Computer, Inc., used an array of Apollo workstations to divide and conquer.

What is the other reason for the spread of Hadoop? We have alluded to the freeware nature of the base software. Of course Hadoop is much like one of our ironic comments regarding the statistical R language: The code is free, but the books to explain it will cost you hundreds of dollars! In the case of Hadoop, a substantial amount of information technology maturity is required to install it efficiently and effectively. Executives and managers should consider outside support when installing and implementing a Hadoop cluster (we discuss vendors later in the book).

POWER THROUGH DISTRIBUTION

The Cold War is remembered as a time of tension between East and West, the Soviet Union with its Warsaw Pact allies and the United States with its NATO allies, communism and capitalism. The world hung in a balance of nuclear terror. This terror had its own delicious acronym, MAD, referring to "mutually assured destruction." Many assumed that a military confrontation was inevitable. Then it ended.

This view contains much truth, but also glaring errors and omissions. From a geopolitical point of view, this version of events ignores the role of Asia, Africa, and Latin America in shaping this conflict. It also ignores the lesson we intend to illustrate here. Decentralization, properly organized, is more dynamic, more resilient, and quicker to respond than centralization is. The Eastern bloc countries, with their all-powerful communist parties, could not respond to changes with the agility of their Western bloc adversaries.

The Western bloc countries, in fact, held specific key advantages that the Eastern bloc could not match: Their economies could adapt more easily. Decentralization became a form of strength; if a key company disappeared, other firms filled the needs created by users and consumers. Freed of the blockage created by centralized control, goods and services moved more efficiently. Multiple small firms operating independently near their customers could deliver their goods more quickly and efficiently than remote, state-run behemoths.

Analogies can be stretched to the point of breaking. Hadoop is not the cure for all computational ills. You definitely do not want to build your company's enterprise resource planning (ERP) around Hadoop. But, for diverse and loosely structured data (and massive amounts of it), Hadoop's advantage derives from strengths that are analogous to those that the Western bloc used to its advantage over the Eastern bloc.

In order to understand this point, let us dig into the structure of Hadoop—how data is stored and used. Let us explore the HDFS (Figure 3.1).

What we see in this instance, we refer to as a "Hadoop cluster." It is a group of servers functioning like a colony of bees. Each server has its role. A program written in distributed frameworks other than HDFS may require large amounts of refactoring when scaling from 10 to 100 or 1000 machines. Imagine writing a 200-page book, then creating the index and table of contents. Now add in another 200 or 400 pages. The changes in the book will go well beyond simply adding the new pages. You will need to change the contents, the index, the numbering, the alignment of where the pages align with the photographs (as photographs usually either appear in special pages in the center of the book or else in sections evenly interspersed throughout the book), and any references to earlier or to upcoming arguments in the book. Now imagine scaling a computer cluster. You add in new machines, and now you must integrate them. This may require rewriting the program several times.

Hadoop, however, is specifically designed to have a very flat scalability curve. Returning to our book example, HDFS is able to function like a program that automatically updates the spacing and references within your text as you write it. Hadoop, then, scales up with minimal effort.

Under a more rigid database structure, fundamental design elements may also put an upper bound on the scale to which the application can grow. Because of its architecture, Hadoop is much easier to scale up without encountering performance issues. After a Hadoop program is written

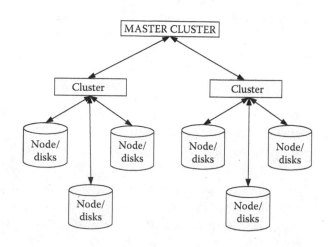

FIGURE 3.1
Hadoop architecture.

and is functioning on ten nodes, very little—if any—work is required for that same program to run on a much larger amount of hardware. Orders of magnitude of growth can be managed with little rework required for your applications. The underlying Hadoop platform will manage the data and hardware resources and provide dependable performance growth proportionate to the number of machines available.

There is a caveat, and that has to do with size. This is not a problem at the macro scale, but rather the micro. Executing Hadoop on a limited amount of data on a small number of nodes may not result in stellar performance. As Hadoop is designed for large-scale data management and analysis, the overhead involved in starting Hadoop programs is relatively high. Other parallel/distributed programming paradigms such as message passing interface (MPI) may perform much better on two, four, or perhaps up to a dozen machines. Though the effort of coordinating work among a small number of machines may be better performed by such systems, the price paid in performance and engineering effort as the system grows will likely increase in a manner disproportionate to the capacity added. If a system is intended to remain small, then Hadoop may not be the best option. If the system will grow, Hadoop is a good bet.

Common sense tells us that as our quantity of data increases, we will need more storage. Since we are storing our data on servers, and data require capacity, more data will require more servers. In that sense, Hadoop's system of storing files across servers is a function of necessity. But it is not merely a function of necessity; it is also the source of Hadoop's power.

We have already discussed striping as it relates to redundant array of independent disks (RAID) storage as well as how Hadoop uses it. That is one source of Hadoop's power. It can read and write data rapidly.

The other way that Hadoop draws power from its structure is that it does not move that data, once it is retrieved, to a central location to process it— instead, it processes data on the servers. Let us back up and examine this. Imagine you have a call center that processes customer service calls every day, and you want to know what percentage of customers who call in hang up before they reach a customer service representative. You will want to slice this number thinly and precisely in order to understand the characteristics of the customers and the characteristics of the call. Examples of this may be:

- Do impatient customers, such as those who press the 0 key on the phone repeatedly, differ from customers who do not, in terms of hanging up early or not hanging up early?

- Do customers who speak Spanish differ from those who do not?
- Do callers who hang up early call back?
- How do the customers who hang up and call back differ in obtaining a successful resolution from those customers who do not hang up? How do they differ in how much time they stay on the phone?

Skillful data analysis will push this line of investigation further, comparing call center results to any possible precursor and follow-up behaviors that tie to customer retention and the costs of keeping or losing the customer. In our example, we will simplify our analysis and just ask what the overall percentage is of customers who hang up the phone before reaching a customer service representative. We will compare two groups: One will be made up of those who receive regular updates, such as, "You are caller number four. A representative will be with you shortly. Your estimated wait time is 45 seconds." The others will be those who hear only easy-listening music.

Around 10,000 calls are received a day, and Hadoop will scour records going back 1000 days to look for the average hang-up rates for each group, comparing about 10 million records. The obvious way to handle such a problem is to call up all of the relevant records, load them into the computer, process them, and then spit out an answer; however, this is not how Hadoop approaches the problem.

Hadoop has a processor on each of its servers. It takes the processing to the data, rather than bringing the data to the processor. Imagine that Hadoop needs to pull this information off four different servers. Each server will have approximately 2,500,000 records in storage. Each Hadoop server in the cluster will break apart each relevant record into those in which the caller heard the recorded voice providing information, and those in which the caller heard the music. We will call these "information" and "music." After separating these calls into their groups, Hadoop will arrive at the mean percent of callers who hang up early for each group as well as the sample size (Figure 3.2).

Then, Hadoop will combine the output into one result that can be used as the basis for making decisions. This process is illustrated in Figure 3.3. The mechanism by which Hadoop delivers quicker results is ingenious.

FIGURE 3.2
Start of activity on Hadoop using MapReduce.

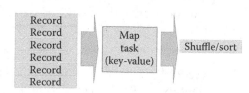

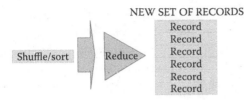

NEW SET OF RECORDS

FIGURE 3.3
Hadoop/MapReduce conclusion.

Instead of extracting data from one storage device, it works with many that operate in parallel. By sending the processing to the data instead of the data to the processing, Hadoop avoids clogging its arteries with data. The processing request travels down, and the result travels up. It also avoids overloading a central server with all of the processing.

This decentralization is also key to how Hadoop scales up so easily. When a new server is added to store more data, more processing power is simultaneously added. The addition of storage results in the parallel growth of processing power. This is the key to multipetabyte server clusters running Hadoop.

Cost Effectiveness of Hadoop

It is easy to think of price as an indicator of quality. That is partially true, but sometimes good things come from inexpensive packages. Think of cars nowadays. There was once a time when Japanese cars were laughed at. In the United States, Toyota was considered a joke when its cars first entered the market in 1957. Remember that this was the year of one of the most recognizable and iconic cars in American history, the famed 1957 Chevy. It took a while for the Japanese import to gain traction in the American market. It did catch on though. And, when it caught on, something important happened. People stopped laughing.

Toyota is forever linked to concept of *kaizen*, a Japanese word translated as "improvement." At Toyota, kaizen was not a buzzword. It was a set of specific practices that have developed into what we now know as lean manufacturing. By the early twenty-first century, this method had conquered the factories of car manufacturers worldwide.

Why is kaizen important to a discussion of Hadoop? It is important primarily through analogy. Toyota showed that one of the lowest-priced competitors could compete on quality by avoiding monolithic manufacturing devices and practices. Hadoop operates on a different set of principles, that of open-source software; yet, the idea of avoiding monolithic computing hardware is a key component of the Hadoop approach.

Hadoop is designed for inexpensive deployment. In fact, Hadoop itself is free (with caveats). It is open source. Open-source software is developed by a community, often administered by a nonprofit organization, and distributed at either no cost or at a minimal cost. This is not to say that there are not costs to running Hadoop. There are. There are just no costs in obtaining your copy of Hadoop from the Apache Software Foundation.

Setting up Hadoop is a quick process compared to putting together a data warehouse. Configuring the data and meshing together the data from different sources is a much quicker process than is the process of planning and implementing a more structured data warehouse. However, just because we *can* implement a loosely structured environment does not mean we *should* implement a loosely structured environment.

Hadoop is designed to run on inexpensive servers often referred to as *commodity servers*. Since the servers used are low cost and therefore often lack the reliability of high-end servers, redundancy is central to Hadoop's organization. These commodity servers do not even need to be uniform. As nodes need to be added to the Hadoop cluster, different models and brands can be integrated.

Earlier in this book, we described the concept of striping. Remember that striping is the splitting up of a file into multiple parts. Each part then resides on a different disk. A large file can be accessed at many points simultaneously and then reassembled, making it possible to pull up and process large files very quickly.

However, without redundancy, a single disk crash would wipe out the usefulness of many files. Again, imagine that you have three disks. Let us say that each disk has one half of a terabyte of capacity. You also have three files, each taking up almost exactly one half of a terabyte. If you have one file per disk and no redundancy, it will take you much longer to access a file than if you stripe a file across disks, but a disk crashing will only destroy one of your files. If you stripe each file across all three disks, with one third of each file located on each disk, a disk crash will destroy all of your files. Therefore, having each file redundantly striped across multiple disks means that a crash will leave your files intact. You will need to replace the lost disk, and it will be repopulated from the other disks that were backing up its information. In Hadoop, files are striped both within a server and across servers, preferably across server racks. As maddening as it is to think of buying multiple disks to replicate the same task, it is not money wasted. Hadoop handles huge amounts of data quickly.

That speed is gained through striping. That striping creates vulnerability to data loss. That threat of data loss leads to redundancy. That redundancy means that the servers need to be inexpensive. Because an inexpensive server may not be as reliable as an expensive server, redundancy is all that much more important. Because of the redundancy, the risk of losing a sufficient number of servers to cost you your data is, barring a freak incident or catastrophe, very small.

And, this is the kicker: Despite the seemingly convoluted logic of this paragraph, the system works. Hadoop is a safe and inexpensive solution when large quantities of diverse and messy data must be held safely and used easily. Hadoop has become nearly synonymous with big data in the minds of many.

NOT EVERY PROBLEM IS A NAIL

If Hadoop is such a panacea, why doesn't everyone use it? Because it is not a panacea. It is a specific tool for a specific job. Just as a hammer is tremendously useful for many things, from separating loose parts that are rusted together, to making noise, to pounding nails, a hammer has its limits. A large enough hammer can break boards, but hammers are useless for cleanly cutting those boards.

Hadoop does not only have its technical limitations, it also has hidden costs. Earlier, we stated that Hadoop is free. That is technically true, but there are still costs involved.

Some Technical Aspects

As powerful as it is, Hadoop and its ecosystem have some issues, good and bad:

Advantages

- HDFS stores large amounts of information.
- HDFS is simple and has a robust coherency model (it should store data reliably).
- HDFS is scalable (growing gracefully), with fast access to information.
- It is also possible to serve many clients by adding more devices to the cluster.

- HDFS integrates with MapReduce (the standard method in big data for a "divide and conquer" method of deconstructing and reassembling data problems), allowing data to be read and computed on locally when possible.
- HDFS provides streaming read performance.
- Hadoop writes data to the HDFS once and then reads it several times.
- The overhead of caching—temporary high speed storage—aids in avoiding rereading from the HDFS source.
- Fault tolerance occurs by detecting faults and applying quick, automatic recovery.
- Hadoop has portability across heterogeneous commodity hardware and operating systems (making hardware and associated operating systems barely relevant).
- Hadoop is economical because it can distribute data and processes across clusters of commodity personal computers.
- It is efficient because it distributes data and the logic to process that data in parallel on nodes where we find the data.
- It has high reliability by automatically maintaining multiple copies of data and automatically redeploying processing logic in the event of failures (we call this redundancy).
- HDFS is a block-structured file system—each file is broken into blocks of a fixed size and these blocks are stored across a cluster of one or more machines with data storage capacity.
- The user has the option to write MapReduce programs in Java, a popular computing language with free and open-source development systems.
- It can be offered as an on-demand service; for example as part of Amazon's EC2 Cluster computing service, a component of Amazon Web Services.

Disadvantages

- It is rough—Hadoop, MapReduce, and HDFS are not polished products because the software is always under active development (we use the Wild West metaphor again for this segment of the information technology universe).
- The programming model can be restrictive—the lack of central data can be a deterrent—particularly if the enterprise requires strict relational databases.

- Joins of multiple data sets are convoluted and sluggish due to the lack of indices in many (but not all) cases.
- Cluster management can be difficult—in the cluster, operations like debugging, distributing software, and collecting logs become more difficult than with the old-fashioned central processing approach.
- It still requires a single master, which requires attention and can limit scaling.
- Managing job flow is not trivial when intermediate data must be retained, particularly if a detailed audit trail is needed.
- The optimal configuration of network nodes may be nebulous; for example, it may not be clear how to configure the mappers, reducers, memory limits, and the assorted impedimenta required for installation.

TROUBLESHOOTING HADOOP

A complex environment such as Hadoop is not going to run all the time. Hence, we need to look for potential issues:

- We must examine our data format, which we may not comprehend at the onset of the project.
- The installation team should test boundary conditions (sometimes called "edge cases") by searching for missing or improperly formatted fields, divide-by-zeroes, big number/little number mathematics, and any other overflows and underflows of which we can conceive.
- The team should verify and validate deployment parameters by checking filenames, code dependencies, and permissions (permissions can be a real pain!).
- The team should look at the scheduling parameters—even though a Hadoop cluster does not represent symmetrical multiprocessing (i.e., it is master-slave oriented), we can still have scheduling challenges.
- The test team must validate the basic logic by using so-called clean ("normal") data (we call this "compliance testing," since we are checking compliance to a specification).
- The team should profile cluster performance execution times.
- If they are using Pig, the MapReduce data language, the team should ensure they are really using Pig and not SQL (it is easy

to confuse these languages) (http://pig.apache.org) (more on this issue can be found at http://www.vertica.com/2010/11/29/how-to-make-pig-for-Hadoop-sql/).

RUNNING HADOOP

One of the nice attributes of Hadoop is the way the designers defined it in such a way that it can be run on any machine supporting Java, which is nearly all current architectures. Given the availability of the Java Virtual Machine (JVM), it is possible to run Hadoop in one of three modes:[5]

1. Local mode: a startup mode that has all Hadoop components run on the same JVM
2. Pseudodistributed mode: different portions of Hadoop run on different Java processors
3. Distributed mode: runs on multiple machines and is the full, industrial configuration for the software

Regardless of our installation, any of these configurations allows us to experiment with the MapReduce component of Hadoop. The MapReduce component can break a task into multiple "streams," execute some work on them, and then produce key-value pairs (basically, we associated some alphanumeric key with a stored value of interest, often in an associative array) using reduce. One of the authors of this book installed Hadoop on a Macintosh iMac successfully and was able to run processes. Of course, this kind of installation defeats the real purpose of Hadoop, which is to distribute the work across multiple nodes.

HADOOP FILE SYSTEM

In order to truly execute MapReduce in the distributed orientation for which it was designed, we set up the HDFS, which is basically a NameNode (one) and a set of data nodes. The HDFS is not a form of storage area network or network-attached storage—it is a mechanism for using tens, hundreds, or thousands of commodity computers to process very large problems. We do not want our computer array pulling simultaneously from the same resource, a situation that could lead to either deadlock or extremely slow performance (compared to performance without everybody pulling data at once). The main features of HDFS are as follows:

- The abundant use of commodity servers
- Oriented toward large streams rather than collections of high-speed reads/writes to speedy drives
- Scalability
- File systems at least into the petabyte range with potential for more
- Graceful failover when a unit drops out of service (i.e., the rest of the system can "heal" the wound)

HDFS is not a part of any operating system that we know about, although we see no reason why it cannot be part of an operating system. Of course, the file system is distributed, since that is a precondition for its very existence. Block sizes can range from 64 megabytes to much higher than that, depending on the potential applications for a specific installation. HDFS replicates each block three times, and these blocks are immutable. In essence, HDFS represents a metafile system. HDFS does not use RAID technology in order to keep the cost of implementation to a minimum, preferring the use of the triple-block system. Because HDFS is an integral part of Hadoop, they work well together, further eliminating the need for the complexities of a RAID disk array.

The NameNode is responsible for metadata, and the DataNodes—as one might expect—are responsible for datablock storage. The NameNode is "aware" of the health and well-being of the DataNodes through the use of a heartbeat metaphor. The user will make use of read and write routines from the Hadoop API library to access the DataNodes. An application programming interface (API) library is a collection of broader commands to facilitate an action using software. For example, an API may carry instructions on two interfacing software applications that would involve a large number of individual commands enacted on a piecemeal basis. In the event a DataNode perishes, the system will take back all packets since the last heartbeat and requeue them, which provides substantial robustness to the file system. Think of these data packets as similar to volumes out of an encyclopedia. Much like the way in which the Internet transfers information in such packets, Hadoop processes and internally transports data packets that are essentially data chunks that are broken down for ease of movement. Returning to our encyclopedia example, moving the data is like wrapping each volume of an encyclopedia in a separate box and sending it so that each volume is easier to handle than the whole. The NameNode will see to it that, by creating a new block on another DataNode, it retains the triple-block system integrity. In later versions of Hadoop, the NameNode itself is also duplicated to enhance robustness (the ZooKeeper application from Apache can be used for this capability).

HDFS is based on a Java-like API. Because of its affinity to such a common language, most large organizations will have staff on hand who can understand it. The user may also employ command-line tools—these resemble UNIX/Linux command lines. The command-line tools documentation is also very much derived from the UNIX-style "man" (short for "manual") page format. In essence, the user is working in a basic shell environment. Again, we are dealing with technology that can be understood by a large percentage of skilled computer staff, but not something that staff whose experience is limited to Microsoft Office will easily adapt to.

MapReduce

On the surface, MapReduce is relatively simple:[6]

- No funky network or processor actions (sockets, threads, or multiprocessing)
- Can use functional programming approaches to eliminate side effects
- No interprocess communication
- Works well with HDFS
- Failover (in conjunction with the overall Hadoop philosophy)

MapReduce in the abstract functions as follows:

1. Read job and split into records
2. Run the map
3. Write out, then sort, intermediate output (here we have our work out on HDFS)
4. Go and get the intermediate output
5. Run the reduce portion of the task
6. Write results to HDFS

FIGURE 3.4
MapReduce generic flow.

Generically, MapReduce looks like Figure 3.4.

The attentive reader will notice that the above sequence bears a suspicious resemblance to batching, and they will be correct. We might also note that MapReduce really only does what we have listed with no options for optimization, no convenient high-level approach, and little warning about problems that are not amenable to parallel processing. Basically, the bulk of the MapReduce implementation is what it is—a series of simple methods to run huge amounts of data on multiple processors, rather than being a highly refined commercial implementation fraught with potential issues and moribund because of its own complexity.

In the Hadoop version of MapReduce (others potentially exist), we use the JobTracker capability as the master controller for all tasking and the TaskTracker to guide processes on their individual processors. Hence, we can say JobTracker sits on the NameNode (the master) and allocates work to the TaskTrackers on the other nodes (the slaves). We may see situations where the child task fails; for example, the heartbeat may stop or we receive an uncaught (Java talk) exception. When this happens, the JobTracker will perform its job and reschedule the task. Unfortunately, we can already see that the failure of the JobTracker is more significant than the failure of the TaskTracker, since we lose all of our jobs when this ghastly event occurs. At the time of writing, no solution exists for this issue. A failure of HDFS is not a MapReduce failure—rather, it is a catastrophic event equivalent to losing the file system on Windows, Macintosh, or any database. More recent installations may see something called the "Yet Another Resource Negotiator" (YARN), which breaks the behavior of the JobTracker into a finer granularity in order to enhance management of large Hadoop clusters (trying to keep track of thousands of nodes with a single JobTracker led to performance issues) (Figure 3.5).

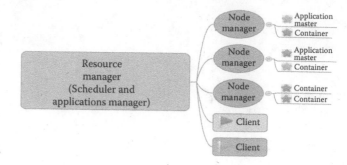

FIGURE 3.5
Structure of YARN.

One example—part of Hadoop (sort of a "hello, world")—is WordCount, which has been implemented in Java (http://wiki.apache.org/hadoop/WordCount):

```
package org.myorg;
import java.io.IOException;
import java.util.*;

import org.apache.hadoop.fs.Path;
import org.apache.hadoop.conf.*;
import org.apache.hadoop.io.*;
import org.apache.hadoop.mapreduce.*;
import org.apache.hadoop.mapreduce.lib.input.
FileInputFormat;
import org.apache.hadoop.mapreduce.lib.input.
TextInputFormat;
import org.apache.hadoop.mapreduce.lib.output.
FileOutputFormat;
import org.apache.hadoop.mapreduce.lib.output.
TextOutputFormat;

public class WordCount {

public static class Map extends Mapper<LongWritable, Text,
Text, IntWritable> {
    private final static IntWritable one = new
    IntWritable(1);
    private Text word = new Text();
    public void map(LongWritable key, Text value, Context
    context) throws
IOException, InterruptedException {
        String line = value.toString();
        StringTokenizer tokenizer = new
        StringTokenizer(line);
```

```
            while (tokenizer.hasMoreTokens()) {
                word.set(tokenizer.nextToken());
                context.write(word, one);
            }
        }
    }
}


public static class Reduce extends Reducer<Text,
IntWritable, Text, IntWritable> {
    public void reduce(Text key, Iterable<IntWritable>
    values, Context
                        context)
    throws IOException, InterruptedException {
        int sum = 0;
        for (IntWritable val: values) {
            sum += val.get();
        }
        context.write(key, new IntWritable(sum));
    }
}


public static void main(String[] args) throws Exception {
    Configuration conf = new Configuration();

        Job job = new Job(conf, "wordcount");

    job.setOutputKeyClass(Text.class);
    job.setOutputValueClass(IntWritable.class);

    job.setMapperClass(Map.class);
    job.setReducerClass(Reduce.class);

    job.setInputFormatClass(TextInputFormat.class);
    job.setOutputFormatClass(TextOutputFormat.class);

    FileInputFormat.addInputPath(job, new Path(args[0]));
    FileOutputFormat.setOutputPath(job, new
    Path(args[1]));

    job.waitForCompletion(true);
}

}
```

PIG AND HIVE

Pig and Hive are effectively metaversions of MapReduce in language form. They transform their own code into MapReduce tasks. This situation is analogous to using C++ instead of assembly code to get the job done.

We use the Grunt shell to write programs in Pig (you have to love these extended metaphors). Pig programs are extremely terse, bordering on cryptic, with the payoff being the automatic and seamless use of mapping and reducing that Pig provides as a service. Here is a silly example from Gates's Pig book[7] using a verse from "Mary had a little lamb" as input:

```
-- Load input from the file named Mary, and call the single
-- field in the record 'line'.
input = load 'mary' as (line);
-- TOKENIZE splits the line into a field for each word.
-- flatten will take the collection of records returned by
-- TOKENIZE and produce a separate record for each one, calling the single
-- field in the record word.
words = foreach input generate flatten(TOKENIZE(line)) as word;
-- Now group them together by each word.
grpd = group words by word;
-- Count them.
cntd = foreach grpd generate group, COUNT(words);
-- Print out the results.
dump cntd;
```

Please notice that Pig is performing a word count with far fewer lines than we observe when we use a language like Java. Pig Latin (the Pig script language) will not reveal any standard control structures such as loops and selections ("if" statements), because the language is a pure dataflow language (we used simple AWK programs like this in the late 1980s and early 1990s). We want our real flow to drop through the nodes in an unrolled form ("unrolling" is a supercomputer term that referred to the tendency of the compiler to convert loops to linear command sequences in order to accelerate the job). The Pig Latin offshoot looks suspiciously like a funky version of an SQL sequence.

INSTALLATION

On an Apple Macintosh computer, Hadoop installation is relatively simple. Reasonably good resources can be found on online, and a good printed source with substantial detail is Eric Sammer's *Hadoop Operations*.[6] Sammer's description provides enough information to install Hadoop "raw" on a UNIX-type system (NetBSD, Linux, etc.).

CURRENT HADOOP ECOSYSTEM

In general, installation of Hadoop will incorporate some or all of the following tools:

Zookeeper: Zookeeper is a centralized service for maintaining configuration information, naming, providing distributed synchronization, and providing group services. All of these kinds of services are used in some form or another by distributed applications.

Mahout: Mahout is Apache's machine learning library containing tools for

- User- and item-based recommenders
- Matrix factorization-based recommenders
- K-means, fuzzy k-means clustering
- Latent Dirichlet allocation
- Singular value decomposition
- Logistic regression classifier
- (Complementary) naive Bayes classifier
- Random forest classifier
- High-performance Java collections

Oozie: Oozie is a work flow scheduler using directed acyclical graphs of actions.

Sqoop: Sqoop allows easy import and export of data from structured data stores such as relational databases, enterprise data warehouses, and NoSQL systems. One can provision the data from the external system on to HDFS and populate tables in Hive and HBase. Sqoop integrates with Oozie, allowing for work flow (read *automation*).

Hive: Hive is data warehouse software that facilitates querying and managing large data sets residing in distributed storage. Hive provides a mechanism to impose structure on the data and query the data using an SQL-like language called HiveQL. Simultaneously, the language allows traditional MapReduce programmers to plug in their custom mappers and reducers when it is inconvenient or inefficient to express this logic in HiveQL.

Whirr: Apache Whirr is a set of libraries for running cloud services. Whirr provides

- A cloud-neutral way to run services
- A common service API
- Smart defaults for services

Flume: Flume is a distributed, reliable, and available service for efficiently collecting, aggregating, and moving large amounts of log data.

Cascading: Cascading is an application framework allowing Java developers to simply develop robust data analytics and data management applications on Apache Hadoop.

Pig: Pig is a platform for analyzing large data sets. Pig's language, Pig Latin, is a simple query algebra that lets the user express data transformations such as merging data sets, filtering them, and applying functions to records or groups of records. Users can create their own functions to do special-purpose processing.

Hue: Hue features

- A file browser for HDFS
- A job browser for MapReduce/YARN
- An HBase browser
- Query editors for Hive, Pig, Cloudera Impala, and Sqoop2

Solr: Solr's major features include

- Powerful full-text search
- Hit highlighting
- Faceted search
- Near-real-time indexing
- Dynamic clustering
- Database integration
- Rich document (e.g., Word, PDF) handling
- Geospatial search

YARN: YARN simplifies and federates the task of executing MapReduce runs by adding a scheduler and an applications manager.

Impala: Cloudera Impala is a massively parallel processing (MPP) SQL query engine that runs natively in Apache Hadoop. The Apache-licensed, open-source Impala project combines modern, scalable parallel database technology with the power of Hadoop, enabling users to directly query data stored in HDFS and Apache HBase without requiring data movement or transformation.

HBase: HBase hosts exceptionally large tables (billions of rows and millions of columns) over the Hadoop distributed architecture.

MapReduce: MapReduce is a software framework for easily writing applications that process vast amounts of data (multiterabyte data sets) in-parallel on large clusters (thousands of nodes) of commodity hardware in a reliable, fault-tolerant manner using a divide and conquer metaphor.

Shark: Shark is an open-source distributed SQL query engine for Hadoop data. It brings state-of-the-art performance and advanced analytics to Hive users.

Drill: Drill is an open-source software framework that supports data-intensive distributed applications for interactive analysis of large-scale data sets. Drill is the open-source version of Google's Dremel system, which is available as an Infrastructure as a Service (IaaS) called Google BigQuery. Drill is an Apache incubator project.

Spark: Spark provides language interfaces for Python, Scala, and Java and works with Shark.

Sentry: Sentry is a highly modular system for providing fine-grained role-based authorization to both data and metadata stored on an Apache Hadoop cluster. Sentry is another Apache incubator project.

Storm: Storm is a distributed, fault-tolerant, and high-performance real-time computation system that provides strong guarantees on the processing of data (Incubator) (Figure 3.6).

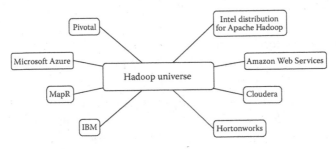

FIGURE 3.6
Hadoop vendor universe.

HADOOP VENDORS

Cloudera

The Cloudera distribution (http://www.cloudera.com/content/cloudera/en/home.html) provides the Hadoop software as well as a substantial collection of support software:

- CDH—Cloudera's 100% open-source, Apache-licensed distribution of Apache Hadoop and related projects
  - Hive
  - Sqoop
  - Flume
  - Pig
  - HBase
- Cloudera Impala—Open-source distributed SQL query engine for interactive/short-cycle analysis of native Hadoop data
- Cloudera Search—Open-source, free-text, and faceted search for native Hadoop data
- Sentry—Provides fine-grained, role-based authorization for Apache Hive and Cloudera Impala
- Cloudera Manager—Console for complete, end-to-end management of CDH clusters

Cloudera also provides "connectors" for database access:

- ODBC Drivers
- ODBC Connector for MicroStrategy
- ODBC Connector for Qlikview
- ODBC Connector for Tableau
- Connectors for Netezza
- Connectors for Teradata
- Quest Data Connector for Oracle and Hadoop

In general, the Cloudera company expects users to run Cloudera under a virtual machine (VM). Regardless of which version the user installs, configuration will generally require substantial editing of shell files and XML support files. Once the user believes all is well, he or she can prove it to themselves by using Bigtop (http://bigtop.apache.org), the Apache tool for the packaging and testing of Hadoop installations (Jenkins [http://jenkins-ci.org], a continuous integration server, is used to run the integration testing).

The user will set up and configure HDFS also, similarly to the main Hadoop installation using XML configuration files. If running, configuring, and tuning a Hadoop cluster sounds intimidating, we now know how Cloudera makes their revenue. Setting up a simple Hadoop example on a single machine is relatively trivial; setting up Hadoop for a large ecosystem of thousands of servers is daunting, indeed. Other topics of concern are fencing (preventing wayward nodes from stomping on their writes), NameNode federation (virtual memory for file system metadata), MapReduce tuning and installation, the hardware configuration, and security for the entire system.

Sammer's book[6] discusses rack topology, which assumes, of course, that we are using a rack. With substantial investment in hardware, it makes sense to use racks, since we can have one enclosure for a large number of nodes, and it simplifies the connections to some extent. Even with control of the hardware, we will use appropriate security software and protocols—Hadoop supports Kerberos for authentication. A discussion of Kerberos is outside the scope of this book; however, we again have a situation where the implementation team/group/customer is probably going to want to hire professional assistance. As with many UNIX-like implementations, we have considerable complexity providing us with considerable power. (As an aside, full-scale use of the EMACS editor is quite complex, given the availability of hundreds of commands, modes, configurations, and views and a seemingly infinite extension capability.)

AMAZON WEB SERVICES (AWS)

AWS appears to insulate the user from much of the heartburn of running a full-scale big data system on their own—if that is what they want. As one might expect with an Internet giant like Amazon, data redundancy is worldwide and many services are available (could this be Big-Data-as-a-Service, BDaaS? And, yes, we know how this would most likely be pronounced!). A big sales point with Amazon is the fact that the user does not need to make the capital investment they might otherwise need to. In effect, we are looking at a subscription service, where a huge amount of risk is borne by Amazon. Amazon indicates:

> WS is more cost-effective than on-premises environments in both short-term and long-term, and at scale, for both variable and steady-state workloads, while also delivering return on agility and enabling new experiences. In early 2012, AWS commissioned IDC to interview 11 organizations that deployed applications on AWS. IDC discovered that the five-year total cost of ownership (TCO) of developing, deploying, and managing critical applications in AWS delivered a 72% savings when compared with deploying the same resources on-premises or in hosted environments. The findings also showed a 626% ROI over five years.[8]

Amazon provides numerous examples of potential uses (http://aws. amazon.com/architecture/):

- Web application hosting
- Content/media serving
- Data-set analysis of various types
- Advertisement servers
- Disaster recovery
- Fault tolerance/high availability
- Massive online games
- Median sharing frameworks
- Financial services
- Time series data (these can become big data quickly!)

With a service, we are very interested in security precautions. Amazon provides a host of tools for access control:

- Encryption (data storage, including hardware encryption)
- GovCloud for US ITAR regulations (this feature is essential for government contractors)
- Multiple levels of authentication
- Firewalls
- Subnets
- VLAN capability
- Trusted advisor—software that responds to brain lapses with notification of potential issues with the existing configuration

- Processes and procedures for penetration testing
- Procedures for security reporting

HORTONWORKS

The founders of Hortonworks were members of the original teams who developed Hadoop and Pig. Many of them worked at Apache and/or Yahoo. Their website (http://www.hortonworks.com) indicates their products are used by Spotify, eBay, Samsung Electronics, Western Digital, Xing, CDW, neustar, Cardinal Health, luminar, and Tagged.

Hortonworks Data Platform (HDP) complements a modern data architecture with a 100% open-source, fully tested and certified Apache Hadoop® data platform. HDP is deeply integrated with strategic data-center technologies and allows the user to reuse existing skills and resources. HDP 2 builds on the massive scale processing and storage of HDP 1.x with a new data-operating system (YARN) enabling multiple workloads, applications, and processing engines across single clusters with greater efficiency than ever before, as well as the latest releases of Apache Hadoop projects for management, data processing, and core operations.

Apache Hadoop YARN is a subproject of Hadoop at the Apache Software Foundation introduced first in Hadoop 2.0, which separates the resource management and processing components. YARN arose from a need to facilitate a broader array of interaction patterns for data stored in HDFS beyond that created by MapReduce. The YARN-based architecture of Hadoop 2.0 provides a more general processing platform that is not constrained to MapReduce.

IBM

The portal to IBM's big data web location is http://www.ibm.com/big-data/us/en/technology/?cmp=usbrb&ct=usbrb301&cr=google&cm=k&csr=41670c aus_bigdata_ep&ccy=us&ck=big_data_solutions&cs=broad&S_PKG=&S_ TACT=USBRB301&mkwid=sOJEylNpH-dc_33828199599_432t5q28552. IBM breaks the ecosystem down into

- Systems
- Privacy
- Governance
- Storage
- Security
- Cloud

IBM focuses strongly on the analytical side of big data (http://www.ibm.com/big-data/us/en/big-data-and-analytics/). We suggest this approach is a wise one. IBM makes a strong case for uses of big data in marketing, dealing with fraud and threats, management, risk control, business modeling, and the evolution of insight. In short, IBM does not assume that the customer who is exploring the big data approach really knows what to do with their newfound technological abilities, and hence, IBM provides substantial reasons for using the big data approach. Let's look at IBM's approach:

- Customer relationships
  - Personalization
  - Profitability
  - Retention
  - Acquisition
- Operations
  - Business process optimization
  - Infrastructure and asset efficiency
  - Counterfraud
  - Public safety and defense
- Management
  - Planning and performance management
  - Disclosure management and financial close
  - Incentive compensation management
  - Human capital management
- Risk
  - Financial
  - Operational risk and compliance
  - Enterprise risk management
- Business models
  - Data-driven products and services
  - Nontraditional partnerships
  - Mass experimentation

- Information technology
  - Data analysis
  - Data governance
  - Optimization of analytical workloads
  - Large variety of analytics

The IBM websites in support of their big data business solutions have tremendous depth and are worthy of investigation on their own merits. IBM provides prompt access to expert assistance as well as a potpourri of case histories and other informative data. We find their website to be a beautiful example of expert marketing, promotion of data value, decision support, and competitive advantage—all music to the ears of executive-level decision makers.

INTEL

Intel's Hadoop solution is at Hadoop.intel.com. The product line includes

- Intel Distribution for Apache Hadoop
- Intel Manager for Apache Hadoop
- Intel Graphbuilder for Apache Hadoop
- Intel HPC Distribution for Apache Hadoop

Not surprisingly, Intel has optimized their distribution of Hadoop for Intel processors, claiming a 30× boost! The Manager tool is designed to simplify management of all aspects of running a Hadoop cluster:

- Deployment
- Configuration
- Management through wizards
- System monitoring
- System logging
- "Health" checking
- Security

Intel also provides training for administrators, developers, and database mavens using HBase. We like the idea of teaching users to become self-reliant. Of course, as with all the other vendors, Intel provides various levels of support (for a fee, of course). Hadoop and the other big data tools are sufficiently complicated that they generally require professional support, even though the bulk of the software is freely downloadable.

MapR

Like Hortonworks, MapR was founded and is led by individuals who have a history with other corporations (Microsoft, Google, etc.) and are well acquainted with what it takes to provide big data services, consulting, and tools. MapR's business model provides for a version of MapR (standard edition) that is available for free download and unlimited production use. Of course, anybody who has tried to bring up a Hadoop cluster on their own realizes that they are probably wiser to employ the services of experts.

MapR supports the basic Apache projects oriented around Hadoop and big data on an advanced technology platform that not only provides enterprise-grade features such as high availability, disaster recovery, security, and full data protection but also allows Hadoop to be easily accessed as traditional network-attached storage (NAS) with read-write capabilities. MapR allows Hadoop to serve business-critical needs for big data applications that cannot afford to lose data, must run all the time, and require immediate recovery from node and site. MapR supports these capabilities for the broadest set of Hadoop applications from batch analytics to interactive querying and real-time streaming.

MapR provides some nice visual tools to help their customers; for example, the MapR HeatMap displays the most critical issues with a readily intelligible green-yellow-red metaphor. It also allows for a quick cluster overview regardless of the trouble.

MICROSOFT

Microsoft's big data platform is Windows Azure. Here is what they have to say about it:

> Windows Azure delivers a flexible cloud platform that can satisfy any application need. It enables you to reliably host and scale out your application

code within compute roles. You can store data using relational SQL databases, NoSQL table stores, and unstructured blob stores, and optionally use Hadoop and business intelligence services to data-mine it. You can take advantage of Windows Azure's robust messaging capabilities to enable scalable distributed applications, as well as deliver hybrid solutions that run across a cloud and on-premises enterprise environment. Windows Azure's distributed caching and CDN services allow you to reduce latency and deliver great application performance anywhere in the world.[9]

HDInsight makes Apache Hadoop (version 2.2 as of February 2014) available as a service in the cloud. It modifies the MapReduce software to become a simpler, more scalable, and cost-efficient Windows Azure environment. Because of this modification, HDInsight itself provides a cost-effective approach to the managing and storing of data using Windows Azure binary large object (Blob) storage.

Installation of HDInsight makes use of Microsoft Powershell. The installation recommends the use of a WordCount program similar to that in the Apache distribution as an initial test engine for the installation. Basically, we are seeing the use of the familiar Windows ecosystem and tools with ancillary support for large-scale operations.

Once the basic installation procedure is complete, we install the familiar Microsoft tools, including the Excel spreadsheet, which is designated a business intelligence (BI) tool by Microsoft (with substantial justice in the more powerful variation of this software). Microsoft's offering can also run Hive if the HDInsight Cluster and Powershell (Windows Azure Powershell) are installed. Furthermore, the Microsoft product also runs Apache Pig, the scripting language we describe elsewhere. The beauty of Pig (a strange thought) is that it provides a layer of abstraction over the MapReduce process and lets us automate the process with a straightforward scripting approach. What follows is the Microsoft example of a Pig Latin job.[10]

Running Pig Latin Using PowerShell

Open a Windows Azure PowerShell console windows. For instructions, see Install and configure Windows Azure PowerShell. Set the variable in the following script, and run it:

```
# Provide the HDInsight cluster name
$subscriptionName = "<SubscriptionName>"
$clusterName = "<HDInsightClusterName>"
```

Run the following script to define the Pig Latin query string:

```
# Create the Pig job definition
$0 = '$0';
$QueryString = "LOGS = LOAD 'wasb:///example/data/sample.
log';" +

                    "LEVELS = foreach LOGS generate REGEX_
EXTRACT($0, '(TRACE|DEBUG|INFO|WARN|ERROR|FATAL)', 1) as
LOGLEVEL;" +
                    "FILTEREDLEVELS = FILTER LEVELS by
LOGLEVEL is not null;" +
                    "GROUPEDLEVELS = GROUP FILTEREDLEVELS by
LOGLEVEL;" +
                    "FREQUENCIES = foreach GROUPEDLEVELS
generate group as LOGLEVEL, COUNT(FILTEREDLEVELS.LOGLEVEL)
as COUNT;" +
                    "RESULT = order FREQUENCIES by COUNT
desc;" +
                    "DUMP RESULT;"
$pigJobDefinition = New-AzureHDInsightPigJobDefinition
-Query $QueryString
```

You can also use the -File switch to specify a Pig script file on HDFS. Run the following script to submit the Pig job:

```
# Submit the Pig job
Select-AzureSubscription $subscriptionName
$pigJob = Start-AzureHDInsightJob -Cluster $clusterName
-JobDefinition $pigJobDefinition
```

Run the following script to wait for the Pig job to complete:

```
# Wait for the Pig job to complete
$Wait-AzureHDInsightJob -Job $pigJob -WaitTimeoutInSeconds 3600
```

Run the following script to print the Pig job output:

```
# Print the standard error and the standard output of the
Pig job.
Get-AzureHDInsightJobOutput -Cluster $clusterName -JobId
$pigJob.JobId -StandardOutput
```

The Microsoft Virtual Academy (http://www.microsoftvirtual-academy.com/training-courses/getting-started-with-microsoft-big-data#?fbid=T2yzFZvxwzi) provides training for the primary tools the average cluster user would be expected to need—MapReduce, Hive, HiveQL, and the .NET interface and how to use the tools operationally.

PIVOTAL

Pivotal can be accessed at http://www.gopivotal.com/. They indicate support for Hadoop, where they refer to testing 1000-node Pivotal Analytics Workbench. As expected, they supply a MPP (distributed) environment, made up of the usual databases (including their own Greenplum). Additional support is available for SQL, Python, Ruby, and Java.

The Pivotal array of product offering is substantial:

- Pivotal CF: The leading enterprise distribution of Cloud Foundry.
- Pivotal One: Comprehensive, multicloud Enterprise PaaS.
- Cloud Foundry: The Open Platform as a Service.
- Pivotal HD: The capabilities of Apache Hadoop in a fully supported, enterprise-ready distribution.
- Pivotal HD with GemFire XD: GemFire XD integrates with Pivotal HD to provide the industry's first platform for creating closed-loop analytics solutions.
- Pivotal Data Dispatch: This delivers faster analytics by enabling self-service discovery and access to data.
- Pivotal Greenplum Database: A platform for large-scale analytic data warehouses.
- The Pivotal DCA: A hardware solution that includes modules for Pivotal GPDB and Pivotal HD for unstructured data.
- Pivotal GemFire: GemFire's in-memory design and unique "shared nothing" architecture delivers improved performance.
- Pivotal SQLFir: A real-time distributed data store that solves the hard problems of distributed systems for you.
- Redis: Keeps all data quickly accessible in memory.
- Pivotal VRP: A best-in-class monitoring solution that helps database administrators monitor the current performance of their database.
- Pivotal Command Center: Web-based interface for deployment, monitoring and management of Pivotal HD.
- Pivotal tc Server: Build and run Java Spring applications.

- Pivotal Web Server: Increase your web tier's performance, scalability, and security while reducing complexity with Pivotal Web Server.
- Pivotal RabbitMQ: An efficient queuing software that makes handling message traffic virtually effortless.
- Spring: A powerful and flexible collection of technologies to improve your enterprise Java app development.
- Fabric Suite: Provides a proven runtime platform for your Spring enterprise Java applications.
- Pivotal Chorus: Provides an analytic platform that enables the team to search, explore, visualize, and import data from anywhere.
- MADlib: An open-source, BSD licensed, scalable, advanced big data analytics library.
- Pivotal GPText: Enables the processing of mass quantities of raw text data into mission-critical information.

REFERENCES

1. Apache Software Foundation. Welcome to Apache Hadoop! 2014. http://hadoop. apache.org/. Accessed April 3, 2014.
2. Chang, F., S. Ghemawat, W. C. Hsieh, D. A. Wallach, M. Burrows, T. Chandra, A. Fikes, and R. E. Gruber. Bigtable: A distributed storage system for structured data. Google Research, 2006, 1–14. http://static.googleusercontent.com/media/research. google.com/en/us/archive/bigtable-osdi06.pdf. Accessed April 3, 2014.
3. Dean, J. and S. Ghemawat. MapReduce: Simplified data processing on large clusters. In *OSDI04. Proceedings of 6th Symposium on Operating Systems Design and Implementation*, San Francisco. 2004. http://blog.csdn.net/jiandanseu/article/details/5321226. Accessed April 3, 2014.
4. Yang, P. Moving an elephant: Large-scale Hadoop data migration at Facebook. July 27, 2011. https://www.facebook.com/notes/paul-yang/moving-an-elephant-large-scale-hadoop-data-migration-at-facebook/10150246275318920. Accessed April 3, 2014.
5. Perera, S. and Thilina G. *Hadoop MapReduce Cookbook*. Birmingham: Packt Publishing, 2013.
6. Sammer, E. *Hadoop Operations*. Sebastopol, CA: O'Reilly, 2012.
7. Gates, A. *Programming Pig*. Sebastopol, CA: O'Reilly, 2011.
8. Amazon Web Services. Economics. Amazon Web Services. 2014. http://aws.amazon. com/economics. Accessed April 3, 2014.
9. Microsoft. What is Windows Azure? http://www.windowsazure.com/en-us/ overview/what-is-windows-azure/. Accessed April 2, 2014.
10. Microsoft. Use Pig with HDInsight. Windows Azure: Microsoft's cloud platform. 2014. http://www.windowsazure.com/en-us/documentation/articles/hdinsight-use-pig/. Accessed April 3, 2014.

4

HBase and Other Big Data Databases

EVOLUTION FROM FLAT FILE TO THE THREE V'S

We have now discussed the evolution of data storage and the growth of processing power, and have also explored some of the data that are now being generated and how they are being used. Now we can dig into the big data phenomenon more deeply. We can now tie this discussion together. Again, we will do so using an evolutionary approach.

Simply put, big data is currently enjoying a positive feedback loop. The Wikipedia definition of this is concise and insightful: "Positive feedback is a process in which the effects of a small disturbance on a system include an increase in the magnitude of the perturbation. That is, A produces more of B which in turn produces more of A. In contrast, a system in which the results of a change act to reduce or counteract it has negative feedback."[1]

An easily visible example of positive feedback is the growth of motor vehicle ownership in the United States and the growth of suburbs and exurbs. Since the early twentieth century, motor vehicle ownership (including both publicly and privately owned vehicles, as well as automobiles, buses, and trucks) has grown from almost zero to the 2010 level of 0.8 vehicles per person. While the exact causes of suburban growth in the United States are still open to debate (city taxes, crime rates, and lower housing costs all play a role), the expansion of motor vehicle ownership has clearly been an enabler. Suburban growth is marked by low population density due to the prevalence of single-family dwellings and the ubiquitous strip malls and stand-alone businesses in single-use zoning. The stereotypical suburban business resides in a single-story building surrounded by its own parking lot and landscaping.

Because of single-use zoning, it is necessary to travel further on a daily basis than one does within a denser urban environment. The low density also makes it difficult to profitably run a public transportation system. Public transportation functions best when there is a high enough population density around the stops to make it possible to walk to those stops. In suburbia, the car is not the convenience (or inconvenience) that it is in the city. It is a necessity. There is a strong argument to be made that the car enabled the growth of the suburbs, and the suburbs made the car a necessity. This is the positive feedback loop.

A similar self-reinforcing process is taking place between the capture and processing of data. As is the case with suburban growth, the relationships creating the positive feedback that is driving the spread of big data are not simple. As is also the case with suburban growth, however, there is clearly an enabling mechanism taking place.

The growth in the quantity of data and the ability to process that data comprise a positive feedback mechanism. There is the ratcheting up of the ability to process data. In this chapter we have explored the growth of data processing, data storage, and data creation.

Organizations have rarely used data to its full, due to difficult data sources. The focus, then, is now as much about making the data processing more able to process diverse data as it is about making data itself easy to use. This additional focus is creating vast new data processing capabilities.

As the share of data that can be processed by newer systems grows, data become more complex and chaotic. This means the tools to handle these data sets need to be ever more sophisticated. However, each innovation in the evolution of data management and processing simplifies the use of large, complex data sets in the short term and opens opportunities for the more intensive extraction of value from data in the long term. This pushes further development of data management systems. The feedback mechanism is clear.

Flat File

The humble flat file is a simple, two-dimensional table arranged in a grid format. An example is the common spreadsheet used to track data. If you have ever put together a mailing list in Excel, with names, addresses, phone numbers, e-mail addresses, and other variables, you have created a flat file. Flat files are not limited to what a user creates. Many automated systems, such as security badge systems and logistics systems, output their data into a flat file.

Let us further examine the flat file. Imagine that you have a start-up packaging business servicing clients throughout your region of the United States. Your business is small, so you track key customer information in Excel. This spreadsheet is a flat file.

What are the advantages of the flat file? First of all, it works well when data are homogeneous and limited in quantity. In the example in Table 4.1, we simply list student names, grade level, identification of courses, sections, and periods. For a small amount of data, this kind of database is acceptable. However, such a simple format will never work with large or big data situations.

A second advantage of the flat file is that you can look at it and understand it without using an external program. The flat file in the example above, while exaggerated in its simplicity, is easy to understand. You do not need a database. More complex flat files also share that trait. If you need to view the characteristics of a manager, you can run your finger down the page until you find the entry you are looking for and then run

TABLE 4.1

Flatfile Database

Student_First	Student_Last	Grade_Level	Course_ID	Section	Period
Lorem	Ipsum	9	V380M-9	2	P1
Dolores	Sit	11	V380M-9	1	P1
Amet	Consectetur	9	V380M-9	3	P1
Adipiscing	Elit	10	V380M-9	1	P3
Morbi	Elit	11	V380M-9	1	P3
Dewey	Faucibus	10	V380M-9	1	P3
Eget	Turpis	10	V380M-9	2	P3
Chris	Fringilla	9	V380M-9	3	P5
Fermentum	Ante	11	V380M-9	3	P5
Integer	Et	9	V380M-9	1	P5
Enos	Faucibus	9	V380M-9	1	P5
Gravida	Ante	10	V380M-9	2	P8
Chris	Lectus	10	V380M-9	2	P8
Donnie	Eusem	11	V380M-9	4	P8

your finger across the page to see all of the data points associated with that manager.

Most of us are familiar with the "freeze panes" function of Excel. With this function, certain rows and columns do not scroll as the rest of the pages scroll. Use of this feature is generally limited to column headings or key-values in the first column or two of a spreadsheet. Think of this feature as a method of making it easier to read a flat file.

What are the disadvantages of the flat file? Let us use an example. Your company is growing. You buy more trucks and hire more drivers. You learn about the insight into your business that data can provide, so you begin to collect more and more data about your drivers, vehicles, suppliers, and customers. Now, the flat file is no longer an efficient solution.

In fact, the flat file's limitations are now becoming painfully clear. You have information that is relatively static in a business file, such as employee names and information about the trucks. These do not change day to day. However, if you wish to track transactional information, such as delivering a shipment to a customer or taking a truck in for maintenance, then your difficulties will begin to grow. Your data are no longer homogenous.

If you decide to stay with a flat file, then it will begin to grow exponentially in size. As you add columns to track more and more fields, you are not only increasing the information that is in those fields, but also adding redundant information as you create one-to-many and many-to-many relationships. There are many circumstances in which one-to-many relationships in the data eat up valuable space without necessarily adding more information.

Imagine that you are creating a spreadsheet to track your friends. You add each friend and his or her cell phone number. Since few people share cell phones, let us assume that this is a perfect one-to-one relationship. Each friend has exactly one cell phone number and each cell phone number tracks back to exactly one friend.

You then add primary addresses. This is still manageable, but will probably not end up as a perfect one-to-one relationship. You have friends who are married and friends who are roommates. In this case, each friend will have one primary address, but a primary address will trace back to more than one friend whenever you have friends who live together. If you decide to include addresses, not just primary addresses, then you break down the one-to-one relationship even further. Friends with beach condos for the winter will have more than one address. We are moving into the territory of many-to-many relationships.

So far the relationships we are using in this example are simple enough that a flat file will not break down, but we can see how the runaway redundancy can occur in a flat file. This redundancy will become unavoidable when a static attribute is paired to a dynamic attribute. A driver will not change his name every day, but will make deliveries every day. His name must therefore be entered with every delivery, and either it or another constant must be entered consistently and correctly in order to accurately analyze the data.

Because flat files tend to be used when the data are simple, they are often used in systems with some degree of manual entry. This is less a weakness of the flat file *per se* than of how the files are used. As an example of the difficulties that arise from such manual entry, imagine that you have a customer, Ajax Dynamite. You supply Ajax with the wooden crates that they use to ship their products. One of your employees typing in an order accidentally enters it as "Jaax Dynamite." It is the largest order of the year and accounts for one-third of your yearly sales to Ajax. When you roll up your yearly report, you incorrectly see that Ajax cut back its purchases to you, so you may very well consider (unnecessary) remedial action to win back its business. These types of problems frequently arise when manual entry is used in data files, even if this example is somewhat extreme for the sake of illustration.

Options do exist for automating information entry, such as bar code scanners, radio-frequency ID (RFID) tags, and the common drop-down menu. In fact, once your firm grows enough to begin automating more and more, you will probably introduce systems to minimize or eliminate this issue. As you automate more, and collect more data, you will face a new problem, however. Your data set will grow more complex and unwieldy. The one-to-many and many-to-many relationships discussed earlier will become more and more common. You will face a decision.

One option to simplify your data entry is to break up your large flat file into multiple tables. You can keep files for trucks, drivers, suppliers, customers, and other business needs. The problem now is tying together all of these different files. You know that insights are hiding there in the data, but it is difficult to pull those insights out without extensive manual data cleansing. The relational database solves exactly this problem. First, though, let us take a detour through another database technology: the hierarchical database.

Hierarchical Database

In your organization, there is probably an organization chart. Workers answer to managers. Managers answer to directors. Going up the chain, we pass through vice presidents, presidents, and the C suite. In a typical organization, a manager has many subordinates, but each subordinate has only one manager.

The hierarchical database, when diagrammed, resembles this organizational chart. There are parent/child relationships in which each parent record may have multiple children, but each child record has only a single parent. Having just discussed the inefficiencies of one-to-many relationships, it is easy to understand the attractiveness of this model (Figure 4.1).

In the early days of this database model, such as IBM's IMS, a record was called a node and no "relations," as we now use the term, existed. This situation would cause substantial heartburn because even a simple invoice/order database had no way to relate products to invoices/orders! While we received the benefit of only having one-to-many relationships, we were also stuck with only this mode of relationship, not to mention the fact that we often had to resort to redundant data to get what we wanted out of the database.

The hierarchical model can be entirely replaced by a relational database using nested sets. However, it still sees application with naturally hierarchical data such as GIS and file systems (but not necessarily organizational charts).

Network Database

Another early approach was the so-called "network" database. With this approach, the database designer would program or use pointers to

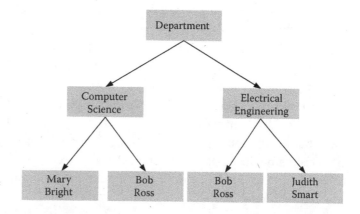

FIGURE 4.1
Hierarchical database structure.

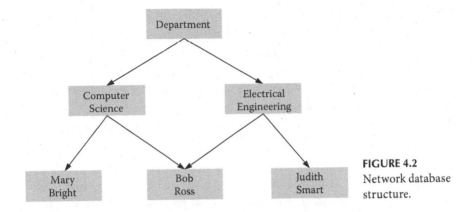

FIGURE 4.2
Network database
structure.

other information in the database, much like pointers in some computer languages. These databases had more flexibility than the hierarchical databases, but they also had a tendency to end up with a welter of quasi-unintelligible pointers. Figure 4.2 shows a very simple version of a network database—commercial versions were significantly more complicated.

Relational Database

A paradox of data management is becoming clear: simplicity through complexity. An astute student of design would object, raising the example of the acclaim and loyalty that Apple has earned through its clean design and ease of use. This is a valid objection, but only to a degree. Yes, Apple's products are elegant, straightforward, and easy to use. But, there is a simple counterargument to this objection: If your iPad breaks, can you take it apart and fix it? The relational database adds a layer of complexity that in turn greatly simplifies the reality of data organization. First laid out by Edgar Codd in 1970, the relational database breaks a large data file into smaller tables. The different rows, or tuples, in a table are tied to related tuples in the other tables by a common attribute, referred to as a primary key. The primary key must be unique to a particular tuple. You have primary keys assigned to you. These include your social security number, your driver's license number, and even your telephone number under some circumstances. As a concrete example, your employer probably has a database entry with your social security number or an employee number as your primary key. Other attributes include your first name, last name, middle initial, street address, city, state, zip code, date of hire, current status, position, salary, and keys that tie your data to other databases.

Your zip code could tie to another table, where it would be tied to state income tax withholding rates. Other identifiers may tie to tables that host security information, the computer assigned to you, and which software is installed on it, or myriad other possibilities.

With your growing crate manufacturing firm, your flat file is no longer sufficient, so we have broken your flat file into three separate tables. Your HR data are now stored on one table, your truck data on another table, and your delivery data on a third table.

Each employee has a unique employee number on his or her badge. It permits access to your offices each morning thanks to an embedded RFID tag. You have a table elsewhere that shows when each employee enters or leaves each day. The badge also has a bar code that each driver scans to check out the bar code scanner, indicating the identity of the driver who made any deliveries scanned by that device that day. The scanner is also tied to a particular truck for that day.

You receive a complaint from Acme Bat Suits that one of your drivers blocked its driveway that morning, leaving the truck there for several hours and delaying one of its outgoing shipments. This sounds strange, but is an easy problem to solve. You search for "Acme Bat Suits" in your relational database. Their customer ID is queried in the delivery table (and both items are on the delivery table).

The delivery table lists who the driver was and what truck he was driving that morning. By backtracking (backing out) through the tabs, we get the driver through his employee identification and call his supervisor, who attests that he has been reliable and has had no disciplinary actions in his 18 years of driving.

However, by tracking back the truck's identification number, you can see on the table dedicated to truck data that maintenance missed a registered complaint several weeks earlier. Furthermore, on the date of Acme's complaint, there is an entry for a mechanical failure that required the truck to be towed off a customer's lot. Thanks to the power of relational databases, the problem is solved.

In real life, the tables of the relational database will not be visible to you, but the names of the databases themselves will be. Relational databases range from Microsoft Access to the broad array of structured query language (SQL) databases to offerings by Oracle, SAP, Teradata, Apache, and IBM. The relational model underpins the enterprise resource planning (ERP) packages that almost all medium and large businesses rely on to coordinate activities and accounting across their firms.

Despite their power, relational databases have important weaknesses. Among these is rigidity. The data in relational databases must be normalized. Normalization is the process of ensuring that the data fit a set format. Relational databases do not cope well with data that do not fit neatly into tables, or even with inconsistently formatted data within tables.

There are key side effects caused by this rigidity. The first and most obvious is the need to normalize data and enact data governance structures to ensure that data stay normalized. The Data Governance Institute defines data governance as, "Data Governance is a system of decision rights and accountabilities for information-related processes, executed according to agreed-upon models which describe who can take what actions with what information, and when, under what circumstances, using what methods."[21] Data governance generally involves set processes, rules, and systems to keep data well organized and in a normal form.

Some of the steps for keeping data usable are straightforward. For example, using drop-down menus with set values eliminates the ability of users to enter variations of a single valuable. "Texas" is "Texas" in all fields for state, not "TX" or "Tejas." Others involve ensuring that a particular class of document is stored in the correct repository and that key databases are updated when they are supposed to be. Often, particular software packages are selected and become the standard for the company.

Data governance has a paradoxical effect on how software is selected and used, and therefore on the data output generated. The tendency of a firm's employees to revert to "shadow information technology (IT)" is one reason why data governance is important. However, data governance practices also act as a driver to such reversion to shadow IT. Shadow IT is the use of software packages, practices, and solutions to solve problems that are exacerbated by the rigidity of IT practices.

For example, imagine that the gold standard software for a particular analysis is not directly applicable to your particular analysis. However, your organization is conducting a slightly different analysis. One of your team members develops a spreadsheet into which you enter key data points and you receive as outputs the key data points that you need for your software package. This is a form of shadow IT.

People, to do their jobs, will improvise and tweak and create roundabout methods to make their software function as they need it to function. Perhaps the software functions just fine, but a system for feeding the output of one employee to another employee to use as input for the next step is grossly user unfriendly. Employees may very well set up a folder on the share drive where the internal folder structure reflects their needs.

IT departments often respond to this problem bureaucratically, inadvertently driving more employees into the arms of their own shadow IT. However, there is a very real problem occurring. Employees need to improvise in order to do their jobs, and IT departments need to keep a lid on this proliferation of systems in order to keep a functional IT system. As the flat file met its match with more complex data sets, the relational database meets its match in the need to maintain normal data in a very nonnormal world.

Object-Oriented Databases

Why have an object-oriented database management system (OODBMS)? In some cases, it makes sense to use object-oriented programming techniques as well as storage; for example:

- Music
- Visual arts
- Video
- Audio

These are often inconvenient for use in other database formats. We tend to consider these systems to be special purpose in nature, and, due to their internal inefficiencies, not suitable for big data.

Relational-Object Databases

The relational-object model is an attempt to merge object-oriented database ideas with powerful relational modality. The beauty of this approach lies in our ability to group like records containing similar objects. Most large relational databases have some capability for object storage.

In school and at work, we are all accustomed to e-mailing a document or carrying a thumb drive (those of us who are a little older remember floppy disks). For larger files, an external hard drive may be used. This is such a common act that we rarely think about it. What we are doing is storing our data and moving it. We work on a document using an application on our computer, save it to a medium of one kind or another, and transport it; then we or someone else use a different program (or a different copy of the same program) to open it up and work with it again.

What do you do with a 15-terabyte file, or a 1-petabyte file? You invert this relationship. You take your software to the data. This does not mean that you move your software around on a thumb drive, but you do install it on the machine where the data reside. The data may take days to move. It is more efficient to install the software where the data is. This leads to the idea of distribution of processing. If you are painting a house, you can paint it alone, but it is much faster if you gather together a group of friends, each of whom paints a section. Likewise, rather than processing all of the data from a central location, big data applications process different sections of data separately, then pull the results back together.

Some applications that need fast processing times for large quantities of data, such as Endeca (now part of Oracle), further speed up processing by keeping the data "in memory." As random access memory (RAM) has become more affordable, this method for storing data has spread, and is not unique to big data applications. There are drawbacks, such as the loss of data in the event of a crash, but there is no wait time for the database to search through hard drives to pull out and process the data.

TRANSITION TO BIG DATA DATABASES

As we have indicated elsewhere in this book, we are currently in the "Wild West" period of big data, where we have a large array of tools, grand new ideas, and new vendors popping up with great regularity. We have also spoken of the history of databases, particularly the ascendancy of the relational database approach and its associated SQL.

HBase, MongoDB, and many others represent either hybrid approaches or completely alternate approaches to the database problem. Part of the rise of these new approaches relates to the difficulty of distributing relational databases while retaining high levels of nearly immediate data integrity. We are aware that some large vendors sell relational products that can be distributed, and we also know that such distribution requires compromises on the part of the relational database. In this chapter we will briefly discuss the relational approach so that we can compare the alternate solutions, the differences and trade-offs being obvious.

What Is Different about HBase?

With a typical relational database management system (RDBMS), we can use rows of data called records, which are further broken down into fields. If we move up the hierarchy, we have row (record)-oriented data organized into named tables. We use this approach because we can achieve a high level of consistency and data integrity.

In its simplest form, HBase is nonrelational and is largely modeled on the Google Bigtable concept. While not a purely column-oriented database, HBase does use the column concept to allow for simpler distribution. Since HBase is not a RDBMS, we might expect that the access language is not necessarily SQL, and such is the case. An alternative to SQL is NoSQL, which does not mean "no" SQL, but really means "not only" SQL; in other words, if SQL is usable, then we can use it, or alternatively, we can use some other method for accessing our data. An excellent resource for information on NoSQL is *Making Sense of NoSQL*,[2] by Dan McCreary and Ann Kelly. Their book goes into great detail about the varieties of NoSQL available. We will discuss NoSQL in greater depth later in this chapter. A good resource for purely HBase is *HBase: The Definitive Guide*[3] by Lars George, which provides extremely detailed information about HBase and how to use it.

HBase, specifically, is supported under the umbrella of the Apache Software Foundation (an organization, by the way, that has done as much as any group to pave the way to rational management of big data). On their website, http://hbase.apache.org/, they list the following features for HBase[4]:

- Linear and modular scalability
- Strictly consistent reads and writes
- Automatic and configurable sharding of tables
- Automatic failover support between region servers
- Convenient base classes for backing Hadoop MapReduce jobs with Apache HBase tables
- Easy-to-use Java API for client access
- Block cache and bloom filters for real-time queries
- Query predicate push-down via server-side filters
- Thrift gateway and a REST-ful web service that supports XML, Protobuf, and binary data encoding options
- Extensible JRuby-based (JIRB) shell
- Support for exporting metrics via the Hadoop metrics subsystem to files or Ganglia, or via JMX

Let's look at a few of these features! We are interested in scalability because we may need to grow our database beyond the bounds of a single, physical platform. Sharding (shared distribution, but we also have the metaphor of broken glass) allows us to put different portions of the database on different physical or logical locations for improved processing performance. Failover support will save us if we one of our physical devices expires. Also, notice how HBase conveniently works with Hadoop and MapReduce—Hadoop includes an open-source version of MapReduce as part of its core capability. Hadoop includes the following modules:

- Common: basic utilities that support other Hadoop modules
- Distributed File System (HDFS): distributed file system that provides high-throughput access
- YARN: job scheduling and cluster resource management framework
- MapReduce: system for parallel processing of large data sets

Hadoop is nondenominational with respect to databases—it can support a variety of types using the appropriate toolboxes, of which we list a few obvious choices:

- Pig: platform for analyzing large data sets
- Hive: data warehouse system for Hadoop with a quasi-SQL language
- Hbase: the topic of this chapter
- Sqoop: designed for efficiently transferring bulk data between Apache Hadoop and structured data stores (think relational database)
- Flume: service managing log data
- Zookeeper: service for maintaining configuration information, naming, providing distributed synchronization, and providing group services. Although the Apache Software Foundation is a nonprofit corporation and generates its own products, it does an amazing job of providing tools and working with tools that support industry.

HBase implementation is widespread. For example, Apache's Hadoop wiki lists the following known users[5]:

- Adobe: 30 nodes running HDFS, Hadoop, and HBase in clusters ranging from 5 to 14 nodes on both production and development
- Benipal Technologies: has a 35-node cluster used for HBase and MapReduce

- BigSecret: a security framework
- Caree.rs: accelerated hiring platform for high-tech companies
- Celer Technologies: uses Hadoop/HBase for storing all financial data for trading, risk, and clearing in a single data store
- Explorys: uses an HBase cluster containing over a billion anonymized clinical records
- Facebook: uses HBase to power their Messages infrastructure
- Filmweb: a film web portal with a large data set of films, persons, and movie-related entities
- Flurry: provides mobile application analytics
- GumGum: an in-image advertising platform
- HubSpot: an online marketing platform
- Infolinks: an in-text ad provider
- Kalooga: a discovery service for image galleries
- NGDATA: a consumer intelligence solution
- Mahalo: "the world's first human-powered search engine"
- Meetup: helps the world's people self-organize into local groups
- Mendeley: a platform for researchers to collaborate and share their research online
- Ning: HBase stores and serves the results of processing user events and log files, allowing for near-real-time analytics and reporting
- OCLC: HBase is the main data store for WorldCat, a union catalog that aggregates the collections of 72,000 libraries in 112 countries and territories
- OpenLogic: stores all the world's open-source packages, versions, files, and lines of code in HBase for both near-real-time access and analytical purposes
- Openplaces: a search engine for travel
- Pacific Northwest National Laboratory: a systems biology data warehouse project that integrates high-throughput proteomics and transcriptomics data sets coming from instruments in the Environmental Molecular Sciences Laboratory
- ReadPath: stores several hundred million RSS items and a dictionary for its RSS newsreader
- resu.me: career network for the Internet generation
- Runa Inc.: offers a SaaS that enables online merchants to offer dynamic per-consumer, per-product promotions embedded in their website
- Sematext: runs search analytics and scalable performance monitoring

- SocialMedia: uses HBase to store and process user events that allows near-real-time user metrics and reporting
- Splice Machine: a full-featured ANSI SQL database
- Streamy: a recently launched real-time social news site
- Stumbleupon and Su.pr: use HBase as a real-time data storage and analytics platform
- Shopping Engine: a web crawler
- Traackr: uses HBase to store and serve online influencer data in real time
- Trend Micro: uses HBase as a foundation for cloud-scale storage for a variety of applications. We have been developing with HBase since version 0.1 and production since version 0.20.0.
- Twitter: runs HBase across its entire Hadoop cluster
- Udanax.org: URL shortener
- Veoh Networks: uses HBase to store and process visitor (human) and entity (nonhuman) profiles
- VideoSurf: "The video search engine that has taught computers to see"
- Visible Technologies: collects, parses, stores, and searches hundreds of social media content sites
- WorldLingo: multilingual archive
- Yahoo!: uses HBase to store document fingerprints for detecting near-duplications
- HP IceWall SSO: a web-based single sign-on solution that uses HBase to store user data to authenticate users

We include this list because it makes it rather obvious the influence Apache has on the marketplace, even though it is incorporated as a nonprofit.

What Is Bigtable?

Bigtable is a distributed storage system for managing structured data, which was originally theorized by Google.[6] Google has used the tool for Google Earth, Google Finance, and web indexing, among others. The tool was designed to scale to the petabyte level.

Bigtable can be accessed by a row key, a column key, and a time stamp. Row keys can be arbitrary strings, which are maintained in lexicographic order. Column keys are gathered in groupings called column families. Generally, the data stored in a family will be of the same type. Access control occurs at the column-family level. Since each "cell" in a Bigtable can contain multiple instances of data, the use of the time stamp is essential to maintaining version integrity. The Google team provided an API, a file system, and a set of standard components: a library, a master server, and multiple tablet servers. Tablets contain metadata to assist in accessing and manipulating user tables.

Bigtable has tools for managing load and availability. It was tested at Google before its existence was made known at the 2006 USENIX OSDI conference. One of the main attractions of the system was the ability to increase capacity simply by adding more machines to the system. One downside is the complexity of installing this system, because Bigtable provides a low-level read and write interface designed to support many thousands of operations per second per server. Of course, this situation may be a reasonable price to pay for the ability to run multiple "threads" of work on systems anywhere on the planet. A review of the original paper will provide an overview of the thought that went into the implementation. To understand the implementation in detail, we would need to look at an implementation—Hbase is a Bigtable-like implementation, while Apache's Cassandra is a Bigtable implementation. Cassandra has nearly as many well-known users as HBase and represents an alternative solution, depending on the needs of the entity making its software choice.

What Is MapReduce?

The name MapReduce results from the conflation of two separate terms:

- Map: splitting our problem into independent components
- Executing some transformation on the components
- Reduce: putting our components in some kind of order so we can retrieve them

At first glance, one might think this approach represents more work than it is worth, and that would indeed be the case for small problems; however, when we are dealing with very large problems, when we have a large quantity of available (usually low-cost) processors, and when we have the computer infrastructure, then it makes sense to "divide and conquer" our data processing problem.

The approach was originally defined in a Google paper called "MapReduce: Simplified Data Processing on Large Clusters."[7] Years later, Ralf Lämmel wrote a rigorous assessment of MapReduce for Microsoft (Figure 4.3).[8]

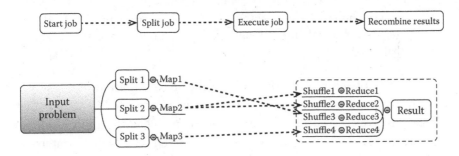

FIGURE 4.3
A MapReduce action simplified.

Here is how MongoDB (2.X) indicates it uses MapReduce with sharding[9] (MongoDB key words are in italics [ours]):

If the "out" field for MapReduce has the sharded value, MongoDB shards the output collection using the _id field as the shard key. To output to a sharded collection:

- If the output collection does not exist, MongoDB creates and shards the collection on the _id field.
- For a new or an empty sharded collection, MongoDB uses the results of the first stage of the map-reduce operation to create the initial chunks distributed among the shards.
- mongos dispatches, in parallel, a map-reduce post-processing job to every shard that owns a chunk. During the post-processing, each shard will pull the results for its own chunks from the other shards, run the final reduce/finalize, and write locally to the output collection.

Note

- During later map-reduce jobs, MongoDB splits chunks as needed.
- Balancing of chunks for the output collection is automatically prevented during post-processing to avoid concurrency issues.

In MongoDB 2.0:

- mongos [*sic*] retrieves the results from each shard, performs a merge sort to order the results, and proceeds to the reduce/finalize phase as needed. mongos then writes the result to the output collection in sharded mode.
- This model requires only a small amount of memory, even for large data sets.

- Shard chunks are not automatically split during insertion. This requires manual intervention until the chunks are granular and balanced.

In the case of MongoDB, MapReduce and sharding are functions built into the software to simplify work for the user. We would like to note that MongoDB is released under the open-source model, with support provide by 10gen, the company that created it. MongoDB is a NoSQL database; HBase, however, while generally classified as a NoSQL database, is quasi-column oriented, rather than document oriented, as with MongoDB.

What Are the Various Modalities for Big Data Databases?

In general, if we go to the websites of the various products, whether open source or commercial, we will see just four basic types[10]:

- Column
- Document
- Key-value
- Graph

We may also see hybrid combinations of the four modalities. The column approach does not mean we have no rows, but it does mean we can use columns as an access mode. When we use document-oriented databases, we may see encodings such as JavaScript Object Notation (JSON) or other standardized formats (most of these have metadata). Graphs express relations in terms of a graph because this modality may naturally arise from that kind of data. Key-values do not require a schema; a great comment on key-values was made by Marc Seeger[11]:

> Key value stores allow the application developer to store schema-less data. This data is usually consisting of a string which represents the key and the actual data which is considered to be the value in the "key -value" relationship. The data itself is usually some kind of primitive of the programming language (a string, an integer, an array) or an object that is being marshalled by the programming languages bindings [*sic*] to the key value store. This replaces the need for fixed data model and makes the requirement for properly formatted data less strict.

In short, each one of our solution approaches allows us yet another way to get at our data while using an access technique that arises naturally from the topology of the data itself.

GRAPH DATABASES

One well-known example of a graph database (a "graphical" database would contain pictorials called "graphs") is Neo4j. Their website indicates that Neo4j is ACID, which means it supports

- Atomicity: A transaction is atomic and must complete in its entirety or the database remains unchanged.
- Consistency: All data meet validation rules.
- Isolation: Concurrent execution is equivalent to serial execution.
- Durability: Transactions are recorded in nonvolatile memory.

At this point, we are still in the "so what" range with regard to databases, since any good relational database will be fully ACID. The Neo4j manual highlights the following features[12]:

- True ACID transactions
- High availability
- Scales to billions of nodes and relationships
- High-speed querying through traversals
- Declarative graph query language

As one might expect, a graph database functions well with highly connected data. A query becomes a traversal. In the case of Neo4j, the database can be made to be fault tolerant by allowing failover (swapping hardware to a redundant processor or cluster) to slave databases (which were created for just this purpose).

How Does a Graph Database Work?

A graph database starts with a node. Relations among pieces of information are modeled with labeled edges (they look like arrows in a drawing; hence, the term digraph or directed graph). A node can be related to subnodes. Graphs can resemble trees, or maps, or other digraph-type structures—in short, we have graph structures as an alternative to the more usual tables.

We navigate graphs using a method called a traversal, going from node to node under the control of an algorithm. An alternative to a traversal occurs when we use an index to go directly to a node of interest.

What Is the Performance of a Graph Database?

Of course mileage will vary depending on the topology of the problem; however, graph databases appear to achieve reasonable performance through caching. However, the book *Graph Database*[13] explains:

> One compelling reason, then, for choosing a graph database is the sheer performance increase when dealing with connected data versus relational databases and NoSQL stores. In contrast to relational databases, where join-intensive query performance deteriorates as the dataset gets bigger, with a graph database performance tends to remain relatively constant, even as the dataset grows. This is because queries are localized to a portion of the graph. As a result, the execution time for each query is proportional only to the size of the part of the graph traversed to satisfy that query, rather than the size of the overall graph.

DOCUMENT DATABASES

Example: MongoDB is free and open-source software, with the usual GNU and Apache-type licensing restrictions. It is perhaps one of the best-known NoSQL databases in general use. One well-known user is Craigslist. MongoDB was designed more for analytics and complex data than it was for tables, ACID compliance, and all the other standards and support requirements that come with relational databases (being probably the most likely database variant in use today)[14]. The MongoDB website lists the following features, which we will discuss in detail[15]:

- Document-oriented storage: JSON-style documents with dynamic schemas
- Full index support: index on any attribute
- Replication and high availability: mirror across LANs and WANs for scale
- Auto-sharding: scale horizontally without compromising functionality
- Querying: rich, document-based queries
- Fast in-place updates: atomic modifiers for contention-free performance
- Map/reduce: flexible aggregation and data processing
- GridFS: store files of any size without complicating the stack
- Professional support by MongoDB: support, training, and consulting available (they are a business)

MongoDB is considered to be a document-oriented database with strengths oriented around websites as well. Another feature, besides the lack of typical transactions, is the philosophy of keeping a copy of itself. These features make MongoDB useful for big data problems, since the database can be distributed.

MongoDB uses a version of JSON called Binary-JSON (BSON) as a data description tool. BSON is an extension of JSON, which uses a length field to enhance the efficiency of scanning. The JSON approach provides less complexity than XML and more information than a comma-delimited file. The JSON world has its own argot, one example of which is the term "embedded document," which occurs when basic information is made more complicated with the addition of more complex information—for example, an array.

MongoDB is also a NoSQL database, which is a part of its nonrelational heritage. Since it makes use of the BSON approach, it always has this metadata to keep things straight; otherwise, data storage would look like one large blob of incomprehensible text. MondoDB will query across various nodes in a network (assuming it has been configured this way!), using keys to find the data needed by the query. The method of distributing information is called sharding (shared database or shards of glass). This sharding approach allows the database to scale to tens and hundreds of nodes.

MongoDB uses an approach called memcached to hold data for higher-speed access, most commonly for websites, allowing for speedy responses to client nodes. The database uses keys to access data; in short, we will search for what we want based on the key we have provided to the database. In MongoDB, the identifiers are unique, such that we do not need to use compound keys.

Mongo DB does not require that every "field" has a value, unlike relational databases. This approach is intuitive; for example, if we expected apartment-type addresses, we would see apartment numbers—if our clients live in houses, they will have addresses but no separate apartment number. MongoDB does not care whether we have a value in this field or not (we don't need to specify a null).

When installing MongoDB, we might consider whether to install it as a 32-bit or a 64-bit version. As we might expect, the 32-bit version is limited to about 2.5 GB per server. We recommend using the 64-bit version whenever it is feasible. The database is available for Windows, Macintosh OS X, Linux, and Solaris, predominantly using the 64-bit version. Once installation is complete, the user can run the MongoDB shell, which is an interesting change of pace from the command-line approach that older users of

MySQL will remember. MongoDB also provides support for a variety of programming languages (controlled through what MongoDB calls drivers):

- Ruby
- Python
- Perl
- PHP
- Java
- C
- C++
- Javascript

MongoDB uses the container metaphor by holding documents within collections, as opposed to the tabular column/row format used in relational databases (Figure 4.4).

The accessible data types are as follows:[16]

- Strings
- Arrays
- Embedded documents
- Dates
- Regular expressions
- Booleans

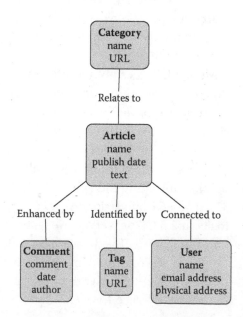

FIGURE 4.4
MongoDB high-level data structure

- Numbers
- MongoDB::OID
- Binary data
- MongoDB::Code
- MongoDB::MinKey
- MongoDB::MaxKey
- MongoDB::Timestamp

The data types in MongoDB are strictly typed. The types "regular expression," "MongoDB::Code," "binary data," "MongoDB::OID" (object identifier), and "date" are extensions to the JSON standard. These data may be embedded in the collection-document or a reference to the required information can be in the collection-document. The first approach forces data to reside within a document, potentially accelerating access.

Unique identification is achieved in MongoDB through the use of the _ id key, an automatic creation of the application. Because the key consists of 12 bytes, we increase the chances that we will be using a unique key (this key is 96 bits!). We can improve performance through the use of indexing, much like we improve the search tools on Windows and Macintosh OS X by allowing the system to index the hard drive. Our experience suggests that when you have the memory, using it for caching and taking the time to index are not losing propositions.

The document/BSON-based format that MongoDB uses makes it useful for geospatial indexing.[14] Locations on the planet are specified with latitude and longitude, so the basic data structure is relatively simple. These locations can be indexed and MongoDB has methods for ensuring that the database software understands that it is dealing with geospatial data. On the occasions when a compound key makes sense (MongoDB supports these), geospatial data can be indexed with a category parameter; for example, suppose we want to sort mountain peaks—this approach would allow us to quickly present the top seven, the top ten, or whatever we chose to retrieve. We could even store our mountain peak data with other attributes, such as elevation. When we query the database for geospatial information, MongoDB has a wonderful query operator called "$near," which allows the user to retrieve data that has some base attitude and longitude, but where the minutes and seconds are not right on that value. The "$within" operator lets the user look for values inside a specified shape. For example, we need only specify two corners of a box and the software will do the rest.[17]

Once we have data to store, we can use the MongoDB shell to create and access the database. On the surface, this approach seems much less formal that the top-heavy table creation used in relational databases. We caution, however, that a modicum of planning is more likely to produce a usable result than any kind of ad hoc creation. We recommend that the potential user considers a review of JSON/BSON and finds a way to model the structure of the database before committing to create a collection and a document. We could do a rapid model using mind-mapping software such as XMind, MindManager, freemind, or one of the others. Such an approach would allow the designer to visualize the structure of the database. If anything, MongoDB makes it—perhaps—a little too easy to create an impromptu database on the fly. Once we have a usable structure, we have no reason to avoid creating the database itself; of course, we can test a new database in the small before we have a major commitment.

Let's assume we have a functional database. At times, we will want to add data to the database by way of insertion (updating the database). MongoDB supplies an "insert" command. While "insert" can be used ad hoc, we do not recommend it (see previous paragraph). If we want to query our database, we would most likely use the "find" command for simple queries. When using "find," we can use key-values to find the data we really want to recall. We can also specify from which fields we want the data. MongoDB has a more complex "dot" notation for querying more complex data structures such as arrays and objects (remember, BSON is an extension of JSON).

Other functions exist to make the query a more useful tool:

- "Sort" will sort the results of the query based on an explicitly declared field.
- We can use "limit" to control the number of results returned by our query.
- We can skip x values using the "skip" command.

By now, we can see that MongoDB provides the necessary tools to make a useful database. Data can occur in the "natural" order of entry (insertion), or the data structure can be modified. We can also limit the size of the database (maybe we have a member database for a membership-limited golf club!). We can use a "validate" function to check the size of our collection; however, we return the number of documents with the "count()"operation. "Count" is a useful function because we can combine it with other functions to provide ourselves with count data regarding returned results.

We really like this database because it has tremendous power for library kinds of data; for example, although it can be scaled to big data standards, it can also be used for a personal book collection of hundreds of volumes or for movie and music collections. Another example would be bibliographies (or, by extension, book and journal collections); for example, the BibTeX structure use in LaTeX documents looks like this:

- Address: publisher's address, most commonly the city
- Annote: annotation for bibliographies requiring this information
- Author: author names separated by "and"
- Booktitle: The title of the book if only a subsection is being cited
- Chapter: chapter number
- Crossref: key of the cross-referenced entry
- Edition: edition of a book in long form (e.g., "second")
- Editor: editor names
- Eprint: electronic publication
- Howpublished: method of publishing, if the publishing method is nonstandard
- Institution: institution involved in publishing
- Journal: the journal or magazine in which the work was published
- Month: month of publication
- Note: miscellaneous extra information
- Number: the issue number of a journal, magazine, or tech report
- Organization: conference sponsor
- Pages: page numbers, when required
- Publisher: publisher's name
- School: school of the thesis
- Series: the series of books in which the book was published
- Title: title of the work
- URL: WWW address
- Volume: volume of a journal or multivolume book
- Year: year of publication

BibTeX types follow an "@" sign and precede the previous detailed information.

- Article
- Book
- Booklet

- Conference
- Inbook
- Incollection
- Inproceedings
- Manual
- Technical documentation.
- Mastersthesis
- Misc
- Phdthesis
- Proceedings
- Techreport
- Unpublished

The point we are making with this example is that we already have formats for structured databases of literary information. The BibTeX format is a natural for input to MongoDB. Here is an example using BSON, making use of the BibTeX approach:

{" type": "book" "support":[{"author" : "Kim Pries and Robert Dunnigan", "editor" : "John the Wizard", "Title" : "Big Data— Big Tools", "publisher" : "CRC Press", "year" : "2014", "volume" : "", "number" : "", "series" : "", "address" : "", "edition" : "first",]}

Since MongoDB works with all the major programming languages, we do not think it is much of stretch to see a BibTeX file converted into database format—let's use what we already have whenever possible.

Of course, MongoDB has the usual commands for renaming portions (collections, documents) as well as a "remove" command to delete the data. Removal exists at various levels:

- "Pop" to remove items from a document
- "Remove" to remove documents or collections

MongoDB is a bit coy about cross-references following a removal, so care is warranted.

We don't intend to provide a tutorial for this database, but we are enthusiastic about the possibilities. We would not be remarking on MongoDB if it were not capable of working in a big data environment. We have already mentioned the term "sharding," a technique for division of labor across multiple processors/computers/platforms.

Given the BSON data structures used by MongoDB, vertical data partitioning will not work. However, since MongoDB is a bit like a file cabinet, we have horizontal partitioning. We accomplish this splitting (sharding) with a sharding key function, which most computer scientists would recognize as the use of a hashing function. Because we can access the information we want across the network, multiple processors/machines function as if they were one large machine (note that we are not speaking of virtual machines *per se*). MongoDB can initiate auto-sharding, which allows the database to manage its own portions and simplifies work for the user. In our library database, we might break things up by genre (we did not use "genre" in our example), or by series/nonseries, or whatever makes sense. As with the structure of the database, we want to use some modicum of thought and design to avoid potential digital train wrecks! It should also be noted that when we don't tell MongoDB the field we want to use to set up the sharding, it will use its own "_id" key, which is arbitrary. This approach is not necessarily deadly to our goal; however, it may affect local caching.

While sharding, it is important to note that MongoDB supports easy cluster growth, is relatively transparent (we do not have to know that much about how things are working in order to function), and has some redundancy to handle a failure at a node. A good big data database should not collapse gracelessly when the inevitable event occurs. If we shard on a given server, we produce subsets of our full database; however, if we shard across multiple servers, we produce copies of the subsets for each server. MongoDB supports automatic balancing and migration as the needs of the database change; for example, the situation can arise where a given shard grows to a suboptimal size—the database will generally take care of this situation for us. We consider this to be a desirable approach, since we do not need the database migrating huge amounts of data while in use.

Of course, sharding involves much more than we intend to cover in this book. A good resource for understanding the scalability of MongoDB is *Scaling MongoDB*.[18]

KEY-VALUE DATABASES

Relational sharding exists; for example, eBay uses this approach to support their big data issue with database queries. We must really understand our database domains well in order to shard a relational database. Another approach would be to use key-values that nicely partition across the various shards. Table-based methods exist as well (effectively, an index). To put things in perspective, let's look at YouTube (Google subsidiary) and the values they posted on their website[19]:

- **Viewership**
  - More than 1 billion unique users visit YouTube each month.
  - Over 6 billion hours of video are watched each month on YouTube—that's almost an hour for every person on Earth, and 50% more than last year.
  - 100 hours of video are uploaded to YouTube every minute
  - 80% of YouTube traffic comes from outside the US
  - YouTube is localized in 61 countries and across 61 languages
  - According to Nielsen, YouTube reaches more US adults ages 18–34 than any cable network
  - Millions of subscriptions happen each day. The number of people subscribing daily is up more than 3x since last year, and the number of daily subscriptions is up more than 4x since last year
- **YouTube Partner Program**
  - Created in 2007, they have more than a million creators from over 30 countries around the world earning money from their YouTube videos
  - Thousands of channels are making six figures a year
- **Monetization**
  - Thousands of advertisers are using TrueView in-stream and 75% of their in-stream ads are now skippable
  - They have more than a million advertisers using Google ad platforms, the majority of which are small businesses
- **Mobile and Devices**
  - Mobile makes up almost 40% of YouTube's global watch time
  - YouTube is available on hundreds of millions of devices
- **Content ID**
  - Content ID scans over 400 years of video every day
  - More than 5,000 partners use Content ID, including major US network broadcasters, movie studios and record labels
  - They have more than 25 million reference files in our Content ID database; it's among the most comprehensive in the world
  - Content ID has generated hundreds of millions of dollars for partners.

Some of these numbers, of course, are what prompted Google to invent MapReduce and other distributed solutions in the first place.

We have looked at a graphic database and a document database—Cassandra is a key-value database, originating at Facebook, but ultimately ending up at the Apache Foundation. Releasing software to the Apache Foundation can encourage further open-source development. A Facebook paper released in 2009 describes the data model[20]: A table in Cassandra is a distributed multidimensional map indexed by a key. The value is an object that is highly structured. The row key in a table is a string with no size restrictions, although it is typically from 16 to 36 bytes long. Every operation under a single row key is atomic per replica, no matter how many columns are being read or written into. Columns are grouped together into sets called column families, in a very similar way to what happens in the Bigtable system. Cassandra exposes two kinds of columns families: simple and super column families. Super column families can be visualized as a column family within a column family.

Not only do we have a key-value, but access requires the name of a table, and in many cases, a column name; hence, like many big data databases, Cassandra is strongly column oriented. At least three large web firms use Cassandra for part of their operations: Twitter, Facebook (not surprisingly!), and Digg.

Cassandra installation is quasi-manual—Apache supplies download versions for Debian Linux, and by default, Apple Macintosh and Microsoft Windows. The fact that the software downloads as a GNU zip file indicates that it does not have an automatic installer. Assistance for installing Cassandra on a Macintosh can be found at http://www.datastax.com/2012/01/working-with-apache-cassandra-on-mac-os-x. Assistance for installing Cassandra on Windows can be found at http://www.datastax.com/2012/01/getting-started-with-apache-cassandra-on-windows-the-easy-way. Datastax makes community versions available (note that the Windows version runs on Windows 7). Because the Macintosh is effectively FreeBSD/NetBSD under the hood (with substantial modifications), installation is similar to installation on Linux. As with most Unix-y systems, we can build the database from source code. Kindly note that we will also have to set some environment variables, alas. These installation issues are not a gigantic hurdle, but it does take more computer knowledge to install successfully.

We test our installation of Cassandra at first through the use of the command-line interface "Cassandra-cli." This approach is reminiscent of MySQL before graphical front ends existed for the database. Table 4.2 shows a list of the top-level commands.

TABLE 4.2

Top-Level Commands for Cassandra Database

Command	Meaning
?	Display this message
Help	Display help
Help	Display command-specific help
Connect/	Connect to thrift service
Use ["password"]	Switch to keyspace
Describe keyspace	Describe keyspace
Exit	Exit CLI
Quit	Exit CLI
Show cluster name	Display cluster name
Show keyspaces	Show a list of keyspaces
Show api version	Show server API version
Create keyspace [with= [and=...]]	Add a new keyspace with the specified attribute and value(s)
Create column family [with= [and=...]]	Create a new column family with the specified attribute and value(s)
Drop keyspace	Delete keyspace
Drop column family	Delete column family
Rename keyspace <keyspace_new_name>	Rename keyspace
Rename column family <new_name>	Rename column family

Do not write this database off because the interface seems primitive! The database is powerful! Rather than a table-oriented approach such as that used by relational databases, Cassandra assigns a name to value, producing a name/value pair—hence the term "key-value pair." Basically, with appropriate planning (much like MongoDB), we can use names that make sense to us, the user. We recommend that users plan any database rather than throwing something together. Planning does not preclude experimentation, and in some cases, test "toy" databases can be used for proof-of-concept explorations. Because many of the big data databases are not table-oriented, it is sometimes easier to create these small experimental stabs at verifying our thinking. One of us used to run experimental versions of databases using MySQL, so even the relational model is not too difficult to use for experimental verification.

If we were extending our book information idea to Cassandra, we would see a family resemblance to what we did with MongoDB. One major difference, however, is the use of column designators and time stamps in Cassandra. In other words, Cassandra maintains something of the tabular orientation we find in relational databases:

- Row keys
- Super column families
- Column families
- Column names

The various levels of columns help the database developer decide how to agglomerate data so it makes sense to the user and eases retrieval.

Another level of structure in Cassandra is the keyspace, which is analogous to a namespace (say, Java), and provides a container for multiple nodes within a cluster of servers. The keyspace will need information, like a cluster name, replication requirements, column information, and more. Think of each of these structural items as if they were containers, and you will get a better picture of how they operate. For example, column families are stored as separate files. In essence, we have a way of storing "clumps" of related (not "relational") information without necessarily having to have a specific column to indicate relatedness.

Users of Cassandra may also know about wide rows (many columns, few rows) and skinny rows (few columns, many rows), as well as hybrids of these structures. A wide row might contain lists, while a skinny row will bear a vague resemblance to a relational database. Wide rows may have sorted columns as well. To manage our columns we will use a structure called a super column.

Keys can be multipart; that is, they are composite keys. These keys are used for queries and can function as an alternative to the super column. Do not expect to find SQL or any real query language for Cassandra, although an API does exist. This database is truly a tool for a master! Data modeling, while potentially important in this context, is probably less significant than query modeling. Query modeling is where we focus on what we want from the database rather than what we put into the database. With our book example, we might want to search from title to author or author to title(s), we might need the ISBN and publisher information, or perhaps we have built in some annotations of interest (e.g., reviews). This information will help tell us how to define our queries and follow that with what goes into the database. With Cassandra, queries drive contents; with a relational database, contents drive queries (in general).

As with any database, we create, read, update, and delete (CRUD) with Cassandra. Consistency of reads is tuneable, based on our defined needs (whatever they may be) to have consistency among nodes. We suspect this feature is more a database administration issue, but the user should be aware of this capability. Also, we can query one node, wait for a quorum of nodes, or query all nodes depending on what we want out of the system.

The point here is that replication can produce problems with multireplicate consistency; hence, at times we may wish to assure ourselves that we are looking at the most recent data. The "all" approach effectively guarantees that we have the most recent data; however, the "quorum" approach may be satisfactory and is likely to be much faster than "all." Writing is symmetrical with reading; that is, we have "one," "quorum," and "all" modes here as well. By now, it should be obvious that Cassandra is eminently tuneable—perhaps a trade-off we receive for the lack of a pretty front end. Also note that one of the major read capabilities for Cassandra is called slicing, which is the method for accessing a range of keys; the other primary method for accessing data is through the use of column tools. In addition, Cassandra has tools for "mass updates" such as "batch mutate," which allow for a collection of insert and update operations.

While Cassandra itself has no front-end *per se*, some third-party approaches exist:

- Chiton (https://github.com/driftx/chiton)
- Cassandra-gui (https://code.google.com/a/apache-extras.org/p/cassandra-gui/)
- Toad (Eclipse plug-in) (http://www.quest.com/toad-for-cloud-databases/)
- Cass-UI (https://code.google.com/p/cassui/)

Toad may provide the most visually appealing interface of these four; however, all of them are relatively primitive compared to a full-blown commercial database administration package. On the other hand, we don't have to pay hundreds of thousands of dollars just for the license to install the software. We feel the real question comes down to user needs; for example, if we only allow database administration professionals to touch the database, then cruder front-end implementations are largely irrelevant! Make no mistake: in our estimation, Cassandra is the high-speed tool of a master.

Thanks to its roots as a large-scale (read "big data") database platform, Cassandra has substantial logging capabilities. Other management tools are available also:

- JMX (Java)
- MBeans (Java)
- JHAT (Java heap analysis tool)
- JMAP (Java memory mapping tool)

Consistent with the rest of the Cassandra ecosystem, these tools are powerful but not really user-friendly in the sense that they are easy to use and understand.

True to its speed-based heritage, Cassandra presents several opportunities for tuning performance. Cassandra protects users and itself by using a high-speed file called the commit log—in the event of a catastrophic shutdown, the system will read the commit log to restore any updates that may not have occurred at the time of the failure. The longer-term, and more standard, database write occurs with a datafile.[21] One of the means of tuning allows the user to decide on the size of these files. The commit log in particular has a synchronizing mode and a nonsynchronizing mode. Our recommendation is that we always use a forced "synch" rather than take the risk that our write does not complete. On the other hand, data integrity is not a very high-level concern (perhaps we have so much data arriving, we have this flexibility), then we might consider taking the risk of not writing to the commit log and thereby increase our performance.

We have mentioned Cassandra's columns. Each family of columns has a data structure called a *memtable* that contains these columns. Since a memtable can become gigantic, choice of size presents yet another opportunity for tuning the database. Memtables can receive a forced write called a *flush* and we, the user, can also determine how long they reside in temporary memory after such a flushing.

Cassandra writes faster than it reads: when it writes, it knows exactly where the data is going; when it reads, it must search to fulfill the query. Reads will generally match the maximum number of hardware-supported threads (e.g., a quad-core system will have eight threads). Cassandra, like most databases, will cache information; in the case of this database, the primary constituents of the cache will be rows and keys, which, given the architecture of the data set, makes a lot of sense. Before setting any cache parameters, we would want to consider the kinds of queries we are likely to employ; once again, we are seeing Cassandra as a query-driven database, perhaps more than any other. Finally, we can also set buffer sizes, relating to indices, data, and slices (portions somewhat similar to slicing in a pivot table in an Excel spreadsheet). We know of other tuning activities that we could use by employing Python or the Java Virtual Machine, but these are outside the scope of this book.

COLUMN-ORIENTED DATABASES

HBase

Initial big data solutions to the tsunami of data involved activities that were time constrained; that is, we would only keep the last x days' worth of data because we didn't have enough storage or processing capability to do anything else.

In a world of real-time responses and lean concepts, we took some steps backward and reexamined the possibilities of using batch processing to solve some data processing issues. In essence, even when it occurs very quickly, that approach is what we are using when we employ Hadoop and MapReduce to solve problems through distributed processing. This method reduces the need for immediate data processing and allows us to analyze the overall problem for potential optimization of processing.

One solution to this data processing issue is the employment of column-oriented databases, where data is grouped by columns (not necessarily the same as those in Cassandra). We can then store these columns on disk in a way that makes for efficient access, which in many cases makes more sense than the row-oriented approach used by relational databases.

HBase is a quasi-column-oriented database that uses efficient storage on disk. HBase employs some level of key-values to access data. If we think about it, we would expect column-oriented storage to provide some benefits, if only for the reason that a specific column will typically hold a specific type of data, even when we use a relational database.

As with some of the other databases we look at in this book, HBase data can be accessed without SQL, although we have seen vendors who provide SQL-like languages for some of the big data alternative databases, presumably to make it easier for those individuals who tend to think in terms of SQL approaches to querying. However, the atomicity, consistency, isolation, and durability (ACID) requirements for consistency are generally not enforceable with high-speed big data databases, since they are largely incompatible with performance and high levels of availability. The alternative to ACID is BASE (basic availability, soft-state, eventual consistency—how long did it take somebody to come up with this humorous alternative?). A database that adheres to the BASE approach is fault tolerant; we know this to be the case because of Brewer's CAP theorem (you can have two out of the three qualities of consistency, availability, and partition tolerance).[22] The CAP theorem appears—empirically—to be the case thanks to the need for scalability in the world of big data processing (the intrepid reader may wish to consider another modality called "resource versioning" at http://code.google.com/apis/gdata/docs/2.0/reference.html#ResourceVersioning and http://www.johndcook.com/blog/2009/07/06/brewer-cap-theorem-base/).

What about database normalization? With a database like HBase (and many of the big data databases), we might want to consider *de*-normalization!. We can denormalize our database by duplicate data—we should remember that normalization is generally the reduction of duplication. When dealing with distributed systems, we simply replicate the data we have in order to remove latency issues on given nodes. Our column orientation and wide tables should remove the need for joins; however, we will most likely proliferate compound keys so that we can access our data expeditiously.

HBase is effectively an open-source instantiation of Google's Bigtable concept: designed for distributed processing and eminently scalable. The fundamental structures of HBase are tables, rows, columns, and cells. Do not be misled by the term "table"—yes, the database has tables and row keys, but it is still oriented around columns for intelligent data storage and high-speed access. Like Cassandra, HBase has column families, which are basically aggregates of columns. Cells are timestamped, which allows for multiple versions of data that is likely to change.

Like MongoDB, HBase has an automatic sharding capability, which allows both splitting and merging (reducing the file count). Pure HBase has no support for SQL, but as with Cassandra, it supports an API. While data in HBase is considered to be immutable, it is possible to mark a key with a delete marker, thus serving the function of record deletion. In addition to pseudodeletion, HBase can compact by either merging (minimal compaction) or rewriting all files (maximal compaction, wherein data marked "deleted" will ultimately disappear).

One sees from Figure 4.5 that HBase is highly hierarchical without being an old-fashioned hierarchical database. In storage, the fundamental structure is the HFile, which consists of blocks, which in turn consist of data, key-values, file information, indices, potential metadata, and a trailer (which points to the file information and the indices). Although HBase can be used with any file system, we suspect that many times the Hadoop file system (HDFS) will be in use even though the block size is 1 K larger than the block size for HBase. MapReduce may be used with HBase,

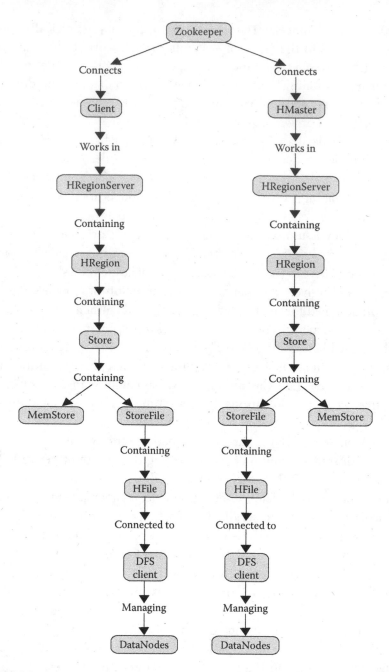

FIGURE 4.5
HBase architecture.

once appropriate configuration steps have occurred (e.g., using a JAR file with the required libraries). Heavily used classes in MapReduce are:

- InputFormat
- Mapper
- Reducer
- OutputFormat

InputFormat splits the input data and returns a RecordReader instance, setting us up for the next method. Mapper will use key-value pairs. Reduce performs the usual recombine activity. OutputFormat writes to files— essentially, HBase tables.

Even though we call HBase a columnar database, it does indeed have key-values, which contain:

- Key length
- Value length
- Row length
- Row
- Column family length
- Column family
- Column qualifier
- Time stamp
- Key type
- Value (at last!)

Key structures are row key and column key, which means sorting order becomes important. Retrieval of information uses key scans and partial key scans.

As with other databases we have examined, HBase protects the user with a log file, which in this case is called a write-ahead log. Sometimes we will see the word "journal," but the concept is the same—we write a "stream of consciousness" (metaphor) of what we ultimately intend to put into the database.

Apache ZooKeeper was developed to maintain an open-source server, thus enabling highly reliable distributed coordination. ZooKeeper is a centralized service that maintains configuration information and naming and provides distributed synchronization and group services. Each time the services are implemented, a lot of work goes into fixing the unavoidable bugs and race conditions. Zookeeper "herds" the various services by distilling the essence of these different services into a simple interface connected to a centralized coordination metaservice, which is distributed and highly reliable. Consensus, group-management, and presence protocols are implemented by the service to ensure that applications do not need to instantiate them by themselves.

Apache Accumulo

HBase is not the only key-value/columnar database in town! Apache Accumulo is a sorted, distributed key/value store that is a robust, scalable, high-performance data storage and retrieval system. Apache Accumulo is based on Google's Bigtable design and is a superstructure to Apache Hadoop, Zookeeper, and Thrift. Apache Accumulo features some improvements to the Bigtable approach in the form of cell-based access control and a server-side programming mechanism that can modify key/value pairs at various points in the data management process.

The feature set of Accumulo is as follows[23]:

- Table design and configuration
  - Iterators
    - Server-side programming mechanisms to encode functions such as filtering and aggregation.
  - Cell labels
    - Additional portion of the key that sorts after the column qualifier and before the time stamp.
  - Constraints
    - Configurable conditions under which writes to a table will be rejected.
  - Sharding
    - Through the use of specialized iterators, Accumulo can be a parallel sharded document store.
  - Large rows
    - When reading rows, this database framework has no requirement that an entire row fits into memory.
- Integrity/availability
  - Master failover
    - Multiple masters can be configured. Zookeeper locks are used to determine which master is active. The remaining masters

simply wait for the current master to lose its lock. Current master state is held in the metadata table and Zookeeper.

- Write ahead log
- Tablet servers send mutations to loggers, which write to the local file system, not HDFS.
    - Each mutation is written to multiple loggers, before being committed, much like in HBase and for the same reason.
- Logical time
    - A mechanism to ensure that server set times never go backwards, even when time across the cluster is incorrect.
- Logical time for bulk import (1.4)
    - Logical time as described above works with streaming (batch) processing, where the tablet server assigns the time stamp. Logical time is also important for bulk imported data, for which the client code may be choosing a time stamp.
- FATE (1.4)
    - Fault Tolerant Executor, for executing operations in a fault-tolerant manner.
- Scalable master
    - Stores its metadata in an Accumulo table and Zookeeper.
- Isolation
    - Scans will not see data inserted into a row after the scan of that row begins.
- Performance
    - Relative encoding
        - If consecutive keys have identical portions (row, colf, colq, or colvis), there is a flag to indicate that a portion is the same as that of the previous key.
    - Native in-memory map
        - By default, written data is stored outside of Java-managed memory into a C++ STL map of maps. It maps rows to columns to values. This hierarchical structure improves the performance of inserting a mutation with multiple column values in a single row.
    - Scan pipeline
        - A long-running Accumulo scan will eventually cause multiple threads to start: one server thread to read data from disk, one server thread to serialize and send data, and one client thread to deserialize and read data. When pipelining kicks

in, it substantially increases scan speed while maintaining key order. It does not activate for short scans.

- Caching
  - Recently scanned data are cached into memory. There are separate caches for indexes and data.
- Multilevel RFile index (1.4) 'RFiles store an index of the last key in each block. For large files, the index can become quite large. When the index is large, a lot of memory is consumed and files take a long time to open. To avoid this problem, RFiles in 1.4 have a multilevel index tree. Index blocks can point to other index blocks or data blocks. The entire index never has to be resident, even when the file is written. When an index block exceeds the configurable size threshold, it is written out between data blocks. The size of index blocks is configurable on a per table basis.
- Binary Search IN RFile blocks (1.5). RFile uses its index to locate a block of key-values. Once it reaches a block, it performs a linear scan to find a key of interest. Starting with 1.5, Accumulo will generate indexes of cached blocks in an adaptive manner. Accumulo indexes the blocks that are read most frequently. When a block is read a few times, a small index is generated. As a block is read more, larger indexes are generated, making future seeks faster. This strategy allows Accumulo to dynamically respond to read patterns without precomputing block indexes when RFiles are written.
- Testing
  - Mock
    - The Accumulo client API has a mock implementation that is useful for writing unit tests for execution against Accumulo. Mock Accumulo is in memory and in process.
  - Mini Accumulo cluster (1.5 & 1.4.4)
    - Mini Accumulo cluster is a set of utility codes that makes it easy to spin up a local Accumulo instance running against the local file system. Mini Accumulo is slower than Mock Accumulo, but its behavior mirrors a real Accumulo instance more closely.
  - Functional test
    - Small, system-level tests of basic Accumulo features run in a test harness, external to the build and unit-tests. These tests

start a complete Accumulo instance, and require Hadoop and Zookeeper to be running. They attempt to simulate the basic functions of Accumulo, as well as common failure conditions, such as lost disks, killed processes, and read-only file systems.

- Scale test
    - A test suite that verifies data is not lost at scale. This test runs many ingest clients that continually create linked lists containing 25 million nodes. At some point the clients are stopped and a MapReduce job is run to ensure no linked list has a hole. A hole indicates data was lost by Accumulo. The Agitator can be run in conjunction with this test to randomly kill tablet servers. This test suite has uncovered many obscure data-loss bugs. This test also helps find bugs that impact uptime and stability when run for days or weeks.
    - Random walk test
- A test suite that looks for unexpected system states that may emerge in plausible real-world applications. Application components are defined as test nodes (such as create table, insert data, scan data, delete table, etc.), and are programmed as Java classes that implement with a specified interface. The nodes are connected together in a graph specified in an XML document. Many processes independently and concurrently execute a random walk of the test graphs. Some of the test graphs have a concept of correctness and can verify data over time. Other tests have no concept of data correctness and have the simple goal of crashing Accumulo. Many obscure bugs have been uncovered by this testing framework and subsequently corrected.
- Client API
    - Batch scanner
        - Takes a list of ranges, batches them to the appropriate tablet servers, and returns data as it is received (i.e., not in sorted order).
    - Batch writer
    - Clients buffer writes in memory before sending them in batches to the appropriate tablet servers.
    - Bulk import
        - Instead of writing individual mutations to Accumulo, entire files of sorted key-value pairs can be imported. These files

are moved into the Accumulo directory and referenced by Accumulo. This feature is useful for ingesting a large amount of data. This method of ingest usually offers higher throughput at the cost of higher latency for data availability for scans. Usually the data is sorted using MapReduce and then bulk imported. This method of ingest also allows for flexibility in resource allocation. The nodes running map reduce to sort data could be different from the Accumulo nodes.

- MapReduce
  - Accumulo can be a source and/or sink for MapReduce jobs.
- Thrift proxy (1.5 & 1.4.4)
  - The Accumulo client code contains a lot of complexity. For example, the client code locates tablets, retries in the case of failures, and supports concurrent reading and writing. All of this is written in Java. The thrift proxy wraps the Accumulo client API with thrift, making this API easily available to other languages like Python, Ruby, C++, etc.
  - Extensible behaviors
- Pluggable Balancer
  - Users can provide a balancer plug-in that decides how to distribute tablets across a table. These plug-ins can be provided on a per-table basis. This is useful for ensuring a particular table's tablets are placed optimally for tables with special query needs. The default balancer randomly spreads each table's tablets across the cluster. It takes into account where a tablet was previously hosted to leverage locality. When a tablet splits, the default balancer moves one child to another tablet server. The assumption here is that splitting tablets are being actively written to, so this keeps write load evenly spread.
- Pluggable Memory Manager
  - The plug-in that decides when and what tablets to do a minor compact is configurable. The default plug-in compacts the largest tablet when memory is over a certain threshold. It varies the threshold over time depending on minor compaction speed. It flushes tablets that are not written to for a configurable time period.
- Pluggable logger assignment strategy
  - The plug-in that decides which loggers should be assigned to which tablet servers is configurable.

- General administration
  - Monitor page
    - A simple web server provides basic information about the system health and performance. It displays table sizes, ingest and query statistics, server load, and last-update information. It also allows the user to view recent diagnostic logs and traces.
  - Tracing
    - It can be difficult to determine why some operations are taking longer than expected. For example, you may be looking up items with very low latency, but sometimes the lookups take much longer. Determining the cause of the delay is difficult because the system is distributed, and the typical lookup is fast. Accumulo has been instrumented to record the time that various operations take when tracing is turned on. The fact that tracing is enabled means that all the requests made on behalf of the user are followed throughout the distributed infrastructure of Accumulo, and across all threads of execution.
  - Online reconfiguration
    - System and per-table configuration is stored in Zookeeper. Many, but not all, configuration changes take effect while Accumulo is running. Some do not take effect until server processes are restarted.
  - Table renaming
    - Tables can be renamed easily because Accumulo uses internal table IDs and stores mappings between names and IDs in Zookeeper.
- Internal data management
  - Locality groups
    - Groups columns within a single file. There is a default locality group so that not all columns need be specified. The locality groups can be restructured while the table is online and the changes will take effect on the next compaction. A tablet can have files with different locality-group configurations. In this case scans may be suboptimal, but correct, until compactions rewrite all files. After reconfiguring locality groups, a user can force a table to compact in order to write all data into the new locality groups. Alternatively, the change could be

allowed to happen over time as writes to the table cause compactions to happen.

- Smart compaction algorithm
  - It is inefficient to merge small files with large files. Accumulo merges files only if all files are larger than a configurable ratio (default is 3) multiplied by the largest file size. If this cannot be done with all the files, the largest file is removed from consideration, and the remaining files are considered for compaction. This is done until there are no files to merge.
- Merging minor compaction (1.4)
  - When a maximum number of files per tablet is reached, minor compactions will merge data from the in-memory map with the smallest file instead of creating new files. This throttles ingest. In previous releases, new files were just created even if major compactions were falling behind and the number of tablets per file was growing. Without this feature, ingest performance can roughly continue at a constant rate, even as scan performance decreases because tablets have too many files.
- Loading jars using VFS (1.5)
  - User written iterators are a useful way to manipulate data in data in Accumulo. Before 1.5., users had to copy their iterators to each tablet server. Starting with 1.5, Accumulo can load iterators from HDFS using Apache commons VFS.
- On-demand data management
  - Compactions
    - This method provides the ability to force tablets to compact to one file. Even tablets with one file are compacted. This is useful for improving query performance, permanently applying iterators, or using a new locality-group configuration. One example of using iterators is applying a filtering iterator to remove data from a table. As of 1.5, users can initiate a compaction with iterators only applied to that compaction event.
  - Split points
    - Arbitrary split points can be added to an online table at any point in time. This is useful for increasing ingest performance on a new table. It can also be used to accommodate new data patterns in an existing table.

- Tablet merging (1.4)
    - Tablet merging is a new feature. Merging of tablets can be requested in the shell; Accumulo does not merge tablets automatically. In 1.5, the METADATA tablets can be merged.
- Table cloning (1.4)
    - Allows users to quickly create a new table that references an existing table's data and copies its configuration. A cloned table and its source table can be mutated independently. Testing was the motivating reason behind this new feature. For example, it can be used to test a new filtering iterator, clone the table, add the filter to the clone, and force a major compaction.
- Import/export table (1.5)
    - An off-line table's metadata and files can easily be copied to another cluster and imported.
- Compact range (1.4)
    - Compacts each tablet that falls within a row range down to a single file.
- Delete range (1.4)
    - Adds an operation to efficiently delete a range of rows from a table. Tablets that fall completely within a range are simply dropped. Tablets overlapping the beginning and end of the range are split, compacted, and then merged.

REFERENCES

1. Positive feedback. Wikipedia. http://en.wikipedia.org/wiki/Positive_feedback. Accessed March 12, 2014.
2. McCreary, D. and A. Kelly. *Making Sense of NoSQL*. Shelter Island, NY: Manning Publications Company, 2014.
3. George, L. *HBase: The Definitive Guide*. Sebastopol, CA: O'Reilly Media, 2011.
4. Apache Software Foundation. Welcome to Apache HBase. http://hbase.apache.org/. Apache HBase. Last modified 2013. Accessed December 4, 2013.
5. HBase/PoweredBy. Hadoop Wiki. Last modified November 11, 2013. http://wiki. apache.org/hadoop/Hbase/PoweredBy. Accessed December 4, 2013.
6. Chang, F., J. Dean, S. Ghemawat, W. C. Hsieh., D. A. Wallach, M. Burrows, T. Chandra, A. Fikes, and R. E. Gruber. Bigtable: A distributed storage system .for structured data. In 7th USENIX Symposium on Operating Systems Design and Implementation, November 6–8, Seattle, WA. http://static.googleusercontent.com/media/research. google.com/en/us/archive/bigtable-osdi06.pdf.
7. Dean, J. and S. Ghemawat. MapReduce: Simplified data processing on large clusters. Google, 2004.

8. Laemmel, R. *Google's MapReduce Programming Model—Revisited.* Redmond, WA: Microsoft, 2010.

9. MongoDB. MapReduce and sharded collections. MongoDB Manual. Last modified 2013. http://docs.mongodb.org/manual/core/map-reduce-sharded-collections/. Accessed December 5, 2013.

10. Tweed, R. and G. James. A universal NoSQL engine, using a tried and tested technology. Creative Commons Attribution CC-BY 3.0. Creative Commons, 2010.

11. Seeger, M. *Key-Value Stores: A Practical Overview.* Stuttgart, Germany: Medieninformatik, 2009.

12. Neo Technology. Chapter 1. Neo4j highlights. *Neo4j: The Graph Database.* Last modified 2013. http://docs.neo4j.org/chunked/milestone/introduction-highlights.html Accessed December 6, 2013.

13. Robinson, I., J. Webber, and E. Eifrem. *Graph Database.* Sebastopol, CA: O'Reilly Media, 2013.

14. Plugge, E., P. Membrey, and T. Hawkins. *The Definitive Guide to MongoDB: The NoSQL Database for Cloud and Desktop Computing.* New York: Springer-Verlag, 2010.

15. MongoDB. http://www.mongodb.org/. Accessed January 7, 2014.

16. MongoDB. MongoDB Perl Driver. Last modified 2013. http://api.mongodb.org/perl/current/MongoDB/DataTypes.htm. Accessed January 7, 2014.

17. MongoDB. 2d index internals. Last modified 2013. http://docs.mongodb.org/manual/core/geospatial-indexes/. Accessed January 8, 2014..

18. Chodorow, K. *Scaling MongoDB.* Sebastopol, CA: O'Reilly Media, 2011.

19. YouTube. Statistics. http://www.youtube.com/yt/press/statistics.html. Accessed January 12, 2014.

20. Lakshman, A. and P. Malik. *Cassandra—A Decentralized Structured Storage System.* Facebook, 2009.

21. Hewitt, E. *Cassandra: The Definitive Guide.* Sebastopol, CA: O'Reilly Media, 2011.

22. Brewer, E. Toward robust distributed systems. PODC Keynote: July 19, 2000.

23. Accumulo. Apache Accumulo notable features. Last modified 2013. http://accumulo.apache.org/notable_features.html. Accessed January 19, 2014.

5

Machine Learning

This chapter is more about what you can do with these tools than it is about covering them from A to Z. In most cases, we will provide a list of tools available at the time of this writing. The wave of big data analysis is just beginning (really!); hence, many of the tools require some technical knowledge in order to use them. For example, the archetype of big data tools for statistics is the statistical language R, which is primarily command-line driven. Figure 5.1 shows a plethora of tools.

MACHINE LEARNING BASICS

What is machine learning? Machine learning is the application of computer software and hardware to recognize patterns and develop actions to respond to these patterns. It is not necessarily the same as using neural networks to learn (although these may be the correct tool in some circumstances), nor is it a traditional expert system.

Why would we use machine learning? We would use machine learning because, if we are able to detect the patterns of interest, the machine can perform the work much more quickly than can the human; or alternatively, the machine can do the work during "downtime" for the human (e.g., sleeping).

When would we use machine learning? We would use machine learning when the cost of the development is less than the cost of doing it ourselves or when the benefit is sufficiently significant to merit this kind of development.

Who would use machine learning? Machine learning covers many areas; however, the most likely candidates are individuals who are being

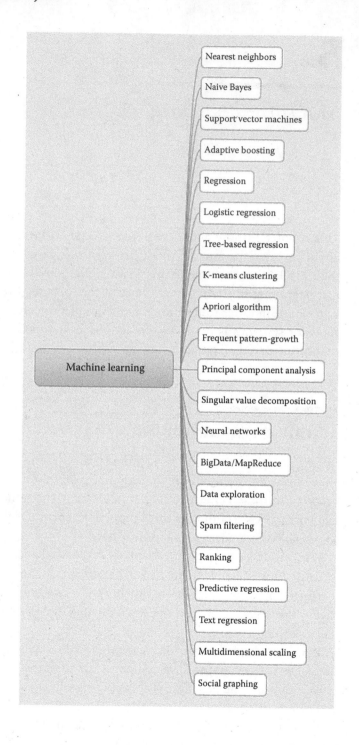

FIGURE 5.1
Machine learning tools.

swamped by influxes of data. We have seen the term "data-driven" proudly touted by educators, but "data" is relatively useless until we convert it into information. That is the rationale for using machine learning: the conversion of data to information.

How do we implement machine learning?   Sadly, we must implement current models of machine learning with some level of trial and error. If we are more sophisticated, we will develop a suite of tests that can drive our decision making; in effect, we, as users, are also learning as we conduct our experiments.

CLASSIFYING WITH NEAREST NEIGHBORS

What is the nearest-neighbors approach?   This algorithm selects a "label" for an item under study. In essence, the algorithm will classify for us based on the criteria we establish for the classification. Clearly, the choices of criteria are critical. A good description of the algorithm from the statistical point of view is available at http://www.statsoft.com/textbook/k-nearest-neighbors/ (Statsoft owns Statistica).

Why would we use nearest neighbors?   We use this algorithm when we have many items to classify and the classification process is tedious and time-consuming. Even with this algorithm, we can expect a fairly high consumption of resources, since we do a substantial number of comparisons.

When would we use nearest neighbors?   We would use this approach when it makes good business sense to do so. We must have tested the criteria with trial data sets and we generally prefer that the criteria be relatively obvious; in other words, we are not looking for a fuzzy solution, unless we define our classification system to have some hybrid forms.

Who would use nearest neighbors?   As an example, we might use word counts or word appearances in Google books to classify them by genre, particularly when we have authors who wrote in more than one genre; for example, Charles Dickens wrote novels, but some of those novels were historical romances, others were oriented around social distress, some were autobiographical, and others were comedies of manners. We could use criteria such as:

- Book length
- Sentence length

- Key words (!!)
- Date of authorship
- Word frequencies (specific words)

We can even classify our books as to whether we agree with the authorship or not, allowing us to potentially detect fakes.

How do we implement machine learning? We are basically comparing our unknown item or items with existing samples of items with well-known criteria. We use a metaphor of location and allow those items with the closest "distance" to vote on the new item—majority rules. Some tools are as follows:

- K-nearest neighbors, a MATLAB® tool (http://www.mathworks.com/matlabcentral/fileexchange/15562-k-nearest-neighbors).
- Another MATLAB tool, knnsearch (http://www.mathworks.com/help/stats/knnsearch.html).
- Lucene (http://lucene.apache.org/): Instructions for using Lucene are available at http://raimonb.wordpress.com/2013/01/02/text-categorization-with-k-nearest-neighbors-using-lucene/.
- allknn (http://trac.research.cc.gatech.edu/fastlab/doxygen/nstutorial.html), a member tool of MLPACK (http://www.mlpack.org/).
- kknn (cran.us.r-project.org/), R tool for weighted k-nearest neighbors.
- knnGarden (cran.us.r-project.org/), R tool for multidistance-based k-nearest neighbors.
- MTSKNN (cran.us.r-project.org/), R tool for multivariate two-sample tests.
- CIShell (http://wiki.cns.iu.edu/pages/viewpage.action?-pageId=1246648): CIShell provides many open-source tools for data analysis.

NAIVE BAYES

What is the naive Bayes approach? The naive Bayes approach, not surprisingly given the name, uses prior probabilities, likelihoods, and posterior probabilities to classify "incoming" data items.

Why would we use the naive Bayes approach? We would use the naive Bayes approach because it is incredibly simple to implement.

When would we use the naive Bayes approach? The naive Bayes approach is suitable for simple filtering and straightforward classification when we want a machine to do the work.

Who would use the naive Bayes approach? For starters, we would expect anyone who uses a "Bayesian" approach to be unprejudiced regarding Bayesian methods. For some reason, the Bayesian approach seems to produce horror in the eyes of some statisticians!

How do we implement the naive Bayes approach? Some software packages already exist to support the naive Bayes approach:

- Apache Mahout (http://mahout.apache.org/)
- Orange (http://orange.biolab.si/): open-source data visualization and analysis for novices and experts; data mining through visual programming or Python scripting; components for machine learning; add-ons for bioinformatics and text mining
- Weka (http://www.cs.waikato.ac.nz/ml/weka/)
- jBNC (http://jbnc.sourceforge.net/): a Bayesian Network Classifier Toolbox
- Naive Bayes
  - TAN: tree augmented naive Bayes
  - FAN: forest augmented naive Bayes
  - STAN: selective tree augmented naive Bayes
  - STAND: selective tree augmented naive Bayes with node discarding
  - SFAN: selective forest augmented naive Bayes
  - STAND: selective forest augmented naive Bayes with node discarding

SUPPORT VECTOR MACHINES

What are vector machines? These approaches are sometimes called support vector networks. This classifier will assign a new value into one category or another, making it a binary tool.

Why would we use vector machines? These routines tend to be quick, thanks in part to the binary classification mechanism.

When would we use vector machines? We would use this tool when our classification needs are straightforward and we are more interested in speed.

Who would use vector machines? The tools we mention below have a formidable list of arguments. The user would do well to explore known practice sets before using the tool.

How do we implement vector machines?

- SVMlight (http://svmlight.joachims.org/), and its brethren SVMperf, SVMstruct, and SVMrank, are implemented in C. Note that this program is free only for scientific use; commercial providers must contact Joachims at Cornell University.
  - SVMstruct is a Support Vector Machine (SVM) algorithm for predicting multivariate or structured outputs.
  - SVMperf is an implementation of the SVM formulation for optimizing multivariate performance measures.
  - SVMrank is an instance of SVMstruct for efficiently training Ranking SVMs.

IMPROVING CLASSIFICATION WITH ADAPTIVE BOOSTING

What is adaptive boosting? Adaptive boosting (sometimes called AdaBoost) is a meta-algorithm in the sense that it is used to increase the performance of other algorithms.

Why would we use adaptive boosting? We can use adaptive boosting as an add-on capability to any classification we may already have performed.

When would we use adaptive boosting? We use adaptive boosting when we are not seeing the performance we would desire from our classifiers.

Who would use adaptive boosting? To some extent, adaptive boosting is partially a "roll your own" situation, where the user would have to possess sufficient knowledge to know how to use the tool.

How do we implement adaptive boosting? We can incorporate the following packages to implement adaptive boosting—we found a "flavor" for just about anybody:

- AdaBoost using the C++ approach (http://codingplayground. blogspot.com/2009/03/adaboost-improve-your-performance.html), by Antonio Gulli

- Icsiboost (https://github.com/benob/icsiboost), open source
- JBoost (http://jboost.sourceforge.net/), includes AdaBoost, logitboost, and boostexter at a minimum
- MATLAB AdaBoost toolbox (http://www.mathworks.com/discovery/adaboost.html)
- adaboostmatlab (https://code.google.com/p/adaboostmatlab/), another MATLAB package
- Milk (http://luispedro.org/software/milk), a Python-based toolkit
- MPBoost++ (http://www.esuli.it/software/mpboost/), a C++ implementation of the original AdaBoost.MH algorithm
- MultiBoost (http://www.multiboost.org/), boosting software implemented in C++ and implementing a multiclass version of AdaBoost (namely AdaBoost.MH) along with several multiclass weak-learning algorithms and cascades
- NPatternRecognizer (http://npatternrecognizer.codeplex.com/), has multiple abilities
- MALLET (http://mallet.cs.umass.edu/), a Java implementation that includes implementations of several classification algorithms, including naive Bayes, maximum entropy, and decision trees
- Ada, adabag, and bagRboostR are several packages for use with R,
- scikit-learn, and Python implementation

REGRESSION

What is regression? Regression involves estimating or predicting a response. Classification is identifying group membership; that is:

- *Regression*: The output variables take continuous values.
- *Classification*: The output variables take categorical or "class" labels.

Why would we use regression? We might use regression techniques (e.g., the general linear model or GLM) when we want to provide ourselves with the option for optimizing our results. This choice is fairly typical with designed experiments, which use analysis of variance (ANOVA) to characterize the impact of the factors, then determine values for those factors, and, finally, use an optimization algorithm to find the sweet spot.

If we are using regression with big data, we are most likely looking for correlations and, possibly, some data serendipity. As always, we want to be cautious with correlations, since large data sets can be prone to specious correlations.

When would we use regression? We are most likely to be using regression in cases where we are looking for factors that influence an output variable. For example, we have seen much information over the years regarding the "signs of impending suicide," but we have seen relatively little analysis of factors from the data. We are not sneering at qualitative assessments, just pleading for some quantitative analysis.

Who would use regression? Anyone interested in determining relationships among data types.

How do we implement regression?

- MRCE (http://cran.us.r-project.org/): multivariate regression with covariance estimation.
- All major statistical packages can do regression (Statistical Analysis System (SAS), SPSS, Angoss, Minitab, Statistica, etc.).

LOGISTIC REGRESSION

What is logistic regression? Logistic regression is poorly named—as used in machine learning, logistic regression is a classifying technique. A quick look at the plot of the function shows how this might work, where we have what can be called a "decision boundary" or a threshold.

Why would we use logistic regression? Logistic regression has some advantages:

- Makes no assumptions about distributions of classes
- Easily extended to multiple classes (multinomial regression)
- Natural probabilistic view of class predictions
- Quick "training"
- Very quick to classify unknown records
- Good accuracy for many simple data sets
- Resistant to overfitting
- Can interpret model coefficients as indicators of feature importance

Disadvantages:

- The linear decision boundary could be an issue

When would we use logistic regression? We might use logistic regression in cases where, for example, we are doing some kind of mortality study, whether of living creatures or of products. Jeff Howbert, in a presentation called "Introduction to Machine Learning," shows a wonderful example of classifying biblical passages as to whether they are poetry or narrative based on the use of the preterite conjugation of the verbs.

Who would use logistic regression? Medical researchers and anybody else who has large, but simple, data sets.

How do we implement logistic regression?

- *Classias* (http://www.chokkan.org/software/classias/): Classias is a collection of machine learning algorithms for classification. Currently, it supports the following formalizations:
  - L1/L2-regularized logistic regression (aka maximum entropy)
  - L1/L2-regularized L1-loss linear-kernel SVM
  - Implements several algorithms for training classifiers:
    - Averaged perceptron
    - Limited memory Broyden-Fletcher-Goldfarb-Shannon (L-BFGS)[1]
    - Orthant-Wise Limited-memory Quasi-Newton (OWL-QN)[2]
    - Primal Estimated sub-GrAdient SOlver (Pegasos)[3]
    - Truncated gradient,[4] also known as FOrward LOoking Subgradient (FOLOS)[5] specialized for L1 regularization
- F# has some programmable examples (http://fsharp.org/machine-learning/): the examples include other techniques we describe in this chapter
  - K-means clustering
  - Simplify data with SVD and Math.NET
  - Recommendation engine using Math.NET, SVD, and F#
  - Setting up F# Interactive for machine learning with large data sets
  - Random forests—first cut
  - Nearest-neighbor classification
  - Decision tree classification
  - Naive Bayes classification

- Logistic regression
- Support vector machine: AdaBoost
- Support vector machines

TREE-BASED REGRESSION

What is tree-based regression? This method is sometimes called *classification and regression tree* (CART) because we use the tree structure to classify data. Typically, regression trees incorporate either/or decision making to build the leaves of the tree. Note also that a true regression tree uses real numbers.

One drawback occurs when a higher-order error propagates down through the leaves. Sometimes, small changes in the data set will magnify themselves in the tree.

Why would we use tree-based regression? Our result is explicit and visual (when small enough). Other reasons to use regression trees are

- They are simple to understand and interpret.
- They require little data preparation.
- Trees can handle both numerical and categorical data.
- It is possible to validate a model using statistical tests, making it possible to account for the reliability of the model.
- Trees are relatively robust.
- They perform well with large data sets within a reasonable amount of time.[6]

When would we use tree-based regression? Regression trees work well when we can handle the idea of only achieving local optima, a by-product of greedy algorithms.

Who would use tree-based regression? Since data mining tools are available, anybody who can handle the drawbacks of this approach can use it.

How do we implement tree-based regression? We can implement regression trees in R, using a package such as itree or tree. We can also use the tool Weka (http://www.cs.waikato.ac.nz/ml/weka/), a data mining tool that also has a data visualizer. Other tools are Orange (http://orange.biolab.si/) and the Eclipse-based KNIME (http://www.knime. org/). R has one more routine, "C50," which is C5.0 Decision Trees and Rule-Based Models.

K-MEANS CLUSTERING

What is k-means clustering? K-means clustering is a relative of principal component analysis (PCA). The k-means clustering algorithm is a simple method for estimating the mean (vectors) of a set of k-groups. A simple explanation of the algorithm is as follows[7]:

1. Initial cluster seeds are chosen (at random).
2. The squared Euclidean distance from each object to each cluster is computed, and each object is assigned to the closest cluster.
3. For each cluster, the new centroid is computed—and each seed value is now replaced by the respective cluster centroid.
4. The squared Euclidean distance from an object to each cluster is computed, and the object is assigned to the cluster with the smallest squared Euclidean distance.
5. The cluster centroids are recalculated based on the new membership assignment.
6. Steps 4 and 5 are repeated until no object moves clusters.

Why would we use k-means clustering?

- With a large number of variables, k-means may be computationally faster than hierarchical clustering (if k is small).
- K-means may produce tighter clusters than hierarchical clustering, especially if the clusters are globular.

When would we use k-means clustering? K-means clustering is useful when we have a substantial number of groups to classify.

Who would use k-means clustering? As with many of the machine learning tools, the user must be technically savvy and understand what they are trying to with the algorithm.

How do we implement k-means clustering? The Java library SPMF (http://www.philippe-fournier-viger.com/spmf/) implements k-means clustering based on the MacQueen[8] approach. Available tools are the following:

Free
- Apache Mahout (http://mahout.apache.org/) k-means. Please note that Mahout currently supports
  - Collaborative filtering

- User- and item-based recommenders
- K-means, fuzzy k-means clustering
- Mean shift clustering
- Dirichlet process clustering
- Latent Dirichlet allocation
- Singular value decomposition
- Parallel frequent pattern mining
- Complementary naive Bayes classifier
- Random forest decision tree–based classifier

- ELKI (http://elki.dbs.ifi.lmu.de/) contains k-means (with Lloyd and MacQueen iteration, along with different initializations such as k-means++ initialization) and various more advanced clustering algorithms.
- MLPACK (http://www.mlpack.org/) incorporates a k-means implementation as part of the library of C++ routines.
- R k-means implements a variety of algorithms:
  - kml
  - kml3d
  - RSKC
  - skmeans
  - sparcl
- SciPy (http://www.scipy.org/), vector-quantization for Python.
- Weka contains k-means and a few variants of it, including k-means++ and x-means.

Commercial
- IDL Cluster, Clust_Wts
- Mathematica clustering components function
- MATLAB k-means
- SAS FASTCLUS

Source code[edit]
- ELKI and Weka are written in Java and include k-means and variations.

APRIORI ALGORITHM

What is the Apriori algorithm? Apriori is an algorithmic solution for frequent itemset mining and association rule learning over transactional (e.g., customer purchase) databases. It functions by identifying frequent individual items in a database and extending them to larger and larger itemsets if those particular itemsets appear often (per criteria or criterion) in the database. We can use the itemsets discovered by Apriori to discern association rules, which emphasize general trends in the database: this has applications in domains such as market basket (that is, what people put in their figurative baskets when they shop online) analysis. Please note that the "market basket" concept is often used to track an economics study item such as inflation. Is Apriori fast enough? We suggest perusal of https://dspace.ist.utl.pt/bitstream/2295/55705/1/licao_10.pdf.

- Basics of Apriori algorithm.
  - Use frequent (k–1) itemsets to generate k itemsets candidates.
  - Scan the databases to determine frequent k itemsets.
  - It is costly to handle a huge number of candidate sets.
  - If there are 104 frequent 1-itemsets, the Apriori algorithm will need to generate more than 107 2-itemsets and test their frequencies.
- To discover a 100-itemset, 2100–1 candidates have to be generated.
  - $2100 - 1 = 1.27 \times 10^{30}$.
  - ...which is several times the number of estimated atoms in the universe!
- Bottleneck of Apriori.
  - Mining long patterns needs many passes of scanning and generates lots of candidates.
  - Bottleneck: candidate-generation-and-test.

Why would we use the Apriori algorithm? We would use the Apriori algorithm when a bottom-up, breadth-oriented search technique is suitable for our problem. The alternative to breadth-oriented searches is depth-oriented searches.

When would we use the Apriori algorithm? We use the Apriori algorithm when we are not particularly concerned about the amount of time it takes to produce a result—Apriori can generate vast numbers of subsets (itemsets) thanks to the bottom-up (but thorough) approach.

Who would use the Apriori algorithm? The user might be someone who is looking for collections of needles in a very large haystack. This algorithmic approach is well suited to processing big data.

How do we implement the Apriori algorithm? We can use any modern programming language to implement Apriori, using the following algorithm:

1. Find all frequent itemsets.
2. Get frequent items.
3. Find items whose occurrence in the database is greater than or equal to the minimum support threshold.
4. Get frequent itemsets.
5. Generate candidates from frequent items.
6. Prune the results to find the frequent itemsets.
7. Generate strong association rules from frequent itemsets.
8. Determine rules that satisfy the minimum support and minimum confidence threshold.

The Java library SPMF (http://www.philippe-fournier-viger.com/spmf/) implements the Agrawal and Srikant approach.[9]

FREQUENT PATTERN-GROWTH

What is frequent pattern-growth?
  Challenges
  • Multiple scans of transaction database
  • Huge number of candidates
  • Tedious workload of support counting for candidates
  • Improving Apriori: general ideas
  • Reduce passes of transaction database scans
  • Shrink number of candidates
  • Facilitate support counting of candidates

Why would we use frequent pattern-growth?
  Benefits of the FP-tree structure:
  • Completeness
  • Preserve complete information for frequent pattern mining
  • Never break a long pattern of any transaction
  • Compactness
  • Reduce irrelevant information—infrequent items are gone

- Items in descending order of frequency: the more frequently occurring, the more likely to be shared
- Never be larger than the original database (not countnode-links and the count field)

When would we use frequent pattern-growth? We use frequent pattern-growth in anticipation of finding frequent patterns! (Not a surprise.) The most common example is the "market basket analysis," which is based on co-occurrence relationships. Clearly, we would see application in retail.

Who would use frequent pattern-growth? The typical user must be technically savvy as well as have the resources to perform this kind of data mining. Retail supermarkets, for example, typically run on slim margins. Probably the archetype for users is Amazon.

How do we implement frequent pattern-growth?

- Mahout (http://mahout.apache.org/), an FP growth algorithm, is a generic implementation; we can use any object type to denote a feature. Current implementation requires us to use a string as the object type.
- Nonordfp (http://ceur-ws.org/Vol-126/racz.pdf) is based on a paper by Balázs Rácz.[10]
- MAFIA (http://himalaya-tools.sourceforge.net/Mafia) is an algorithm for mining maximal frequent itemsets from a transactional database—especially efficient when the itemsets in the database are very long.
- FP-Growth (http://adrem.ua.ac.be/~goethals/software/) is based on the Han et al. algorithm.

PRINCIPAL COMPONENT ANALYSIS (PCA)

What is principal component analysis? PCA (sometimes known under the more general term of "factor analysis") is a tool for defining the underlying structure among variables in whatever we choose to analyze. Each component we find is sorted on the magnitude of the variance in descending order, with the assumption that we are most interested in the variable (factor) that has the greatest impact on variation.

Why would we use principal component analysis? We would use PCA when we feel that our understanding of a specific data set is lacking with regard to interrelationships. Principal component analysis helps establish which factors seem to be primary to a data set.

When would we use principal component analysis? PCA is a reasonable choice for data discovery, since we use it to liberate interrelationships among variables; this leads to the definition of sets of variables that closely correlate, which we call "factors."

Who would use principal component analysis? Anyone looking for fundamental constructs will use PCA as a primary tool.

How do we implement principal component analysis? At least nine R packages are available to assist with PCA (http://cran.r-project.org/web/packages/available_packages_by_name.html). We suspect R is an excellent choice for PCA. The user will want to take advantage of any opportunity to visualize the data. Most of the other statistical packages (commercial) can support PCA. Other tools are the following:

- Mathematica
- The NAG Library, in which PCA is implemented via the g03aa routine
- MATLAB Statistics Toolbox, in which PCA is implemented via the functions princomp and pca
- GNU Octave, a free software computational environment mostly compatible with MATLAB, in which the function princomp gives the principal component
- R, in which PCA is implemented via the functions princomp and prcomp
- SAS, in which PROC FACTOR offers principal components analysis
- Weka, which computes principal components
- Orange (software), which supports PCA through its Linear Projection widget (http://orange.biolab.si/docs/latest/widgets/rst/unsupervised/PCA/).

SINGULAR VALUE DECOMPOSITION

What is singular value decomposition? Singular value decomposition is related to principal component analysis and is most frequently used for pattern recognition. In its rawest form, it is composed of a collection of techniques for manipulating arrays. Bear in mind that we will need to consider the resources necessary if we need to handle large arrays, particularly if we are dealing with a true big data problem.

Why would we use singular value decomposition? We would use singular value decomposition because it is well supported by numerous packages and because it works with natural language processing, a big data problem.

When would we use singular value decomposition? Interestingly, SVD has been used in weather prediction algorithms. The technique has also found use in natural language analysis.

Who would use singular value decomposition? SVD would be used by a practitioner with the mathematical maturity to properly code the matrix manipulations. We have seen a journal article where the data were conditioned using logistic regression and then treated with SVD.[11] Another article showed how SVD could be used to classify NetFlix movies.[12]

How do we implement singular value decomposition?
Libraries that support complex and real SVD:

- LAPACK, the Linear Algebra Package. The user manual gives details of subroutines to calculate the SVD.
- LINPACK Z Linear Algebra Library. It has officially been superseded by LAPACK, but it includes a C version of SVD for complex numbers.
- SLEPc, which computes partial SVD decompositions of large, sparse matrices on parallel computers.
- For the Python programming language:
  - NumPy (NumPy is module for numerical computing with arrays and matrices).
  - SciPy (SciPy contains many numerical routines).
- NMath (NMath SVD Documentation), math and statistics libraries for.NET.
- Armadillo, a linear algebra library for the C++ language, supporting full and reduced SVDs.
- ScaLAPACK, supported distributed block-cyclic matrix SVD in both complex and real.

Libraries that support real SVD:

- GNU Scientific Library, a numerical C/C++ library supporting SVD
- For the Python programming language:
  - NumPy (NumPy is a module for numerical computing with arrays and matrices)
  - SciPy (SciPy contains many numerical routines)

- Gensim, an efficient randomized algorithm on top of NumPy; unlike other implementations, allows SVD of matrices larger than RAM (incremental online SVD)
  - Sparsesvd, Python wrapper of SVDLIBC
  - SVD-Python, pure Python SVD under GNU GPL
- ALGLIB, includes a partial port of the LAPACK to C++, C#, Delphi, Visual Basic, and so on
- JAMA, a Java matrix package provided by the NIST
- COLT, a Java package for High Performance Scientific and Technical Computing, provided by CERN
- SVDLIBC, rewriting of SVDPACK in C, with minor bug fixes
- SVDLIBJ, a Java port of SVDLIBC (also available as an executable.jar similar to SVDLIBC in the S-Space Package)
- SVDLIBC#: SVDLIBC converted to C#
- For the R programming language:
- pbdDMAT, provides real SVD on distributed block-cyclic matrices

NEURAL NETWORKS

What is a neural network? A neural network is a computer simulation of the way some individuals believe the mind works, using an interconnected web of simulated neurons. In essence, the system adapts during a learning phase, which may take considerable time. We assess the working capability of the neural network by testing it with a variety of data sets and "teaching" it which items are correct and which are not correct.

Why use a neural network? Neural networks have been used in control and robotics. As with most of the machine learning toolbox, neural networks can also serve as data classifiers. As part of the classification scheme, neural networks have seen use for facial recognition and as a diagnostic tool for cancer.

When would we use a neural network? We can use a neural network when we have the time to train the system. Additionally, if we have a sufficient array of processors with which we can go significantly parallel, neural networks would make a great deal of sense. We need to remain aware that many neural network applications are really simulations, and that the use of multiple processors more closely approximates the neural network itself.

Who would use a neural network? The short list of companies providing neural network software is not so short:

- AND Corporation: Provider of application development services and software systems and licensor of the Holographic/Quantum Neural Technology (HNeT).
- Alyuda Research: Provides neural network software for forecasting and data analysis as well as consulting and research services in neural networks and data mining.
- Applied Analytic Systems: An operations research and artificial intelligence consulting and software development company specializing in neural networks, statistical modeling, and mathematical optimization.
- Applied Neurodynamics: Consulting design of neurocomputing hardware and Neuromorphic aVLSI bus infrastructure and support for wet lab research.
- Attrasoft: Provider of a number of neural network–based products for image and sound recognition/retrieval, trend prediction, and data mining.
- BioComp Systems Inc.: A consulting and software development firm specializing in neural networks and genetic algorithms.
- HiTech Analytics, LLC: Sells financial indicators based on neural networks and consulting services.
- Jurik Research: An Excel add-in that enhances forecasts with the power of neural networks.
- Lester Ingber Research: Conducts research in applying neural networks to EEG analysis and trading and combat analysis, and provides consulting services in areas of expertise.
- NeuralWare: Provides neural network–based analysis products and engineering services, which help business, government, industry, and universities solve data mining, classification, prediction, and pattern-recognition problems.
- NeuroDimension, Inc.: Provides NeuroSolutions, neural network software based on backpropagation. Also provides additional software to embed NeuroSolutions in Excel and to produce DLLs implementing neural networks created with NeuroSolutions.
- Nonlinear Solutions Oy: Services based on nonlinear modeling, particularly neural networks, including process models and models for material behavior. Provides tailor-made software, simulators based on nonlinear models, experiment design, and industrial courses.

- Vesta Services, Inc.: Develops neural network modeling software for forecasting, recognition, and general data-handling tasks.
- Ward Systems Group, Inc.: Develops software for prediction, classification, and optimization based on neural networks and genetic algorithms.
- hav.Software: Sells software implementations of feedforward and recurrent networks trained with backpropagation and feature maps.

How do we implement a neural network?   Not surprisingly, many neural network tools exist, both commercial and open source—the methodology has been around for years and the technology has improved as machine speeds and multiple cores have improved.

- Alyuda (http://www.alyuda.com/) (commercial): neural network software and Excel add-ins for forecasting and data analysis
  - Alyuda NeuroIntelligence: neural network software for experts, designed for intelligent support in applying neural networks to solve real-world forecasting, classification, and function-approximation problems
  - Alyuda Forecaster XL: an easy-to-use Excel add-in allows you to instantly apply the forecasting capabilities of neural networks to your Excel data, while retaining all of the Excel data manipulation and formatting tools
  - Alyuda NeuroFusion: general-purpose neural networks library written in ANSI C++ and compiled with Visual C++ 6.0; for both regression and classification problems
  - Plug&Score: credit scoring systems for consumer and SME lending that can be effectively used for application, collection, and behavioral scoring and fraud detection
  - Alyuda Forecaster: neural network software for forecasting, data analysis, and classification
  - Alyuda NeuroDienst: a server-side application, used to process requests to neural network models, created using Alyuda NeuroIntelligence
  - Alyuda BrokerBOOSTER: white label, feature-rich, customizable online trading software platform
- Amygdala (http://amygdala.sourceforge.net/): open-source software for simulating spiking neural networks in C++

- Annie (http://annie.sourceforge.net/): originally used for facial recognition
- NARIA (http://naria.karasuma.net/): open-source project about creating or simulating humanlike intelligence with the help of neural networks, with the main objective being to copy the functions of the human brain in an efficient way onto normal home computers
- Cortex (http://cortex.snowcron.com/): a backpropagation neural network application
- DELVE (http://www.cs.utoronto.ca/~delve/): standard environment for evaluating the performance of learning methods
- EasyNN (http://www.easynn.com/) (commercial): neural network software for Windows with numeric, text, and image functions
- Fast Artificial Neural Network (FANN) (http://leenissen.dk/fann/wp/): neural-network library implemented in ANSI C:
  - Multilayer artificial neural-network library in C
  - Backpropagation training (RPROP, Quickprop, Batch, Incremental)
  - Evolving topology training that dynamically builds and trains the ANN (Cascade2)
- Genesis (http://genesis-sim.org/): general-purpose simulation platform that was developed to support the simulation of neural systems ranging from subcellular components and biochemical reactions to complex models of single neurons, simulations of large networks, and systems-level models
- Lightweight Neural Network++ (http://lwneuralnetplus.sourceforge.net/): free software project including a multilayer perceptron neural network, backpropagation training, and SuperSab (Self Adaptive Backpropagation) training
- NNSYSID Toolbox (http://www.iau.dtu.dk/research/control/nnsysid.html): MATLAB tools for neural network–based identification of nonlinear dynamic systems
- NetMaker (http://www.ire.pw.edu.pl/~rsulej/NetMaker/): developed for classification for CERN experiments, which includes Bayesian network capability
- Netlab (http://www1.aston.ac.uk/eas/research/groups/ncrg/resources/netlab/links/): library of MATLAB functions for simulating neural network algorithms
- Neural Network Toolbox for MATLAB (http://www.mathworks.com/products/neural-network/): a neural network simulator for MATLAB

- NeuralWorks (http://www.xanalys.com/products/link-explorer/): Professional II/PLUS, a neural network development environment, available for Windows and Unix; Predict, a neural network tool for solving prediction and classification problems, available for Unix or as an Excel add-in for Windows
- NeuroShell Predictor (http://www.wardsystems.com/index.asp) (commercial): forecasting and estimation software based on neural networks; products include NeuroShell Predictor, NeuroShell Classifier neural net software, and GeneHunter genetic algorithm (GA) software
- NeuroSolutions (http://www.neurosolutions.com/) (commercial): icon-based neural network development software; available by itself or supporting Excel and/or MATLAB
- NeuroXL (http://www.neuroxl.com/) (commercial): Microsoft Excel add-ins based on neural networks. Designed for predicting, classification, and financial forecasting. Add-ins include:
  - NeuroXL predictor
  - NeuroXL classifier
  - OLSOFT neural network library
  - PredictorCMD
- Neuroph (http://neuroph.sourceforge.net/): Java open-source neural network framework, primarily for Windows and Linux
- Neuropilot Project (http://freespace.virgin.net/michael.fairbank/neuropilot/): Java applet demo of a trained neural network piloting a lunar-lander type spacecraft over landscapes of various complexity
- Simbrain (http://simbrain.sourceforge.net/): a free Java-based neural network simulation kit
- Torch (http://www.torch.ch/): provides a MATLAB-style environment for machine learning algorithms
- Tradecision (http://www.tradecision.com/): uses neural networks as a tool for discovering nonlinear dependencies, rather than as a trade predictor
- Xerion (http://www.cs.toronto.edu/~xerion/): neural network simulator based on C and Tcl
- libF2N2 (http://libf2n2.sourceforge.net/): an open-source neural network library. Classes for C++ and PHP; save and load neural network weights and biases to a common format; multilayer perceptron neural network; backpropagation training with momentum; sigmoidal activation function; implements a Gaussian mutation function for use in neuroevolution

BIG DATA AND MAPREDUCE

What is MapReduce? MapReduce, which we describe in more detail elsewhere, is a programming approach, the best known version of which was developed by Google. It is widely used for processing large data sets in parallel. Its primary feature is that if a task can be constituted as a MapReduce, the user can actualize it as a set of parallel processes without writing parallel code. The practitioner develops serial functions that operate on portions of the data set individually. The data movement and other parallel operations can be performed using an application-independent approach.

"Map" is the activity that applies a given function to each element of a list, returning a list of results. "Reduce" is the activity that analyzes a recursive data structure and recombines it through the use of a predefined combining operation and gives the results of recursively processing its constituent parts, building up a recombinant value. Basically, we "sow" and then we "reap."

Why would we use MapReduce? We use MapReduce because we can increase throughput by intelligent use of parallelism on multiple processors, platforms, and hardware. We may even have scenarios where we use multiple locations.

When would we use MapReduce? We would use MapReduce any time a parallel solution makes sense:

- The problem can be decomposed.
- Ample resources are available.
- The technical ability to perform this approach is on hand.

Who would use MapReduce? MapReduce is a critical component of most Big Data solutions, so any practitioner with substantial data needs would potentially use MapReduce. As we indicate elsewhere in this book, the use is likely to see an entire big data ecosystem of Hadoop, special databases, and other equipage associated with the size of the problem.

How do we implement MapReduce?
- MapReduce-MPI (http://mapreduce.sandia.gov/index.html): This is an open-source implementation of MapReduce.
- Hadoop (hadoop.apache.org): Hadoop is a free, open-source implementation of MapReduce and perhaps the most popular implementation.

- Nutch (nutch.apache.org): This is an extensible and scalable open-source web-crawler software project.
- Pentaho (www.pentaho.com): This provides open-source data integration (Kettle), analytics, reporting, visualization, and predictive analytics directly from Hadoop nodes. Pentaho does not stop at MapReduce; it is a major data mining implementation with both commercial and free components.
- Datameer (www.datameer.com): This product is about data source integration, storage, an analytics engine, and visualization, presenting an integrated solution to customers.
- Apache Accumulo (accumulo.apache.org): This approach/product is a sorted, distributed key/value store, representing a scalable data storage and retrieval system. Apache Accumulo is based on Google's BigTable design and is built on top of Apache Hadoop, Zookeeper, and Thrift. Apache Accumulo has cell-based access control and a server-side programming mechanism that can modify key/value pairs at various points in the data management process. Basically, we have a secure BigTable that is integrated with the other big data Apache tools.
- HBase (hbase.apache.org): HBase is the Hadoop database, a distributed, scalable, big data store that is not a relational database.
- Hypertable (http://hypertable.org): HBase alternative.
  - Scalability: Hypertable is based on a design developed by Google to meet their scalability requirements.
  - Wide range of applications: Hypertable keeps data physically sorted by a primary key, and it is well suited to a broad set of applications.
  - Cost savings: By choosing to do the implementation in a compiled language that does not incur the performance and stability costs of garbage collection and runtime interpretation, Hypertable can deliver equivalent database capacity on a fraction of the hardware.
  - Performance: Reduces overall request latency.
  - Clean semantics: Hypertable was designed to be consistent from the start rather than using eventual consistency, as with other big data databases.
- Apache Cassandra (cassandra.apache.org): This data model offers column indices with the performance of log-structured updates, support for normalization and materialized views, and built-in caching on top of Hadoop.

- HPCC (hpccsystems.com): HPCC implements data refining and clearing through clustering.
- Sector/Sphere (http://sector.sourceforge.net): Sector/Sphere supports distributed data storage, distribution, and processing over large clusters of commodity computers, either within a data center or across multiple data centers.
- MongoDB (http://mongodb.org): MongoDB is an open-source document database, and the leading NoSQL database written in C++. It supports document-oriented storage, full index support, replication and high availability, auto-sharding, querying, fast-in-place updates, and MapReduce.

DATA EXPLORATION

What is data exploration?   Data exploration is related to ideas of the great statistician, John Tukey.[13] Despite the frequentists' assertions, hypothesis testing is not the only game in town, and exploratory data analysis tools generally provide for strong visualization capabilities.

Why would we use data exploration?   The very name implies that we are not completely sure what we are looking for, so we become cognitive explorers, hacking our way through a jungle of data. In many cases, dedicated tools such as GGobi allow the practitioner to zoom in on specific anomalous points and investigate them.

When would we use data exploration?   We would use data exploration any time we have the goal of data serendipity, in which we discover relationships and situations hitherto unconsidered. The book *Freakonomics* is full of examples of unexpected relationships.

Who would use data exploration?   As with many of the tools we discuss in this chapter, we would expect our explorers to be fairly sophisticated and well able to use the tools that are available, which we describe in our implementation section.

How do we implement data exploration?

- Most major software tools—R, Statistica, SAS, SPSS, and others—provide substantial visualization capabilities.
- GGobi (http://www.ggobi.org) is written specifically to enhance data visualization and is derived (at least figuratively) from XGobi; it also

works hand-in-hand with R (rggobi). It has versions available for Windows, Macintosh, and Linux.

SPAM FILTERING

What is spam filtering? We hesitate to include spam filtering as machine learning, but that is, in fact, exactly what many of these tools will do for the user. Many of them implement a Bayesian classification filter that "learns" as the user indicates which e-mail is spam and which is not.

Why would we use spam filtering? We use spam filtering to declutter our e-mail of useless advertising, sexual promotions, and other trivia in the net-verse. Similar algorithms can also be used to separate other kinds of data.

When would we use spam filtering? Any time we decide we have had enough garbage is the right time to implement a spam filter.

Who would use spam filtering? Anybody who is unafraid to allow a machine to assist with classification is a good candidate for these tools. Many of the implementations do not require very much technical knowledge.

How do we implement spam filtering?
- SpamAssassin (http://spamassassin.apache.org): Perl-based system available for Windows and Linux/Unix systems; installable on Macintosh, but needs substantial operating system knowledge
- SpamBayes (spambayes.sourceforge.net): Python-based system that works most easily with Windows programs; a statistical antispam filter
- Spam Bully (http://www.spambully.com): a commercial program that uses a Bayesian spam filter and is Windows-only
- Spamchek (http://www.spamchek.ch): appears to be somewhat out of date
- Spamfighter (http://www.spamfighter.com): a commercial product supporting only Windows
- Spam Reader (http://www.spam-reader.com): base version is free; pro version is commercial and appears to be Windows-only
- Spam Arrest (http://www.spamarrest.com): commercial; uses a unique approach requiring sender verification to an automatic replay system

RANKING

What is ranking?   Instead of dividing our data into two bins with a classifier, we might wish to get somewhat more sophisticated and rank data in terms of importance. We can rank words, documents, searches (Google!), equations, numbers, and so on.

Why would we use ranking?   As we indicated, simple binary classification may not be the solution to certain problems. Ranking provides an alternative, although we can expect more processing. And, yes, we know we can rank using force comparisons with binary approaches.

When would we use ranking?   The search engines provide the most obvious examples of why ranking might be useful. We can let the machine help us organize our data to improve their usefulness.

Who would use ranking?   Anybody who needs a system for scoring data would use ranking techniques. We see this when translating natural language, in biology, and in brute force optimization.

How do we implement ranking?

- http://research.microsoft.com/en-us/groups/mldept/ is an entire department devoted to research on machine learning.
- Dynamic ranking (http://dynamicranking.joachims.org) is a tool that tries to resolve the opposing goals of result diversity and high coverage. Dr. Thorsten Joachims's site (http://www.cs.cornell.edu/people/tj/) is a good place to go for state-of-the-art software and documentation.
- TreeRank (https://r-forge.r-project.org/projects/treerank/) is an R-package for building tree-based ranking rules through the tree induction method.

PREDICTIVE REGRESSION

What is predictive regression?   In essence, predictive regression uses regression techniques to perform forecasting. Some heavy-duty mathematics is involved due to the desire to reduce error, particularly in the financial industry.

Why would we use predictive regression?   We could use this method when we have substantial data (big data) and no better way to establish a forecast.

When would we use predictive regression? Since we are writing about a regression model, we are interested in short-range projections rather than in a long-range approach based on seasonality.

Who would use predictive regression? This method is dominated by the financial industry.

How do we implement predictive regression? This approach appears somewhat more esoteric than others. We found almost no dedicated software and only a few companies.

- Logit Research (http://www.logitresearch.com): They call their version correlated component regression analysis (CCR). They created CCR as a solution for "noisy data" caused by high-dimensional data sets, but they discovered it also delivers more reliable predictions in conventional applications. Among the specific benefits are maximizing out-of-sample performance; producing simpler and/or very robust models; and big data benefits, including high performance and suitability for otherwise unusable data sets.
- LiblineaR   (http://cran.us.r-project.org/web/packages/LiblineaR/index.html): A package for R.
- PredictiveRegression   (http://cran.us.r-project.org/web/packages/PredictiveRegression/index.html): Another package for R.

TEXT REGRESSION

What is text regression? Text regression, in most cases, uses regression techniques to determine a predictor (really, a classifier) based on strings found in text. As with most models, a training period must occur until the system understands which strings are meaningful.

Why would we use text regression? Clearly, we are going to use this technique to take a step beyond the purely subjective and come up with a quantitative result, based on relatively qualitative input.

When would we use text regression? A nice example has been provided in a paper by Joshi et al.,[14] in which they use sentiment expression with text regression to develop a model that predicts movie revenue. They achieved an R^2 of 0.521 for gross revenues, which is enough to be significant.

Who would use text regression? We suggest that any group, from the National Security Agency and others, would find text regression useful as an aid to predicting certain behaviors. The method can also be used with authorship problems.

How do we implement text regression?

- OpenNLP (http://opennlp.apache.org) can be used with R.
  - KoRpus: A package for text analysis
  - Maxent: Low-memory multinomial logistic regression with support for text classification
  - Textir: Inverse regression for text analysis
  - TextRegression: Predicts continuous-valued outputs associated with text documents
- BBR, BMR, and BXR (http://www.bayesianregression.com): These open-source packages include
  - BBRtrain: Trains binary (i.e., 2 class) logistic regression models from labeled data. Ability to train from instances in group label format (whether or not hierarchical modeling is actually used).
  - BBRclassify: Applies models trained by BBRtrain to new data. Capabilities currently not present in BXRclassify:
  - BMRtrain: Trains polytomous (2+ class) logistic regression models. Capabilities not present in BXRtrain:
    - BMRclassify: Applies models produced by BMRtrain to new data. Capabilities not present in BXRclassify:
    - BXRtrain: Provides a range of new capabilities, particularly with respect to ease of use.
    - BXRclassify: Provides a range of new capabilities, particularly with respect to ease of use.

MULTIDIMENSIONAL SCALING

What is multidimensional scaling (MDS)? Multidimensional scaling is one of a suite of techniques used when data appear in more than one dimension, hence the name. We might resort to this technique in cases where PCA is not working well. In general, the techniques either reduce dimensionality or they produce a graphical representation of the data— even then, analysis can be difficult. It should also be noted that these approaches are overwhelmingly based on topological concepts; the methods that do not contain "mapping" in their name still map implicitly. A list of techniques in this family looks like

- Mapping types
  - Sammon's mapping
  - Kohonen maps
  - Isomap
  - Laplacian eigenmaps
  - Diffusion maps
  - Relational perspective map
  - Nonexplicit mapping types:
    - Locally linear embedding (LLE)
      - Hessian LLE
      - Modified LLE
  - Principal curves and manifolds
  - Autoencoders
  - Gaussian process latent variable models
  - Curvilinear component analysis
    - Curvilinear distance analysis
    - Diffeomorphic dimensionality reduction
    - Manifold alignment
    - Local tangent space alignment
    - Local multidimensional scaling
    - Maximum variance unfolding
    - Data-driven high-dimensional scaling
    - Manifold sculpting
    - RankVisu
    - Topologically constrained isometric embedding

Why would we use MDS?   As we mentioned, we have most likely already attempted standard PCA and achieved mediocre or worse results. In MDS, we work in n-space and locate "objects" as naturally as possible. We might consider MDS to be a "sample space" approach to problem solving.

When would we use MDS?   In essence, we would use MDS when the n-dimensional mapping makes sense; for example, with perceptual mapping in marketing.

Who would use MDS? A common application of MDS relates to the manipulation of geospatial data.

How do we implement MDS?

- XLSTAT Pro (http://www.xlstat.com/en/products-solutions/feature/multidimensional-scaling-mds.html): XLSTAT uses the SMACOF (scaling by majorizing a convex function) algorithm.
- Quick-R (http://www.statmethods.net/advstats/mds.html): This Web page shows how to do MDS with R.
- NewMDSX (http://www.newmdsx.com): A commercial tool developed in part by Anthony Peter Macmillan Coxon, one of the foremost proponents of this approach.
- Multidimensional scaling for Java (http://www.inf.uni-konstanz.de/algo/software/mdsj/): A free Java library.
- ALSCAL (http://forrest.psych.unc.edu/research/alscal.html): ALSCAL performs metric or nonmetric multidimensional scaling and unfolding with individual differences options. It can analyze one or more matrices of dissimilarity or similarity data. The analysis represents the rows and columns of the data matrix as points in a Euclidean space.
- High-throughput multidimensional scaling (http://dig.ipk-gatersleben.de/hitmds/hitmds.html): Dimension reduction, reconstruction of data dissimilarity relationships (matrix) in the Euclidean output space, conversion of one metric space into Euclidean space, and dealing with missing data relationships.
- GGobi (http://www.ggobi.org): An open-source visualization program for exploring high-dimensional data, providing highly dynamic and interactive graphics such as tours, as well as familiar graphics such as the scatterplot, bar chart, and parallel coordinates plots.
- Visual statistics system (ViSta) (http://forrest.psych.unc.edu/research/index.html): A somewhat dated, but free, program that contains MDS.
- Dr. Mark Steyvers's libraries (http://psiexp.ss.uci.edu/research//programs_data/mdszip.zip): A free program; Dr. Steyvers is a professor at UC Irvine.
- orngMDS module (http://orange.biolab.si/doc/modules/orngMDS.htm): A subset of the Orange machine learning libraries.

SOCIAL GRAPHING

What is social graphing?   Social graphing is synonymous with social networking; however, we are not directly writing about Facebook, LinkedIn, Twitter, or other implementation of social software, but rather about the analytical approaches we take to investigate networks. Most of the software packages will produce a visual graph (a graph is really a mathematical object), making it easier to see relationships. In some cases, the user can define distances to reflect how relationships will appear.

Why would we use social graphing?   Social graphing sometimes allows us to see relationships that were not initially obvious.

When would we use social graphing?   The method can be used anywhere we have a network:

- Computer networks
- Word networks
- Family relationships
- Journal article citations
- Parts lists

Who would use social graphing?   This is useful for visualization of data analyzed by MDS. Alternatively, we may see exploratory investigation of a given network; for example, cliques in organization settings such as companies or educational institutions.

How do we implement social graphing?   We found a substantial number of network tools for social network analysis (social graphing). We will cover only a few; for more detail, please use http://en.wikipedia.org/wiki/Social_network_analysis_software as a starting point. From the length of the list, it is apparent that substantial interest exists in this area of research as well as in product development. Here is our list:

- Pajek (http://pajek.imfm.si/doku.php?id = pajek): a well-documented, freely available program for large network analysis. Macros can be recorded to perform repetitive tasks. Data can be sent directly to R, to calculate additional statistics.
- AllegroGraph (http://franz.com/agraph/allegrograph/): AllegroGraph is a graph database. It is a disk-based, fully transactional OLTP database

that stores data structured in graphs rather than in tables. AllegroGraph includes a Social Networking Analytics library.

- C-IKNOW (http://ciknow.northwestern.edu/): C-IKNOW is a powerful web-based software tool for social network analysis investigation. It has been designed around real-world problems, and it can store and analyze virtually any type of network data. The documentation provides a basic step-by-step walk-through of how to get started on a C-IKNOW project as well as more advanced support, including the C-IKNOW Question-Type Primer. C-IKNOW's visualization and analytics suite allows both administrators and users to access visualizations, recommendation tools, and analytical measures for their networks. The website indicates that it is no longer under active development.
- CFinder (cfinder.org): A software tool for finding and visualizing overlapping dense communities in networks, based on the clique percolation method. It enables customizable visualization and allows easy exploration of the found communities. The package contains a command-line version of the program as well, which is suitable for scripting.
- Commetrix (http://www.commetrix.de): Commetrix is a software framework and tool for dynamic network analysis and visualization. It provides easy exploratory access to network graphs and has been applied to study coauthorship, instant messaging, manual social network analysis (SNA) surveys, e-mail, newsgroups, and so on. Each node and each linking event can have properties, for example, types of messages or rank of nodes, but also types, topics, or time stamps. This allows animations of network growth, structural change, and topic diffusion. A short introductory video is available on the website.
- CoSBiLab Graph (http://www.cosbi.eu/index.php/research/prototypes/graph): CoSBiLab Graph is an application for visualization analysis and manipulation of networks. It provides a highly customizable graphical representation of networks based on local properties. Nodes can be aggregated and arranged on the space manually or by choosing from a list of predefined layouts. A set of indices is provided for measuring the positional importance of nodes in the network, and they can be combined to define new mathematical expressions. The manual and a set of examples are available on the website.

- Cuttlefish (http://cuttlefish.sourceforge.net/): Cuttlefish is a network workbench application that visualizes the networks with some of the best-known layout algorithms. It allows detailed visualizations of the network data, interactive manipulation of the layout, graph edition, and process visualization as well as different input methods and outputs in tex using Tikz and PSTricks (Tikz and PSTrick are tools used with the LaTeX publishing program). It is developed by the chair of systems design of ETH Zürich, a research group that applies a complex system approach to investigate economic and social networks.

- Deep Email Miner (http://deepemailminer.sourceforge.net/): A software solution for the multistaged analysis of an e-mail corpus. Social network analysis and text mining techniques are connected to enable an in-depth view into the underlying information.

- Detica NetReveal (https://www.deticanetreveal.com/en/): A platform that can process billions (often at national scale) of multiformat data sources and builds social networks. In doing so, a single view of entity (customer, business, telephone, bank account, vehicle, address, citizen, etc.) can be generated across multiple, poor-quality data sources. Social networks and entities can be scored using a range of powerful analytics and a full free text entity centric search is available across all records. The platform includes network visualization tools, work flow, and a real-time rules engine to score incoming events in real time.

- DEX (http://sparsity-technologies.com/): DEX is a high-performance graph database written in Java and C++. One of its main characteristics is its performance storage and retrieval for large graphs, in the order of billions of nodes, edges, and attributes, allowing the analysis of large-scale networks.

- EvESim (http://sourceforge.net/projects/evesim/): The EvESimulator provides a simulation framework for biologically inspired P2P systems—the evolutionary environment (EvE) as a part of the digital business ecosystem (DBE). Although its focus is on the EvE, the EvESimulator simulates a DBE. In addition, the EvESimulator constitutes a collaborative platform for interdisciplinary research acting as a framework for understanding, visualizing, and presenting the DBE concepts to contributors.

- FNA (http://www.fna.fi): Financial network analytics (FNA) is an analytics platform that helps financial institutions and regulators manage and understand financial data with network analysis and visualization. It is particularly suited for the analysis of large transaction, trade, or link databases in finance and for monitoring continuous data via dashboards. You can use FNA for free online at the website.

- Gephi (https://gephi.org/): Gephi is an interactive visualization and exploration platform for all kinds of networks and complex systems, and dynamic and hierarchical graphs. It is a tool for people that have to explore and understand graphs. The user interacts with the representation, manipulating the structures, shapes, and colors to reveal hidden properties. It uses a 3D render engine to display large networks in real time and to speed up the exploration. A flexible and multitask architecture brings new possibilities to work with complex data sets and produce valuable visual results.

- Graph-tool (http://graph-tool.skewed.de/): Graph-tool is a Python module for efficient analysis of graphs. Its core data structures and algorithms are implemented in C++, with heavy use of Template metaprogramming, based on the Boost Graph Library. It contains a comprehensive list of algorithms.

- Graphviz (www.graphviz.org): Graphviz is an open-source graph visualization framework. It has several main graph layout programs suitable for social network visualization.

- Idiro SNA Plus (http://www.idiro.com): Idiro SNA Plus is the market-leading SNA platform for telecoms, with a particular focus on churn prediction, viral marketing, acquisition, and family unit identification. Idiro SNA Plus takes social network analysis from academia and into the realm of business, where the focus is on deriving real value from the application of SNA to real-world problems.

- igraph (igraph.sourceforge.net/): igraph is a C library for the analysis of large networks. It includes fast implementations for classic graph-theory problems and recent network analysis methods like community structure search, cohesive blocking, structural holes, dyad and triad census, and motif count estimation. Higher-level interfaces are available for R, Python, and Ruby.

- InFlow (http://www.orgnet.com/inflow3.html): InFlow is intended for business users and is designed for ease of use, multiple networks per node set, and what-if capabilities. Network data can be entered via (1) CSV files, from data bases and spreadsheets; (2) automated survey tools such as NetworkGenie, Optimice, and so on; (3) data entry screens with paper surveys; or (4) drawn by hand with mouse, using node and link tools in a graphics window. Most popular network metrics include Density, Geodesics, Freeman Centralities, Watts-Strogatz Small World, Structural Equivalence, Cluster Analysis, Krackhardt E/I Ratio, and Krebs Reach and Weighted Average Path Length. Metrics are executed based on current network view—you measure what is mapped. Many network layouts are possible using automated algorithms and geometric layouts (arcs, lines, etc.), resulting in an unlimited number of custom views. Different actions can be taken on selected nodes versus unselected nodes.

- Java Universal Network/Graph (JUNG) Framework (jung.source-forge.net): JUNG is a Java application programming interface (API) and library that provides a common and extensible language for the modeling, analysis, and visualization of relational data. It supports a variety of graph types (including hypergraphs), supports graph elements of any type and with any properties, enables customizable visualizations, and includes algorithms from graph theory, data mining, and social network analysis (e.g., clustering, decomposition, optimization, random graph generation, statistical analysis, distances, flows, and centrality [PageRank, HITS, etc.]). It is limited only by the amount of memory allocated to Java.

- Jerarca (http://sourceforge.net/projects/jerarca/): Jerarca is a suite of hierarchical clustering algorithms that provides a simple and easy way to analyze complex networks. It is designed to efficiently convert unweighted, undirected graphs into hierarchical trees by means of iterative hierarchical clustering. Moreover, Jerarca detects and returns the community structure of the network.

- KrackPlot (https://www.andrew.cmu.edu/user/krack/krackplot.shtml): KrackPlot is a program for network visualization designed for social network analysts.

- KXEN Social Network (KSN) (http://www.kxen.com/Products/Social+Network+Analysis): KSN is a social network analysis module designed for extracting many social networks from call detail records (CDRs), extracting many attributes from a social network, integrating social network attributes into the customer's database, and exploiting social network attributes to build predictive models.

- libSNA (http://www.libsna.org/): libSNA is a widely used open-source library for conducting SNA research. Written in the object-oriented programming language Python, libSNA provides a simple programming interface for applying SNA to large-scale networks. libSNA is built on top of the open-source library NetworkX; without NetworkX, libSNA would not be possible.

- Meerkat (http://www.aicml.ca/node/41): Meerkat allows interactive visualization of networks and provides facilities and algorithms for community mining, filtering on edge and node properties, network statistics, and node metrics. In particular, it provides dynamic network community mining or community evolution event analysis, which allows abstraction and better understanding of changes to communities across timeframes for dynamic networks.
- Neo4j (www.neo4j.org): Neo4j is a graph database. It is an embedded, disk-based, fully transactional Java persistence engine that stores data structured in graphs rather than in tables.
- NetMiner 4 (http://www.netminer.com/index.php): NetMiner is a software tool for exploratory analysis and visualization of large network data. NetMiner 4 embeds an internal Python-based script engine, which is equipped with an automatic script generator for unskilled users. Then the users can operate NetMiner 4 with existing GUI or programmable script language.
- Network Genie (https://secure.networkgenie.com/): Network Genie is used to
  - Design complete, egocentric, and hybrid social network surveys using a wide variety of survey question formats.
  - Manage social network projects, including a collaborative team who have privileges defined by a project coordinator.
  - Collect social network data using online forms.
  - Download and export data to the social network analysis program of your choice. Registration is free.
- Network Overview Discovery Exploration for Excel (NodeXL) (http://nodexl.codeplex.com/): NodeXL is a free and open Excel 2007, 2010, 2013 add-in and C#/.Net library for network analysis and visualization. It integrates into Excel 2007, 2010, 2013, adds a directed graph as a chart type to the spreadsheet, and calculates a core set of network metrics and scores. It features multiple network visualization layouts and reads and writes Pajek, UCINet, and GraphML files.
- NetworkX (http://networkx.github.io/): NetworkX (NX) is a toolset for graph creation, manipulation, analysis, and visualization. User interface is through scripting/command-line provided by Python.

NX includes several algorithms, metrics, and graph generators. Visualization is provided through pylab and graphviz.

- ORA (http://www.casos.cs.cmu.edu/projects/ora/): ORA is a dynamic meta-network assessment and analysis tool containing hundreds of social network, dynamic network metrics, trail metrics, procedures for grouping nodes, identifying local patterns, comparing and contrasting networks, groups, and individuals from a dynamic meta-network perspective. ORA has been used to examine how networks change through space and time, contains procedures for moving back and forth between trail data (e.g., who was where when) and network data (who is connected to whom, who is connected to where…), and has a variety of geospatial network metrics, and change detection techniques. ORA can handle multi-mode, multi-plex, multi-level networks. It can identify key players, groups and vulnerabilities, model network changes over time, and perform COA analysis. It has been tested with large networks. Distance based, algorithmic, and statistical procedures for comparing and contrasting networks are part of this toolkit.

- R (http://www.r-project.org/): R contains several packages relevant for social network analysis:
  - Igraph is a generic network analysis package.
  - Sna performs sociometric analysis of networks.
  - Network manipulates and displays network objects.
  - Tnet performs analysis of weighted networks, two-mode networks, and longitudinal networks.
  - Ergm is a set of tools designed to analyze and simulate networks based on exponential random graph models.
  - Bergm provides tools for Bayesian analysis for exponential random graph models.
  - Hergm implements hierarchical exponential random graph models.
  - "RSiena" allows the analysis of the evolution of social networks using dynamic actor-oriented models.
  - Latentnet has functions for network latent position and cluster models.
  - Degreenet provides tools for statistical modeling of network degree distributions.
  - Networks provides tools for simulating bipartite networks with fixed marginals.

- Sentinel Visualizer (http://www.fmsasg.com/products/sentinelvisualizer/): Sentinel Visualizer is a Windows-based program that provides data visualization, analysis, and knowledge-base management within one product. Sentinel Visualizer produces interactive dynamic link charts, timelines, and geospatial views and provides a variety of analysis tools including Social Network Analysis, temporal analysis, and entity and relationship weighting. Sentinel Visualizer includes a multiuser knowledge base for efficiently and economically storing analysis data.

- SNA-Forte (http://www.forteconsultancy.com/): SNA-Forte is a social network analysis solution using raw telecommunications CDR data as its input. It automatically identifies communities of customers, as well as segments of these communities and roles of individuals in each community, based on selected parameters and weights. The algorithm is implemented as an open-source solution in SAS and is already in use in the commercial environment.

- Social Networks Visualizer (http://socnetv.sourceforge.net/): Social Networks Visualizer (SocNetV) is an open-source graphical application, developed in C++ language and the cross-platform Qt toolkit. The user interface is friendly and simple, allowing the researcher to draw social networks or plain graphs by clicking on a canvas. SocNetV computes basic network properties (i.e., density, diameter, shortest path lengths), as well as more advanced statistics, such as centralities (i.e., closeness, betweeness, graph), clustering coefficients, and so on. Various layout algorithms are supported. For instance, nodes can be automatically positioned on circles or levels according to their betweeness centralities. Random networks and small world creation are also supported. SocNetV can handle any number of nodes, although with a speed penalty when nodes are more than 3000 or the graph is quite dense (many edges).

- Sociomapping (http://www.sociomap.com/en/): An all-in-one social network analysis tool with built-in questionnaire design, data collection, data visualization, and statistics. Find case studies and other application possibilities at https://www.sociomap.com

- SocioMetrica (http://www.casos.cs.cmu.edu/computational_tools/tools/sociometrica_pop.html): This is a set of applications for interview-based gathering of egocentric data (EgoNet), linking of data records through matching of node attributes (LinkAlyzer), and visualization (VisuaLyzer). VisuaLyzer also provides prototype functionality for analysis using a relational algebra model. A relational programming language, RAlog, derives and analyzes representations in this relation algebra.

- StOCNET (http://www.gmw.rug.nl/~stocnet/StOCNET.htm): StOCNET is a software system for the advanced statistical analysis of social networks, focusing on probabilistic (stochastic) models. The program consists of several statistical models for network analysis. In the present version, six modules are implemented: BLOCKS (stochastic block modeling of relational data), p2 (analysis of binary network data with actor and/or dyadic covariates), PACNET (constructing a partial algebraic model for observed multiple complete networks using a statistical approach), SIENA (analysis of repeated measures on social networks and MCMC-estimation of exponential random graphs), ULTRAS (analysis of binary undirected network data using ultrametric measurement models), and ZO (simulation and enumeration of graphs with given degrees).

- Tulip (http://tulip.labri.fr/TulipDrupal/): Tulip is an information visualization framework dedicated to the analysis and visualization of relational data. Tulip aims to provide the developer with a complete library, supporting the design of interactive information visualization applications for relational data that can be tailored to the problems being addressed.

- UCINET (https://sites.google.com/site/ucinetsoftware/home): A comprehensive package for the analysis of social network data as well as other 1-mode and 2-mode data. Can handle a maximum of 32,767 nodes (with some exceptions), although practically speaking many procedures get too slow at around 5,000–10,000 nodes. Social network analysis methods include centrality measures, subgroup identification, role analysis, elementary graph theory, and permutation-based statistical analysis. In addition, the package has strong matrix analysis routines, such as matrix algebra and multivariate statistics.

- UrlNet (https://code.google.com/p/urlnet-python-library/): UrlNet is a Python class library for generating networks based on Internet linkages. In the simplest case, UrlNet creates a tree by harvesting the outlink URLs from the page referenced by a root URL (Level 0), retrieving each of those pages (Level 1) and harvesting their outlink URLs, retrieving those pages (Level 2) and harvesting their outlink URLs, and so on, to a caller-specified depth. UrlNet can also create "forests," the union of multiple tree networks. Specialized classes are provided for the generation of networks from search engine result sets (six search engines are currently supported). UrlNet can also utilize URL-based web service APIs to generate networks. Current examples include Technorati's Cosmos API and three types of networks utilizing APIs provided by the National Center for Biological Information (NCBI).

- visone (http://visone.info/): Interactive graphical tool for manipulating, analyzing, and visualizing social networks. Analysis methods include centrality indices, clustering, cliques, components, and centralization. Generic graph layout algorithms and tailored network visualizations are available. Visone supports many graphical properties and generates high-quality images in PNG, PDF, and so on.
- VisuaLyzer (socioworks.com/productsall/visualyzer/): Interactive tool for entering, visualizing, and analyzing social network data. Users can create nodes and links directly in VisuaLyzer, or import data from Edgelist/Edgearray, Excel, or GraphML formats.
- Xanalys Link Explorer (http://www.xanalys.com/products/link-explorer/): Interactive visual analytics tool combining data acquisition and querying with link analysis, temporal analysis, and spatial analysis (GIS) techniques. Integrates with other desktop applications and services such as Excel and Bing mapping.

REFERENCES

1. Nocedal, J. Updating quasi-Newton matrices with limited storage. *Mathematics of Computation* 35(151): 773–782, 1980.
2. Andrew, G. and J. Gao. Scalable training of L1-regularized log-linear models. In *Proceedings of the 24th International Conference on Machine Learning*, 2007. http://research.microsoft.com/en-us/um/people/jfgao/paper/icml07scalable.pdf. Accessed March 26, 2014.
3. Shalev-Shwartz, S., Y. Singer, and N. Srebro. Pegasos: Primal estimated Sub-GrAdient SOlver for SVM. In *Proceedings of the 24th International Conference on Machine Learning*, Corvallis, OR, 2007. http://ttic.uchicago.edu/~shai/papers/ShalevSiSr07.pdf. Accessed March 26, 2014.
4. Langford, J., L. Li, and T. Zhang. Sparse online learning via truncated gradient. *Journal of Machine Learning Research* 10(2009): 777–801
5. Duchi, J. and Y. Singer. Efficient online and batch learning using forward-backward splitting. In *Proceedings of Neural Information Processing Systems*, Vancouver, BC, Canada, 2009. http://www.cs.berkeley.edu/~jduchi/projects/DuchiSi09_folos.html. Accessed March 26, 2014.

6. Anonymous. Decision tree learning. Wikipedia. July 3, 2013. http://en.wikipedia.org/wiki/Decision_tree_learning. Accessed March 27, 2014.

7. Templin, J. K-means clustering. Class lecture. Lawrence, KS: University of Kansas, March 27, 2014.

8. MacQueen, J. Some methods for classification and analysis of multivariate observations. In *Proceedings of 5th Berkeley Symposium on Mathematical Statistics and Probability*, vol. 1, pp. 281–197. Berkeley, CA: University of California Press, 1967. http://www-m9.ma.tum.de/foswiki/pub/WS2010/CombOptSem/kMeans.pdf. Accessed March 27, 2014.

9. Agrawal, R. and R. Srikant. Fast algorithms for mining association rules. In *Proceedings of the 20th VLDB Conference*. Santiago, Chile. 1994. http://cs.stanford.edu/people/chrismre/cs345/rl/ar-mining.pdf. Accessed March 27, 2014.

10. Racz, B. Nonordfp: An FP-growth variation without rebuilding the FP-tree. In *Proceedings of 1st Frequent Itemset Mining Implementations (FIMI) Workshop*. Budapest, Hungary: Computer and Automation Institute of the Hungarian Academy of Science, 2004. http://ceur-ws.org/Vol–126/racz.pdf. Accessed March 27, 2014.

11. Fallucchi, F. and F.M. Zanzotto. Singular value decomposition for feature selection in taxonomy learning. In *Proceedings of the International Conference RANLP 2009*, pp. 82–87. Borovets, Bulgaria, 2009. http://aclweb.org/anthology//R/R09/R09–1016.pdf. Accessed March 27, 2014.

12. Sali, S. Movie rating prediction using singular value decomposition. Technical paper no. 242. University of California, 2008. http://classes.soe.ucsc.edu/cmps242/Winter08/proj/serdar_report.pdf. Accessed March 27, 2014.

13. Tukey, J.W. *Exploratory Data Analysis*. Reading, MA: Addison-Wesley, 1977.

14. Joshi, M., D. Das, and N.A. Smith. Movie reviews and revenues: An experiment in text regression. In *Proceedings of NAACL-HLT*. Pittsburgh, PA: Carnegie-Mellon University, 2010. http://www.dipanjandas.com/files/joshi.das.gimpel.smith.naacl10.pdf. Accessed March 27, 2014.

6

Statistics

STATISTICS, STATISTICS EVERYWHERE

In our modern world, statistics are everywhere. They comprise the famous infographics found in almost any newspaper (but most closely associated with *USA Today*). When we purchase a car, we look at its "stats." How much horsepower does it have? Is the gas mileage acceptable? Kids (and many adults) regularly absorb the numbers underlying that most statistical of games: baseball.

Though we are familiar with statistics, we often fail to absorb its intricacies. Statistics may be intended to describe surface phenomena or to dig into an underlying relationship. They may be used to inform or mislead. They may summarize averages or elaborate on the underlying distributions. The discussions surrounding statistics are much like the other points pondered in this book. The question is not whether big data is valuable, or whether hypothesis testing is valuable. The question is, "How can my organization use these tools most effectively? What is my strategy for capturing their value while minimizing the characteristics of these tools capable of being misleading? The integration of statistics is no different.

A close cousin of statistics is the field of probabilities. Statistics can be descriptive, quantitatively illustrating a phenomenon. Statistics, in the form of hypothesis testing, also provide a structured approach to asking and answering questions. Probabilities are used to establish the level of uncertainty a certain situation will hold in the future.

In this chapter, we will start at a basic level, with the different kinds of data, before moving into the mean, median, and mode and then on to distributions. Distributions are how data fall when charted. When we count the values in our data, what does the diagram look like? Is it roughly symmetrical? Is there a great deal of variation, or are all the values close together? If the diagram is not symmetrical, is it at least regular?

This approach provides a gateway into hypothesis testing. Hypothesis testing is simply a way to measure either one variable against another or against a set of expectations to determine whether an underlying assumption is valid. Although we went from the technical to the vague, we will see that hypothesis testing is conceptually simple and widely applicable.

We will include tests, such as the chi-square test, used to determine if discrete nonnumeric values fall outside of a random distribution. We will also examine Bayes's theorem, which is used to hone in on a probability. If you, the reader, get butterflies in your stomach thinking about these areas, you are not alone. Statistics can be daunting at first. But not to worry. We will keep our discussion at an intuitive and conceptual level.

We will also cover concepts that will enable us to ask analysts probing questions when they present us with their results. The unfortunate reality is hypothesis testing can present us with false or weak conclusions. We do not condemn hypothesis testing, and, in fact, hypothesis testing enables the flourishing of science and unprecedented management of risk. However, its usefulness does not make it perfect, as retracted scientific studies and counterproductive risk control strategies will attest. Finally, we will examine different software packages used for our organizations. These range from Minitab to SPSS to the freely available R.

Statistics, hypothesis testing, and probability are powerful tools to enable us to better understand our businesses. However, they require a great deal of detail to properly describe. Most of the good statistics books are as thick as this book, and that is without the chapters dedicated to particular big data tools or to the data itself. A standard strategy for teaching MBA students about accounting is to do so at a sufficient level that the student, when he or she is a manager, can ask detailed questions and spot problems; the student does not become an accountant. In our discussion, we will generally avoid formulae. We endeavor to present sufficient information to better understand what capabilities are available. We highly recommend that everyone read at a detailed level how statistics and hypothesis testing may mislead, and how we can improve our chances of obtaining meaningful results.

A final point about the level of statistical difficulty we cover: all of these methods are common knowledge for certified Six Sigma Black Belts. As Six Sigma matured in the fields of quality and efficiency, we find it still associated with those themes. However, the tools of Six Sigma are, effectively, the tools of science. We use the same hypothesis testing techniques with a different emphasis. If our organizations employ Six Sigma resources, they have the ability to investigate and check the results gleaned from our company's data and delivered to us by our analysts.

By treating the data analysis results with skepticism, we are not casting doubt on the value of data or the value of integrating the lessons we learn into our operations—we imply nothing of the sort. Science demands replication and so should data analysis in a business setting. Mistakes occur often. Even when mistakes do not occur, we often draw results based on statistical artifacts rather than true relationships derived from the underlying data. Replication is a tool to minimize the risk of mistakes and false conclusions. Skepticism is not being difficult, but it is prudent.

Finally, a few words on terminology: while hypothesis testing and statistics overlap, they are not completely congruent. Regardless, the word "statistics" will generally be used to refer to both unless we discuss a practice that is clearly just statistics or clearly just hypothesis testing. There is sufficient overlap in practice.

DIGGING INTO THE DATA

First, in looking at the data we need to understand whether we are looking at a population or a sample. A population is composed of every single entity or instance making up a particular category. A sample occurs when we select a subset of a population, which we measure and log.

An entire population can sometimes be measured. *The Dukes of Hazzard* was a popular TV show in the United States., which ran from 1979 to 1985. In its seven seasons and 145 episodes, its recognizable orange 1969 Dodge Charger became one of the most famous emblems of the show. The Charger, named the General Lee, was famous for jumping over obstacles such as roadblocks and rivers. Theoretically, it would be possible to estimate the length of each jump and to create a distribution for distance covered. The number of episodes filmed was not overwhelming, so it would be realistic to watch three episodes per week and estimate each jump over the period of a year. This assessment would be a measurement of the *population*, since it would leave no episode uncounted.

If we wanted to measure the maximum distance traveled by Canadian geese from their nest of birth to the furthest point on their migration, we know of no practical way for us to track down and tag every goose. We would instead capture and tag enough geese to infer the behavior of the population overall. The majority of geese in any migration would not possess one of our beacons, but if we were diligent in setting up our study, we would be able to derive meaningful information about the flight patterns of the population based on those geese we tagged. We call this approach a *sample*.

Statistical studies of populations are relatively rare, a phenomenon often related to the core constraints of cost and duration. More common is the use of a sample to infer the characteristics of a population. It is common practice to infer the sentiments of the population by asking a sample of people about their opinions. In most cases, we choose several thousand randomly selected individuals for samples such as this. This sampling always includes some level of error, something that cannot ever be eliminated due to sampling and measurement imperfections, but it is a valid way to achieve insight. A common question heard when a political poll is released is, "What can they really tell about how people are voting by such a small sample?" The answer is: a lot, really. That is why the results of these tests tend to converge (though there are differences created by how questions are framed and which locations are polled).

Sampling is used to test products for quality. It is necessarily the method used when we require destructive testing, such as crash testing or crushing. A company relying on destructive testing of a statistical population would not have any product left to sell. It would destroy each product that rolled off its assembly lines and would promptly become penniless.

The statistics behind sampling are powerful, but we must sample with care or we can bias our results. We discuss sampling bias more than once due to its significance.

Once we have our sample, we will need to understand what kind of data we have. This will let us know what types of analyses we can use with the data:

- *Attribute or Nominal*: Data represented by category or identity, such as name, country of origin, gender, or ownership. They can be used for numbers whose importance is not the representation of a measurable quantity *per se*, but rather, the count of how many we have of each attribute. Attribute data also include binary data, such as pass/fail and on/off.

- *Discrete*: This is a form of ordinal data that use only integers and would include counts and ratings. For example, the number of children a family has will be an integer. Even if the average number of children is 3.5, families will have 2 or 4 or 6 or another round number of children. Ordinal data are likewise discrete data. Ordinal data would include numerical ratings. On Amazon, we rate products with a number of stars. We rate teachers on a scale of 1–5 or 1–10.

- *Continuous*: Numeric data on a scale with no jumps from one possible value to the next possible value. As an example, the Federal Reserve Bank of New York has a scale in its basement to measure gold bars they transfer, internally or externally. This highly precise scale provides comfort to the countries whose gold they store. Despite a design for staggeringly heavy loads, the needle of the scale moves when as little as a dollar bill drops onto it. The data that come from this precise instrument are *continuous*. A precision level of pounds plus several decimal places would be realistic with this instrument. There is no rounding off to integers. Often, finely sliced discrete data, or pseudocontinuous data, such as dollars and cents, are treated as if they were continuous data.

This is a simplified list, but it provides an illustration of how data differ by type. As we progress, we will see how data type influences which hypothesis tests we must use as well as how slicing data poorly can create faulty results. Sometimes the data we need are not available, so we rely on surrogates. For example, many standard medical screening tests cannot detect whether we have a condition, but rather they detect what levels of a certain biochemical marker appear. This biochemical marker correlates well with the condition for which we screen. Other factors can cause this marker to increase or decrease, causing false-positives and false-negatives, but such tests are an effective way to diminish the number of patients on whom medical professionals should focus, particularly when they may need more detailed tests and treatments. In our big data analytics, we will likely need to use proxy attributes in some of our calculations. How we select and slice this surrogate data, or for that matter where we draw thresholds with our data in general, can have a more compelling effect on our results than our choices of statistical tools.

When approaching a variable in a data set, a common approach is to estimate the magnitude of the values addressed. For example, if we were the CEO of a chain of stores, we would want to know whether a typical customer visits our store six times a year or once every 6 years. We cannot use such basic information to draw solid conclusions, but unless we understand the central tendencies of the data as well as the dispersion, we find it difficult to understand the significance of the phenomena we measure.

Measures of central tendency provide some idea of which values are common and which are not. Using a measure of central tendency to examine home prices in our communities does not tell us much about either the mansions or the lower-income neighborhoods, but it does provide a useful measure of the general affluence of the community.

There are three primary measures of central tendency. These are the mean, median, and mode. Of these, the mean and median are the two most important. We use the mode less frequently.

The mean is a familiar concept. It is often called the "average," which is a synonym. The arithmetic mean is the sum of all values for a particular set divided by the number of values in that set. The mean of discrete ordinal data need not be discrete itself. If we roll a single, unloaded six-sided die 100 times, the mean value of the numbers we roll should be approximately 3.5. Or, take this Wikipedia article about the baby boom, "Family size increased sharply throughout the baby boom: the average woman bore 3.09 children in 1950 which increased to 3.65 children per family in 1960; the peak was in 1957, when the figure stood at 3.77."[1] Clearly, no women have ever given birth to 3.09, 3.65, or 3.77 children.

Although the mean is a most common and useful measure, we should remember it is really a mathematical abstraction (the examples in the previous paragraph). If we work for 5 days/week on billable hours, earning $100/hour and working a mean of 8 hours/day, we can quickly figure out that in a typical 5-day work week, we will earn gross pay of $4000. Some weeks will be more and some will be less, but the average is clear.

This is meaningful. If we value income more than free time, we know we would rather be on a job where we work a mean of 8 hours/day than one where we can bill 6 hours/day at the same rate during a typical 5-day work week. Instead of having a mean, or average, gross pay of $4000, we would bring home a mean weekly paycheck of $3000 with 6-hour workdays. We can begin to make life decisions using this information, but we should never forget that a mean without a measure of dispersion, usually the standard deviation (to be discussed later in this chapter), provides little information about what to expect when examining specific cases. We consider it wise to also calculate the median, which is less sensitive to outlying data.

The median is a similar measure to the mean in use, but we base it on a different calculation possessing different strengths and weaknesses. The median is simply the number in the center when we order the numbers from low to high or high to low; that is, ordinally. When we have an even number of values, we use the mean of the two values in the center. I roll a die 10 times, and then order the results from low to high. An analysis of the table of the results illustrates the difference between mean and median:

$$2\ 3\ 3\ 3\ 4\ 5\ 5\ 5\ 6\ 6$$

The mean of this string of numbers is 4.2. I calculate this by adding the string of numbers, arriving at a sum of 42, and then dividing the sum by 10. The 10 represents the number of times I rolled the die.

The median is 4.5. As the table above contains an even number of values, the two centermost values were selected. These are the fifth and sixth values, which are a 4 and a 5. The midpoint between the two is 4.5.

The third measure of central tendency is the mode. This is simply the most frequent value. In our example, we see two modes. Those are 3 and 5, each number of which appears 3 times. Normally, there is one mode. Sometimes, there is none. The mode is the only central tendency measure used for attribute or nominal data, and it is also useful for discrete data. For continuous data, it is rare to see repeating values. For the purposes of our discussion, we feel little need to discuss the mode further.

The median is often used in discussing attributes, such as house values or income, that can easily be skewed by extreme values. Imagine we live in a small town with five houses:

- A run-down older house worth $50,000
- A middle-class house worth $150,000
- A middle-class house worth $210,000
- A larger middle-class house worth $300,000
- A mansion worth $900,000

The mean price of houses in this town is the sum of these numbers divided by the number of houses, or $322,000. This is a skewed data set.

Notice that the mansion drags up the price much more than the run-down house drags the price down. It is exceedingly rare (though not impossible!) for a house to have a negative value. The run-down house cannot realistically decline to a value below zero, so it has zero as a floor. We have no such hard and fast upper limits to house values. The mansion has much more room to affect the mean value than does the run-down house. We can see this in the fact that the mean value of houses in this town is higher than the value of the second most valuable house. When we use the median price, or $210,000, we see the value is much more closely in line with what a typical house in town is worth.

As is the case with housing prices, multimillionaires and billionaires have much more power to skew mean income upward than someone at minimum wage has to skew the mean income downward. For this reason, median income is typically used instead of mean income.

STANDARD DEVIATION: THE STANDARD MEASURE OF DISPERSION

The central tendency measures of a data set are most definitely helpful in gaining an understanding of the topography of the data. If we were recent college graduates, knowing we would be stepping into a career with a mean starting salary of $80,000 per year (after changing majors)—as opposed to a career track with a mean starting salary of $55,000—is comforting. More often than not, we made a good choice. The important missing element here is the distribution of salaries. Rarely will someone who steps into either career earn the mean salary in either career choice. The most common measure of how the data points disperse around the mean we call the standard deviation.

Although we wish to avoid an excessive number of formulas, this formula is important. Notice that while the standard deviation is functionally used as if it were simply the mean distance of each value from the mean itself, that is not what the formula is. The formula for the standard deviation is

$$s = \sqrt{\frac{1}{N-1}\sum_{i=1}^{N}(x_j - \bar{x})^2}$$

(6.1)

TABLE 6.1

An Illustration of the Repeated Operation of Finding the
Difference between Each Value and the Mean of the Values

Value	Mean	Difference
2	4.2	−2.2
3	4.2	−1.2
3	4.2	−1.2
3	4.2	−1.2
4	4.2	−0.2
5	4.2	0.8
5	4.2	0.8
5	4.2	0.8
6	4.2	1.8
6	4.2	1.8

This looks worse than it is. First of all, notice the uppercase Greek letter sigma (Σ). This symbol means we repeat the operation for all cases. The "$(x - \bar{x})$," pronounced "x minus x-bar," means we subtract the mean value from each individual value. In short, the standard deviation is not the average distance between individual values and the mean, but it functions similarly.

In our above example of the string of numbers with a mean of 4.2, we would process it as shown in Table 6.1.

Intuition tells us we would simply take the mean of the differences, but we do not. First, we divide by the number of values minus one (or $n - 1$). More importantly, we square all of the differences and then take the square root. Since squaring a number and then taking the square root brings us back to the same number, this step seems like a waste of time. However, it serves a vital role. Note that one half of the differences in the table above are negative. This step eliminates the negative values, giving us the absolute value (the positive value) of the differences, since a negative times a negative results in a positive.

THE POWER OF SHAPES: DISTRIBUTIONS

We mentioned distributions—what exactly are they? Ever since the brilliant French philosopher and mathematician, Rene Descartes, developed analytical geometry, the power of plotting values on an x axis and a y axis

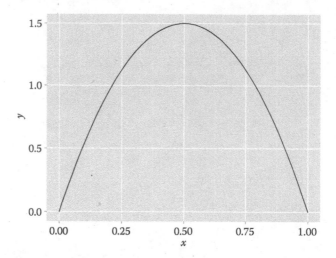

FIGURE 6.1

The beta distribution is used to model probabilities. An example would be the probability of a part failing under particular circumstances. The beta distribution can be used to model what is expected based on historical data of similar parts, then adjusted as further tests refine the probabilities. Notice that with probability distributions (this and others), the x axis runs from zero to one.

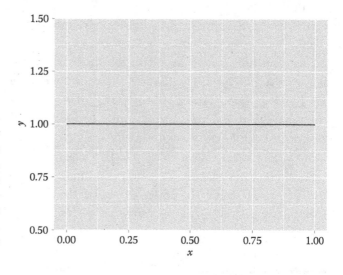

FIGURE 6.2

The uniform distribution for probability assumes all outcomes are equally likely. This would be akin to the odds of any particular value when rolling a single die. Again, the x axis runs from zero to one.

has been amply demonstrated. The grid has become a standard part of everything from trigonometry to calculus to analyzing statistical distributions. Distributions are simple.

The idea behind a distribution is to plot either observed phenomena or expected phenomena, then use the plot as a lever to pry into the

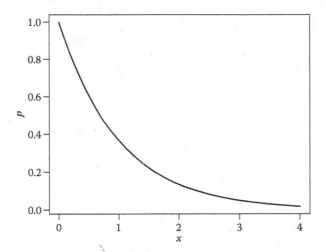

FIGURE 6.3

The exponential distribution is usually used to describe the time or length between indepen-dent events that occur at a constant rate. For example, if a customer has not been through your door for an hour, the average time until the next customer arrives will be shorter than if you just had a customer walk through, all else being equal. Because more customers arrive at some times than others, this distribution only works well for homogenous chunks of time (e.g., from 2:00 to 4:00 pm rather than one lunch hour and one non-lunch hour). Note that the number of possibilities is not finite, so the x axis does not run from zero to one.

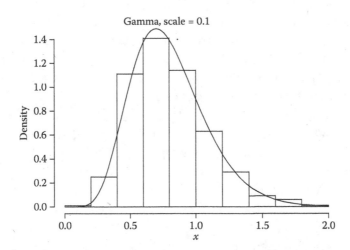

FIGURE 6.4

The gamma distribution is ideal for describing phenomena with a natural boundary such as rainfall and elapsed times for an activity. The rainfall and times cannot be negative, so they have a natural cutoff at zero or higher (nobody will run a mile in a minute, so a cutoff of zero is meaningless in that case). The curve in the example is superimposed on a histogram, so would be describing real data rather than simply describing probabilities.

probabilities involved. This sounds more complex than it is, and we will see how it works shortly. In a sense, it is a form of sleight of hand, but it is one that has proven its usefulness time and time again.

The distribution can be plotted based on experience, such as plots of length of employment, or a strongly grounded estimate, such as a casino determining the frequencies of different payouts from gambling machines. Then we can develop expectations—probabilities—from those calculations. What represented concrete examples or perhaps models firmly grounded in mathematics now becomes a set of expectations. In other words, when we plot our observed results or our mathematically determined expectations, we create a model of how we expect future events to unfold. The distribution is a precise way to draw abstract rules from specific occurrences.

When we move into hypothesis testing, we will see how important this conceptual interplay truly becomes. It has been one of mankind's crowning achievements in gaining understanding of the natural world and wrestling some degree of control of it away from chance and circumstance.

The familiarity of distributions can be deceiving, however. Those who know some theory of distributions well can easily fall prey to misusing them. It is not a lack of mental ability or ignorance that causes this result. The popular press, when it even bothers to mention distributions, emphasizes the standard normal distribution. In reality, we can calculate and plot many other distributions, from fat-tailed bell curves to skewed distributions to logarithmic distributions to flat distributions to distributions that simply appear misshapen. The entire actuarial profession uses a variety of probability distributions to ply its trade.

One of the authors was once asked by a colleague to help create a spreadsheet to analyze a large data set. The individual asking for the data set was highly intelligent and competent with numbers. He wanted to see the distribution, stating, "It will probably be a bell curve clustering around such-and-such a number."

We knew the data set was numerically dominated by the smallest values, with the largest values being comparatively rare. We suspected a logarithmic distribution would be the result. Although the result was actually an irregular distribution, it did bear a similar shape to the logarithmic distribution.

An important note about distributions is that they are, at best, approximations of how data really fall. When we collect and plot data, the "real" distributions (regardless of which distribution is being discussed) almost never match the abstracted elegance of the theoretical curves. This situation by no means detracts from the usefulness of these curves, as long as we do not overfit the data. We will discuss overfitting—the shoehorning of reality to perfectly to meet an expected set of results. Theory in the service of facts is a wonderful intellectual tool; facts in the service of theory are a perpetual source of grief.

DISTRIBUTIONS: GAUSSIAN CURVE

As we discussed, a distribution is essentially a series of values on the x (horizontal or abscissa) axis and the frequency with which those values appear on the y (vertical or ordinal) axis. Now we dig into a fascinating topic: the Gaussian curve and the central limit theorem. The most famous form of Gaussian curve is the standard normal distribution.

Carl Friedrich Gauss, the mathematician in whose honor this distribution was named, lived in what is now Germany during the late eighteenth and early to mid—nineteenth century. His contributions span across mathematics. In fact, along with Leonhard Euler (pronounced "oiler") he is one of the greatest mathematicians to have lived.

So, what exactly is the Gaussian curve? It is more famously known as the bell curve. The bell curve is a symmetrical bell-shaped plot with distinct mathematical characteristics. For our purposes, we will use the terms bell curve and Gaussian curve (or Gaussian distribution) interchangeably. It is the distribution most often used to describe the heights of individuals, the variations existing in manufactured products, and the results of standardized test scores. It is also the distribution that describes IQ scores, leading to this distribution being dragged into the limelight because of its use as the title of the controversial book entitled *The Bell Curve* by Richard Herrnstein and Charles Murray. Figure 6.5 shows an example of this distribution.

Because this curve is symmetrical, the mean and the median are approximately equal. As we discussed earlier, in reality, a distribution merely approximates data. Theoretically, the mean, median, and mode are exactly equal if we are using a Gaussian distribution. Because of this, the bell curve is known as "unimodal." All three measurements of central tendency occupy one location on the distribution.

When we collect and analyze real experiments and fit this distribution to the data, we always distinguish variability. The reason for this alignment of the mean and the median is clear when we observe the curve

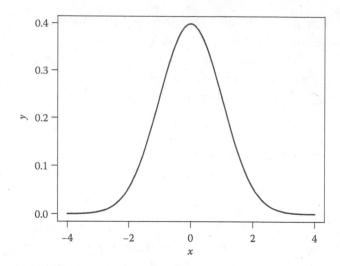

FIGURE 6.5
Normal distribution.

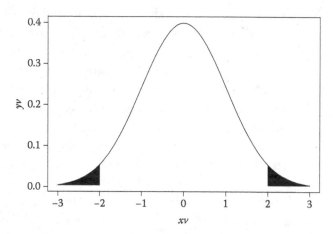

FIGURE 6.6
A normal distribution with the tails high-lighted. The tails are the thinnest parts of the curve, describing the least likely occur-rences. For this rea-son, they are key to hypothesis testing.

carefully. The average occupies the center—a function of the symmetry. As the average is in the center of the distribution with one-half of obser-vations falling above and one-half falling below the mean, the median by necessity falls onto the mean (again, theoretically).

We find rare events on the extreme left- and right-hand sides of the graph. As these are thin and trail off, they are called the graph's "tails." The left tail represents improbable events of a low value, while the right tail represents improbable events of a high value.

Let us return to our previous example of rolling a single die. There is a one in six chance of rolling any number. If we were to roll this die all day, we would have a result similar in shape to the histogram of the frequencies generated in Figure 6.7.

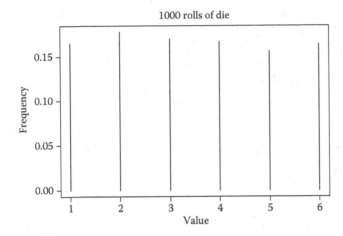

FIGURE 6.7
A simulated series of rolls of a single die. Note that while the distribution is not perfectly flat (almost no graph will perfectly match up to its probability distribution), it closely approximates the uniform distribution of Figure 6.2.

We can tell from this flat distribution we have a more or less equal chance of rolling any one of the values. Real life has a tendency to be trickier, though. We rarely have such neat casino odds. Instead, a single event is made up of several factors or components. Some of these factors work for us while others work against us. When we drive across a major city, sometimes all of the stop lights are green and sometimes all of them are red, but usually we run across a combination of green, yellow, and red lights. We can represent this in a hugely simplified form by using dice. Rolls of the dice are independent of each other, just as the chances are of hitting separate lights on green or red. Imagine that rolling a one is arriving at a light just as it is too late to pass through yellow, four is arriving several seconds before it turns green, and six is sailing through green comfortably. If you think of it in this way, the distribution obtained by rolling dice is much like the distribution obtained by measuring travel times to work.

We now move from the rolls of a single die to the realm of multiple dice. When using simple logic to create probabilities, the distribution of these probabilities will resemble the bell curve distribution that results frequently (but not always!) when measuring real-life phenomena. There is a little sleight of hand here as we are looking at this distribution based on calculated rather than observed probabilities. Much of the logic carries over, but in most big data applications of examining probabilities, we will estimate future probabilities based on past observations.

To conduct our analysis, we will take a look at three values: how many dice we have; how many different values we can roll; and how many different ways there are for us to roll any particular value. Table 6.2 shows the number of combinations one can roll with two dice. We can see

TABLE 6.2

An Example of How the Distribution Changes from Flat to the Peak Shape of Figure 6.8 When the Values on the Dice Are Added Together.

Roll 1	Roll 2	Sum
1	1	2
1	2	3
2	1	3
1	3	4
2	2	4
3	1	4
1	4	5
2	3	5
3	2	5
4	1	5
1	5	6
2	4	6
3	3	6
4	2	6
5	1	6
1	6	7
2	5	7
3	4	7
4	3	7
5	2	7
6	1	7
2	6	8
3	5	8
4	4	8
5	3	8
6	2	8
3	6	9
4	5	9
5	4	9
6	3	9
4	6	10
5	5	10
6	4	10
5	6	11
6	5	11
6	6	12

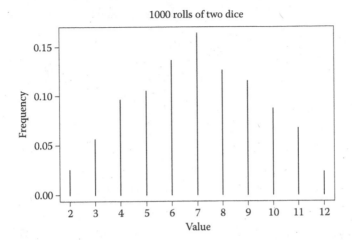

FIGURE 6.8

This graph illustrates simulated random throws of two dice at a time (the distribution of Table 6.2). Note that the most likely value is seven. This is because there are more ways to roll a seven with two dice than there are any other number. For example, a six and a one, a five and a two, etc.

immediately we have one 2, one 12, and six 7s. The distribution is no longer flat. If we look at Figure 6.8, we get a good visual grasp of the probabilities involved (here we run a simulation in R with two fair dice for 1000 experiments).

What we see is an approximately straight line running up from 2 to 7, then straight back down to 12. The distribution is peaked like the roof of a house. What happens if we add a third die and roll three dice? The third die adds a twist in the relationship and a curve to the distribution.

What we are seeing is that as we add more dice, the probabilities of the extreme values become smaller more quickly than do the larger values. What happens when we use five dice? The most unlikely results to roll when using all five are 5 and 30. To roll a 5, all five dice must land with a 1. To roll a 30, all must land with a 6.

If we examine how many ways we can roll a 6, we have five ways to roll that number. Four of the dice must land with a 1, and any one of the five may land with a 2. Once we look at the combinations enabling us to roll a 7, we can perceive 15 ways. We detect 10 different combinations of two dice that may roll a 2, with all of the rest rolling a 1. There are also five different combinations of four dice rolling a 1 and one die rolling a 3.

Once we look at how many ways to roll an 8, we see 35 possibilities, and for rolling a 9, there are 70 possibilities. The number of possible

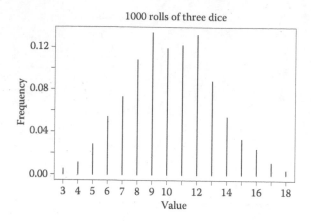

FIGURE 6.9

This graph of the simulation of random throws of three dice at a time demonstrates the distinct bell shape beginning to form. Notice that the tails are forming on the left and right side of the graph. There is one oddity to this simulation, however. It looks like a volcano, with the lines representing 10 and 11 being lower than those for 9 and 12. This is atypical and best used as an illustration of how the curve is at best an approximation of real life rather than a shoehorn that forces a particular shape on the world.

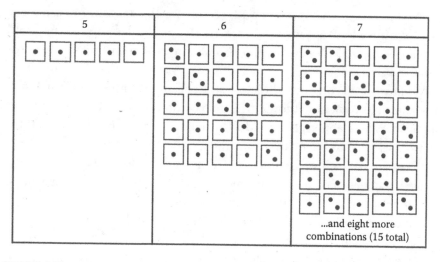

FIGURE 6.10

Note what is referred to as a combinatorial explosion. When there are five dice rolled at a time, there is only one way to roll a five, five ways to roll a six, and fifteen ways to roll a seven. The number of combinations increases until we reach 780 combinations to roll a 17 or 18, then decreases until we reach only a single combination that rolls a 30 (five sixes). This illustrates why the events in the tails are so unlikely. Much of hypothesis testing relies on this unlikelihood to filter out chance results from real effects. If the probability of a phenomenon is unlikely to land in the tails by chance, yet it does land in the tails, then it is more likely to be the result of the variable being tested.

combinations explodes (in fact, we call this behavior a "combinatorial explosion"). As we move nearer to the number of combinations allowing us to roll a 17 or an 18, we see this explosion in possibilities tapers off and reaches its peak. It is easy to roll either one. In fact, for both, 780 possible combinations of five dice will yield 17 or 18 as a result.

When we are looking at rolling a 5, all the dice must yield the same number and all must yield a 1. When we are looking at rolling an 18, a huge quantity of combinations can yield that result.

In fact, 17 and 18 are the two integers on either side of 17.5, which is an important value; it is the mean of all of the possible results of five dice being rolled:

$$5 \times 6 = 30, 5 \times 1 = 5, 30 - 5 = 25$$

One-half of 25 is 12.5. If we subtract 12.5 from 30, or add 12.5 to 5, we will end up with 17.5.

The number 17.5 is also the median, halfway between the two values in the center of the distribution. It is also the mean value of the values on a single die—remember this is equal to 3.5—multiplied by five dice.

This result, in fact, ties directly into a key component of the standard normal distribution (which we have called the Gaussian distribution). We refer to this component as the *central limit theorem*. When we sum a well-defined set of variables repeatedly, the distribution of those sums will follow the distribution we developed in this example. The distribution of dice thrown individually is a uniform (flat) distribution—all probabilities are equal. The distribution when we cast more dice converges progressively to

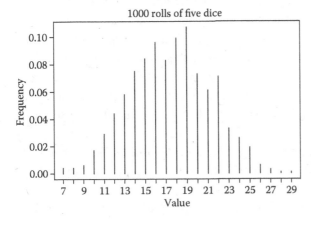

FIGURE 6.11
This graph illustrates the results of random throws of five dice a time, with the value graphed being that of the sum of the dice. Note again an atypical result, with 17 being abnormally low, even though it is more probable than 16. However, the tails are becoming very clearly visible.

the standard normal distribution. This trend occurs even when we analyze a highly skewed distribution of individual occurrences.

Now, we had some sleight of hand mentioned earlier. We based our examples of probabilities on Excel models running through all possible combinations that could result from throwing one, two, three, four, or five dice.

So, how does the standard normal distribution work when we are not working with anything as simple as dice? Think of the factors leading to the standard normal distribution in describing the heights of individuals within a population. The reality is we cannot begin to quantify the factors causing someone to be 6 ft., 3 in. in height while another person only reaches 5 ft., 7 in. We do know, however, different factors influence height, including nutrition, genetics, and childhood stress among others. A newer field of study, known as epigenetics, shows that nongenetic factors actively influence how genes express themselves. When discussing genetics alone, we find many genes that affect height, much the same as we have for skin color. Imagine the difference that occurs in the height of an individual if most of these factors influence in the same direction as opposed to having tall parents, but living through a stressful famine during one's years of growth. Imagine we have a tall parent and a short parent, and those genes mix (incomplete dominance). In fact, most phenomena are the result of a variety of factors. These factors may not be as mathematically neat as rolls of the dice, but they will probably not all regress with the same trend. They will most likely regress the height of any one person toward the center of the distribution.

The Gaussian distribution is also familiar in another famous curve, the sigmoid curve often used to represent the adoption of a new technology. To see how these two curves relate, let us imagine the length of time necessary for people to adopt a new technology, such as electricity and telephones. The diffusion of many of these technologies follows a sigmoid curve. The sigmoid curve is also known as the S curve, as much because it is shaped like the letter *S* as that the letter is also first letter of the word "sigmoid." Figure 6.12 makes much sense because we expect our adopters to accumulate, and this is a graph of the cumulative distribution function of the normal distribution.

As can be seen in the above graph, the sigmoid curve shows that a few people adopt a new technology early in the life cycle, then provided the technology is successful, its rate of dissemination increases. Increasing numbers of people begin to use the technology and incorporate it into

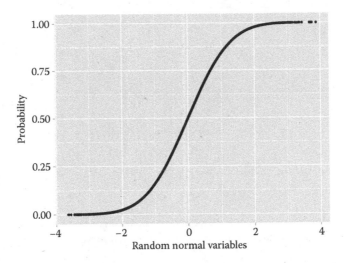

FIGURE 6.12

The sigmoid curve often describes the adoption of technologies. For example, the lower left side would be a good indicator of the adoption of cell phones when they were released to the public, with the upper right side indicating market saturation. The x axis in that case represents time. This chart, however, indicates a phenomenon to the left or right of a point zero.

their lives. Part of this effect occurs due to how technological knowledge disseminates. Part of what happens results from network effects. Part of it results from seeing the technology as more normal by seeing others use it (social modeling).

Regardless of the reasons for the spread of the technology, its rapid rate of acceptance continues but then begins to taper off as the market saturates. A technology may surpass 100% of the population only if measured by devices per person. If measured by the percentage of the population who use the device, it can never exceed 100%, and it will probably never reach 100% of the population. Instead, it will probably hit an asymptote somewhere near full acceptance but never hitting full acceptance.

What are we discussing here? We are discussing a distribution where we have a few early adopters and a few late adopters. The period where the rate of saturation grows the most quickly is the period during which the largest proportion of the population is adopting the technology.

This situation sounds like we are discussing the same phenomenon as we see with the Gaussian distribution but with a key exception. We can use the Gaussian distribution to explore the rate at which people integrate

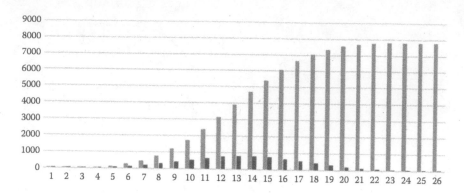

FIGURE 6.13

The relationship between the bell curve and the sigmoid curve. At each bar the sigmoid curve grows by the amount of the adjacent bar of the bell curve.

the technology into their lives. The sigmoid curve describes the proportion of the population that has accepted it across time.

In fact, what happens if we take our rolls of the dice and add the quantity of rolls that equal a particular number, then add this quantity to the cumulative number of rolls that came before it? We can see this in Figure 6.13.

These concepts are ideal for discussing many business phenomena. By tying them together, we look past what is common sense to better grasp the underlying factors. Nevertheless, the Gaussian curve is not the *ne plus ultra* of distributions.

DISTRIBUTIONS: WHY BE NORMAL?

Our thought experiment with dice seems to be a solid demonstration in favor of the soundness of the standard normal distribution, and, to a large degree, it is. Nevertheless, the standard normal distribution also has its weaknesses. A central weakness is it describes tendencies that are commonly found in the external world, not a mold into which the world fits itself. Inappropriate application of this distribution is an invitation to misadventure. Investors tend to discover these setbacks whenever the market makes sudden movements astronomically improbable according to the normal distribution. The fiascos are not limited to sudden downward movements, as many of those who short stocks or commodities have also learned painful lessons when there is a sudden upward movement.

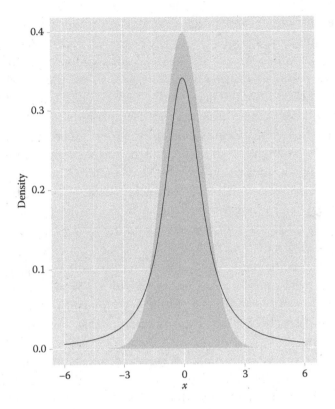

FIGURE 6.14

Gaussian (shaded) and *t*-distributions overlaid (dof=1.5). Note that the *t*-distribution is shorter and wider, with fatter tails, than the Gaussian distribution. This is because the Gaussian represents a population and the *t*-distribution represents a sample. As the sample size increases, the *t*-distribution becomes taller and narrow, resembling the Gaussian distribution more and more. Remember also that the width of the distribution is a function of the standard deviation. The effect of the division by *n*–1 instead of *n* is visible in this phenomenon of the narrowing of the *t*-distribution with increasing sample size.

What are the characteristics of the values we generated in our thought experiment? First, each time we roll the dice, it is an independent event. For example, what are the odds of rolling a 5 using five dice? The answer is approximately 0.01268%, or $(1/6)^5$. Imagine we roll a 5. What are the odds of it happening on the next roll? They remain unchanged; the odds are still 0.01268%. The human mind has a tendency to assume that if an uncommon event occurs, it is less likely to occur again. In events such as coin flips and rolls of the dice, this assumption is an illusion. In reality, these events are independent.

Some events are not independent; examples include cigarette smoking and lung cancer or any other case where we can show a mechanism of cause and effect. Pedestrians across grassy fields are unlikely to take random trips across once a path is worn. The path is a function of which areas around the field feature the most traffic, such as gates and buildings, and we generally refer to these human-created features as *desire lines*. Once the path forms, then it also begins to shape the route taken by future pedestrians. Other examples of nonindependent occurrences include fashion, as well as popular music and movies. People tend to buy what is trendy and popular. Anyone with a taste for underground or international movies and music can attest that it is not quality that keeps their favorites obscure. It is often a lack of marketing and the want of a snowball effect leading to obscurity.

Coin flips, on the other hand, are independent. If we flip a coin that lands heads eight times in a row (an event with a 0.391% chance of occurring if it is an isolated series of eight flips), the odds it will land heads on the ninth flip are still 50%, or the same chance that it was on each other individual flip.

The importance of independent occurrences versus those not independent is the tendency for nonindependent occurrences to be more extreme. Movements in the market are not independent events, (although the market is effectively a random walk from a predictive aspect). If we see the bottom dropping out of the stock market, we are likely to sell off our stocks to avoid further losses. Our act of abandoning the market makes a small but real contribution to the downward pressure on stock prices. When many people react this way, the contribution to the depression of stock prices accumulates. In other words, unlike our hypothetical example, events such as the movement of investments interconnect.

A related gap between reality and our model is what Nassim Nicholas Taleb refers to as the Ludic Fallacy. Taleb has expressed his irritation with attempts by publishers to use symbols of gambling, such as dice, on his books when they translate and publish his books in other languages. Why? Aside from psychological games such as poker, gambling can be broken down into calculable and well-established probabilities—real life is rarely so neat.

Casinos can tailor their probabilities to consistently earn money. This is part of the reason they consider card counters, cheaters, and others who alter these probabilities as such a grave threat. Those who consistently win draw extra attention because their behavior is highly improbable in these games with well-defined probabilities, which the casino deliberately sets in its own favor.

Firms that build cars and smartphones and distribute goods through their supply chains suffer difficulties in marketing and operations that casinos do not face. Who could predict one of the best-selling cars of all time would be the underpowered, air-cooled early generation of the Volkswagen Beetle? Who could predict VHS would beat Sony Betamax in the market, fending off challengers such as the videodisk, only to be toppled by the DVD (itself falling prey to Blu-ray and Internet streaming)? None of these odds could be calculated using the methods casinos utilize or create. We find no way to fit these events into a standard distribution. In fact, they are impossible to calculate.

On the other hand, we know of many other phenomena, such as the movements of stock prices and commodity prices, which we describe without using a Gaussian distribution. For the moment, let us consider a slightly misshapen Gaussian curve—a fat-tailed curve. It strongly resembles the standard normal distribution, but to confound the two is dangerous.

To see why, let us step back and remember our discussion of tails. The tails represent improbable events. The area under a particular portion of the curve is proportional to the probabilities that lie under it (contained within that area). When the tail fattens, the probability of an extreme event increases, and, likewise, the probability of a nonextreme event decreases somewhat. If we accurately consider this probability, then we can profit thereby. If we underestimate it, perhaps by using the mathematics of the standard normal distribution in our analysis, we risk losses and possible ruin.

It is easy to see how this scenario presents a problem. Let us imagine we insure agricultural crops against both drought and drown-outs. This policy requires, among other things, that we construct actuarial tables around how precipitation affects our clients. Since our example is a simplified thought experiment, we will assume that the tails past two standard deviations in either direction represent the effects of extreme weather, although reality would almost never be this simple. In other words, on either tail, 2.2% of our policyholders will be outliers who collect insurance. Those on the left side of the distribution will suffer events that will qualify as crop disaster from droughts. Another 2.2% of our policyholders will suffer events on the other side of the distribution; this rightmost 2.2% will represent crop disasters resulting from drown-outs.

We will assume all of our policies are written for $1 million, and reinsurance is not an option. The expected payout on any given year will be $44,000 for each $1 million in crops insured. We price our policy at $61,600 ($44,000×1.4) to be able to cover disasters yet still be able to pay staff and keep our investors happy. If we underestimate our risk and we have an especially disastrous year costing us double or triple what a normal year would cost us, then we witness a calamity. If the same event happens many times over a couple of decades, then we are probably using the wrong distribution as a tool for prediction. This series of infelicities occurred in finance, especially in the 2007–2008 economic debacle. There are several price movements of the stock market since the 1980s that would probably happen only once in the age of the universe—underestimated risk if we use a normal distribution!

A paper by Dan diBartolomeo of Northfield Research pinpoints the folly of using a standard normal distribution to explain the movements of markets:

> Some articles have suggested that extremely rare events (e.g. seven to ten standard deviations) have been observed on several occasions between August and today in various markets. This explanation is paradoxical because it simultaneously asserts that these large return events are very, very rare and yet have occurred frequently between September 2007 and March 2008. Clearly, something is wrong with this explanation.[2]

Events better represented by fat tails are just one way a user can err by relying on the standard normal distribution. Another occurs when we have a skewed distribution. A skewed distribution is one in which the mean and median are separated, as we have a constrained tail on one side while the other is not. Let us put this into more concrete terms.

If we are the owner of a franchise fast-food restaurant, we might fret about customers who may be upset about the length of service in the drive-through. This leads us to measure the interval between when a given customer drives away from the speaker where they place the order and when we physically hand off the order to the same customer.

We can arrive at a method to track all orders surreptitiously, so we do not cause our staff to alter their practices while accommodating the measurement. From opening to closing, all day every day, we measure each order for a period of 7 days. We enter our measurements into a spreadsheet and then graph them. Will our observations form a symmetrical bell curve; that is, a normal distribution? Probably not.

Why? Let us imagine the mean time for delivery is 90 seconds. As we understand from experience and from our previous discussion, almost no particular instances will be 90 seconds. Will there be any instances where the measured duration exceeds 3 minutes? Probably. Imagine one hamburger of a particular style remains, and we give it to a customer inside the restaurant before our drive-through customer can get it. Imagine a school bus with a sports team on board arrives, and our restaurant fills with kids. All of our French fries are burned while staff scrambles to move 30 kids through the line promptly. It is not difficult to imagine several scenarios that will cause the waiting time for our drive-through customers to double, triple, or quadruple. That is why we have coupons for a free meal our staff can give to upset customers, along with an apology and a smile.

It is easy to imagine situations that would cause an extra 90 seconds (or 180 seconds, or 270 seconds, or 360 seconds) in waiting time for our customers. Now, imagine scenarios that would cause our customers to have food in hand in 90 seconds or more below the mean. That would be 0 seconds or even a negative number of seconds. This would mean our customer would literally move from the speaker to the window and receive the food instantaneously, or our staff gets food into a customer's hands before the customer has even decided on the order. Once we trim any fraction of a second from the original 90 seconds, we are dealing with time travel. Hedge fund management or sports betting would be a better outlet for this talent than fast-food delivery. The reality is we will have no zero-second deliveries and vanishingly few 30 second deliveries. In fact, a realistic distribution would look like the one in Figure 6.15.

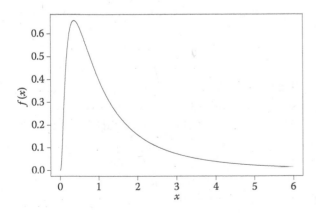

FIGURE 6.15
Highly skewed distribution.

DISTRIBUTIONS: THE LONG ARM OF THE POWER LAW

Criticism of Malcolm Gladwell has become a form of intellectual trophy hunting of late. This criticism ranges from thoughtful methodological criticism to mindless sniping at a journalist who has attained tremendous popularity. In reality, although his methods could sometimes be more systematic, Gladwell has done a tremendous service in bringing complex concepts to intelligent, interested readers whose education may not have included those concepts. An example of this is a 2006 essay discussing how the majority of instances of a particular phenomenon often are the result of a minority of contributors. In plain English, a minority of cars cause the majority of air pollution. A minority of police officers attract the majority of citizen complaints.

In discussing a post–Rodney King investigation of the Los Angeles Police Department (LAPD) by a commission headed by Warren Christopher, Gladwell writes that

> Between 1986 and 1990, allegations of excessive force or improper tactics were made against eighteen hundred of the eighty-five hundred officers in the L.A.P.D. The broad middle had scarcely been accused of anything. Furthermore, more than fourteen hundred officers had only one or two allegations made against them—and bear in mind that these were not proven charges, that they happened in a four-year period, and that allegations of excessive force are an inevitable feature of urban police work. (The N.Y.P.D. receives about three thousand such complaints a year.) A hundred and eighty-three officers, however, had four or more complaints against them, forty-four officers had six or more complaints, sixteen had eight or more, and one had sixteen complaints. If you were to graph the troubles of the L.A.P.D., it wouldn't look like a bell curve. It would look more like a hockey stick. It would follow what statisticians call a "power law" distribution—where all the activity is not in the middle but at one extreme.[3]

The power law Gladwell describes is a statistical distribution called a Pareto distribution. It describes the number of links different websites have, the numbers of fatalities from wars, the sizes of earthquakes, and the movements of financial markets. It is the probability distribution that describes the apportionment of wealth in a society, and it is the reason we use median and not mean when we describe the income of a city or a state. A few extremely wealthy individuals can badly skew the mean for wealth

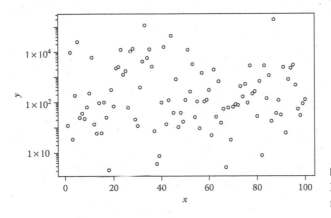

FIGURE 6.16
Logarithmic scale with
random data.

in a society. The power law version of this distribution—known as Zipf's law—is also behind the famous, and poorly named, as we shall see, 80/20 rule.

So what is the power law? The power law is a scale invariant distribution in which the number of cases decreases from the most common to the least common following a logarithmic scale. Before we translate this to plain English, let us look at the example in Figure 6.16. This chart shows random data on a logarithmic scale. The value of those points to the right of 1×10, or 10. Those to the right of 1×10^4 indicate a value of roughly 10,000. The y axis does not grow at a linear rate but rather an exponential rate.

When we are dealing with a power law distribution, we are dealing with a distribution that finds itself at home in a world of extremes. In fact, Taleb, whom we have discussed elsewhere, has called the world inhabited by the power law distribution *Extremistan*. This is the opposite of the world inhabited by the Gaussian distribution, a world he calls *Mediocristan*.

This is the world of the "winner takes all." Wal-Mart is by far the largest brick-and-mortar retailer by sales in the United States in terms of market penetration. Other large retailers not in the size range of Wal-Mart include Target, Kohl's, JC Penney, and Sears. Although we do not observe a huge number of such retailers, they are numerous compared to retailers as large as Wal-Mart, and they are still large enough to be household names. These retailers would be off to the left side of this distribution. As we move to the right, we will see commonplace stores, but these businesses would have less revenue and would be less recognizable. Examples of these merchants are stores such as the Body Shop or the Gap that we find in malls throughout the country. As we move further to the right, we note the emergence of regional retailers. Moving further right, we find shops that are community

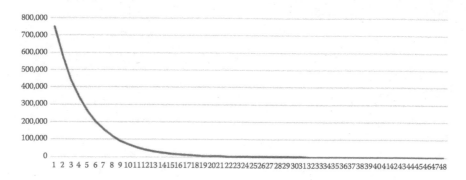

FIGURE 6.17

The logarithmic distribution. Notice how rapidly the graph increases toward the left side. The values at the left are significantly more likely than the values even slightly to the right.

institutions but with limited sales and located within one or two counties. Such stores are everywhere—and almost every region has them. As we reach the far right side of the distribution, we reach those family-owned stores which have a single location. Almost every community in the country that has a large enough population base to support retail merchants has these. These are the "Joe's Hardware" and "Ed's Menswear" stores that help make small-town main streets charming.

We also begin to see the idea underpinning the phrase we used earlier: scale invariance. What scale invariance means is this: as we move across the distribution, whether from right to left or left to right, the rate of change stays the same. In other words, in Figure 6.17, the number of cases logging in at 1 second divided by the number of cases logging at 2 seconds is equal to the number of cases logging in at 32 seconds divided by the number of cases logging in at 33 seconds. Let us examine this:

For this example, we assumed there were 10 cases logged in at 60 seconds, 13 cases at 59 seconds, and 16.9 cases at 58 seconds (again, a distribution at a conceptual level is an approximation). The formula used, running from right to left, is the previous number multiplied by 1.3. However, the power law cannot be scale invariant, correct? After all, look how it rises slowly from right to left and then takes off. If we lop off everything to the left of where it begins to rise rapidly, we will just end up with the slow growth we see when we move from right to left up until the point of rapid growth, correct? Not at all. That acceleration is the result of the scaling of the graph. As an example, take a look at what happens when we do lop off that section (Figure 6.18).

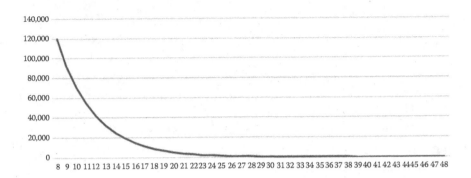

FIGURE 6.18

This is an example of scale invariance, but look closely. Note that the values of one through seven have been removed from the graph. In Figure 6.17, it is around eight that the rate of change from one value to the next appears to diminish (the line flattens), but this is an optical illusion. The steepest part of this graph is around eight and it appears to flatten around 15 or 16. We could continue to cut off values on the left side of the chart but, as long we keep adjusting the y axis to take up the same space, then the appearance of the chart will remain constant.

With a readjusted scale, the graph appears the same. Another interesting feature of the power law approach is the curve will become a straight line if it is plotted on a logarithmic scale. In plain English, the curve we saw in the above examples is what we see when we use a scale where each unit on the left axis is of an equal value, such as the 10 million incidents used in the above examples. When the scale instead increases by one order of magnitude, or one power of ten, then the curve becomes a straight line (Figure 6.19).

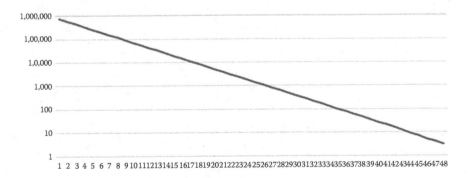

FIGURE 6.19

This is a key feature of a true logarithmic distribution: when it is charted with a logarithmic y axis, the curve becomes a straight line. The only difference between this chart and that in Figure 6.17 is that this one has a logarithmic scale on the y axis. The values are the same.

We can see the scale runs from 1 to 10 to 100 to 1000 and so on up to 100 million. This is logarithmic growth. Even though it looks like the line of our curve reaches nearly to 100 million, it really only reaches to somewhere short of 53 million. The logarithmic scale also applies to the space between the horizontal markers on the graph, so we are witnessing an optical illusion.

Playing with a spreadsheet can have nothing to do with the real world, though. Right? Wrong. The power law has everything to do with the real world, including finance.

The famed French mathematician, Benoit Mandelbrot, created the field of fractal geometry. Most of us are familiar with fractal screensavers and colorful tee shirts. If we have seen a graphic similar to the one in Figure 6.20, we have seen fractals.

The idea behind fractals is the repetition of phenomena across scales. For example, consider a fern. The leaves of a fern look like little ferns. If we were building a dollhouse, we could passably plant ferns in the front yard by plucking the leaves off ferns in front of our own house and placing them in front of the dollhouse. Or, we can think of trees. In Figure 6.21, is it easy to guess the length of the branch that was used as the model for the following drawing? Is it measured in inches (or centimeters,) or feet, or (or meters)? Once we guess the approximate scale, can we guess more specifically?

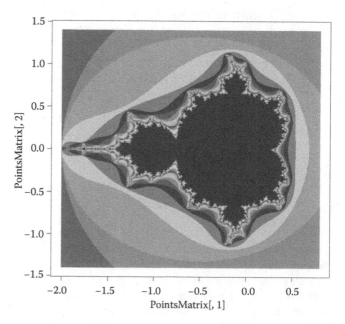

FIGURE 6.20

Fractal image from Mandelbrot set.

FIGURE 6.21
Tree branch: What
size is it?

The odds are that we cannot. The reason is the structure of trees follows a fractal structure. A smaller section resembles a larger section. The image of the fractal image shown in Figure 6.20, of the kind found on tee shirts and dorm wall posters, itself repeats across scales. If we look up videos featuring fractal geometry, we can see that it is possible to zoom into a fractal landscape indefinitely and see the same patterns repeating endlessly.

The way this ties into the power law is simple. As was argued, the power law distribution is scale invariant. We lopped off one end of the distribution and rescaled it, and it did not change in appearance. In fact, as we discussed earlier, we created the graph using a formula that remained constant. Each occurrence on our graph we declared to be 1.3 times as frequent as the value to its right.

Mandelbrot's expertise in such scale invariance, it turns out, is exactly what was needed to study markets. Beginning with research into the cotton market, Mandelbrot was able to demonstrate that markets tend to follow a scale invariant power law distribution. In discussing this discovery, Mandelbrot describes the appearance of his price charts in his brilliant 2004 work, *The (Mis)behavior of Markets*:

A month looks like a day, one set of days like another. In fact, at a first approximation, you could not readily tell without the labels which line was which. That clicks with something else. Having acquired an interest in financial markets after my move to New York, I started chatting with the Wall Street pros. There is something funny, one told me: In the newspaper, all price charts look alike. Sure, some go up; some go down. But daily, monthly, annually—there is no big difference in the overall look of it. Strip off the dates and price markers, and you could not tell which was which. They were all equally wiggly.[4]

An uncomfortable component of the scale invariance of the power law, from a risk management point of view, is that extreme outliers are assumed to occur and can be gargantuan. They are still rare, but not so rare they can be ignored or treated as controllable using formulas and concepts designed for the standard normal distribution. Huge financial movements, such as the Great Depression and the Great Recession of 2008, are extremely improbable when examined from the point of view of the standard normal distribution. The power law, however, easily accommodates them.

There are two key phenomena directly related to the power law distribution, and they are closely related. The first of these is the Pareto principle. The second is Zipf's law.

The Pareto principle is named after the late Italian economist, Vilfredo Pareto, who lived from the middle of the nineteenth century through the first quarter of the twentieth century. Pareto discovered about 20% of the population held about 80% of society's wealth, hence the other name for the Pareto principle: the 80/20 rule. This rule has been generalized all the way from wealth distribution to no end of social phenomena, such as a small number of customers accounting for a large percentage of a firm's revenue to items such as social networks.

The 80/20 rule is an unfortunate name for a simple reason. The breakdown is a generalization about a minority of cases having the majority of the effect. The breakdown may be 70/30, or 75/25. There is one further unfortunate side effect to referring to the Pareto principle as the 80/20 rule: there is no reason why the two numbers must add up to 100. It is common when referring to this rule to use two numbers that add up in such manner (and our use such numbers earlier in this paragraph was deliberate). In reality, 23% of customers may account for 84% of sales.

The Pareto principle also highlights another characteristic of the power law distribution. We have discussed the heightened risk existing in situations described by the power law. Extreme outliers are more common than they are when a bell curve holds. Risk is not the only side of the story, however, and we can also find opportunity. Remember the example from Malcolm Gladwell's discussion of citizen complaints against police officers in Los Angeles. The majority of the officers had no complaints against them. The majority of the officers with complaints against them had one. When the 80/20 rule is applicable, then we may address the majority of cases of concern while focusing on a small subsection of cases overall. We may address sources of 87% of our revenue while only formulating a strategy for 34% of our customers. We may focus our efforts using the leverage we see in the power law.

Let us imagine our company is losing corporate customers, so we conduct a data assessment. We find certain characteristics indicate a heightened risk of losing them, such as an expensive payment plan to which they are contractually bound. They feel cheated, so when their contract runs out they leave us regardless of any incentives we might offer.

We find that the largest 10% of our customers by volume account for 70% of our revenue, but they do not cost significantly more to take care of than those who pay for fewer services. Using the Pareto principle, we can begin to find which among those customers have the priciest services, then begin to work with them to offer them complementary services, charge them a little less, and make more profit.

Intimately related to the power law discussion is Zipf's law, named after linguist George Kingsley Zipf. Zipf noticed that the ratio of the frequency of usage of the most common word compared to that of the second most common word is roughly equal to the usage ratio of that second most common word to the third most common word, and so on. This holds not only for word freqency but for phenomena ranging from the population size of cities to the number of links to Internet sites of varying popularity. A difference between Zipf's law and the Pareto principle does exist, but it is extremely subtle. One way to simplify the difference is to think of Zipf's law as defining the relationship between pairs of points in the graph, whereas the Pareto principle addresses the relationships of areas on that graph. In other words, Zipf's law addresses the prevalence of usage of "the" versus "then," whereas the Pareto principle addresses the number of times the 20 or 25 or 42 most common words are used as compared to all other words.

THE UPSHOT? STATISTICS ARE NOT BLOODLESS

"Numbers do not lie" is a cliché we hear frequently. Nevertheless, author Darrell Huff, working with artist Irving Geis, produced a brilliant book by the name *How to Lie with Statistics*[5] over a half century ago. In fact, it is easy to use statistics to fool others and to fool oneself.

The reality is statistics are often poorly used. We suggest some guidelines to lead the reader to spot poor usage. When managing analysts or contracting with a firm showing off the results it has attained with data, it is worth asking questions such as

- Are we basing our analysis on the mean or median? (And remember that the mean can lose a great deal of its meaning if the distribution is not symmetric!)
- Is our distribution based on individual data points or collections of points (think of the example with dice)?
- What distribution did we use?
- What is the dispersion of the data?
- If there is a threshold past which the data indicate an unacceptable situation, what is the percentage of data crossing that threshold (such as dangerously high blood pressure on an experimental drug)?
- Can we demonstrate that the data fit that distribution? (Again, remember the central limit theorem that will allow even extreme distributions to become bell curves.)
- How do our assumptions and recommendations fit with the distribution that we are demonstrating?

FOOLING OURSELVES: SEEING WHAT WE WANT TO SEE IN THE DATA

As a quick thought experiment, how many people can we think of who gain most of their news from sources that disagree with them? In other words, how many on the right obtain their news from MSNBC, or how many on the left obtain their news from Fox News? For people outside the United States., the former interprets events in a left-leaning tone, while the latter interprets them in a right-leaning tone. There is a minor industry in complaining that the news media is biased rightward (if one is on the left) or leftward (if one is on the right).

Anyone with a Facebook account and a politically diverse circle of friends will notice we can assemble data to support diverse viewpoints. On any topic, whether it is gun control, economic policy, or international trade, both sides of the argument readily deploy statistics to their defense. We can also do this with business data. It is second nature to seek confirmation of our opinions, and we often do this through subtle framing tricks. In a business setting, however, to do this is risky.

Let us look at some brief examples. Both of us are US citizens, so we will draw our illustrations from our country's political discourse, that of the United States of 2014. As so much of current-day politics revolves around blame, we will take two examples from the question of who is responsible for the national debt run up by the government of the United States.

According to left-leaning website *Politicus USA*, Ronald Reagan raised the debt ceiling 18 times for a 67% increase in debt during his time in office, as opposed to President Obama's six increases in the debt ceiling for a total of a 31% increase in the national debt during his term in office.[6]

Rick Ungar of *Forbes*, who writes from an acknowledged left-leaning viewpoint, writes of President Obama's first year in office, "where the federal budget increased a whopping 17.9%—going from $2.98 trillion to $3.52 trillion." He then states this is due to Bush's actions in his last year in office. Mr. Ungar then goes on to argue that in percentage terms, Obama did less to increase spending than any president since Eisenhower.[7]

If we move from the left side of the spectrum to the right, the focus changes. The right-leaning CNSnews.com argues that under Obama, "the federal debt has increased by $4.212 trillion—more than the total national debt of about $4.1672 trillion accumulated by all 41 U.S. presidents from George Washington through George H.W. Bush combined."[8]

In a *Wall Street Journal* op-ed, Karl Rove, a former advisor to the second President Bush, states, "the debt held by the public grew $3 trillion under Mr. Bush—to $6.3 trillion from $3.3 trillion at a time when the national economy grew as well." He then argues that by the end of President Obama's first 20 months, he will have overseen as great an increase the deficit as President Bush oversaw in 8 years, and "Mr. Bush's deficits ran an average of 3.2% of GDP, slightly above the post World War II average of 2.7%. Mr. Obama's plan calls for deficits that will average 4.2% over the next decade."[9]

As neither of us wants nor intends to stand on a political soapbox, we will not take sides. Instead, we ask the reader to look at these excerpts from different opinion pieces and examine what assumptions were made. How was the issue framed? Was it in absolute numbers or in percentages? What time frames were used? What rationales were given for slicing the information in a particular way? Note that the different sides chose the interpretation that fit the case they were trying to make, rather than lay out the numbers and fit the interpretation to those numbers.

Much of the analysis we receive in a business setting will try to influence us in a particular direction. We will observe it used much the way in which a lawyer arranges facts rather than in the practice in which a scientist—ideally—seeks an answer. However, the analysis will appear scientific. As a manager, we probably run across biased information and know this intuitively. A statistical argument is like jargon. It can create great precision unattainable with standard usage of language, or it can be used to obfuscate the truth.

Even the most honest and impartial of analysts can create multiple meanings from the same data, though. The difficulty in selecting the most appropriate metric is illustrated by a thoughtful article by David Ropeik, an instructor at the Harvard School of Public Health. In his article, Mr. Ropeik discusses the dilemmas in calculating meaningful metrics of risk, in this case using the example of the risk of dying in an airplane crash.

In asking whether the risk of flying should be calculated based on a per capita basis, a per flight basis, or a per mile basis, Mr. Ropeik points out

> They all produce accurate numbers, but which one is most relevant to you depends on your personal flying patterns. Some fliers take lots of short flights and some take longer ones, for example. Since the overwhelming majority of the few plane crashes that do occur take place in connection with takeoffs and landings, the risk is less a matter of how far you fly and more a matter of how often. If you're a frequent flier, then the risk per flight means more. For occasional long-distance fliers, the risk per mile means more. A frequent, long-distance flier would want to consider both.[10]

He then also points out a neglected aspect of drawing a measurement: Over what period is the measurement being drawn? The September 11, 2001, attacks skewed the deaths from air travel upward for that year. Changes in safety practices make numbers from 5 or 10 years beforehand obsolete. Yet, single year numbers are volatile because a plane crash is a catastrophic event.

Let us put the above discussions into a business framework. As a manager, we are interested in increasing margins, as this influences how analysts view our business, which in turn affects our company's stock. We have been tasked to analyze the issue and recommend solutions.

Our analysts run through the different data sources in the company and tell us one division of our company, the one making Ajax safe-cracking kits, is suffering from poor performance, and a better allocation of expenses would probably indicate the division is not turning a profit.

Aside from one cartoon coyote, most customers do not become repeat customers. Previous attempts to rescue this division have failed miserably in a cross fire of accusations.

A sentiment analysis using Twitter feeds related to our product shows customers see a gap between how we present the product and how it works. Our marketing division has been stung multiple times by trying to broaden the appeal of this product, with occasional firings as well as voluntary staff turnover. They see the Twitter feeds as an indication the business line is hopeless and should be discontinued. Marketing further points out that its methods work well across other areas of the company. The numbers bear this out. Why would it fail on this one product?

The division to which this product line belongs wants to keep the product, blaming customer discontent on false expectations created by careless marketing. Management in this division sees this product as a vital part of Ajax's offerings. They also receive bonuses that are, in part, based on the sales of the safe-cracking kit. They point out the success of their other products, all of which are considered outstanding successes. Why would this one product be a dud?

We are looking at a business example of the ability of data to deliver up what the viewer wants to see. People can cherry-pick results and find what they want in the data but, does the ability of two divisions to argue, while both citing the data, invalidate the utility of big data? No, it does not.

When the analyst hands off the results of his analysis to us, we are not listening to an infallible oracle. Instead, we are holding a first draft. The report in our hands is not offering definitive answers; it is giving us a recommendation on how to better pinpoint further questions.

As a manager, a good approach would be to bring in the analyst and representatives of marketing and the division that runs the safe-cracking business line and discuss the following:

- What data points were used?
- Over what interval were they collected?
- What were the sample sizes?
- From which data sources were they extracted?
- What formulae were used for calculated statistics, (such as hours and miles to create miles per hour)?
- Which statistical analyses were used?
- What were the strengths and weaknesses of these statistical methods?
- Were these statistical tests appropriate to the questions being asked?

- What would be alternative calculations and formulae that would better address the needs of the company in improving sales?

On a more specific note, it would be worthwhile to ask the following:

- Did the woes of the safe-cracking kit hit at a particular time that may have influenced performance (e.g., did the firing of a manager in marketing coincide with the rollout of a new marketing campaign)?
- Did a new product come out (whether it be a better safe or a better safe-cracking kit) that affected perceptions of Ajax's offering?
- Were there any glitches in quality that went undetected?
- Did another part of the company contradict the messaging of the marketing department?

We can see from the questions listed here that a rather detailed and illuminating conversation can be driven forward based on what is in the analyst's report. The questions above allow us to cut through both deliberate obfuscation with the data as well as honest differences in measurement and assessment. By tying a solid thought-provoking line of questions to the results of big data, we gain insights into our business we could not otherwise attain.

WE CAN LEARN MUCH FROM AN OCTOPUS

The Sea Life Center in Oberhausen, Germany, was home to a notable resident. Until his untimely death in 2010 at the age of 2 years old, Paul the octopus was famous for his ability to accurately pick the winners of football matches (soccer in the United States) during the 2010 World Cup held in South Africa. Few would have taken Paul seriously as a true psychic but his record truly was impressive. When given food to choose from in two containers, each of which contained the flags of the countries in an upcoming match, Paul correctly chose the winner 11 out of 13 times. He was correct nearly 85% of the time. What drove Paul's predictive abilities? The Wikipedia entry on him contains a clue:

> Some other German oracles did not fare so well in the World Cup. The animals at the Chemnitz Zoo were wrong on all of Germany's group-stage games, with Leon the porcupine picking Australia, Petty the pygmy

hippopotamus spurning Serbia's apple-topped pile of hay, and Anton the tamarind eating a raisin representing Ghana... Mani the Parakeet of Singapore became famous for correctly predicting the results of all four quarterfinal matches. Mani contradicted Paul by picking the Netherlands to win the final, resulting in some media outlets describing the game as an octopus-versus-parakeet showdown.[11]

Simply put, there were many animal oracles. Any oracle that could not prove its accuracy slid into obscurity. From the sheer number of animal oracles, probability suggests some would be accurate; chance is all that is necessary. Reducing Paul's results to luck rather than skill or divine guidance should not detract from the fun he brought to the world, attracting the attention of the press and even of heads of state.

Taleb has an insightful thought experiment we alluded to elsewhere, but it bears repeating. He imagines we create a cohort of 10,000 incompetent fund managers whose luck is based on drawing colored balls from an urn. They lose $10,000 with a 55% probability or gain $10,000 with a 45% probability in any given year. This is an average loss of $1000 per manager per year.

Any time a fund manager loses money, he is culled from the game. Each year the number diminishes. After 5 years, we observe only 184 managers still in the game. This remnant, somewhat less than 2% of the originating team, seems brilliant for having earned money consistently even though the results are purely luck.

This phenomenon is called survivorship bias and is discussed in greater detail in the chapter on data. Its relevance here is as a habit of thought. The survivorship bias as discussed in the case of Paul the octopus or Taleb's fund manager thought experiment illustrates how a result that only occurs with a small percentage probability can have an outsized impact. We laud fund managers who consistently generate returns, but are they really more skillful? In addition to asking our analysts the above questions, we need to be sure we are getting the whole truth:

- What other statistics were collected and what other tests were run?
- Was there any attempt, formal or informal, to filter out inconclusive tests or contradictory results?
- What other hypotheses could invalidate the current results if true?
- Were these other hypotheses tested? If not, can they be tested?

We now move into the heart of this chapter, that being analysis and hypothesis tests.

HYPOTHESIS TESTING: SEEKING A VERDICT

When we begin to study the effects of medicines or the role played by a new marketing campaign, we are entering a messy area of analysis in which the underlying result must be inferred from what we see in the data. Medicines almost always affect more than just the disease they are designed to treat and often are rendered less effective by interactions with other medicines or foods. The success of marketing campaigns depends on the attractiveness of the product or service being marketed, the willingness of consumers to spend money, the marketing campaigns and the offerings of the competition, the time of year, and myriad other factors. What medicines and marketing campaigns have in common is the lack of a one-to-one relationship between the independent variable (the medicines and the campaigns themselves) and the dependent variable (their effectiveness toward reaching the specified goal).

The intellectual structure behind testing such hypotheses revolves around the null hypothesis and the alternate hypothesis (or hypotheses). This structure is common and forms the basis of the scientific method. It is likely also in our organizations even now. It is the basis for the statistical side of the Six Sigma tool kit.

The null hypothesis is usually the status quo ante or possibly the lack of a relationship between the variables being tested. A common hypothesis test affecting everyone who has at any point taken medicine is the clinical trial. One stage of clinical trials concerns the efficacy of the medicine being tested in living patients (yet other steps ensure the potential medicine in fact works at a theoretical level and on animals, and other steps ensure the medicine is safe for human consumption). At this stage, the medicine is compared to an inert look-alike referred to as the placebo. The null hypothesis, usually denoted H_0, would be that the effect of the medicine and that of the placebo are equal.

We are trying to see whether the medicine is effective. If it is only as useful as the placebo, our customers will have little use for it—it is the medicines having real and documented effects that keep pharmaceutical companies in business. The alternate hypothesis, with the notation H_a, would be that we detect a significant improvement of the performance of the medicine over that of the placebo. We could write it as this:

H_0: medicine=placebo; H_a: medicine>placebo

A common analogy for the way hypothesis testing functions is the courtroom during a criminal trial. Under the common law system used in the United States., a verdict is either "guilty" or "not guilty." There is no such thing as an "innocent" verdict, but there is a presumption of "innocent until proven guilty." In this case, the presumption of innocence is equivalent to a null hypothesis of not guilty. The alternate hypothesis is that the defendant will be found guilty. In the notation we used above:

H_0: not guilty; H_a: guilty

The trial is to determine whether the evidence of guilt has achieved a level of being beyond a "reasonable doubt." It is incumbent on the prosecutor to establish this guilt by relying on evidence and testimony that comply with the rules of admissibility established by the court. Think of this as the equivalent of good data quality and sound methodological design in our analysis.

The test in the above example of the clinical trials is what we call a one-tailed test. The name derives from the fact that if we were to find the medicine was significantly less effective than the placebo (in other words, if it somehow undeservedly slipped out of the toxicity trials despite being poisonous—a highly unlikely event), this information would not be captured by the test. At this stage of trials, there are only two real possibilities, which are that the medicine does or does not work on human subjects, so the test is only seeking to find whether the medicine is more effective than the placebo or not. We can see an illustration of the one-tailed test in Figure 6.22 (for this discussion, we will assume our data is parametric; that is, fits a known distribution model).

A key concept in the area of hypothesis testing that seeks to establish a causal relationship (as opposed to a correlation) is the role of the independent variable and the dependent variable. The independent variable, when changed or manipulated, affects the dependent variable when there is a relationship between the two. In other words, when we reject the null hypothesis and we have no false-positive, then the independent variable may *cause* the observed change in the dependent variable.

A-B analysis is the deliberate manipulation of characteristics of a website—presenting these variations at random to different audiences and then comparing reactions. Do more people donate when we use one logo versus another? Does greater streamlining or greater user control lead to

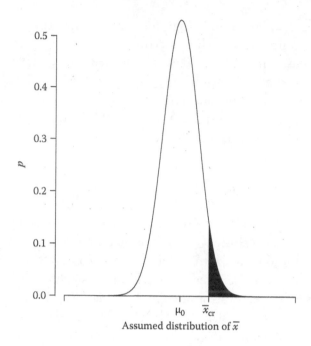

FIGURE 6.22
Bell curve with $p = .05$ rejection region highlighted.

Assumed distribution of $\bar{x}$

higher sales? In this case, the version of our website the user sees is the independent variable. The user's reaction is the dependent variable.

There are two types of error that can arise in our hypothesis testing: Type I and Type II errors.

As can be seen in Figure 6.23, a Type I error is what happens when a positive result is found between the independent and the dependent variables despite no real relationship existing between the two. Imagine we run a trial of a medicine and find it is useful, even though our result is due to contamination caused by a poorly designed study or possibly even just a statistical artifact. The chance the results obtained in a test are a Type I error has a name. It is called the *p value*. The *p* value is expressed in a

		Actual relationship between variables	
		Related	Not related
Test result	H0 Rejected	Correct result	Type I error: false-positive
	H0 Not rejected	Type II error: false-negative	Correct result

FIGURE 6.23
Type I and Type II errors.

decimal format rather than a percentage, but it is otherwise equivalent. A *p* value of 0.032 on a statistical test means we calculate a 3.2% chance the result is not due to a real relationship between the variables, but rather, it is the result of other factors.

The Type II error is the lack of a positive result between the independent and the dependent variables even though the two are linked in reality. The causes of a Type II error are the same as those for a Type I error, with one additional possible cause. That possible cause is an insufficiently large sample. The ability of a hypothesis test to avoid a Type II error is its statistical *power*. Statistical power is important, but it is less commonly used in communicating statistical results than is the *p* value.

For most hypothesis testing, a *p* value of .05 is the threshold between what is considered statistically significant and what is not. The range of possible results of a hypothesis test is shown in Figure 6.24, with the statistical area at which the null hypothesis is rejected shown for both

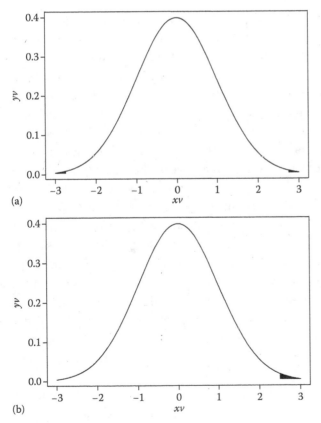

(a)

(b)

FIGURE 6.24
Bell curve for (a) two-tailed test and (b) one-tailed test. For both, the significance level of $p = .05$ stipulates that 5% of the area under the curve results in rejecting the null hypothesis. In the two-tailed test, this area is split between the right and left tails. This means that the phenomenon being measured may be in either direction, but the relationship must be stronger since the rejection region under the tail is only 2.5% of the area on either side.

one-tailed and two-tailed tests. Statistical *significance* is the threshold value that divides an effect large enough to consider the null hypothesis rejected and one with a sufficient likelihood of occurring due to chance it is safer to leave the null hypothesis in place.

This threshold for statistical significance is somewhat arbitrary. For psychology, the social sciences, and medical studies, the previously discussed p value of .05 (5%) is the standard threshold for statistical significance. Such a threshold is called the significance level. In hard sciences, for which more linear and direct cause and effect relationships are normal, p values of .01 (a 1% chance of the event occurring through chance) or .005 (a probability of 0.5% the result is due to chance) are common.

A common misconception is that a p value measures the odds a particular outcome would occur by chance, but this is not the case. Rather, it is the case that this particular outcome or one more significant would occur by chance.

If we have a hypothesis test using .05 as the significance level, then a p value of .032 on our test will mean we reject our null hypothesis and we accept the alternate hypothesis test. In other words, if we are testing the efficacy of a medicine and our statistical software indicates a p value of .032 on our test, there is a 3.2% chance we could receive our actual results or results even more meaningful by chance. As a 3.2% chance is less than a 5% chance, we can reject the null hypothesis that our medicine is no more effective than a placebo and provisionally accept the hypothesis that our medicine works. We cannot rush it to market, as there are problems we will explore that occur in hypothesis testing, but we can justify further exploration of the relationship between the variables.

If our test p value is not smaller than our significance level, we cannot reject our null hypothesis and we must assume for the time being we can find no relationship between the independent and the dependent variables. If our test p value were still small, perhaps .061, then we would be justified in conducting a new study with a larger sample size (sample size influences the p value) to see if we can find a relationship too small to be detected by our previous test. If our test p value is .52, we have a better than even chance (52%) our results were not due to a real relationship between our independent and dependent variable. In our clinical trials, we would probably be better off cutting our sunk costs and moving on to trials of a different drug.

Let us explore this more concretely. If we flip a fair coin, the odds the coin will land heads up are one in two, or 50%. No conclusion can be drawn from such a result. The odds three coins in a row land heads up are 50% × 50% × 50%, or 12.5%. It would not be wise to bet against the coin if we have no further information, but such results are not outside the realm of everyday life and are not statistically meaningful.

The odds of six throws of the coin landing heads up would be 12.5% × 50% × 50% × 50%. This is slightly better than a 1.56% chance the results occurred absent a weighted coin. Our trials do not provide conclusive proof the coin is unfair, but it is certainly reasonable to suspect that it is not. This is expressed in our test p value of .0156.

Coin flips are easy. Calculating the p value in most hypothesis tests is not so simple. We calculate a p value for other tests we will be going over shortly, such as the t-test, the chi-square tests, correlations, and other tests. The methods used to calculate these p values are significantly more complex than the one for calculating the p value for coin flips, but they are almost always automatically calculated in today's computerized world. Their importance to us is not in the method used to derive them, but in understanding what they represent.

In summary, the p value is a calculation of the probability such a result, or a more extreme result, could occur by chance. We calculate the probability either abstractly (think of our ability to calculate probabilities around coin tosses or throws of the dice) or through applied mathematics, as is the case with scientific experiments or large-scale observations such as demographic trends. The p value does not and cannot tell us whether our hypothesis is correct. What it can tell us is whether there is *probable cause* to reject the null hypothesis and crown the alternative hypothesis as a likely alternative.

So, what influences the p value?

- The size of the effect: A pronounced change in the dependent variable whenever the independent variable is changed will drive down the p value (remember a lower p value is stronger than a higher p value). This is intuitive. If we flip a fair coin 100 times, we would not suspect anything amiss if we flipped 53 heads and 47 tails, but we would be suspicious if we flipped 79 heads and 21 tails. The latter case is a more pronounced result and is less likely to be due to chance.
- The size of the sample: It is easy to see an effect with a small sample. Chance will often create it. Returning to our coin flip example, imagine that we flipped seven heads out of 10 tries. Such a result would not be entirely surprising. It is only two more heads than one would expect by calculating probabilities mentally. If we can maintain this ratio of

heads to tails with 100 flips, the odds turn overwhelmingly against us unless our coin is biased. Chance creates utter chaos with small samples but creates predictability with large samples. This is why the games of chance at a casino do not drive the casino out of business and why exit polls usually have sample sizes above 1000 participants.

Two-Tailed Testing

Returning to our hypothesis tests, we will move away from the one-tailed test to what is called a two-tailed test. A two-tailed test is different from a one-tailed test. To create a concrete example, let us imagine we are conducting an analysis of marketing efforts for a retailer. This retailer recently introduced a new strategy that seemed sound but led to utterly unexpected results. Sales for some products grew tremendously while sales dropped severely for others. As this strategy was neither an unambiguous success nor an unambiguous failure, it will neither be kept nor abandoned, but it will be applied more selectively and retested. Before redesigning, it is necessary to separate the effect of the new marketing campaign from other factors affecting our stores. What we will need to do is to examine sales before and after our new strategy for each product line.

To gain a better understanding of the different factors at play, we should also run similar analyses between those product lines in stores that implemented the new strategy and those that did not. To understand why, imagine our analysis shows sporting goods sales dropped significantly both from last month to this month, and from this time last year to now in those stores with the new marketing strategy. Would we call this scenario a clear case of failure?—Maybe, but not necessarily. What if our sales dropped more precipitously in those stores that did not implement our new strategy? Defining or measuring a simple cause and effect is inadequate. We may have an aggressive new competitor eroding our sales in sporting goods, and our new marketing strategy may have slowed the downswing without stopping it. While this strategy is hardly an unqualified success, it would not be prudent to abandon it for sporting goods without replacing it or augmenting it with something better. Returning to our test, let us put our first tests into notation (as there is little to be gained by analyzing the notation for each variation we will be testing) and then consider what it means:

H_0: sales before new strategy=sales after new strategy; H_a: sales before new strategy≠sales after new strategy

The null hypothesis is we will detect no difference in sales before and after we unveil and implement the new strategy. With alternate hypotheses, we expect to distinguish a difference, without regard to whether the difference is an increase or a decrease. Compare this to our clinical trials, in which our alternate hypothesis implied more pronounced results when study participants received our medicine than when they received a placebo. In the real world, worse-than-placebo results would mean the medicine was causing harm and we would terminate the study. From a hypothesis testing point of view, though, anything not producing results better than the placebo would mean there is no reason for the medicine to go to market so we would probably use a one-tailed test.

The difference between a one-tailed and a two-tailed test is real not only from the standpoint of what is being tested, but also from the standpoint of establishing whether the threshold has been met. A significance level of $p = .05$ on a one-tailed test is not as rigorous as a significance level of $p = .05$ on a two-tailed test. To understand why, let us again highlight the bell curve with the region in which we reject the null hypothesis highlighted. In this case, though, we have two bell curves. One represents our rejection region for the one-tailed test and one represents it for the two-tailed test.

It is possible to game a two-tailed test that barely misses the $p = .05$ threshold by rerunning it as a one-tailed test with the alternate hypothesis likewise redefined. We inveigh against this practice; we can counteract it by using $P = .025$ as the significance level for two-tailed tests and .025 for one-tailed tests.

HYPOTHESIS TESTING: A BROAD FIELD

Our above discussion may not be sufficient for us to go out and run a study but it should be enough for us to be able to ask questions of our analysts. However, we have merely covered the conceptual basics of hypothesis testing. Our examples are clearly insufficient tools to validate the results of any possible result presented by our analysts. Not to worry, though. Hypothesis tests exist to answer many other kinds of questions:

- What happens if I need to know about nonnumerical variables? In other words, what if I want to determine the relationship between which products a consumer purchases and whether that consumer returns it?

- What if I just want to know whether I am in compliance with a set value, and I do not want to compare two different conditions?
- What if my independent variable has three or more different values that I need to compare? In other words, what if, instead of conducting A-B testing on my website, I am comparing responses to A, B, and C and need to test all of them?
- What if I do not care about the cause, but I just care about the correlation? After all, if a certain behavior indicates higher revenue, why should I care about why that is the case? I just want to jump on the opportunity.

We suggest another question that may not be as obvious, which is how to deal with data that does not conform to the standard normal distribution or some other well-known probability distribution function (e.g., β, γ, Weibull, exponential)? In other words, what if my data is not parametric? What if it is nonparametric?

MOVING ON TO SPECIFIC HYPOTHESIS TESTS

Richard Feynman was the epitome of a great mind. Aside from being an accomplished physicist, he was known for his playfulness and wisdom. Speaking to the 1974 graduating class at Caltech, he stated, "The first principle is that you must not fool yourself—and you are the easiest person to fool. So you have to be careful about that. After you've not fooled yourself, it's easy not to fool other scientists. You just have to be honest in a conventional way after that."[12] Let us keep the great Mr. Feynman's words in mind as we move forward.

Now, we can see some of the issues involved in hypothesis testing, and we understand the importance of asking strong questions and demanding replicable answers. To ask good questions means understanding the specific hypothesis tests involved. Rather than memorizing the different hypothesis tests, we will instead understand how they work and have the grounding to ask the right questions when necessary. When someone displays a PowerPoint presentation explaining how an analysis of the data from our system indicates we should take a particular course of action, we can cut past the jargon and ensure the presenter knows what he or she is talking about. If someone suggests we incorporate a particular criterion into the decision trees for our software, we will be able to target our questions toward understanding the underlying logic, unintimidated by mathematical formulae.

If a salesperson or supplier presents results that seem to defy common sense, it could be for one of two reasons: first, the results are correct and common sense has yet to catch up; second, the results are bunk. A minor industry has arisen devoted to finding unexpected results in sets of data. The validity of these surprises is not always well established. When a firm advertises such surprises, we consider it wise to ask many questions.

Even more insidious is when the analyst tells us what we want or expect to hear when the grounds for a conclusion are questionable. The degree to which this phenomenon is present in data analytics for business is unclear but we observe it often in analyses of economic data by politically motivated participants. It is every bit as important to interrogate the data when it tells us what we want to hear as when the conclusions are frustrating or disheartening, and perhaps more so.

As we present our hypothesis tests, recall our discussion of distributions. Those used when we assume the data roughly fits a standard distribution are called parametric. Those tests used in the absence of such an assumption are called nonparametric. Generally speaking, parametric tests are more intuitive to interpret for someone who does not work with statistics on a regular basis. They tend to be less likely to result in Type II errors than are nonparametric tests. However, using a parametric test on data we cannot model with a standard distribution (e.g., β, lognormal, etc.) will most likely give us meaningless results. Aside from whether a set of data is parametric, it may also be important whether or not the variance between the samples is consistent. The variance is the square of the standard deviation.

We avoid formulae in our exploration of hypothesis tests in Table 6.3. This table is intended to provide us with an overview of the different kinds of hypothesis tests available. There is no need to know how to calculate all of these, and there is no need to remember what each of them does. What is important is to know what can be done with these tests and some of the factors that can compromise the accuracy of the results. By knowing what these tests can do, we can ask detailed questions of those who present their analysis. Even if we based the analysis on complex analytical algorithms greatly exceeding these hypothesis tests in complexity, these tests can be used as a "sanity check" ("Do these results really hold up?"), as well as a method to return to the same variables later in order

TABLE 6.3

A Very Basic Overview of Questions That Can Be Posed, Then Answered with the Right Data and Right Hypothesis Test

Description
One sample against a target mean or median. An example of this would be a sample of crash tests compared to what the mean would need to be to meet regulations.
Two samples against each other. Does our product perform better in crash tests than does the competitor's product?
More than two samples against each other. We are showing each customer one of three versions of a website and then comparing click-through rates.
Testing the variance (the standard deviation squared) between samples. This could be used to test whether results are more consistent using one or another method, or can be used to judge the suitability of the above tests.
Correlations in which causation is not examined. We want to determine whether certain purchasing habits by customers indicate later increases or decreases in purchasing.

to replicate the presented results using a different set of equivalent data. This may be a different sample or a calculation of the same attributes collected at a different time. If we can clearly reject the null hypothesis multiple times, we can make a strong case for the presence of a meaningful difference.

With this in mind, let us explore the realm of hypothesis tests (Table 6.4). In addition to the common parametric and nonparametric hypothesis tests shown in Table 6.4, there is also the chi-square test, which compares whether different nominal, nonquantitative, variables are independent of each other. An example of where this may be used is in seeing whether residents of different states have different preferences for different brands that our business has. An example is shown in Table 6.5. In this case, there is an equal sample size of customers (100) taken from each state and an assumption that preferences will be evenly distributed in each state. In reality, no such assumption is necessary for the chi-square to function. The above test results in a p value of .36, so there is no statistically significant difference. If we have a sample size of 1000 from each state and maintain the same distribution, we end up with a p value of .00, with many more zeroes that follow before we see any other digits. Sample size does matter.

As a manager being approached by our analysts with the results of our machine learning or data mining initiatives, it is prudent to ask for several months of results broken out by month or week, if we have sufficient data points, to see whether we are really viewing a trend. If we do not have sufficient data points, and we have time to wait, it is prudent to

TABLE 6.4

A Description of Parametric Tests, in the Left Column, with Their Nonparametric Counterparts in the Right Column

Parametric	Nonparametric
One-sample *t*-test (against a sample mean).	One-sample sign test (against a sample median).
Two-sample *t*-test (two sample means compared to each other). Note: There are different *t*-tests depending upon whether the variances (the standard deviation squared) are equal for the two samples.	Mann–Whitney test (Contrary to popular belief, this is not a test of medians, but rather involves a comparison of ranks of values.) Note: The Kruskal–Wallis and Mood's median tests (below) can be used for two samples.
One-factor ANOVA (multiple sample means, compared on a single attribute). Note: We use a two-factor ANOVA when we have multiple attributes that may interact.	Kruskal–Wallis (similar to the Mann–Whitney test, and used when the distributions are similar between the samples) Mood's median test (used when there is greater variability between the samples)
f-test (for two samples); Bartlett test (for three or more samples)	
Pearson correlation	Spearman correlation

TABLE 6.5

An Example of a Hypothesis for Which the Chi-Square Test Is Ideal. Do Preferences (a Non-Numeric Variable) Differ by State (another nonnumeric variable)?

	Brand A	Brand B	Brand C
North Dakota	35	32	33
Texas	42	29	29
Michigan	33	32	35
Louisiana	28	31	41

ask for follow-up. If we are purchasing services from a supplier that has found newsworthy relationships in the data, it is prudent to ask deeper questions. Counterintuitively, if we are presented with results that make perfect sense, we should treat them with the same skepticism we use for results that appear nonsensical.

Remember relationships requiring immensely powerful computers and advanced algorithms to discover them most often can then be simplified for testing in the future. When double-checking the results delivered to us by analysts, we should ask

- What was the sample size for the specific result? I may be testing millions of customers of an online media vendor, but a test of those who prefer both Bollywood movies and documentaries on design will be but a tiny fraction of that total. For any given result, ask what the sample size was as opposed to the overall sample size.
- How significant was the result? A large sample is more sensitive than a small sample. If we have a sample measured in the thousands, our test may be sensitive enough to detect a relationship that is practically meaningless. If we have a reliable vendor who goes the extra mile, but our analysis indicates we have a statistically significant but practically insignificant increase in our margin with a backup vendor who is more problematic, it may still make no sense to switch from one vendor to the other.
- How was the appropriate statistical test decided on? Does it in fact fit the shape and the variance in the data? If an external vendor is selling us a service by showing us results, have an internal analyst on hand to ask difficult questions. If it is an internal analyst whose results require deeper questioning, bring together a group of analysts and keep the atmosphere friendly yet inquisitive.
- Was the statistical test the best possible one to use? If we are seeking a root cause, we will not use a correlation. If we are comparing multiple parametric variables with more or less the same variance, we will want to see our analysis conducted using ANOVA rather than a series of *t*-tests. A significance level of .05 with ANOVA means .05, whereas there is an additive increase in Type I errors when multiple *t*-tests are used to accomplish the same thing. If this sounds confusing, do not worry, as it will be clarified later in this chapter.
- How was the sample drawn? Look for potential sources of bias (described in greater detail in Chapter 10).
- Were there any results on other tests of the same variables that showed no relationship? What was similar and what was different between the two tests and data sets?
- Were there any results not statistically significant but nearly so? If so, keep an eye on the attributes tested. If there is potentially a practical significance to this relationship, then revisit it with a larger set of data that may allow for the requisite sensitivity in the test. However,

never push and push until we obtain the result we want. Remember to guard against spurious relationships. They may be satisfying in the short term but costly in the long term.

REGRESSION AND CORRELATION

The lesson we need to cover now is the difference between correlation (including that derived from regression analysis,) and causation. As this is commonly one of the first points covered in statistics or research methods courses, as well as in quantitative reasoning courses at business schools, we will not belabor the difference here, but we will offer some implications. Once we detail the nature of the regression and correlation, we will outline some of the characteristics of the tests involved. We can say this about regression analyses: correlation is more suggestive than conclusive.

Causation discussions are a quick trip to controversy: philosophers have worried about this topic for millennia. Perhaps John Stewart Mill, in *A System of Logic*, put together the most practical set of considerations regarding causation (we discuss his idea in more detail later):[13]

- "If two or more instances of the phenomenon under investigation have only one circumstance in common, the circumstance in which alone all the instances agree, is the cause (or effect) of the given phenomenon."

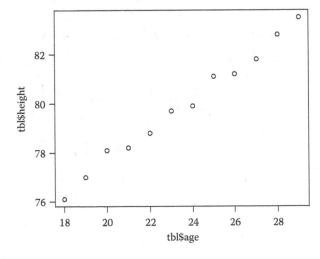

FIGURE 6.25
Scatter plot.

- "If an instance in which the phenomenon under investigation occurs, and an instance in which it does not occur, have every circumstance save one in common, that one occurring only in the former; the circumstance in which alone the two instances differ, is the effect, or cause, or an necessary part of the cause, of the phenomenon."
- "If two or more instances in which the phenomenon occurs have only one circumstance in common, while two or more instances in which it does not occur have nothing in common save the absence of that circumstance; the circumstance in which alone the two sets of instances differ, is the effect, or cause, or a necessary part of the cause, of the phenomenon."
- "Subduct from any phenomenon such part as is known by previous inductions to be the effect of certain antecedents, and the residue of the phenomenon is the effect of the remaining antecedents."
- "Whatever phenomenon varies in any manner whenever another phenomenon varies in some particular manner, is either a cause or an effect of that phenomenon, or is connected with it through some fact of causation."

An example of mistaking correlation for causation would be the following: I know my company's sales may have increased since my brilliant strategy was rolled out firm-wide, but I forget that this increase in sales may have simply been due to my competitor's unanticipated implosion or a new regulation that made my technology mandatory. This is not far from the common example of correlation versus causation.

So let us take a look at a correlation. Figure 6.26 shows a chart called a scatter plot. We can observe values along each of the axes, the *x* and the *y*. Each point on the field of the scatter plot is a particular data point, and we determine its location by *the x and y* coordinates that describe that data point.

In fields where we use statistics to justify and bolster an established point rather than as a guide to more effective action, this difference between correlation and causation is purely academic—not a sarcastic comment. If we are an attorney arguing to win on behalf of our client, we probably will not highlight that his actions may have nothing to do with the benefits gained. If we did, our client would fire us. If we are a partisan news commentator supporting a particular political party, we will probably not weigh the benefits of the opposing party's voting record fairly. For good or for ill, politics has entered a realm in which image is king and the role of partisan commentators is to

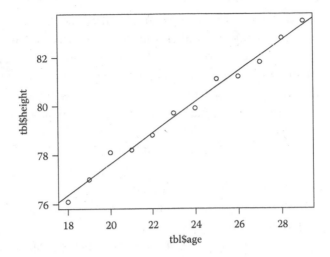

FIGURE 6.26
Regression on a scatter plot. The line is referred to as the regression line. This is the line for which the square of the distance in the horizontal direction between each point and the line is the smallest. This is not important for our purposes, but the line measures the strength of the relationship between the variables represented on the *x* and *y* axes. The regression line can be used to estimate the value for one variable if only the other variable is known.

scrub the image of their preferred candidates and throw mud on the image of their opponents. If we check our history, we can see this has always been so, but now, we find it so much easier to disseminate politically oriented venom.

In the real world, this reasoning does not cut it. Being able to understand exactly what the data indicates is a requirement in order to survive and thrive. If we are an aircraft engineer, a CEO with investors breathing down our neck, a data analyst helping law enforcement better target its police work, or a manager in a private equity fund, the consequences of being wrong are real and painful. They can even be deadly. In setting a course of action, knowing the difference between correlation and causation is an actual and vitally important need.

Discovering a correlation in the data does not tell us the cause, so it is tempting to treat correlations as less important than hypothesis tests seeking causation; but it is wrong to jump to such a conclusion, as sometimes a correlation is sufficient.

Imagine that we are driving to work on a Monday morning and traffic begins to slow noticeably. Often that means nothing as traffic irregularly slows down then speeds up again, with a net delay of a minute or so. It is difficult to attribute a direct cause to this. It could be a near accident with someone slamming the brakes and this effect cascading backward through traffic. The delay could also be more serious. A stalled car, a police officer pulling someone over, or a car accident could cause it. In that case, the delay could be more serious and slow traffic down to a crawl for several minutes, or maybe longer. We usually have no idea why traffic acts as it does, but we do know that it often makes us late for work. There is a correlation between a certain behavior—traffic slowing—and a certain result—arriving late for work. In this case, is it relevant to understand the cause? If we are a doctor, a business executive, or an attorney, it probably does not. We know a correlation exists between noticing this particular phenomenon and our timeliness in arriving at work. We know we associate one variable with the unpleasant outcome of another variable. If we can get off the main road and reroute using side roads, we should.

If we are the mayor or are otherwise involved in the smooth functioning of the city (even as a journalist!), we have a reason to care. If the traffic is snarled up because of an on-ramp that meets the main road at too abrupt an angle and lacks an acceleration lane, we can propose a change. If the cause is a car accident, we can see whether the root cause is an abrupt lowering of speed limits, bicyclists who should not be riding on the shoulder of the road, or some other cause. We can do something to improve the situation and the cause does matter.

So, is correlation used in the absence of causation to make decisions in the business world? Yes, as this article from Bankrate.com demonstrates:

> The Insurance Information Institute, a trade association for insurers, says drivers at the bottom of the credit heap file 40 percent more claims than drivers at the top of the pile. The institute doesn't have such statistics yet for homeowners' insurance claims.

> "A consumer with bad credit is going to pay 20 to 50 percent more in auto insurance premiums than a person who has good credit," says Clarence Smith, former assistant vice-president at Conning & Co. On the other hand, having sparkling credit could land you lower rates so you should shop around if you've got a glowing report.

> Elizabeth Mosley, of Ill., says, "Insurance is based on risk, and research has shown that individuals who tend to not pay their bills on time—and then get low credit scores—file more claims, and that those claims are more

expensive." When insurers get stuck with a bad risk, she adds, other policy-holders end up footing the bill.[14]

Let us pull apart this article. The author points out that insurance companies, whose businesses live or die on an understanding of statistics, use the credit scores of potential policyholders to determine insurance premiums. Why? Insurance companies have found a correlation between credit scores and the risk that policyholders will be filing claims. The role of an insurance company is to attract policyholders who will not file claims and raise the price of the premiums for those who are at a higher risk of filing claims—so as to not lose money through them.

The article is interesting in that nobody interviewed could identify a causal mechanism for why credit scores should reflect the risk that an insurance company assumes. In fact, that inability is one of the objections raised. An entirely plausible explanation could be that people who are careless with their credit are careless in other aspects of their lives, such as taking care of their homes or driving prudently. That is plausible but unproven. It is a hypothesis, and it fails to capture those with damaged credit as the result of a job loss or a catastrophic medical emergency that the health insurance company chose not to pay. If the irresponsibility hypothesis turned out correct, it is clear that charging more to those whose credit was bad for reasons beyond their control would make no sense and would be unjustified. However, without further analysis, it is difficult to determine the relationship between these two variables, so it is probable that much high-value information is lost in this correlation and

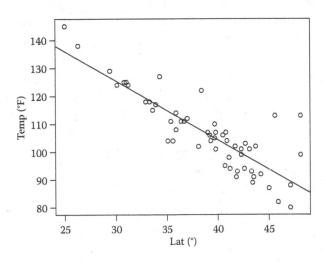

FIGURE 6.27
Negative correlation of temperature and latitude.

that linking the two variables is a crude and imprecise way of controlling risk. This is not to say that a crude measure is without value. If it saves money for the insurance company, it is valuable to the company. The decision on where to draw the line is a business and regulatory question, not a statistical question, until further research is available on the underlying causal variable.

Unlike insurance premiums, which can have an undeservedly punitive effect on low-risk individuals who fall into a high-risk category, the detection of credit card fraud involves correlating certain shopping habits with later reports of fraud or challenges to charges. The downside of falsely flagging a transaction is low (unless someone is late to the airport and finds his or her card rejected at the gas pump while in transit, for example). The credit card company can call and ascertain the validity of the charge and the cardholder continues with daily activities, provided that no fraud has occurred. In the event of fraud, this use of correlation is a lifesaver. Based on the correlation, we can infer with a high degree of certainty that certain characteristics indicate an elevated risk that fraud is ongoing.

We ran across the difficulties of unconfirmed root causes firsthand when working on a data set that tied the characteristics of particular assignments to meeting performance targets and the individuals responsible for the assignment. Some individuals were not meeting expectations and the enterprise asked us to identify them so that measures such as additional training or oversight could help them meet targets. In this case, the organization initially assumed the important relationship between variables was between individual employees responsible and whether they met the target.

We were able to demonstrate, using other data in the set that, in fact, those who missed their targets were consistently the same people, but they were also those who consistently had the most difficult assignments. In other words, the most likely problem was that the same people kept going out on the most difficult assignments. In this case, identifying the root cause meant that the strategy to help these individuals meet targets had to change.

In these examples, we discussed situations in which there is a hidden variable influencing a correlation. This is akin to the correlation between hand size and foot size in the same person through the life span. Generally, at later stages of life both the hands and feet are larger than in infancy and childhood. Hand size does not drive foot size and vice versa. It is general growth that drives both. In some cases, we may find a risk for reverse causality. Reverse causality occurs when one of the variables is the cause, yet it is treated as the effect.

With this background in mind, let us dig into correlations a little bit deeper. Think back to Figure 6.26. We notice a positive correlation coefficient, which we can see by the upward trend from left to right on the plot. If we had a negative correlation coefficient, there would be a downward trend from left to right, as we can see with the example scatter plot in Figure 6.28.

The most common calculation measuring correlation is the Pearson correlation coefficient. This is a stand-alone number—it has no units—that varies between –1 and +1. A value of one means there is a perfect, lock-step movement between one variable and the other. If the correlation

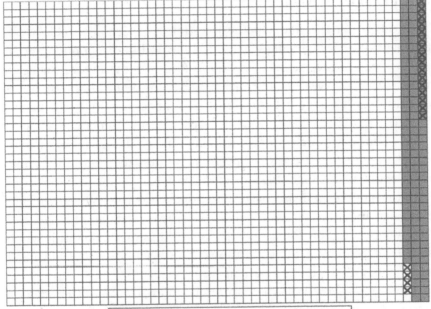

Variables related, null hypothesis rejected, correct result
Variables related, null hypothesis not rejected, Type II error
Variables not related, null hypothesis rejected, Type I error
Variables not related, null hypothesis not rejected, correct result

FIGURE 6.28

Distribution of Type I and Type II errors on a grid of 2000 instances. This graph illustrates how a significance level of $p = .05$ can deliver primarily incorrect results when the prevalence of the underlying phenomenon being tested is extremely low. Even though the hypothesis test will only reject the null hypothesis by chance roughly 5% of the time, this is still significantly more likely than the chance that we are testing a valid relationship. If this was a data set from our business that we were data mining, we would probably catch around 16 of the valid relationships and miss 4, while rejecting the null hypothesis incorrectly 99 times. This is how data mining can result in swamping the user with incorrect results.

coefficient is –1 or +1, all the points on the scatter plot will fall on the same line.

A value of 0 means that the two variables have no relation. A negative coefficient indicates a high value for one variable trends with a low value for the other. An example of a negative correlation would be vehicular speed and fuel efficiency.

p VALUE IN HYPOTHESIS TESTING: A SUCCESSFUL GATEKEEPER?

The fields of statistics and hypothesis testing have been invaluable in controlling risk and advancing science. If a medical intervention has at any point saved our life, we have hypothesis testing to thank for proving the value of that intervention and eliminating many others that were useless or harmful. That hypothesis testing is useful does not imply it is perfect. In fact, hypothesis testing begins to expose its limits under the particular circumstances in which our firm will likely use it. The conversation in the popular and business press has begun to address this, but in a fatalistic manner that undermines the improved use of big data.

The goal of the following pages is to discuss why there is concern being expressed about the results being obtained by big data and then to point to a way out. As was the case with the previous discussion, this will be somewhat technical. However, a grasp of these technical issues will greatly enhance our ability to manage a big data project.

A threshold of $p = .05$ has been a useful standby, but it has been shown as clearly inadequate when (1) we observe a large number of variables being compared to each other, perhaps dozens or hundreds, and (2) the likelihood that there is any relationship between any two or more variables occurring is low.

Remember that the significance level of .05 implies a 5% chance that random fluctuations or statistical artifacts could deliver a result of the same or a greater magnitude, incorrectly leading to a rejection of the null hypothesis and delivering a Type I error. This scenario relates to a single hypothesis test. In a single scientific study, we find at most only a few hypotheses under test. However, remember from our discussion earlier in this book about the differences brought about by big data that this technology inverts the old paradigm of formulating and then testing a hypothesis.

In our popular culture, it is common to dismiss an old paradigm as some sort of anachronism. In reality, the old paradigm for data analysis was an extremely valuable filter against wrong information. Whereas big data is tremendously valuable in exploring dozens of relationships between variables, it defeats the protections offered by the old paradigm. Its method for defeating these protections is to analyze large numbers of relationships without formulating any hypothesis. The odds of spurious relationships grow rapidly. It is like a car overriding its braking and steering capabilities.

Let us step back and explore this issue by looking to science, particularly the cohort or longitudinal study. A longitudinal study is one in which a large group of participants is studied for years or decades. Health habits such as smoking, drinking, diet, and occupation are compared to medical tests and causes of death. If we are running an epidemiological analysis in a longitudinal study to see what factors affect cancer rates, we will probably find that most of our relationships are spurious. Just think of the different reports we read in the popular press about a behavior causing cancer one year but preventing it the next. These news reports create a great deal of skepticism about science among the general population, not due to any weakness in the scientific method, but rather because of the scientific illiteracy of the reporters writing the stories. Longitudinal studies are not meant to provide irrefutable truths but rather to illuminate potential areas for further study. As such, it is no surprise they churn up a lot of questionable relationships, in part because they are covering so many variables from the beginning.

Functionally, the sheer number of scientific studies, not just longitudinal in nature, illustrate a similar issue at the macro level of science overall, as we will see shortly when we discuss the work of John Ioannidis. With thousands of scientists plugging away on health studies worldwide, each producing multiple studies each year, the p value is not functioning as an adequate gatekeeper against Type I errors. It is being overwhelmed. This explains why there are so many odd study results reported in the popular press that are then proven to be wrong. When we dig into scientific research, we will see that this glitch in scientific practice is directly relevant to big data in organizations.

A concrete example will illustrate this. Let us say that I have a sudden hunch that a particular chemical in bananas can be extracted and then processed in a certain way and then added to fish food to significantly increase the lifespan of the fish. I buy 50 aquariums and have paid assistants put five random fish in each aquarium from a single batch of fish I bought from the same supplier. I communicate nothing to them to guide the pairing of fish and fish tank. In this way, we introduce no systematic bias regarding which fish would go into which aquarium.

I buy 50 identical fish food cartons and number them. I then place 25 black marbles and 25 white marbles into an urn. Walking past each carton of fish food, a second assistant of mine sets a randomly drawn marble next to it. The assistant records which color marble went with a particular fish food carton. He then fills all those that had a black marble next to them with the experimental fish food and all those with the white marble using the standard fish food. The experimental fish food is the leading brand but with my chemical sprayed on it. Other than my treatment, the control food and the experimental food are identical and come from the same batch.

A third assistant, who has no idea which fish have consumed which food, feeds the fish in each aquarium using the box of fish food matched to that aquarium and records the life span of the fish. She runs the calculations of fish life spans by tank and discovers that in half the tanks the fish lived longer on average. These are the tanks with fish we fed with our experimental fish food. The results are messy but indicate with a p value of exactly .05 that my hypothesis about fish living longer is correct (reality is not so binary; p values rarely fall exactly on the significance level).

I have just conducted a methodologically sound study that delivered a positive result. Based on market knowledge, we suspect that turning this idea into a company would cost about $2 million, but that within 5 years, fish enthusiasts would have time to see the longer lives of their fish and would flock to my new brand. We estimate that we could sell the company for $8 million at the end of those 5 years. We have $1 million to invest to become a half-owner of the company and limited time to decide. Others also want to invest with us. If we do not decide within a few days, the opportunity is gone. What would we do?

What do we know? My research methods were sound. There is a 5% risk that my results were due to chance because of $p = .05$. If my results were due to chance, then the fish food does not work to a statistically significant level, the company will face a difficult future, and we may lose our investment. Ignoring the time value of money, this is what our weighted average calculation will be:

$$-\$1 \text{ million} + \big((0 \times 0.05) + (\$4 \text{ million} \times 0.95)\big) = \$2.8 \text{ million}$$

A simplified version of the assumption might read: Our $1 million investment has a 5% chance of being worth nothing at all and a 95% of being worth \$4 million (remember, we only receive half of the \$8 million). Of course, there are many questionable assumptions in our example. Many sound scientific discoveries flop despite the best efforts of the entrepreneurs who drive them to market. Sometimes inferior ideas beat superior ideas in the market. Other people work on new technologies that quickly supersede the previous state of the art. We ignored many areas of risk, so the example is overly simplified in order to keep it mathematically intelligible.

The above assumptions mask deeper issues. We assumed that our idea and experiments were an isolated case. That 5% chance of losing our investment could be significantly higher if what we witnessed was not an isolated experiment. How is this the case?

Imagine that I have tried this experiment several times before and failed. Let us say that I had hunches about different fruit-based chemicals and have tested nine of them already. My experiences with apples, oranges, kumquats, durians, kiwis, and others have failed to turn up any positive relationships between the chemical used and a longer fish life span. On my tenth try, I hit pay dirt. My fish lived longer. What are the odds that a methodologically impeccable study yields a false-positive among my attempts? If we were to run 10 studies of unrelated variables, there would be a nearly 40% chance of a false-positive. Our decision whether to invest has just become more complicated. Now, let us step back and see how similar the situation can be with the results we gain from our analysis using our big data system.

Imagine we have 10 relationships between variables that we wish to test, and we know that none of them is in fact related to each other. If we use a significance level of 0.05, the probability that our result will not reject the null hypothesis on a single test is 0.95, or 95%. Just as the probability that two coin flips will land heads is 0.5 times 0.5, or 0.25, the probability that we will not reject the null hypothesis on either of two tests of variables unrelated to each other is 0.95 times 0.95, or 0.9025. To calculate the probability of 10 tests of unrelated variables not having a Type I error, we need to do the following:

$$0.95^{10} = 0.5987 = 59.87\%$$

If we run 20 independent hypothesis tests of unrelated variables, there is only a slightly better than 35% chance that no Type I error will appear. If we are running 40 independent hypothesis tests, that drops to less than

13%. In other words, the probability of having at least one Type I error tops 87%. In fact, we probably have more than one such error. By the time we have 100 independent hypothesis tests, then the odds of having at least one Type I error exceed 99%. In fact, we can expect somewhere around five (100 trials times 5% of a Type I error).

The outcome of our statistical test can be conceptually similar to the odds of winning the lottery. The odds of winning the Powerball (a US-based lottery) grand prize are 1 in 175,223,510.[15] The odds of being struck by lightning, in comparison, are 1 in 280,000.[16] Most people do not know anyone who has been struck by lightning, yet the odds of being struck by lightning are approximately 625 times greater than the odds of winning the Powerball grand prize. Nevertheless, people keep winning the "big one." Often, we observe more than one winner, because the odds stated above are the odds of a single ticket played in a single drawing being the winner, not the odds that someone will win the lottery. If only one individual played the lottery, a win would be a miracle. Chances are there would not have been a single win in the history of civilization. As so many people are playing, however, it is a certainty that we have winners.

It can be difficult to find the number of tickets sold, but it is certainly safe to say that the number is well into the millions. If 100 million numerically distinct tickets are sold, the probability that one of them will be a winner is approximately 57%. Once the number of tickets with distinct numbers sold matches the number of possible combinations, a winning ticket was certainly sold somewhere.

The numbers and probabilities involved in looking at p values and those that arise when we discuss the lottery are drastically different, although the concepts are similar. When we reject the null hypothesis in a single hypothesis test, we expect to find a relationship. When many hypothesis tests are run, the odds that the results are meaningful are more hit-and-miss. If we run a large number of trials, our odds of a false-positive become a near certainty.

Currently, we see much self-examination occurring among scientists and medical researchers—a phenomenon caused by the publication of irreplicable results, which is, in turn, the result of a similar phenomenon to the one that occurs with big data. As data analysis within an enterprise is usually confidential, whereas most science is open, our discussion will now turn to what science has found. It begins with a medical researcher in Greece who found flaws in presentations of medical research. These flaws are consequential.

John Ioannidis, whose medical career has spanned between his native Greece and the United States, is as of this writing a professor of health research and policy as well as the C. F. Rehnborg Professor of Disease Prevention at Stanford University. He published a now famous paper in the online journal *PLoS Medicine* in August of 2005, the title of which is provocative: "Why Most Published Research Findings Are False." It has gone on to become one of the most read research papers in medical science. It has led to write-ups of Dr. Ioannidis in *The Atlantic* and discussions of his work in *The Economist* and in a noted *Wired* article by Taleb.

Dr. Ioannidis discusses a set of conceptually different issues that together cause the phenomenon of irreplicable research. This situation is consequential because we base so much of scientific enterprise on the ability of other researchers to recreate an experiment and verify that the results are meaningful and true. For this reason, well-written scientific papers do not merely cover conclusions and theories, but also discuss the sample size, how it was drawn, the conduct of controls, the dependent and independent variables, the types of statistical techniques used, and the results. Before publishing the paper, a panel of other experts in the field reviews it to assess the quality of the research. This system is by no means foolproof, as Dr. Ioannidis points out, but the concepts behind it are intended to foster transparency and a freewheeling discussion that weeds out the incorrect results and fosters the spread of correct results. A major point of Dr. Ioannidis is that bias does creep in and affects results. That is important, and it has been discussed in this chapter. There are many ways to gently nudge results in the desired direction even though doing so is detrimental to the accuracy of the results.

The most important point that Dr. Ioannidis makes, for the purpose of this book, is that in a standard study even a statistically positive result may very well not be a meaningful indicator of the true relationship between the variables being explored. This situation brings us into a counterintuitive yet vital discussion of Bayes's theorem. Named after the Reverend Thomas Bayes, who was responsible for developing it conceptually, this indispensable intellectual achievement became a quantitative, probabilistic tool in the able hands of the revolutionary-era French mathematician Pierre-Simon Laplace. Bayes's theorem looks like this:

$$P(A|B) = \frac{P(A)P(B|A)}{P(B)} \tag{6.2}$$

It looks fearsome, but it is not. Bayes's theorem lets us calculate a posterior probability using prior information—which we are more likely to have. Put another way, using imperfect information that we do have, we can focus on a more accurate probability that we cannot discern directly.

In the way that Bayes's theorem is usually discussed, repeated applications of Bayes's theorem should drive the posterior distribution to more closely resemble the "real" distribution. More fundamentally, Bayes's theorem does with probabilities what golf clubs do with golf balls. It moves the ball closer to the hole (well, one of us is a golfer who is not always so good at moving the ball in the right direction). With each stroke, the golf ball should be in a better location than it was previously. With Bayes's theorem, each application to the same problem to be solved should bring the calculated probability more in line with the underlying reality.

Bayes's theorem is often unfairly treated as merely a way of creating a quantitative façade over subjective speculation. A false dichotomy exists between frequentist statistics and Bayesian analytics. Frequentist statistics are effectively those we use most commonly with our firms' data sets; for example, we can roll up the data set and see 17% of our customers spent on average more than $200 per month in our store last year and our Cleveland office has the best employee retention rate. The hypothesis testing we have discussed is a frequentist technique. Bayesian analysis is something different, and as we will see using one of John Ioannidis' examples, it can shed much light on how strong is the conclusion we can draw from our hypothesis test.

Dr. Ioannidis posits a thought experiment using research involving gene polymorphisms related to schizophrenia. He argues that out of 100,000 polymorphisms, it is realistic to expect we can tie 10 of those to risk of this disease. That means that there is a 10/100,000, or 1/10,000, chance that any one of these polymorphisms indicates heightened susceptibility. Our study has 60% specificity (also known as detection rate or statistical power), or in other words it detects 60% of cases. This also means that there is a 40% (1 − 60% or 100% − 60%) Type II error rate where the test fails to reject the null hypothesis when it should be rejected. Our significance level is .05. As we have discussed, this means that approximately 5% of the time we can expect the test to incorrectly result in a rejection of the null hypothesis.

Let us plug in some numbers to calculate the probability that our rejected null hypothesis was correctly rejected. First, we calculate the numerator or the part of the equation above the line. This value is the probability that any given polymorphism is indicative of a heightened schizophrenia risk multiplied by the statistical power, or detection rate. When we calculate we get 0.01% multiplied by 60%, or 0.006%.

$$0.0001 \times 0.60 = 0.00006 = 0.006\%$$

Next, we calculate the denominator, or the part of the equation below the line. The first part of this equation is exactly the same as the calculation for the numerator. This is then added to the p value multiplied by 1 minus the probability that a polymorphism is indicative of a higher risk. We add 0.006% to the product of 5% multiplied by 1 minus 0.01%, or 99.99%. This gives us a value of approximately 5.006%. Here is the equation:

$$0.00006 + (0.05 \times 0.9999) = 0.050055 \approx 5.006\%$$

When we divide the numerator by the denominator, we end up with 0.12%.

$$0.00006 / 0.050055 = 0.001198 \approx 0.0012 = 0.12\%$$

Figure 6.28 illustrates this point using different values. As you can see, a highly improbable phenomenon remains improbable even after a hypothesis test, correctly applied, is used to reject the null hypothesis. This result means that 12 times out of every 10,000 tests in which we rejected the null hypothesis on a test of polymorphisms, we rejected it correctly. The other 99.88% of those times will have been a Type I error.

Something is clearly amiss. The challenge is that the probability we correctly rejected the null hypothesis is the result not only of the precision of the test, but also the probability we should reject the null hypothesis in the first place. The problem is not that a p value of .05 is bad or that hypothesis testing is a fatally flawed practice. The problem is that hypothesis testing faces an issue of resolution. In plain English, think back to the last time we viewed a satellite photo of our house. It was probably interesting and enlightening. The level of detail was impressive because of all we could see. However, could we recognize individual models of car? Could we recognize people? We could almost certainly not. The resolution was wrong. To take a useful photo of our car or of people, we need finer resolution. A coarse resolution allows us to see our entire house. A finer resolution allows us to see individual people or details of our house. Think of the difference between microns and miles as a different example. Measuring our family trip in microns would be meaningless, as would measuring molecular structures in miles. Hence, the resolution of the units we use matters.

A significance level of .05 is commonly used in the social and biological sciences because it makes a Type I error reasonably unlikely while still not casting the net too narrowly and missing valid findings. The balance is not always the right one, however. Let us use Bayes's theorem to take a look at the example from Dr. Ioannidis' paper using different significance levels. If we take the same study with the same results, but we use a significance level of 0.01, we find the probability that our rejection of the null hypothesis was correct is 0.6%. We can also set the significance level at .001, in which case the probability moves to 5.66%. It is important to note, however, that we are tightening the significance level in this example without adjusting the statistical power. Remember that statistical power is the ability of a test to correctly avoid Type II errors (false-negatives). It closely relates to detection rate or sensitivity in laboratory testing, which measures the percentage of positive cases detected. If we assume the statistical power drops to 20% when we raise the significance level, we can still only assume that 1.96% of our rejected null hypotheses are correct, according to Bayes's theorem.

We obtain a trade-off between false-negatives and false-positives, assuming we are using the same test and sample for both. We cannot get something for nothing, but we can improve the quality of our results by obtaining a larger sample as long as that sample remains demonstrably random. In many ways, laboratory tests are analogous to statistical tests and may form a part of our analyses. In such cases, improved methods can improve both sensitivity (resistance to Type II errors) and specificity (resistance to Type I errors). These are akin to statistical power and significance level. An example is the move from testing biochemical marker levels in the body toward the examination of DNA markers. This shift in methodology simultaneously improved both sensitivity and specificity.

When the phenomenon we examine is not so rare, however, the looser significance level is more likely to catch a meaningful connection. Let us say that we are studying fuel injection settings for their effect on fuel economy. We find a high probability that the two factors are related, so the looser significance level may be appropriate. Let us say that we know the settings we are making will cause a difference of 5 miles/gallon or more about 25% of the time. We will place the statistical power at 80%, a reasonable level. A test p value that exactly reaches the significance level of $p = .05$ will reach the correct result nearly 85% of the time; this is resolution.

We can see a fundamental tension in hypothesis testing. The more resistant a test is to Type I errors, the less sensitive it is; in other words, the more likely it is we will miss real relationships too weak to cross the threshold set by the significance level. A real relationship may hit $p = .006$, and if our significance level is set at $p = .005$, we will reject that real level. However, if we set a looser threshold as our significance level, such as $p = .05$, then we will churn up more trivial results that will clog our analytical resources at best and lead us to propose action based on false conclusions at worst.

The same phenomena—provoking self-examination among scientists and readers of scientific news—are at play in interpreting the results of big data. Big data systems essentially invert much of the scientific method by finding answers and then enabling the user to seek out the questions. We discussed this issue earlier. The strength of this method is that connections that would otherwise remain submerged can surface. The weakness of this method is that false conclusions can just as easily emerge. In fact, when using the scientific method, we abhor running a plethora of related studies, reporting only those offering positive findings. The issues involved in running data analysis in this manner are different, but the practice is problematic in science because it facilitates *the publication of incorrect results*. We understand the value of this approach for management when drawing conclusions from an organization's data, so rather than condemning this practice in a business setting, we instead urge due caution.

What are we to do in a business setting? Again, we turn to science for guidance. The work of thousands of scientists churning away on their separate analyses provides a meaningful parallel for big data practitioners. When a false link between variables arises, it is almost never replicable in a disciplined setting. If such an association is a fluke, it is unlikely to keep appearing in subsequent experiments, and this is exactly what happens. Our organizations should maintain a record of inconclusive or negative results for particular studies. First, if our research keeps finding that variables A and B are not related, and then one day they are, we have the ability to investigate whether conditions changed in a way that would influence our results, or whether the results were in fact a fluke. Second, a corollary of this is that results should be subject to repeatability. When we find significant results, we should be able to examine those results with the same methods or with other hypothesis tests (remember the list of tests earlier in our discussion, which can be used to reexamine relationships found through other, more complex, analyses to see if they can be repeated).

One of our metaphorical "friends" is a common statistical tendency that filters our results for us. It is called regression to the mean. Think of a dartboard: if we throw darts with reasonable accuracy, a few will hit the bull's-eye, a few will hit the wall next to the dartboard, and most will hit a cluster roughly around the middle of the dartboard. This result occurs because the area of the dartboard that is not the bull's-eye makes up the preponderance of the board. Likewise, the area of a roughly normal distribution is much larger toward the middle than it is at the extremes. As a result of the central limit theorem we discussed during our tosses of the dice, this is true even when the distribution of underlying events is nonnormal (so long as we are plotting the means of samples).

If we hit only green lights on our way to work, we will arrive quickly. If we hit only red lights, we may arrive late. However, it is unlikely that we will usually hit all green lights or all red lights. The odds are against that. Most days, we will hit a random selection of each. If we hit all green lights on Monday, it is a safe bet that our commute on Tuesday will take longer. We have more ways to hit a combination of green and red lights than we have to hit all one or all the other. Likewise, if our data show a relationship between hail damage and the percentage of convertible cars involved in accidents in different regions—and such relationships are not unlikely due to the statistical factors described above—we have good reason to be skeptical unless such a link shows up year after year. Hail damage and accidents for these cars will almost certainly regress to the mean. If they do not, then we may have a trend.

In our discussion of epidemiological and medical research, we brought up a concept we can redefine, repackage, and make useful for big data. Broad environmental studies often examine large numbers of factors, with scientists poring over data to seek out correlations they then appraise further, seeking either more finely sliced studies of the data or else experimental studies to isolate causes. Many specious relationships will arise in these studies. They make the news and cause panic, but scientists know beforehand such studies often shine light on conjunctions among variables that will not stand the test of time. It is the nature of the beast. What these uncovered relationships do is provide greater focus to researchers in looking for more conclusive proof.

A study of cancer patterns may look at 100 connections and find seven statistically significant relationships highlighting areas for further research. Five of those relationships may turn out to be specious, but two of them may result in significant findings that save lives. The scientists can then go on to observe the data for Texas, North Dakota, and California, followed by Sweden and Japan. Does this trend appear in all populations or just some? What other factors break it down further? If the same occupational hazard or medical treatment results correlate highly with the same disorder across populations, then we may have reason to take such an affinity seriously.

Ideally, we can then launch experimental research in which scientists manipulate an independent variable to observe changes in the dependent variable (or, more efficiently, use a designed experiment with several factors and measurable effects). In a business setting, this approach would involve executing a partial rollout based on the results of statistical analysis to see whether our expected results were in fact realized. Reflect on our thought experiment about the market plan that partially succeeded and partially failed. When it succeeded, its successes were significant enough that it was inadvisable to throw it away despite its equally significant failures.

Just as a large-scale scientific study is followed up by more precise studies, in our example of the mixed results following our new marketing strategy, we could follow up with more precise analysis. An example of analyses that could be conducted, in addition to those discussed earlier, include

- Sales of specific items over different days of the week and times of day, by geographical area, before and after the shift in sales strategy
- Changes in practices by HR or other internal actors that would affect employee morale or incentive structures
- Competitors' sales efforts and offers as pitched on their social media sites and as they appear on coupon websites
- Geographical distributions of these offers (perhaps automatically pulled from their corporate website)
- Comments alluding to our firm on social media, as well as any relevant segmentation of those commenters
- Comments citing our firm on influential websites, as well as the known segments who may use those websites
- The demographics of the areas where our affected stores are located

We can begin to see possible connections between particular customer segments and sales trends and then delve deeper into them. Perhaps our new strategy was successful in attracting a younger crowd but left our older and more affluent customers feeling out of place in our stores. Perhaps we joined our sales strategy to an advertising blitz that was not offensive and did not generate much negative publicity but partially alienated a significant segment of our customers. It is possible our goal for getting our sales staff more involved in assisting customers was welcomed by those buying sporting goods but uncomfortable for those who pop in and out after work for laundry detergent and soda.

When conducting these analyses, the complex algorithms used will generate less complex results. These results are ripe for the hypothesis testing we discussed. Our analytics may unearth a relationship between the presence of skateboarding equipment and decreased sales of expensive kitchenware. Our analyst may speculate this occurs because the appearance of teenagers sporting goth fashion scares off older, more traditional customers attracted to a kitchenware brand. However, such speculation is without value unless we can pull apart and confirm that finding. Did the drop-off in kitchenware sales occur only in stores with skateboarding equipment? Did we spot discussion of this item on social media or in news stories? Did it happen in all stores, or was there a particular region where it occurred? In other words, can we

- Replicate this finding temporally
- Replicate this finding across locations
- Find supporting information through other sources
- Detect significant contradictory information from any source

To make a proper decision on whether or not we need to address the potential tension between skateboarding equipment and our kitchenware sales, we need to determine whether that relationship is real or if it is a statistical artifact arising because a certain percent of random, unrelated attributes will show a correlation by chance. Reflect on our discourse about hypothesis tests. Our analysts identified the relationship between the presence of skateboarding gear and decreased sales of our high-margin cookware. We arrived at our results through a substantial decision tree generated by our Hadoop cluster. Does this mean we need to replicate those results that way?—No, it does not.

Before we change our strategy in a way that could have a negative impact on our sales, we pull out the statistically significant results from our decision tree analysis. We then ask our analysts to design a query that will pull the data for different stores and different periods (different weeks or different months). We then have the before and after data analyzed using one of the statistical software packages described later in this chapter to verify that this link holds across time and across our stores. It is possible sales dipped because of some unrelated factor, such as a negative news story about a celebrity who endorses this cookware or because with summer approaching more people cook outdoors than in their kitchen.

If we find complaints about skateboarders on Facebook posts that refer to our store and we see a sudden and sustained drop of cookware and other items bought by similar customers, then perhaps we have a problem we will need to address.

Both the popular and industry press latch onto findings similar to this hypothetical relationship and report them without investigating the backstory necessary to determine whether the result is even valid. This approach is entirely similar to how they report on scientific announcements. It is also why we emphasize prudence before deciding the use of a particular web browser by a job applicant is indicative of future job performance based on data analysis. Without knowing the replicability of this finding, and under which specific circumstances it applies, it is impossible to judge its validity. It may be a counterintuitive yet practical and money-saving finding, but unless we know how well it holds up and which tests it may have failed, we should not take it at face value.

If we can replicate our results for the specific successes and specific failures of our new marketing strategy independent tests for our different locations, then we have a strong basis for examining what went wrong. We may not know why it went wrong, but we know how to verify our results and dig into the data to find meaningful results rather than broad-brush generalizations. Remember, we also considered the possibility that what registered as a failure when examined partially was in fact a success when we examined *all* of the data. Sales decreased in some stores with the new marketing strategy but decreased even more in those stores without the new strategy. Using partial experiments to test what went wrong and what can remedy the situation allows us to manipulate independent variables to observe dependent variables. In other words, it allows us to use intelligent, planned trials.

The partial roll-out is also a way to control risk. A counterproductive strategy need not bring down our business, and in fact it may even become a productive strategy if tweaked and adjusted by motivated staff members. We must measure those tweaks and adjustments along with their results. They form an experiment and shine light into behaviors that consumers may not even know they have.

SPECIOUS CORRELATIONS AND OVERFITTING THE DATA

Dr. David Leinweber, who is now the head of the Center for Innovative Financial Technology at Lawrence Berkeley National Laboratory in Berkeley, California, wrote an unpublished paper in 1995 based on some data mining he conducted. It was a joke paper, so it therefore remained unpublished. He rewrote "Stupid Data Miner Tricks: Overfitting the S&P 500" in 2000 and circulated it again in 2007, when it was published in the *Journal of Investing*. The paper points to the hazards of data mining. In so doing, it touches on many of the points we articulated: false-positive results, cherry-picking, and finding results that resist replication. However, the reason for using it in the current example is different.

Dr. Leinweber did something interesting. He wanted to find data that correlated with the Standard & Poor's 500 (S&P 500), a common stock market index in the United States, tracking 500 major companies traded on the country's two major stock exchanges: the New York Stock Exchange and the NASDAQ. In so doing, he knew that if he used data from other US stock market indices he would end up with an R-square (correlation coefficient) value of nearly 1.0, which means the real data and the predictive ability of the model coincide.

The R-squared measures the relationship between two variables on a scale of 0–1. Two variables with an R-squared value near 0 have no relationship to each other. An example would be our driver's license number and our grade point average in high school. Two variables with a relationship near 1 would be the example above of different stock market indices in the US. As an example of an intermediate R-squared, Dr. Leinweber uses body weight and height, estimating that the value would be 0.75. In this sense, it is similar to the correlation coefficient, with a key conceptual difference being that the correlation coefficient has a scale of –1 to 1. A negative correlation coefficient would measure two values that are related but trend an opposite directions. One example would be income and the percentage of income dedicated to food purchases.

In his search for clearly specious but significant R-squared values related to the S&P 500, Dr. Leinweber turned to a CD-ROM of international statistics compiled by the United Nations. He found the elusive connection he was seeking in the butter production of Bangladesh. The R-squared value for the relationship between Bangladeshi butter production and the S&P 500 was about 0.75, or it was able to "explain" about 75% of its movement.[17]

Describing 75% of the S&P 500 was insufficient. He needed to gain better explanatory power, so he sought other variables that could enhance the model in addition to this particular South Asian dairy product. He succeeded in doing so. By adding the US butter and cheese production to the Bangladeshi butter production, he was able to explain 95% of the movement of the S&P 500. Still, he found this inadequate. To make his model fit the S&P 500 data even better, he searched for another variable, and he found that also. By adding the movements of the Bangladeshi sheep population, he pushed the R-squared to 0.99.

Dr. Leinweber's paper is ridiculous and that is its brilliance. It is absurd, yet mathematically sound. By writing something so technically thorough yet so outrageous in its conclusions, Leinweber created a rich example that anyone working with data should read and absorb, which explains its cult status. Like a Monty Python movie, the paper is entertaining yet contains truth on a variety of levels.

We are seeing a specious correlation gained by comparing a prodigious number of variables. As we argue in many places, if we have a sufficient number of variables to compare, we will find a relationship somewhere. Some might call this the "there is a pony in here somewhere" syndrome. With big data systems, this event occurs frequently and is a by-product of the strategy of looking for insights in the data by comparing a large number of variables and then highlighting those that show a relationship, rather than proposing a hypothesis and testing it. More often than not, when we investigate dozens of variables, a connection will appear as a function of the probabilities of the statistical tools and not as a result of the underlying data or a related mechanism.

An analogy to this would be an inexpensive camera that one of us used to carry in the days of film photography. While traveling, we carried a top-of-the-line Canon 35 mm SLR for the bulk of photography but an inexpensive point-and-shoot camera for photos in another format. For example, if the SLR had color film, the point-and-shoot had black and white, or vice versa. One day, we saw a haunting statue ideal for a black and white photo. When we processed the film, we noticed an odd, light colored shape floating in front of the statue. While the statue was haunting, it was certainly not haunted. Under certain conditions, the camera would in fact leave such shapes in the photos. They were artifacts of the camera, not the external scene. We also see random artifacts in big data analyses, a product of our method of investigation.

Likewise, when Dr. Leinweber found the relationship between the stock index and the production of a food product halfway around the world from the stock markets on which the index is based, the correlation was an artifact of the statistical tools used. These statistical tools are accurate the vast majority of the time, and they are indispensible to most analytics. However, they have the limitations covered in the discussion of p value and statistical power. The nature of data mining evokes these limitations.

Without going too far into the technical side of Dr. Leinweber's analysis, what he found is that he could demonstrate an impressively strong but completely spurious result by adding irrelevant variables to an analysis that is based on the premise that by comprehending the movement of one variable, he could understand something about another variable. When properly used to uncover valid relationships, this is akin to knowing something about the value of someone's home as a function of his or her salary. There is no neat one-to-one relationship and plenty of exceptions exist, but generally the higher someone's salary is, the more his or her house will be worth. If someone has an expensive home, that person more than likely has a large salary to pay for it.

Let us assume that knowing a salary allows us about 50% predictive ability with regard to home values. This is good enough information to be able to more accurately target advertisements for high-end landscaping, for example, but our predictive ability is still limited. More information would help us better predict home values, provided the information adds something new.

I could add in take-home pay as a variable. Take-home pay is simply salary minus withholdings. In other words, take-home pay will highly correlate with salary, with some wiggle room because some people choose to deduct more taxes than others, while others have payments for health insurance or retirement accounts. Still, if we know someone's salary, we will not discover much new information contained in his or her net pay.

What about investment income? This provides new information. Although we observe some overlap between who invests much and who invests little—someone who is stuck with a low wage job will simply not have money to invest—we will expose different spend-versus-save patterns, different risk appetites, and different instance of happenstance driving divergent investment incomes for distinct individuals with similar salaries. Another example of an alternate source of information with explanatory power may be debt load. Someone with student loans who overspent for a marginally affordable car may need to scale back on house payments to compensate. This result is a source of information that will diverge from the results derived from salary. Determining what these factors are provides us the ability to derive insights into plausible housing prices, so we can fine-tune our analyses. Each new variable should provide more information we can use to develop a probable range for home values.

Dr. Leinweber showed how easy it is to make irrelevant information fit the data as if the information provided real and valid insights. Obviously, the irrelevant data is only fitting the past data. It will be worthless for prediction. Fitting past data does not guarantee the correctness of an extrapolation.

Dr. Leinweber did not stop at simply plugging in irrelevant data, however. He overfitted the data. What is overfitting? Overfitting relates closely to the finding of irrelevant variables just discussed, but it is different in scope. Even when the independent variables are truly related to dependent variables, overfitting can undo the utility of a model. To understand why, consider our home value example.

In most cases, factors are present that prevent our predictive capability from reaching any high degree of accuracy. Some people like houses and some like townhouses or condominiums. There are people who find homeowner associations to be irritating and some who like having a wall around the neighborhood. Some people like trees and some people do not care either way. Some people move to select a particular school district and some people do not have kids. We find folks who like suburbia and those who chafe within it.

All of these factors affect the values of homes. These factors will also provide decision criteria that have nothing to do with income or debt or other numerical values. Any attempt to drive further predictive ability—the higher R-squared we discussed—using quantitative measures will surpass the capability of the tool while possibly attaining the illusion of such a capability. This is overfitting. Adding in miles driven to our analysis may increase the R-squared of our analysis while lowering it for most future analyses. It is the ability to create a model valid for generalization that is important, not the attainment of the highest possible fit for a single sample.

In the social sciences, our models will have noise inexplicable with the data that we could realistically attain in any circumstance. It would be good if we could later explain some of that noise in a replicable manner. If that is not possible, let the noise be noise. In overfitting, perfection becomes the enemy of the ability to generalize.

So, what is the lesson? Our big data system is a powerful tool, but one that requires thoughtful use. Dr. Leinweber puts it succinctly:

> Unlimited computational resources are like dynamite. Used properly, you can move mountains; used improperly, you can blow up your garage, or your portfolio. The easy access to data and tools to mine it has given new meaning to Mark Twain's admonition about "lies, damn lies, and statistics."

One of the reasons why "Stupid Data Miner Tricks" is a classic is that it is fun to read. Nevertheless, the seriousness of its message should not be lost. An astute student of statistics and data quality should see how dangerous is this ability to derive statistically sound conclusions from nonsense. What if our analysis concludes that we can increase our margins by eliminating efforts to retain a certain segment of customers? What if a firm tells us that potential hires with certain characteristics tend to be unreliable employees? The conclusions may be utter nonsense, but they will have impressive numbers and formulae lending them an air of authority.

As has been shown by no end of mistakes and meltdowns, danger lurks with intelligent people accommodating to the same human nature that usually serves well, but doing so at the wrong time. The collapse of Long-Term Capital Management required the intervention of the Federal Reserve and 14 financial institutions and a $3.6 billion bailout. The parties responsible for this collapse included the former head of bond trading at the Salomon Brothers investment bank and two recipients of the Nobel Memorial Prize in Economic Sciences. There was adequate brainpower behind the doomed hedge fund but an inadequate respect for the nuances of risk.

In December 2013, *The Atlantic* ran an intriguing article by Jennifer Richler with the odd title, "How to Read about Science." Anyone who reads the news reads about science. What new tidbit of knowledge could Ms. Richler deliver? In the article, Ms. Richler notes:

> Getting the most out of science writing takes work, but it's vital, and similar to the attention we devote to consuming other products: We check the labels on food packages at the supermarket. We pore over online reviews before making even minor purchases. We should put the same care into the way we absorb scientific information, which has the power to shape the way we live.

In other words, gaining knowledge by reading about science is an active pursuit. The reader must assess what is being written. The conclusions may not be the most important part of the article. Ms. Richter then points out:

> Even a good study has limitations and weaknesses. Usually the researchers are direct about these in academic papers, and do a decent job of explaining how they might detract from the study's conclusions. Look for science writers to be similarly frank. Examples of weaknesses include: samples that are either very small (which makes it difficult to find a statistically significant difference) or very large (which means tiny, basically meaningless effects might still be statistically significant), or are somehow unrepresentative of the population they're trying to understand (studying animals to learn about human diseases, for example).[18]

The author of this article emphasizes a key point that this book makes. The result of a study is not a direct window to truth. It is part of a puzzle, the goal of which is to tease out an accurate description of an underlying reality. Sample size, statistical methods, research methods, characteristics of the data, and the size of the measured effect all play a role in how a reader should interpret science writing. This lesson must also be applied to interpreting the results delivered by our data analytics system.

A SAMPLE OF COMMON STATISTICAL SOFTWARE PACKAGES

Minitab

We can find several common software packages available for statistical analysis, ranging in price from free to thousands of dollars. Among Six Sigma practitioners, the dominant product is probably Minitab. Designed to be user-friendly and intended for use on a laptop or PC, Minitab has become so ingrained into Six Sigma culture that many Six Sigma instruction books and courses default to it in their instructions and homework problems. Minitab features a broad feature set for quality professionals, with capabilities for descriptive statistics, hypothesis testing, experiment design, and quality control features such as control charts. A single license for the current version, Minitab 17, costs $1495 on the Minitab website, so it is good value for businesses, if a little pricey for individual users.

Minitab can handle a data spreadsheet of roughly 150 million cells, which may not be adequate for enormous data sets, particularly given the limitation of 4000 columns. The website for Minitab gives no indication of strategic direction for big data analysis. We are keeping our fingers crossed with this product because of its traditional ease of use.

SPSS

Statistical Package for the Social Sciences (SPSS) was once, as its name indicates, a statistical program for the social sciences. It has since extended its reach beyond those fields. The software has become a serious business statistics package, however, as we can discern from IBM's 2009 purchase of the company. Some of its high-end capabilities move into the realm of machine learning, and there is the ability to include custom scripts. The price range is significantly higher, with single-user licenses starting over $2,000 for a basic level and reaching over $16,000 for a premium version on IBM's website. IBM SPSS has components (e.g., data modeler) designed to work with big data support products such as IBM InfoSphere BigInsights, Cloudera, Hortonworks, and Apache Hadoop. The IBM package collection for SPSS looks like this:

- IBM Analytic Answers
- IBM Analytical Decision Management
- IBM Social Media Analytics
- IBM SPSS Data Collection
- IBM SPSS Modeler
- IBM SPSS Statistics
- Predictive analytics for big data
- Customer analytics
  - Customer acquisition
  - Customer lifetime value
  - Customer loyalty

- Profitability
- Social media analytics
- Operational analytics
  - Inventory management
  - Predictive maintenance
- Threat and fraud analytics
  - Fraud prevention
  - Public safety

IBM is one of the big players in the big data arena, so we are unsurprised at its substantial involvement in big data analysis.

R

R is probably the most important development in statistical software; it is really a statistical programming language. What it lacks in user-friendliness, it makes up in sheer value and capability. We discuss it because it is free and powerful, it works well with other big data tools such as Hadoop, and it has special libraries for big data manipulation. Although it is not immediately user-friendly, its basics are easy to learn, its graphics are great, it is supported by over 4000 user-submitted packages, and it works on every significant and readily available operating system. Some of the other statistical players have taken notice and decided to work with R rather than against it (we believe this strategy is wise!).

One reason for using R is the fact that the price is right! However, if that were the only reason, it would be insufficient for professional use. R, *per se*, has been around since 1997. Version 1.0 appeared in 2000, and, as of this writing, the current version is 3.0.1. Some quick arithmetic indicates R is 17 years old, which is sufficient to provide the maturity needed to believe in the results; in short, developers have already ironed out egregious defects.

Additionally, the use of R is so widespread that other development groups have designed, coded, and tested alternate tools that work in tandem with R; for example, the data mining, machine learning, and predictive analytic tool, Weka, can use R. Many others are available. R is also available for at least three platforms:

- Windows-based systems
- Apple Macintosh
- Linux

Enterprising souls have also developed "front ends" for R to simplify use for users unenthralled with the command-line interface (if we learned to use a PC in the days of MS DOS, we are familiar with this interface). The best known of these tools is R-Commander.

Ultimately, we feel that power users will most likely revert to the command line in order to truly understand how R meets their needs. For common statistical tests, the R command line is not particularly any more difficult than working one's way through a menu system.

So how much data can R handle? R is available in 64-bit versions, suggesting an address space of 18,446,744,073,709,551,616 or greater than 18 quintillion bits. Obviously, in-memory calculations will be limited by the amount of memory on the computer; for example, we are writing part of this text on a 32 GB iMac with an Intel i7 quad-core processor. To expand beyond the RAM level requires that we use tool design to break the problem into digestible components—defeat in detail, as the military phrase goes.

In concert with IBM, Revolution Analytics, a commercial company, produces a variant of R that works with Hadoop. In effect, this ability means the size of the data set is only limited by the number of available nodes on the network, memory limitations, and the quality of the job partitioning.

Revolution Analytics provides commercial support for their big data products. Users of other big data packages would have to resort to World Wide Web queries in order to resolve issues with the code. We should base our choice among these possibilities on the needs of the user. For example, here are some simple *t*-tests on small data sets:

Paired *t*-test
    t.test(yone,ytwo,paired = TRUE) # yone & ytwo are both numeric

One-sample *t*-test
    t.test(y,mu = 4) # Ho: mu = 4

Independent two-group *t*-test
    t.test(y_x) # y - numeric; x is a binary factor

Independent two-group *t*-test
    t.test(y1,y2) # y1 and y2 are numeric

One of the most common approaches when analyzing big data is multiple regression modeling, either with the general linear model or one of the many others (see our discussion on machine learning). The yield should be correlation in many cases, perhaps multiple correlations. Of course, with vast quantities of data it is entirely possible to derive specious correlations, as we indicated; that is to say, variable B appears to change in a meaningful way with variable A. As we discussed, we would call variable A the independent variable and variable B the dependent variable, suggesting B is somehow related to A. It should be clear that we should use common sense, intuition (gut feelings), and any other component of understanding we can bring to bear on our bBig dData problems.

"Garbage in, garbage out" is a problem during large data analyses. Robert Muenchen, also at the R-bloggers site, noted:

> While the vast array of functions in R covers most data analysis situations, they have been completely unable to handle data that bears no actual relationship to the research questions at hand. Robert A. Muenchen, author of R for SAS and SPSS Users, has written a new ggply function, which can adroitly handle the all too popular "garbage in, garbage out" research situation. The function has only one argument, the garbage to analyze. It automatically performs the analysis strongly preferred by "gg" researchers by splitting numeric variables at the median and performing all possible cross tabulations and chi-square tests, repeated for the levels of all factors. The integration of functions from the new pbdR package allows ggply to handle even Big Garbage using 12,000 cores.[19]

The algorithm applies what is called a backpropagational Bonferroni algorithm to control for error. Do not worry about the jargon. What is important is that it controls for error.

SAS

Big Data Analytics

Here are some offerings from SAS (http://www.sas.com):

- SAS In-Memory Analytics: With SAS In-Memory Analytics solutions, organizations can attack problems using big data and analytics rapidly.
- SAS Visual Analytics: SAS Visual Analytics is an in-memory solution for exploring huge amounts of data expeditiously.

- SAS Social Media Analytics: This product integrates, archives, analyzes, and enables organizations to act on intelligence gleaned from online conversations on professional and consumer-generated media sites, bringing big data techniques to qualitative/quantitative data analysis.
- SAS High-Performance Analytics Server: An in-memory solution that allows us to develop analytical models using complete data, not just a subset, to potentially increases our insights. We can run frequent modeling iterations and use powerful analytics.

SAS was an early large-scale player in the analytics domain. They offer an array of existing capability similar to the capabilities list from IBM:

- Analytics
- Business analytics
- Business intelligence
- Customer intelligence
- Fraud and security intelligence
- High-performance analytics
- Information management
- Performance management
- Risk management
- Supply chain intelligence
- Sustainability management

Hadoop Integration

SAS can work with Hadoop to partition the problem into solvable components, which is what Hadoop is all about. Keep in mind that in-memory solutions will still need sufficient memory to operate, although we can expect accelerated run times.

Angoss

Angoss delivers predictive analytics and business intelligence software to businesses looking to improve performance across sales, marketing, and risk. Angoss can use Hadoop as a data source and as a deployment platform for models designed with KnowledgeSTUDIO, providing big data capability for those companies with Hadoop installations. Data scientists are able to import and prepare massive amounts of data—both structured and unstructured—into memory with 64-bit addressing; and perform in-database analytics using enormous data sets and numbers of predictive variables so customers can mine and analyze data faster and more accurately. "In-database" analytics means Angoss tools work directly within a database rather than a copy.

The product list looks like this:

- KnowledgeEXCELERATOR: a visual data discovery and prediction tool for business analysts and knowledge workers.
- KnowledgeSEEKER: a business intelligence software solution with data mining and predictive analytics capabilities.
- KnowledgeREADER: visual text discovery, sentiment analysis and predictive analytics for marketers and customer intelligence professionals.
- KnowledgeSTUDIO: advanced modeling and predictive analytics capabilities for high-performance business users and data analysts.
- StrategyBUILDER: a module in KnowledgeSEEKER, KnowledgeREADER and KnowledgeSTUDIO that allows data analysts and business analysts to work together to build and deploy predictive strategies using strategy trees.
- Big Data Analytics: In-database analytics driver for data mining and predictive analytics directly on data stored in our enterprise data warehouse.
  - Data preparation
  - Data profiling
  - Decision trees
  - Model analyzer
  - Strategy trees
  - Text analytics

Angoss also works with R.

Statistica

Capabilities

The Statistica solution possesses the following capabilities:

- Leading-edge predictive analytics: This package uses sophisticated algorithms to build models based on big data in order to provide high accuracy.

- Enterprise-wide solution: This multiuser, role-based, secure Statistica enterprise platform permits a cooperative environment to build, test, and deploy possible models for predictive analytics.
- It performs model, reporting, and general analytic templates and life cycle management.
  - An ability to institute version control and life cycle management for all analytic reporting, modeling, scoring, and other analytic processes means we *manage* our work.
  - Life cycle management is effectively large-scale configuration management—in this case, being used to manage the models and data.
- Reflexive models for real-time needs: The Statistica feature *Live Score* processes new data as they arrive and updates predictions in real time, using scoring models centrally managed through the enterprise platform.
- Integrated Workflow: The Statistica *Decisioning Platform* provides a work flow for rules-based predictive analytics where business rules and constraints appear in conjunction with advanced analytics to build models, and it then scores these efficiently over multiple parallel processors, or in real-time.

We note that Statistica also integrates with R. In essence, a user will run R programs to produce output into Statistica as spreadsheets and graphs, which we can then manage in Statistica workbooks and save into Statistica reports. Statistica uses its own programming language, Statistica Visual Basic, which supplies the flexibility needed for the two packages to work together when customer solutions demand them.

SUMMARY

This chapter covered a lot of ground. First, understanding our data starts with the basics of comprehending its shape, central tendencies, and dispersion. Different data sets, and various attributes within the same data set, generate alternate distributions. The distribution is important to understanding the behavior of the attribute, such as the volatility of the values or whether the majority of the cases will cluster in the center of the distribution or towards a tail. Mean and standard deviation are typical ways of analyzing our data, especially when the data fit one of the standard probability distribution functions, although we sometimes use the variance (we take the square root of the variance to calculate the standard deviation). The mean is the most common measure of central tendency but we will often use the median and the mode, particularly when the coincidence of these measures suggests we can model our data using the normal distribution.

When we use this information with big data, we compare a large quantity of attributes. Much of the value of big data is the result of its ability to surface an enormous number of attributes from a variety of sources and then look for links; it brings one huge advantage and one huge disadvantage absent from traditional data analysis. That we can find relationships where nobody thought to look for them is an advantage. The disadvantage is in so doing we find specious dependencies. The probabilities behind these pretenders mean it is entirely possible the false-positives will inundate the true-positives. This is especially the case when the phenomena being sought are rare, in which case any positive relationship is likely to be a false-positive. We saw this in our discussion of Bayes's theorem. Tightening the significance level also presents problems because it increases the probability of encountering Type II errors, or false-negatives.

We could throw our hands up and capitulate. Popular discussion of big data tends to discuss the promises of big data or the dangers of these false-positives. Due to the promise of big data for business and the dangers these erroneous conclusions present to this promise, the fatalism of much of the current discussion is unacceptable. If we move beyond big data and check in on the science and medical arenas, we find a healthy awareness of these problems. Finally, science is a cooperative effort involving the comparison of vast numbers of attributes, and for which flawed conclusions remain costly.

In medical research, the use of cohort studies and other large-scale epidemiological studies find relationships between variables, which are explored in greater detail to determine the validity and nature of the relationship. For example, investigators suspected the common sweetener aspartame of being a carcinogen based on a study, but it was later shown to be safe in follow-up studies. We have no easy way to eliminate false-positives and false-negatives in statistical hypotheses, but this mathematical practice promises applicability to big data applications. When a regression, decision tree, or other algorithm returns a list of relations, we should not accept these as a statement of factual ties between variables. What our result should do is incite further examination using a tighter, hypothesis-driven series of tests. If a series of these follow-up tests indicates a connection is probable, then it should be safe enough to make a business decision using this information. If the dependencies are unsustainable, then we were probably dealing with an error that could have been costly if used as the basis for making decisions.

The same sophisticated algorithms used to find these relationships are unnecessary to confirm them. Once we determine the query used and the attributes compared, we may use simpler hypothesis tests. We provided a list of hypothesis tests and their applicability. We feel no need to commit any of this to memory, but a solid understanding of how hypothesis tests are designed and applied enables a manager to ask probing questions of analysts or of salespeople selling a data-related service. Many organizations have the requisite people to understand and interrogate data, and these individuals are often Six Sigma Black Belts and Master Black Belts.

A manager faces the judgment call in when to apply these higher standards to their analysis. It is probably not necessary in A-B analysis and induces damaging paralysis in cracking down on new forms of credit card fraud; however, it can prevent costly mistakes when applied to considered changes in sourcing, logistics, strategy, and marketing.

We wrapped up the discussion by covering common statistical packages. All these products are useful, but not all statistical packages are equal for the same jobs. As a manager, we need to understand how data analysis will be integrated into our organization and how we confirm results. Many high-quality options are available, however.

REFERENCES

1. Wikipedia. Post–World War II baby boom. Wikipedia. http://en.wikipedia.org/wiki/Post%E2%80%93World_War_II_baby_boom. Accessed October 28, 2013.
2. diBartolomeo, D. Fat tails, liquidity limits and IID assumptions. Northfield Research. March 2008. http://www.northinfo.com/Documents/536.pdf. Accessed May 18, 2014.
3. Gladwell, M. Million-Dollar Murray. Gladwell.com (originally published in *The New Yorker*). February 13, 2006. http://gladwell.com/million-dollar-murray/. Accessed December 3, 2013.
4. Mandelbrot, B. *The (Mis)behavior of Markets: A Fractal View of Risk, Ruin, and Reward*. New York: Basic Books, 2004.
5. Huff, D. and Geis, I. *How to Lie with Statistics*. New York: Norton, 1954.
6. Jones, S. Republican myth busted: Reagan raised the debt ceiling 3 times more than Obama. Politicus USA. January 17, 2013. http://www.politicususa.com/2013/01/17/ronald-reagan-raised-debt-ceiling-times-1960.html. Accessed November 16, 2013.

7. Ungar, R. Who is the smallest government spender since Eisenhower? Would you believe it's Barack Obama? *Forbes*. May 24, 2012. http://www.forbes.com/sites/rick-ungar/2012/05/24/who-is-the-smallest-government-spender-since-eisenhower-would-you-believe-its-barack-obama/. Accessed November 16, 2013.

8. Jeffrey, T.P. Obama has now increased debt more than all presidents from George Washington through George H.W. Bush combined. Cnsnews.com. October 5, 2011. http://cnsnews.com/news/article/obama-has-now-increased-debt-more-all-presidents-george-washington-through-george-hw. Accessed November 16, 2013.

9. Rove, K. Obama versus Bush on spending. *Wall Street Journal*. January 21, 2010. http://online.wsj.com/news/articles/SB10001424052748704320104575015072822042394. Accessed November 16, 2013.

10. Ropeik, D. How risky is flying? Nova. October 17, 2006. http://www.pbs.org/wgbh/nova/space/how-risky-is-flying.html. Accessed November 16, 2013.

11. Wikipedia. Paul the Octopus. Wikipedia. http://en.wikipedia.org/wiki/Paul_the_Octopus. Accessed December 25, 2013.

12. Feynman, R. Cargo Cult Science. Commencement address to 1974 graduating class at Caltech. http://neurotheory.columbia.edu/~ken/cargo_cult.html. Accessed December 24, 2013.

13. Mill, J.S. *A System of Logic*, pp. 454–470. New York: Harper, 1858.

14. Cruise, C. How credit scores affect insurance rates. Bankrate.com. September 23, 2003. http://www.bankrate.com/brm/news/insurance/credit-scores1.asp. Accessed May 14, 2014.

15. Powerball.com PowerBall—Prizes and odds. Powerball.com http://www.powerball.com/powerball/pb_prizes.asp. Accessed May 6, 2014.

16. National Lightning Safety Institute (NLSI). Lightning strike probabilities. NLSI. http://www.lightningsafety.com/nlsi_pls/probability.html. Accessed May 6, 2014.

17. Leinweber, D.J. Stupid data miner tricks: Overfitting the S&P 500. *Journal of Investing*. 2007, 16(1): 15–22.

18. Richler, J. How to read about science. *The Atlantic*. December 6, 2013. http://www.theatlantic.com/health/archive/2013/12/how-to-read-about-science/281855/. Accessed December 6, 2013.

19. Muenchen, B. R tackles big garbage. R-bloggers. http://www.r-bloggers.com/r-tackles-big-garbage/. Accessed July 2, 2013.

7

Google

![BIG DATA GIANTS section divider]

BIG DATA GIANTS

We suggest that looking at market cap (shares outstanding times dollar value thereof) is one quick way of ascertaining the "gianthood" of a corporation. Table 7.1 shows some of them in a tabular format (March 2014).

With nine companies, we are looking at nearly $2 trillion in market capitalization. With some of these firms, their market cap is small because they focus on one or two capabilities (LinkedIn) rather than becoming a one-stop center for all things (Amazon). The Google presence is interesting because their business is dominated by services, whereas Apple sells software and hardware as well as some services.

In this chapter, we will explore some of these giants to see how large they really are. In addition, some of them seem to be engaging in multifront economic warfare with their competitors, betting on their technical prowess to win the day.

Some of these vendors—Google and Amazon come to mind immediately—have the advantage of using big data in all their transactions, thereby providing themselves with the benefit of their own masses of data converted to information. An example of data converted incompletely to information (data are data and information is processed data) is Zillow.com, where real estate values are estimated and features of domiciles are presented in a terse, tabular format. If we were to see the data more obviously converted to information, we might expect to see where a given house lies on a distribution based on a specific area, say the zip code or even the neighborhood. Zillow does provide some perspective—when one of us took a look at the "value" of our house, we found much more under the detail heading (not surprisingly) as well as a graphical comparison of this home value versus the general neighborhood (as defined

TABLE 7.1

Corporate Value by Market Cap for Select
Companies

Corporation	Market Cap ($ billion)
Apple	469.84
Google	408.09
Microsoft	313.6
IBM	196.01
Facebook	178.34
Oracle	174.72
Amazon	170.82
Twitter	29.45
LinkedIn	25.03
Total	1965.9

by Zillow) and the overall value for the city in which we live. Zillow also provides some information regarding foreclosure activity—which can have an effect on home prices by driving them down. Our point is that simply presenting numbers is often insufficient for decision support and we would like to see more perspective on what our data might really mean.

GOOGLE

The first step in understanding Google and big data is to realize how corporately large Google really is (as of Spring 2014):

North America

- United States
  - Google Inc.—Mountain View, CA
  - Google Ann Arbor—Ann Arbor, MI
  - Google Atlanta—Atlanta, GA
  - Google Austin—Austin, TX
  - Google Boulder—Boulder, CO
  - Google Boston—Cambridge, MA
  - Google Chicago—Chicago, IL
  - Google Detroit—Birmingham, MI
  - Google Irvine—Irvine, CA
  - Google Kirkland—Kirkland, WA

- Google Los Angeles—Los Angeles, CA
- Google Madison—Madison, WI
- Google New York—New York, NY
- Google Pittsburgh—Pittsburgh, PA
- Google Reston—Reston, VA
- Google San Francisco—San Francisco, CA
- Google Seattle—Seattle, WA
- Google Washington DC—Washington, DC

Asia Pacific

- Australia
  - Google Sydney
- Mainland China
  - Google Beijing
  - Google Guangzhou
  - Google Shanghai
  - Google Hong Kong
- India
  - Google Bangalore
  - Google Gurgaon
  - Google Hyderabad
  - Google Mumbai
- Japan
  - Google Japan—Minato-ku, Tokyo
- Asia, other countries
  - Google Seoul—Google Korea LLC, Seoul, South Korea
  - Google Malaysia—Kuala Lumpur, Malaysia
  - Google Auckland—New Zealand
  - Google Singapore—Google Asia Pacific Pte. Ltd., Singapore
  - Google Taipei—Taiwan
  - Thailand—Google (Thailand) Company Limited—Bangkok, Thailand

Africa

- Kenya—Google Kenya Ltd., Nairobi, Kenya
- Ghana—Google Ghana, North Ridge, Accra
- Nigeria—Google Nigeria, Lagos, Nigeria

- Senegal—Google Senegal, Dakar, Senegal
- South Africa—Google South Africa, Bryanston, Johannesburg
- Uganda—Google Uganda, Kampala

The Google story is the raw material for Internet legend: two enterprising guys who found a better solution to network searching and hit the market at the right time with a better product than anything the competition had at the time. Larry Page and Sergey Brin were students at Stanford University who met in 1995. By 1996, they had produced a search engine to determine the importance of individual web pages.[1] The name is based on the mathematical term *googol*, which is 1 followed by 100 zeros. The company itself was formed in 1998. Over the years, they have released some signal products:

- AdWords in 2000
- Gmail in 2004
- Google Maps and Google Earth in 2005
- YouTube (through acquisition) in 2006
- Android mobile operating system (OS) in 2007
- Google Chrome browser in 2008
- Google+ in 2011 as an entry into the social networking marketplace

Early on, Google put out a kind of manifesto (note that we quote verbatim to avoid misstating Google's approach)[2]:

1. Focus on the user and all else will follow.
   Since the beginning, we've focused on providing the best user experience possible. Whether we're designing a new Internet browser or a new tweak to the look of the homepage, we take great care to ensure that they will ultimately serve you, rather than our own internal goal or bottom line. Our homepage interface is clear and simple, and pages load instantly. Placement in search results is never sold to anyone, and advertising is not only clearly marked as such, it offers relevant content and is not distracting. And when we build new tools and applications, we believe they should work so well you don't have to consider how they might have been designed differently.
2. It's best to do one thing really, really well.
   We do search. With one of the world's largest research groups focused exclusively on solving search problems, we know what we do well, and how we could do it better. Through continued iteration on difficult problems, we've been able to solve complex issues and

provide continuous improvements to a service that already makes finding information a fast and seamless experience for millions of people. Our dedication to improving search helps us apply what we've learned to new products, like Gmail and Google Maps. Our hope is to bring the power of search to previously unexplored areas, and to help people access and use even more of the ever-expanding information in their lives.

3. Fast is better than slow. We know your time is valuable, so when you're seeking an answer on the web you want it right away—and we aim to please. We may be the only people in the world who can say our goal is to have people leave our website as quickly as possible. By shaving excess bits and bytes from our pages and increasing the efficiency of our serving environment, we've broken our own speed records many times over, so that the average response time on a search result is a fraction of a second. We keep speed in mind with each new product we release, whether it's a mobile application or Google Chrome, a browser designed to be fast enough for the modern web. And we continue to work on making it all go even faster.

4. Democracy on the web works.

   Google search works because it relies on the millions of individuals posting links on websites to help determine which other sites offer content of value. We assess the importance of every web page using more than 200 signals and a variety of techniques, including our patented PageRank™ algorithm, which analyzes which sites have been "voted" to be the best sources of information by other pages across the web. As the web gets bigger, this approach actually improves, as each new site is another point of information and another vote to be counted. In the same vein, we are active in open source software development, where innovation takes place through the collective effort of many programmers.

5. You don't need to be at your desk to need an answer.

   The world is increasingly mobile: people want access to information wherever they are, whenever they need it. We're pioneering new technologies and offering new solutions for mobile services that help people all over the globe to do any number of tasks on their phone, from checking email and calendar events to watching videos, not to mention the several different ways to access Google search on a phone. In addition, we're hoping to fuel greater innovation for mobile users everywhere with Android, a free, open source mobile platform. Android brings the openness that shaped the Internet to the mobile world. Not only does Android benefit consumers, who have more choice and innovative new mobile experiences, but also it opens up revenue opportunities for carriers, manufacturers and developers.

6. You can make money without doing evil.

Google is a business. The revenue we generate is derived from offering search technology to companies and from the sale of advertising displayed on our site and on other sites across the web. Hundreds of thousands of advertisers worldwide use AdWords to promote their products; hundreds of thousands of publishers take advantage of our AdSense program to deliver ads relevant to their site content. To ensure that we're ultimately serving all our users (whether they are advertisers or not), we have a set of guiding principles for our advertising programs and practices:

- We don't allow ads to be displayed on our results pages unless they are relevant where they are shown. And we firmly believe that ads can provide useful information if, and only if, they are relevant to what you wish to find-so it's possible that certain searches won't lead to any ads at all.
- We believe that advertising can be effective without being flashy. We don't accept pop-up advertising, which interferes with your ability to see the content you've requested. We've found that text ads that are relevant to the person reading them draw much higher click through rates than ads appearing randomly. Any advertiser, whether small or large, can take advantage of this highly targeted medium.
- Advertising on Google is always clearly identified as a "Sponsored Link," so it does not compromise the integrity of our search results. We never manipulate rankings to put our partners higher in our search results and no one can buy better PageRank. Our users trust our objectivity and no short-term gain could ever justify breaching that trust.

7. There's always more information out there.

Once we'd indexed more of the HTML pages on the Internet than any other search service, our engineers turned their attention to information that was not as readily accessible. Sometimes it was just a matter of integrating new databases into search, such as adding a phone number and address lookup and a business directory. Other efforts required a bit more creativity, like adding the ability to search news archives, patents, academic journals, billions of images and millions of books. And our researchers continue looking into ways to bring all the world's information to people seeking answers.

8. The need for information crosses all borders.

Our company was founded in California, but our mission is to facilitate access to information for the entire world, and in every language.

To that end, we have offices in more than 60 countries, maintain more than 180 Internet domains, and serve more than half of our results to people living outside the United States. We offer Google's search interface in more than 130 languages, offer people the ability to restrict results to content written in their own language, and aim to provide the rest of our applications and products in as many languages and accessible formats as possible. Using our translation tools, people can discover content written on the other side of the world in languages they don't speak. With these tools and the help of volunteer translators, we have been able to greatly improve both the variety and quality of services we can offer in even the most far-flung corners of the globe.

9. You can be serious without a suit.

Our founders built Google around the idea that work should be challenging, and the challenge should be fun. We believe that great, creative things are more likely to happen with the right company culture–and that doesn't just mean lava lamps and rubber balls. There is an emphasis on team achievements and pride in individual accomplishments that contribute to our overall success. We put great stock in our employees–energetic, passionate people from diverse backgrounds with creative approaches to work, play and life. Our atmosphere may be casual, but as new ideas emerge in a café line, at a team meeting or at the gym, they are traded, tested and put into practice with dizzying speed–and they may be the launch pad for a new project destined for worldwide use.

10. Great just isn't good enough.

We see being great at something as a starting point, not an endpoint. We set ourselves goals we know we can't reach yet, because we know that by stretching to meet them we can get further than we expected. Through innovation and iteration, we aim to take things that work well and improve upon them in unexpected ways. For example, when one of our engineers saw that search worked well for properly spelled words, he wondered about how it handled typos. That led him to create an intuitive and more helpful spell checker.

Even if you don't know exactly what you're looking for, finding an answer on the web is our problem, not yours. We try to anticipate needs not yet articulated by our global audience, and meet them with products and services that set new standards. When we launched Gmail, it had more storage space than any email service available. In retrospect offering that seems obvious–but that's because now we have new standards for email storage. Those are the kinds of changes we seek to make, and we're always looking for new places where we can make a difference. Ultimately, our constant dissatisfaction with the way things are becomes the driving force behind everything we do.

This Google manifesto is brimming with enthusiasm and optimism. The question we must ask ourselves arises when we question the power that is possessed by a company who knows what we are looking for. It is perhaps too easy to come up with Orwellian scenarios related to the all-seeing Big Brother, but how do we or anybody else restrain them? Ultimately, in this book, we want to ascertain the use of Google's capabilities for business purposes, particularly with respect to big data.

Go

Go is a computer programming language that Google created in 2007 and announced in 2009. One of its creators is Ken Thompson (of Thompson and Ritchie C language fame). Its goals include safety and speed.

The Go language specification resides on http://golang.org/ref/spec. The documentation positions the language as a systems language as opposed to an application language. As with many computer languages, this demarcation appears to be based on wishful thinking rather than on any limitation in the language itself. Not surprisingly, Go has a look that is reminiscent of C. The documentation describes Go as:

> Go is expressive, concise, clean, and efficient. Its concurrency mechanisms make it easy to write programs that get the most out of multicore and net-worked machines, while its novel type system enables flexible and modular program construction. Go compiles quickly to machine code yet has the convenience of garbage collection and the power of run-time reflection. It's a fast, statically typed, compiled language that feels like a dynamically typed, interpreted language.[3]

Go has some peculiar functions when compared with a typical programming language:

- Defer allows the programmer to push function calls onto a list, which allows for some convenience when using "cleanup" functions.
- Panic allows a routine to issue a panic call, which effectively forces functions to complete activities on the stack and execute everything in the routine before executing a crash.
- Recover regains control after a panic call and is only useful in deferred functions.

In essence, these functions make for a quick version of Java's try, catch, and finally methods. Note also that Go effectively supports a functional programming style while maintaining strong typing.

Go can be used to build web applications using Google's App Engine. As of this writing, the dominant method to present a graphical user interface (GUI) with Go is to use a browser app or to use the old standby, the tk user interface library common to Unix flavors and systems that have the tcl language. We will not waste our time with a meaningless "Hello, World" program, since this kind of example would hardly provide us with a clue about the general behavior of the language. To us, Go looks like a terse, C-like language that is waiting to blossom with some really good GUI libraries. Also, because Go is designed for distributed processing from the very beginning, it makes a good candidate for use in large, distributed processing scenarios; that is, it may end up being a killer application for development on big data systems.

Android

Released in 2008, Android (www.android.com) exists under the permissive Apache license model. Samsung has, to date, used Android as the OS for their cell phones and tablets. Almost three-quarters of all mobile users are using Android on their cell phones/tablets.[4] Interestingly, it appears that Android is largely based on C, C++, and Java:[5]

- C: approximately 40%
- C++: approximately 24%
- Java: approximately 18%
- The rest: 28%

We find the lack of functional languages (e.g., Scala) to be interesting. The list of languages actually used with Android seems to reflect popularity and knowledge rather than a careful study of the benefits of eliminating side effects. Any claim that a functional language takes up too much memory is absurd when a person can buy a 32 GB smartphone. The software development kit (SDK) for Android uses a complete Java integrated development environment (IDE) called Android Studio (built on IntelliJ IDEA), so the Java presence is not particularly surprising. It appears that Android can also use the services of the existing IDE, Eclipse.

The Android website provides the tools for Android development, which are free to download. It is obvious that we are not looking at a "baby" OS, but rather a full-scale mobile system designed to proliferate through a growing market. Unlike Apple's iOS OS and its associated iTunes and App Store, Android is an open system. Of course, with an open ecosystem comes responsibility; for example, it is not clear how malware can be controlled in the Android sphere, whereas Apple applies some modicum of control through their closed system.

Google Product Offerings

- Web
  - Web Search
    - Search billions of web pages
    - Big data
  - Google Chrome
    - A browser built for speed, simplicity, and security
    - Application, not big data
  - Toolbar
    - Add a search box to the browser
    - Browser app, not big data
  - Bookmarks
    - Access bookmarks and starred items
    - Browser feature, not big data
- Mobile
  - Mobile
    - Get Google products on a mobile phone
    - Management of these is a big data issue
  - Maps for mobile
    - View maps, your location, and get directions on a phone
    - Big data
  - Search for Mobile
    - Search Google wherever an individual is located
    - Potentially big data
    - Big data if number of users is considered
- Media
  - YouTube
    - Watch, upload, and share videos

- Undeniably big data
- Google Play
  - Your music, movies, books, and Android apps available anywhere
  - Big data in terms of storage
- Books
  - Search the full text of books
  - Potentially big data
- Image Search
  - Search for images on the web
  - Big data
- News
  - Search thousands of news stories
- Video Search
  - Search for videos on the web
  - Big data
- Picasa
  - Find, edit, and share photos
  - Application, not big data *per se*
- Geo
  - Google Offers
    - Get amazing offers at the best places to eat, shop, and play
    - Possibly big data
  - Maps
    - View maps and directions
    - Big data
  - Earth
    - Explore the world from a computer
    - Big data
  - Panoramio
    - Explore and share photos of the world
    - Storage is big data
- Specialized Search
  - Blog Search
    - Find blogs on your favorite topics
    - Management is big data
  - Custom Search
    - Create a customized search experience for your community

- Not big data *per se*
- Patent Search
  - Search the full text of US patents
  - Not big data *per se*
- Google Shopping
  - Search for products to buy
  - Potentially big data
- Finance
  - Business information, news, and interactive charts
  - Potentially big data
- Scholar
  - Search scholarly papers
  - Potentially big data
- Alerts
  - Get e-mail updates on the topics of your choice
  - Potentially big data
- Trends
  - Explore past and present search trends
  - Potentially big data
- Home and Office
  - Gmail
    - Fast, searchable e-mail with less spam thanks to a strong spam filter
    - Uses the Google search engine
    - Substantial online storage for the individual user
    - Storage is big data
  - Drive
    - Create, share, and keep all your information in one place
    - Storage is big data
  - Docs
    - Open, edit, and create documents
    - Management is big data
  - Sheets
    - Open, edit, and create spreadsheets
    - Management is big data
  - Slides
    - Open, edit, and create presentations
    - Management is big data
  - Forms

- Building free surveys tied to an online spreadsheet (among several options) is a major purpose for this tool
- We suspect that this tool could be easily used as a form of formative assessment with students, with results recorded
- Not big data
- Drawings
  - Create diagrams and flowcharts
  - Appears to be in its infancy—not big data
- Sites
  - Create websites and secure group wikis
  - Management is big data
- Calendar
  - Organize your schedule and share events with friends
  - Storage is big data
- Translate
  - Instantly translate text, web pages, and files among and between over 50 languages
  - Surprisingly, the algorithm for this self-cleansing translator may be a big data project
- Voice
  - One number for all your phones, online voicemail, and cheap calling
  - Not big data yet
- Google Wallet
  - Make your phone your wallet
  - Storage is big data
- Google Cloud Print
  - Print anywhere from any device
  - Management is big data
- Google Keep
  - "Save what's on your mind"
  - Management is big data
- Social
  - Google+
    - Real-life sharing, rethought for the web
    - At over half a billion users this is undeniably big data
  - Blogger
    - Share your life online with a blog—it is quick, easy, and free
    - Storage and management is potentially big data

- Groups
  - Create mailing lists and discussion groups
  - Unknown
- Hangouts
  - Conversations that come to life; anytime, anywhere, for free
  - Unknown
- Orkut
  - Meet new people and stay in touch with friends
  - Managed by Google Brazil, where most of the activity occurs (33 million users)
- Innovation
  - Fusion Tables
    - Visualize, combine, host, and share your data tables
    - Spreadsheet/database with hundreds of thousands of rows
    - Charting, mapping, network graph capabilities
    - The search engine can search other tables for table "mashups"
    - Appears to be an application, storage could potentially become a big data issue
  - Code
    - Developer tools, application programming interfaces (APIs), and resources
    - Google's developer alternative to SourceForge.net
    - Not big data *per se*
- Advertising
  - AdWords
    - Provides advertising copy on web pages
    - Undeniably a big data item
    - Controlled by Google in the Google-verse
    - Cost per impression
    - Cost per click (CPC)
  - AdSense
    - Targeted advertising and definitely a big data item
    - User choices drive what a user sees based on:
      1. Content
      2. Feeds (e.g., really simple syndication [RSS]), which allows web-based news collection for subscribers
      3. Search
      4. Mobile content

      5. Domains
      6. Video
    – Uses tracking cookies
- Demo Slam
    – A website for demonstrating Google products
- Google Analytics
    – Big data
    – Customer measurements
      1. Websites
      2. Mobile
    – Audience analysis
      1. Advanced Segments
      2. App-Specific Metrics and Dimensions
      3. Audience Data and Reporting
      4. Custom Dimensions
- Filters

Of course, one of the questions to consider when talking about Google is whether any action that is taken with Google or a Google product is not always implicitly a big data item. Let us hover a bit on Google Analytics.

Google Analytics

Google Analytics is part of taking incoming raw data and converting them into information. The Google Analytics product offering is an archetypal example of the use of big data to drive decisions.

Advertising and Campaign Performance

- Advertising Reports: Advertising reports for search, display, social, e-mail, and more to view conversion rates and returns across all digital channels. This feature has AdWords integration.
- Campaign Measurement: See which of your marketing campaigns are really paying off with this detailed real-time report. Engagement and conversion activity are included for any link that you tag (even on e-mail and banners) and can be segmented by channel. Off-line campaigns that send users to your site can also be measured.
- Cost Data Import: The enterprise can import cost data from any digital source: paid search and display providers, affiliates, and social

and even organic traffic. The data appear in a Cost Analysis report in Traffic Sources and also in the Attribution reports. As the company compares how digital marketing channels are doing, it will make better decisions about your marketing programs.

- Mobile Ads Measurement: What if the enterprise is running mobile ads or using mobile applications? Google Analytics helps follow the singular performance issues and trends for both. Mobile Ads breaks down data by device, and then optimizes the results using metrics such as time on site, bounce rate, and conversion rate.

- Remarketing: Enterprise marketing groups can find clients who have shown an interest in their products and services, and then show them pertinent ads for those particular products as they surf the web, due to integration with the Google Display Network (GDN).

- Search Engine Optimization (SEO): The SEO reports in Google Analytics help marketing and sales understand how Google Web Search queries led visitors to the website.

Analysis and Testing

- Advanced Segments
  - Advanced Segments lets marketing departments isolate and analyze subsets of web traffic, such as paid traffic or visits that led to conversions. Then, they can compare segments together, or apply them to current or historical data. The conversions concept is important because we would otherwise be trying to base our decisions on vanity metrics such as the number of visits and the number of unique visits to a website. The goal is to look at the results of a cohort, say the group for this week, and see what they do with regard to actually spending money over some previously defined duration.
- Annotations
  - Annotations let employees leave shared or private notes directly on the reporting graphs. That makes it easy to remember what caused traffic spikes or other unusual issues. This approach is analogous to annotating statistical control charts for assignable causes.
- Content Experiments
  - Content experiments aid in purging speculation from website design. Developers test variations of pages to learn which designs

bring in the most conversions. Content experiments are relatively simple to set up: the developer looks under Experiments in the content section of their Google Analytics account. Experiments are one of the most powerful means that we have to convert data to information, as long as we define the purpose of the experiment before we commence. To initiate an experiment without a purpose and while silently hoping (praying) for data, serendipity is most likely not a suitable course to success in terms of marketing and customer conversions.

- Custom Reports
  - Custom reports can be built in minutes, and they are painless to share with coworkers. Hence, all vendors can have immediate access to the numbers that really count for their business. Custom reports can be a form of data-to-information transformation. Clearly, a report is a product of big data, but it is not big data itself.
- Dashboards
  - Dashboards provide a summary of many reports on a single page. These can be popular with upper management. The development team starts with a dashboard with the most important performance indicators ("company key performance indicators [KPIs]"), and they then create detailed dashboards for other important topics such as SEO. Dashboards use drag-and-drop widgets for fast, easy customization with preexisting tools.
- Real-Time Reporting
  - The vendor can see how many people are on his or her site immediately, where they came from, and what they are viewing. With real-time reporting, the vendor will know which new content is popular, how much traffic today's new promotion is driving to his or her site, and which tweets and blog posts draw the best results. Real-Time Reporting is information.
- Audience Characteristics and Behavior
  - Audience Data and Reporting
    - Focus on the enterprise's audience: the kinds of people they are, where they come from, how they find the company's web content, and how loyal and engaged they are. The difficulty here lies with deciding whether these results are simply data or actual information that is sufficient to drive a meaningful decision.

- Browser/OS
  - PC or Mac or Linux? Chrome, Firefox, Internet Explorer, Opera, or Safari? The Browser/OS report indicates what tools people are using to view specific sites, so the team can make smarter decisions about site layout and design. This information may be important to fine-tuning a website but it is otherwise not particularly useful, at least not in the big data sense.
- Custom Dimensions
  - This product can handle user data such as demographics or purchase history, content data such as page categories or product information, and even behavioral data about those who use certain site tools. Purchase data can become purchase information when we are able to understand the levels of conversion as well as what is driving the conversion.
- Flow Visualization
  - Flow Visualization reports let us see and analyze the path that a visitor takes on our site. We can see where he or she came from, the pages he or she moved through, and where he or she exited our site. This visual approach is clearly information, particularly if we are able to discern confusion on the part of our potential customer.
- Map Overlay
  - With a clear map view and visitor stats broken down by continent, country, and city, we can comprehend the actual origins of our traffic and find the best places to invest for new opportunities. At the beginning, this approach is much like Zillow and represents raw data with a visual interface where we probably really want to see some information regarding the meaning of the geographical area.
- Mobile Traffic
  - Should we build a separate mobile site, create a mobile app, or implement responsive design? As mobile computing continues to boom and consumer preferences shift, the Mobile Traffic report helps us analyze and optimize for improved results. These data are more important to tweaking our website presentation.
- Social Reports
  - Social Reports show the impact that social media has on our business goals and sales conversions. Integrated web and

social data offer a holistic view of our content and community. This is clearly information and may lead to decisions regarding the efficacy of the social media usage or a marketing campaign or both.

- Traffic Sources
  - How do people find the vendor's website? Vendors use Traffic Sources to evaluate the effectiveness of their referrals, direct traffic, organic (unpaid) search key words, and custom campaigns. These are data.
- Cross-device and cross-platform measurement
  - Universal Analytics is a feature of the Google product.
  - The multiscreen, multidevice world is the new standard. Universal Analytics measures digital platforms beyond websites and applications, so we can connect off-line conversions with online activity.
- Data Collection and Management
  - API
    - Applications, plug-ins, and other customizable features will help us to integrate Google Analytics into our team's existing work flows. We can use third-party solutions or build our own applications using the Google Analytics API. This is not information, but rather a means for improving our own presentation.
  - Filters
    - Filters help us to limit and modify the traffic data that appear in any given report view. Do we want to exclude traffic from certain domains (or from inside our own company) or focus on particular types of traffic? Filters make data reduction straightforward. Filters can be an easy way to convert data to information because we control the content of the data stream, so presumably we know something about what we are looking at.
  - User Permissions
    - User Permissions lets vendors choose the appropriate levels of access for different users of the Google Analytics account. It allows some people to manage the entire account, while others can simply view and analyze. This is not information. Access control can become a form of information in itself, because we will now know who thinks they need to access particular portions of our data or information.

- Solely for mobile applications
  - App Profiles
    - We can get the full power of Google Analytics reporting—dedicated to apps. App Profiles gives us access to app-specific metrics, dimensions, and features—collectively designed to help us understand user acquisition, behavior, and conversion. This is a feature.
  - App-Specific Metrics and Dimensions
    - We can access the metrics and dimensions that truly count when using our app. Screen views, sessions, app versions, and screen size are just a few of the app-specific concepts that we can find in Google Analytics for Mobile Apps. These data could readily become information if we use them to inform our decision making.
  - Crash and Exception Reporting
    - Our customers generally will not enjoy or use a defective app. Using built-in crash and exception reporting, Google Analytics lets the user triage and prioritize the issues that are affecting users, improving the user experience (UX).
  - Google Play Integration
    - This exclusive integration with the Google Play Store gives us consummate visibility into how users are finding our application. We can peek inside the Play Store and see how well the content is driving installations and new users. This feature provides for information supporting decision making.
  - iOS and Android SDKs
    - Google Analytics is known for ease of use—the native iOS and Android SDKs make it easy for us to measure user interaction with our app by tracking vital events and activities.
- Product Integrations
  - AdSense
    - AdSense gives content publishers and bloggers a way to earn money with relevant advertisements placed on websites, mobile sites, and site search results. Google Analytics can import AdSense data directly to help the development team display their advertisements in the best possible position on the website. AdSense drives decisions and is therefore information.

- AdWords
  - Google Analytics can import AdWords data seamlessly, to bring in essential information about what visitors do after they have clicked on an advertisement. We can gain deeper insights into how our advertisements and campaigns are performing. AdWords drives decisions and is thus a form of information.
- Google Display Network
  - Google's integration with the GDN means that the user can employ AdWords to create and manage campaigns and then insert Google Analytics tags on GDN marketing campaigns to gauge their success. Also, we can link accounts to see our GDN campaign data within Google Analytics.
- Google Tag Manager
  - Google Tag Manager lets us add or update website tags and mobile applications easily and without necessarily involving the information technology part of the enterprise. Also, it is free. We can configure our tags for Google Analytics (and for many other online marketing tools) from one uncomplicated user interface.
- Google+
  - Google+ is the Google approach to a social network, analogous in some ways to Facebook, yet permeated with the Google design philosophy. Google+ provides for the latest updates about products, upcoming events, interaction with analytics industry experts, or relating to the broader community. Google+ is really a product and is not information *per se*. It is not clear yet if the social network analytical tools that we can use on Facebook are really available for Google+, although it would be surprising if they were not.
- Wildfire
  - Wildfire by Google lets us easily publish social content (such as pages and posts) and measure the engagement, leads, web visits, and revenues driven by our social marketing. There are multiple integration points with Google Analytics. If Wildfire truly works with Google+, it may provide enough computation to convert data into information.
- Sales and Conversions
  - Attribution Model Comparison Tool
    - Gives the right amount of credit to all the digital marketing interactions that affect sales or conversions. We can evaluate

the impact of different channels, referral sources, campaigns, and key words—then use what we learn to enrich our marketing. This tool converts data to information.

- Data-Driven Attribution
  - Google's sophisticated modeling approach assigns values to marketing touch points across the customer experience. The vendor will see a more complete and actionable view of which digital channels and key words perform best. Data-Driven Attribution is only available in Google Analytics Premium, an upgrade to the product.
- E-commerce Reporting
  - E-commerce Reporting is used to identify the best-selling products and the most powerful promotions. The vendor will see what customers buy and how they do it, whether with complex transactions or one-click purchases. The user can trace transactions down to individual key words, understand shopper actions, and adjust the enterprise shopping cart to build loyalty and sales. Not only does this tool help convert data to information, it is also clearly a big data approach.
- Goal Flow
  - This tool allows the vendor some level of visibility into customer preferences on a vendor website. Visitor conversion paths show where they enter, where they get stuck, and where they leave. The vendor can see the strengths and weaknesses of the site navigation, and learn where adjustments are needed to the site and the marketing plan.
- Goals
  - We can assess sales, downloads, video plays and conversions, or define business goals. We can tailor reporting to suit the desired goals or objectives and find the visitor actions that are most likely to help the vendor meet his or her targets.
- Multi-Channel Funnels
  - Multi-Channel Funnels shows a vendor the impact of all his or her digital marketing activities: searches, displays, social activities, affiliates, e-mails, and more. Because this tool is clearly information, the vendor can use it to drive marketing campaigns. If we consider carefully all the offerings we have seen so far, it becomes obvious that Google has positioned

themselves as the "go-to" vendor for advanced marketing analytics insofar as the marketing involves the Internet (old-style newspaper, television, and radio marketing are more difficult to measure, since Google does not have a direct presence in these media).

- Site and App Performance
  - Alerts and Intelligence Events
    - Google Analytics monitors a vendor's website traffic to detect significant statistical variations, and then generates alerts called Intelligence Events when they occur. A closer look brings insights that we might otherwise have missed—for example, a spike in traffic from a particular city or from a referring site. The actual statistical variation is information—the alerts are really a form of data in the form of flagging potential issues. We would still want to understand why we are receiving an alert.
  - Event Tracking
    - How do visitors actually interact with vendor pages? The vendor can use Event Tracking to measure activities such as downloads, video plays, mobile ad clicks, gadgets, Flash elements, and AJAX embedded elements. This tool provides data; the tool also requires some technical understanding of the components of a web page.
  - In-Page Analytics
    - Vendors use In-Page Analytics to see how users really interact with vendor pages. To make analysis easier, Google Analytics includes a variety of charts to display information just as you want to see it. The charts are a means to convert the data to information.
  - Site Search
    - When visitors cannot find what they want on a vendor site, they search. Site Search reporting in Google Analytics helps the vendor to see what visitors are really looking for, to spot missed opportunities, and to speed up time to conversion. This tool provides information.
  - Site-Speed Analysis

If we surveyed a host of people, we would guess that we would find that most associate Google primarily with the search engine. It is clear that

Google has leveraged its search technology to create other businesses; however, this relation begins to fray at the edges when we look at tools such as Android, the Go language, and Google Documents. If the Google strategy is not market domination, then what is it? We are not even sure the question is rhetorical!

FACEBOOK

Available from the Facebook corporate page,[6] the numbers appear as follows:

Third Quarter 2013 Operational Highlights

- Daily active users (DAUs) were 728 million on average for September 2013, an increase of 25% year-over-year.
- Monthly active users (MAUs) were 1.19 billion as of September 30, 2013, an increase of 18% year-over-year.
- Mobile MAUs were 874 million as of September 30, 2013, an increase of 45% year-over-year. Mobile DAUs were 507 million on average for September 2013.

It should be obvious from these numbers that Facebook deals with big data problems on a daily basis. Notice also the 18% year-over-year growth in monthly active users, which presents its own problems—especially when dealing with scalability.

Facebook also presents a "year in review" summary, an indication of their own big data analyses of their social networking platform, for example[7] (the lists that follow are from this reference and are archetypical examples of the use of big data):

The U.S. Year in Review
In addition to our global data, we've also curated lists about activity on Facebook specific to the U.S.

Most Talked About Topics in the U.S.

1. Super Bowl
2. Government Shutdown
3. Boston Marathon
4. Syria Crisis

5. Harlem Shake
6. Pope Francis
7. George Zimmerman
8. Royal Baby
9. Nelson Mandela
10. Presidential Inauguration
11. NBA Finals
12. Kim Kardashian
13. Miley Cyrus
14. James Gandolfini
15. Meteor Sighting

Most Talked About By Topic in the U.S.

Sports—Super Bowl
Movies—The Conjuring
TV Shows—Scandal
Music—Get Lucky by Daft Punk*
Books—"Happy, Happy, Happy: My Life and Legacy as the Duck Commander" by Phil Robertson
Games—Criminal Case by Pretty Simple Games
Public Figures—Peyton Manning
Politics—Government Shutdown
Technology—Instagram
Viral Moments—Harlem Shake
Internet Memes—Giraffe
*Most Played on Facebook via Spotify

Top Check-Ins in the U.S.

1. Disneyland and Disney California Adventure (Anaheim, CA)
2. Times Square (New York, NY)
3. Epcot–Walt Disney World (Lake Buena Vista, FL)
4. Dodger Stadium (Los Angeles, CA)
5. AT&T Park (San Francisco, CA)
6. Rangers Ballpark (Arlington, TX)
7. Universal Studios Hollywood (Universal City, CA)
8. Fenway Park (Boston, MA)
9. MGM Grand Hotel and Casino (Las Vegas, NV)
10. Houston Livestock Show and Rodeo (Houston, TX)

Top Life Events in the U.S.

1. Added a Relationship
2. Got Married

3. Got Engaged
4. Traveled
5. Moved
6. Ended a Relationship
7. Had a Baby
8. Expecting a Baby
9. First Met
10. Lost a Loved One

Facebook also provides information about their infrastructure:[8]

- Facebook is one of the largest users in the world of memcached, an open source caching system, and we have one of the largest MySQL database clusters anywhere.
- We store more than 100 petabytes (100 quadrillion bytes) of photos and videos. We've built storage and serving technologies, such as Haystack, which allow us to efficiently serve and store data.
- The engineering team developed Hip Hop for PHP - a way to transform PHP source code into highly optimized C++ code. HipHop offers significant performance gains when compared to traditional PHP.
- Apache Hive is our data warehouse infrastructure built on top of Hadoop, which provides tools to enable easy data summarization, *ad hoc* querying and analysis of large datasets.

Once again, it is clear that Facebook is using the big data tools: Hadoop, memcached, and Apache Hive. What is surprising is that they are able to use the MySQL database, which is a more traditional SQL form of database. The key word is MySQL "cluster," which means that Facebook is using a version with auto-sharding, multisite clustering, scalability, and management. Interestingly, despite "SQL" appearing in the name, the cluster version database can be accessed via NoSQL APIs.[9]

NING

Created in 2005, Ning is a platform for creating social networking platforms, so it is really a metaplatform. Up through version 3.0, Ning was a free platform. As of 3.0, Ning went after premium customers and began charging for the use of the platform. In September 2011, the product was purchased by Glam Media. A look at the history of Ning indicates a rather stormy presence over the 9 years of its existence.

TABLE 7.2

Social Media from Non-U.S. Countries

Nation	Social Platform
China	Tencent QQ
	Tencent QZone
	Sina Weibo
Estonia	Skype (owned by Microsoft)
Japan	LINE
Russia	Odnoklassniki
	VKontakte
The Netherlands	Nimbuzz

NON-UNITED STATES SOCIAL MEDIA

The US-based social media sites are not the only communities available. For example, the breakdown in Table 7.2 indicates country of origin.

Tencent

Tencent QQ is available internationally at http://www.imqq.com/. Its website makes it clear that they intend to play the market multilingually by supplying social media in English, French, Japanese, German, and Korean, with more on the way.

Tencent's leading Internet platforms in China—QQ (QQ Instant Messenger), WeChat, QQ.com, QQ Games, Qzone, 3g.QQ.com, SoSo, PaiPai, and Tenpay—are China's largest Internet community. The company's products are designed to meet the various needs of Internet users including communication, information, entertainment, e-commerce, and others. As of December 31, 2012, the active QQ users' accounts for QQ IM amounted to 798.2 million, while its peak concurrent users reached 176.4 million.[10]

Tencent Qzone, on investigation, appears to be Chinese only, given that the pages show up in the Chinese language rather than the choice of English or other languages.

LINE

LINE is oriented toward instant messaging, as well as a line of apps and games. From its website presence, LINE appears to play to English speakers, at a minimum, while also providing support for Vietnamese, Melayu, Hindi, Turkish, Russian, German, Spanish, Indonesian, Portuguese, Italian, and French speakers. It also appears to be able to present in Devanagari, Chinese, and Korean characters. European languages use either Roman or Cyrillic characters.

Sina Weibo

Weibo (www.weibo.com) is a Twitter-like web application that seems to make minimal effort to present a European face to users. In short, it is basically Chinese only.

Odnoklassniki

Odnoklassniki (www.odnoklassniki.ru) supports Russian, German, and English as far as the presentation of their corporate information applies. It supplies e-commerce tools, media projects, navigational services, e-mail, instant messaging, social networking, and games. Its website indicates 13 million users of instant messaging and 115 million users of its mail service. It indicates that it is the largest Russian online game provider, with at least 34 massive multiplayer online games. It also supports services in English, Russian, Uzbekistan, Azerbaijan, Romania, and a few others.

VKontakte

VKontakte appears very much like a Facebook application, with over 100 million active users. It is headquartered in St. Petersburg, Russia.

Nimbuzz

Nimbuzz (http://www.nimbuzz.com/en/) provides instant messaging aggregation for smartphones, tablets, and personal computers. Its website indicates that it provides support for Android, iPhone, Blackberry, Windows, Nokia, Java, and Kindle Fire. In addition, Nimbuzz provides chat rooms. It appears that a portion of the service is very similar to Skype, providing for both dialing out and receiving telephone messages as well as the transfer of data.

N-world is a subdivision of Nimbuzz that provides gifts, avatars, chat buddy, and games. The software is available for Linux, Macintosh, Windows, and nearly every phone platform.

Nimbuzz: Pulse of the Nation! (http://nimbuzz.org/) is a subdivision that deals specifically with the Indian subcontinent. It provides for opinion polls and has over 25 million users.

RANKING NETWORK SITES

The primary source for web ranking is Alexa. A quick look at Alexa's top 25 websites (www.alexa.com/topsites) appeared in March 2014 as follows:

1. google.com
2. facebook.com
3. youtube.com
4. yahoo.com
5. baidu.com (Chinese search engine)
6. wikipedia.org
7. qq.com
8. linkedin.com
9. taobao.com (customer-to-customer marketing, Chinese)
10. twitter.com
11. live.com (Microsoft search engine)
12. amazon.com
13. sina.com.cn
14. google.co.in (Indian Google)
15. hao123.com
16. blogspot.com
17. weibo.com
18. wordpress.com
19. yandex.ru
20. yahoo.co.jp
21. bing.com
22. tmall.com (Chinese online shopping)
23. 360.cn
24. vk.com (VKontakte)
25. ebay.com

One item of immediate interest is the presence of Google in more than one location in the top 25 (YouTube is a Google product).

Alexa itself is a big data vendor, providing website analytics for its customers. Its ranking derives from 30 million websites across the world, which is not exhaustive, but probably represents the 30 million top websites (assuming a Pareto distribution of website activity). Alexa uses a rolling classification system that bases its results on data derived from the most recent quarterly traffic. We should also note that Alexa is domain-name dependent; in short, it picks up on all subdomains of a given domain. Some of Google's divisions, for example, have their own domains, particularly if they were acquired through purchase.

Alexa itself is an Amazon company and has been since 1999. It retains its own president and management staff, most of whom have strong technical backgrounds educationally as well as in terms of career development. Alexa is cautious regarding measurement biases because rankings are tied to the use of its toolbar. It makes note that accuracy improves with the volume of visitors, and users should not put a whole lot of credence in very small site rankings. As of 2008, Alexa claims that it uses more data sources than the toolbar.[11]

NEGATIVE ISSUES WITH SOCIAL NETWORKS

One issue that one of us has witnessed personally is the vituperative presence of "cyberbullies" on Facebook in particular (although Twitter is open to this problem as well). In the particular instance to which we refer, the individual committed suicide after announcing in somewhat misleading language that this was the individual's goal. Further investigation—before the pages were taken down—indicated that this individual was "dishing it out" as well as taking it. In the United States, issues like commentary on social networks are theoretically protected by the First Amendment to the Constitution; however, the United States also has laws regarding slander and libel. One question, then, regards the nature of privacy: does the social network provider have the responsibility to track communication on its own social network using big data tools such as machine learning? We suggest that some of these issues will ultimately go to the US Supreme Court for elucidation. On the other side of the coin, we suggest that the market may be the most effective means of control for these kinds of hurtful shenanigans.

LinkedIn took steps to control "stalking" on their network by implementing privacy controls.[12] We know this situation had become an issue when one of our wives inadvertently accepted a link from someone trolling for unhappy women. LinkedIn made their decision in February 2014, while under pressure from a group of individuals who felt that they were victims of cyberstalking. A portion of LinkedIn's announcement reads as follows:

> Hi everyone, my name is Paul Rockwell, and I head up Trust and Safety at LinkedIn. We know members have requested a blocking feature on LinkedIn. I come to you today to assure you that your concerns were heard loud and clear. We built this feature not only because it was a feature our members requested, but because we also knew it was the right thing to do. I'm pleased to share that we are rolling out a new Member Blocking feature today to all LinkedIn members.
>
> While on the surface this may seem like a simple feature to develop, it was not. There were many different use cases to consider, products and features to integrate, as well as a user interface we had to create.
>
> In addition to Member Blocking, there are also a number of other LinkedIn settings that you may want to consider such as:
>
> - *Disconnecting*: This provides you with the ability to remove any existing connection to another member in your network.
> - *Customize Your Public Profile*: This provides you with control over the profile content that's discoverable by search engines.
> - *Activity Broadcasts*: This provides you with control whether others can see updates to your profile, recommendations made and companies followed.
> - *Photo Visibility*: This provides you with control over who can see your profile photo.
> - *Profile Viewing*: This alters what others see when you visit their profile.
>
> Before you decide to block another member, we recommend you enable anonymous profile viewing (the last bullet listed above).[13]

The primary source of complaints about LinkedIn's step to implement blocking is related to "anonymous" viewing, a feature of their free Basic account. Those with paying accounts can generally see who has viewed their profile and when. It is also important to note that LinkedIn appear to be the only significant social network that alerts users to the fact that they have been scanned over by others.

AMAZON

Amazon has become a true big data vendor, both in providing services via Amazon Web Services and using big data approaches itself. Amazon has gone from online bookstore to general store:

- Automotive
- Books
- Camera and photo
- Contractor supply
- Desktops and servers
- Exercise and fitness
- Gift cards
- Gourmet gifts
- Grocery
- Industrial and scientific
- Laptops and netbooks
- Magazines
- Movies and TV
- Musical instruments
- Office products and supplies
- Paper store
- Printers and ink
- Software
- Tools and home improvement
- TV and video
- Video games

Amazon started in business (http://phx.corporate-ir.net/phoenix. zhtml?c=97664&p=irol-faq) circa 1995. We were aware of it even then, since the bookstore made available a much larger array of titles than was available at Waldenbooks, B. Dalton, and Barnes & Noble as well as others, many of which have fallen by the wayside. Amazon.com went public in 1997 at \$18.00 per share. Current Amazon share prices run well over \$300.00. The only significant decline occurred during the 2001–2002 dot-com bust. If we invested \$18.00 in 1997, 17 years later we would have increased our portfolio by 2000%!!! Amazon has expressed their philosophy as follows:

- *Focus relentlessly on our customers.*
- *Make bold investment decisions in light of long-term leadership considerations rather than short-term profitability considerations.* There is more innovation ahead of us than behind us, and to that end, we are committed to extending our leadership in e-commerce in a way that benefits customers and therefore, inherently, investors—you can't do one without the other. Some of these bold investments will pay off, others will not, but we will have learned a valuable lesson in either case.
- *Focus on cash.* When forced to choose between optimizing the appearance of our GAAP accounting and maximizing the present value of future cash flows, we'll take the cash flows.
- *Work hard to spend wisely and maintain our lean culture.* We understand the importance of continually reinforcing a cost-conscious culture.
- *Focus on hiring and retaining versatile and talented employees, and weight their compensation to significant stock ownership rather than cash.* We know our success will be largely affected by our ability to attract and retain a motivated employee base, each of whom must think like, and therefore must actually be, an owner.[14]

Amazon's focus on cash reflects a conservative approach to growth. The use of stock ownership as an incentive makes employees literally invested in the business, effectively making them into capitalists. It is clear from this almost-manifesto that Amazon's philosophy is oriented toward long-term profitability rather than pleasing Wall Street pundits.

Much like Wal-Mart Corporation, Amazon has had an influence on logistics, building massive distribution centers in 14 of the 50 United States, not to mention offices for subsidiaries such as Alexa, Zappos, IMDb, and others. Other locations for what Amazon calls "fulfillment" centers are located in:

- Canada (2)
- Luxembourg (1)

- Germany (7)
- Ireland (1)
- The Netherlands (1)
- Italy (1)
- Romania (development center)
- Slovakia (corporate office)
- Spain (1)
- Sweden (Amazon Web Services)
- United Kingdom (8), corporate offices, two development centers, and one customer service center
- China (8) plus a corporate headquarters and a customer service center in Beijing
- India has three development centers and one customer service center
- Japan (9), a corporate headquarters, and two customer service centers
- South Africa has a development center
- Egypt has a book depository in Alexandria (the irony lying in the fact that this city was the location of the largest Mediterranean library of ancient times)
- Morocco has one customer service center
- Costa Rica has two customer service centers
- Brazil has a data center
- Australia has two sets of corporate offices

As with Google, Amazon's presence is truly global in its reach. Also, to some extent, the number of fulfillment centers can be an indication of the health of that country's economy. While most of us might consider Barnes & Noble to be Amazon's primary competitor, it is obvious that Amazon has competitors on many fronts: clothing, shoes, toys, games, sporting equipment, home goods, food, appliances, and more.

Even if we only look at the bookselling part of the Amazon business, we might conclude that Amazon's bestseller listings are probably more meaningful than those of the *New York Times* or any other source simply because Amazon receives their data in real time and because their presence is huge.

In addition, Amazon has purchased other online vendors; for example:

- 6pm: deals with fashion brands
- Abebooks: rare books and textbooks

- Afterschool.com: kids' sports, outdoor, and dance gear
- Alexa: actionable analytics for the web
- Amazonfresh: groceries and more right to your door
- Amazon local: great local deals in your city
- Amazonsupply: business, industrial, and scientific supplies
- Amazon Web Services: scalable cloud computing services
- Audible [sic]: download audiobooks
- Beautybar.com: prestige beauty delivered
- Book Depository: books with free delivery worldwide
- Bookworm.com: books for children of all ages
- Casa.com: kitchen, storage, and everything home
- Createspace: indie print publishing made easy
- Diapers.com: everything but the baby
- DPReview: digital photography
- East Dane: designer men's fashion
- Fabric: sewing, quilting, and knitting
- Imdb: movies, TV, and celebrities
- Junglee.com: shop online in India
- Kindle direct publishing: indie digital publishing made easy
- Look.com: kids' clothing and shoes
- Myhabit: private fashion designer sales
- Shopbop: designer fashion brands
- Soap.com: health, beauty, and home essentials
- Tenmarks.com: math activities for kids and schools
- Vine.com: everything to live life green
- Wag.com: everything for your pet
- Warehouse deals: open-box discounts
- Woot!: discounts and shenanigans
- Yoyo.com: a happy place to shop for toys
- Zappos: shoes and clothing

We were stunned when we began our research to see how vast both Google and Amazon have become. Interestingly, a look at Amazon's cash flow reporting shows the Christmas season effect, with over $2 billion in free cash flow in 2013. The return on invested capital is 13% and net sales approached $26 billion for the fourth quarter of 2013. Amazon does not issue dividends on their common stock, preferring to retain earnings for further investment in their business.

SOME FINAL WORDS

By now, it should be obvious that the single most significant impact of big data occurs through Google, with Facebook probably a distant second. We say this because Google provides applications, white papers that have shaped an industry (MapReduce), methods, tools, companies, links, and more. The influence of Google is vast. Android, for example, has eclipsed all other mobile OSs, with an 80+% market share. Highlight Press made the following comment in November 2013:

> Android's unstoppable rise is proving to be exactly that, with the world-leading mobile OS having broken through the 80% market share threshold for the very first time. Or, in other words, for every 10 Smartphones now shipped on a global basis, no less than eight are running Google's Android operating system.
>
> Yesterday brought the release of the latest Worldwide Quarterly Mobile Phone Tracker by IDC, which includes a detailed breakdown of global Smartphone sales activity for Q3. An impressive 261.1 million Smartphone sales were recorded during the three months, of which a staggering 81% were running one of the many builds of Android currently doing the rounds.[15]

Android also runs on touch-screen notepad computers. The advent of Android becomes even more interesting when we note that it is primarily installed on systems driven by ARM processors and not the Intel x86 family of processors that dominated the small computing market for over 20 years.

Other Google tools may result in great changes; for example, the Go language represents a high-performance native code compiler with relatively straightforward syntax and simple installation. While Go may be restricted to developers, it remains to be seen where developers will take this tool. In general, languages seem to take off when they accrue enough libraries to support moneymaking activities: games, enterprise applications, security, and so on.

Google is also clearly a huge component of Internet advertising, particularly with AdSense, AdWords, and Google Analytics.

Amazon runs a close second to Google in swing power. Just about anything that these companies do becomes significant. It is clear, however, that Google will occasionally clear the air and drop a product or product line that is not doing well; for example, Google dropped their RSS reader for reasons unknown to most users.

REFERENCES

1 Google. About company: Google. 2014. http://www.google.com/about/company/. Accessed March 21, 2014.

2 Google. Ten things we know to be true. http://www.google.com/about/company/philosophy/. Accessed February 22, 2014.

3 The Go Programming Language. Creative Commons. http://golang.org/doc/. Accessed March 15, 2014.

4 Vision Mobile Ltd. Developer economics Q3 2013. http://www.visionmobile.com/product/developer-economics-q3-2013-state-of-the-developer-nation/. Accessed February 22, 2014.

5 Black Duck Software. Android. The Open Source Project on Ohloh: Languages Page. 2014. http://www.ohloh.net/p/android/analyses/latest/languages_summary. Accessed February 22, 2014.

6 Facebook. Investor relations. SEC filings. 2013. http://investor.fb.com/sec.cfm. Accessed January 26, 2014.

7 Facebook. Newsroom. 2013 year in review. 2014. http://newsroom.fb.com/Trends/770/2013-Year-in-Review. Accessed January 26, 2014.

8 Facebook. Newsroom. Infrastructure. 2014. https://www.facebook.com/ServerWarrior/posts/491198350922120. Accessed January 26, 2014.

9 Oracle. MySQL cluster: Scalability. MySQL. 2014. http://www.mysql.com/products/cluster/scalability.html. Accessed January 26, 2014.

10 Tencent. About Tencent. 2013. http://www.tencent.com/en-us/at/abouttencent.shtml. Accessed March 6, 2014.

11 Hickey, M. Alexa overhauls ranking system. TechCrunch. April 16, 2008. http://techcrunch.com/2008/04/16/alexa-overhauls-ranking-system/. Accessed March 6, 2014.

12 Warzel, C. LinkedIn finally tries to fix its stalker problem. BuzzFeed. February 21, 2014. http://www.buzzfeed.com/charliewarzel/linkedin-tries-to-fix-its-stalker-problem. Accessed March 6, 2014.

13 Rockwell, P. LinkedIn announces member blocking. LinkedIn Help Center. February 20, 2014. http://community.linkedin.com/questions/156990/linkedin-announces-member-blocking.html. Accessed March 6, 2014.

14 Amazon. Amazon.com investor relations: Corporate governance—Message to shareholders. 2014. http://phx.corporate-ir.net/phoenix.zhtml?c=97664&p=irol-govHighlights. Accessed March 7, 2014.

15 Harper, T. Android tops 80% global smartphone market share—Windows phone up 156% year on year. Highlight Press. November 13, 2013. http://www.highlightpress.com/android-tops–80-global-smartphone-market-share-windows-phone-up–156-year-on-year/6708/tharper. Accessed March 6, 2014.

8

Geographic Information Systems (GIS)

We suggest that geographical information systems (GIS) are either big data situations or have the potential to become a big data tool. We know from global positioning system (GPS) use that a lot of data can be compressed and used in relatively small memory. However, most GPS use is regional, which cuts down on some of the data storage requirements. Even if we blanket the globe with degree-minute-second information for latitude and longitude, we still may not be looking at a true big data problem.

Our calculations appear in Table 8.1. The use of degrees is relatively trivial and, most likely, not too useful since a degree of latitude is roughly 69 miles and a degree of longitude is roughly 69 miles, as well (at the equator). At seconds, we come within a few meters of what we want (at worst). The size of the problem at worst is approximately 840 trillion units, which is at least a quasi–big data situation. We suggest that it quickly becomes a big data situation when we store any support data at all:

- Elevation
- Type of surface (e.g., rock, loam, sea)
- Population
- Roads
- Rivers

Clearly, a full-scale GIS database enters the realm of big data quickly. If we start cataloging other objects (moon, planets, and so forth), we expand on our problem, but we leave the world of "geo," which means "earth."

We should note that surveillance, for example, also enters the realm of big data because if we are using a GIS, we are recording location data, times, dates, individuals or license plates observed, and whatever else the cameras can pick up, including the images themselves. Hence, any

TABLE 8.1

Granularity of Geographical Units

Type	Degrees	Minutes	Seconds
Latitude	180	10,800	648,000
Longitude	360	21,600	1,296,000
	64,800	233,280,000	839,808,000,000

significant GIS implementation that includes more than simple location data moves into the big data universe.

It is also possible for GIS use to be dynamic; for example, a realty company might use a GIS and update sales numbers on the hour to try to and detect hot spots in the region (the alternative being to find cold spots where no sales seem to occur. Other dynamic information uses would be

- Border crossings
  - Drug interdiction (hot spots!)
  - Illegal immigrant movement
  - Routine crossers
- Train movement
- Aircraft location
- Utility information
  - Voltage and current values
  - Water pressures
  - Gas pressures
- Air quality
  - Pollen
  - Pollution
  - Dust storms

GIS IMPLEMENTATIONS

As computers have become more sophisticated, we have seen an increase in GIS implementations:

- Autodesk (commercial) (http://www.autodesk.com/products/autocad-map-3d/overview): This is an enterprise spatial data (GIS) server providing data integrity, management, and analysis capabilities for enterprises that need multiple users (tens to hundreds) to work concurrently on a single spatial database that can also store nonspatial data.

- Cadcorp (commercial) (http://www.cadcorp.com): This is a UK firm that provides GIS/web mapping software, as well as spatial information management.
- Capaware (http://www.capaware.org): This open-source three-dimensional geographical framework is available for Linux. Instituto Tecnologico de Canarias (ITC) developed it in concert with the commercial company InventiaPlus.
- Chameleon (http://chameleon.maptools.org/index.phtml): This tool is built on MapServer and is a development environment for web mapping applications.
- Deegree (http://www.deegree.org): Open-source software for spatial data infrastructures and the geospatial web; it includes components for geospatial data management, including data access, visualization, discovery, and security.
- Erdas Imagine (commercial) (http://www.hexagongeospatial.com/products/remote-sensing/erdas-imagine/overview): Currently owned by Intergraph, this has been around in one form or another since the 1970s.
- Esri ArcGIS (commercial) (http://www.esri.com/software/arcgis): Esri is a major player, supplying mapping support to numerous municipalities in CompStat types of implementation. In 2013, France TVsport used ArcGIS to show the progress of the Tour de France bicycle race as well as tie locations to photographs.
- GeoBase (commercial) (http://www.geobase.ca/geobase/en/): GeoBase is a Canadian federal, provincial, and territorial government initiative, overseen by the Canadian Council on Geomatics (CCOG). It is apparently not open source, but it makes data available at no cost and with no restrictions to users.
- Geomajas (http://www.geomajas.org): Geomajas is a free and open-source GIS framework that integrates server-side algorithms into the web browser and includes features such as
  - Integrated client–server architecture
  - Geometry and attribute editing
  - Custom attribute definitions
  - Advanced querying capabilities (CQL)
  - Out-of-the-box security
  - Extensible plug-in mechanism
  - Multiple front-end technologies
  - Cross-browser support, without the need for browser plug-ins

- GeoNetwork (http://geonetwork-opensource.org): This tool is a catalog application to manage spatially referenced resources, with a web interface and substantial support for international standards.
- GeoServer (http://geoserver.org): GeoServer is an open-source software server written in Java that allows users to share and edit geospatial data. GeoServer is the reference implementation of the Open Geospatial Consortium (OGC) Web Feature Service (WFS) and Web Coverage Service (WCS) standards, as well as a high-performance certified compliant Web Map Service (WMS). GeoServer forms a core component of the Geospatial Web.
- GeoTools (http://www.geotools.org): GeoTools is an open-source Java library that provides tools for geospatial data.
- GRASS (http://grass.osgeo.org): GRASS GIS, referred to simply as Geographic Resources Analysis Support System (GRASS), is free GIS software used for geospatial data management and analysis, image processing, graphics and map production, spatial modeling, and visualization.
- gvSIG (http://www.osgeo.org/gvsig): gvSIG is a GIS for capturing, storing, handling, analyzing, and deploying any kind of referenced geographic information. gvSIG is known for being able to access the most common formats, both vector and raster.
- ClarkLabs IDRISI (commercial) (http://clarklabs.org): IDRISI is a software system for the analysis and display of spatial data: GIS, image processing, surface analysis, vertical application for land change analysis, and earth trends exploration. IDRISI appears to have a strong seasonality analyzer.
- IBM ILOG JViews Maps (commercial) (http://www-01.ibm.com/software/integration/visualization/jviews/maps/):
  - Customizable map display components
  - Point-and-click tools
  - Background map data from all major formats
  - Handles very large data sets
  - Ready-to-tailor map application
  - Software development kit included
  - Deployable as Java desktop clients, inside an Eclipse application, or as applets or Ajax-enhanced thin clients
- ITC ILWIS (http://www.itc.nl/Pub/Home/Research/Research_output/ILWIS_-_Remote_Sensing_and_GIS_software.html): ILWIS

comprises a complete package of image processing, spatial analysis, and digital mapping. It is easy to learn and use; it has full online help, extensive tutorials for direct use in courses, and 25 case studies of various disciplines. It is a product of the Faculty of Geo-Information Science and Earth Observation at the University of Twente.

- OpenJUMP GIS (http://www.openjump.org): OpenJUMP is an open-source GIS written in the Java programming language. It is developed and maintained by a group of volunteers from around the globe. OpenJUMP started as JUMP GIS, designed by Vivid Solutions.
- Saig Kosmo (http://www.saig.es): A Spanish firm (Saig) developed Kosmo. The Kosmo Project is a free GIS platform.
- LandSerf (http://www.soi.city.ac.uk/~jwo/landserf/): LandSerf is a freely available GIS for the visualization and analysis of surfaces. Applications include visualization of landscapes, geomorphological analysis, gaming development, GIS file conversion, map output, archaeological mapping and analysis, surface modeling, and many others. Since it is Java-based, it runs on any platform that supports Java.
- MapDotNet (commercial) (http://www.mapdotnet.com): A variety of municipalities and real estate and other organizations use this software. MapDotNet appears to be well integrated with various Microsoft toolboxes: SQLServer, Silverlight, and more.
- Manifold System (commercial) (http://www.manifold.net): Manifold GIS is a combination of mapping, CAD, database management systems, and image processing.
- Google Earth (earth.google.com): Google Earth does not directly provide the level of manipulation of many GIS packages, but it is perhaps the most readily available GIS for general users. The "pro" version of Google Earth supports distance measurements, area measurement and three-dimensional measurements, as well as commercial property analysis.
- Pitney Bowes MapInfo (commercial) (www.mapinfo.com): Pitney Bowes's software division provides multiple GIS products targeted at the desktop, the server, and the web. Pitney Bowes uses a wonderful neologism: "location intelligence."
- UMN MapServer (mapserver.org): MapServer is an open-source platform for publishing spatial data and interactive mapping applications to the web. It was originally developed in the mid-1990s at the University of Minnesota.

- Caliper Maptitude (commercial) (http://www.caliper.com/maptovu. htm): Maptitude is a full-featured GIS implementation, presenting both maps and table tools to accelerate development.
- Caliper TransCAD (commercial) (http://www.caliper.com/tcovu.htm): This Caliper product is designed to support transportation analysis.
- Caliper TransModeler (commercial) (http://www.caliper.com/trans-modeler/): Transmodeler is used in traffic simulation. It is truly a GIS tool because two-dimensional and three-dimensional GIS data can be used.
- MapWindow GIS (http://www.mapwindow.org): The MapWindow GIS project includes a free and open-source desktop GIS with an extensible plug-in architecture, a GIS ActiveX control, and a C# GIS programmer library called DotSpatial. This project is C++-based and uses ActiveX controls, so we are talking Windows-only software.
- Microsoft MapPoint (commercial) (http://www.microsoft.com/map-point/en-us/home.aspx): Microsoft advertises MapPoint for North America and Europe. The product appears to be targeted at personal users and small commercial enterprises.
- ThinkGeo Map Suite (commercial) (http://thinkgeo.com): The ThinkGeo product is Windows-based, with use of the "ribbon" for editing and basic mapping tools as well as GPS integration.
- Oracle Spatial (commercial) (http://www.oracle.com/us/products/database/options/spatial/overview/index.html): The Oracle Spatial and Graph option for Oracle Database 12c includes advanced features for spatial data and analysis; physical, network, and social graph applications; and a foundation to help location-enable business applications. Not surprisingly, Oracle support is dominated by the database, providing the foundation for other GIS implementations.
- Mapdiva Artboard (commercial) (www.mapdiva.com): Mapdiva Artboard is an adjunct to Ortelius (if desired) for the Apple Macintosh and it provides vector graphics. (We include it here because it works with other Mapdiva products.)
- Mapdiva Ortelius (commercial) (www.mapdiva.com): This tool appears to be a map publishing tool available specifically for the Apple Macintosh.
- Panorama (commercial) (http://www.gisinfo.net/): Panorama consists of products for Windows and Linux, which include
  - Professional GIS Map 2011
  - Desktop GIS Map 2011

- GIS WebServer
- Professional vectorizer Panorama-editor
- Block of geodetic calculations
- Program of construction of orthophotomaps Photopian 2005
- Surface editor
- GIS view
- Realty (for some detail because it shows the possibilities inherent in GIS)
  - Inventory of property and resources of realty
  - Information support for acceptance or rejection of administrative decisions
  - Optimization of work of municipal and public services
  - Improvement of interfaces and relationships of state and commercial structures
  - Increase of tax collections on property, taxes with operations with the realty, and payments for municipal services
- GIS Toolkit (Windows)
- Panorama Mobile
- PostGIS (http://postgis.net/): PostGIS extends PostgreSQL, which is a hybrid object-relational database (while the SQL orientation suggests this approach is not oriented around bBig dData, PostgreSQL has a project—AXLE—designed specifically to implement big data algorithms, and the AXLE updates are expected in 2014).
- Quantum GIS (www.qgis.org/en/site): Quantum GIS (QGIS) is an open-source GIS licensed under the GNU General Public License; QGIS is an official project of the Open Source Geospatial Foundation (OSGeo), and it runs on Linux, Unix, Mac OS X, Windows, and Android and supports numerous vector, raster, and database formats and functionalities. It uses PostgreSQL.
  - QGIS Desktop
  - QGIS Browser
  - QGIS Server
  - QGIS Web Client
  - QGIS Android
- RegioGraph (commercial) (http://www.regiograph.de/en/homepage. html): RegioGraph is a product for visualizing customer locations and analyzing data, sales territories, and decision support. Currently, it does not appear to support big data applications because it works specifically with "personal" databases (e.g., Microsoft Access).

- RemoteView (commercial) (http://www.transvoyant.com/technology/spatialfx/): RemoteView for international customers is a solution among imagery and GIS users for the import, viewing, analysis, and reporting of commercial remote sensing data. RemoteView combines high-speed processing chain technology with a carefully refined user interface to enhance work flow and boost productivity on the largest images, videos, and data sets. Overwatch has other spatial products for the military intelligence market. It is a specialized vendor.

- Smallworld (http://www.gedigitalenergy.com/GIS.htm): Smallworld is the brand name of a portfolio of GIS software provided by GE Energy, a division of General Electric. Not surprisingly, the tool has strong support for the utility industry: electric, gas and pipeline, water supply and drainage, and telecommunications. The website claims substantial savings for each form of utility and documentation clearly identifies Oracle Spatial as one major resource. The software will also work with Google Maps. The variety of product offerings and solutions appears to be substantial.

- SpatialFX ObjectFX (commercial) (http://www.transvoyant.com/tag/spatialfx/): TransVoyant provides tools for security and intelligence uses, (their website does not make it clear if it supports massive data sets).
  - Health care and life sciences
  - High tech
  - Homeland security and public safety
  - Manufacturing and industrial
  - Mobile applications
  - National security and intelligence
  - Retail and consumer marketing
  - Supply chain and logistics

- SpatialRules|ObjectFX (commercial): SpatialRules is another TransVoyant (see above) product designed for use with the intelligence community, making it clear to which niche TransVoyant markets.

- SPRING (http://www.dpi.inpe.br/spring/english/): SPRING is a state-of-the-art GIS and remote sensing image processing system with an object-oriented data model that provides for the integration of raster and vector data representations in a single environment. SPRING is a product of Brazil's National Institute for Space Research, among others. Unfortunately, the website shows 2008 as the last date for an update.

- TerraLib TerraView (http://www.terralib.org/): TerraLib is a GIS classes and functions library, available from the Internet as open source, permitting a collaborative environment for the development of multiple GIS tools. Its purpose is to enable development of a new form of GIS applications, based on the technological advances on spatial databases. TerraLib is free software. TerraLib is being developed by the image processing division (DPI) at the National Institute for Space Research in Brazil (INPE), Tecgraf, the Computer Graphics Technology Group of PUC-Rio (the Pontifical Catholic University of Rio de Janeiro in Brazil), and FUNCATE (Foundation for Space Science, Applied Research and Technology). Terralib appears to be the up-to-date follow-on to SPRING.
- MicroImages TNTmips (commercial) (http://www.microimages. com/products/tntmips.htm): TNTmips is MicroImages's flagship product for geospatial analysis. TNTmips is a professional system for fully integrated GIS, advanced image processing, CAD, triangular irregular networks, desktop cartography, geospatial visualization, geospatial database management, and more. The product works with MySQL Spatial, PostGIS, and Oracle Spatial. uDig (http://udig. refractions.net/): uDig is an open-source (EPL and BSD) desktop application framework, built with Eclipse Rich Client (RCP) technology. The name is an acronym:
  - User-friendly, providing a familiar graphical environment for GIS users
  - Desktop located, running as a thick client, natively on Windows, Mac OS X, and Linux
  - Internet-oriented, consuming standard (WMS, WFS, WPS) and de facto (GeoRSS, KML, tiles) geospatial web services
  - GIS ready, providing the framework on which complex analytical capabilities can be built and gradually subsuming those capabilities into the main application
- AvisMap GIS Engine (commercial) (http://www.avismap.com/): AvisMap GIS Technologies is a GIS company in Asia, specializing in the development of GIS, including GIS mapping software, maps, mapping, GIS, GIS software development kits, developer GIS, geographic information systems, executives, IT professionals, developers, GIS practitioners, desktop GIS, server GIS, developer GIS, mobile GIS, spatial database, and spatial database engines.

A GIS EXAMPLE

We have chosen to focus on Esri, the developer of ArcGIS. ArcGIS is a successful product that has been used in some CompStat implementations as well as many other areas. The Esri website indicates the number of industries that use their product (www.esri.com/industries):

- Aid and development
  - Humanitarian aid
  - Sustainable development
- Business
  - Insurance
  - Retail
  - Real Estate
  - Banking
  - Marketing
  - Media
- Defense and intelligence
  - Defense and force health protection
  - Enterprise GIS
  - Geospatial intelligence
  - Installations and environment
  - Military operations (command, control, communications, computers, intelligence, surveillance and reconnaissance [C4ISR])
- Education
  - Libraries and museums
  - Schools (K-12)
  - Universities and community colleges
- Government
  - Federal, state, local
  - Architecture, engineering, and construction (AEC)
  - Economic development
  - Elections and redistricting
  - Facilities
  - Land administration
  - Public works
  - Surveying
  - Urban and regional planning

- Health and human services
  - Public health
  - Human services
  - Hospital and health systems
  - Managed care
  - Academic programs and research
- Mapping and charting
  - Aeronautical
  - Cartographic
  - Nautical
  - Topographic
- Natural resources
  - Agriculture
  - Climate change
  - Conservation
  - Environmental management
  - Forestry
  - Mining
  - Oceans
  - Petroleum
  - Water resources
- Public safety
  - Emergency call taking and dispatch
  - Emergency/disaster management
  - Fire, rescue, and emergency Medical Services
  - Homeland/national security
  - Law enforcement
  - Wildland fire management
- Transportation
  - Aviation
  - Highways
  - Logistics
  - Railways
  - Ports and maritime
  - Public transit
- Utilities and communications
  - Electric
  - Gas
  - Location-based services

- Pipeline
- Telecommunications
- Water/wastewater

One of us is working on a (slow) project to see if mapping of student incidents in a school district can identify problem areas, much like the way CompStat systems identify areas where crimes seem to be concentrated. Esri indicates that its GIS tools are used in academic institutions, but we see more use for GIS as a support for CompStat operations. Examples of how we think GIS could be used in a school district are as follows:

- Bus routes (and optimization thereof)
- Crimes
- Building locations
- Fire station locations versus school locations
- School location versus supermarkets, fast-food restaurants, and others
- High school, middle school, elementary school feeder patterns
- Poverty demographics
- Scholarship demographics
- Utility maps
  - Gas lines
  - Electric
  - Phone
  - Water
- Customs and border protection issues, (if in a border town)
- Police stations
- Religious institutions
- Fund-raising opportunities and history

The previous list is a quick assessment of possibilities attainable with a sophisticated GIS connected to a well-kept database.

Esri provides a really nice example of 4H students mapping a cemetery (http://www.directionsmag.com/articles/4-h-community-mapping-the-story-of-a-local-cemetery-project/197461) using GPS and a mapping tool as well as modification of legacy data from a DOS-based system into a Microsoft Excel spreadsheet. The online article indicates some lessons learned from the activity:[1]

1. As with any project, planning is imperative. All stakeholders need to be in the planning session, including 4-H youth and potential project mentors.
2. Open and ongoing communication needs to be established from Day 1.
3. Start with skill-appropriate projects to reduce frustration. Marking a trail using GPS may take a day or two and use 150 records, while a cemetery project requires a longer-term, continuing commitment and may include more than 25,000 records.
4. The right mentors and project partners may mean the difference between a project that frustrates and fails and one that satisfies and succeeds.
5. Not all youth come into a project with the same interest level. Try to develop backup activities for those youth whose interest wanes. For example, some youth may enjoy doing tombstone rubbings of interesting markers or researching some of the people buried in their local cemeteries. Others may take an interest in restoring or maintaining forgotten cemeteries.

The point we are making is that GIS use is only limited by the imagination. We also suggest it is truly a big data issue because it takes special tools to process the data and, in the case of school districts and other government entities, the amount of data can easily soar to millions of records and, in the state of Texas, possibly much more.

GIS TOOLS

Professional GIS workers can use a mature tool like ArcGIS in a variety of venues:

- ArcGIS Online
- ArcGIS for Desktop
- ArcGIS for Mobile
- ArcGIS for Server

Location analytics provides data visualization and geographic intelligence for business analytics systems:

- Esri Maps for Office
- Esri Maps for IBM Cognos
- Esri Maps for SharePoint
- Esri Maps for Dynamics CRM
- Esri Maps for MicroStrategy
- Esri Business Analyst
- Esri Community Analyst

Note that these capabilities are available "out of the box."

Esri also has connections to the OpenStreetMap project (www.open-streetmap.org), a user-created web map that is freely available. It does not appear to have the resolution of Google Maps, but it does maintain a library of GPS traces, which is useful for bicyclists, runners, and serious walkers, among others.

Getting to Know ArcGIS[2] provides an overview of GIS principles, as well as a highly detailed introduction to ArcGIS. The principles, which apply to any GIS, are

- GIS maps contain layers.
- Layers contain features or surfaces.
- Features have the attributes of shape and size.
- Surfaces are composed of numeric values rather than shapes (elevation, slope, temperature, rainfall, and more)
- Features have locations.
- We can display features at different sizes (degrees of magnification)
- Features are linked to information. (aha!)
- Features have spatial relationships.
- New features arise from regions of overlap.

In one of the examples in the book, we see a small table with 256 records with 11 attribute columns. The example is intended for learning, not production use. If we were to look at a simple database of school districts in Texas, we would find the following column headers:

- OBJECTID,N,9,0
- DISTRICT,C,6
- DISTNAME,C,42
- CAMPUS,C,10
- CAMPNAME,C,42

- STREET_MAI,C,50
- CITY_MAIL,C,50
- ZIP_MAIL,C,10
- STREET,C,50
- CITY,C,50
- ZIP,C,10
- COUNTY,C,3
- CNTYNAME,C,25
- REGION,C,2
- GRADERANGE,C,50
- GRADEGRP,C,1
- VERIFY,C,1
- INSTR_TYPE,C,30
- STREET_M_1,C,50

This database has fewer than 8500 records, sufficient to list every school district and school in the state of Texas. Now let us take a look at the size of the problem, whether it is a big data problem, and how we might find value in using data with a GIS. We take a look at data pulled from the National Center for Educational Statistics (Tables 8.2 through 8.6).

We have, in Texas, roughly speaking, 5 million students and 335,000 teachers (current) in grades preK–12. If each teacher puts in 20 years of receiving one paycheck per month, we have 240 paychecks times the number of current teachers, which is roughly 80.5 million records (of course, we are assuming all the current teachers remain in their current positions and we are also disregarding, for the moment, the total number of

TABLE 8.2

Elementary and Secondary Education Characteristics

Item	Texas	United States (Average)
Total number of schools	9,332	1,988
Total students	4,935,715	970,278
Total teachers	334,996.94	60,766.56
Pupil/teacher ratio	14.73	15.97

(Data from U.S. Department of Education Institute of Education Sciences. State education data profiles. National Center for Education Statistics. 2012. Accessed December 25, 2013. http://nces.ed.gov/programs/stateprofiles/sresult. asp?mode=short&s1=48.[3])

TABLE 8.3

Elementary and Secondary Education Finance

Item	Texas	United States (Average)
Total revenues ($)	50,045,607,224	11,715,409,205
Total expenditures for education ($)	53,838,221,095	11,906,580,615
Total current expenditure (public, elementary to secondary) ($)	42,621,885,838	10,303,880,343

(Data from U.S. Department of Education Institute of Education Sciences. State education data profiles. National Center for Education Statistics. 2012. Accessed December 25, 2013. http://nces.ed.gov/programs/stateprofiles/sresult.asp?mode=short&s1=48.)

TABLE 8.4

Postsecondary Education

Type of Institution	Texas	United States (Average)
Total Title IV degree-granting	252	90
Public	108	32
Private, not-for-profit	57	31
Private, for-profit	87	25

(Data from U.S. Department of Education Institute of Education Sciences. State education data profiles. National Center for Education Statistics. 2012. Accessed December 25, 2013. http://nces.ed.gov/programs/stateprofiles/sresult.asp?mode=short&s1=48.)

TABLE 8.5

Demographics

Item	Texas	United States (Average)
Total male population	10,335,430	2,704,238
Total female population	10,516,390	2,813,837
Average household size of all occupied housing units	2.74	2.59

(Data from U.S. Department of Education Institute of Education Sciences. State education data profiles. National Center for Education Statistics. 2012. Accessed December 25, 2013. http://nces.ed.gov/programs/stateprofiles/sresult.asp?mode=short&s1=48.)

TABLE 8.6

Public Libraries

Item	Texas	United States (Average)
Number of central libraries	553	177
Number of Branch Libraries	298	147
ALA-MLS librarians (FTE)	1,571.60	603.08
Total librarians (FTE)	2,168.60	885.95

(Data from U.S. Department of Education Institute of Education Sciences. State education data profiles. National Center for Education Statistics. 2012. Accessed December 25, 2013. http://nces.ed.gov/programs/stateprofiles/sresult.asp?mode=short&s1=48.)

already-retired teachers in the Teacher Retirement System of Texas, TRS). Furthermore, we can expect an expansion of records for those individuals who start working younger and stay until they are old, taking in 40 years of records, for example. These records include pay rates, contributions to the TRS, insurances, federal tax information, and all the rest of the typical paycheck detritus found in most employment in the United States. At this stage, we have a large database, but not necessarily a big data problem, although we could enhance processing using techniques we describe in this book, such as machine learning, distributed operations, and advanced statistics.

The TRS currently administers retirement for 1.3 million members[4] (We are now looking at somewhere in the vicinity of 312 million records, assuming 20 years for each retiree and potential retiree.) Additionally, the TRS manages health coverage for 233,000 retirees. Perhaps we cannot really call this big data, but we are certainly headed in that direction. Once we start to tally the probable number of fields in addition to the back-of-the-envelope calculation of records, we are looking at a very large database, which may or may not be managed as a relational database, but which could certainly be managed with one of the appropriate choices from Chapter 4.

How might we use this information with a GIS? We can imagine some examples:

- Typical locations for retirees
- Locations of members and types of members
- Gender

- Ethnicity
- Race
- Disabilities
- Health insurance
- Retirement status
- Death rates
- Accidents
- Salaries in a general sense (This information might generate an interesting surface overlaid on the map, given previous attempts at more equitable distribution of monies in the state.)

Another example involves the use of GIS for bus systems; in this case, ArcGIS. The New York City (NYC) Department of Education's (DOE) Office of Pupil Transportation (OPT) manages the transportation needs of NYC schoolchildren, with busing overseen by OPT, although the buses are owned and operated by private companies. To simplify and ease a new transportation contract bidding process, OPT generated a web-based mapping system that permits potential bidders to see pre-K schools service area boundaries, pricing tiers, and historical attendance data. Previously, bus enterprises bid on each school as a unique entity. The new system allows for cost analyses that were previously unavailable, not to mention route optimization.

Subsequent to implementing a new service area–based system for awarding contracts, the OPT received feedback from its vendors that a census estimate of student attendance at each facility was insufficient to provide for a safe profit margin, part of a competitive bid. Under the new system, initiated in 2011, the city was divided into 43 service areas, indicating neighborhood and transportation path characteristics. Pre-K busing to all schools within a service area would be awarded to the same vendor. However, since pre-K students often attend school in a service area other than the one in which they live, the city was also divided into different pricing tiers to indicate the varying distances to each target region. Pricing tiers are composed of one or more service areas that share common routing opportunities.

Other variables can complicate the routing process. Special populations have disabilities that influence the transportation service selection. Costs associated with different issues have substantial variance. Bus companies are asked to provide an estimate for each of three classes of pupils—ambulatory, non-ambulatory (children in wheelchairs), and Early

Intervention (a special program for pre-pre-K students under the age of three)—from each PT to the target service area. One pupil in a far-flung PT who requires a wheelchair ramp or lift can dramatically increase the cost to the vendor of serving that area. If this information is not known at the time of the bid, it could make an entire route unprofitable for the vendor. Thus, the new system, which was designed to reduce costs by consolidating busing to each service area, could end up having the opposite effect if vendors began bidding on contracts based on potential but unknown worst-case scenarios.

Simply stated, if lower per-pupil bids were to be achieved, the DOE needed to provide a better means for vendors to estimate their true costs. The solution the DOE proposed was to provide three years of student historical data by location for each disability class. Potential bidders can see the number and location of pre-K students, categorized by disability class, for the past 3 years.[5]

The DOE provided this data as a web-based map, where bidders could visualize service areas, pricing tiers, and pupil distribution patterns that would help them make informed bids. Pre-K schools were also geocoded. The data sets were uploaded to ArcGIS for Server and a web-based application built to display the data and provide users with query capability.

The resultant website hosts a mapping system that shows

- Boundaries of the service areas
- Pricing tiers for each service area
- Schools
- Children who attended those sites for the prior 3 years
- Disability status of children

A critical function of the application is that service area or school can query the data. This allows bus vendors to more accurately base bids on historical patterns as they transition from the old system of individual school routes to the new system of service areas. This example shows how costs can be contained using GIS.

Information for programs such as ArcGIS is stored in geographical databases called geodatabases, in which we find spatial information in the form of geometric objects. The Open Geospatial Consortium specifies a substantial amount of information in their standards, available at http://www.opengeospatial.org/standards/is. Examples of GIS operations and information are

- Spatial measurements, including line length, polygon area, the distance between geometries, and more.
- Spatial functions used to modify existing features to create new ones
- Spatial predicates, which allow true/false queries about spatial relationships between geometries
- Geometry constructors, which allow the creation of new geometries
- Observer functions, which provide for queries that return information about a feature

In the case of ArcGIS, we expect use of similar functions; however, this program uses a combination object and relational database to manage spatial references. The program has made use of Microsoft Access and SQLServer databases over the years.

Given the power of freely available and open-source tools such as Cassandra and the R Project, we wondered if such a capability was available for GIS. Such a list could look like this:

- FGIS: http://www.digitalgrove.net/fgis.htm
- GRASS: http://grass.ibiblio.org/index.html
- OpenJUMP: http://www.openjump.org
- OpenEV: http://openev.sourceforge.net/
- Quantum GIS (QGIS): http://qgis.org/
- Thuban: http://thuban.intevation.org/
- uDig: http://udig.refractions.net/

Several of these packages do little to mention database support in their literature (JUMP, OpenEV), while presenting substantial material regarding rendering of map images. QGIS uses small personal computer databases. JUMP and Thuban appear to be in a state of stalled development. uDig indicates that they are a "framework" for a GIS. QGIS integrates with GRASS. For this reason, we suggest that GRASS is probably the GIS of choice for open-source developers.

A major open-source version of a GIS is Geographic Resources Analysis Support System (GRASS), an OSGeo project. Downloads for Apple Macintosh, Microsoft Windows, and Linux are available at http://grass.osgeo.org/. The US Army Construction Engineering Research Laboratories (USA-CERL), starting in the early 1980s, created the tool. With the advent of the twenty-first century, the project came under a steering committee and involves a multinational team of developers.

GRASS GIS capabilities include[6]

- *Raster analysis*: Automatic rasterline and area to vector conversion, buffering of line structures, cell and profile data query, colortable modifications, conversion to vector and point data format, correlation/covariance analysis, expert system analysis, map algebra (map calculator), interpolation for missing values, neighborhood matrix analysis, raster overlay with or without weight, reclassification of cell labels, resampling (resolution), rescaling of cell values, statistical cell analysis, surface generation from vector lines
- *3-D-Raster (voxel) analysis*: 3-D data import and export, 3-D masks, 3-D map algebra, 3-D interpolation (IDW, regularized splines with tension), 3-D visualization (isosurfaces), interface to ParaView and POVray visualization tools
- *Vector analysis*: Contour generation from raster surfaces (IDW, splines algorithm), conversion to raster and point data format, digitizing (scanned raster image) with mouse, reclassification of vector labels, superpositioning of vector layers
- *Point data analysis*: Delaunay triangulation, surface interpolation from spot heights, Thiessen polygons, topographic analysis (curvature, slope, aspect), LiDAR
- *Image processing*: Canonical component analysis (CCA), color composite generation, edge detection, frequency filtering (Fourier, convolution matrices), Fourier and inverse Fourier transformation, histogram stretching, IHS transformation to RGB, image rectification (affine and polynomial transformations on raster and vector targets), ortho photo rectification, principal component analysis (PCA), radiometric corrections (Fourier), resampling, resolution enhancement (with RGB/IHS), RGB to IHS transformation, texture oriented classification (sequential maximum a posteriori classification), shape detection, supervised classification (training areas, maximum likelihood classification), unsupervised classification (minimum distance clustering, maximum likelihood classification)

- *DTM analysis*: Contour generation, cost/path analysis, slope/aspect analysis, surface generation from spot heights or contours
- *Geocoding*: Geocoding of raster and vector maps including (LiDAR) point clouds
- *Visualization*: 3D surfaces with 3D query (NVIZ), color assignments, histogram presentation, map overlay, point data maps, raster maps, vector maps, zoom/unzoom function
- *Map creation*: Image maps, Postscript maps, HTML maps
- *SQL support*: Database interfaces (Table 8.7)
- *Geostatistics*: Interface to "R" (a statistical analysis environment), Matlab[7]
- Erosion modeling
- Landscape structure analysis
- Solution transport
- Watershed analysis

Please note the SQL-support part of the list. MySQL is now owned by Oracle, although a community version still exists as of 2014. PostgreSQL indicates[8] that database size is unlimited, but maximum table size is constrained to 32 TB. Neither of these databases can be considered to be big data databases in our estimation; however, it is possible the open-source team supporting GRASS may decide to support one of the distributed databases as the product continues to mature. It is also possible that an interface to Postgres-XC may arise—Postgres-XC supports multimaster replication. A least one version of the database has worked on a system with 64 cores.

The choice of supporting database is important because the GIS environments can only be expected to grow as enterprises and individuals

TABLE 8.7

Database Extensions Used for GIS

Extension	File Type	URL
dbf	DBF files. Data are stored in DBF files.	http://shapelib.maptools.org/dbf_api.html
sqlite	SQLite embedded database (GRASS 7 default DB backend)	http://sqlite.org/
pg	PostgreSQL RDBMS	http://postgresql.org/
mysql	MySQL RDBMS	http://mysql.org/
mesql	MySQL embedded database	http://mysql.org/
odbc	UnixODBC (PostgreSQL, Oracle, etc.)	http://www.unixodbc.org/

discover the power of spatial representation. For example, we already know that John Deere uses what they call an agricultural management solution (AMS) guidance system to control the movement of their products (especially combines). Let us take a look at this industrial application of map and geospatial location technology:

- *AutoTrac system choices*: AMS, John Deere tractors in field
  - Choose the signal for your integrated, automatic AutoTrac guidance system solution based upon the accuracy you need for your applications.
  - AutoTrac SF1 uses the FREE SF1 signal and is a starting point for tillage, spraying, and grassland applications.
- AutoTrac RTK System gives high-level accuracy for planting row crops, bedding, strip till, drip tape, and any controlled traffic operation.
- *AutoTrac SF1 & SF2*: John Deere SPFH and tractor AutoTrac SF1 uses the FREE SF1 differential correction signal, which is useful for
  - Tillage, spraying, and grassland applications, for example, slurry or fertilizer spreading.
  - AutoTrac SF2 uses the highly accurate SF2 differential correction signal.
- AutoTrac RTK System uses a ground-based RTK station as "point of reference" for repeatable accuracy for farming operations, using a ground-based correction signal to eliminate or mitigate GPS drift; other benefits include
  - Highly accurate, repeatable guidance in curves and straight tracks
  - One base station for multiple machines and RTK networks
  - Productivity and efficiency benefits
  - Reduced soil compaction
  - Increased operator comfort
  - Work in low visibility situations
  - RTK-Extend feature
- *AMS*: John Deere RTK SystemPerfect repeatability: high-precision farming using guidance accuracy: AutoTrac & RTK Systems
- *Hassle-free RTK System*: RTK systems can be dealer- or self-installed
- *RTK Extend*: maintains the performance and full functionality of RTK System even when temporary line of sight obstructions occur

Notice how the John Deere system combines map technology with extremely accurate GPS location data to provide the information necessary for the tractor or combine to perform automated farming. In addition, corrections to fertilizer deposition and seeding can be made based on historical data.[9] Both John Deere and Monsanto have initiatives in place to use private data as part of a larger framework for the benefit of regional farmers. Such data, apparently protected from competitive tampering, would allow the following:

> Monsanto thinks it can help farmers come up with the perfect prescription of seeds for their soil and weather because the company will have more data than any one farmer can collect or analyze. It will have more detailed soil maps and information from many other fields with similar soil conditions.

> Eventually, it will have field-by-field weather predictions from a high-tech venture called the Climate Corporation, which Monsanto bought last year for $1 billion.[10]

The purpose of large-scale big data, collection is to optimize work with the soil. If Monsanto and Deere can obtain a bigger picture of soil trends, theoretically, everybody will benefit. Furthermore, map technology could allow for detection of alluvial deposits, yield declines, changes in hydrological patterns, and more.

We discussed Monsanto twice. The May 24, 2014, edition of *The Economist*[11] discusses ownership of information. The Climate Corporation uses remote sensing and any other available cartographic means to map fields and then add weather information. The article suggests yield could rise from 160 bushels/acre to upwards of 200 bushels/acre, a 25% increase. So far, the vendors have provided access control to farming data, making it challenging for unauthorized individuals to access potentially proprietary information.

GIS DATABASES

What about GIS databases? Where do we get the information? One source, commercial, is www.geocomm.com. They provide several services:

- Spatialnews: online news
- GIS data
  - US Geological Survey (USGS) digital raster graphic data
  - USGS digital elevation models (DEM)

- USGS orthoimagery
- Federal Emergency Management Administration (FEMA) flood data
- Vector map information usable by multiple software programs (including ArcView GIS)
- Geoimaging
  - Imagery sources
  - Imaging software (the USGS Landsat 7 Image Viewer)
  - Hardware
  - Educational resources
- Software
  - Surveying software
  - SuperGIS
  - Reviews
  - Articles
- GeoBids: online service for requests for proposal (RFP) and procurement
  - Submission of RFP
  - Latest RFP
  - Archived RFP

A large list of GIS data resources is available at http://en.wikipedia.org/wiki/List_of_GIS_data_sources, including US, regional, and global sources of data. USGS itself provides access to some of their data at http://webgis.wr.usgs.gov/globalgis/. Most of this data will run on the Esri ArcView Data Publisher software and includes the following regions:

- Central and South America
- Africa
- South Asia
- South Pacific
- North Eurasia
- North America
- Europe

USGS is a treasure trove of information; for example, at http://water.usgs.gov/maps.html, we can find substantial information regarding water resources, especially in the United States, although some other regional information is available as well. In fact, USGS supports data and news for the following items:

- Climate and land use change
- Core science systems
- Ecosystems
- Energy and minerals
- Environmental health
- Natural hazards
- Water. Another US government resource is the FEMA map service center at https://msc.fema.gov/webapp/wcs/stores/servlet/FemaW elcomeView?storeId=10001&catalogId=10001&langId=-1. A large concern of FEMA regards issues with floods, including historical flood maps. The interested user can find historical information at the National Historical Geographic Information System (NHGIS; at https://www.nhgis.org/), free of charge.

We must bear in mind that these free "databases" are really structured files and we will need some kind of formal database in order to really make use of the information.

REFERENCES

1. Stevens, D. and J. Akers. 4-H community mapping—The story of a local cemetery project. *Directions Magazine*. September 1, 2013. http://www.directionsmag.com/articles/4-h-community-mapping-the-story-of-a-local-cemetery-project/197461. Accessed March 28, 2014.
2. Law, M. and A. Collins. *Getting to Know ArcGIS for Desktop*. Redlands, CA: Esri Press, 2013.
3. U.S. Department of Education Institute of Education Sciences. State education data profiles. National Center for Education Statistics. 2012. Accessed December 25, 2013. http://nces.ed.gov/programs/stateprofiles/sresult.asp?mode=short&s1=48.
4. Wikipedia. Teacher retirement system of Texas. Wikipedia. December 12, 2013. http://en.wikipedia.org/wiki/Teacher_Retirement_System_of_Texas. Accessed March 28, 2014.
5. Jenkins, K., T. Calabrese, J. Laroussi, and H. Orr. Optimizing New York City's school bus contract bidding process. Spring 2012. http://www.esri.com/news/arcnews/spring12articles/optimizing-new-york-citys-school-bus-contract-bidding-process.html. Accessed September 27, 2014.
6. GRASS Development Team. GRASS GIS. General Overview. GRASS. November 13, 2012. http://grass.osgeo.org/documentation/general-overview/. Accessed March 28, 2014.

7. GRASS Development Team. GRASS GIS Manual: SQL Support in GRASS GIS. 2014. GRASS. http://grass.osgeo.org/grass70/manuals/sql.html. Accessed March 28, 2014.

8. The PostgreSQL Global Development Group. About PostgreSQL. The PostgreSQL Global Development Group. 2014. http://www.postgresql.org/about/. Accessed March 26, 2014.

9. Charles, D. Should farmers give John Deere and Monsanto their data? NPR. January 22, 2014. http://www.npr.org/blogs/thesalt/2014/01/21/264577744/should-farmers-give-john-deere-and-monsanto-their-data. Accessed March 28, 2014.

10. Deere & Company. Guidance and machine control. John Deere Agricultural Management Solutions. 2014. http://www.deere.com/wps/dcom/en_INT/products/equipment/agricultural_management_solutions/guidance_and_machinecontrol/guidance_and_machine_control.page. Accessed March 28, 2014.

11. Anonymous. Digital disruption on the farm. *The Economist*. May 24, 2014. http://www.economist.com/news/business/21602757-managers-most-traditional-industries-distrust-promising-new-technology-digital. Accessed June 2, 2014.

9

Discovery

Our recent discussions of big data solutions center on what are becoming the "traditional" big data systems, to the extent that we have anything traditional in a new field. By traditional big data, we refer to predictive analytics, machine learning, and other such technologies we have discussed. In comparison with these technologies, discovery is distinct. It pulls together the data from different sources, both structured and unstructured, and creates a single environment in which users can find the data they need and explore trends for further analysis. Discovery is an ideal technology when our staff members need the flexibility to explore data across source systems, assemble data, and use it in their daily work. Discovery is, most of all, user-friendly.

Perhaps the most effective way to summarize discovery is that it delivers two key abilities and ties them together so that the whole becomes greater than the total of its component parts. These two abilities are

- The ability to tie together diverse data sources into a coherent whole
- The ability to search data easily using an input that is like a more flexible version of the humble search engine but with an output that brings significantly more meaning to the data

When we combine these two abilities, the result is a significant amount of our organization's data at our fingertips with an easy path to follow in order to obtain even more information and context. Imagine that our accounting package has accounts receivable information detailing what we sold, as well as for how much, and billing addresses for our clients, whereas the system in our warehouse has the number of shipments that went out, the difficulty in fulfilling them, and the shipping address. By combining these data sources, we can start to map patterns on what would not otherwise be visible. For example, do clients in more expensive areas purchase more or less at once? Theory could go either way and questionnaires may not be helpful. When we say that we can map patterns, we mean this both literally and figuratively. We can create heat or pin maps to add color and data to maps so our clients' actions speak for them in a manner directly visible to us. The implications for creating meaningful customer segmentation should be clear.

Among the most famous discovery systems are Endeca, an Oracle product, and the Lucene and Solr package by Apache, the same open-source Apache Software Foundation responsible for Hadoop. We may have already used Endeca without even knowing it. Named after the German verb "entdecken," meaning "to discover," Endeca was founded in Cambridge, Massachusetts, as an independent company in 1999.[1] Before its purchase by Oracle in 2011, Endeca had two primary offerings named Endeca InFront and Endeca Latitude. It is Endeca InFront, now called Oracle Endeca Commerce, that underpins Wal-Mart's website and those of companies such as Boeing, Hallmark, Ford, IBM, the Census Bureau, the Environmental Protection Agency, and the late, great Borders books.[2] The concepts we cover here apply to Oracle Endeca Information Discovery, the business intelligence tool that used to be called Endeca Latitude.

Solr is the brainchild of Yonik Seeley, born of necessity at CNET to enable search capability within the website. In 2006, the source code was donated to the Apache Foundation.[3] Since then, Instagram, Digg, reddit, Whitehouse.gov, and FCC.gov have adopted it, as have aspects of the corporate websites of Sears, Ticketmaster, Netflix, and Zappos.

FACETED SEARCH VERSUS STRICT TAXONOMY

To define the outline of what discovery is, we need to define faceted search. Almost all of us have certainly used faceted search, which is defined by Wikipedia as:

> ... a technique for accessing information organized according to a faceted classification system, allowing users to explore a collection of information by applying multiple filters. A faceted classification system classifies each information element along multiple explicit dimensions, enabling the classifications to be accessed and ordered in multiple ways rather than in a single, pre-determined, taxonomic order.[4]

In a structured data set, these facets may be name, city, telephone number, product number, ISBN, and any other such attribute. In unstructured data, such as e-mail records, PDF files of research papers, and web searches, these facets may be key information pulled out by searching for terms or inferred through an analysis of the text (such as sentiment analysis). Very frequently, the data pulls together from a mix of structured, unstructured, and semistructured sources. An example of semistructured information is a formalized table in a report that always follows a set format internally while the reports themselves are scattered across servers and disk drives within the organization. Our upcoming thought experiment will illustrate the power of faceted search and demonstrate exactly how complex it is, even though it will also seem extremely familiar. It is so pervasive we do not even think about it.

The strict taxonomic order is more difficult to use in exploring data, but it is easier to grasp because we learn about it in school and use it to impose order on our own knowledge. Carl von Linné, better known as Carolus Linnaeus in the Latin that he used to write his works and his name, created the basis of one system of taxonomy that we still use. Though there are variations on this system, a common version is

- Kingdom
- Phylum
- Class
- Order
- Family
- Genus
- Species
- Subspecies

As we move down the list, the gradations involved become finer. We may have a *Felis domesticus* (common house cat) in our home and a *Picea pungens* (blue spruce) in our backyard. The first word in each pair is the genus and the second is the species, with the pair together comprising the scientific name. We know the cat and the tree are not closely related because, in the hierarchy of the taxonomic system developed from Linnaeus's original work, one is from the kingdom Animalia and the other from the kingdom Plantae. We usually use the kingdom as the most basic level of taxonomic classification of life. We know our cat and a rainbow trout are connected more closely than our cat and a tree—aside from common sense—because the cat and the trout are both from the kingdom Animalia, although they are not from the same genus (the trout is *Oncorhynchus mykiss*). Both animals are from the phylum Chordata because they both have spinal columns. This seems like a characteristic of all animals, but many such as jellyfish and sponges are related more distantly and do not have spinal columns and are therefore not from the same phylum as fish and cats.

Even more closely related to the house cat than the fish is the lynx (*Lynx lynx*), which, like the house cat, is from the family Felidae, though from a different genus and species. Other wildcats more closely related to the house cat, however, fall within the same genus *Felis*, such as the sand cat (*Felis margarita*).

What does this have to do with business intelligence? A lot. The taxonomic order underlies how we organize information on our hard drives. Think of our folder structure, which may be first broken down by client, then by project, then by date ranges. When we create dashboards with key performance indicators (KPIs), we often distinguish these taxonomically. We can classify these KPIs first by the company as a whole, then by division, then by office. Drilling down into detail allows vital insights, but other insights remain hidden by the barriers between different departments, business lines, or offices created by the taxonomy.

The analogy between the nomenclature created by Carolus Linnaeus and the folder structure on our hard drive is of course imperfect. A folder for our client Acme or Ajax in our North American Division folder will probably address the same Acme or Ajax within our South American Division folder. A domestic dog is not directly comparable to a domestic cat. We define a less explicit but even more rigid taxonomic system for the characteristics of data sources. A relational database stores and processes data that we cannot efficiently load into a spreadsheet or PDF research paper. Even two relational databases may not play well together if different divisions operating on different assumptions that created them. They rely on different organizational principles, or taxonomies, to provide structure. This is not an explicitly intended taxonomy, but a real one nonetheless. If we ask our information technology (IT) department, they may not have thought about it in that way. If we ask them to seamlessly splice our different systems, we will see they cannot simply do that for us without considerable effort.

We can partially overcome the taxonomy behind folder structures by using the search feature of our operating systems. The de facto taxonomy created by different data sources is not so easily overcome, but discovery tools are an effective way of "taming" it and making it yield to our organizational needs.

The strength of taxonomy is that it is intuitive to create, and it grows naturally within a business intelligence setting. With living creatures, the taxonomy usually aligns neatly with common sense and the creation of viable offspring. It is easy to see that a house cat and lynx are more similar to each other genetically than either is to a trout, and the cats and fish are closer to each other than either is to a sponge or a tree. Taxonomy is a powerful tool in its proper context.

For example, obtaining information on a particular division may be a simple case of rolling up each of its constituent parts. A corporate body may include human resources, finance, and other divisions. Finance may include finance and accounting. Accounting may include accounts payable, accounts receivable, tax, and other departments. Accounts receivable may include standard receivables and delinquent accounts. An understanding of any one level of the organization is simply a matter of rolling up those divisions under it.

Outside of that context, taxonomy is limiting. As was noted, such a taxonomy is rigid. If we discovered a new and strange species, we could fit it into Linnaeus's scheme, but imagine trying to fit sentiment analysis (subjective trending) from analyzing Twitter feeds into a standard dashboard of charts measuring KPIs. For that matter, trying to fit such slippery concepts we now measure into any taxonomy is not easy and is likely to fall apart as data sources grow, die, and evolve. A taxonomic system projects stability, but stability can stifle adaptation. Going back to our use of Acme and Ajax in our firm's North American and South American operations, our firms may in fact use entirely different systems that do not play well together. In trying to call up information on Acme and Ajax, we may need to query different systems and worry that we are missing something. We may also find that missing information greatly complicates our ability to aggregate information. As an example of this, a different key identifier may be used to refer to the same customer between divisions, creating difficulties in linking the data. This is especially likely to be the case if one division was acquired separately from another. Even if a new accounting package is rigorously implemented immediately on a newer division, then there is a break between new, postacquisition data and old, preacquisition data.

Second, a taxonomic system makes it difficult to draw out hidden relationships in the data. Using the Target example from an earlier discussion, if we do not think to aggregate a particular segment with purchases of particular items not related to babies, we will not discover we can figure out which customers are pregnant and will not know whether to market to them. Drawing together different systems measuring completely different attributes can be tricky and time-consuming if we do not break the taxonomic mindset. This is not to say that a discovery system based on faceted search will be a panacea. The weaknesses of a taxonomic system are outweighed by its strengths when using an ERP system. However, to explore in your organization's data and to draw lessons, a discovery system may be ideal.

FIRST KEY ABILITY: BREAKING DOWN BARRIERS

We may observe a real situation at play in which companies fail to develop a repository of institutional knowledge. Real-world examples abound of companies not knowing what they have already developed. Items may be re-invented, multiple divisions may compete with each other or send mixed signals to customers, and opportunities may simply vanish because nonobvious connections do not occur. Our own organizations, if they are of sufficient size, probably have similar horror stories of angry clients, waste, and frustrated employees who see their efforts amount to naught. One of us is familiar with a case in which someone negotiated a payment plan on a medical bill, was paying on time, and was then sent to collections for part of the bill that ended up separated and processed separately while nobody properly communicated to either the party making the payments or the employee responsible for negotiating the plan. This other part of the bill had a different customer number as the key identifier and so the system treated it as a separate account not covered in the payment plan, unbeknownst to the parties making the arrangements.

These problems arise for many reasons, such as the acquisition of another firm with its own data management systems or the growth of shadow IT. Shadow IT is information technology that we find developed in the parts of the company that cannot answer the needs of employees with the speed or efficiency the employees need; hence, they create workarounds and improvisations that are effectively highly customized, and occasionally incorrect, variations. IT departments strike a balance between the flexibility required of them to be useful in a business setting and the rigidity required to prevent the same splintering.

Discovery aggregates diverse data sources into a usable format. In a sense, it is like a search engine such as Bing, DuckDuckGo, Yahoo, or Google, only it brings the data into tables, graphs, and maps. Whereas a web search will deliver results that include websites, PDF files, Word files, videos, songs, and other files based on their contents, discovery will pull in these disparate files and join them, provided the necessary key identifier or identifiers are in place.

To better understand this ability, imagine we are a firm in a commodity market. We incur fierce competition from our competitors, but customers also maintain loyalty to those vendors who are reliable. In this market, we really want to evaluate which customers require the least effort per dollar of margin so we can concentrate our efforts on them. We will slowly cut loose our more difficult customers by maintaining higher prices and sales fees than our competitors while offering enhanced service and better prices for major customers who purchase in large quantities and at a price that we could reduce while still maintaining a reasonable margin for our firm. We would also use time we free up for our staff to seek new customers.

We have our enterprise resource planning (ERP) software, our customer relationship management (CRM) package, saved e-mail messages, and a purchased set of industrial economic data for across the country. Using an internal customer number and internal invoice number, we can tie together the details of the sale and other customer data into a coherent data set. We can then display our results on maps and charts, and in tables. For nontabular data such as e-mail strings, we can index and make searchable the data so that we have access to context in order to decide whether or not a customer is worth the trouble.

Aggregating diverse data with different levels of structure suggests we will have "jagged and dirty data." To understand jagged data, imagine we need to create a database dossier on ourselves and on all of our neighbors (we do not intend this example to be creepy but to rely on common attributes that almost everyone understands). Most likely all of us will have driver's licenses from the state in which we live, but someone who lives between locations may have a license from a different state. The credit card information among us will be different (let us assume that there is no limit to the information we may access). Some will have American Express cards, some will have Visa cards, some will have MasterCard, and some will have Discover. Most will have some combination of these. Each card company uses some industry standard data and some proprietary measures. Each neighbor uses different banks, belongs to different social clubs, and pays for different insurance and mortgages. If we were to create a single database, there would be a mishmash of formats, terminology, and exact metrics. This result is jagged data, and it is a phenomenon that exists when any organization tries to pull together disparate data sets.

Dirty data is data with errors and poor standardization. Incorrect numbers are difficult to overcome, but we have many ways to make such data visible. Incorrect latitudes or longitudes will often be obvious when using the mapping capabilities. We can roll nonstandard spellings of a term together using the data uptake process and by enabling the simultaneous selection of multiple similar values on the search and navigation tools, to be discussed later. It is clearly a problem to have such data quality issues, but with a discovery system's capabilities, these data issues need not be paralyzing.

Data cleansing, or normalization, is the process of making data less jagged and less dirty. It is a mix of manual and automated processes. Discovery does not eliminate the need for cleansing, but it minimizes the need.

After we discuss faceted search in greater detail, we will aggregate this fusion of data with the flexibility to demonstrate how discovery applies to the goals and needs of our organization.

_____

SECOND KEY ABILITY: FLEXIBLE SEARCH AND NAVIGATION

Discovery enables the user to drill down to a detailed level in the data. This is the faceted search mentioned at the beginning of this chapter. We use faceted search on a nearly daily basis, so it no longer seems remarkable. However, let us walk through a faceted search using Endeca on a common e-commerce site and see how remarkable this feature can be if applied to business. To show how discovery works, we provide an extended example related to personal purchasing.

Imagine we are in the following situation: today is February 13. Valentine's Day is tomorrow, and we have not yet purchased a gift for our Valentine. We have 2 hours of free time between our other commitments, such as work and Zumba and doing a favor for a cousin. We only have time to shop online but have to pick up the item in person; otherwise, it will not arrive on time. Our Valentine loves the outdoors, and the two of us enjoy sipping wine in the backyard. Patio furniture seems nice but does not strike us as the perfect gift.

We face a unique set of logistical constraints in mutual competition. We more or less know what we want, but not exactly. In other words, we are human beings who should not procrastinate but do. We have competing issues that cannot be neatly prioritized, unlike the neatly defined avatars used in modeling perfectly rational behavior. Making decisions by running up and down the branches of a taxonomic system is inefficient. In real life, we draw inferences and use information found in one context to shape our decision seconds later by a process of analogy. We use a process not unlike faceted search.

Taxonomy is not useless. It is an ideal way to ensure that we focus on the outdoor items we seek rather than a distraction such as clothing. People do this in real life. If they look for the perfect outfit for a job interview, they go to the formal wear section in a department store and compare blazers with slacks to suits and one color of shirt against another. They use taxonomy to narrow their options, then a less formal decision-making process, heuristics, to decide exactly what they want within that category.

To find the perfect gift for our Valentine, a perfect place to turn would be Walmart.com. We can narrow down our search to outdoor items and then browse. All the while, we make sure to look within items available in our nearest store so we can go pick up our gift within our time window. This is interesting, but how does it tie into our discussion of big data? Simple. Walmart.com uses Endeca.

We type www.walmart.com into our favorite browser and see a list of categories down the side of the web page. Among these are Home, Furniture, and Patio; and Sports, Fitness and Outdoors. Our Valentine is an outdoors enthusiast, so these are two ideal places to start. We think patio furniture is a good idea, so we click on Home, Furniture, and Patio, but keep the other category in mind just in case. When we move our mouse over that category, there is a Patio and Garden section. Under that, we go to click Patio Furniture, but instead we notice Grills and Outdoor Cooking. Our Valentine's grill has seen better days, but our Valentine still has good patio furniture.

So far, we are navigating using the old taxonomic method of working from the trunk of the tree out to smaller and smaller branches. We are focusing in on one area, and this is where the power of faceted search comes into play. On the left side of the screen, there are different categories with check boxes next to them. We can drill down into the selection of grills by many different attributes:

- Kind of grill: Gas, charcoal, electric, and so on
- Brands: Black & Decker, Brinkmann, Weber, Kingsford, and so on
- Color: Black, silver, red, multicolored, and so on
- Price ranges: Under $10, $10–$20, and so on (We can also enter our own price range in the boxes there.)
- Whether the grill is available in a store or needs to be shipped
- Which shipping offer we prefer
- Customer rating: One through five stars (though why we would want to buy a grill rated one star is puzzling, unless we and our Valentine just had a falling out)
- Retailer: Other online retailers sell through Wal-Mart's website, and we can order from one of them.
- Special offers that are available: Rollback, online-only, and reduced price
- Size: Medium, large, 100 quart, 7 quart, and so on

Each of these categories is an attribute, and any selection for that attribute is a value. For you, "name" is an attribute, but our name is a value in this approach. We notice each selection has a number in parentheses next to it. This number indicates the number of grills available that fit an attribute based on what we already selected.

As we will need to pick up a grill at a Wal-Mart near us, we go to the top of the page and enter our zip code at the Store Availability section.

If nothing else is yet selected, we will see "(98)" next to gas grills and "(105)" next to charcoal grills under Category. Each other category of grill likewise has such a number next to it. That number of different models is available for each of those categories.

Under Type, we see "(85)" next to portable grills and "(84)" next to nonportable grills. Each other type of grill also has such a number. Under Free Store Pickup, we see 139 models we can find at the Wal-Mart nearest us if we walk into the store today.

Let us assume that we know our Valentine sometimes likes to pack up the grill and go camping, so we select only charcoal and gas grills, as electric grills and fryers are not so convenient out in the wilderness. After we check the boxes next to gas and charcoal, we see that most of the numbers in parentheses change. We now see 76 models available today at the

Wal-Mart nearest us. We detect 67 portable and 54 nonportable models, regardless of whether they can be picked up.

What this means is that there are 67 models that are portable that use either gas or charcoal. Among these models, some will be available in the store and some will not. A large grill is difficult to take camping, so we click the check box next to portable grills.

The numbers in parentheses change again. We now see 34 gas grills and 33 charcoal grills. These add to 67, the number of portable grills. There are 34 models available in the Wal-Mart down the street from us that are portable and use either gas or charcoal as their fuel. We now click the check box representing those 34 models.

Next to Available Today, we see "(34)" that are both portable and available today: we find 20 gas grills and 14 charcoal grills. Of these, 22 models earned four stars in the customer reviews, four earned three stars, and one earned one star.

We can glean some information from this. We detect no portable gas or charcoal grills of the models available in the Wal-Mart down the street that earned five stars or two stars, and we find ratings only for 22 + 4 + 1, or 27 different models. Some models are unrated.

We select only four-star models, then only those models in the $100–$150 price range. This leaves us with three models from which to choose. We find a nice Weber gas grill that is compact, buy it, and pick it up on our way home.

This is a common act that seems unremarkable. We do something similar almost any time we shop online, whether at Amazon, Barnes & Noble, Target, or Wal-Mart. Let us break down how we approached it. We used a taxonomic system to find more or less what we were looking for. We started seeking patio furniture but then changed direction and looked for grills. Once we were in barbecue grills, however, we used *faceted search*. The grill had to be available for same-day pick-up. We knew what price range fitted our needs, what fuels and characteristics would make it useful in the back yard and out in the wilderness, and we knew that a four-star rating meant that it would probably be a better grill than one with a lower rating.

Discovery brings this same flexibility to business intelligence. It enables finely tuned examinations of our organization's data, drilling into a particular salesperson's performance in one state or another, last year or this year. Whereas we were once limited to KPIs we needed to define in advance, we are now able to explore our data. If we find an intriguing

Taxonomic (hierarchical) classification

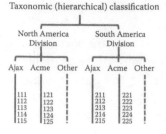

Faceted search (based on faceted classification)

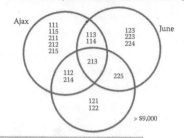

Invoice number	Supplier	To which division	Date	Amount
111	Ajax	North America	4-May	$ 5,500
112	Ajax	North America	24-May	$ 10,500
113	Ajax	North America	12-Jun	$ 6,250
114	Ajax	North America	22-Jun	$ 8,000
115	Ajax	North America	2-Jul	$ 4,000
121	Acme	North America	18-May	$ 13,000
122	Acme	North America	22-May	$ 9,750
123	Acme	North America	5-Jun	$ 2,250
124	Acme	North America	5-Jul	$ 5,000
125	Acme	North America	8-Jul	$ 7,500

Invoice number	Supplier	To which division	Date	Amount
211	Ajax	South America	20-May	$ 6,250
212	Ajax	South America	25-May	$ 9,250
213	Ajax	South America	9-Jun	$ 11,500
214	Ajax	South America	2-Jul	$ 13,750
215	Ajax	South America	13-Jul	$ 4,250
221	Acme	South America	18-May	$ 7,000
222	Acme	South America	30-May	$ 8,750
223	Acme	South America	15-Jun	$ 3,000
224	Acme	South America	18-Jun	$ 6,750
225	Acme	South America	21-Jun	$ 9,250

FIGURE 9.1
Taxonomy versus faceted search.

graph, we can tunnel into the data on which it is built and find connections that we might have otherwise overlooked. Figure 9.1 illustrates the difference between these two approaches.

The previously mentioned graphs, tables, and maps function are outputs presenting the data to us to visualize, and all business intelligence software does this. However, discovery is unique in how easy it is to aggregate and compare information across many different sources.

This scenario raises an obvious question: "What has taken so long for this to arrive?" The answer is that this simplicity of search is only possible because of remarkably sophisticated technology. The more difficult old taxonomic system we use to find what we need is actually logically simpler in computer terms than the more intuitive faceted search.

Endeca and Solr are designed for ease of use. Their search components guide the user to relevant attributes that can be used to refine a search. Many of the output components can be used as inputs as well. These include tag clouds, bar and pie charts that narrow by a criteria when the user clicks on one of the bars or slices, and tables in which the user can click on a particular value and add that to the criteria used in the selection.

Search is similar to the search box found on a search engine such as Bing, Yahoo, or Google, and it features a similar predictive function. If we enter "wheel," we could pull up product lines with "wheel" as part of the name, suppliers and vendors, even if they are unrelated to the main line of business, such as a Wagon Wheel Café, if our organization pays such

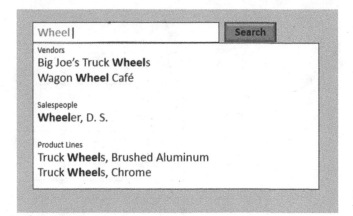

FIGURE 9.2
Wheel search.

a restaurant for functions and has it listed as a vendor, employees who have a last name such as Wheeler, and anything else with "wheel" as part of one of its attributes that is part of one of the ingested data sets. This is illustrated in Figure 9.2.

Navigation can also guide the user by breaking the search into distinct categories that each has its own input. Numeric and nominal attributes can be made to use different inputs. For example, numeric attributes can be selected using sliders or manual input of the minimum and maximum values needed. Nominal attributes can drop down a menu and allow the user to narrow the search by typing part of the name until the desired search term appears in the box. This latter method is similar to the auto-fill search used on common search engines to anticipate what the user is searching for. Figure 9.3 shows the appearance of a search box in such a guided format.

We touched on dirty data earlier. The navigation allows a user to work around dirty data in multiple ways. Through the use of synonyms, data can be "cleaned" without changing the underlying source data. This is because your discovery system will upload a full set of the data to be explored (with the exception of some links to external files such as PDF documents or e-mail messages), but also serves to maintain the integrity of your source data systems. Let us imagine that we supply truck wheels to customers worldwide. In looking at our data, we may be aghast to find we sell "truck wheels," "lorry wheels," "truckwheels," "trick wheels," and other variations according to our data. This is an artifact of data problems and not of different product lines. A discovery system can be configured to map all of these variations to one category, such as simply "truck wheels." If a user discovers that there are "Truck Wheels" and "truck wheels," he or

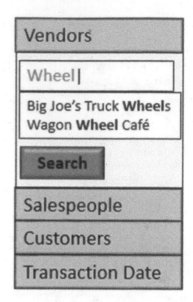

FIGURE 9.3
Focused wheel search.

she merely needs to select both to view the total results for both of them until the mapping can be improved to remove the duplication.

UNDERLYING TECHNOLOGY

The engine underlying Endeca is called the MDEX, an application that stores the data set in both secondary storage (the hard drive) and primary storage (RAM). In the Solr world, Lucene fills the role of the MDEX in Endeca. The amount of memory needed depends on the task, but 256 GB is not unheard of.

As Endeca is used, and a cache is built up in primary memory from users' queries, the system becomes faster. The cache is an in-memory repository of the heavy lifting done by Endeca, thereby speeding up the results of later queries. This necessitates that the RAM available is larger than the portion of the data set that is held within it. When the server hosting the MDEX is rebooted or power is cut, the prior queries are erased with the loss of power. This is comparable to how the data on the clipboard of our PC is lost when we reboot our computer or we are hit by a power outage. When the MDEX is brought up again, the data from the hard drive is loaded into the RAM but does not fill the capacity of the RAM. The leftover room is where the recent queries are stored. This leads to two interesting traits of Endeca. First, the more that Endeca is used after being started up, the faster it runs. Second, the lack of sufficient RAM for caching previous queries becomes a bottleneck to the efficient functioning of the application. When we first start up Endeca, we need to run it for a while to build up the cache, which in turn will allow it to run faster.

THE UPSHOT

Discovery is a tremendously powerful tool that can do much to unlock a firm's human capital. It uses search to pull together data from across the organization and uses graphical representations to display the shape of that data. In less than a minute, a skilled user can drill down through a variety of attributes to create a specialized query. Very few software packages can do this. It is a demonstration of the power of discovery. It can also be misleading if due care is not taken.

The first and most obvious problem is that narrow searches are also susceptible to small data sizes. We may start with millions of records, but this does not guarantee a quality result if our queries narrow the number of selected records, for example, to 12. The user of a system built around a discovery system has access to metrics describing the size and likely the quality of the data set that is left over after the query, as measured by the number of missing or flagged variables (such as N/A). It is extremely important to monitor data size and, where possible, data quality when using discovery to draw conclusions.

Likewise, a user of discovery must use the tool in a structured manner to understand the reasons patterns in the data exist as they do. Just finding the patterns is not sufficient. Imagine finding that sales are dropping in the midwestern United States for a particular product. That alerts the user that there may be a serious threat, but it does not provide enough information to draw a conclusion.

A quick selection of the data may well show that the sales are declining for the territory of a particular salesman, but a valid conclusion requires digging deeply. During the growth of hydraulic fracturing as a method for stimulating production of petroleum and natural gas, suppliers purchased trucks and trailers at a booming rate. Now that fracturing is a mature practice, they purchase transport rigs more slowly. If the parts for which we are witnessing a decline were being sold largely for use on these trucks, it is likely that no salesman could sustain sales as before. The requirements for drawing valid conclusions from traditional big data systems apply equally to results found in discovery.

There may be economic changes that affect the Midwest differently than other regions. There may be problems with a salesman not doing his job properly. There may be a concerted marketing effort by a new competitor centered in that region that is eating into sales. A key client may have moved its headquarters westward, driving sales from the Midwest sales region to the Rocky Mountain sales region. To understand what is happening and why it is happening, it is imperative to break down the problem in different ways and explore the scale of the problem and its limits. Discovery is a tool that helps illuminate what is in the data. It does not eliminate the necessity of diligent, structured, and rigorous analysis.

As is also the case with other big data solutions, discovery systems read from data that has been brought into their resident database. The term for this is data that has been "ingested." This means we will need to create another instance of all data that is included in our discovery system. Source data will remain where it resides and will be only read by our discovery system. This requires new hardware, a system to automate ingestion and ensure that it is done accurately, and security measures that will be just as important as those of the source systems.

As is the case with other big data systems, our discovery system will not become our system of record for accounting or managing customer relationships. What it will do is to enable our staff to break through barriers between functions and divisions and to shine a light into valuable data that our firm has not utilized to its potential. Discovery can be integrated with other, more traditional big data functions, but on its own it is intended more for a more human experience in confronting large quantities of diverse data.

SUMMARY

The needs of web-based data repositories have led to the creation of a technology sometimes called discovery. The best known of these systems are Solr (sometimes referred to as Lucene, which is the name of its underlying engine) and Endeca, an Oracle product.

Discovery is a more manual and more flexible, and less known, corner of the world of big data. Discovery delivers two primary abilities. It draws together diverse sources of data into a largely coherent whole and it makes that data searchable in an intuitive manner that also permits a high degree of refinement. A key aspect of the ability of discovery to draw together all of this data is its ability to cope with "jagged" data and "dirty" data. Jagged data is the result of data that does not fit together neatly in a tabular form and, in fact, when placed in a table, the missing attributes will be immediately noticeable. Dirty data are data that are incorrect or use multiple manners of indicating the same thing, such as different units of measure or multiple spellings for the same word.

Although discovery pulls together diverse data sources and creates a seamless experience navigating across data sources, it is no more capable of making diverse data deliver only the correct results than are systems such as Hadoop. However, by pulling together so much data from so many sources and enabling the user to explore them as if they were a single source, discovery is a key tool in converting different systems and forgotten folders on servers into an institutional knowledge base. It also brings to users the ability to create insights that would never have been possible if these different data sources remained distinct from each other.

REFERENCES

1. Wikipedia. Endeca Technologies Inc. Wikipedia. http://en.wikipedia.org/wiki/Endeca. Accessed August 27, 2013.
2. CrunchBase. Endeca. CrunchBase, San Francisco. http://www.crunchbase.com/company/endeca. Accessed August 27, 2013.
3. The Apache Software Foundation. CNET code contribution. Apache Jira ticket SOLR-1. The Apache Software Foundation. https://issues.apache.org/jira/browse/SOLR-1. Accessed May 29, 2014.
4. Wikipedia. Faceted search. Wikipedia. http://en.wikipedia.org/wiki/Faceted_search. Accessed August 26, 2013.

10

Data Quality

![section divider]

KNOW THY DATA AND THYSELF

Imagine an airline hires us to consult as to why its customers are unhappy according to survey data. We have strong reason to doubt that our client, the airline, attracts especially grumpy passengers. After applying the statistical lessons we learned earlier in this book, we note the complaints about bad flight crew service are coming from a particular cross section of airports. We notice the same aircrews and airplanes cycle through other airports, with few passenger satisfaction problems. The problems are with these airports in particular. How could this be?

On a hunch, we suspect something is causing late departures from these airports, and angry passengers then feel less satisfied with the rest of the flight. We obtain a data set showing on-time and late departures and find the flights in question depart on time over 80% of the time. So much for our hypothesis. Now what?

What is the definition for on-time departure? According to the US Department of Transportation, "A flight is counted as 'on time' if it operated less than 15 minutes later than the scheduled time shown in the carriers' Computerized Reservations Systems (CRS)... Departure performance is based on departure from the gate."[1]

Let us examine our data more carefully. The definition is based on when the aircraft leaves the gate, not when the wheels break contact with the tarmac. There is leeway for the aircraft to be late in practice without being late in definition. The definition of an on-time departure specifies that it is a particular computer system, which belongs to the carrier, on which the rest of the definition relies.

We now know our data better. We can form new hypotheses. Maybe we have the following situations:

- The carrier's CRS provides too little turnaround time to account for bottlenecks in the problem airports.
- There is a bottleneck on the runway and our planes push back from the gate on time but then sit on the tarmac waiting a long time, perhaps 20–30 minutes, to take off.
- Something is causing an abnormal number of planes to push back 12–14 minutes after their scheduled time, so they are technically on time yet still cause frustration for the passengers.

It could be more than one of these, or it could be none. What we can see now, though, is that it is possible to depart late and still technically be on time. If our data have a built-in bias, measure the wrong thing, shift method of measurement somewhere in the middle, are inexact, or are ambiguous as to what they should be measuring in the first place, we will have problems. This problem will not go away, but awareness of it will help us minimize complications. Welcome to the world of data.

Data are messy. Data need to be defined. Data are often wrong. Yet, data are becoming one of the greatest assets to the modern company. Companies often fail to extract the true value residing in their data. How can these seemingly contradictory statements all be true?

For those of us who must wear glasses, we become frustrated when we must navigate without them. Think of those moments walking from the outdoor furniture to the pool, or when something splashes onto the lens and we must take off our glasses until we find something to cleanse them. The shapes and outlines of the world are still present and discernable— they are just blurry. The fine-grained resolution we would like to have is not there. Still, blurriness is preferable to not seeing at all. Data are likewise blurry. The details may seem obscured, but by enabling us to see the outlines of a situation they are providing a service to us.

A major component of the science of geology involves the study of rock strata. Rock strata are a permanent record of past events. Where there is coal, there was once a swampy area. Where there are seashells, the area used to lie under a body of water. If the stratum has an acute curve, significant compressive pressure along the horizontal axis in that area caused the earth to fold. Data likewise maintain the fingerprint of the environment in which we recorded them.

A common misconception is that data have their own voice. This misconception holds even among those who know at a deeper level this is not so. Data are not an oracle providing direct insight into a deeper truth, but they do provide a more solid foundation for decision making than any another option available. They are superior to untested theory. An apocryphal saying attributed to quality improvement pioneer W. Edwards Deming reads: "In God we trust, all others bring data." There is no paradox in data-driven decision making being the gold standard in effective navigation of business and policy issues, and the fact that data are imperfect. Data are power, but they are misleading if not well managed.

Think of a log of visitors to a website. It is a simple data file showing when someone visited, from whence they clicked to arrive at the website, some characteristics of their operating system and browser, and their location (which is determined though their internet protocol [IP] address.) However, sometimes erroneous data make it through. One of the authors needed to use a website designed to identify his computer's IP address for troubleshooting purposes. The IP address was correct, but some of the other location information that arrived was just plain wrong. The server to which he connected was not in the same city as he was.

By design, some users of the Internet rely on proxy servers to mask their identifying information. The proxy server masks the location of the user. Someone in California may appear to be in Texas and someone in Asia may appear to be in the United States. This is one reason hackers are difficult to catch, but it is also a common practice among security-minded individuals. When someone using a proxy server accesses a website, the identifying information recorded on the web server's log files is erroneous.

Most people know someone who has had incorrect information on a credit report. One of the authors spoke of someone who missed the opportunity to refinance his house at a better rate because of erroneous information on his report. Maybe it has happened to us. The cause may be reporting errors, clear fraud, or honest mistakes such as incorrect billing addresses in a creditor's database (yet another data error).

Data quality is central to useful analysis, and it is therefore the subject of this chapter, but it matters more in some instances than in others. To illustrate, let us consider two distinct possibilities. The first is the use of click-through data on different versions of our website that we are floating to different users. Imagine an electronic commerce website has different variations shared at random with different shoppers, with shopper response measured and incorporated into new designs that are then offered up to shoppers in an ongoing iterative approach. In the other example, a police chief uses crime statistics to help officers anticipate crime and get out ahead of it. In both cases, error can be anticipated. In the latter, however, the consequences are arguably more serious.

Why? There are several reasons. In the former case, the processing of the data is generated as part of an iterative process and therefore can be designed to test the same pages multiple times, thereby enabling analysts to isolate flukes in the data. In the latter case, it is more difficult to tease out confounding variables in the data and correct for them.

Think of it this way: when we are testing click-through rates, we can more or less directly measure how customers react. Yes, the data will be messy, but they will be meaningful. It is possible that the options we test the day after a stock market crash will appear less successful simply because our customers are keeping their wallets closed. It is also possible we did not optimize our page for a common browser, and our team missed this fact, causing customers who view our page to look elsewhere. Now we have a complication, but one we can understand and correct. When we are a police officer analyzing crime, does the lower crime reporting in a particular neighborhood reflect the fact we have less crime, or does it reflect that the residents of this neighborhood are less likely to report crime than residents in other neighborhoods? This intricacy is not so easy to tease apart.

We have a less obvious yet vitally important answer to this question. This is the "so what?" of the analysis. How will we use the results? The expenses of testing variations on a website are not minor, but they are also not permanent and rarely require huge capital outlays. They are certainly not as expensive as an action like wasting police resources because the beats the officers patrol are incompatible with optimized beats. We waste much money when we misallocate such a resource. If we decide where to place our next precinct headquarters based on misleading crime data, then we are taking away resources from where they can do the most good and essentially wasting them, creating facts on the ground that are often difficult to change later.

Finally, we have other, more profound risks at play. In the first case, the risk is lower. Unless our web design is an unusable disaster, the odds are low it will destroy our business or push us into a situation where we need to lay off large portions of our workforce. In the latter case, crime can literally be a life or death situation. In particularly high-crime areas, there are all-too-common heart-wrenching stories of families with multiple murdered children. Even burglary and auto theft can be a financial disaster for their victims. The stress of high-crime neighborhoods tears apart the social fabric and the trust upon which educational and economic success often depends.

We are building on the foundation we created in our discussion on statistics. The statistics we discussed rely on what is reported in the data. Many of the statistics, such as descriptions of central tendency and the standard deviation, are direct descriptions of the underlying data. It is unavoidable that we have overlap between these two chapters, but the focus is different. This chapter will delve into how the quality of data may be affected by issues that do not necessarily show up in statistics. It will also discuss how statistics can be misused, often inadvertently, or misinterpreted. Our analysis may be impeccable but based on a misreading of the statistics we are using.

One of the reasons classical authors of Greece and Rome are still read today is because they lived in a vastly different world (and Greece and Rome were not merely different from today's world, but from each other as well), but they addressed many of the same issues as we do in the modern world. The thoughtfulness of those authors whose work has risen to immortality, and the fact that they applied their intellect to similar problems, yet with a cultural twist to reflect the world in which they lived, makes it worthwhile to read them. Plato died more than 23 centuries ago, yet Nassim Nicholas Taleb, who has been mentioned many times in this book, still criticizes Plato's work. We suspect Mr. Taleb would not do so if Plato were not still influential today.

Likewise, we discern value in stepping outside the world of big data in discussing data. Just as the Greek and Roman world is different from our own, but teaches us a tremendous amount about our own world, the world of science is different from the world of big data, yet it teaches us about big data. In fact, the authors would argue that the scientific community is ahead of the big data community in wrestling with difficult topics in data. For this reason, we will learn the lessons from science (and some from journalism) and then apply them back to big data.

STRUCTURED, UNSTRUCTURED, AND SEMISTRUCTURED DATA

Let us revisit the types of data processed by a big data system. The enterprise resources planning (ERP) system with which we work every day manages structured data. It may allow us to view an image of important documents, with little processing of the data in those documents. Overall, ERP data are structured data like the relational database model discussed earlier in this book.

Unstructured data include scanned and indexed reports, information found by a program searching the Internet seeking information about our product, call center calls that have been translated to text and indexed, analysis of Twitter feeds to see who is influencing who, and patterns detected in company e-mail messages to seek patterns of behavior signifying fraud. Such information is not easy to place into rows and columns. Unstructured data are not merely messy data, they are data that simply do not conform to the patterns of a traditional database.

Semistructured data might well be in rows and columns, but even so, they are still not easy to push into the tabular format. The oil industry uses a specific format to log oil and gas wells known as Log ASCII Standard (LAS). A LAS file possesses significant amounts of identifying information about an oil or gas well, such as the American Petroleum Institute (API) number (in the United States), location, owner, and so forth. This information is in a row-and-column format at the beginning of the file when viewed with a text reader such as Microsoft Notepad.

Not all LAS files measure the same thing, and not all of them label the same readings in the same way. However, LAS files incorporate a real structure. We find a series of columns of readings taken at different depths as the equipment that is logging the data is moved through the well. These columns, with measurements taken every foot or every several feet, have values for such measurements as gamma rays, acoustic data, or other such measurements that assist engineers to comprehend the characteristics of the rock into which they drilled the well.

LAS files are a classic example of semistructured data. The internal structure of a LAS file is altogether understandable and consistent. Trying to put together several LAS files to gain a better understanding of the geology of an area is more difficult because each file can be quite different from others.

DATA INCONSISTENCY: AN EXAMPLE FROM THIS BOOK

Data are not an unbiased and abstract Platonic form; rather, data reflect the decisions and systems that formed them. The form of data varies depending on our assumption and how we collect them and make our calculations. Let us reach back to the discussion of positive feedback loops and the concurrent growth of suburbs and car use as an example. It is an example that draws us into data definitions and the confusion that this entails, yet it has a clear resolution.

If we look at the Table 10.1, we will see that one data source is used to derive the number of motor vehicles on the road during the years between 1900 and 1990[2] and another source for 2000 through 2010.[3]

Let us dive into the first data set, covering the earlier years. This chart, compiled by the Federal Highway Administration, divides motor vehicle registrations into automobiles, buses, trucks, and all motor vehicles (the sum of the other three columns). How we define a motor vehicle affects which figures appear in the results. In this case, the example uses the total number of registered motor vehicles. However, for each type of motor vehicle, the figures are broken out into private and commercial vehicles on the one hand and publicly owned vehicles on the other. The figures in our chart include both categories.

In other words, our example uses the most inclusive definition available, based on the Federal Highway Administration chart, to estimate the number of registered vehicles that existed in the United States for the years listed. In 1900, this dubious figure was the rounded number 8000, and in 1990, the figure was 188,797,914.

TABLE 10.1

Initial Look at Motor Vehicle Data

Year	DOT Vehicles	Statista Vehicles
1900	8,000	
1910	468,500	
1920	9,239,161	
1930	26,749,853	
1940	32,453,233	
1950	49,161,691	
1960	73,857,768	
1970	108,418,197	
1980	155,796,219	
1990	188,797,914	193,057,380
2000		225,821,240
2010		250,070,050

As the former chart, compiled in 1997, does not include figures for 2000 or 2010, we needed another data source to fill in those years covering the period from 1990 to 2010. Although it is from a website, Statista, which also drew from the Federal Highway Administration's figures, the number of registered vehicles found on Statista shows a discrepancy with the number found on the Federal Highway Administration's own website (Table 10.2).

We find 1 year of overlap between the two charts, which is 1990. Whereas the Federal Highway Administration site shows the 1990 number of total registered vehicles as 188,797,914, the Statista chart shows 193,057,000. The two numbers came from the same data source, and the smaller number was the most complete number available on the chart where we found it. All the other columns added together composed this number. The Statista chart shows a single figure rather than the breakdown by vehicle type and ownership.

We think it is clear the data is not speaking for itself. We find nothing self-evident in the numbers provided. The only way to solve this conundrum is to dig in and play with the data to comprehend what is happening. First, we need to look at the notes provided with the figures. The earlier figures, taken directly from the government source, state

TABLE 10.2

Updated Look at Motor Vehicle Data

Year	DOT Vehicles	Statista Vehicles	Difference	DOT Motorcycles	Adjusted
1900	8,000				8,000
1910	468,500				468,500
1920	9,239,161				9,239,161
1930	26,749,853				26,749,853
1940	32,453,233				32,453,233
1950	49,161,691				49,161,691
1960	73,857,768				73,857,768
1970	108,418,197				108,418,197
1980	155,796,219				155,796,219
1990	188,797,914	193,057,380	4,259,466	4,259,000	188,797,914
2000		225,821,240		4,346,000	221,475,240
2010		250,070,050		8,010,000	242,060,050

1. This table was compiled principally from information obtained from State authorities, but it was necessary to draw on other sources and to make numerous estimates in order to present a complete series. It includes Alaska and Hawaii for 1959 and subsequent years.
2. Trucks include pickups, panels and delivery vans. Beginning in 1985, personal passenger vans, passenger minivans and utility-type vehicles were no longer included in automobiles but are included in trucks.
3. For the years in which no entries are given for buses and publicly owned vehicles, the available data on the relatively small number of such vehicles were not in sufficient detail to make possible reliable segregation by vehicle types.

The Statista figures include the following note:

This statistic represents the number of registered vehicles in the United States from 1990 through 2010. In 2000, there were approximately 225.82 million registered passenger cars, motorcycles, trucks, buses, and other vehicles in the United States.

A possible explanation lies in those definitions. One clear difference in the definition of a motor vehicle between the two data sets is that the Statista data include motorcycles whereas the other data set does not. We need to determine if this is the root cause of the discrepancy. To do so, it is necessary for us to find the number of registered motorcycles for 1990 and see whether it matches the difference between the two figures for registered motor vehicles for that year. Another source from within the Department of Transportation, the Bureau of Transportation Statistics, has a chart with the number of motorcycles registered in 1990 enumerated in its own cell.[4] The number we find is 4,259,000 motorcycles, close to the difference between the number of motor vehicles registered in 1990 according to the Statista source and the chart published directly by the Federal Highway Administration.

The figures used in the example of a positive feedback loop earlier in this book are therefore adjusted to make them equivalent. They come from multiple sources. Without our adjustment, the two data sets do not measure the same thing. They will provide misleading information, independent of what statistical analyses we run, regardless of our level of care, and regardless of how carefully the statistics were compiled in the first place.

THE BLACK SWAN AND INCOMPLETE DATA

Before continuing with the discussion of specific pitfalls found in data, we think it important to return to the concept of the "black swan." First popularized in the 2001 book by Nassim Nicholas Taleb, *Fooled by Randomness*, before being further elaborated upon in the eponymous 2007 book, *The Black Swan* has become a popular culture icon, often abused and misunderstood.

Taleb's definition of a black swan is

> First, it is an outlier, as it lies outside the realm of regular expectations, because nothing in the past can convincingly point to its possibility. Second, it carries an extreme impact. Third, in spite of its outlier status, human nature makes us concoct explanations for its occurrence after the fact, making it explainable and predictable.[5]

He derives the name of this phenomenon from the black swans of Australia. Swans are defined in the minds of many by all of the stereotypical characteristics often associated with a swan, such as a long neck, graceful poise, and white feathers. An individual encountering a black swan while in Australia will find his definition of a swan challenged by the encounter. There is no way to foresee this challenge for someone unaware of the existence of such an unexpected species of swan.

Attempts to foresee and anticipate black swans are doomed to fail. The terror attacks of September 11, 2001, are a classic case of a black swan, but we know of other notable examples. The Asian tsunami in December, 2004, and the Japanese earthquake and tsunami of 2011 are both egregious examples. The Black Monday stock market crash on October 19, 1987, was a black swan, as was the flash crash of May 6, 2010. Improved seismic monitoring and modeling may someday render earthquakes less of a shock by improving reaction time, and the use of the proper statistical distribution will prevent investors from being so unprepared for crises. For now, the events themselves (as opposed to their statistical likelihood) are not predictable. They remain black swans.

We suggest it is a human tendency to look backwards after a black swan and to see the chain of contingencies. It is rarely that easy, however. Even now, investors have seen nothing in the data before the stock market crash in 1987 or the flash crash of 2010 that conclusively identify the cause. Whereas markets are quick to respond to new information, the bond markets failed to respond to the triggering events of what we now know was a jolting disaster in the making.

This discussion appears to lead us away from the topic of data sets, but it is in fact directly relevant. If we detect no identifiable precedent in the data for an event, we will not catch it. This is not because our statistical tools are not good enough, and it is probably not because we were careless in collecting data. It is fiendishly difficult to systematically collect the needed data when the relevant precursors to the event to be forecasted are not even known. Without the relevant data, we will not be able to identify, much less predict, such events. It is possible to become buried in less than useful data leading to false relationships between variables. It is possible to fall into analysis paralysis. We can manage this paradox, but ridding ourselves of it in whole is difficult or impossible. We can control risk; we cannot banish it.

HOW DATA CAN FOOL US

Ambiguous Data

Data are not always as obvious as they seem. It may look obvious, but in order to prevent pitfalls, it is important to speak to those knowledgeable about the process that generated the data. Who fixes the sensors? Who calibrates the system? Who has read all the technical manuals for any of our new logistics systems? In some ways, the term "ambiguous data" is a misnomer. All data are to some degree ambiguous. It is the responsibility of the researcher analyzing the data to root around and understand the degree of ambiguity. It is likewise incumbent to understand the structure of the data, the specific definitions of the different variables, and the measurement used for each variable.

One of the authors of this book—while on a Six Sigma project—fell into the trap of analyzing a data set based on false assumptions. The results were not merely useless but outright misleading. It seemed to him at the time that he exercised due care, but he did not penetrate to the right level within the organization to speak with the staff members who generated that data. The staff members who helped him define the data were acting in good faith and were supremely competent, but they were one step removed from the process being measured. This situation made all the difference.

The measurement of time caused the problem. The data were broken out by day, then by employee, then by discrete intervals during which the employee was signed into the system. The employee could sign in for 30 seconds or several hours (or more than a week if he or she forgot to exit the system when leaving work). During each interval when the employee signed in, the system provided instructions requiring fulfillment. As the employee fulfilled each instruction, he or she scanned a bar code, and logged the event as a data point (Figure 10.1).

Discussions with the author's counterparts on the client side informed the author's interpretation of the data. Each time the employee signed in and out equaled one period; a shift could have many periods, and it was the number of events within each period that determined efficiency (each logged event was essentially the same).

The project entered a lull during which the recommended changes were enacted but data were sparse due to unforeseen circumstances. When, several months later, the data were again available, it appeared as if the firm's efficiency dropped. This inauspicious event seemed unlikely, as the changes enacted were clearly an improvement in the workspace (Figure 10.2).

As a result of these troubling results, we scheduled a meeting with one manager who directly oversaw the system data used for the project. The author and the manager dissected the technique systematically. This manager explained how the assumption of different periods of work within each shift was misleading and recommended that the author rework the data set to cover only events per shift, not events per each discrete period within the shift. When we executed this approach, the data told a

Employee 1				Employee 2		
Start	Stop	Time worked		Start	Stop	Time worked
9:02	9:41	0:39		**9:03**	10:08	1:05
9:47	9:49	0:02		10:20	10:21	0:01
9:55	10:03	0:08		10:23	10:26	0:03
10:04	10:09	0:05		10:27	10:28	0:01
10:16	10:27	0:11		10:30	10:33	0:03
Etc.	Etc.	4:42		Etc.	Etc.	4:39
4:34	**4:56**	0:22		4:53	**4:58**	0:05

Total hours	**6:09**		**Total hours**	**5:57**

FIGURE 10.1
The data were originally organized as the sum of all periods worked.

Employee 1				Employee 2		
Start	Stop	Time worked		Start	Stop	Time worked
9:02	9:41	0:39		**9:03**	10:08	1:05
9:47	9:49	0:02		10:20	10:21	0:01
9:55	10:03	0:08		10:23	10:26	0:03
10:04	10:09	0:05		10:27	10:28	0:01
10:16	10:27	0:11		10:30	10:33	0:03
Etc.	Etc.	4:42		Etc.	Etc.	4:39
4:34	**4:56**	0:22		4:53	**4:58**	0:05
	Total hours	7:56			Total hours	7:55

FIGURE 10.2
The data were reorganized to calculate time worked as the period from the original check-in to the final check-out.

different story. The recommended changes had, in fact, been impressive. Performance did not decrease; it significantly increased.

On another occasion, one of the authors confronted data from multiple systems with overlapping functions. Essentially, individuals could log their data into one system, which we will call system A, or into another system, which we will call system B, or both. We found some highly useful data automatically reported by the system along with dubious data that were manually entered. The author was not the first person to wrestle with what exactly each attribute measured. The author finally had to break down and draw a map outlining the relationships within the data contained within the system in question.

Even after all of the work put into this analysis of exactly what the system measured, it was clear we were not going to eliminate the ambiguity. We produced enough clarity, though, that the data could be the basis for analyzing the recorded performance. Later, the data yielded meaningful results.

Finally, data ambiguity will be a major component of any unstructured data that we use. As our system parses and interprets unstructured data, it will always do so with a certain error rate. Computers are generally poor at interpreting sarcasm. Imagine, for example, that our system scans and interprets Twitter feeds to seek tweets about our product and it processes this: "My Acme Flying Bat Suit was just great! It lasted a whole 2 hours!" Sarcasm and double meanings are susceptible to misinterpretation.

Even parsing unembellished text can be touchy. If we have ever witnessed an embarrassed colleague react to a web search by saying something like,

"I didn't know this phrase meant THAT!" we have seen what often happens when a computer misinterprets language. Just before we wrote this passage, one of the authors struggled with a common software product, typing in a natural speech question into his favorite search engine and turned up an abundance of results, the vast majority of which were completely irrelevant.

As medical records—largely a hold-out against digitization trends—move truly into the digital realm, their ambiguity will become a challenge. The percentage of hospitals that have adopted electronic health records increased from 9% in 2008 to 44% in 2012, with a somewhat less dramatic increase in adoption by individual physicians. Nonetheless, privacy regulations hamper the increased use of big data in health care.[6]

Even if we overcome these obstacles, we will still suffer difficulties with interpreting the data because of substantial intrinsic ambiguity in the health data. For example, the body mass index often used to determine obesity is notoriously inexact. Highly muscular, athletic individuals are routinely judged obese because they are heavy for their height. The self-reporting of symptoms is also problematic; not only do patients hide embarrassing symptoms, but even sincere reporting is often more sentiment than fact. Does a patient report a cough as a symptom? If the patient attributes it to allergies, then it is likely it would not be reported. If the patient relates it to another illness—one of concern—then he or she is more likely to report it.

Medical records mix the precision of direct numerical measures, such as height, weight, and blood work results, with impressionistic observations by medical professionals. As patients do not usually obtain and read their own medical records, errors go undetected and uncorrected, and then there are misdiagnoses. This is not a criticism of the doctors who do misdiagnose, although carelessness may be a component. Although many doctors are diligent, they still face highly ambiguous data in conducting the tests that constitute patient records. As we saw in our discussion of statistics, a certain rate of false positives is impossible to eliminate.

What this means is the use of medical records will require a certain level of care in how we interpret the data because the level of uncertainty remains high. Reporting rates among patients, the imperfection of measures and indices, the evolving nature of medical knowledge itself, and simple mistakes of interpretation will persist as concerns in any attempts to use big data to analyze medical records.

To see how big data could meet its match with medical records, let us conduct a thought experiment: imagine the use of optical character recognition (OCR) technology to convert a doctor's handwriting into computer text; then imagine using big data to scan the same text looking for key words related to symptoms for a profound analysis of the reporting of symptoms and outcomes. Now, consider a patient who thought that the symptom was unimportant, but who is now reconsidering the symptom because the doctor is specifically asking, "Have you felt a pain in your side in the last month?" The patient does not understand whether the symptom is internal or is at the level of the muscle, and the patient may have been getting back into shape by running hard—which can also cause a pain in the side (a "stitch").

If we have a sample of patients—some misdiagnosed—used in a big data study of the importance of early reporting of symptoms in relation to reduced health-care expenses, it is easy to see how the study could go badly, even without false positives resulting from statistical artifacts. The data would be phenomenally messy, with the quality of diagnoses, the characteristics of the patients, and other external factors working against us in trying to come up with quality results. Medical records can be ambiguous and contain errors in patient reporting, the doctor's recording, and movement from paper to computer. A study such as that outlined in the previous paragraph may also suffer from overlooked factors. Later in this chapter, we will cover how one important variable that affected patient headaches when recovering from anesthesia escaped detection for decades, only to finally be identified due to a doctor's hunch. The cause of the headaches was surprising to say the least. It was definitely not the wearing off of the anesthetics.

Big data will have a role in improving health care, especially in areas where less nebulous data such as age, chemistry, and genetics as well as geography, income levels, and unemployment periods can be used in analyses. Analysts will need to handle this role with tremendous care; the studies will require replication to improve the interpretation and reduce the error. Medicine treats people, and people will always be imprecise creatures.

This discussion should not discourage our organizations from considering the use of unstructured data. Extremely powerful work is being done using such data sources (e.g., web searches). Companies can gain a solid impression of what consumers think of certain features of their products and can better target their marketing to appropriate segments of consumers. By watching who is quoting who, we can map who influences who. By analyzing sentimental words and my specific history of such words when quoting others, computers can gain some knowledge of whether I am probably quoting you to criticize you or because I like what you said. When we use unstructured data this way, the lack of sensor-like precision in the data becomes irrelevant. The computer is conducting a powerful analysis that was impossible even a decade ago. Still, when considering a potential project based on unstructured data, we think it is definitely worthwhile to consider whether the intended task matches the nature of the data. Moreover, there are methods being developed to assist in the judgment of ambiguous and unstructured data. Some of these are discussed later in this chapter.

Aging of Data or Variables

Data age. An interesting experiment for those who have lived in the same community for many years is to take an old telephone book (itself becoming a relic) and look up the names of friends and acquaintances, as well as their parents, aunts, and uncles. Maybe we can look up old businesses—a surreal experience. A telephone book is clearly a printed work that goes out of date, but something similar happens with electronic data even though it is theoretically easier to update.

This is not to say that old data are without value; they just need to be understood as such. To use an example from credit reports, we find no problem with having old addresses on file, as long as we all understand that none of these addresses is current.

A paper by Benjamin Skalland of the University of Chicago and Meena Khare of the National Center for Health Statistics demonstrates an instance of variable aging in the use of telephone records to determine geographically specific data in the national 2009 H1N1 flu survey. As area codes relate to specific areas, which can vary from covering neighborhoods within a city—New York City alone has six—to covering an entire state, they serve as a resource when polling in order to draw conclusions regarding the geographical distribution of the results. Unfortunately, with changes in the law, cell phone numbers are often kept when their owners move from one location to another. The authors found that

> Unlike with landline telephone numbers, the geographic information associated with cell-phone numbers is often not accurate at the state level or at

smaller geographic levels. We estimate that 11.5 percent of U.S. cell-phone-only adults reside in a state that differs from their sampling state based on the area code of the cell-phone number, and that this sampling inaccuracy varies considerably from state to state.[7]

An article written by Leah Christian, Michael Dimock, and Scott Keeter of the Pew Research Center, and cited by Skalland and Khare, finds that 43% of their sample of those reachable only by cell phone did not have an area code from the same county as their zip code, whereas only 7% of those reachable only by landline did not have a matching area code and zip code. The same phenomenon existed at the state level, but to a lesser extent.[8] Without a doubt, a major factor contributing to these results is the movement of people who keep their cell phone numbers with them as they relocate. This is an example of the aging of data.

As this chapter was being written, one of the authors visited the website of the US Department of Transportation (DOT) to determine how on-time departures were calculated and to find a baseline figure for a good, but not outstanding, percentage of on-time flights. The DOT does a solid job at publishing intriguing statistics. For the tables that contain information about on-time departures and arrivals, "The report is usually issued during the first week of each month."[9]

However, we found this message when we accessed the website during July of 2013: "This page was last updated on September 17, 2012, and the most recent data are from July 2012." Alas, sometimes it is necessary to rely on data that are not current. Insights are available, but the researcher needs to exercise caution when arriving at conclusions.

Sometimes the problem of the aging of data is not simply the data itself becoming stale, but rather the data fermenting in a way that affects its utility. A colleague of one of the authors once worked on a project where the equivalent data were being reported on different cycles for different regions. The cycles would be of different durations, usually between a week and a month, and even those that were equivalent intervals ended on different days. As this disorder was the result of a situation external to his client, there was no way to simply change the reporting system to create a more orderly schedule. Clearly, in this situation, the most recent data are a resource for analyzing trends within a region, but not between regions. Comparing the most recent data for two different regions would be comparing apples and oranges, not because the data were inconsistent, but because the reporting schedule was incompatible. Once all of the data were in for all regions, however, trends across regions would be useful for investigation.

Missing Variables May Change the Meaning

To see how an unconsidered variable may acutely change an interpretation, we need look no further than the headaches caused by anesthesia subsiding. A 1991 study by Fennelly and Galletly in the journal *Anesthesia & Analgesia* decided to explore one particular mechanism of this headache: "One of the most frequent postoperative side effects of general anesthesia is headache…, and, although often ascribed to the effect of anesthetic drugs, this symptom could be the result of caffeine abstinence."[10] If we study only what is in front of us—anesthesia and the headaches that occur as the anesthetic wears off—the relationship between the two seems obvious, until we take caffeine into account.

Fennelly and Galletly approached 300 postoperative patients who had been placed under general anesthesia for minor procedures between 3 and 6 hours prior and, with their consent, administered a questionnaire asking about consumption of alcohol, food, caffeine, tobacco, and analgesics in the period prior to their surgery. They also asked about how frequently they experienced headaches and any postoperative symptoms, such as dizziness, headache, nausea, and so on, that they were experiencing.

What the authors uncovered was a clear relationship between postprocedural headaches and general caffeine consumption. The mean calculated daily intake of caffeine for the subjects in the study was 397 mg, with 96% of the subjects being consumers of caffeinated beverages. The range of calculated daily caffeine consumption was between 0 and 2120 mg. They found no correlation between daily caffeine consumption and the administered anesthesia. The researchers found

> A significantly higher caffeine consumption was found for patients reporting the symptom of headache both for the preoperative and postoperative periods. No significant relationship was observed between perioperative headache and the patients' sex, age, or surgical category, the anesthetic agents or adjuvants used, or previous frequency of headache.[10]

For each 100 mg increase in caffeine consumption, they calculated a 12% increase in the odds of a preoperative headache and a 16% increase in the odds of a postoperative headache.[10]

Other studies confirm this result, including a 1995 study in the *Canadian Journal of Anaesthesia*. In this study, 40 nonsmokers between the ages of 20 and 65 years old who reported at least 200 mg of daily caffeine intake and no more than one headache per week were selected to abstain from caffeine for 16–18 hours before a medical procedure. Blood tests corroborated their abstinence. The researchers divided the sample into two groups: to one they administered caffeine equal to reported daily consumption, and to the other they administered a placebo identical in appearance twice on the day of the procedure and again on the day after.[11]

Despite finding no statistically significant difference in normal daily caffeine intake (both with a mean of around 400 mg) or surgical conditions between the two groups, and despite the small sample size, they discovered a significant difference in reported headaches between the recipients of caffeine tablets and the recipients of placebos. They observed no reported headaches among those who received the caffeine pills either before the procedure or at 6:00 p.m. on the day of the procedure. At 9:00 a.m. the day after, only one recipient of the caffeine pills reported a headache. This is 0%, 0%, and 5% for the 20 subjects selected to receive caffeine. For the 20 subjects who received a placebo, the number who reported a headaches were one, seven, and ten, respectively. This is 5%, 50%, and 35%.[11]

The lesson is clear for business users of big data: an important relationship may well be hidden because it is unexplored. Fennelly and Galletly demonstrated that not only may the underlying cause be nonobvious, it may not even be in the data set until there is a specific reason to look for it. That missing attribute of the data may lead to erroneous conclusions, such as the old commonsense judgement that it was the anesthesia causing the headache rather than caffeine withdrawal. We discuss some brainstorming techniques later in this chapter that may be helpful in teasing out some of these obscure influencers of the data.

Imagine, for example, we analyze lost high-value customers, those in our top 10% according to sales, and we discover over two-thirds of those lost customers were trucking firms. We also see in our data these lost customers had one particular sales contact, Edward. Our analysts run a statistical analysis and confirmed that Edward, who specializes in trucking firms, does indeed have a statistically significant relationship with lost customers. We give Edward until the end of the day to clean out his desk. Furious, Edward finds a job with a competitor a week later and poaches several of our best salespeople.

What we are looking at in this example is, in fact, a variation on our "correlation does not equal causation" discussion from our chapter on statistics. However, in this case, we do not even have all of the history in our data. E-mail streams that we did not read because they were not analyzed or made available to us, and a database that was not linked to our big data system, would tell us that a competitor offered a new and better service at the same price as ours. Edward, in fact, waved his arms and jumped up and down trying to bring this state of affairs to the attention of management, but we missed this communication. As our customers began to defect, Edward found an innovative way to package multiple services together and offer these to our defecting customers. Just under half of them decided that this was a better offer than what the competitor was offering and chose to stay. Yes, we lost some margin, but we saved our customers and came out money ahead thanks to Edwards's efforts. However, that was not in our data because we did not combine systems. Edward was our best salesperson and was dealing well with an adverse situation. He is now gone, taking his knowledge, colleagues, and contacts to benefit our competitor.

We cannot include every variable and every data source in every analysis (as we discussed with black swans)—our business is not an infinite set. It does make sense to fill in missing data about our business when possible. When we have a tentative conclusion that may or may not be accurate, we should refer to this ancillary data. Missing variables do matter to business, just as they do to patients suffering from a headache while recovering from surgery.

Inconsistent Use of Units and Terminology

An exchange rate establishes a ratio between two currencies (€1 euro was equal to $1.31 as we wrote this sentence). This factor fluctuates from day to day, and even throughout the day. More permanent conversion factors exist. One centimeter is equal to 0.3937 inches. One kilogram is equal to 2.2046 pounds. Or not.

In fact, kilograms and pounds do not measure the same thing. Under most circumstances, such as shipping 100 pound bags of potatoes from the United States to a country on the metric system, this does not matter. For space exploration, however, the difference is important. Someone who weighs 100 pounds on Earth weighs less than 17 pounds on the moon and over 200 pounds on Jupiter, assuming it were possible to stand on Jupiter. Someone who is 45 kilograms on Earth is 45 kilograms on the moon and 45 kilograms on Jupiter.[12] This is because a kilogram measures mass and a pound measures weight. Merriam-Webster defines mass as

...the property of a body that is a measure of its inertia, that is commonly taken as a measure of the amount of material it contains, that causes it to have weight in a gravitational field, and that along with length and time constitutes one of the fundamental quantities on which all physical measurements are based.[13]

An object's mass is a property intrinsic to that object. An object's weight is a function of the object's mass and the strength of the gravity upon it. The English system's equivalent of the kilogram is the slug, which is equal to 14.5939 kilograms.

A conversion that has much more room to create confusion here on Earth is barrel of oil-equivalent (BOE). This measure is intended to permit comparisons of the energy contained in a resource by setting it against the number of British thermal units (BTUs) created by burning a barrel of oil. The Internal Revenue Service sets the definition of BOE as 5.8 million BTUs. When measuring natural gas, it most often means anything between 6000 and 6500 cubic feet.[14] Hence, when working with data sets involving measurements of BOE, a clear definition is needed.

A related problem occurs when people use inconsistent terminology, as we touched upon in the discussion of rolling up data under different file types. A common example is that of place names. We can find separate entries for England, Great Britain, and the United Kingdom, which are not exactly synonymous, though London resides in all of them, or for the Netherlands and Holland. North Dakota may be ND, N. Dak., Nodak, or North Dakota.

In May of 2008, political commentator Kevin Phillips published an exposé in *Harper's* covering how the administrations of different presidents changed the way in which they calculated key economic indicators. Tracing number tinkering across Democrat and Republican presidents from John F. Kennedy to George W. Bush, Mr. Phillips (a former advisor to Richard Nixon's campaign and current politically independent analyst) points out how tinkering here and there to make economic trends look better than they are has made recent numbers mean something different from their counterparts from decades ago. This tinkering includes

- Removing discouraged job seekers from the rolls of the unemployed to hide true unemployment numbers
- Lumping together nondiscretionary Social Security figures with discretionary spending in a "unified budget" so the surplus of the former would mask the deficit of the latter

- Removing high-inflation factors such as food and energy from inflation figures to create a "core inflation" that was in fact an artificially lowered version of the true rate
- Substituting "owner equivalent rent," or what a homeowner might gain by renting out a house, to artificially lower inflation in housing
- Reclassifying military personnel as "employed" rather than outside of the labor force to lower the unemployment rate
- Counting only those who had been looking for a job for less than a year as unemployed (a continuation of the removal of discouraged job seekers from the unemployment numbers) to lower official unemployment figures even further
- Substituting lower-inflation goods for higher-inflation goods or reweighting high-inflation goods with the rationale that these higher-inflation goods will be used less and therefore should influence inflation figures less

All of these points involve redefining values such as inflation, unemployment, or deficits through redefinition. With each presidency, the definitions of these values change in a directional manner to make economic indicators appear more positive than they otherwise would. Mr. Phillips states "Based on criteria in place a quarter century ago, today's US unemployment rate is somewhere between 9 and 12 percent; the inflation rate is as high as 7 or even 10 percent; economic growth since the 2001 recession has been mediocre"[15]

In contrast with the previous statement, the Bureau of Labor Statistics reports, "The unemployment rate rose from 5.0 in April 2008 to 5.5 percent in May 2008."[16] The official figure for the CPI-U (consumer price index for urban consumers) was 4.2% for May 2008.[17]

An interesting variation of this problem, in historical texts, is discussed in a TED talk given by Erez Lieberman Aiden and Jean-Baptiste Michel in July 2011.[18] The authors discuss the use of Google's digital repository of books to conduct analyses, demonstrating how everything from censorship and propaganda to fads in the use of "argh," "aargh," "aaargh," and "aaaargh" can be seen in graphs of the frequency of these words in the text Google stores. Through the use of the publishing date, language, and other metadata, researchers find it possible to shine the light of data analysis on cultures and eras.[18]

One key point for the purpose of discussion is what they find when they look for the word "best." Going back to around 1800, its use drops off precipitously. It is not that the word did not exist before 1800 though—it is because it was more often spelled "beft" in keeping with the use of the letter *F* to convey the sound of *S* during that time. (Using Google's Ngram Viewer as this book was written, with an undoubtedly changed data set and without the data scrubbing described in the talk, the prior use of "beft" is still visible but does not supersede "best" in common usage before 1800.)[18]

This data problem is uncommon when a well-functioning, automated system is running and recording data. The sensors in a temperature-sensitive warehouse will generally not switch from Fahrenheit to Celsius spontaneously, and a device for monitoring the weight of bags of produce will not shift from pounds to kilograms. These inconsistencies will usually creep into a data set when

- We have manual data entry, including the use of unstructured data, now more common with the ability of big data systems to analyze such data. Unstructured data, by definition, does not fit into a normal form, neatly scrubbed. Some users will likely rely on one set of units and one set of terminology whereas other users will rely on another.
- We have many different types of equipment or sensors in use—resulting from any number of causes, such as a merger between two companies who use different equipment to generate their data or the still-incomplete phasing out of one type of equipment in favor of a new one. If the proper conversions are not in place before we feed the data into the data set, then we will have internal inconsistencies.
- Two or more data sets are being combined—occurring at the level of the data sets used rather than the equipment generating the data. Different organizations default to different measurements. One of the strengths of big data systems is just this ability to create a unified whole out of diverse data sets at a reasonable cost. This creation of a composite analysis from different data sets means the analyst must be more aware of units and terminology than ever.

When examining the data, it may or may not be sufficient to merely convert units. The conversion between two measures of length, such as meters and inches, is straightforward. So are conversions of different measures used to effectively convey the same information, such as mass and weight on the surface of the earth (although for aerospace uses, the pounds and kilograms clearly represent related but different concepts).

With measures of unlike units, such as volume and weight, we can effectively convert from one to another if they are measuring a consistent and well-defined substance—distilled water being a good example. Such conversions are much less effective when used to describe highly variable substances, such as the soil removed from a construction site (which will contain combinations of sand, clay, rock, and topsoil, each of which is highly variable) and mineral ores.

The most difficult conversions are those such as the BOEs from earlier in this discussion, for which we have no clearly defined measure. In fact, both oil and most substances with which we compare it can vary greatly in quality and composition. Derived units such as BOE are useful for understanding the magnitude of what we examine, such as approximately how many years of production remain in a reservoir, but they will lack the precision to be useful in measuring finer causes and effects.

In the petroleum industry, another factor affecting data is how the states report their production data. Different state agencies, such as the Railroad Commission of Texas and the North Dakota Industrial Commission, require the reporting of oil production within their states. These data extend beyond production to include other well characteristics, and petroleum and service companies use this information to gain awareness of the general state of the industry. Among the leaders in processing and reporting these data is the firm IHS. As IHS notes, however, not all states report at the level of an individual well. In a PowerPoint presentation available on its website, the company discusses the reporting of lease-level production in Texas and Louisiana.[19] As the unit being reported is larger than a single well, this reporting requires that the production be allocated to wells. Although IHS is renowned for its diligence in reporting data, and allocation to wells within a lease is the best option available to provide data on individual wells, allocation is not the same as reporting directly at the well level.

BIASES

Sampling Bias

When we cannot measure all members of a population, we take a sample. The term *population* not only refers to populations of people in this context, but it also can refer to other living creatures, inanimate objects, or events such as sales or emergencies. Sampling leads to a common bias, which is named in a straightforward enough manner: *sampling bias*. Any time we decide not to report an issue to avoid bureaucracy, consequences, or wasting time, we witness a form of sampling bias in action.

Cases where such a bias is common include reporting fender benders, filing an insurance claim for minor injuries, and calling the police for minor pranks against property. In all of these cases, we might make an argument that it is advantageous to avoid reporting smaller incidents we can resolve outside of the reporting mechanism.

Imagine running an analysis on car accidents using insurance data. What we will find is that smaller fender benders—especially those where the persons involved will incur higher insurance rates that outrun the cost of the repairs if a claim is filed—are absent from the data set. This means the number of fender benders in the data set will be smaller than the overall number of accidents involving customers of the insurance company whose data we analyze. If we calculate the average dollar amount of the damage from automobile collisions, the result will appear artificially high. All of those smaller amounts missing from the data set will also be those the least expensive to repair. Also, the standard deviation will be unnaturally low, as it will be those small-dollar outliers that will be underreported. If we are using insurance data, as analysts we must be clear that we are measuring insurance claims from a particular company, and our results do not reflect car accidents in general.

Another example occurs when reporting sales leads. Imagine we have a firm that bids for construction contracts. Our business development staff builds relationships and develops sales. These tend to be larger sales that involve negotiation and multiple contacts between our firm and our clients. Due to the complexity of these sales we must nurse along, it is beneficial to log all contacts into a customer resources management (CRM) database.

Now, our business is making a strategic decision about which sectors to focus on and which clients are the most valuable versus those who cost more to maintain than they deliver in profit. We may tap into the CRM data, and it will provide important insights, but it may just as easily mislead us. How does this happen?

There are several ways. In an earlier chapter, we discussed shadow information technology (IT). Shadow IT is the phenomenon where different parts of the business develop their own solutions that are not officially sanctioned components of the central IT system. We may have other databases, of which management may not even be aware, that log business development activities. The data found in these systems may well be absent from our centralized CRM system.

If we have a division—we shall call it the Red Division—that specializes in small, quick projects that are often requested by clients who do not pass through a bidding system, then this division may well close these deals without logging them the CRM system. These deals are not nursed along until a sale is made.

If a different division, which we will call the Blue Division, has larger projects and a director who ties bonuses to accurate reporting of potential sales, then this division may log an abnormally high number of lost sales or sales that drag along slowly.

Is the director of the Blue Division a less effective director than the director of the Red Division? If we compare CRM data, he may well appear to be the inferior director regardless of the underlying truth.

If we see managers whose bonuses depend on their portion of the profit and loss statement run away from cost center projects, it is often related to just this kind of bias being built into the data. Selection bias can have real consequences and drive behavior in perverse directions.

Sometimes a sampling bias is deliberate. Within the United States, the television and online news sources of choice are more and more selected so as to confirm the political views of the viewer. Commentators often host polls, inviting viewers or readers to log in or call to vote on a particular issue. Those issues for which there is a strong polarization along partisan lines, such as abortion or gun control, will be deeply swayed by which core audience is responding to the poll. The audience for a politically slanted news source will have self-selected.

Sampling bias may be innocent in intent if not in results. This bias has become a concern in polling now that more homes have dropped their landline phones. Why would this matter? If there are different characteristics on average between households which have cell phone access only versus those which also have landlines, the results of the polling will be skewed. The Centers for Disease Control adjusted its telephone polling in 2011 to include both cell phones and landlines but expressed concern about the different rates of answering between cell phones and landlines.[20]

Data may also be withheld for valid reasons, yet still create a de facto sampling bias. This situation may happen to protect confidentiality, perhaps in the event of a small sample that all but reveals to which person or organization the data point refers. Imagine we have a health study that breaks out cases of a particular disease that carries some stigma and does so at community level. Even if the identity of a sufferer of the disease remains confidential, a nefarious researcher can determine that person's identity if our example individual lives in a small or sparsely populated community.

A simple consideration underlies the withholding of economic information, such as the production statistics for a particular industry. If a producer has the only production facility, field, or well in a particular county, even anonymized data communicate the firm's secrets and promote legal problems for the possessor of the data. This situation need not result in poor quality data, but it may occur if the data are only withheld in those circumstances where they could prove problematic. For example, in our discussion of withholding information on a disease, we stated it could prove a problem in small or sparsely populated communities. Withholding it in those cases would lead to a misleading statistical artifact, indicating smaller communities are largely avoiding this disease.

Bias is also often introduced by the replication of some entries multiple times. A frustrated individual may manually introduce this situation by thinking a computer is malfunctioning when it is not, and by repeatedly hitting the submit button. It may be the computer itself is incorrectly replicating some entries. It may also be a person manually entering data into multiple systems due to a misunderstanding, not knowing that the systems automatically share every entry with each other. Regardless of the cause, data replication is maddeningly common and biases the data simultaneously.

Incorrect information may be the result of outright fraud. The Sarbanes-Oxley Act of 2002 became the law of the United States after a series of public-company scandals, including those involving Enron, WorldCom, and Tyco. The misleading information issued by these companies was a driver of the law, which requires among other actions that company officers sign off on financial statements issued for any firm whose shares are listed in the United States. Whereas the fraud that led to the Sarbanes-Oxley Act would clearly have revealed errors for those using those firms' data in their calculations, those calculations also have the power of uncovering fraud—in essence, a double-edged sword. The field of forensic accounting does just this. If this is a concern in an organization, the authors of this book recommend that specialized and qualified legal or law enforcement personnel trained in detecting fraud are utilized.

Publication Bias

Publication bias is a variant of sampling bias, affecting which unstructured data (e.g., publications) become available. Sampling bias distorts the inputs used in a study; publication bias distorts which studies readers can access. Studies not drawing the preferred conclusions may never reach publication. This statement seems vaguely conspiratorial, but often the reasons we do not see a publication are simply because the researchers find a greater reward in uncovering an exciting result than in showing no significant results exist. We see no need for any malfeasance to explain this bias. In a system that archives and scans scientific literature, this would clearly be a concern.

However, this bias extends beyond the scientific literature. Imagine using Internet conversations to develop a risk map of different countries as part of our international diversification strategy. Clearly, biased news coverage or hostile information operations would have the potential to distort our results. Just consider how rigidly held opinions regarding the land dispute between Israel and Palestine filter into more general discourse. Nuance disappears and hyperbole dominates both sides of the argument. We see exaggerated or falsified news, and each side is unwilling to demonstrate unbiased behavior. The acumen of the assemblage that we are trying to harness drowns in noise. Instead of alerting us to easily overlooked but underreported threats to our investment, our system will inundate us with nonexistent or exaggerated threats.

Survivorship Bias

The Wikipedia definition of the survivorship bias, which includes a summary of why it is important, is succinct and insightful:

> the logical error of concentrating on the people or things that "survived" some process and inadvertently overlooking those that did not because of their lack of visibility. This can lead to false conclusions in several different ways. The survivors may literally be people, as in a medical study, or could be companies or research subjects or applicants for a job, or anything that must make it past some selection process to be considered further.[21]

Survivorship bias, just as with selection bias, relates to data that were once part of the data set, but are no longer a part because they did not survive. Nassim Nicholas Taleb contributed greatly to introducing this bias to the general population in his book *Fooled by Randomness*. One of the discussions in his book centers on how survivorship bias causes the illusion that mutual fund managers can outperform the market. The superior performance of some actively managed mutual funds is, argues Taleb, luck. How can this be?

Survivorship bias is in many ways more cruel to those who understand statistics than those that do not, and for a counterintuitive reason. Consider the odds of outperforming the market for, say, 6 consecutive years. If we assume that the odds of beating the market are exactly 50% (they are not, since we are dealing with averages and averages do not break down so neatly), then the odds are 1:64. In the real world, this could work out to a sizeable proportion of fund managers usually beating the market. Statistically literate individuals appreciate the unlikelihood of so many managers beating the market just by chance, so the idea that chance alone could boost a manager to a consistent winning streak seems ridiculous on the surface. If chance is so much less likely than what is observed in the market, it must be skill. What is less appreciated is how selection bias can highlight the winning managers and bury the losing managers where the data do not find them.

Perhaps the best way to ease us into understanding this bias is a thought experiment. Imagine there is a 50% chance of beating the market due to pure luck for 1 year and an equal chance of underperforming the market. As with a coin that lands on its edge, let us discount the chance of performing exactly at the level of the market.

A fund manager's chance of beating the market for 1 year is 50%; for 2 years running, it is 25%; for 3 years it is 12.5%. By the time we reach 6 years, only 1.56% of the original sample will have beaten the market on a regular basis. The survivorship bias will tend to keep those positive outliers, even if their performance is due only to luck.

Let us start with a cohort of 200 fund managers and monitor their performance. If we dismiss any manager who underperforms the market for a year and keep any manager who outperforms the market for the same duration, we can expect to employ 100 managers as we start the second year and 50 as we start the third. We will retain four remaining managers after the sixth year (let us round up for any fractions, even if this introduces our own small bias into our sample), and by the ninth year, we will find just one manager.

Each year, we will introduce another 200 managers. What will happen by the time we reach our ninth year is, just by chance, we will admire one legend who has beaten the market for 9 years running. We will have just over 400 fund managers in total, including the 200 in their first year who have not yet failed and 200 who experience some history of survival.

If we eliminate those not yet tested in their first year, reducing our sample size to just over 200, and then calculate the average number of years that they beat the market, we will arrive at approximately 4 years—even though an unbiased sample, in which those who lose are not eliminated, would arrive at an average of one half of a year. Survivorship bias is real, and it is easy to overlook. We have just explained superior performance through simple mathematics, where we need no real recourse to skill.

In reality, the math is much messier than what we used in the 50/50 thought experiment above. How does this play out in real life? Let us start with the work of two giants in the world of finance—names forever engraved in the intellects of business school graduates worldwide.

Eugene Fama, an economist at the Booth School of Business at the University of Chicago, and Kenneth French, a professor of finance at Dartmouth College's Tuck School of Business, published a study in *The Journal of Finance* in 2010 demonstrating that managed funds do not outperform simulated funds. The authors compared the results of 10,000 bootstrap simulations of funds against a sample of actively managed funds with primarily investments in US equities between 1984 and 2006.

An important financial concept used in this simulation is alpha (α). Investopedia defines alpha, the first letter in the Greek alphabet as

> A measure of performance on a risk-adjusted basis. Alpha takes the volatility (price risk) of a mutual fund and compares its risk-adjusted performance to a benchmark index. The excess return of the fund relative to the return of the benchmark index is a fund's alpha.[22]

Investopedia then clarifies this definition with the following explanation, "A positive alpha of 1.0 means the fund has outperformed its benchmark index by 1%. Correspondingly, a similar negative alpha would indicate an underperformance of 1%."[22]

Fama and French set α to zero. In other words, they ran their simulation so their results would perform no better and no worse than the market itself. These results were then compared to the results obtained by actively managed mutual funds. According to the authors, they allowed for some room for skill, both positive and negative, among active mutual fund managers, but we do not need to invoke skill to explain the vast majority of managed fund performance. While Fama and French do leave the door open for skill, it need not be any more than a minor player in explaining fund results.

A 2002 study by Mark Carhart of Goldman Sachs, Jennifer Carpenter and Anthony Lynch of New York University, and David Musto of the University of Pennsylvania demonstrated empirical evidence of survivorship bias.

> Evidence suggests that funds disappear following poor multi-year performance... [W]e demonstrate both analytically and empirically that this survival rule typically causes the bias in estimates of average annual performance to increase in the sample length, at a declining rate.[23]

The authors point out that the relationship is complicated (the world is messier than thought experiments and theories), and they do warn, "Researchers forced to use survivor-only samples need to consider carefully the likely impact of using such samples on the test statistics of interest."[23]

Financial researchers take the survivorship bias as a serious concern. The Center for Research in Security Prices at the University of Chicago's Booth School of Business went so far as to create a database designed to avoid survivorship bias.

In the event one must work with a data set in which the survivorship bias is present, what to do? As we can see in the study by Carhart and his colleagues, this bias can cause meaningful distortions in the results of an analysis. The authors point out

> many areas of finance run cross-sectional regressions with performance as the independent variable. The use of a survivor-only sample may seriously bias such regressions. For instance, researchers often relate cross-country differences in equity market performance to cross-country differences in equity market characteristics. Our data suggest that data unavailability for failed equity markets can have important ramifications for such comparisons, particularly if the characteristics in question are related to survival. Similarly, many finance studies sort stocks on firm characteristics. When survival criteria are related to these characteristics, survivor conditioning can bias the return on the spread portfolios.[23]

In other words, real studies of real data can disseminate misleading results because of this bias.

DATA AS A VIDEO, NOT A SNAPSHOT: DIFFERENT VIEWPOINTS AS A NOISE FILTER

In its August 2012 issue, *The American Conservative* magazine arrived in mailboxes and on newsstands with the controversial headline "Race, IQ, and Wealth: How Political Bias Distorts the Facts" splashed across the cover. The cover was sensational, but the article referenced was a thoughtful rebuttal of theories of inherent racial differences in intelligence.

The author, Ron Unz (who is also the magazine's publisher), began his article by discussing the debate around the controversial study *IQ and the Wealth of Nations* by Richard Lynn and Tatu Vanhanen, who had argued that immutable genetic differences in intelligence quotient (IQ) between different national populations explained their wealth or poverty. Unz points out

> Correlation does not imply causality, let alone the particular direction of the causal arrow. A traditional liberal model positing that socio-economic factors strongly influence performance on academic ability tests would predict exactly the same distribution of international results found by Lynn and Vanhanen.[24]

The approach Unz uses is to look for movement in the data in order to tease out what happens through time. In other words, if the differences in IQ are related to inherent ethnic differences, these differences between groups should not change over time. If we observe movement in the data during the period under study, then the differences are mutable. Unz is taking a movie view of the data as opposed to a snapshot view. Unz states

> Critics have often suggested, not without some plausibility, that when Western-designed IQ tests are applied to Third World peoples, the results may be distorted by hidden cultural bias. There is also the possible impact of malnutrition and other forms of extreme deprivation, or even practical difficulties in administering tests in desperately impoverished nations...[24]

Unz's critique makes sense. Many evolving factors could skew IQ results between groups. Consider the challenges to performing difficult intellectual tasks when the tasks are unfamiliar or when we suffer distress. Additional factors not mentioned by Unz may also play a role.

One is education. A better educational system will provide the population with a broader intellectual toolkit with which to approach difficult problems. Another is interest. In countries where the IQ test is well known, a high IQ is a bragging point. Why would anyone in a country where IQ is not well known and rarely discussed even care about an abstract problem that involves choosing which drawing does not belong? What does it matter if one thinks through a problem with care or just says what seems correct at the start?

Finally, there is a high probability of a bias built in for certain forms of intelligence. The Flynn effect, named after James Flynn, who did much to draw attention to it, is the constant upward drift in IQ scores by approximately three points per decade that is taking place worldwide and across tests. IQ test scoring needs to be periodically reset so that a score of 100 remains the mean and the standard deviation remains at 15. Ulric Neisser wrote in a 1997 *American Scientist* article:

> Greater sophistication about tests surely plays some role in the rise, but there are other possible contributing factors: better nutrition, more schooling, altered child-rearing practices and the technology-driven changes of culture itself. Right now, none of these factors can be ruled out; all of them may be playing some part in the increasing scores. Whatever the causes may be, the sheer size of the gains forces us to reconsider many long-held assumptions about intelligence tests and what they measure.[25]

In other words, an IQ score that measures an immutable, genetic intelligence without any ambiguity should not drift upward like this.

John Medina, a molecular biologist who is also the author of the brilliant book *Brain Rules*, lists exercise, sleep, interest, and other malleable factors as the main factors influencing cognitive ability. Medina only asserts what passes the MGF, or Medina Grump Factor. For any study to be included in his book, it must be published in a peer-reviewed journal and replicated.[26]

One of the authors of this book once applied for a job online that unexpectedly kicked him over into a cognitive test right after he woke up and before he needed to leave for another commitment. Needless to say, situational factors affected his performance. To whoever read the results and where the cognitive ability is the signal, the noise of sleepiness and time pressure clearly buried the outcome. The recipient had no way of seeing that and only saw the aftermath was suboptimal. At another time, the same author took another examination for a different company in the midafternoon. He was well rested and comfortable, and he logged one of the highest scores that tester had seen. The difference between his performances on these two tests cannot logically be grounded on innate intelligence.

Unz takes two actions to ensure he actually measures the signal—the existence, or lack thereof, of innate differences in IQ across groups—and not the noise of cultural biases or factors such as nutrition and home-country education. First, he limits himself to exploring countries that are similar. Second, he attends to movements in IQ scores. In other words, he focuses on the dimension of time.

Unz then demonstrates that genetically indistinguishable populations, such as East and West Germans (prior to reunification), Croats and Austrians, and Turks and Greeks, demonstrated IQ differences that were reflective of the economic circumstances of their countries at the time of testing. The yawning chasm in the tested IQ, "perhaps as large as 25 points," between American Jews (primarily the Ashkenazi who immigrated to the United States from Europe) and Israeli Jews (also primarily from the same population, who left Europe at the time the data were generated) would be difficult to explain genetically, but it could well be the result of the large difference in per capita income between the United States and Israel at the time the numbers were drawn.

If IQ is determined by genetics, then it should not be asymmetric between similar groups. Nevertheless, it is, and scores are converging. As Ireland evolved from a poor rural country to a booming center of technology:

> During the early 1970s, a huge national sample had placed the Ireland IQ at 87, the lowest in all of Europe, but today Ireland's [Programme for International Student Assessment] scores are about average for the continent and roughly the same as those for France and Britain, while Irish per capita incomes have pulled a little ahead.[24]

Croatian IQ scores went from being 12 points lower on average than Austrian scores to nearly the same values. This growth is not the Flynn effect simply bringing up all scores equally, but rather, it represents the astonishing reduction of a gap. The magnitude of this diminution of difference is a powerful argument against inherent differences in IQ between groups.

Using proxies for IQ, Unz points out that as Latinos in the United States become an economic power in their own right, and as they close the gap in educational attainment, any gaps in measures of "intelligence" are likewise narrowing. This outcome is no longer speculation; it is visible in the data. (As a side note, in a separate article, Unz also debunked charges that Latinos in the United States are a major crime risk. By using data sources to control for mean age differences and immigration-related offenses, Unz demonstrated that Latino incarceration rates are in line with those of non-Hispanic whites—careful data analysis is a useful antidote to careless TV punditry.[27])

By using time as a dimension and by treating data as diachronic (a video) rather than as synchronic (a snapshot), Unz is able to demonstrate "proof" of differences in IQ between ethnic groups does not stand up. In common data analysis parlance, advocates of inherent racial IQ differences are mistaking the noise for the signal. They are reading situational factors and interpreting them as genetic. This is why arguments for inherent differences use static arguments. When he introduces time and measures dynamic movements, the arguments become unsound.

Think of static on the radio on a long-distance car trip. As we move away from population centers, the radio station we were listening to becomes harder to hear. The sound quality deteriorates and more static passes through our speakers. If we are one of those drivers who cannot live without music and forgot to bring any recorded music, we may have experienced listening to music overwhelmed by noise, picking out whatever music we can whenever we can. The signal-to-noise ratio varies with our distance from the radio transmitter, the weather conditions, signal interference, the choice of modulation, and any obstacles, such as mountains, that are in the way.

This signal-to-noise ratio also exists in data. If one thinks of a transmission as being comprised of data, the comparison between the two is not merely an analogy; it is a comparison of two forms of the same phenomenon. Usually, though, noise is more difficult to directly perceive in the data of our data set than it is on the radio. Even if we never heard a particular song before, we know the sound of different instruments and the human voice enough to know the "tshshsh" of radio static is not part of the song.

In other data, discerning the noise may not be easy. The whole reason we analyze the data is to calculate the trend. We do not already know the appearance of our trend, or even to what degree it exists. Furthermore, the noise and the signal may be so entwined we cannot tease them apart. To understand how this is the case, we need to step back and reexamine the case of radio static.

With the radio transmission of a song, we have two broad components that differ qualitatively. We have the song that exists as it is and we have the act of broadcasting the song.

With the arrival of digital recordings, the ticks and crackles of records and the decline of sound quality through loss of magnetism on tapes are no longer issues. The quality of sound is preserved, provided the medium remains undamaged. When we are listening to the broadcast of a song, and the quality of the broadcast deteriorates badly due to static, we are not hearing noise that is inseparable from the data. If we buy a copy of the song to which we are listening and play it on our computer, the static will be gone.

It is the process of the radio signal leaving the broadcast station and arriving at our radio that introduces the noise, due to the factors we already mentioned. This is important. It means a version of the data that does not contain that noise is available. We can isolate the noise and determine exactly what is noise and what is signal.

Now, try to do the same with stock market data or political polling data. Both the daily movements that amount to next to nothing in aggregate and the major shifts are made up of the same thing: people buying and selling stocks or reporting their preferences of candidates. We know of no way to neatly isolate the signal from the noise. The best that one can do is to observe the trends over time and see what develops over a longer interval.

This situation then raises the question of what is noise in such a circumstance. Noise is the movement whose cause is difficult to designate. However, over time in watching these trends, the deterioration of a company will differentiate itself from the havoc caused by day traders panicking from a subtle downtick in the market. The loss of trust in a candidate will differentiate itself from the electorate responding to the press panicking over a moment of honesty (usually referred to as a "gaffe").

In Mr. Unz's work, the evidence of a connection between IQ and ethnicity did not withstand a dynamic, time-elapsed examination separating the noise from the signal. That the IQ scores varied with national development but converged when this difference no longer pushed IQ scores apart is quite convincing evidence that IQ and ethnicity are not tied strongly by any immutable factors. The most we can see is a transient relationship. The signal and noise become separate.

This is not just an academic issue related to social trends. The difference between signal and noise can strongly affect our business. When using data to seek stable characteristics such as "The performance of managed mutual funds when compared to index funds," it is in our firm's best interest to observe and record the data across time and across circumstances, as did Ron Unz with IQ differences. Time is a useful filter to differentiate noise and signal.

With stock market data, we anticipate daily fluctuations. The majority of these do not constitute a trend and are unworthy of worry. We have all seen people glance nervously at their phone or computer screen and mutter something like, "Oh my God! I am down $1150 today!" Does that matter? Maybe yes, but most often no. The price fluctuates. If the stock price continues on an upward trend, in general, then our investor friend will be fine. It is, however, a good idea to not withdraw money in a slump. These slumps, however, are different from the small and transient common stock price drops that happen to stocks every trading day.

Nassim Nicholas Taleb stated:

> As I am writing these lines I see the following headlines on my Bloomberg:
>
> - *Dow is up 1.03 on lower interest rates.*
> - *Dollar is down 0.12 yen on higher Japanese surplus.*
>
> and so on for an entire page. If I translate it well, the journalist claims to provide an explanation for something that amounts to *perfect noise* [emphasis in the original]. A move of 1.03 with the Dow at 11,000 constitutes less than a 0.01% move. Such a move does not warrant an explanation. There is nothing there that an honest person can try to explain; there are no reasons to adduce.[28]

The consequences of mistaking signal for noise in investing are obvious; an investment that makes sense grounded on information based on a meaningful signal we know to be correct becomes at best a risk when what appears to be a signal is instead really noise. The same goes for marketing data, logistics data, and fuel prices.

Richard Lynn, a coauthor of the study Ron Unz was responding to in the example above, stated in an interview that while working as a professor at the Economic and Social Research Institute in Dublin, Ireland, he thought much about the problem of the country's poverty at the time and how it should be handled.

> I settled down to investigate the economic and social problems of Ireland and think about what contribution I could make to finding public policies that would help solve them. The major problem was the economic backwardness, and when I researched the literature it was not long before I discovered that the Irish had a low average IQ. So I formulated the theory that the low IQ was likely a significant reason for the economic backwardness.

The solution for this problem was obvious. What was needed was a set of eugenic policies that would raise the Irish IQ.[29]

Lynn was in no position to implement a eugenics program, but the lesson we can draw is clear. The morality of eugenics aside, the simple fact is that Ireland boosted its gross domestic product (GDP), became a world-class technology hub, and raised the average IQ of its population on its own while respecting the rights and freedom of its own population. It did so through education and raising the standard of living. A eugenics program would have been a tragedy, delivering palpable misery on a population that had its own hopes and dreams. It would have been even more of a tragedy because it would have been utterly unnecessary.

WHAT IS MY TOOLKIT FOR IMPROVING MY DATA?

There are several methods for improving the quality of one's data. Some of these are quantitative and some are qualitative. Some are time-consuming and are best for data analysis whose results will result in significant investment. Others are simple and straightforward and can be applied to many circumstances.

First, having the team that is most knowledgeable about the data brainstorm potential problems is valuable. Whether or not there are data quality problems, just having the team be aware of any potential problems and able to report them is valuable. As certified Six Sigma Black Belts, both authors are familiar with brainstorming tools. Brainstorming often has a reputation as being a waste of time ("let us go through this formality so we have a work product to show, then get back to our real work"); this need not be the case. In Six Sigma, brainstorming is structured and goal oriented.

To gain an idea of how brainstorming can be used on data quality, we will use a real example from a project one of the authors conducted. The session started out as a traditional brainstorming session, then became confusing when it was clear different users had different ideas of how the data gathering and reporting systems functioned. These were intelligent, well-informed users. Their day-to-day jobs did not require them to necessarily understand every single nuance of the systems in question, but they did work with the systems.

Part of the brainstorming session involved mapping the systems. Who were the users of each system? What system fed information into which other system? What kinds of data were fed? How were the data reported? What was measured and which units were used? How was it measured? For user-reported data, which incentives had an impact on how data were reported? How did the different systems overlap? How often were systems updated?.

Next, the team began to brainstorm the new system to replace it and how to improve data quality. In a big data project, such improvements will likewise be central to quality reporting from then on. However, danger lurks. If data quality abruptly improves, then an artificial discontinuity between the old data and the new arises. The process we measure may not necessarily change in efficacy, but the before and after data may well indicate significant differences because they measure various things or because they use diverse methods of measurement.

The results of these brainstorming sessions will be helpful to the team designing and implementing the big data project that our firm is planning. The benefits expand beyond simply identifying computer systems and variables, however. By understanding the expertise of the brainstorming team, the big data project team can also anticipate other important aspects of the project such as

- Who are the internal owners of different data systems?
- Which attributes come from which source?
- Which attributes are calculated, and which formulae and which other attributes are used in the calculation?
- Which attributes caused the most data quality headaches?
- What are potential sources of error in data collection, data transmission, and data storage?
- What are the refresh schedules for the different data sources? How often is a data refresh needed? How often are the data in fact available?
- Since we are partially starting anew, what is the wish list of future users and what data must be available to make that a reality?
- How large are the data repositories, both in standard data storage measurements and by the number of records?
- What legal and policy issues are affected by accessing the data?
- What sources of data have been traditionally overlooked? Often, we will overlook unstructured data due to the difficulty of dealing with it. Big data, however, can make it useful.

Two examples of specific brainstorming methods are the KJ method and the Ishikawa diagram, also known as the fishbone diagram. The KJ method is a more focused alternative to what is known as affinity diagramming. Affinity diagramming is the use of free brainstorming of ideas, one each on a sticky note, with the notes then organized into natural groupings by the team afterward. The group will tend to stay on task and the tool is excellent at reducing wasted time, effort, and distractions.

The team should be multidisciplinary. If we have multiple individuals in the same department who have different approaches to similar problems, we prefer the participation of both. Furthermore, we prefer participation of the members of the data implementation team, including both internal resources and external consultants. The idea of brainstorming is to cast a wide net to pinpoint problems and seek solutions, and then to present the product as a consensus document to the parties responsible for delivering results.

We can perform the process with groups of arbitrary size, often in less than an hour. Two or more colors of notes (sticky notes or 3×5 cards) should be used to keep different categories distinct. We recommend using a room with much wall space, such as a large meeting room or auditorium (although auditoria possess some drawbacks, such as odd acoustics). This form of brainstorming works best with a facilitator, along with supplies such as whiteboards, flipcharts, and projectors.

The process starts with what is called the "focus question." This question drives the brainstorming, and every session revolves around a question. Sample focus questions are

- What is the purpose of our data?
- How is our use of data suboptimal and what can we do to better apply our data?
- What characteristics of our data prove problematic in how we use our data?
- What did we learn from previous studies?
- What are the biggest obstacles to getting what we want?

Once we decide on the focus question, the team will work for around an hour. A multidisciplinary team is better than one with a common background among the team members. The team puts data onto the sticky notes, one item per note. We will place these notes—which should be in random order—on the wall.

After all team members add their sticky notes to the wall, the facilitator directs them to group similar items on another wall. Team members may move items into existing groups or create new ones. Up to now, we permit no discussion, since it is often counterproductive when we attempt to interact without moving toward conformity of opinion. We finish this stage once we group all of the sticky notes.

We mentioned using two colors of sticky notes. The second color provides headings for each group; if we use more colors, we can do likewise. Often, the more concise we make the name on the note, the better. Each team member should read every group sticky note and every group name.

As this stage is all about priorities, we want team members to rank their choices. They can mark their choices by priority (3 being highest) or use sticky dots on the second colored sticky notes (the names). We endeavor to avoid discussion thus far during our session. Until we prioritize, we do not want to waste time discussing topics of little import; hence, the significance of voting.

Once we tally the votes, we discuss how the groups arrived at their results. Dissenting voices are important, even though at this stage they do not have the power to alter the consensus.

The strengths of this approach should be clear. We are pulling together a team based on individuals with a diverse array of experiences and talents. These individuals have encountered different problems and different opportunities. They dredge up a broad array of potential issues before any surprises arise. Knowing we have an arcane legal issue—regarding a subset of data—as the project is beginning makes it possible to begin addressing the problem immediately so it does not become a roadblock to later progress.

Ishikawa Diagram

It is easy to sneer at a wholly qualitative tool with a high cuteness factor like the Ishikawa diagram, also known as the fish bone diagram (templates exist to fit the "fish bones" of the Ishikawa diagram into a fish-shaped body complete with fins and head), but it has become an indispensable troubleshooting tool in the world of Lean and Six Sigma. The power of this tool is illustrated in yet another name it has: the cause-and-effect diagram. The example in Figure 10.3 illustrates the general layout.

The genius of the Ishikawa diagram is that it takes a desired end state, such as "improved consistency in data quality" or "a higher rate of compliance with the internal reporting of job data," and structures the discussion to encourage participants to broaden the factors they consider. The tool

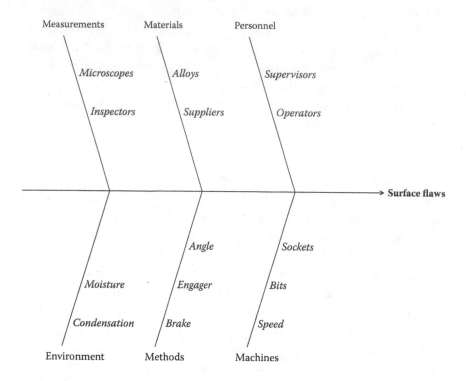

Cause and effect diagram

FIGURE 10.3
Ishikawa diagram.

encourages this approach by placing the primary attribute being discussed (or, to use statistical terms, the dependent variable) as the head of the fish and each of the attributes that affect it (or the potential independent variables) on a separate "bone." The shape of the diagram makes it obvious the bones function as inputs to the head of the fish, preventing the conversation from moving astray. Putting these categories in separate boxes instead of on fish bones would enable the participants to deviate from the goal they are trying to reach. As a rule, the six major "bones" have been

- Man (or manpower or person)
- Machine
- Measurement
- Method
- Materials
- Environment

The reason these are the traditional bones is because the Ishikawa diagram has its roots in the worlds of Lean and Six Sigma, and it has been a central tool for identifying the potential root causes of quality and efficiency problems. The use of the five "M"s and one "E" is by no means a requirement. The point is that we put a problem or opportunity in the "head" of the fish, major categories on the bones, and then brainstorm possible causes under each major bone. Other categories can include, but are not limited to, the following:

- People
- Policies
- Premises
- Transport
- Finance
- Information technology (IT)
- Management (another "M")
- Education
- Supply
- Demand
- Lead time
- Reorder point

Well-chosen categories help during the brainstorming sessions. The purpose of the categories is to spark creative thinking with regard to the problem-solving at hand. If a participant works in IT and sees everything through the lens of IT needs and IT policies, the Ishikawa diagram forces this participant to imagine the problem from the points of view represented on the other bones, such as finance. It enables the participant to discover and record connections that would be lost if each participant were not forced to look beyond his or her own functional silo.

How can we apply the Ishikawa diagram to data quality? Suppose our "fish head" is "data quality." We could include some factors in our chart such as the following:

- Quantity
- Outliers
- Probability distribution function
- Data dependencies
- Incentives (official and unofficial)

- Categorization
- Source
- Measurement

The outputs of a brainstorming session using the Ishikawa diagram are useful in and of themselves, but they become even more useful when used as the basis for further discussion. We should also remain cognizant of the need for high-quality participation and investment in the Ishikawa process; otherwise, this qualitative tool wastes times and yields products of minimal value.

Interrelationship Digraph

The interrelationship digraph is appropriate for simple cause and effect modeling, such as would be useful for ironing out annoying data quality issues in which different parts of the problem reinforce other parts. It is also an ideal follow-up to the two previous methods of brainstorming discussed in this section, because it ties together the causes and effects and how they relate to each other.

As a child, one of us was a fan of a now defunct magazine called *CARtoons*, targeting car enthusiasts with *Mad Magazine* styled drawings and humor, but with an automotive twist. One cartoon featured a man examining the wreckage of a car from all different angles. Afterwards, he hit the car once with a hammer in a location he carefully selected and all of the dents popped out, leaving the car looking like new. The interrelationship digraph will not permit quite this degree of precision in problem solving, but it will illuminate which factors, when targeted for improvement, have a higher likelihood of delivering success to our efforts. It brings precision to our other results (Figure 10.4).

A digraph is a directed graph, which means the arrows show the direction of interest. A good tool to use for this diagram, aside from the pervasive sticky notes, is the program Graphviz (http://www.graphviz.org), a high-quality freeware product originating with Bell Labs (AT&T).

Use of the interrelationship digraph reinforces nonlinear thinking, the exploration of relationships, and the root causes of problems. An ideal situation for using the interrelationship digraph would be something like this:

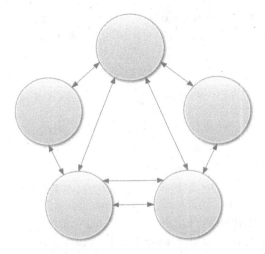

FIGURE 10.4
Interrelationship digraph template.

Suppose our organization purchased a world-class data storage and reporting system and it is failing miserably. Our closest competitor uses the same system, and employees from our competitor who have come to our firm absolutely loved this system when they used to work with it. We know our intended use of the system is in line with what our competitors do with it. They draw insights from it and win over customers that are barely in our field of awareness. They earned tens of millions of dollars and gained market share. We tried to do likewise and lost 17% of our customer base. When we tried to make better use of our system, our employees did not take it seriously and still scarcely used it. A survey of employees showed those who would benefit most from our system did not use it because it contained little data, and what there was tended to be junk. To boost usage of the tool, our organization required that a certain quantity of cases be entered each month. Then, we discovered that employees responded by entering the requisite quantity of data, but usually junk data, right before each month's deadline. This situation is a variant of both student and quota syndromes, where people wait until the end of the process to execute tasks that should already be complete.

We are facing a complex issue with a self-reinforcing abuse of the system occurring. How can we break this problem and generate the large quantities of high-quality data that drive improved business performance? An interrelationship digraph will allow our team to discuss technological issues and use issues, incentives, technical glitches, and countless other factors that are coming into play. The act of completing the exercise will almost certainly bring forward "a-ha!" moments of realization that will create a more holistic systems view of other data issues plaguing our firm.

Force Field Analysis

Force field analysis derives from the work of the late Gestalt theorist/practitioner, Kurt Lewin. The simple variant involves drawing a "T" diagram and putting positive forces (drivers) and negative forces (stallers) on each side of the vertical bar. The force field analysis seems simple to the point of being absurd, but one should not jeer at this tool. Experience has shown it is an effective follow-up to KJ, affinity diagrams, or Ishikawa work, and it is certain to stimulate critical discussions when used instead of, or maybe even as a supplement to, the interrelationship digram. Adding a semi-quantitative approach, wherein a numerical value is applied to each driver and each staller, provides further discipline to the method. This semi-quantitative approach can enhance the interrelationship diagram by providing context to the arrows connecting the different boxes. Figure 10.5 shows the standard appearance.

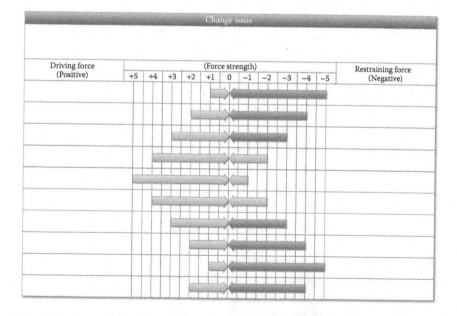

FIGURE 10.5

Force field diagram. Force field analysis is a management technique developed by Kurt Lewin, a pioneer in the field of social sciences, for diagnosing situations.

DATA-CENTRIC METHODS

In most cases, it is improbable to have a simple, single cause for data quality problems in a data set. We emphasize the point because the temptation exists to assume that all is well once we manage the troublesome data. However, keeping reliable data is a ceaseless process. Once we resolve an obvious problem, a less obvious problem often lies in wait.

We can treat the most obvious data quality problems by looking for senseless data. This could comprise a mismatch between a postal code and the matching state or province or it may be as simple as a silly value, such as a negative length, area, or weight. It may be a portion of a road that is longer than the road itself or a world record shipment speed across the Pacific Ocean—perhaps a few hours.

Flagging such visibly incorrect data as unreliable is straightforward. Note that we argue that big data systems are competent when dealing with messy data (mostly due to a plethora of automated tools involving machine learning). This is not a discussion of messy data, but rather wrong data. When wrong data are not obviously wrong, however, the issue becomes more nuanced.

To deal with incorrect or questionable data, having a data quality policy and data correction process in place is advisable. This should answer questions such as

- Who is in charge of data quality?
- How is incorrect internal data to be treated? Will it be pulled out? Will an attempt be made to correct it? Under what circumstances will the data be corrected? As we will see, sometimes the underlying problem in a data point can be easily determined and sometimes the solution is less obvious than the problem. An across-the-board policy may not be the best.
- How is incorrect purchased data to be treated? The issues involved are similar to those for internal data, but it is necessary to decide whether or not to report this incorrect data to the party that compiled it. After all, a more accurate version of the data than our competitors have can be a competitive advantage.
- What is the data reporting process? What information is to be collected and through which system is it to be reported?
- Will the original, incorrect data also be maintained in case it must be re-interpreted?

To better understand, imagine we have a sales district that is more difficult than others and often reports sales numbers much lower than the other districts. If an error causes the report to be within one half of a standard deviation of the mean sales level for other districts, it will not appear suspect to any data filtering algorithm that weeds out outliers. We would need a sharp-eyed user to spot the anomaly and to report it.

Our organization will need to decide the level of control that it will grant users in signaling unusual data. Type I errors may be a factor in signaling data if uncontrolled. To avoid losing good data unnecessarily, our policy will need to address the verification and escalation process for "flagging" or removing questionable data.

Flagging filters can be programmed into the system to allow users include or exclude debatable data. Another way of dealing with data interpretation is to allow the big data system to float potential matches for data, allowing users to approve or reject the interpretation. This approach is helpful in teaching the system how to better interpret textual data, or at least to manually confirm or deny the accuracy of a recommendation even if no teaching is taking place. One example of this is GeoDeepDive, a collaborative project at the University of Wisconsin at Madison. This system uses textual documents such as journal articles (circa 36,000 as of late 2012) to fill in geological information. The computer program interprets the text and displays the information. The display allows the geologist to see the context of the interpreted passage and either approve or reject the interpretation. In this way, articles that are not in a row-and-column database-style format can lend their data to a particular rock formation, visualized on a map.[30]

Troubleshooting Queries from Source Data

When we develop a reason to suspect data quality problems, we should troubleshoot those problems. We already presented several brainstorming methods to find and eliminate data quality issues. Our focus here is to consider some of the methods that delve into the data directly. The first of these is to ensure data pull correctly from the correct source. This data source may be a subscription service for which we purchase download rights. The data source may be something our organization does on its own, such as scanning for and downloading online comments about our product. The source could also be a purely internal system, such as a series of sensors on our production line.

To a manager with experience, installing an ERP system or other traditional data solution that possesses a clear right or wrong answer, determining the accuracy of data for a big data system may be frustrating. Often, we have no answer as straightforward as a simple right or wrong value for current assets such as we can see with an accounting package. We think it likely that a developer or administrator needs to query a source data system and then compare the results to those within the installed system. This method may be time-consuming and require examination of a large quantity of data.

The simple case of requiring a reference to a data set occurs when a reported (as opposed to calculated) attribute is the cause for concern. The process of verifying the data often involves little more than querying that data in the source system and then comparing the result to what is reported in our big data tool.

The problem becomes trickier when our data analysis involves calculations or filters involving a data source cross-tabulated (similar to an Excel pivot table) but with another data source. As a more concrete example, imagine we have job ID numbers and customer ID numbers as fields in our database. If we have a data source behaving reliably with job ID numbers, but which misses several customer ID numbers, our system may use another data source to fill in those missing customer ID numbers by tying them to job numbers or other identifying information. For an example, see Figure 10.6.

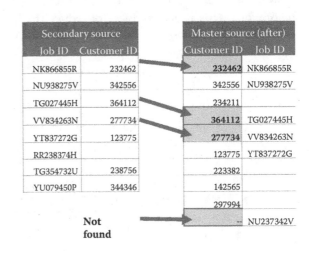

FIGURE 10.6
Records table example.

If we need to connect this table to the source systems, even a perfectly executed data set in our system may not relate properly back to the source data. As the data in our system are bringing together two other systems, the logic determining what we see displayed in our big data system is important. If our big data system is designed only to store and analyze records for which there is both a customer ID and a job ID, it will most likely not match with either system from which it pulls data.

In order to comprehend this situation, imagine that we have 1 million records from source system A. Eighty percent of these records have the job ID number available and half of those records include a customer ID number also. This scenario means that we have a job ID number, but not a customer ID number, for 400,000 records, but we have another 400,000 records that are fine as they are. We must throw out 200,000 records because we cannot link them to any concrete identifying information (our example is an oversimplification, but conceptually realistic).

Using source system B, we can fill in the missing customer ID for 300,000 of those records that had a job ID number but lacked the customer ID number. We found 100,000 records in source system B, which had both the job ID numbers and the customer ID numbers, but just for jobs for which the information was already complete when pulled from source system A. We were unable to use these records. We also found another 100,000 records from source system B too incomplete to use at all (Figure 10.7).

The difficulty that may exist in querying information from the source system and linking it to the data displayed in the big data system should be obvious. This situation does not reduce the importance of linking with these data and it does not make it impossible. What it does mean, though,

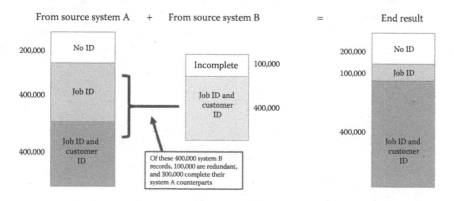

FIGURE 10.7
Combining different systems.

is that as a manager, we will need to understand the difficulties involved so we can provide meaningful oversight and work with our development team to provide enough staffing to ensure that quality assurance and system development can occur concurrently.

As an aside, we find another issue arises when we combine data sources. This issue revisits our conversation on bias, and it presents a dilemma. Imagine we have a data source that we will call Source 1 that has a certain degree of inaccuracy. Perhaps these data are a purchased data source for our industry or a broad internal data source. We have another much more accurate but more limited data source, which we will call Source 2, whose data can partially replace the data of the first data source. An example of this scenario would be using an industry-wide database but replacing data about our own firm's activities with internally generated, and hence more accurate, data.

If we chose to replace the less accurate data within the larger data set with the more accurate data from our internal source, we will increase the overall accuracy of the data set. If we need to find a particular data point, we will improve the chance that the data point we need is correct. We will also introduce a bias into the data. If we wish to run a study on our company's performance versus that of the industry as a whole, it is entirely likely we will draw false conclusions because the data specific to our own firm will be different from the data of other firms, independent of real-world differences. This presents a dilemma: our more accurate data set may also be more misleading for certain analyses because we introduced this bias.

An effective way to deal with this is to draw one attribute from Source 1, draw one from Source 2, and draw one preferentially from Source 2, but uses Source 1 when a value is not available from Source 2. This does not eliminate the bias created by blending data sources, but it does minimize it. Another option is to rely only on the broader data set when conducting analyses that compare your firm to others. This will require careful thought and coordination with your data experts.

The particular attribute we use will depend on what we need it to do, and this approach involves discussions with our data scientists.

Troubleshooting Data Quality beyond the Source System

Problems that may occur in our data have formed the bulk of our discussion in this chapter. Many of these, such as ambiguous data and biased data, will not be amenable to the solutions discussed here because such problems are not immediately visible (unless we have access to accurate and trustworthy benchmarks). The brainstorming methods discussed earlier are the best methods available to identify and resolve such issues.

However, some data quality problems are immediately visible. For example, we have the negative 47 tons of ore we processed through our machines; we have the 13.6 fluid ounces we fit into each 12 ounce can. Also, the job we completed that was almost three times as long as the world record, or the per-instance mean revenue which is less than the lowest possible lower bound. In short, we can use checks based on reality, where we know the bounds of sensible data.

If we are using a system that permits flexible data discovery (Oracle Endeca and Apache SOLR are perhaps the most famous), we can already begin drilling down into troublesome data. However, the old standby in this case is to have an analyst back out how calculations are being made. This approach requires exporting the data and pulling it apart in Excel or a specialty program such as OpenRefine.

Without delving into different techniques, it is often possible to pinpoint exactly what is defective with the data. Sometimes, such as when we reverse the numbers we calculate, creating negative values instead of positive values, a course of correcting the erroneous data may be constructive. At other times, corrections are not so easy or advisable, such as when a value is abnormally large through augmentation with an extra digit. (How do we know which digit is the incorrect one?)

Do not forget, though, sometimes outliers really are outliers, and eliminating them outright will bias our data. An oversimplified but illustrative example would be the charting of the net worth of all of the participants at Steve Jobs's famous 2005 commencement address at Caltech. Mr. Jobs's net worth would have been an outlier, but throwing it out would have introduced an error rather than eliminating one. The decision about what to do with extreme outliers is subjective. Whenever possible, the cause of the outliers should be identified (and there may be several causes) and used as the filter rather than using the value of the outliers themselves. In all cases, outlier management requires appropriate documentation of the decisions made.

In addressing noise in the data, with a large enough data set, we can often dismantle it and compare the pieces to see which trends survive the decomposition and which do not. This approach is simpler than it sounds, and it functionally replicates the passage of time in filtering the noise from the signal. Imagine our data fit the graph in Figure 10.8.

Which of those movements are signal and which are noise? The signal should appear in the data regardless of how we slice it; the noise should

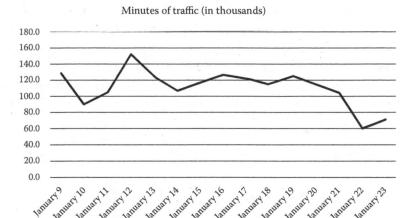

FIGURE 10.8
Whole data set.

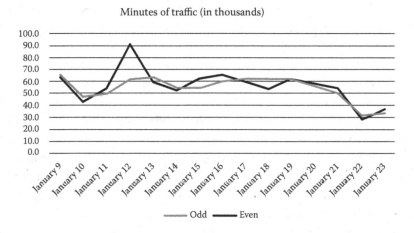

FIGURE 10.9
Halves of data set broken out for comparison.

not. If we break out the data by customer number, even numbers in one group and odds in the other, and then compare the two groups, we begin to detect similarities. Try breaking them out in a different manner, perhaps alphabetically by customer name, and then compare the groups (Figure 10.9).

Just as we discussed the regression to the mean in the chapter on statistics, the noise will regress. Only the signal, which is being pushed into its state by the variable that interests us, will remain.

As we argue, sometimes the fine points of data and statistics are of central importance and sometimes of lesser importance—it all depends on context. When the quality of data is key, and when users access our big data system on a daily basis to run their own queries, they need to *know* their data. They need to understand what specific attribute they pulled from which source system, and by using which data and which formula to derive a calculated statistic—big data analysis is not an unmindful exercise. We recommend that data sources and formulae receive full explanations and documentation. End users who shift from the varied sources throughout our organization will have more confidence if they understand from whence their numbers derived.

Using Our Hidden Resources

Depending on the size of our organization and the centrality of data to its operations, we may hire dedicated data scientists. Data science is set, like big data, to become a new buzzword thrown about in this emerging quantitative world. Like big data, this is a meaningful buzzword—not one that causes so much confusion and consternation in serious business settings.

Still, we consider it wise to use the full scope of our data-literate workforce to seek opportunities to use our big data system, to seek out and recommend corrections to errors or bias, and to communicate the value of our initiative to the broader workforce.

The Six Sigma approach is famous for addressing quality and efficiency. It does so through data and statistics. As practitioners, both of the authors saw promise in this book because concepts with which we work and in which we have trained have direct bearing on the debate over big data. With awareness of data and statistics, the promises of big data can be accentuated and the danger of spurious results can be controlled.

Like big data, the scientific world is also currently addressing these issues. The discovery of the probable prevalence of false-positives has been embarrassing for the scientific profession. However, like true scientists are supposed to, practitioners have been stepping up and helping to resolve the problem. That is the power of science: it is a self-aware and self-cleansing enterprise.

If we have a highly qualified Six Sigma staff or an internal research and development practice with scientists trained in statistics, then we have a broader team that can help us in the successful implementation of our big data project. Not only that, they are also among its natural beneficiaries.

Our organization likely has more talent to apply to the success of big data than we realize.

SUMMARY

Data converted to information is the strongest possible basis for more rapid and precise decision making, but it also contains flaws we must appreciate and control. Data are susceptible to ambiguity, bias, missing variables, and noise. Whereas falsified data are a threat to good science, we did not address it here because it is a specialized issue, indirectly related to big data. For information on this area, we recommend the reader speak with staff qualified in forensic accounting and fraud detection, such as we might find in a large organization's internal audit department.

No matter how good our data are, however, we cannot predict a black swan. Some occurrences are simply unpredictable until they occur. Once they occur, then maybe the knowledge and data based on research will exist to render them predictable in the future. Attempting to foresee everything, however, can lead to analysis paralysis and our signal being overcome by noise. Remember the lesson we learned in the chapter on statistics about how we will always face meaningless results. When we try to anticipate everything, we drastically raise the risk that these meaningless results will bury any meaningful information we uncover such that we cannot differentiate one from another. Balancing this risk against the risk of missing important information, as in our case discussing the fictional salesperson named Edward, is not easy but it is part of effective analysis. Just as with statistics, Type I and Type II errors must be balanced.

Data quality problems are not usually fatal, however. We discussed several practices involving both brainstorming and direct analysis of the data that can help our organization mitigate risks and enhance the promise of our data. Different brainstorming techniques have distinct strengths and weaknesses in illuminating data quality issues. We can use a variety of techniques to directly analyze our data for quality and to recognize exact defects. None of these techniques stands by itself. In fact, an organization can be much more effective at understanding its data through the use of multiple brainstorming techniques, following with a direct examination of the data.

We need policies for dealing with data quality issues. These will involve striking a balance between sensitivity (wanting users to report bad data) and accuracy (not wanting good data to be reported as bad). There are also technological solutions to helping manage data quality, such as filters to include or ignore data flagged as questionable, as well as the option for knowledgeable users to review and accept or reject conclusions made by the system regarding the applicability of data.

Finally, we discussed the statistical and data-literate talent that many organizations possess that can help us better use data, diagnose problems, and assist other staff members to use these data to their full potential. This talent will include Six Sigma practitioners and scientists trained in statistical methods. Not only can they help our organization use its data better, they can also benefit from it.

REFERENCES

1. US Department of Transportation. Airline on-time performance and causes of flight delays. US Department of Transportation, Research and Innovative Technology Administration. http://www.rita.dot.gov/bts/help/aviation/index.html. Accessed July 20, 2013.
2. US Department of Transportation. State motor vehicle registrations, by years, 1900–1995. US Department of Transportation, Federal Highway Administration. http://www.fhwa.dot.gov/ohim/summary95/mv200.pdf. Accessed June 29, 2013.
3. Statista. Number of registered vehicles in the United States from 1990 to 2010 (in 1,000s). Statista. http://www.statista.com/statistics/183505/number-of-vehicles-in-the-united-states-since-1990/. Accessed June 29, 2013.
4. US Department of Transportation. Table 4–11: Light duty vehicle, short wheel base and motorcycle fuel consumption and travel. US Department of Transportation, Bureau of Transportation Statistics. http://www.rita.dot.gov/bts/sites/rita.dot.gov.bts/files/publications/national_transportation_statistics/html/table_04_11.html. Accessed June 29, 2013.
5. Taleb, N. N. The black swan: The impact of the highly improbable. *New York Times.* April 22, 2007. www.nytimes.com/2007/04/22/books/chapters/0422-1st-tale.html?pagewanted=all&_r=0. Accessed May 8, 2014.
6. Bipartisan Policy Center. A policy forum on the use of big data in health care. Bipartisan Policy Center. June 25, 2013. http://bipartisanpolicy.org/sites/default/files/Use%20of%20Big%20Data%20in%20Health%20Care.pdf. Accessed April 9, 2014.
7. Skalland, B. and Khare, M. Geographical accuracy of cell phone samples and the effect on telephone survey bias, variance, and cost. American Statistical Association. http://www.amstat.org/sections/srms/proceedings/y2012/files/400225_500647.pdf. Accessed July 10, 2013.
8. Christian, L., Dimock, M., and Keeter, S. Accurately locating where wireless respondents live requires more than a phone number. The Pew Research Center. July 9, 2009. http://www.pewresearch.org/2009/07/09/accurately-locating-where-wireless-respondents-live-requires-more-than-a-phone-number/. Accessed July 10, 2013.

9. Research and Innovative Technology Association. Table 6: Ranking of major airport on-time departure performance year-to-date through November 2013. Bureau of Transportation Statistics. November 2013. http://www.rita.dot.gov/bts/subject_areas/ airline_information/airline_ontime_tables/2013_11/table_06. Accessed May 12, 2014.

10. Fennelly, M. and Galletly, D.C. Is caffeine withdrawal the mechanism of postoperative headache? *Anesthesia and Analgesia*, 1991, 72(4): 449–453.

11. Hampl, K.F., Schneider, M.C., Rüttimann, U., Ummenhofer, W., and Drewe, J. Perioperative administration of caffeine tablets for prevention of postoperative headaches. *Canadian Journal of Anaesthesia*, 1995, 42(9): 789–792.

12. Your Weight on Other Worlds. http://www.exploratorium.edu/ronh/weight/. Accessed July 12, 2013.

13. Mass. Merriam-Webster. http://www.merriam-webster.com/dictionary/mass. Accessed July 12, 2013.

14. Internal Revenue Service. Part III—Administrative, procedural, and miscellaneous: Nonconventional source fuel credit, §29 Inflation adjustment factor, and § 29 Reference price—Notice 99–18. Internal Revenue Service. http://www.irs.gov/pub/ irs-drop/n-99-18.pdf. Accessed July 12, 2013.

15. Phillips, K. Numbers racket: Why the economy is worse than we know. *Harper's Magazine*. May, 2008, pp. 43–47.

16. Bureau of Labor Statistics. Increase in unemployment rate in May 2008. Bureau of Labor Statistics. June 9, 2008. http://www.bls.gov/opub/ted/2008/jun/wk2/art01.htm. Accessed April 8, 2014.

17. Bureau of Labor Statistics. CPI in May 2008. Bureau of Labor Statistics. June 18, 2008. http://cc.bingj.com/cache.aspx?q=cpi+may+2008&d=4508286758421938&m kt=en-US&setlang=en-US&w=i7GSL63eZdACIY2lMjLhpeA5-rToG76X (cached page, original was unavailable). Accessed April 8, 2014.

18. Aiden, E.L. and Michel, J. What we learned from 5 million books. TED. July, 2011 (posted September, 2011). http://www.ted.com/talks/what_we_learned_from_5_ million_books.html. Accessed July 13, 2013.

19. IHS. Allocated production Texas and Louisiana. IHS. September, 2010. https:// penerdeq.ihsenergy.com/dynamic.splashscreen/papers/Allocated%20Production. pdf. Accessed April 8, 2014.

20. Centers for Disease Control. Statistics and surveillance: Adding households with cell phone service to the National Immunization Survey (NIS), 2011. Centers for Disease Control. http://www.cdc.gov/vaccines/stats-surv/nis/dual-frame-sampling-08282012.htm. Accessed July 10, 2013.

21. Wikipedia. Survivorship bias. Wikipedia. http://en.wikipedia.org/wiki/Survivorship_ bias. Accessed April 2, 2014.

22. Investopedia. Alpha. Investopedia. http://www.investopedia.com/terms/a/alpha.asp. Accessed July 16, 2013.

23. Carhart, M., Carpenter, J., Lynch, A., and Musto, D. Mutual fund survivorship. *The Review of Financial Studies*, 2002 15(5): 1439–1463.

24. Unz, R. Race, IQ, and wealth: What the facts tell us about a taboo subject. *The American Conservative*. August 2012. http://www.theamericanconservative.com/ articles/race-iq-and-wealth/. Accessed July 19, 2013.

25. Neisser, U. Rising scores on intelligence tests: Test scores are certainly going up all over the world, but whether intelligence itself has risen remains controversial. *American Scientist*. September–October 1997. http://www.americanscientist.org/ issues/id.881,y.0,no.,content.true,page.1,css.print/issue.aspx. Accessed July 19, 2013.

26. Medina, J. *Brain Rules*, p. 5. Pear Press, 2009.
27. Unz, R. His-Panic: Talk TV sensationalists and axe-grinding ideologues have fallen for a myth of immigrant lawlessness. *The American Conservative*. March, 2010. http://www.theamericanconservative.com/articles/his-panic/. Accessed July 20, 2013.
28. Taleb, N. *Fooled by Randomness: The Hidden Role of Chance in Life and in the Markets*, p. 196. New York: TEXERE, 2004.
29. Lynn, R. and Nyborg, H. Helmuth Nyborg interviews Richard Lynn. Personality and individual differences (reprinted on Inductivist). May 24, 2012. http://inductivist.blogspot.com/2012/05/helmuth-nyborg-interviews-richard-lynn.html. Accessed July 20, 2013.
30. GeoDeepDive. GeoDeepDive. http://hazy.cs.wisc.edu/hazy/geodeepdive/. Accessed May 8, 2014.

11

Benefits

We know that big data has benefits; otherwise, we would not see companies jumping on the bandwagon to participate in big data analytics. Figure 11.1 shows the potential expenditures on big data next year (2015)[1] to highlight the benefits of big data. We will deal with concerns regarding big data in Chapter 12.

DATA SERENDIPITY

Data serendipity occurs when we find new insights that we did not expect to find during our initial investigation. Since we recommend defining our task before we start, how do we allow for fortuitous discoveries? We should be aware that we have four kinds of "serendipity":

- *Serendipity*: fortuitous discovery
- *Bahramdipity*: fortuitous discovery suppressed by the powerful and mighty[2]
- *Zemblanity*: unfortuitous discovery (Richard Boyle referring to William Boyd and his novel *Armadillo*[3])
- *Penicillindipity*: making a discovery and not knowing what we are looking at (We invented this one—penicillin's effects were known since 1877, but it was not really used until 1939, 62 years later.)

In a paper entitled "Fostering Serendipity through Big Linked Data,"[4] the authors propose some preconditions:

- Data volume
- Data variety

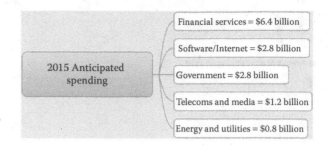

FIGURE 11.1
Anticipated 2015 spending on big data by industry sector.

- Data velocity
- Usability
- Value
- Functionality

They chose the PubMed database for its 23 million publications and because it has a useful interface. The authors also noted:

> One of the most prominent challenges in delivering and using data-driven solutions for any type of human process is the provision of data visualization/summarization tools that are intuitive and easy to use for the experts at whom the datasets are targeted. Summarizing and displaying the evidence that these experts need for making informed decisions, reusing the results in new contexts, and addressing their own challenges is the main task of such data visualization tools. The current method by which physicians look for information on the web is through peer-reviewed publications. However, with the indexing of over 10,000 papers in PubMed every year, keeping current with the literature and using this knowledge to derive new research questions has become a herculean task.[4]

They developed their own tool to facilitate review, called the *Visual Analytics Platform*, using directed graphs to link various tumor typologies.

CONVERTING DATA DRECK TO USEFULNESS

How do we take a mess and make it into something useful? We accomplish part of this goal when we use the methods that we suggested in Chapter 10—in short, we define what we need. The perspicacious reader will note that we have somewhat of a conflict between data serendipity and knowing where we are going and defining that objective.

As we have indicated elsewhere, data are so abundant in the case of big data that we can look at a large river metaphor and consider how we would select portions of our river for analysis, all the while being careful to avoid selection bias—in other words, we select with our eyes open and do not pretend that we are looking at a truly random sample when we are not!

Luckily, we can count on support in our data analyses from a variety of suppliers:

- R project for statistics
- Apache Foundation for tools
  - Hadoop, a distributed cluster/node tool
  - Hbase, a columnar database
  - NoSQL, which is "not only SQL"
- A variety of geographical information systems (GIS) suppliers, some free and some not
- Large-scale pivot table tools for certain versions of Microsoft Excel (PowerPivot)

We really have no excuse for data dreck with the availability of both commercial and open-source tools to partition the work, put it back together, and make the best use of resources. For example, we can use the MapReduce component of Hadoop to handle job mapping, per comments from the Apache Foundation:

> A MapReduce job usually splits the input data-set into independent chunks, which are processed by the map tasks in a completely parallel manner. The framework sorts the outputs of the maps, which are then input to the reduce tasks. Typically both the input and the output of the job are stored in a file-system. The framework takes care of scheduling tasks, monitoring them and re-executes the failed tasks.[5]

The Hadoop framework is written in Java; however, Apache ensured that other application program interfaces (APIs) can access and use MapReduce, including shell utilities. MapReduce uses a key system to keep control of the "inventory" so that the user ends up with useful results from all of this work. Hence, we have components of MapReduce alone that look like:

- Mapper
- Reducer

- Partitioner
- Reporter
- OutputCollector (!)

MapReduce is sufficiently complex that the documentation begins to look more like we are describing an operating system than a utility—and, in a sense, we really are documenting a network "operating" system, so this appearance is not surprising. Apache provides a simple example of using the tools at https://hadoop.apache.org/docs/r1.2.1/mapred_tutorial. html#Source+Code-N110D1.

SALES

One example of Big Data in the sales business is Salesforce.com, which started in 1999 (presumably when the World Wide Web became mature enough to support data-intensive applications based through browsers). Salesforce. com has over 100,000 customers and 2.1 million subscribers. One of many subsidiary (acquisition and merger) components of Salesforce.com is data. com, a business data firm. For example, the data.com prospecting tool taps directly into Dun & Bradstreet profiles (220 million companies worldwide as of December 2012 derived from the SEC Form 10-K that they file)[6] and provides the information through the browser. With information and details from 220 million firms, this product is very much a big data solution.

In a 2013 white paper, Intel Corporation ran a proof-of-concept experiment in predictive analytics and achieved the following results:

> The predictive analytics engine identified three times as many potential high-volume resellers substantially faster in the Asia-Pacific region compared to what the sales organization could identify using manual methods. Automation is making the sales organization more efficient and strengthening customer relationships.[7]

The Intel document also took a look at increased sales:

> … incremental revenue estimates increased by USD 3 million as a result of the Intel sales organization's efforts using the ranked list developed by our predictive analytics engine. Since the PoC was conducted in the Asia-Pacific online sales center in Q4 2012, the predictive analytics engine has

also been rolled out in the Europe, Middle East, Africa, and North America regions. The annual estimates for increased incremental revenue for the Asia-Pacific and Europe, Middle East, and Africa regions equal approximately USD 14 million.[7]

To get an idea of the kind of access big data provides, we can look at the Globus department store (37 retail stores, so not gigantic), which uses the SAP Hana platform. The retailer does offer 800,000 products with a network of 3500 suppliers. The website (2013) explains:

> "Previously, it took 22 minutes to generate a basic slow-seller report that did not include the whole product line," says Alexander Weiss, team leader, processes and business warehouse at the company. "Access to these reports had to be planned in advance because of the processing it. [*sic*]"[8]

After implementing the in-memory database system, Globus can generate a slow-seller report for the entire product line in just 17 seconds. Sales promotion reports, which once took 7 minutes to complete, can be produced in just 60 seconds. As a result, Globus can improve its point-of-sale analytics and the management of slow-selling items.

In a *Washington Post* article, Mohana Ravindranath indicated that Brooks Brothers had secured an outsource solution to their big data marketing problems (500 outlet stores):

> Brooks Brothers is hardly alone. A new market has developed for companies that can digest and analyze all the "big data" that retailers and others collect. Some, like Nordstrom, have invested in internal data analysis, creating what it calls the Nordstrom Innovation Lab. Others use software provided by giants such as Oracle, IBM and Microsoft, or start-ups such as Domo. Corporate business intelligence and analytics software generated $13.1 billion in revenue last year, according to Gartner, an information technology research company.[9]

We are only beginning to see the advent of analytics, and already substantial money is involved in the retail marketplace! To continue this thread, *Forbes* (July 22, 2013) says

> Some companies are already turning that Big Data promise into reality. Those that use Big Data and analytics effectively show productivity rates and profitability that are 5–6 percent higher than those of their peers. McKinsey analysis of more than 250 engagements over five years has revealed that companies that put data at the center of the marketing and

sales decisions improve their marketing return on investment (MROI) by 15–20 percent. That adds up to $150–$200 billion of additional value based on global annual marketing spend of an estimated $1 trillion.[10]

Again, on the *Forbes* website, Piyanka Jain, in an article called "The 80/20 Rule of Analytics Every CMO Should Know" says

- Bring more "future" customers to the door in the most cost-effective manner by:
  - Increasing marketable universe by identifying new channels based on existing customer profile. (aggregate analysis, sizing/estimation)
  - Targeting messages and offers based on past marketing campaign to increase response (A/B testing, correlation analysis)
  - Optimizing channels to increase ROI and decrease cost of customer acquisition (correlation analysis)
- Convert more of those who come to the door into customers by:
  - Identifying conversion drivers: do certain fulfillment options, user experiences, reviews options, cart options, payment options, offers, and promotions drive incremental conversion? (A/B testing, correlation analysis)
- Keep the current customers "buying" by:
  - Segmenting the base to drive engagement (simple segmentation based on past product usage or RFM or similar).
  - Launching engagement campaign, customized by segments to drive "buying."
  - Understand Engagement drivers (like certain offers, discounts, bundling, loyalty memberships etc.) for each of the customer segments (correlation analysis)
  - Campaign analysis—what resonates with customers and what doesn't (A/B testing, aggregate and correlation analysis)
  - Understanding drivers of Churn—factors that make customers leave your business (correlation analysis)[11]

These tools can be balanced against the use of more sophisticated tools: time series analysis, segmentation, and predictive analytics.

RETURNED MERCHANDISE

One of the heartbreaks of being in business occurs when engineering or manufacturing or both has made an error and we start to see returned product. One of the problems with being a reliability engineer lies in the fact that we can only make intelligent assessments of how bad the situation is as we begin to accumulate significant amounts of data. For small- to medium-sized companies, this scenario is not a big data issue. However, when we look at very large companies (say, automotive), the amount of detail that can be available can at least resemble a big data problem. Of course, proprietary information is not going to be readily available to all comers, so sales returns may never result in being a true big data problem.

How big is the problem? In the online article at enterrasolutions.com, Stephen DeAngelis quotes AP reporter Jennifer Kerr as saying:

> Each year, consumers return about $264 billion worth of merchandise, or almost 9 percent of total sales, according to industry estimates. Many buyers aren't aware that some returns, with and without receipts, are being monitored at stores that outsource that information to a third-party company, which creates a "return profile" that catalogs and analyzes the customer's returns at the store. [12]

In this type of data tracking, when a "serial returner" is identified, the goal is to challenge those who use, wear, and sometimes steal items and then return them for a refund later.

One of the largest players in return tracking is The Retail Equation, a specialized outsource for retail companies. On their website,[13] they claim to have saved retailers well over $1 billion by preventing fraudulent and abusive returns. They break their solution formula into four parts:

- Revenue optimization
- Return optimization
- Return authorization
- Financial benefits

This firm attempts to drive a fine path between return leniency and return limiting, both of which can lead to a reduction in revenues and margin. They also note that their service ultimately provides a positive impact on the consumer, since any reduction in "shrinkage" or returns will most likely result in a reduction in cost to the consumer. By managing the return process, The Retail Equation indicates increases in objectivity, reduced return rates, and identification of high-value customers.

SECURITY

Perhaps the first instance of the power of big data surveillance occurred immediately after the 2005 London bombings. It became clear that at least some of the individuals involved had been captured on closed-circuit television (CCTV) as events led up to the bombings (one example can be seen at the BBC website).[14] More images are available at the *Guardian* website.[15] Of course, the tragedy of these images lies in the fact that the police work occurs after the horrible event—that is, we currently do not have adequate technology to support meaningful and focused interdiction of extreme acts, which in this case resulted in the deaths of 52 civilians.

Let us look at some more mundane uses for big data/security:

- Password control and updates
- Penetration detection (cameras, sensors)
  - Buildings
  - Vehicles
  - Parking lots
  - Bridges
  - Toll roads
  - Military facilities (some are so vast that it becomes difficult to provide human support all the time)
- Copyright violation (including the pirating of music online)
- Patent violation
- Just-under-the-detection-limit money transfers
- Material possessions versus stated income

Big data tools provide a method to use our machines for tasks that would be too boring for human beings; for example, various kinds of guard duty. Over the years, the United States has tried to use technology for border interdiction—usually before the technology was sufficiently mature. We suspect that the government could follow the example of Google and use relatively cheap hardware technologies with a failover mechanism and proceed to achieve real-time detection of border incursions without the manpower-heavy issues of border patrol initiatives such as Operation Hold the Line.

How about flight school checks for individuals pursuing training who never get their pilot's license after substantial training? We also suspect that we are at the very beginning of the age of vehicle tracking through telematics and devices such as electronic tachographs (these record speed, distance, and, sometimes, driver activities). Tachographs are used in the European Union and in Brazil. People who support tachograph use see it as a method to keep large and small corporations from abusing their drivers with excess mileage and hours on the road. Drivers see tachographs as unwarranted intrusion by management. We see them as a sword that can cut either way; on the other hand, we do not suffer much heartburn relative to firing or arresting really bad drivers. It is not entirely obvious how such an instrument would fare in an unregulated, truly free marketplace.

Big data techniques can also be used with election fraud—after the fact, of course. A beautiful journal article on this topic is Klimek et al.,[16] which shows color models of the actual voting statistics, models them, and then shows what the model would have looked like if the election had been fair. It is also possible to detect clusters of indignant voters as well as differences between regions within the same country. We think that the monitoring of elections by impartial third parties using advanced analytics is most likely a benign approach at worst and a good thing at best.

MEDICAL

Revolution Analytics has this to say about big data and the insurance industry:

> Big Data is driving immediate changes in the insurance industry that will have long-term effects well beyond its industry impact. Reacting to pressure from competitors and shareholders, insurance companies around the world are working to improve their analytical capabilities to deliver innovative and personalized products to both acquire new customers while ensuring the profitability of all their customers remains high.[17]

The same article points out that Tesco—a company similar to Wal-Mart with over 6000 stores—makes their loyalty card information available to their insurance business.

The PriceWaterhouseCoopers LLC report, "The Insurance Industry in 2012," says the following:

> "Big data" is a powerful combination of (a) sophisticated technologies and devices—all of which are communicating seamlessly with each other in

real-time—and (b) the use of unstructured multi-media (e.g., audio, video) data. Fully exploiting the big data trend requires "smart" predictive and simulation analytics that analyze real-time dynamic data to project the future. Properly done, this can result in a variety of high business-impact scenarios; for example, if a driver unwittingly re-routes his/her path to work through congested and accident-prone areas, then the car's mobile tracking device will immediately alert the driver's insurance company, which can potentially adjust the premium. In addition, the company can inform the driver of any risks he/she might be facing and suggest safer alternate routes. In this and many similar ways, big data and smart analytics are starting to help insurers improve their overall performance by facilitating greater pricing accuracy, deeper relationships with customers, and more effective and efficient loss prevention.[18]

The report goes on to look at the following:

- Use of sensors
- Identification and prediction
- Increasing effectiveness and efficiency of marketing and outreach campaigns
- Increased use of telematics
- Leveraging of unstructured data
- Greater availability of medical and behavioral data[18]

Issues related to big data and insurance include, "Additional challenges associated with big data will revolve around architectural changes necessary to retrieve data trapped in legacy core business systems...." as indicated by www.businessinsurance.com.[19] At some point, the actuaries will have a field day; however, the analytics staff should be prepared to deal with a glut of data the likes of which they have never seen before.

Strategy Meets Action put out a white paper in August 2012 to discuss the effect of Big Data on insurers.[20] They break their considerations down into key areas:

- Customer-centric
  - Segmentation
  - Prospecting
  - Campaigns
  - Cross- and up-selling
  - Customer retention

- Lapsed customers
- Lifetime value
- Risk-centric
  - Product design
  - Product pricing
  - Underwriting
  - Telematics (vehicle computer networks)
  - Catastrophe modeling
  - Fraud
  - Reserving (carrying cash to settle claims)
- Finance-centric
  - Capital asset pricing models
  - Asset and liability matching
  - Portfolio optimization
  - Financial modeling
  - Econometrics

We suspect that small insurance companies hardly exist anymore! In order to have the necessary resources, an insurance company must have the critical mass or be able to afford an external service provider to do the analytics for them.

TRAVEL

Cell phone tracking can be accomplished in at least two ways: (1) by triangulating among at least three cell phone towers or (2) by using a global positioning system (GPS) processor built into the phone. The GPS functions by communicating with some subset of approximately 30 satellites sent aloft for that purpose. Realistic accuracy is on the order of 20–30 cm, although surveyors can use a special signal to achieve greater accuracy.

As of this writing, websites and software are available that permit the tracking of a GPS-enabled cell phone. Some sites even tout the ability to track the location of teenage phone users.

Lodging

Given a 20–30 cm accuracy, it is quite possible to track the movements of an individual through a hotel, including his or her altitude, and estimate his or her location by room, hallway, and floor. BigData-Startup.com makes mention of the InterContinental Hotels Group (IHG) as one example of a big data collector in the hospitality industry:

> With 4,602 hotels across the globe and 675,982 hotel rooms, the InterContinental Hotel Group is collecting massive amounts of data across its seven brands. Since a few years [sic], IHG has embraced the use of advanced analytics. They moved from a structured dataset with about 50 variables in it to a big data solution analyzing both unstructured and structured data in real-time. Today they use up to 650 variables from different sources such as information about its hotels, as well as its competitors, guests, and other internal and external data.[21]

We should note that IHG currently manages:

- Intercontinental Hotels and Resorts
- Hualuxe
- Crowne Plaza
- Hotel Indigo
- Even Hotels
- Holiday Inn
- Holiday Inn Express
- Holiday Inn Club Vacations
- Staybridge Suites
- Candlewood Suites

We think it is fair to say that IHG has a substantial presence in the hospitality marketplace.

The potential benefits, aside from the marketing aspect, of big data analyses in the hospitality industry are as follows:

- Personalized rooms
- Smoking preferences
- Beverage preferences
- Duration analysis
- Restaurant preferences
- Type of customer (business, vacation, etc.)

Large-scale analyses allow a vendor to acknowledge the presence of a customer at levels previously unknown—no need for a 3×5 card system!

The traveler can use tools such as Olset (www.olset.com) to assess online postings about hotel attributes. Once the user specifies what he or she wants, Olset recommends three hotels. Olset is an organized front end and uses, for example, unstructured information form tools such as TripAdvisor (www.tripadvisor.com) to assess hotel behaviors. Also note that TripAdvisor provides comments about hotels, flights, vacation rentals, and restaurants—other possibilities for big data analyses exist.

The benefits to the vendor are a little different from those of the potential lodger:

- Quicker, more intelligent booking
- Expense management
- Staffing versus lodger satisfaction
- Supply chain management
- Bedding analyses
- Food supply
- Room rates
- Discounting
- Service usage

Vehicle

The 20–30 cm accuracy of a GPS is perhaps even more critical for vehicle location. With big data applications, we are less concerned with providing a trip service to individuals than we are with tracking and asset recovery.

Important vendors in the tracking and asset recovery marketplace are

- TLO
- MVTRAC
- Vigilant Solutions
- Digital Recognition Network (DRN)

Gil Aegerter of NBC News wrote, "But private industry also has put the technology to work, most prominently in recovering vehicles from deadbeat borrowers. As the new TLO service demonstrates, private use of LPR data for other purposes is expanding rapidly." The gist of the article was the ability of private firms to capture license plates through video recognition technology (frame grabbing) and sell that information to lenders and insurance companies. In general, these data will include the following:

- Location
- Time stamp (date, hour, minute) of observation
- Image itself

In the same article, the CEO of MVTRAC indicated that the technology for tracking employees, scouting rival politicians, and watching babysitters was at least a decade away, suggesting 2023 before this level of service becomes commonplace. MVTRAC is one of the two main license plate recognition vendors in the United States.

With regard to privacy, Chris Metaxas, the CEO of DRN has indicated

his company adheres to best practices laid out in federal driver's privacy laws for access control, encryption and security of its data. "DRN's data does not contain private information about individuals," he said.

" We do not retain any identifiable information related to owners of those license plates," he said.[22]

Meals

Just as we have big data firms for tracking information related to motor vehicles, we have much the same in the food industry. An example is Food Genius,[23] a technology and services company that delivers big data analysis to the food industry. They currently track over 50 million menu items from over 87,000 unique menus at 350,000 restaurant locations. Food Genius use web technologies and custom tools to generate data and insights for an array of commercial uses. Food Genius customers can access their data in several ways, by

- Percentage of menu item
- Percentage use of ingredients
- Type of preparation
- Competition tracking
- Segment
- Type

Analysis provides information regarding the meeting of standards and protocols.

Another approach is that of Applied Predictive Technologies (APT), working with leading restaurant companies to improve the profitability of their critical marketing, capital expenditure, operations, and network planning decisions. APT use testing and analysis to enable decision makers to understand the incremental value of an initiative before they roll it out. Much like Food Genius, they provide menu analysis. They are also involved in the analysis of remodeling and capital expenditures (new restaurants, rebuilt old ones) as well as assessments of operational capabilities such as kitchen and server technologies with an eye on the "value-add." Interestingly, they also provide analysis for media and advertising, a traditional area for big data analysts.

Another supplier of big data is Avero. Their website (www.averoinc.com) indicates that they supply data for over 4000 food and beverage operators across the globe. Part of their business is processing checks (370 million), so they have substantial fodder for data mining. Avero (http://www.averoinc.com/benefits) do a nice job of illuminating the benefits to big data analysis:

- *Selling more*: Identifying what is driving sales; for example, specific days of the week, hours of the day, menu categories, or individual items
- *Reducing prime costs*: Defining trends for purchasing and preparation, improving scheduling, and reducing overtime
- *Improving the service team*: Pinpointing top performers and best practices and uncovering those in need of training and support
- *Saving time*: Making better decisions (decision support with data)
- *Uncovering fraud and theft*: Uncovering fraudulent or sloppy point-of-sale behaviors

Also consider the big data possibilities of a vertically integrated business such as McDonald's:

McDonald's is a massive global food service retailer with more than 34,000 local restaurants serving more than 69 million people in 118 countries each day. Their daily customer traffic is 62 million customers and they sell approximately 75 burgers every second. With annual revenue of $27 billion and over 750,000 employees McDonald's is a huge company. Americans alone consume one billion pounds of beef at McDonald's in a year.[24]

GEOGRAPHICAL INFORMATION SYSTEMS

Perhaps one the most successful uses of GIS has been the advent of computerized mapping of criminal hot spots. Most of the very large cities in the United States use some kind of mapping system.

Not all CompStat systems involve the use of GIS. For example, the city of Philadelphia appears to use CompStat in its format of a scrum-like (scrum is a high-speed, high-intensity form of project management) review activity, with the emphasis on a solution to the immediate problems. Philadelphia saw an improvement in their crime rates by applying relatively low technology. On the other hand, New York City, Chicago, Baltimore, and Los Angeles took the high-technology approach and they too can point to improvements in their crime rates.

New York City

The archetype of all GIS-based anticrime management systems is the CompStat model of New York City, developed by the New York Police Department (NYPD) in the early part of the 1990s. While the reporting and statistical components—as well as the mapping—are perhaps the best-known features of the CompStat system, there are other factors:

- Flattening of organizational structure
- An initiative toward organizational learning
- Information sharing (rather than a rigid hierarchy)
- Decentralization[25]

O'Connell indicated that the dramatic 1990s decline in crime in New York City is attributable to the use of CompStat. That the crime rate diminished is indisputable; that CompStat was the primary cause of this decline is probably arguable. If, in fact, CompStat was the source of the reduction in the crime rates, it is also possible that this change may have been more the result of organizational alterations than the result of any technology.

The four tenets of the CompStat approach are as follows:

1. Accurate and timely intelligence to ensure the most complete analysis possible
2. Rapid deployment of resources to quickly address city problems

3. Effective tactics and strategies to ensure proactive solutions
4. Relentless follow-up and assessment to ensure that problems do not reoccur

Determining "effective tactics and strategies" is nontrivial—we know this from our involvement in an educational system that prides itself on being data driven—yet many of the "best practices" are really components of lore and not necessarily factual or even "best." Rapid deployment is measurable if we baseline our initial measurements. What is "timely" intelligence? We agree with relentless follow-up; however, we have seen manufacturing corrective actions that were effectively "tampering" (á la W. Edwards Deming) and did not lead to the elimination of problems.

The key features of the CompStat management approach are as follows:

- Strategic planning meetings fortnightly with concomitant improvements in interregional communications
- Assembly of crime data by ward, region, and city
- Subsequent monitoring of data trends

As with high-stakes testing, not only does "what gets measured, gets done," but "what gets measured, lends itself to corruption." Jiggering the numbers is probably the weakest feature of the CompStat system, since it must largely rely on an honor system.

Chicago CLEARMAP

Chicago's system is Citizen Law Enforcement Analysis and Reporting (CLEARMAP), which began as Information Collection for Automated Mapping (ICAM) in 1995.[26] ICAM provided a relatively primitive but suggestive interface and probably resulted in more of these systems coming into being, particularly as the technology improved. ICAM could generate maps and, in particular, maps of hot spots. ICAM morphed into CLEARMAP. They have won some awards:

- 2007 Innovations in American Government
- 2005 Esri Special Achievement in GIS Project Summary
- 2004 CIO Enterprise Value—Grand Winner

One example of CLEARMAP's capabilities is the Sex Offenders web application, which allows citizens to search the Chicago Police Department's (CPD) database of registered sex offenders. The CPD maintains a list of sex offenders residing within the City of Chicago who are required to register under the Sex Offender Registration Act. The data are updated daily. The user can search using an address, a community area, a ward, a police beat, or a district, and around a school or park. Other services provided by CLEARMAP are:

- Crime incidents
- Crime summary
- Registered gun offenders
- Community concerns
- Block clubs

A crime incidents report can contain the following items—identified on a map:

- Homicide—first and second degree
- Involuntary manslaughter
- Criminal sexual assault
- Robbery
- Aggravated assault
- Aggravated battery
- Burglary
- Larceny
- Motor vehicle theft
- Simple assault
- Simple battery
- Arson
- Forgery and counterfeiting
- Fraud
- Embezzlement
- Stolen property
- Vandalism
- Weapons violation
- Prostitution
- Criminal sexual abuse

- Drug abuse
- Gambling
- Offenses against family
- Liquor license
- Disorderly conduct
- Miscellaneous nonindex offense

The list of capabilities of one map category in CLEARMAP is incredible. One of us was able to quickly generate a report down to one-eighth of a mile resolution (for 220 years). When a user requests a report such as a crime incidents report, he or she will also see a tabular output providing more detail. The web user can print reports as well.

Community concerns include the following items:

- Gangs
- Narcotics
- Prostitution
- City services
- Trouble developing (that is, a potential "hot spot" in the making)
- Other

These can have the following status:

- Accepted
- Assigned
- Closed
- Investigation complete
- Not accepted
- Submitted

The user applies a data range and a geographical selection before launching the map application. Advocates of these systems are likely to tout their benefits, and detractors are most likely to raise the specter of 1984 and Big Brother. We suggest "by their fruits ye shall know them," and we recommend external oversight on large-scale policing systems with the potential for intrusion on privacy. While the right to privacy is not guaranteed by the Constitution, it has shown up over the years, particularly under the authorship of Louis Brandeis (former justice of the supreme court).

Baltimore

Baltimore, Maryland, uses a big data system called *CitiStat*. The Henderson report indicated that:

> The program is designed to increase the performance of Baltimore City government by requiring agencies to generate data on key performance and human resource indicators every two weeks for review by the mayor's CitiStat staff. Through intensive meetings with the Office of the Mayor, agencies are asked to account for agency performance and are offered support to improve performance when necessary. Because the process encompasses federal and state-funded programs and policies managed by city agencies, CitiStat makes an important contribution to the achievement of the strategic goals and objectives of federal and state agencies by increasing accountability through city agencies. A unique feature of CitiStat is the combination of strict accountability for the management of employee absences, sick leave, accident leave, and workers' compensation, and the analysis of employee performance on key policy mandates of the agency.[27]

On their website, Baltimore says:

> In 1999 Baltimore City instituted a new style of management called CitiStat in order to "make City government responsive, accountable and cost effective." Modeled after a similar program in the New York City Police Department, the Baltimore City Police Department initiated weekly CompStat meetings (short for "computerized statistics") to improve crime-fighting efficiency. CitiStat represents the extended application of the same basic principles to the management of all municipal functions. The program was designed to maximize personal accountability by requiring City agencies to provide CitiStat analysts with metrics representing performance. During monthly and bimonthly meetings with the Office of the Mayor, each agency must examine sub-standard performance and propose solutions that can be carried out in an efficient manner.[28]

CitiStat evaluates the policies and procedures practiced by Baltimore city departments for delivering all manner of urban services from criminal investigations to pothole repairs. Their analysts check out data and execute investigations to identify areas for improvement. City agencies are required to participate in a special presentation format that is designed to maximize accountability. Agencies are supposed to answer appropriately any question that is raised by the mayor or the city cabinet at CitiStat sessions, which are held every four weeks. CitiStat allows both government employees and citizens to see where issues are prevalent for many areas of concern:

- Sanitation
- Crime
- Environmental citations
- Property taxes
- Vacant buildings
- Parking citations
- Fire
- Recreation and parks
- Gross salaries
- Heat maps (crime maps similar to the old stickpin models)
- Police CCTV locations
- Hurricane inundation zone
- Shopping center locations
- Vacant lots
- Narcotics arrests
- Multiuse trails
- Bicycle facilities
- Bicycle lanes
- Bus zones
- Firearm use "heat" map
- Permit activity
- Floodplain mapping

The Baltimore implementation has 790 web pages of information! Those with maps provide for zoom in and zoom out capability with some level of detail about the crime. In some case, the city has provided special reports for certain areas. A key component of making this level of data presentation a benefit is the fact that the information is readily available to any citizen with access to a computer and to the World Wide Web. Baltimore shows the warts as well as the beauty marks in a tremendous show of open information. We see no reason why this would hinder citizen engagement in the governance of a city.

Baltimore works hard to indicate success with their CitiStat program (including supporting reports):

- Year 1: CitiStat helps the City of Baltimore save $13.2 million, of which $6 million was in overtime pay
- Year 3: Overtime falls by 40% and absenteeism by as much as 50% in some agencies
- Year 4: CitiStat saves the City of Baltimore over $100 million
- Year 5: CitiStat is presented with the Harvard Innovation in Government Award, a prestigious award that recognizes and promotes excellence and creativity in the public sector
- Year 7: CitiStat saves the City of Baltimore $350 million[29]

At the start of the twenty-first century, Baltimore crime rates had fallen to a 10-year low.

San Francisco

A look at the San Francisco implementation shows strong similarities to that of Baltimore (they both use ArcGIS software). The approach is not particularly user-friendly, although the data are generally freely accessible to the patient user. Once into the mapping system, the software is relatively easy to use and quite responsive. Although the map can zoom in to building-level detail, the crimes are marked with very similar blue circles with a white circumference—clicking on these icons will yield some detail about the crime itself.

Using the visualize menu choice opens a menu that provides little guidance as to its purpose and capabilities. On the other hand, much like Baltimore, the San Francisco system will provide information about many nonpolice events such as:

- Filming locations
- Spending
- Registered businesses
- City lots
- Pipeline maps
- Zoning districts
- Campaign finance
- Schools

- Restaurant scores
- Bicycle parking
- Many more

In effect, San Francisco has 756 pages of choices for the citizen to assess. What we see is a trade-off between usability and wealth of information.

Los Angeles

The Los Angeles (LA) CompStat system, which was initiated in 2002, is based on four fundamental principles:

1. Accurate and timely intelligence
2. Effective tactics
3. Rapid deployment
4. Relentless follow-up and assessment[30]

These principles are effectively identical to the CompStat system in New York City, an indication that the CompStat system has made it across the 48 states, East to West Coast.

The LA system has the goals of improvement in:

- Patrol operations
- Detective operations
- Crime analysis
- Crime prevention efforts
- Management and supervision

The LA CompStat system is quite straightforward, with its primary categories being:

- Homicide
- Rape
- Burglary
- Aggravated assault
- Robbery
- Burglary/theft from a vehicle
- Personal/other theft
- Auto theft

At the top level, LA CompStat lets the user cut to the chase and go straight to his or her general geographical area

1. Central
2. Rampart
3. Southwest
4. Hollenbeck
5. Harbor
6. Hollywood
7. Wilshire
8. West LA
9. Van Nuys
10. West Valley
11. Northeast
12. 77th
13. Newton
14. Pacific
15. North Hollywood
16. Foothill
17. Devonshire
18. Southeast
19. Mission
20. Olympic
21. Topanga

Interestingly, we find LA CompStat a bit more convenient than that of Baltimore or Chicago. In exchange for a bit less granularity on crime categories, the information is presented very quickly with a semitopographical map and crime icons (these are a little opaque). With LA CompStat, we can generate a printable version of what we see, a trend report, and a detailed report; paste a link in an e-mail or other document; and send a message (icon driven). The LA CompStat system has a strong customer/client/protectee orientation and it is relatively pleasant to use.

LA CompStat provides a link to the book *Crime Mapping Case Studies: Successes in the Field*,[31] which shows empirical support for the use of mapping when dealing with individuals who are guilty of serial crimes. LA CompStat also presents some statistics covering the period from 1992 to 2010, which indicate substantial improvements, although it would be wise to remember the possibility of a *post hoc* logical fallacy, since the

Los Angeles Police Department was doing many other things during this period.

Tucson, Arizona, University of Arizona, and COPLINK

The city of Tucson and the University of Arizona worked together to add an artificial intelligence component to police work in the city. An IEEE article indicated that:

> The Coplink project attacks several problems existing in many law enforcement agencies by developing a model-integrated system that lets law officers access and share information with other agencies. Coplink has the additional goal of developing consistent, intuitive, and easy-to-use interfaces and applications that support specific and often complex law enforcement functions and tasks.[32]

COPLINK is also capable of providing a sample of mug shots based on certain parameters, such as an alias or a location. The main functionalities of the system include the monitoring of data on an entity or using search queries, locating officers in other units who work on related cases, and sharing useful information for investigation. The Knowledge Computing Corporation currently manages the software, after transitioning from the University of Arizona Artificial Intelligence Laboratory. The software is capable of the following items (not an exhaustive list):

- Terrorism Knowledge: A search engine intended precisely for terrorism research.
- COPLINK Collaboration Agent: The main functionalities of the system include monitoring data on an entity or a search query, locating sergeants/detectives in other units who work on related cases, and sharing useful information for investigation.
- COPLINK Hyperbolic Tree Visualization: This tool uses a graphical representation of a tree structure as well as line weighting to indicate the relationship of an entity (person or organization) to other entities.
- SpatioTemporal Visualizer: This tool provides multiple views of a scenario:
  - Periodic view
  - Time line view
  - GIS view

- BorderSafe: The project aims to leverage data from participating agencies to develop a test bed for research and analysis on cross-jurisdictional data.
- Criminal Network Analysis: As one might expect, this tool uses social network analysis methods and graphical representations to assist in police work and intelligence.
- Deception Detection: This tool uses data mining to provide an officer with a collection of information that can be used to assess the level of deception of a potential perpetrator.
- Authorship Analysis: This tool uses substantial artificial intelligence and machine learning to assess the authorship of a document.

COPLINK is probably a bit of a look into the future thanks to the artificial intelligence component in the software.

SOCIAL NETWORKING

Let us look at some numbers for major social networks (assuming nobody is falsifying any data!):

- *Facebook*: Monthly active users (MAUs) were 1.11 billion as of March 31, 2013[33]
- *Twitter*: 200 million users as of March 21, 2013[34]
- *LinkedIn*: As of January 9, 2013, "LinkedIn now counts over 200 million members" as per their website in 2013[35]
- *Google+*: 540 million[36]

These are some familiar names. Less familiar to US readers are the following:

- Tencent QQ—China
- Tencent Qzone—China
- Tumblr—United States
- Odnoklassniki—Russia

A cursory overview of the statistics for these services indicates a probable membership of over 1 billion users.

Social networking is not always what is obviously a social network. For example, we would suggest that eBay, Craigslist (partially owned by eBay as of 2004), and Angie's List also belong under this heading because each one of these services provides their own communities. eBay provides the framework for running one's own business under their umbrella. Craigslist is often used for freelancers looking for work or individuals and companies looking for freelancers looking for work. Craigslist claims that they service 60 million US citizens alone and reach 50 billion page views per month.[37] Craigslist has over 700 local sites in 70 countries as of November 2013.

So, what can we say about social networking? We suggest the following:

- Connections made easily (one of us has over 850 LinkedIn connections)
- Ability to passively stay "connected" to individuals we know in life rather than "losing" them
- Potential for business
- Data analysis (social network analysis using tools such as Pajek)
- Nonprofit fund-raising
- Massive gaming
- Massive learning

The last item in our list relates to massive open online courses (MOOCs). Examples of these at well-known institutions are as follows (web addresses included):

- Udemy Free Courses: http://www.udemy.com/; Udemy connects with multiple universities as sources for faculty
- ITunesU Free Courses: http://www.apple.com/education/itunes-u/
- Stanford Free Courses: http://see.stanford.edu/see/faq.aspx
- UC Berkeley Free Courses: http://webcast.berkeley.edu/
- MIT Free Courses: http://ocw.mit.edu/index.htm
- Duke Free Courses: http://itunes.duke.edu/
- Harvard Free Courses: http://www.extension.harvard.edu/open-learning-initiative
- UCLA Free Courses: https://www.uclaextension.edu/r/search.aspx?c = free+courses
- Yale Free Courses: http://oyc.yale.edu/
- Carnegie Mellon Free Courses: http://oli.web.cmu.edu/openlearning/

Another well-known location is Coursera (https://www.coursera.org/), which claims (as of November 29, 2013) to have 5,603,381 Courserians and 545 courses from 107 partners. Courses are in multiple languages (English, Chinese, French, Russian, Spanish, and a smattering of others) and cover everything from market analyses to guitar instruction. Coursera categories appear as follows:

- Arts
- Biology and life sciences
- Business and management
- Chemistry
- CS: artificial intelligence
- CS: software engineering
- CS: systems and security
- CS: theory
- Economics and finance
- Education
- Energy and earth sciences
- Engineering
- Food and nutrition
- Health and society
- Humanities
- Information, tech, and design
- Law
- Mathematics
- Medicine
- Music, film, and audio
- Physical and earth sciences
- Physics
- Social sciences
- Statistics and data analysis
- Teacher professional development[38]

We include this list as an indication of the sheer massiveness and availability of coursework for a student community that is global. The next section of this chapter more explicitly addresses educational issues.

EDUCATION

General Educational Data

Educational entities across the world maintain records. In the United States, substantial record keeping is a requirement for meeting the No

Child Left Behind Act (NCLB) of 2001. At a minimum, state testing scores must be part of the record, since these scores allegedly permit "accountability," measures of improvement, and important information about the capabilities of students.

One of us works in a school district with roughly 40,000 students and 6000 staff members. While we are not discussing billions of records in this case, this particular school district has been a legal entity since 1936. The other two large regional school districts together have roughly 100,000+ students also.

We would suggest that unless a district makes a concerted attempt to digitize older data, most digital data start in the 1970s and really gain traction in the 1990s. Even with these limitations, we are looking, in the region that we are using for an example, at roughly 190,000 students during any given snapshot. If we say that we are looking at approximately 24 years of data, then we would expect to see records for at least one-third of a million students (a student takes approximately 12 years to graduate from high school, so 24 years gives us roughly two cohorts).

While the number of records for a quarter of a century may not seem particularly astonishing, we should also consider the number of fields, which can greatly enlarge the number of possibilities.

Legacy Data

We mentioned digitizing data: this situation is a big data problem of a concrete kind. The overwhelming bulk of educational information is still contained on decaying paper records. One of us attempted to recover some information that should have been filed since the 1960s in Arizona and the records effectively did not exist. Here are some potential issues:

- Handwritten or typed
- Format changes over the years
- Letter grades, numerical grades
- Fields no longer used
- Deportment
- Penmanship
- Paper changed color
- Colored paper (from the start)
- Ditto machine output
- Stapled

- Bound
- Missing data
- Inconsistent field use
- Inability to convert nicely to a spreadsheet or database format through sophisticated scanning

Grades and Other Indicators

Each district (in the United States and presumably elsewhere) maintains a database of grades that have been entered as students demonstrate academic performance. Along with high-stakes testing scores, we would anticipate a huge volume of data. For example, one of us produced 360 grades for each of 90 students during one school year for a total of 32,400 grades! Let us say that we are looking at a high school with 1200 students and 200 grades per student; our resulting total number of grades is 240,000 grades for 1 year alone. Even in a district with 40,000 students, it is easy to produce 1.5+ million individual grades for the high schools alone. We are suggesting that roughly eight million grades per year are not particularly difficult to achieve. If we multiply that by the age of one of our districts (77 years), we get 616 million records of grades alone.

Other typical indicators that are recorded by teachers are tardies (late to class), absences, and behavioral notifications. If teachers input these values consistently and rigorously, we have a data set for some large-scale analysis. Additionally, it would be an improvement if we could use these indicators in close-to-real-time mode so we can determine the need for interventions, both academically and behaviorally. Analyzing school data to establish some level of prediction with regard to untoward events such as suicides, neglect, beatings, and other felonies and misdemeanors is extremely difficult.

Testing Results

We see no reason why testing results and subsequent "success" in life should not be analyzed. A big data analyst should be able to determine the benefits or costs of high-stakes testing with relation to school performance, postsecondary education performance, and general life performance (e.g., salary).

Consider the idea that it may now be possible to follow the careers and educational choices of individuals after they have taken the government-required, high-stakes state tests. We think it would be valuable to assess the predictive value of these expensive examinations—not to mention looking at their diagnostic value also. Testing is big business—one of us lives in Texas where the state paid Pearson a total of $468 million for a 5-year contract[39] and an estimated $1.2 billion for the period 2000–2015. Supposedly, these examinations provide some kind of putative accountability, but we think a rethinking of high-stakes testing is long overdue. We suggest tracking (with the permission of the trackees) a random sample of former students to assess the benefits of high-stakes testing. Additionally, it would make sense to see if we could measure other factors that contribute to some level of well-defined "success."

Alternatively, assuming we accept the existence of high-stakes testing, we could use big data approaches across the nation to check for the presence of fraud. We could also have our systems apply Benford's law (as pictured in Figure 11.2) (see also Refs. 40 and 41 for last digits), which looks at the distribution of first digits in the real world—in short, we would partition out suspicious data for further review and use other classifiers (machine learning techniques). Note also that we can calculate values for second digits and so on. As we have seen in other venues (returned merchandise), fraud detection is a large component of big data work.

Addresses, Phone Numbers, and More

A big data analyst with full access to the data of a school district could run some exploratory analyses; for example:

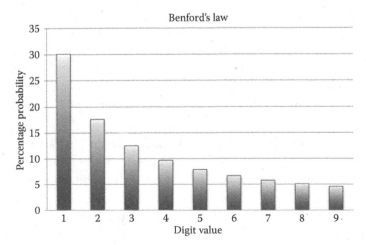

FIGURE 11.2 Benford's law.

- Suicides versus address, zip code, telephone exchange
- Suicides versus income
- Hostile behavioral issues
- Drop-out potential using multiple factors
- Success after high school using multiple factors
- Benefits or costs of athletics to students
- Benefits or costs of programs such as Reserve Officers' Training Corp (ROTC) to students
- Effect of academic after-school programs
- Effect of artistic programs on student results
- Effect of career and technology programs on student results
- Early warning of special education issues
- Learning disabilities
- Intellectual disabilities
- Autism spectrum disorder
- Other health indications
- Anomalous behaviors
- Probable high-stakes testing cheating

We also have access to massive communities through tools such as Edmodo (http://www.edmodo.com), which also provides automatic grading for objective tests (true/false and multiple choice as well as the exact answer).

CONCLUDING COMMENTS

Basically, we have provided a brief survey of this brave new world of big data and what it can do for business. The biggest benefits, not surprisingly, pertain to business and large business—at this time—more than to small business, although we would anticipate outsourcing becoming more cost-effective as capabilities and competition proliferate.

A recent article, first seen in *Fortune* magazine,[42] refers to big data and how the National Football League (NFL) will harness its power to improve the game. We can expect increased use of video plus the addition of sensors in helmets, shoulder pads, and along the sidelines, which all goes to show what we have known all along—the NFL is a business and not a sport. The same issue interviews the chief financial officer (CFO) of Starbucks,

Troy Alstead, wherein he observes that Starbucks is approaching 20,000 stores and 70 million people visit the stores in a given week and he is quite open about the fact that Starbucks has a startling amount of customer data.[43] Also of note in the article is the fact that Starbucks purchased a significant interest in a product called Square, allowing customers to have the option of automated payment. That means that companies such as the following have a substantial incentive to maintain big data analytics (number following name is the number of locations):

- McDonald's (31,000)
- Dunkin' Donuts (15,000)
- Kentucky Fried Chicken (13,000+)
- Pizza Hut (13,000+)
- Subway (40,000)
- Wendy's (approaching 7,000)

Our next chapter looks at some of the potential dark sides to big data analytics. We have seen the shadows of some these concerns in this chapter. Surveillance is a heavy hitter on both the benefits side and the concerns side. Furthermore, vast amounts of quantitative data are not always going to provide a meaningful answer to our problems. While data serendipity is advantageous when it occurs, we do not feel that it is prudent to bank on this event occurring with any level of regularity.

REFERENCES

1. Pearson, T. and R. Wegener. Big data: The organizational challenge, Bain & Company. September 11, 2013. http://www.bain.com/publications/articles/big_data_the_organizational_challenge.aspx. Accessed December 16, 2013.
2. Sommer, T. "Bahramdipity" and scientific research. *TheScientist.* February 1, 1999. http://www.the-scientist.com/?articles.view/articleNo/19271/title/-Bahramdipity--and-Scientific-Research/. Accessed December 16, 2013.
3. Boyle, R. When serendipity becomes Zemblanity. *The Sunday Times,* Wijeya Newspapers Ltd. July 25, 2009. http://www.sundaytimes.lk/090726/Plus/sundaytimesplus_24.html.
4. Saleem, M., M.R. Kamdar, A. Iqbal, S. Sampath, H.F. Deus, and A-C. Ngonga. Fostering serendipity through big linked data. Last modified September 21, 2013. Digital file. http://publicationslist.org/data/muhammad-saleem/ref-4/SWC_ISWC2013.pdf.
5. Apache Software Foundation. MapReduce Tutorial. Hadoop, Apache Software Foundation. 2008. https://hadoop.apache.org/docs/r1.2.1/mapred_tutorial.html. Accessed November 30, 2013.

6. Dun & Bradstreet Corporation. FORM 10-K: Annual report pursuant to section 13 and 15(d), Securities and Exchange Commission. 2012. http://pdf.secdatabase.com/2492/0001115222-13-000004.pdf. Accessed November 29, 2013.

7. Ronen, E., K. Burns, and A. Chandramouly. *Using Big Data Predictive Analytics to Optimize Sales*. Santa Clara, CA: Intel Corporation, 2013.

8. Soudagar, R. How retailers use big data to spot hot shopping trends. *Forbes*. Last modified November 25, 2013. http://www.forbes.com/sites/sap/2013/11/25/how-retailers-use-big-data-to-spot-hot-shopping-trends/. Accessed December 16, 2013.

9. Ravindranath, M. Brooks Brothers, national retailers analyze "Big Data" from sales to adjust marketing. *The Washington Post*. Last modified September 22, 2013. http://www.washingtonpost.com/business/on-it/brooks-brothers-national-retailers-analyze-big-data-from-sales-to-adjust-marketing/2013/09/22/639601d0-1ef4-11e3-b7d1-7153ad47b549_story.html. Accessed December 16, 2013.

10. Gordon, J., J. Perrey, and D. Spillecke. Big data, analytics and the future of marketing and sales. *Forbes*. Last modified July 22, 2013. http://www.forbes.com/sites/mckinsey/2013/07/22/big-data-analytics-and-the-future-of-marketing-sales/. Accessed December 14, 2013.

11. Jain, P. The 80/20 rule of analytics every CMO should know. *Forbes*. Last modified May 26, 2013. http://www.forbes.com/sites/piyankajain/2013/05/26/the-8020-rule-of-analytics-every-cmo-should-know/. Accessed December 16, 2013.

12. DeAngelis, S. Getting a handle on returned merchandise. Enterra Insights Blog, Enterra Solutions. Last modified September 26, 2013. http://www.enterrasolutions.com/2013/09/getting-a-handle-on-returned-merchandise-2.html. Accessed December 12, 2013.

13. Retail Equation. Why the retail equation? Retail Equation, Inc. Last modified 2011. http://www.theretailequation.com/Retailers/. Accessed December 10, 2013.

14. BBC News. Image of bombers' deadly journey. *BBC MMIX*. Last modified July 17, 2005. http://news.bbc.co.uk/2/hi/uk_news/politics/4689739.stm#. Accessed September 29, 2013.

15. Guardian News and Media. In pictures: The London bombers. Guardian News and Media. Last modified 2005. http://www.theguardian.com/gall/0,,1530933,00.html. Accessed September 29, 2013.

16. Klimek, P., Y. Yegorov, R. Hanel, and S. Thurner. Statistical detection of systematic election irregularities. *Proceedings of the National Academy of Sciences USA*, 109:16469–16473, 2012.

17. Peruvankal, J. Big data disruption in the insurance industry. *Revolutions*, Revolution Analytics. Last modified August 28, 2013. http://blog.revolutionanalytics.com/2013/08/big-data-disruption-in-the-insurance-industry.html. Accessed November 29, 2013.

18. PricewaterhouseCoopers. Top issues: The insurance industry in 2012, An annual report, vol. 4. Last modified March 6, 2012. PDF.

19. Kenealy, B. Insurers must overcome storage issues to capitalize on big data technology. Business Insurance, Crain Communications. Last modified March 13, 2013. http://www.businessinsurance.com/article/99999999/NEWS040105/399999706?tags=|59|331|76#full_story. Accessed November 29, 2013.

20. Smallwood, D. and M. Breading. *What Does Big Data Really Mean for Insurers?* Boston, MA: Strategy Meets Action, 2012.

21. van Rijmenam, M. Big data empowers the InterContinental Hotel Group. *SmartData Collective*, Social Media Today LLC. Last modified March 27, 2013. http://smartdatacollective.com/bigdatastartups/113976/big-data-empowers-intercontinental-hotel-group-service-oriented-data-driven. Accessed November 11, 2013.

22. Aegerter, G. License plate data not just for cops: Private companies are tracking your car. NBC News. Last modified July 19, 2013. http://www.nbcnews.com/news/investigations/license-plate-data-not-just-cops-private-companies-are-tracking-v19548772. Accessed November 5, 2013.

23. Food Genius, Inc. Big data and insight solutions for the food industry. *Food Genius*, Food Genius, Inc. Last modified 2014. http://getfoodgenius.com/food-genius-reports. Accessed March 13, 2014.

24. Big Data Startups. From big data to Big Mac; How McDonalds leverages big data. Big Data Startups. Last modified 2013. http://www.bigdata-startups.com/BigData-startup/from-big-data-to-big-mac-how-mcdonalds-leverages-big-data/. Accessed November 28, 2013.

25. O'Connell Paul, E. *Using Performance Data for Accountability*. Arlington, VA: PricewaterhouseCoopers Endowment for the Business of Government, 2001.

26. Rich, T.F. *The Chicago Police Department's Information Collection for Automated Mapping (ICAM) Program*. Washington, DC: National Institute of Justice, 1996.

27. Henderson, L.J. *The Baltimore CitiStat Program: Performance and Accountability*, p. 6. Arlington, VA: IBM Endowment for the Business of Government, 2003.

28. City of Baltimore. CitiStat/Learn about CitiStat. City of Baltimore. Last modified 2010. http://www.baltimorecity.gov/Government/AgenciesDepartments/CitiStat/LearnaboutCitiStat.aspx. Accessed March 14, 2014.

29. Anonymous. CitiStat/Learn about CitiStat/Highlights. Baltimore. Last modified 2010. http://www.baltimorecity.gov/Government/AgenciesDepartments/CitiStat/LearnaboutCitiStat.aspx. Accessed March 14, 2014.

30. The Los Angeles Police Department. CompStat. LAPD. Last modified 2014. http://www.lapdonline.org/crime_mapping_and_compstat/content_basic_view/6363. Accessed March 14, 2014.

31. Lavign, N. and J. Wartell (eds.), *Crime Mapping Case Studies: Success in the Field*. Washington, DC: Police Executive Research Forum, 1998.

32. Hauck, R.V., H. Atabakhsh, P. Ongvasith, H. Gupta, and H. Chen. *Using Coplink to Analyze Criminal-Justice Data*. New York: IEEE Computer Society, 2002.

33. Facebook. Investor relations. Facebook. Last modified May 1, 2013. http://investor.fb.com/releasedetail.cfm?ReleaseID=761090. Accessed November 29, 2013.

34. Wickre, K. Celebrating #Twitter7. Twitter Blog, Twitter. Last modified March 21, 2013. https://blog.twitter.com/2013/celebrating-twitter7. Accessed November 29, 2013.

35. Nishar, D. 200 million members!. LinkedIn Official Blog. Last modified January 9, 2013. http://blog.linkedin.com/2013/01/09/linkedin-200-million. Accessed November 29, 2013.

36. Google. Google+ hangouts and photos: Save some time, share your story. Google Official Blog. Last modified October 29, 2013. http://googleblog.blogspot.com/2013/10/google-hangouts-and-photos-save-some.html. Accessed November 29, 2013.

37. Best, S. Factsheet. Craigslist/about, Craigslist. Last modified 2014. http://www.craigslist.org/about/factsheet. Accessed March 14, 2014.

38. Coursera Inc. Courses. Coursera Inc. Last modified 2014. https://www.coursera.org courses. Accessed March 14, 2014.

39. Cargile, E. Tests' price tag $90 million this year: Standardized tests cost $1.2 billion since 2000. kxan In-Depth-Investigative, LIN Television of Texas. Last modified May 2012. http://www.kxan.com/news/staars-price-tag-90-million-this-year. Accessed November 29, 2013.

40. Scott, P.D. and M. Fasli. Benford's Law: An empirical investigation and a novel explanation. Technical report no. 349. Colchester, UK: Department of Computer Science, Essex University, 2001.
41. Preece, D.A. Distributions of final digits in data. *Statistician*, 30(1):31–60, 1981.
42. Leahey, C. The NFL's plan to tackle big data. *CNN Money*, Webutation. Last modified November 21, 2013. http://money.cnn.com/2013/11/21/technology/nfl-big-data.pr.fortune/index.html. Accessed December 13, 2013.
43. Colvin, G. Questions for Starbucks' chief bean counter. *Fortune*, December 9, 2013, pp. 78–82.

12

Concerns

Notice how our concerns mirror our benefits! Like most things in life, we are faced with trade-offs, and for each benefit, we have cost. Investigators were able to use *in situ* camera storage to help isolate the Boston marathon bombers, but Edward Snowden revealed that the National Security Agency (NSA) has been using subpoenas to access domestic phone records and, perhaps, accessing phone records surreptitiously.

Let us take a look at a couple of articles from the Universal Declaration of Human Rights. Please note that commentary outside the block quotes is our verbiage and not that of the United Nations. Article 12 states

> No one shall be subjected to arbitrary interference with his privacy, family, home or correspondence, nor to attacks upon his honour and reputation. Everyone has the right to the protection of the law against such interference or attacks.

Article 18 states

> Everyone has the right to freedom of thought, conscience and religion; this right includes freedom to change his religion or belief, and freedom, either alone or in community with others and in public or private, to manifest his religion or belief in teaching, practice, worship and observance.[1]

In short, the United Nations considers privacy to be a fundamental human *right*.

In the case of the United States, we have Article 1 of the Bill of Rights:

> Congress shall make no law respecting an establishment of religion, or prohibiting the free exercise thereof; or abridging the freedom of speech, or of the press; or the right of the people peaceably to assemble, and to petition the Government for a redress of grievances.

We also have Article 4:

> The right of the people to be secure in their persons, houses, papers, and effects, against unreasonable searches and seizures, shall not be violated, and no warrants shall issue, but upon probable cause, supported by oath or affirmation, and particularly describing the place to be searched, and the persons or things to be seized.[2]

The US constitutional amendments do not explicitly recognize personal privacy; however, we feel that privacy is implicit in Articles 1 and 4.

The United States has also enacted many data privacy laws; for example, the following:

- Americans with Disabilities Act (ADA): primer for business
- Cable Communications Policy Act of 1984 (Cable Act)
- California Senate Bill 1386 (SB 1386): chaptered version
- Children's Internet Protection Act of 2001 (CIPA)
- Children's Online Privacy Protection Act of 1998 (COPPA)
- Communications Assistance for Law Enforcement Act of 1994 (CALEA)
- Computer Fraud and Abuse Act of 1986 (CFAA) law summary
- Computer Security Act of 1987: superseded by the Federal Information Security Management Act (FISMA)
- Consumer Credit Reporting Reform Act of 1996 (CCRRA): modifies the Fair Credit Reporting Act (FCRA)
- Controlling the Assault of Non-Solicited Pornography and Marketing (CAN-SPAM) Act of 2003 law overview
- Electronic Funds Transfer Act (EFTA) Summary
- Fair and Accurate Credit Transactions Act (FACTA) of 2003
- Fair Credit Reporting Act
- Federal Information Security Management Act (FISMA)
- Federal Trade Commission Act (FTCA)
- Driver's Privacy Protection Act of 1994
- Electronic Communications Privacy Act of 1986 (ECPA)
- Electronic Freedom of Information Act of 1996 (E-FOIA)
- Fair Credit Reporting Act of 1999 (FCRA)
- Family Education Rights and Privacy Act of 1974
- Gramm-Leach-Bliley Financial Services Modernization Act of 1999 (GLBA)
- Privacy Act of 1974

- Privacy Protection Act of 1980 (PPA)
- Right to Financial Privacy Act of 1978 (RFPA)
- Telecommunications Act of 1996
- Telephone Consumer Protection Act of 1991 (TCPA)
- Uniting and Strengthening America by Providing Appropriate Tools Required to Intercept and Obstruct Terrorism Act of 2001 (USA PATRIOT Act)
- Video Privacy Protection Act of 1988

Please note that the legislation listed relates to privacy, but these laws may not, in fact, do much to enforce privacy. For example, the notorious USA PATRIOT Act actually permits substantial incursions on personal privacy, such as vetting of private bank accounts. The law about non-solicited pornography relates to abusive commercial e-mail, false and misleading e-mails, a do-not-e-mail registry, and various rules about enforcement. All of these apply to big data usage as well.

In addition, in the United States, we see individual state laws also listed by the National Conference of State Legislatures, dealing with

- Access to employee/student social media passwords
- Reader privacy
- Websites or online services that collect personal information: policies required
- False and misleading statements in website privacy policies
- Privacy of personal information held by Internet service providers (ISPs)
- Notice of monitoring of employee e-mail communications and Internet access
- Privacy policies: government websites[3]

In the European Union (EU), we also have some stabs at privacy legislation. One example is the data protection directive (Directive 95/46/EC). Article 7 of the directive states that

Member States shall provide that personal data may be processed only if:

1. The data subject has unambiguously given his consent; or
2. Processing is necessary for the performance of a contract to which the data subject is party or in order to take steps at the request of the data subject prior to entering into a contract; or

3. Processing is necessary for compliance with a legal obligation to which the controller is subject; or

4. Processing is necessary in order to protect the vital interests of the data subject; or

5. Processing is necessary for the performance of a task carried out in the public interest or in the exercise of official authority vested in the controller or in a third party to whom the data are disclosed; or

6. Processing is necessary for the purposes of the legitimate interests pursued by the controller or by the third party or parties to whom the data are disclosed, except where such interests are overridden by the interests for fundamental rights and freedoms of the data subject which require protection under Article 1 (1).[4]

In addition, we have the Organization for Economic Co-Operation and Development (OECD) *Guidelines on the Protection of Privacy and Transborder Flows of Personal Data*. The OECD recommendation appears thus:

PART TWO: BASIC PRINCIPLES OF NATIONAL APPLICATION

Collection Limitation Principle

7. There should be limits to the collection of personal data and any such data should be obtained by lawful and fair means and, where appropriate, with the knowledge or consent of the data subject.

Data Quality Principle

8. Personal data should be relevant to the purposes for which they are to be used, and, to the extent necessary for those purposes, should be accurate, complete and kept up-to-date.

Purpose Specification Principle

9. The purposes for which personal data are collected should be specified not later than at the time of data collection and the subsequent use limited to the fulfillment of those purposes or such others as are not incompatible with those purposes and as are specified on each occasion of change of purpose.

Use Limitation Principle

10. Personal data should not be disclosed, made available or otherwise used for purposes other than those specified in accordance with Paragraph 9 except:
    a. With the consent of the data subject; or
    b. By the authority of law.

Security Safeguards Principle

11. Personal data should be protected by reasonable security safeguards against such risks as loss or unauthorised [*sic*] access, destruction, use, modification or disclosure of data.

Openness Principle

12. There should be a general policy of openness about developments, practices and policies with respect to personal data. Means should be readily available of establishing the existence and nature of personal data, and the main purposes of their use, as well as the identity and usual residence of the data controller.

Individual Participation Principle

13. An individual should have the right
    a. To obtain from a data controller, or otherwise, confirmation of whether or not the data controller has data relating to him;
    b. To have communicated to him, data relating to him within a reasonable time; at a charge, if any, that is not excessive; in a reasonable manner; and in a form that is readily intelligible to him;
    c. To be given reasons if a request made under subparagraphs (a) and (b) is denied, and to be able to challenge such denial; and
    d. To challenge data relating to him and, if the challenge is successful to have the data erased, rectified, completed or amended.

Accountability Principle

14. A data controller should be accountable for complying with measures which give effect to the principles stated above.[5]

Another European document is Directive 2002/58 on privacy and electronic communications, more familiarly known as the e-Privacy Directive.

This document is well aware of web tools such as "cookies" and other Internet jargon. Like the items we have looked at thus far, this directive hedges, in part because of lack of control over member countries. For example, Article (11) states

> (11) Like Directive 95/46/EC, this Directive does not address issues of protection of fundamental rights and freedoms related to activities, which are not governed by Community law. Therefore it does not alter the existing balance between the individual's right to privacy and the possibility for Member States to take the measures referred to in Article 15 (1) of this Directive, necessary for the protection of public security, defence[*sic*], State security (including the economic well-being of the State when the activities relate to State security matters) and the enforcement of criminal law. Consequently, this Directive does not affect the ability of Member States to carry out lawful interception of electronic communications, or take other measures, if necessary for any of these purposes and in accordance with the European Convention for the Protection of Human Rights and Fundamental Freedoms, as interpreted by the rulings of the European Court of Human Rights. Such measures must be appropriate, strictly proportionate to the intended purpose and necessary within a democratic society and should be subject to adequate safeguards in accordance with the European Convention for the Protection of Human Rights and Fundamental Freedoms.[6]

In the final analysis, it would appear that US rules, when followed, are not so bad after all. Of course, the revelation in 2012–13 of NSA activities by contractor Edward Snowden casts some doubt on the efficacy of privacy legislation. One of the most critical revelations is the existence of XKeyscore, a NSA computer system designed to collect World Wide Web metadata from the files and e-mails of millions of individuals. In particular, the Snowden documents revealed through Glen Greenwald of *The Manchester Guardian* indicate that

- Microsoft helped the NSA to circumvent its encryption to address concerns that the agency would be unable to intercept web chats on the new Outlook.com portal.
- The agency already had pre-encryption stage access to e-mail on Outlook.com, including Hotmail.
- The company worked with the Federal Bureau of Investigation (FBI) this year to allow the NSA easier access via Prism to its cloud

storage service SkyDrive, which now has more than 250 million users worldwide.

- Microsoft also worked with the FBI's data intercept unit to "understand" potential issues with a feature in Outlook.com that allows users to create e-mail aliases.
- In July 2013, 9 months after Microsoft bought Skype, the NSA boasted that a new capability had tripled the amount of Skype video calls being collected through Prism.
- Material collected through Prism is routinely shared with the FBI and the Central Intelligence Agency (CIA) with one NSA document describing the program as a "team sport."[7]

As US citizens, we have a touch of ambivalence; on the one side, we are somewhat proud of our intelligence services for their incredible computer hacking and surveillance skills; on the other side, we are horrified by the level of ruthless incursions by this faceless agency.

The NSA is about big data, perhaps more than any Google or Amazon in existence. Not only does it have supercomputers availability, but it can also support server farms all over the United States. It would probably be a waste of paper to list all of the Snowden revelations, but a quick summary is available at http://en.wikipedia.org/wiki/2013_global_surveillance_disclosures. The sheer magnitude of NSA surveillance is incredible; of course, we will probably never know whether it used Hadoop, Hbase, and other big data tools.

LOGICAL FALLACIES

Fundamental logical fallacies occur whether we are looking at relative tractable data sets or "big data." Some logical fallacies can be rather subtle; hence, we must be alert to potential flaws in our thinking. In any case, logical fallacies can occur when we are analyzing big data, as with any data, and then we must consider potentially damaging cognitive biases also.

In short, both logical fallacies and cognitive biases represent what the psychologist Albert Ellis would call "stinking thinking." We want to knowingly remove cognitive distortions from data analyses, which is not the same as eliminating outlier data. Removing cognitive distortions is more fundamental than any kind of data manipulation.

Affirming the Consequent

The logical fallacy of "affirming the consequent" can be found in business books and reviews. The fallacy occurs when the investigator tries to work back from effects to causes; hence, this fallacy often reveals itself as the fallacy of "reasoning from effects to causes." The main point is that any given effect may have a plethora of causes and simply reasoning back to some preferred causes is really bad form, as that cause may not be the actual cause of the observed effect.

If we combine affirming the consequent with sample bias, we have a recipe for improperly grounded conclusions. Let us say we want to investigate the success of millionaires or billionaires (which can also rear its ugly head as the halo effect), or we want to compare "great" companies against merely "good" companies. We gather a sample of the appropriate entities (e.g., millionaires or great companies) and we look at our sample to see what is common among entities. Unfortunately, both of these approaches resulted in best-selling books, and yes, they also represent textbook examples of affirming the consequent.

When we look at data sets such as millionaires or great companies, we should take time to do some factor analysis and then analyze those factors for effect. Simply assuming that commonality represents a significant factor is inadequate. The primary statistical tools would be principal component analysis followed by analysis of variance. Even if we performed these analyses with these particular data sets, we still have to deal with sample bias.

It seems more likely in the case of the millionaire study that the books sold because "millionaires are just like us!" than because of any particular validity to the research (although we would have to analyze this statement!). In essence, this particular bestseller was effectively little more than hand waving.

In the case of the "great companies" analysis, we see a sample selection issue, but this time, the selection was more sophisticated. The author looked at great as well as merely good companies and endeavored to divine the factors that mattered. This particular author has a wonderful sense of the trenchant phrase ("right people on the bus") without really saying anything. Writing about using the "right" people is useless if we have no mechanism for determining who these "right" people are.

Is reasoning from effects to causes always an error? We suggest that we can overcome this serious flaw if we can prove that such is the case through an explicit revelation of intermediate mechanisms. Even so, we consider it wise to remember this particular fallacy and proceed only with the greatest prudence.

Denying the Antecedent

"Denying the antecedent" is related to "affirming the consequent." In essence, we say that effect B will not happen if cause A is not present. Once again, we are in the position of ignoring the possibility that effect B may have other causes. As with affirming the consequent, denying the antecedent can be surprisingly subtle. For example, we might see the phrase in the first premise that suggests a condition is a "necessary" part of some state. Denying such a condition (implicitly or explicitly) results in a logical fallacy. We will sometimes hear the phrase "absence of evidence is not the same as evidence of absence," which is particularly significant in quality assurance and medicine, where simply looking away can produce absence of evidence (we would much rather have evidence of no cancer than no evidence of cancer). This situation where we have absence of evidence can become an issue when we assume that in a big data scenario, we do not expect to see a paucity of evidence because we have so much data for analysis—it is still a logical fallacy.

When we are assessing correlation and covariance, we must pay particular attention to affirming the consequent and denying the antecedent because we are using logic to try to move from mere relation to actual cause and effect.

Let us follow up on cause and effect by looking at John Stuart Mill's statements on this issue. His first statement runs as follows:

> If two or more instances of the phenomenon under investigation have only one circumstance in common, the circumstance in which alone all the instances agree is the cause (or effect) of the given phenomenon.[8]

Unfortunately, this statement by itself resembles affirming the consequent, which is odd, given the incisiveness of Mill's mind. We will need more than this particular consideration to progress in our analysis.

Mill's second statement appears as follows:

If an instance in which the phenomenon under investigation occurs, and an instance in which it does not occur, have every circumstance save one in common, that one occurring only in the former, the circumstance in which alone the two instances differ is the effect, or cause, or a necessary part of the cause, of the phenomenon.[8]

Mill's second statement makes a stronger argument than does the first. Note how he hedges his bets by indicating we may be looking at a "part of the cause."

Mill's third statement is:

If two or more instances in which the phenomenon occurs have only one circumstance in common, while two or more instances in which it does not occur have nothing in common save the absence of that circumstance; the circumstance in which alone the two sets of instances differ, is the effect, or cause, or a necessary part of the cause, of the phenomenon.[8]

With this comment, Mill seems to be adding strength to his second statement. The difference is subtle; in essence, a given apparent cause appears with one event set that includes a particular subevent, and when that apparent cause is removed, the subevent disappears as well.

Mill's fourth statement is:

Subduct from any phenomenon such part as is known by previous inductions to be the effect of certain antecedents, and the residue of the phenomenon is the effect of the remaining antecedents.[8]

The fourth statement seems to be reverting to potentially affirming the consequent. Also notice the use of the term induction, which is fraught with its own difficulties (all the way back to Hume and *A Treatise on Human Nature*). Nassim Taleb (*The Black Swan*[9] and *Antifragile*[10]) has pointed out more than once the difficulties with making decisions based on history as an alternative to probability or robustness.

Mill's fifth statement is:

Whatever phenomenon varies in any manner whenever another phenomenon varies in some particular manner is either a cause or an effect of that phenomenon, or is connected with it through some fact of causation.[8]

The fifth statement is weak because it is merely a text statement of correlation/covariance, although it can be suggestive in the sense that it relates a change in magnitude to another change in magnitude. We find Mill's second statement to present a potential argument for causation. As we can see, proving causation is a nontrivial task. A reasonable discussion of Mill's canons is available at http://www.philosophypages.com/lg/e14.htm.

Ludic Fallacy

When the ludic fallacy occurs we might assume we have a perfect statistical model, or one without a flaw, when, in fact, we do not (we are not sure such a beast can even exist!). Nassim Taleb coined the term in *The Black Swan*.[9] In short, we may see a plethora of real situations where the independently distributed data concept is violated. Note that inadequate understanding of the ludic fallacy may look suspiciously like the bogus "law of average" when, in fact, it really means we need to look at our situation systemically rather than reductively and dogmatically.

The ludic fallacy suggests a modicum of empirical spleen is warranted during moments of statistical bliss. This situation is very much like working with the elements of Euclid and then realizing the wood we are building our shed with is actually severely warped and all of our nice, straight line diagrams go out the window as we introduce a modicum of improvisation to our work (the difference between a carpenter and an engineer!).

COGNITIVE BIASES

Cognitive biases are sometimes even subtler than logical fallacies are. We can look at our data and make decisions while remaining unaware of the distortions occurring in our own minds.

Confirmation Bias

Confirmation bias can occur during any of our data forays. We should be especially aware of this bias when the data seem to confirm what we think we already know. A course of rigorous self-examination might make sense when practiced on a daily basis. Whereas the formation of a statistical hypothesis seems to support the idea of looking for confirmation or disconfirmation, the choice of terms is perhaps less than wonderful. Our approach must always be to see what is there insofar as we are capable of doing this, even if it means going over our presuppositions with a check-list of potential fallacies and biases.

Our first step might involve making statements that are capable of fal-sification; that is, if we have no way of attacking a statement, it cannot be falsified, thus leading to potential grandiose and quasi-religious affirma-tions rather than challenging our own thinking process. Confirmation bias occurs when we see what supports our preconceptions and explain away that which does not. We can see this happen when a huckster tries to sell us something by basically repeating back to us what we have already said to this individual. We will often see confirmation bias at work dur-ing extremely dogmatic and polarized scenarios, such as gun ownership disputes in the United States.

We can also view confirmation bias as a type of *apophenia*, wherein the observer discerns imaginary patterns, with the situation worsened by the presence of cognitive influence even before the study begins. The purpose of our data analyses is illumination, not domination. To the extent that we drift from this objective, we fail in our fundamental mission of ascertain-ing some kind of truth through the analysis of data.

We can see confirmation bias even during objective laboratory experi-ments. In the early 1980s, one of us was conducting metallurgical experi-ments with samples whose change in electric potential was being measured through a salt bridge. One day, we began to exercise the sample using a very powerful MTS mechanical testing device. As we uniaxially loaded the speci-men, we observed our strip chart recorder (remember the early 1980s) evinc-ing a sinusoidal plot in synchrony with the loading—we thought we had a really great journal paper to write. Unfortunately, when we disconnected our experiment but left the MTS on and the strip chart recorder on, it contin-ued to record a sinusoidal output, thus indicating that the MTS machine was radiating enough electromagnetic noise to drive a sensitive recording device.

Other biases can relate to confirmation bias; for example, the false con-sensus effect occurs when others agree with the hypothesis. "Others" can mean other data also. We may also see references to something called a self-fulfilling prophecy, wherein the world seems "jiggered" to confirm our prophecy. If we predict a data outcome and that outcome arrives, we are set up to disregard other possibilities.

The system justification effect and its cousin, the *status quo* bias, are also related to confirmation bias. We can "justify" the existing system (or even a new system), and we have a natural tendency to look for that which justifies the status quo.

Notational Bias

Notational bias occurs when we induce a bias through the classification system we use. For example, the bulk of the biota classification system (kingdom, phylum, class, order, family, genus, species, subspecies) related initially to sexual viability—what could reproduce with what else and were the results neuter or could they, in turn, reproduce? However, we could have broken down our system into air, land, marine, or other classifications. What occurs when we have species that reproduce sexually under some circumstances and reproduce asexually under other circumstances?

Notational bias can occur in such venues as the education system. Special education has all sorts of categories in which an individual may fall, including more than one. Our classification may be based on empirically observed characteristics but have no real theoretical underpinning—the biota classification system currently uses DNA as the primary determinant rather than the more primitive and obvious classifier based on sexual results. In fact, the notational bias arose through the generation of spurious natural laws based on inadequate classification. We also note how fingerprints have long since superseded the Bertillon biometric system for purpose of criminal identification, with DNA analysis now on the rise.

Selection/Sample Bias

Selection and sample bias occurs when we do not make positive efforts to choose a random sample. To consider an obvious example, let us contemplate the situation where we have selected our millionaires for analysis. Had we selected a random sample, we might have discovered that a large proportion of the rest of the sample basically exhibited the same behaviors as what we deemed important in the case of the millionaires. In short, because this particular author did not take a random sample, he really has not any idea of what factors were significant to the monetary situation of the millionaires.

We consider sample bias to be pernicious because it leads to faulty conclusions based on slanted subsets of real data; in short, it is false data parading as real data—a wolf in sheep's clothing. We have enough difficulty keeping fallacious concepts out of random data, so why would we make it even worse with a bad data set? Consequently, if we are using machine-learning techniques to separate out data, we need to understand what we are doing before we start. When dealing with very large data sets, our computer programs function largely as redirecting filters—as if we were selecting out parts of a great river (e.g., Mississippi or Amazon) with special gates and directing that flow where we want it to go. The river flows ever on much as the data continue to flow.

The formulation of hypotheses is important because the hypothesis itself represents a preconception—we know of no random hypothesis generator. In a sense, we must consider the quality of our questions before we begin our investigation, analyses, or experiments. Misconceptions can be magnified by large data, particularly when it is easy to produce illusory correlations.

Halo Effect

The halo effect occurs when we attribute some (generally positive) value for an entity that is not necessarily the case. In the case of the business book *Good to Great*, we have affirming the consequent, a variation of sample bias, and the halo effect.

When the halo effect is active, we have a tendency to overlook negatives (we assume the negative alternative would be the "horn effect") and see only the positives. With *Good to Great*,[11] at least two of the firms later went into bankruptcy. One might argue that "greatness" is not necessarily related to sustainability, but we suggest that is not only splitting hairs but is rather disingenuous also.

A typical example of the halo effect can be seen in the mythos surrounding the late chairman of Apple, Steve Jobs. We tend to overlook his quirks. It appears he may have died prematurely due to some poor medical decisions. Nonetheless, the effect of the aura of Steve Jobs is difficult to shake. Oracle's CEO, Larry Ellison, stated:

> Raising his hand above his head, presumably to indicate the rise of Apple's fortunes during Jobs' initial reign, Ellison said: "We saw Apple with Steve Jobs."
> Then he lowered his hand: "We saw Apple without Steve Jobs." In other words, the period following Jobs' ouster, when the company's revenues declined and it launched whole portfolios of consumer products that failed.
> "We saw Apple with Steve Jobs," Ellison continued, raising his hand above his head again—this time, to suggest that incandescent period following Jobs' return to the company, when it released the iPod, iPhone, iPad, and a variety of bestselling PCs.
> "And now, we're going to see Apple without Steve Jobs," he finished, and his hand fell.[12]

One of us feels uncomfortable even using the term halo effect in the case of Jobs and the fortunes of Apple, and yet, we know that current chief executive officer Tim Cook, Jonathan Ive, and a host of other individuals, both celebrated and not, helped make Apple what it is today. Furthermore, the media have yet to present any statistical analysis of Apple's fortunes, so we have no indication of the effect of random actions. We have seen books on presentation style, the "inner workings" of Apple, and quotes and pointers from Steve Jobs. We have also seen these kinds of works with regard to Bill Gates of Microsoft, the Google pair, Jeff Bezos of Amazon, and many more. Occasionally, we will see this effect also referred to as outcome bias, because we are affixing the halo due to the fortuitous outcome.

From the big data aspect, we can see this hero worship when we see references to Warren Buffett ("the oracle of Omaha") and his sidekick, Charles Munger. We can also see the halo effect occur when a new coach takes over a sagging team, with its fortunes suddenly shifting (other factors are ignored). The influence of experts can be pernicious to our analyses if we go into our data work with preconceived notions.

Any time we deal with an individual, we may be looking at a complex array of factors that lead to effects. We would suggest, in fact, that these arrays of factors are unique to individual entities, be they companies, individuals, or other creatures. We may be able to analyze for the aggregate, but working from a single data point (this entity) seems particularly unsound and imprudent. Let us say, for example, we want to implement a corrective action based on what appears to be the challenge with a production line based on substantial data analysis: How do we know we are making things better and not worse (or neutral)? How do we know this change is what made the purported difference?

Consistency and Hindsight Biases

Both the consistency and the hindsight biases may relate to confirmation bias. Either one can affect our interpretation of data, particularly if we have an investment in consistency. Of course, hindsight bias may occur when we produce a set of results and assume that was what we thought all along.

Alternatively, we might have the Semmelweis reflex and reject anything that conflicts with what we think we know. The Semmelweis reflex is a metaphor for the reflex-like tendency to ignore or reject new evidence or new knowledge because it contradicts established paradigms. Ignaz Semmelweis was a physician who discovered that childbed fever mortality rates diminished by a magnitude when doctors washed their hands with an antiseptic chlorine solution between patient visits. Semmelweis's contemporaries unscientifically rejected his hand-washing suggestions. In a sense, the Semmelweis reflex is a tendency to reject that which disconfirms previously held beliefs. The word "belief" itself has difficulties—belief will always appear in the presence of ignorance, since the alternative to belief is knowledge, which involves gnosis, not ignorance.

Congruence Bias

With congruence bias, we go ahead and test our hypothesis directly, thereby avoiding any attempt at potential falsification, not to mention possibly discovering something new by looking at alternative hypotheses. If we only separate or search for specific items during our big data analyses, we may run into this bias.

Congruence bias generally is equivalent to endeavoring to prove oneself right. This approach suggests endeavoring to confirm our ideas (congruency), rather than searching for the best answer (note that this approach is not even meeting basic requirements, the method whereby we stop looking once we meet our requirements). So even if your test boosts closings at sales, we may have eliminated a more effective solution or omitted the actual reason for a change in the behavior of potential clients.

Von Restorff Effect

The Von Restorff effect is also called the isolation effect—it predicts that an extreme data item (called distinctive encoding) is more likely to be recalled than other data items. The unique, the unusual, and the bizarre are more memorable. When a student marks seemingly important information in notes with a highlighter, he or she is unknowingly attempting to engage the Von Restorff effect by hoping the highlighted information will stand out.

We will always run into a similar situation when we discover outliers in our data. Outliers will literally "stand out" and move to the foreground of our perception. Even when we use statistical techniques to modify out the outliers, we will have a sneaking suspicion we are missing out on something important.

DATA SERENDIPITY

We always hope for a "lucky" find while data mining; we can also end up with specious relations, a topic we alluded to when we discussed correlations and covariance. Interestingly, we know about a Palo Alto firm whose very name is "Serendipity". It is a data analytics company.

Converting Data Dreck to Usefulness

As we think we are converting really bad data into something useful, we need to reflect on what we are really doing, with special attention paid to our goals. As we have indicated all through this book, we consider it prudent to establish our goals for analysis from the very beginning of each exercise or experiment. It may be that we are unable to improve data quality to the point where we achieve satisfactory results.

We need to remember that consumption of big data can be costly if our goals are nebulous and our techniques are poorly considered—we will consume resources for no purpose.

SALES

The archetype for sales data collection has to be Amazon. They provide their own big data platform with their Amazon Web Services (AWS) product. They also have somewhere between 150 million and 200 million customer accounts—sufficient to provide a basis for big data analytics. The positive side to this approach allows Amazon to appropriately provide customer representatives with ready-to-hand information to handle their calls; the negative side to all of this might be considered intrusive if it were not for the fact that customers must provide some information for the transaction to occur at all. According to the BigData-Startups (updated in 2013) website:

> However, there is more. Amazon also uses big data to monitor, track and secure its 1.5 billion items in its retail store that are laying around it 200 fulfillment centres around the world. Amazon stores the product catalogue data in S3. This is a simple web service interface that can be used to store any amount of data, at any time, from anywhere on the web. It can write,

read and delete objects up to 5 TB of data each. The catalogue stored in S3 receives more than 50 million updates a week and every 30 minutes all data received is crunched and reported back to the different warehouses and the website.[13]

Amazon is not the only player in large data analytics—Salesforce owns the following purchased entities:

- Radian 6 (social media measurement)
- Buddy Media (social media management)
- ExactTarget (cloud-based marketing)
- EdgeSpring (business intelligence and analytics)[14]

The big vendors are not the only business intelligence activities in the marketplace, for they largely serve only themselves. Some examples of alternative resources are

- DataLogix
- Acxiom
- Epsilon
- BlueKai
- V12 Group

Acxiom, for example, touts the Acxiom Audience Operating System (AOS) as a tool that allows marketers, agencies, and publishers to plan, buy, and optimize audiences across channels, devices, and applications.[15] AOS can incorporate many legally usable data elements, first-party, third-party, or others. The data layer offers the necessary context to safely and securely understand their audiences, including attributes required for rich segmentation, the match data used for campaign deployments and Acxiom predictive models that provide further context for selection and refinement. We are not suggesting that companies such as Acxiom are evil in themselves; however, we are concerned at the level of customer targeting available in the marketplace. Acxiom defines "layers": audience operations, applications, and data.

Similarly, BlueKai[16] can deal with the high volume of data generated across channels to create a unique challenge for the data-driven marketer through the Data Activation System (DAS). The DAS is an enterprise-level, cloud-based platform that manages data assets and provides a common data management system for all their customers' marketing and customer interaction programs. The DAS is made of three products that work together, allowing one to centralize, acquire, monetize, and get insights on all of their data assets: data management platform, audience data marketplace, and audience analytics suite.

Epsilon documentation online indicates

Epsilon provides solutions to 15 of top 20 leading advertisers and dozens of Fortune 100 companies, including

- 7 of top 10 insurance companies
- 8 of top 10 retailers
- 9 of top 10 consumer packaged goods companies
- 9 of top 10 financial institutions
- 10 of top 10 healthcare companies
- 10 of top 10 automotive companies

By sheer volume of consumer connections, they are market leader for:

- Loyalty: They have 300 million loyalty members worldwide.
- Data: They have information on 130 million households representing 250 million consumers in the US market and 22 million businesses.
- E-mail: They are the global leader in reach delivering tens of billions of e-mails annually in 115 countries.
- Engagement: They enable tens of billions of conversations across addressable channels including direct mail, e-mail, mobile, display, social media, and point of sale.[17]

The V12 Group[18] provides data and cross-channel digital marketing that allows organizations of all sizes to communicate with prospects and customers individually or through a combination of e-mail, mobile, social media, direct, and digital display ads. V12 Group's marketing automation platform provides a suite of integrated applications that enable marketers to plan, automate, deliver, and optimize data-driven marketing and real-time communications to drive new and existing customer engagement, increase sales, and improve return on marketing investment. In short, the V12 Group provides a similar product line to those of its competition.

DataLogix has made it a mission to use the power of purchase-based audience targeting to drive measurable online and off-line sales.[19] Their data include nearly every US household and more than $1 trillion in consumer transactions.

Again, we want to caution the reader that we are not making broad claims about "evil" vendors of data. We suggest, however, that it behooves the intelligent customer/citizen to be aware of just how vast the data collection capabilities of independent vendors can be. We suspect that most of us would not be surprised at the extent of data collection by Google, Amazon, and other large online vendors (Target, Walgreens, etc.), but these other firms provide services regarding purchases that are made outside of the corporate bounds.

MERCHANDISE RETURNS

We are selling when we persuade a buyer to purchase our product. If our product is such that it can be returned due to customer dissatisfaction, inadequate performance, or because it is simply broken, then we have a case for big data analytics regarding returns.

Cost/benefit analyses based on data (even big data) can become notorious sources for litigation. One obvious example refers to the cost-driven decision Ford Motor Company management made regarding the fiery propensities of their Pinto line. In a paper by Christopher Leggett at Wake Forest University, he examines the Ford decision and the surrounding litigation. He comments:

> Although Ford had access to a new design which would decrease the possibility of the Ford Pinto from exploding, the company chose not to implement the design, which would have cost $11 per car, even though it had done an analysis showing that the new design would result in 180 less deaths. The company defended itself on the grounds that it used the accepted risk/benefit analysis to determine if the monetary costs of making the change were greater than the societal benefit. Based on the numbers Ford used, the cost would have been $137 million versus the $49.5 million price tag put on the deaths, injuries, and car damages, and thus Ford felt justified not implementing the design change. This risk/benefit analysis was created out of the development of product liability, culminating at Judge Learned Hand's BPL formula, where if the expected harm exceeded the cost to take the precaution, then the company must take the precaution, whereas if the cost was liable, then it did not have to. However, the BPL formula focuses on a specific accident, while the risk/benefit analysis requires an examination of the costs, risks, and benefits through use of the product as a whole.

Based on this analysis, Ford legally chose not to make the design changes, which would have made the Pinto safer. However, just because it was legal doesn't necessarily mean that it was ethical. It is difficult to understand how a price can be put on saving a human life.[20]

The BPL formula (derived from the case US v. Carroll Towing[21], involving the drifting of a barge and adjudicated by Judge Learned Hand) looks like this:

$$B < PL$$

where:

B is the burden of being prudent (precautionary actions)
P is the probability of loss
L is the magnitude of the loss

As indicated in Leggett's comments, determining the loss value of a human life can be difficult. The wife of one of the authors remembers the cost of killing a sheep in an automotive accident in Turkey in the 1970s—which included a formula for descendants of the given sheep and a monetary value set upon that number!

Unfortunately, the calculus of returned material may ultimately involve the use of intangibles, which by their very nature are impossible to calculate. For example, Pennsylvania State University has attempted to settle with the alleged victims of former and convicted coach, Jerry Sandusky, rather than deal with each alleged victim by going through the torts process, in spite of the relative lack of physical evidence (Sandusky may be guilty, but little physical evidence was presented at the trial, as far as we can tell from news reports). Penn State has presumably decided the intangible damage of going to court is not worth the risk.

SECURITY

CompStat

Preeti Chauhan and Lauren Kois of the John Jay College of Justice Research and Evaluation Center (City University of New York) took a recent look at the decline in crime in New York City in the 1990s, as well as during the first decade of the twenty-first century. Politicians and police administration have touted the benefits of CompStat, the data-driven police information system. Chauhan and Kois did not definitively deny the effect of CompStat, but they did review the data.

> The modest relationship between misdemeanor policing and homicide rates may be explained by the fact that not all high crime areas uniformly received misdemeanor policing. This further explains why effects dissipate when broken down by age and race. Moreover, some precincts that did not experience a significant "dose" of misdemeanor policing still experienced significant reductions in homicides, which suggests that other factors were influential in lowering crime rates. Thus, multivariate models must include other relevant covariates (e.g., cocaine consumption).[22]

Misdemeanor policing was an offshoot of broken windows theory, introduced by social scientists James Q. Wilson and George L. Kelling in 1982. Broken windows theory has received criticism for being unscientific (notably, David Thacher in 2004).[23] Additionally, Harcourt and Ludwig summarized their 2006 research paper[24] as follows:

> Yet understanding the ability of a broken windows policy to affect disorder and crime is important for both legal and scientific purposes. The notion that broken windows policing might reduce crime is plausible because many of the behavioral mechanisms underlying this policing strategy are at least in principle consistent with existing models of social contagion. Since the Almighty has so far resisted the temptation to publish in scholarly journals, our results help answer Wilson's question in the interim. Our bottom line is that there appears to be no good evidence that broken windows policing reduces crime, nor evidence that changing the desired intermediate output of broken windows policing—disorder itself—is sufficient to affect changes in criminal behavior.

Chauhan and Kois found some difficulties when dealing with data-skewing outliers.

> The results highlight that city-level trends can lead to biased results given that they often mask within-city differences. Moreover, a few precincts may be driving the citywide and multivariate results (i.e., Harlem, Mott Haven/Melrose and Marcus Garvey). Future multivariate research should test whether the results are sustained when highly influential precincts (i.e., outliers) are removed from causal models.[22]

Note that Chauhan and Kois carefully and correctly indicate the research must show the influence of certain areas of the city on overall data analyses and conclusions.

As with any system, CompStat is open to corruption. For example, Radley Balko writes

> But according to a survey of high-ranking NYPD retirees conducted by Long Island's Molloy College, police commanders faced heavy pressure from higher-ups to reduce felonics to misdemeanors—or in some cases to not report crimes at all—in order to make the numbers look prettier. An officer from Brooklyn's 81st Precinct then came forward to complain about constant pressure from commanders to downgrade felonies, talk victims out of filing reports, and even simply refuse to take reports at all. CompStat critics predicted much of this. Even data-heavy crime tracking, it turns out, can fall prey to public choice theory.[25]

Balko also adds, "Critics of broken windows counter, among other arguments, that many big cities that did not adopt the policy, including San Diego, Washington, DC, and Houston had more significant decreases in the homicide rate over about the same period."

On the other hand, Heather McDonald writes in the *City Journal*:

> NYPD foes can put away their party hats. Nothing in the survey discredits Compstat or its crime-fighting accomplishments. Eterno's claim about a decreased emphasis on crime-data integrity in the Compstat era is demonstrably false. It is ludicrous to suggest that a department where the top brass did not even get crime data until six months after the crime and then did nothing with them—as was the case in the pre-Compstat era—cared more about the accuracy of crime statistics than one in which every deployment decision is made based on the minute-by-minute reality of crime on the streets. Nor does the study, which has several design flaws, cast any doubt on the city's record-breaking crime drop. Given the enormous efforts that the NYPD makes to ensure the validity of its statistics, the study ultimately comes down to a dangerous argument against accountability systems per se.[26]

It appears, then, that CompStat has been a mixed blessing at best. Leery police officers, data-corrupted administrators, and potential lack of efficacy have affected initial enthusiasm. What seems should be effective may not be effective in the long run. What is surprising is how difficult discerning cause and effect can be; however, please note that crime science is complex.

Medical

Some level of surveillance pertains to medical issues, particularly in the case of epidemiology. Our readers can review the freely available Centers for Disease Control and Prevention justification of estimates for appropriation committees, put out by the US Department of Health and Human Services, to see the amount of money put into epidemiological tracking. We do not feel that this kind of tracking/surveillance is a consideration for the average citizen.

More troubling is the data collected by health insurance groups, which they can legitimately do for individuals as these persons exercise their health insurance through claims. A document by McKinsey suggests that "An era of open information in healthcare is now under way." The authors also identify sources of data:

- Clinical
  - Electronic medical records
  - Medical images
- Claims and cost
  - Payers
  - Providers
  - Utilization of care
  - Cost estimates
- Pharmaceutical
  - Clinical trials
  - Screening libraries
- Patient behavior and sentiment
  - Retail purchase history
  - Exercise data in running shoes

The document goes on to discuss information sharing and other "benefits" of this so-called revolution, which is supported by the US Government legislatively with the following:

- Open Government Directive (2009)
- Affordable Care Act (2010)
- Health Information Technology for Economic and Clinical Health (HITECH) Act (2009)

The point here is that these legislative acts permit aggregation and relation of data from such agencies as the Centers for Medicare and

Medicaid Services, the Food and Drug Administration, and the Centers for Disease Control. The American Recovery and Reinvestment Act (ARRA) authorized up to $40 billion to move toward electronic medical records.

TRAVEL

Lodging

How much of our global positioning system (GPS) information is available to licit and illicit onlookers? For example, Brickhouse Security advertises the following potential questions "I need to know..."

- If my teenager is driving too fast
- If my child is home from school
- If my possessions are safe
- If my spouse made it to work on time

Brickhouse Security indicates it can track a person, a car, some property or employees.[27] A quick check on the Internet using a Google search reveals these tracking websites:

- www.liveviewgps.com
- www.spyassociates.com
- www.vehicle-tracking.com

These websites are just a sample of suppliers of surveillance software and tools. GPS surveillance can apply to lodging as well as vehicular movement of any kind (train, bus, car, and airplane if allowed).

Also note that tagged photographs can be correlated to GPS log data. If we need serious surveillance, we would use a GPS "pusher" that sends updates at some meaningful interval, allowing for mapping of movement and location. In the circumstance of commercial vehicle use, it might make sense to track vehicles to eliminate vehicle and time clock abuse. We can see minimal ethical issues with delivery trucks, large-scale haulers, taxicabs, and commercial vehicles in similar businesses. We also have no heartburn with wildlife tracking when used for scientific studies (we expect our fearless nimrods to track the traditional way!).

Vehicle

What we have stated in the lodging section applies even more to vehicular movement. Consider something as mundane as clothing detergent: GPS devices were added to Unilever's Omo brand in Brazil with the alleged basis for this invasion of privacy being the award of a pocket video camera to those with the special boxes. Only 50 boxes were implanted with the GPS device (not enough for a representative statistical analysis), but we wonder how far this kind of vehicle-tracking marketing can go.

In some cases, criminals have received electronic tags that permit surveillance of their location. Of course, the question will always arise as to how much surveillance is too much surveillance. We feel this situation is a question of civil liberties.

So far, we have addressed GPS surveillance, which is not necessarily a big data problem unless done on a vast scale. However, we also have public video surveillance, which can also track the movement of vehicles by capturing snapshots of license plates. As of 2008, an ACLU report examining data from 2000 to 2008 indicated:

- Meta-analyses (studies that average the results of multiple studies) in the UK show that video surveillance has no statistically significant impact on crime.
- Preliminary studies on video surveillance systems in the United States show little to no positive impact on crime.[28]

The paper used the Los Angeles CompStat system to determine before and after numbers for several areas in the city (p. 5). Interestingly, surveyed citizens in the UK were generally favorable towards the surveillance, even though the numbers do not support efficacy.

A 2002 UK study found a reduction in vehicle crimes in such areas as parking garages but no reduction in violent crime. Welsh and Farrington summarized their research as follows:

> The studies included in the present review show that CCTV can be most effective in reducing crime in car parks. Exactly what the optimal circumstances are for effective use of CCTV schemes is not entirely clear at present, and needs to be established by future evaluation research. But it is interesting to note that the success of the CCTV schemes in car parks was limited to a reduction in vehicle crimes (the only crime type measured) and all five schemes included other interventions, such as improved lighting and notices about CCTV cameras.

Conversely, the evaluations of CCTV schemes in city centres and public housing measured a much larger range of crime types and the schemes did not involve, with one exception, other interventions. These CCTV schemes, and those focused on public transport, had only a small effect on crime.[29]

We feel that at least two issues are present in the case of video surveillance:

1. Privacy and civil liberties
2. Cost for a system that has little effect

Additionally, we may have more effective methods for both vehicular and foot movement in the form of foot patrols by uniformed officers. Another UK study found a 16% reduction in personal robbery, while the rest of the force saw an increase of 5%.[30]

In a research paper on the proliferation of surveillance cameras in California, the ACLU made the following suggestions:

Recommendation 1: Cease deploying surveillance cameras.

Reducing crime and apprehending criminals are worthy goals, but the evidence suggests that video cameras are generally ineffective in achieving them. Given surveillance cameras' [sic] limited usefulness and the potential threat they pose to civil liberties, the ACLU recommends that local governments stop deploying them.

For cities considering cameras:

Recommendation 2: Evaluate other alternatives.

The ACLU recommends that local governments fully evaluate other crime reduction measures before spending limited public safety dollars on video surveillance systems.

Recommendation 3: Fully assess any proposed system's effectiveness and impact and establish a process for open public debate.

No city should deploy a technology without fully debating and considering its impact on members of the community. The ACLU recommends that any proposed video surveillance program be subjected to intense public scrutiny, and that the city conduct a full assessment of the system's effectiveness and impact on privacy and free speech before proceeding with the installation of cameras.[31]

Do we really need surveillance, especially when surveillance has no preventive value? What about catching speeders? We know from a US Department of Transportation report that compliance to speed limits is weak to nonexistent, despite claims by local governments that they investigate "speed of traffic" before assigning speed limits.[32] Stuster and Coffman also noted that crash risk is generally lowest near the average speed of traffic and that crash risk also increases for both those moving more quickly than the average and also for those moving more slowly than the average. Of course, once a crash occurs, speed is a factor related to the level of severity of the ensuing results. A 2009 report indicates that "Visible and active enforcement reduces operating speeds but the effect diminishes as the distance and time from the enforcement increases."[33] Hence, instead of big data enforcement through surveillance technology, we once again see the benefit of physical police presence.

Meals

Any meal purchase with a credit card will be stored and is potentially searchable by big data systems. The only rational means of avoiding this situation is through the use of cash.

With geographic information systems (GIS), some companies will use the increasingly pervasive traffic camera system (as well as others) for data collection purposes. For example, TLO Online Investigative Systems claims they can verify and locate with regard to individuals:[34]

- Names, aliases, and social security numbers
- Bankruptcies, foreclosures, liens, judgments, and criminal history
- Current and historical addresses
- Phone numbers, including listed and unlisted landlines, cell phones, and utilities data
- Relatives, neighbors, and associates
- Assets, including property, vehicles, and more
- Licenses, including professional, driver, IDs, and more
- E-mail addresses and social networks
- Vehicle sightings

Additionally, the TLO website indicates these capabilities and more for business searches.

A competitor to TLO is MVTRAC, which claims they are "home to The Intelligent Data Network, a motorist/vehicle information network between the public and private sector designed to promote transportation safety, recover delinquent collateral, detect fraud and deter criminal activity."[35] MVTRAC specializes in license-plate-reading technology, indicating that law enforcement could scan vehicles as they drive along the roadway.

Yet another alternative is Vigilant Solutions,[36] whose website indicates they, too, have automated license plate recognition (ALPR). Their website indicates they "create intelligence by merging previously disparate data sets such as fixed and mobile license plate recognition, public records, facial recognition, and more."

SOCIAL NETWORKING

Before we get deeply into social networking, we should note that numerous personal intelligence firms operate in the marketplace. Some of these are as follows:

- Intelius (intelius.com): "Intelius helps you live in the know with instant people search, background check, and reverse phone lookup results."
- Spokeo (spokeo.com), which "is a people search engine that organizes White Pages listings, Public Records and Social Network Information to help you safely find and learn about people."
- PeopleFinders (http://www.peoplefinders.com), which considers themselves a source for finding people and obtaining public records about them (name, phone number, address, or e-mail).
- BeenVerified (http://www.beenverified.com), whose publicly stated "mission is to make public records easy and affordable for everyone."

The previously mentioned photograph to GPS log correlation can apply to social networking also. With Facebook, for example, a user might consider turning off this feature. Also note that since 2010, the NSA has been "mining" Facebook; for example, Pamela Brown noted that "In addition to phone records and e-mail logs, the National Security Agency uses Facebook and other social media profiles to create maps of social connections—including those of American citizens."[37] Brown also noted

The surveillance began after a policy change in November 2010.

Prior to then, the "chaining" of a foreign person's contacts had to stop when it reached an American citizen or legal resident.

The policy change was intended to help the NSA "discover and track" connections from a foreign intelligence subject to an American citizen, the leaked documents show.

It allows NSA analysts to use social media, geolocation information, insurance and tax records, plus other public and private sources to enhance their analysis of phone and email records.[37]

We find this very interesting, given that US President Obama has been considered by some to be a "liberal."

Tools using R are available for both Twitter and Facebook:

- twitteR [*sic*] for Twitter
- RFacebook for Facebook

RFacebook requires a Facebook developer account, which is not difficult to achieve if one already has a Facebook account. Once we have a developer account, we can begin to query Facebook about friends, and perhaps more importantly, their relations (on Facebook) to our other friends. The reader can take a quick look at what RFacebook can do at http://blog.revolutionanalytics.com/2013/11/how-to-analyze-you-facebook-friends-network-with-r.html.

EDUCATION

In the education business (and business it is) the powers that be seem to be hung up on two ways of looking at the mass of numbers they purportedly analyze:

- How many students passed a criterion-based examination (usually expressed as a percentage)?
- What is the arithmetic mean?

Another issue is the one of so-called "accountability," where the US government has decided that student performance can be directly tied to teacher performance. In other words, the government says we can measure a surrogate value (student performance) and somehow divine the quality of the teaching. Once we know we have a "bad" teacher, we can hold him or her accountable. We are not sure that teachers were not accountable before this mishmash of confused testing concepts; furthermore, we have seen no scientific evidence that student performance is an adequate surrogate for estimating teacher performance. The government website states:

> No Child Left Behind is designed to change the culture of America's schools by closing the achievement gap, offering more flexibility, giving parents more options, and teaching students based on what works.

> Under the act's accountability provisions, states must describe how they will close the achievement gap and make sure all students, including those who are disadvantaged, achieve academic proficiency. They must produce annual state and school district report cards that inform parents and communities about state and school progress. Schools that do not make progress must provide supplemental services, such as free tutoring or after-school assistance; take corrective actions; and, if still not making adequate yearly progress after five years, make dramatic changes to the way the school is run.[38]

The madness does not end with these statements; for example, the American Speech-Language-Hearing Association summed things up as follows:

> Accountability is the centerpiece of NCLB. The Act requires states to implement statewide accountability systems covering all public schools and students. These systems must be based on challenging state standards in reading and mathematics, annual testing for all students in grades 3–8, and annual statewide progress objectives ensuring that all groups of students reach proficiency within 12 years. The Act requires a single statewide accountability system that will be effective in ensuring that all districts and schools make adequate yearly progress.[39]

One can see that this system is open to corruption, particularly when faced with punitive measures related to the unrealistic expectation of adequate yearly progress (AYP). For example:

> School districts and schools that fail to make AYP toward statewide proficiency goals will, over time, be subject to improvement, corrective action, and restructuring measures aimed at getting them back on course to meet state standards. The statute grants flexibility to state and LEAs [author

note: LEA = local education agency] to direct resources and tailor interventions to the needs of individual schools. Schools that meet or exceed AYP objectives or close achievement gaps will be eligible for State Academic Achievement Awards.[40]

As big data analysts, with open minds about cognitive biases and logical fallacies, we must be cautious when setting standards, achievement goals, and, most of all, corrective actions that are not evidence-driven, but are more likely based on hand-waving behaviors called "best practices." Apparently, the US government does not understand the normal distribution (assuming this distribution applies and is not just an artifact of the measurement system), preferring to change standards to ensure that students "graduate" from high school, thereby diluting the meaning of a high school diploma. No, we are not anti–special education, but if we are going to set standards, then let us set real standards and let the chips fall where they may. Since a severely intellectually disabled child can receive the same diploma as any other student, we practice a style of basic dishonesty, not to mention deceiving potential employers who use the high school diploma as a basic filter.

The National Center for Education Statistics produces an annual report called *The Condition of Education*, the most recent as of this writing being for 2012. An example of the phraseology is as follows "For geography, the score for 12th-grade students was lower in 2010 (282) than in 1994 (285)."[41] We suggest that this statement does not really pass the "so what?" test and that they are expressing data as results and results as conclusions. We suggest that a statistical test might tell us if we are looking at a significant change or just random variation. We shudder at the thought that politicians are making policy decisions based on noninformational statements such as the one above. If we continue on this tenor and look at another web page,[38] we see that the dropout rate for blacks, whites, Asian/Pacific islanders, and American Indian/Alaska natives has not changed appreciably over the 20 years from 1990 to 2010. However, the rate for Hispanics has improved from roughly 35% to roughly 15%, and we do not need a statistical test to assess a monotonic decline in undesirable results! Unfortunately, *The Condition of Education* does not provide any analysis whatsoever. Of concern to the big data analyst in this quagmire of "information" would also be the definition of dropout, since some students choose to "drop in" at a later opportunity.

One example of potential data issues (as well as big data issues) occurs when every student is forced to take an exam such as the Scholastic

Assessment Test (SAT). When those who do not really qualify for college are added to the population of measured students, we would expect to see scores fall on average (the reader can see the real values in Figures 12.1 and 12.2, which represent the mean scores for the four decades). We can see some issues with these scores:

- Mathematics scores are higher than in the past.
- Reading/verbal scores are lower.
- The combined scores circulate around a mean of 1011.2.
- The median of the means is 1010.

Given the hundreds of thousands, if not millions, of students who have taken this examination over the years, how do we make a statement as to whether things have gotten better or worse? We have something like 50.1 million K-12 students in 2013,[38] so we are looking at big data. Also note that mathematical ability clearly falls into Jean Piaget's final category of abstract operational, a classification that is not necessarily reached by all individuals.

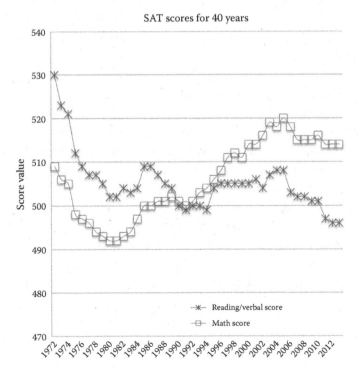

FIGURE 12.1 Four decades of SAT scores.

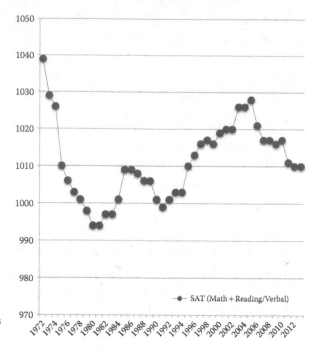

FIGURE 12.2
Four decades of SAT scores total.

One would think the US educational system would be a treasure chest (albeit, rather large) for data on just about everything. Unfortunately, for the data to truly have value, we have to ask the correct questions. Here are some suggestions.

- Use standards that are tied to real-world needs (are we serious about teaching geography?).
- Do not assume raising standards somehow will be met as a quest.
- Always identify the median, the standard deviation, and the most likely distribution in addition to obscure references to proportions and means.
- Realize that the purpose of any test is to identify undesirable situations, which must be defined beforehand.
- No test verifies knowledge, but some tests may demonstrate lack of knowledge.
- Do not call anything a "best practice" unless it has been proven to be a best practice.
- All "programs" must be falsifiable. (In short, we cannot use "raising awareness" as some kind of basis for awarding funding, time, resources, etc.)

- Realize that accountability starts at the top of an organization, not at the bottom.
- Verify any surrogate is a meaningful surrogate. (Students are much like horses in that "you can lead them to water, but you cannot make them drink.")
- Always identify, to the best of one's ability, whether a change is statistically meaningful and take the time to explain the terminology to the common citizen (do not assume everyone is stupid or ignorant).
- Consider applying Six Sigma methods, lean tools, and pull systems to the education system by cultivating a culture of experimentation.

Our final comment on this education quagmire relates to missed opportunities. How can we gather so much information about our student population but produce largely useless reports? Yes, we understand that the average citizen may not understand statistics, but then why would we report a value like the mean (which is generally less useful than the median due to sensitivity to outlying data points). Furthermore, when we have a collection of mean values (and, presumably, the other moments), why not analyze our results with one-way analysis of variance or some other statistical tool to see if the changes we observe are random variation or meaningful? Of course, we would need enough information to run the test (or the Kruskal-Wallis nonparametric test, assuming requirements for either of these tests are satisfactory).

MAKING YOURSELF HARDER TO TRACK

People who are paid to find other people who do not want to be found are often called "skip tracers."[42] They are tracing or looking for traces of somebody who has "skipped" town. Law enforcement may call this "fugitive recovery." We are not advocating violating the law; however, many of the techniques used by individuals to "skip" can also be used to reduce the impact of surveillance (big data in particular) on the individual. Not all individuals who are trying to fade away are criminals; consider whistle blowers, crime witnesses, and some varieties of libertarians. We suggest that some modicum of digital invisibility can reduce the chances of an identity thief getting our information.

As an example, one of us received an interesting notification one day from our credit card carrier; a rather large and unusual purchase had been made with our number at a fabric store we never frequented. The credit card algorithm correctly identified this action as an anomaly (a positive use of big data). Of course, we did not respond directly to the text message we received, but instead we called the credit card company directly, agreed that the purchase was illicit, and had a new credit card issued under a new number. In addition, we purchased wallets that have embedded metal in order to function as Faraday cages—enclosures of conducting material that blocks external electrical fields (the downside is that Faraday cages do not block slowly altering magnetic fields). We have also set our various cards to send alerts every time they are used. We are suggesting that users be aware of the issues associated with credit cards, especially the technologically backwards type of card used in the United States. The recent Target security breach attacked cards that only use a magnetic strip; other countries use cards with an embedded processor to provide another level of encryption. We might mention that another alternative is to use a secured card; that is, a card that only contains the money put into the account. That way, if the "bad guys" drain the account, the damage is limited to only what was in the account at the time of the intrusion.

We will discuss credit cards further, but any kind of digital footprint becomes a source for surveillance and tracking:

- Loyalty cards at supermarkets and department stores
- Social media
- Phones, especially phones receiving e-mail and texts
- Insurance information
- Tax information
- Filings with other government entities (property deeds, titles, etc.)

Misinformation

We supply misinformation when we unintentionally provide false or inaccurate information. A gray area exists between misinformation and disinformation when we can control circumstances sufficiently that our intended audience draws incorrect inferences; in other words, they fail because they make assumptions.

We also have misinformation when we make our own sets of assumptions. However, in this section of the book, we are primarily concerned with reducing our profile to data gatherers, be they governments, businesses, or nonprofits. An example of misinformation occurs when we see what is ostensibly "news," but some relevant data are missing. A common version of this kind of misinformation occurs when an apparently unusual event occurs and the news media jump on it as if it were common—they never provide any data to indicate whether we are really looking at an anomaly.

Disinformation

We supply disinformation when we intentionally provide false or inaccurate information. Disinformation is very much a part of the espionage business. We can remember many times when a variety of service functions have asked for our information; for example, a recent paper mail document arrived at home that requested drug interaction information. The insurance provider for subscriptions supplied this document. How much do they really need to know? Does providing such information add to yet another database and provide evidence for a pre-existing condition?

If we know our data will be used for some nefarious purpose, we are on the moral high ground when we provide disinformation. The moral nature of our personal information becomes problematic when we really do not know the purpose to which the information will be put. For example, when we fill out a warranty registration, are we simply providing information a vendor can sell to other vendors? I suspect many of us (in the United States) have filled out cards indicating our interests. We suggest these were clearly being used for marketing to targeted groups. Furthermore, we would suggest that a receipt with the product clearly marked on it should be sufficient evidence for warranty usage.

So how far do we go? Possible disinformation could consist of:

- Incorrect address
- Wrong name
- Date of birth changed
- Use of nicknames
- Use of post office (PO) box to remove home address from many lists (this probably is not really disinformation)
- Wrong family members listed or incomplete list
- Incorrect telephone number (with cell phones, these shift around)

- Obscured information on résumés (we are personally uncomfortable about this.)
- Wrong information on loyalty cards
- Racial obscurity
- Incorrect previous addresses

Reducing/Eliminating Profiles

Social Media

With social media, we can either log on with minimal information or we may not be members at all, with the second choice being the stronger of the two. The problem is that the moment we publish information about any of our personal details, we open ourselves to marketers, criminals, political groups, and nongovernmental organizations (usually charities). If we are irresponsible enough to put phone numbers and addresses online, that information becomes available to these parties as well.

Self Redefinition

One of the easiest physical changes to make is to use a PO box rather than a home mailbox. Such an approach makes it more difficult for criminals to remove mail from mailboxes. One of us has been able to walk up to the mail man as he delivers the daily mail and have him hand us our mail, although he did not know whether we really live at that address.

Another option is to hide ourselves behind a limited liability company (LLC). We can use the LLC name rather than our personal name. Yes, our real names are presumably part of the public record, but this approach will make it at least slightly more difficult for annoying entities to get our information. One of us was stunned when, after years of ignoring an alumnus organization and never leaving a mailing address, we started to receive mail from these people—and this was before the Internet era.

Another more painful option involves how we handle money:

- Use prepaid cell phones only.
- Use prepaid charge cards only and only when a card is necessary.
- Use cash—without a loyalty card, it is effectively untraceable.
- Obviously, do not use loyalty cards.
- Do not send in warranty mail.

- Do not register your products.
- Send all bills to your PO box.
- Send all subscriptions to a PO box and use the LLC name.
- Do not feed insurance companies your private information (especially health insurance).
- Put yourself on a do-not-call list.
- Remove yourself from the various mailing lists.
- Do not maintain debt—it reduces interest from creditors in your location

Identity Theft

Identity theft occurs when other individuals use your name and personal information to pose as you; that is, they are an impostor. We can reduce the possibility for identity theft with some planning and preparation. We recommend some simple steps:

- Use a Faraday cage wallet/billfold.
- Shred any document with your name on it when done.
- Do not mail documents with your real name and address on the return address.
- Use a doing-business-as (DBA) or LLC as the return address, preferably with a PO box instead of a physical address.
- Use UPS or FedEx (yes, it is generally more expensive, but consider the consequences).
- Deposit mail at the US Post Office, their blue boxes, or an alternative supplier such as the UPS store.
- Pick up your mail at a PO box.
- Be extremely careful with your online presence, whether it is personal or corporate.
- Make sure all financial transactions are sent to you as a text or an e-mail as close to real time as possible.
- Buy Internet purchases with a prepaid charge card.
- Never click to something you pay for from an e-mail since this approach is one of the primary tactics of "phishing."
- Check state laws (in the United States) to see if you can use a PO box as an address.
- Be cautious with pet information also.
- Consider the rules regarding voter registration.

The point of this discussion is to take simple steps to at least make it somewhat more difficult for the "bad guys" to capture your personal information. Bear in mind that personal information is sold by corporations as part of their business practices and effectively constitutes a product for them.

Besides a PO box, we can set up ghost addresses. This approach is "hard core" and we should be considering all applicable laws before using an alternate location as a mailing address:

- Motels (for a fee)
- Offices of relatives
- Offices of friends
- Charitable organizations (for a fee)

If you are truly trying to submerge from obvious tracking, you should remove your house number information. Where one of us lives, it is common for painting services to market door to door—they paint your house number on the curb by the driveway. Furthermore, many people display the house address by the garage or carport. Some of this can be obviated by the intelligent use of a PO box. Do not have packages delivered to your house. How do you know if that is really the UPS or FedEx delivery person? We suggest that our comments are not paranoid but rather a symptom of our times.

Who holds evidence of our identity? We suggest the following entities, at a minimum (in the United States):

- Family and friends
- Acquaintances
- Professional societies
- Social organizations
- Religious organizations
- City records
- County records
- State databases
- Internal Revenue Service
- Other governmental services
- Financial institutions
  - Banks
  - Credit card carriers

- Insurance
  - Life
  - Vehicular
  - Health
  - Lawsuit umbrella
- Loyalty cards (department stores and so forth)
- Service providers
- Search engines
- Social networking
- Work records at various companies and institutions

We suggest that it is extremely difficult to disappear. The highest leverage and simple act is to take a PO box in the name of a DBA or LLC where the ownership is not obvious. The level of "protection" this affords from identity thieves is difficult to quantify.

When using the Internet, anonymity is not particularly easy either. Some browsers support a privacy mode that provides minimal protection by not leaving large digital footprints. Another alternative is software known as Tor,[43] which uses a circuitous path through a variety of routers as well as encryption to try and provide some level of privacy from governments and ill-doers alike. *Bloomberg BusinessWeek* notes that Tor has received substantial support from the US government while simultaneously providing a means for blunting the incursions of the US NSA. The Bloomberg article claims Tor can defeat NSA spying, but we are not sure how it can prove this statement. What we do know is that the use of anonymizing software will certainly make spying more difficult—the disadvantage is that some sites that rely on Internet entities such as "cookies" will cease some functions. As with most of the options we have discussed in this section, citizens are faced with trade-offs, much like everything else in life. We must decide for ourselves how invisible we desire to be and act accordingly. At a minimum, we again suggest the PO box option is relatively painless and decouples our mail from our home address.

Facebook

At the time of this writing, Facebook is easily one of the most popular social networking tools on the planet, if not the most popular. The issue with any social networking tool is privacy, as well as identity control. If we are using the tool as an alternative and asynchronous means for staying in touch with our "friends," then disguising our identity seems to contradict the essence of the social network.

Visits to a brick-and-mortar bookstore such as Barnes & Noble show at least 10–20 titles that claim to provide knowledge about marketing your business with a social networking tool. Submerging below a DBA or an LLC is presumably less problematic than openly using your personal name and providing your personal information.

Facebook targets advertising, games, and quizzes at users. Once a member uses one of these applications, they open up their information for use and abuse by the vendor. We are not claiming Zynga (Farmville) is an evil empire, but we suggest some modicum of awareness when taking part in ostensibly "free" activities in a social network.

The privacy settings in Facebook are not exactly transparent—they are visible. The Facebook user needs to understand the ramifications of each choice. Chop too much off, and you defeat the ostensive purpose of the social network; leave too much open, and you reveal too much information about your private life. LinkedIn has some of these issues also. We have seen a lovelorn UK citizen attempt to make connections with married women on what is supposedly a business-oriented social network!

Do we need Facebook? How many real friends do we have in our lives? We do not think these are curmudgeonly questions but rather fundamental when we are trying to reduce our profile with big data vendors and governments. Business connections may make some kind of sense, so the stated purpose of LinkedIn seems to have meaning.

In our experience, postings on Facebook are often of this order:

- Narcissistic photographs
- Passing on of "cute" pictures
- Political, often offensively so
- Personal information and status we do not really need to know from people who are effectively tangential in our lives
- Out and out business
- Facebook advertising (want it or not)

Do people even think before they post some of this material? We suggest that Facebook is easily a social network that most likely yields a minimal return and poses significant privacy issues. We also see the same kinds of issues with tweets from Twitter. We may change our generally positive impression of LinkedIn if they do not police some of the more predatory behavior on the social network (in LinkedIn's defense, we note that a user can indicate to LinkedIn that a connection is inappropriate).

Drop Facebook. Drop Twitter. Use LinkedIn cautiously, if at all. Create a PO box that is not close to home. Do not use your personal name. Be cautious with driver's license, passport, and other official forms of identification.

Data ownership is a particularly difficult aspect of the explosion in data that we see around us, and the issue will not become easier any time soon. Remember that this book has argued that data is one of your organization's most valuable assets? Well, it is also a valuable asset for others as well. Think of your trade secrets, your client lists, your financial statements, the discounts you offer to your most valuable clients (how far you really can bid down), the performance numbers of your newest product, the new market whose growth you can see in your data but whose importance has been missed by competitors and the press—you get the idea.

An article in *Salon* from the end of 2013 discusses concern among farmers about data being collected by Monsanto[44] (we discussed some of this in another chapter). As an aside, it is difficult to know exactly how Monsanto uses the data it collects. Firms are often extremely respectful of customer data, segregating it and protecting it. There are cases of corporations abusing customer data but it would be grossly unfair to paint all firms with such a broad brush. Client data may well be segregated and heavily restricted. Monsanto is an organization that has often been maligned unfairly in the past, so a healthy skepticism against anti-Monsanto paranoia is in order.

However, despite the need to step back and avoid maligning Monsanto, concerns in general about how user data are stored and used by firms are timely, prudent, and defensible. We are entering a new and worrisome period in history. Just as the Internet promised to be a liberating technology that in fact can also very easily be subverted (think of 2013's string of NSA scandals involving spying against US citizens), such is also the case with big data. The situation our society faces is unprecedented. The technological trends that affect your privacy also affect your company's ability to protect its data.

The *Salon* article discusses a topic that this book has touched upon: precision farming. There is a common prejudice that farming is an unsophisticated and backwards occupation. A flipside to this stereotype is that the farm offers a peaceful lifestyle that gets away from technology, back to an older set of roots. The latter offers some truth about the joys of being alone in a field on a calm day but misses how high-tech farming truly is. Many crops are at the cutting edge of biotechnology, tractors now largely drive themselves guided by GPS satellites, databases guide pesticide and fertilizer application to maximize efficiency, and farmers are perhaps the most voracious consumers of financial and weather data after professional traders.[45]

Much of the value in agricultural data derives from the fact that farmers are not just passive consumers of data, but they are also active producers of huge quantities of data. As the benefits of precision farming become more widespread, these data will increase in importance. The *Salon* article states

> The big question is who exactly will end up owning all this data, and who gets to determine how it is used. On one side stand some of the largest corporations in agriculture, who are racing to gather and put their stamp on as much of this information as they can. Opposing them are farmers' groups and small open-source technology start-ups, which want to ensure a farm's data stays in the farmer's control and serves the farmer's interests.
>
> Who wins will determine not just who profits from the information, but who, at the end of the day, directs life and business on the farm.[44]

Knowledge is power, and just as the ability of Standard Oil to gain control of railroad routes gave it tremendous market leverage over its competitors, control of data can grant tremendous leverage over smaller competitors in agriculture and other industries, for that matter.

The cause for concern provided in the article is the movement of Monsanto and a partnership of John Deere and DuPont into the gathering and storage of data from farms throughout the United States. The services provided by these firms are indeed valuable. Monsanto, through its acquisition of the Climate Corporation, has become a major player in big data acquisition.

The Climate Corporation is a firm founded by Silicon Valley technical talent from firms such as Google that uses data to help farmers control risk. The Monsanto press release announcing the acquisition states, "The Climate Corporation's expertise is in data science. The company turns a wide range of information into valuable insights and recommendations for farmers. For example, recommendations may be planting a few days earlier or changing an irrigation schedule."[45]

The acquisition of The Climate Corporation is part of a general technological strategy being pursued by Monsanto, but one providing little grounds for controversy. One innovation being rolled out by Monsanto in 2014 is FieldScripts. Unlike the use of weather data from The Climate Corporation, FieldScripts involves the sharing of specific information about a field by the farmer with Monsanto so Monsanto can help choose the proper seeds for the conditions as well as help the farmer control planting density on a custom basis that varies from one part of a field to another. The data are processed by Monsanto and delivered to an iPad app. The iPad is then connected to a monitor inside the cab of the tractor to control planting for optimal yields. The service includes regular assistance to the farmer throughout the year, including at this stage, "The dealer captures farmer harvest data and submits it to Monsanto to further optimize next season's prescription."[46]

The title of the *Salon* article that raises this issue is, "Monsanto's scary new scheme: Why does it really want all this data?"[44] The reality is that what Monsanto is offering will almost certainly prove to be a valuable contribution to agricultural productivity. Few individual farmers will have the resources to create big data clusters and aggregate sufficient data of high quality on their own. The uncomfortable truth is that a large corporation with access to huge quantities of data that are collected through a standardized system (and therefore more or less akin to comparing apples to apples) is capable of extracting value from these data that individual farmers on their own will not be able to do. Thus, Monsanto is able to provide a valuable service to farmers that they could not obtain on their own.

This does not mean that farmers have no cause for concern. As this book has emphasized, data is an asset. Providing more data to a supplier has a high likelihood of providing greater insight into the farm's operations to an external party. Few companies think this is a good idea, which is why they jealously protect their data. No good negotiator gives away his or her intimate details to a future negotiating partner.

A likely motive behind Monsanto's move into data, aside from moving into a field that is likely to become a progressively more valuable line of business as big data takes root profoundly in agriculture, is that by knowing its customers more intimately, Monsanto will be able to target more relevant services to those customers. Moreover, farmers whose strategy is dependent on Monsanto's services will find it increasingly difficult to move elsewhere.

It is tempting to put a sinister spin on this strategy, but it is unjustified. Most of us have similar relationships with other companies that use a similar strategy. Do you use Amazon Prime, enjoying its recommendations to you based on your prior purchasing habits? Do you purchase Apple or Android products because you have a sunken cost in music or apps from one or another of these platforms? Do you use free e-mail that supports itself by advertising to you? Do you belong to a loyalty program, such as airline miles or hotel points, which occasionally offers you prizes or coupons? Have you resisted switching from the Kindle to the Nook (or vice versa) because you would lose all of your books?

All of these are examples of business strategies designed to create loyalty through offering benefits that create path dependence. Path dependence, according to Wikipedia, "explains how the set of decisions one faces for any given circumstance is limited by the decisions one has made in the past, even though past circumstances may no longer be relevant."[47] The data that Monsanto has gathered will enable it to continue to market valuable customized solutions that other firms without that data will be unable to offer. The cost of entering such a relationship is some loss of independence. Whether this is a worthwhile trade-off depends on the goals and values of the individual farmer.

As data make such strategies more feasible, it will be increasingly important to understand their effects. For example, companies that do not provide their data may find themselves at a competitive disadvantage to those who do. The court actions against Microsoft in the 1990s were in large part because Microsoft's dominance of the operating system market enabled it to bend consumer behavior in a way that consumers would more likely have selected against, absent the said market dominance. Standard Oil was able to coerce its competitors to behave to their own detriment because of its dominance of the petroleum infrastructure. The dominance of data analysis by major firms will have the potential for destructive, coercive actions against smaller firms if data processing capabilities are overly centralized. Such a concentration of power is not a foregone conclusion and not necessarily a disastrous outcome should it occur. After all, Bell Telephone's monopoly created tremendous public goods and Microsoft's dominance had the upside of creating standards for computing. Still, firms should understand the risks of such dominance and should create contingency plans in the event such consolidation occurs in their industries.

One possible drawback is that the data belonging to an individual or an organization could result in them being shared against the will of the owner. Many farmers rent their land. A landlord could likely find his closely held secrets ending up in the hands of a third party if one of his tenants uses a service that requires the kind of reporting that FieldScripts requires to be successful. Clearly, legislation will be needed to adjust to this brave new world. Until the law itself converges to the big data reality, the language of contracts will be the best protection of any individual who wishes to avoid having his or her data falling into the possession of parties who have no legitimate need for it.

This is also an issue due to a topic discussed earlier in the book, which is one of the drivers of the growth of big data: the spread of sensor technology. In the case of agriculture, an article from the *Grand Forks Herald* covered an unexpected angle involving the use of drones:

> Though drones are already being used by some farmers, mostly to monitor their acreage, [North Dakota Agriculture Commissioner Doug] Goehring said UAVs could be on the verge of being used on a wider scale for advanced disease detection, pest mitigation, crop mapping and to develop complex algorithms, all in an effort to maximize yields and improve productivity.[48]

Some of the uses imagined for drones listed in the article include identifying weeds via the optical signature obtained by light refractivity so herbicides can be better targeted, monitoring crop nutrition, and tracking livestock. Clearly, there are data ownership issues that will arise as such solutions take their first baby steps toward broad and accepted implementation.

Will a third party own and monitor such data? To what degree will losing control of one's own information affect business decisions and negotiations? Will the way that interpretive algorithms are written affect—fairly or unfairly—land valuations? Will it create differential values between the product of one producer and the product of another (humorously: "From this photo, it looks like farmer Joe has a viral infection in his crops.")? Will new incentives created by such transparency cause farmers to game the system in new ways? What is measured affects what actions are taken, often to nonsensical effect.

This book has used the example of big data in hiring decisions to illustrate several points. As this technology becomes more embedded in deciding who is hired for what job, as well as which career tracks an employee should take once inside a company, it seems more than likely that a small industry will arise to game the system. Methods to improve the probability of being hired will almost inevitably arise, without these methods necessarily making better employees.

Psychometric tests are valuable measurements that have a long and useful history in research and treatment. While some of the measures of potential employees or contractors are not explicitly psychometric, such as those that measure performance on video games and draw conclusions from that, many do have the explicit question and answer format associated with psychometric testing. Psychometrics, like many other measurements such as consumer sentiment, are fuzzy because of the nature of what they are measuring. It is much more difficult to quantify intellectual horsepower than it is to the measure the mass or length of an object.

What we have seen and can see is that psychometrics functions "good enough" to make an impact on turnover, poor performance, and other problems that plague companies with a large number of employees. To use round numbers, imagine that the authors of this book offered a service that decreased first-year employee turnover by 20% for an annual fee of $400,000. It costs you $10,000 in direct and indirect costs to bring a new employee on board. You have 2000 employees and an annual turnover rate of 25%.

You are losing 500 employees per year. Hiring their replacements costs you $5 million per year. If you can lower that turnover by a measly 20%, you actually save $1 million per year before calculating in the $400,000 fee that we charge. Your net savings are $600,000 per year. In this example, we are wrong far more often than we are right. Remember that we are only lowering your turnover by 20%, with 80% of the employees that will leave within 1 year slipping right past our system. Although it is far more difficult to measure, we are probably also filtering out a lot of potential star employees. Despite our high error rate, it is difficult to argue with the tangible results of our testing. It will create difficulty for those who potentially great employees who are erroneously filtered out, but you need to satisfy shareholders or pay back your business loans.

If you are a potential employee, it is easy to see what your incentives are. You want to be hired. If you find a better opportunity before a year is up, that is the business's problem, not yours. You will want to game the system, and this is achievable provided that the test is meaningful. It is fairly easy to see through many of the more reliable tests. There are pages online with varying levels of detail that teach potential employers how to beat the tests. The most basic summary of the strategy for answering a psychometric question on a pre-employment examination is this sentence from one of the articles: "Ask yourself what it is that the company is looking for and not necessarily how that question makes you feel."[49] More specific information is also available. As testing becomes more pervasive, it is probable that more testing training will likewise become available, just as has occurred with training for college admission tests such as the SAT, ACT, GMAT, and others has occurred.

A fascinating article from *Wired* describes how a mathematician whose love life was lacking reverse-engineered the process used by OKCupid to narrow down the kinds of women he wanted to date, then used that knowledge to make his profile match theirs.[50]

Another danger is a flipside to this in that employers will create self-fulfilling prophecies that lock eager and diligent employees into dead-end jobs that fit their profile but not their character and promise. Remember that a putative strength of big data is that it takes away decision-making capability from flawed human judgment. As we have argued in this book, this does not mean big data should be trusted blindly. The famous Pygmalion study by Robert Rosenthal and Lenore Jacobson created random intelligence test results that were then reported to teachers.[51] In so doing, they found the expectations that they created among teachers resulted in different increases in students' IQ tests. The results of this study have generated substantial controversy since their 1968 publication and have been challenged. Two researchers, Lee Jussim and Kent Harber, published a paper in 2005 discussing the controversy surrounding Rosenthal and Jacobson's work. What they found was decidedly more qualified and can be summarized in two of the paper's paragraph headings: "Self-fulfilling prophecies in the classroom are real" and "Self-fulfilling effects are typically small."[52]

The reason a real, but typically small, effect is important is the mechanism that makes it such. Self-fulfilling prophecies are real, but they are held in check by something. A 1982 paper by Jere Brophy also followed up Rosenthal and Jacobson's work and in the process made a tremendously important finding. It is worth quoting at length (citations and references have been removed for readability):

> Expectation formation studies in which subjects are given only carefully controlled information about, and little or no opportunity to interact with the "students" (usually fictional) about whom they are asked to make predictions typically show that expectations can be affected significantly by information about test performance, performance on assignments, track or group placement, classroom conduct, physical appearance, race, social class, ethnicity, sex, speech characteristics, and various diagnostic labels. Ultimately this list could be could be extended to include any factor that is known or believed to be associated with student achievement, or indeed any factor likely to induce a positive or negative halo image of the student being described.[53]

However, the fact that experimental subjects working with very limited information sometimes develop expectations based on inappropriate evidence does not mean that teachers typically do the same.[54]

Teachers work daily with students and they care about students. After all, that is why most teachers become teachers. In their daily activities, they adjust course because they see the strengths and weaknesses of students. This is not to say that the halo effect does not occur. There is ample anecdotal evidence to suggest that it does exist. That is part of human psychology. Teachers, however, are motivated to help students succeed. In so doing, they course-correct. Brophy continues:

> ...it should be noted that the potential for particular teacher expectations to exert self-fulfilling prophecy effects on students depends not so much on the degree to which the expectations are initially accurate or reality based as on the degree to which expectations remain open to corrective feedback (emphasis in the original) and thus flexible or adjustable in view of current events... A variation on this point is that even initially justified expectations can lead to self-fulfilling prophecy effects if those expectations are rigidly maintained despite upward or downward trends in the student's performance levels that should dictate a change in those expectations.[54]

The lesson for the use of big data in hiring and promotion is clear if we generalize Brophy's ideas. Big data can improve decision making in hiring and promotions to some degree, but the human judgment that can be so troublesome at times is indispensable in others. Feedback—high-quality feedback that measures variables other than those used to arrive at the original decision—is imperative in order to ensure results are accurate and that they remain accurate. By all means, big data can create a hiring process that is fairer to prospective employees and less of a burden for companies, but when big data becomes a fetish, when it is viewed as an oracle, it will fail.

Big data shines most brightly when dealing with constant patterns or smooth trends. It deals poorly with abrupt shifts, unless predictable signs precede those shifts. We must remain cognizant of big data limitations, including issues with nonlinearity, when we use the results of our analyses to make decisions.

A feedback mechanism will allow an escape hatch for employees who want to move to the fast track but who are initially selected out. It will relieve the stress of employees who have modest goals but who were scored as potential whiz kids. It will enable employees to try a new job that they never considered, which uses their talents and that they only discovered by accident while speaking with a coworker in the company cafeteria.

The applicability of this lesson to education, social work, crime prevention, and myriad other areas where misperceptions carry consequences, should be clear. One of the key advantages of big data is that it unlocks unused potential by identifying it. The paradox is that the careless acceptance of a computer-generated score as our fate, and absent continuous and meaningful corrective feedback, threatens to lock up that same potential that it is meant to unlock.

One of the authors of this book understands this very clearly. With an interest in commodities and international trade, he once told a flatmate in graduate school, in all honesty, that he found information technology to be of no interest and he had no intention of seeking a career in that field. He expected to work for a giant agribusiness firm. Through a series of life accidents, he went on to coauthor the book you are now reading.

Having third parties who aggregate data is not necessarily a problem. Companies such as IHS and Drillinginfo use public data to create useful data sets that are then purchased by companies operating in the petroleum sphere. By law, certain information on wells that are drilled must be reported to state agencies such as the Railroad Commission of Texas (despite the name, it is the state agency in charge of petroleum production), the North Dakota Industrial Commission, and the counterparts to these agencies in other states. Canada has its own reporting requirements.

The reported data are voluminous. They covers well locations, geometries, statuses, and production levels. Since the data are self-reported rather than automatically generated, they can be messy. These companies that aggregate the data serve a very valuable function by cleaning it and offering it up on a subscription basis.

As these data are public, and those companies selling the data for a profit are adding value to that public data, any information asymmetry that forms is not one that can be easily exploited by one party over another. This is a very different phenomenon from that caused by one party accumulating data on its customers.

A main theme of this book has been the issues of data quality and how we react to it. A book review of *Uncharted: Big Data as a Lens on Human Culture* in *Pacific Standard* discusses some of these points. The book has a clever premise that builds on a TED talk given by the authors of *Uncharted*,

Erez Aiden and Jean-Baptiste Michel, that was mentioned earlier in this book. The review argues that scholarship using big data is not necessarily deep scholarship:

> Ngram [the tool created by Google to analyze the content of books, which was heavily influenced by Aiden and Michel] counts the number of books in which a term was used, but it doesn't consider the context in which the term was used within an individual book, nor how widely a book was read. And what about the influence of other media—television, film, radio, newspapers—in word usage? [55]

As big data is being treated more and more as a fount of wisdom, the consequences can be more severe than the lack of a probing examination of a scholarly issue. The author of the *Pacific Standard* piece argues what we have argued in this book:

> In academia, overenthusiasm for suggestive correlations makes for shoddy scholarship. Out in the wider world, it affects lives, as when the government puts you on a no-fly list because the latest algorithm says your digital profile resembles that of a terrorist, or when a mortgage company denies you a loan based on patterns in your social media presence.

We have discussed the use of big data to create customer loyalty from the point of the view of the customer. This would include the Amazon Prime customer who likes the perks and finds it onerous to switch to a different company. After all, Amazon provides free e-books for the Kindle, access to streaming video, and carefully customized recommendations based on past purchasing behavior. You simply allow Amazon to collect your browsing and purchase history.

It would also include the example of Monsanto's FieldScripts service. Monsanto provides a valuable service that allows farmers to farm more efficiently. The farmers simply provide data about their fields.

Retail is now a commodity service. Brick-and-mortar stores that lost their way, such as Kmart and Sears, have lost tremendous market share to Wal-Mart. Wal-Mart—a paragon of the use of data in logistics—can track sales and shelf space to a degree that few other physical retailers are able to match. Along with its massive bargaining position, its efficiency enables it to profitably drive down prices below what its competitors can easily match. Target has thrived in this new environment by staying lean and affordable while also emphasizing high-end design by celebrity designers such as Michael Graves and Philippe Stark. Wal-Mart competes on price and variety. Target keeps its foothold by differentiating itself, but it still stays in Wal-Mart's price range and maintains a wide array of products.

Amazon has pushed prices into a realm where brick-and-mortar stores cannot compete. The ability of consumers to try out products at Best Buy and then purchase them on Amazon is considered a major factor in the precipitous decline of Best Buy. A similar behavior among readers is thought to have contributed to the demise of Borders. The wisdom of Amazon founder and leader Jeff Bezos is in knowing full well that no company remains invulnerable. Most major brick-and-mortar retailers have an online presence, including Wal-Mart, as we saw in our discussion of Endeca. Plus, there are other popular sellers such as NewEgg.com, Half.com, and myriad others.

In a commodity market, suppliers are price takers rather than price makers. This also means that suppliers remain vulnerable. What Amazon is doing is entrenching itself, and it is doing so using data. It is safe to assume that low prices will remain Amazon's strategy, but the ability of the company to provide additional services will protect Amazon from other online retailers that match its prices.

Companies that use big data as an active measure to serve customers will be more successful than competitors that do not have that vision. Yes, this is obvious, but it is forgotten. Pick up an article about using big data in business strategy. The odds are high that it will discuss how big data can be used to identify high-potential customers or to identify potential hires. Big data is wonderful for these activities, but it is also a tool to use to interact with customers. A firm that has big data resources has a service that it can offer to its customers. In using big data to recommend products, Amazon is removing itself from the realm of a mere e-commerce site to also be the provider of a value-adding service. In using big data to help farmers, Monsanto is providing a value-adding service on top of its business of just selling seeds.

Customer data cut both ways though. As this passage was being written, hackers stole the information of tens of millions of customers from Target and Nieman Marcus. If your firm is holding customer data, there is almost certainly someone trying to steal them. As has been emphasized at several points in this book, data are an asset; they are increasingly becoming one of the most important assets an organization possesses. Thieves will want these data. In some cases, so will spies. However, this is not the same as shoplifting or embezzling. It is worse. It is more dangerous. If a customer shoplifts from your store, your store loses the value of that product. If an employee embezzles money from you, your firm suffers that particular loss. These are closed-ended losses.

When a thief or a spy steals data from your firm, then very possibly customer information will be lost. The loss extends beyond you to directly affect others. As your firm acquires and retains customer data, it also takes on additional legal obligations and liability risks. A write-up in *USA Today* by Eric Cernak, a vice president at the insurer Hartford Steam Boiler states

> A Ponemon Institute survey for insurer Hartford Steam Boiler found that 55 percent of small businesses had a data breach and 53 percent of those businesses had multiple breaches. Yet, surprisingly, only 33 percent of the businesses notified the people affected, even though 46 states, the District of Columbia and Puerto Rico require that individuals be contacted when their personal information is compromised.[56]

Just as travelers who know better than to drink the water when overseas need to be reminded sometimes not to eat the ice, Mr. Cernak points out that firms who outsource payroll, payments, or websites should negotiate that the firm handling these third-party services should assume liability for breaches that occur under its control. It also highly important to know the trustworthiness of employees who have access to data as well as have the ability to properly dispose of old computers and data storage devices. Finally, as Mr. Cernak emphasizes, if your organization suffers a data breach, the company should not ignore it and hope for the best. It is best to get the issue into the open, notify customers immediately, and help customers prepare to mitigate consequences.

Many firms are turning toward cloud storage. Cloud storage firms are very often experienced in protecting customer data. After all, much data is aggregated on their servers. Nonetheless, it is incumbent that a firm wishing to use cloud storage for its data should understand very well the security measures in place and run these past a properly trained and accredited data security professional.

Understanding how data that your organization possesses are susceptible to a data breach, you should also keep in mind that firms with whom you do business are likewise susceptible. As has already been emphasized in this discussion of data breaches, a firm should negotiate where the liability falls when a firm relies on third-party suppliers. However, data can leak out in other ways aside from breaches, such as our example of the potential use of drone aircraft in monitoring fields used in agriculture.

Among the secrets released by a whistleblower and former NSA contractor is that the US and British intelligence services found ways to use applications such as Angry Birds and Google Maps to monitor users at a highly invasive level. Referring to a 14-page NSA slideshow that was leaked:

> It wasn't clear precisely what information can be extracted from which apps, but one of the slides gave the example of a user who uploaded a photo using a social media app. Under the words, "Golden Nugget!" it said that the data generated by the app could be examined to determine a phone's settings, where it connected to, which websites it had visited, which documents it had downloaded, and who its users' friends were. One of the documents said that apps could even be mined for information about users' political alignment or sexual orientation.[57]

This invasion of individual privacy is not *per se* directly applicable to your organization, as it is an attempt to catalogue the characteristics of particular individuals. Nevertheless, it is conceptually applicable to your business in that you may end up using telephone and tablet applications as these become more ingrained in daily business practices and customer interactions.

If it were simply the NSA trying to collect information about you and your firm, that would be one thing. The NSA's motivations are not to steal your credit card logs to go shopping on your customers' dime. It is highly unlikely that the NSA will post your customer list online to embarrass anyone. The questions raised by the NSA's actions instead revolve around the role of safety versus individual liberty and whether it is the interest of the citizen or the state that should take precedence.

Private firms are also after your company and your individual data. Google has raised questions about its practices of storing so much customer data for so long, as well as its opacity in what it does with these data. Some of these data are voluntarily handed over, such as when a user opens a Google+ account (not unlike handing information over to Facebook, Amazon, or the iTunes store when opening an account). Some of these data is not, however.

Google raised eyebrows in 2012 when the *Wall Street Journal* caught the company bypassing safety protections in the Safari web browser installed as standard on Apple iPhones. The *Journal* explains:

> To get around Safari's default blocking, Google exploited a loophole in the browser's privacy settings. While Safari does block most tracking, it makes an exception for websites with which a person interacts in some way—for

instance, by filling out a form. So Google added coding to some of its ads that made Safari think that a person was submitting an invisible form to Google. Safari would then let Google install a cookie [a small file to track user behavior—authors] on the phone or computer.[58]

Taking privacy assurances at face value can be risky. Even if the system with which you are directly interacting is being run in a transparent and completely ethical manner, computer systems interact with each other. If a firm hosts advertisements on my website, no matter how well it adheres to its stated privacy practices, your privacy is directly impacted by the policies and practices of the firm hosting the advertisements.

The previously mentioned cookies are one way of tracking user behavior. Criminal groups will also use viruses and other malware (harmful software) to extract information from your computer system. This malware can be used to access those consumer data that you are trying to protect.

Respectable companies will probably not resort to malware to obtain your information, but the use of web browsing history can be used to glean information. One of the authors is familiar with the case of an individual who was making payments on a medical bill. Due to a clerical error, the account on which the payments were being made was sent to collections. There was an unwillingness on the part of the medical office to pull the account out of collections, so this person conducted a web search on a non-Google search engine on how to apply legal pressure to force the hand of the medical office. The user's Gmail account was dominated afterward by advertisements aimed at those with financial problems and accounts in collections. Even after deleting all cookies on the computer, the advertisements remained. It was necessary to go back and delete the web browsing history to make the advertisements disappear. We presume this practice is not isolated.

Your browsing history will probably not be used to steal large quantities of data from your firm, but it can provide intelligence about it to others. Likewise, if you research your competition using the Internet from your organization's computers, it is very likely that your competition can track your movements through monitoring your internet protocol (IP) address on their internal logs aside from using just cookies and browsing history. The power behind monitoring IP addresses is that it is possible to trace traffic back to the computer being used. Unless the IP address is disguised through the use of a virtual private network (VPN) or other anonymizing proxy server, the location of the computer with that address, along with the Internet service provider, can be determined.

The use of an IP address look-up almost undid one of the largest criminal investigations into the use of stolen credit card numbers. In his disturbing, impactful look at this area of Internet crime, *DarkMarket*, the journalist Misha Glenny describes the incident. One of the hackers involved in the administration of the website CardersMarket, using the alias Iceman, hacked into his website's competitor, DarkMarket, and began to examine the IP addresses of the administrators. Seeing one that looked suspicious, Iceman traced it back to a company, Pembrooke Associates. Little information was available about the company except its phone number and address, 2000 Technology Drive in Pittsburgh, Pennsylvania. He recognized this address from a document that one of his colleagues had found online. It belonged to the National Cyber-Forensics and Training Alliance.[59]

In the age of big data, these fingerprints left by your systems can, and probably will, be used to find out about your firm or you personally. Security countermeasures are beyond the scope of this book, but if your organization is conducting sensitive research online and is worried about leaving behind such digital traces or preventing the tracking of its browsers, it is worth discussing this with qualified security professionals. Sometimes, however, you cannot avoid having your information collected.

CONCLUDING COMMENTS

We are not particularly surprised at any of the data incursions, from NSA surveillance, to traffic cameras, to business intelligence gathered by the likes of Google, Amazon, IBM, and any other large World Wide Web firm. In the United States, it has become virtually impossible to drop out of sight, even with the use of cash.

We can think of a variety of opportunities for companies to track citizens:

- Insurance policies (health, life, auto, home)
- "Loyalty" cards at vendors
- Credit cards
- Social Security
- Medicare/Medicaid

- Military
- Online purchases of any kind
- Hotel/motel room rental
- Auto rental
- Air travel
- Anything involving a card with a magnetic strip
- Public utilities
- Cable TV and data lines (probably satellite TV also)
- School records
- Law enforcement
- Hospital and doctors' offices

The list could go on, but we think the reader gets the point by now. In effect, our world has become contaminated by surveillance by businesses, government agencies, and even nongovernmental organizations.

Just because we can collect vast amounts of data and convert these data into statistics does not mean in all cases that we should do so. It appears that legislation is ineffective when the government itself wants access to information. Anything that can identify anybody is fodder to data collection from license plates on cars to facial recognition packages.

We recommend some simple ideas:

- Continue to legislate.
- Negotiate with allies.
- Take steps to become "invisible" when feasible.
- Use cash.
- Drop the loyalty cards.

Ultimately, we have done all of this to ourselves.

An article in *Wired* demonstrates just how "big data" the NSA has become. Hadoop was used by the agency in its location tracking efforts, with individual users' locations nabbed by accessing the location data of individual cell phones. Remember that cell phones track both the GPS coordinates of individual users as well as which cell towers they access. Another open-source software package leveraged by the NSA is OpenStack, a cloud computer package that enables the NSA to use virtual machines across servers just as Amazon does. However, when the agency decided that it needed a system with greater security than was easily available, it built Accumulo, which is based of Google's BigTable paper and is similar in many ways to HBase. Due to the difficulty of building its security features into HBase, though, it was easier to build it from the ground up.[60]

REFERENCES

1. United Nations. The Universal Declaration of Human Rights, UDHR, Declaration of Human Rights, Human Rights Declaration, Human Rights Charter, the UN and Human Rights. UN News Center. 2013. Accessed November 27, 2013. http://www.un.org/en/documents/udhr.
2. US Congress. United States Bill of Rights. Ratified 1791.
3. National Conference of State Legislatures. State laws related to internet privacy. 2014. http://www.ncsl.org/research/telecommunications-and-information-technology/state-laws-related-to-internet-privacy.aspx. Accessed March 16, 2014.
4. Publications Office of the European Union. Directive 95/46/EC of the European Parliament and of the Council of 24 October 1995 on the protection of individuals with regard to the processing of personal data and on the free movement of such data. Publications Office of the European Union. November 23, 1995. http://eur-lex.europa.eu/LexUriServ/LexUriServ.do?uri=CELEX:31995L0046:EN:HTML. Accessed November 27, 2013.
5. OECD (Organization for Economic Cooperation and Development). Recommendation of the council concerning guidelines governing the protection of privacy and transborder flows of personal data. *Information, Computer and Communications Policy*. July 11, 2013. http://www.oecd.org/internet/ieconomy/oecdguidelinesontheprotectionofprivacyandtransborderflowsofpersonaldata.htm, Part Two. Accessed November 27, 2013.
6. Cox, P. and T. Pedersen. Directive 2002/58/EC of the European Parliament and of the Council. PDF. Brussels, Belgium: Official Journal of the European Communities, July 12, 2002.
7. Greenwald, G., S. Ackerman, L. Poitras, E. MacAskill, and D. Rushe. Microsoft handed the NSA access to encrypted messages. *The Guardian*. July 12, 2013. http://www.theguardian.com/world/2013/jul/11/microsoft-nsa-collaboration-user-data. Accessed November 27, 2013.
8. Mill, J. S. *A System of Logic: Ratiocinative and Inductive, Being a Connected View of the Principles of Evidence, and the Methods of Scientific Investigation*. London: John W. Parker, 1846.
9. Taleb, N. N. *The Black Swan: The Impact of the Highly Improbable*. New York: Random House, 2007.
10. Taleb, N. N. *Antifragile: Things That Gain from Disorder*. New York: Random House, 2012.
11. Collins, J. C. *Good to Great: Why Some Companies Make the Leap—and Others Don't*. New York: HarperBusiness, 2001.
12. Kolakowski, N. Larry Ellison believes Apple is doomed. *Slashdot*. August 13, 2013. http://slashdot.org/topic/cloud/larry-ellison-believes-apple-is-doomed/. Accessed November 25, 2013.

13. Big-Data Startups. Big data best practice: How Amazon is leveraging Big Data. BigData-Startups RSS2. 2013. http://www.bigdata-startups.com/BigData-startup/amazon-leveraging-big-data/. Accessed November 27, 2013.

14. Hughes, D. Big data is the only way to compete with Google. *AllThingsD*. July 18, 2013. http://allthingsd.com/20130718/big-data-is-the-only-way-to-compete-with-google. Accessed November 27, 2013.

15. Acxiom. Acxiom audience operating system. 2014. http://aos.acxiom.com/. Accessed March 16, 2014.

16. BlueKai. BlueKai: Big data for marketing. Bluekai. 2013. http://www.bluekai.com/. Accessed March 16, 2014.

17. Epsilon. Where intelligence ignites connection. Epsilon. 2013. http://www.epsilon.com/about-us/our-story. Accessed November 28, 2013.

18. V12 Group. V12 Group explained. V12 Group. 2014. http://www.v12groupinc.com/. Accessed March 16, 2014.

19. DataLogix. It's all about the data. DataLogix RSS. 2014. http://www.datalogix.com/about/. Accessed March 16, 2014.

20. Leggett, C. The Ford Pinto case. Spring 1999. http://users.wfu.edu/palmitar/Law&Valuation/Papers/1999/Leggett-pinto.html. Accessed March 16, 2014.

21. *United States et al. v. Carroll Towing Co., Inc., et al.*, 1 (1947) (testimony of Learned Hand).

22. Chauhan, P. and L. Kois. Homicide by neighborhood: Mapping New York City's violent crime drop. Research and Evaluation Center. July 2012. http://johnjayresearch.org/. Accessed November 27, 2013.

23. Kelling, G. L. and J. Q. Wilon. Broken windows. *The Atlantic*. March 1, 1982. http://www.theatlantic.com/magazine/archive/1982/03/broken-windows/304465/. Accessed March 16, 2014.

24. Harcourt, B. E. and J. Ludwig. Broken windows: New evidence from New York City and a five-city social experiment. *University of Chicago Law Review*, Winter 2006, 73:271–320.

25. Balko, R. The other broken windows fallacy. *Reason.com*. March 8, 2010. http://reason.com/archives/2010/03/08/the-other-broken-window-fallac. Accessed March 16, 2014.

26. McDonald, H. CompStat and its enemies, *City Journal*. 17 February 2010. http://www.city-journal.org/2010/eon0217hm.html. Accessed November 25, 2013.

27. Brickhouse Security. GPS trackers instantly locate anyone or anything. *GPS Tracking*. 2013. http://www.brickhousesecurity.com/category/gps%2Btracking.do. Accessed November 27, 2013.

28. Biale, N. What criminologists and others studying cameras have found. Report. June 25, 2008. https://www.aclu.org/files/images/asset_upload_file708_35775.pdf. Accessed March 17, 2014.

29. B. C. Welsh and D. P. Farrington. Development and statistics directorate. Crime prevention effects of closed circuit television: A systematic review. United Kingdom Home Office. August 2002. http://www.popcenter.org/Responses/video_surveillance/PDFs/Welsh&Farrington_2002.pdf. Accessed March 17, 2014.

30. Jones, B. and N. Tilley. The impact of high visibility patrol on personal robbery hot spots. Report. London, UK: Home Office, 2004.

31. Schlosberg, M. and N. A. Ozer. Under the watchful eye: The proliferation of video surveillance systems in California. California ACLU Affiliates. 2007. https://www.aclunc.org/docs/criminal_justice/police_practices/under_the_watchful_eye_the_proliferation_of_video_surveillance_systems_in_california.pdf. Accessed March 17, 2014.

32. Stuster, J. and Z. Coffman. Synthesis of safety research related to speed and speed management. US Department of Transport. Federal Highway Administration. July 1998. http://www.tfhrc.gov/safety/speed/spdtoc.htm. Accessed March 17, 2014.

33. US Department of Transportation. Speed concepts: Informational guide. FHWA-SA-10-001. Federal Highway Administration. Washington, DC: USDOT, 2009.

34. Transunion TLO. People searches & business searches with TLOxp®. 2014. http://www.tlo.com/reports.html. Accessed March 17, 2014.

35. MVTRAC. MVTRAC: The intelligent data network. 2013. http://mvtrac.com/. Accessed March 17, 2014.

36. RIP Media Group. ANPR/LPR—Video analytics—Facial recognition. Vigilant Solutions. 2014. http://vigilantsolutions.com/. Accessed March 17, 2014.

37. Simpson, D. and P. Brown. NSA mines Facebook for connections, including Americans' profiles. CNN. September 30, 2013. http://edition.cnn.com/2013/09/30/us/nsa-social-networks/index.html?hpt=ibu_c2. Accessed March 17, 2014.

38. US Department of Education, Institute of Education Sciences, National Center for Education Statistics. Fast facts. 2013. http://nces.ed.gov/fastfacts/display.asp?id=372. Accessed March 14, 2014.

39. American Speech-Lanaguage-Hearing Association. No Child Left Behind Act fact sheet on accountability. ASHA. October 15, 2008. http://www.asha.org/uploaded-Files/advocacy/federal/nclb/NCLBFactsAccountability.pdf. Accessed March 17, 2014.

40. US Department of Education, Institute of Education Sciences, National Center for Education Statistics. 2012 Spotlight. The condition of education. 2012. http://nces.ed.gov/programs/coe/analysis/2012-section4.asp. Accessed March 17, 2014.

41. US Department of Education, Institute of Education Sciences, National Center for Education Statistics. 2012 Spotlight. The condition of education. 2012. http://nces.ed.gov/programs/coe/analysis/2012-section5.asp. Accessed March 17, 2014.

42. Wikipedia. Skiptrace. Wikipedia. March 16, 2014. http://en.wikipedia.org/wiki/Skiptrace. Accessed March 17, 2014.

43. Lawrence, D. The inside story of Tor, the best internet anonymity tool the government ever built. *Bloomberg Business Week.* January 23, 2014. http://www.businessweek.com/articles/2014-01-23/tor-anonymity-software-vs-dot-the-national-security-agency. Accessed March 17, 2014.

44. Khan, L. Monsanto's scary new scheme: Why does it really want all this data? *Salon.* December 29, 2013. http://www.salon.com/2013/12/29/monsantos_scary_new_scheme_why_does_it_really_want_all_this_data/. Accessed December, 29, 2013.

45. Monsanto. Monsanto acquires The Climate Corporation. Monsanto corporate website. http://www.monsanto.com/features/Pages/monsanto-acquires-the-climate-corporation.aspx. Accessed January 7, 2014.

46. FieldScripts. Monsanto corporate website. http://www.monsanto.com/products/pages/fieldscripts.aspx. Accessed January 7, 2014.

47. Wikipedia. Path dependence. Wikipedia. 2014. http://en.wikipedia.org/wiki/Path_dependence. Accessed January 7, 2014.

48. Horwath, B. Drones have "unlimited potential" in ag, Goehring says. *Grand Forks Herald.* December 30, 2013. http://www.grandforksherald.com/event/article/id/281228/group/News/. Accessed December 30, 2013.

49. Smith, T. How to take a personality test. *Yahoo Voices.* February 1, 2011. http://voices.yahoo.com/how-take-personality-test-7674614.html. Accessed January 24, 2014.

50. Poulsen, K. How a math genius hacked OkCupid to find true love. *Wired.com*. January 19, 2014. http://www.wired.com/wiredscience/2014/01/how-to-hack-okcupid/. Accessed March 17, 2014.

51. Rosenthal, R. and L. Jacobson. Newman Study Site Rosenthal. September 14, 1999. http://www.sagepub.com/newman4study/resources/rosenthal1.htm. Accessed March 17, 2014.

52. Jussim, L. and K. Harber. Teacher expectations and self-fulfilling prophecies: Knowns and unknowns, resolved and unresolved controversies. *Personality and Social Psychology Review*. 2005, 9(2): 131–155.

53. Brophy, J. Research on the self-fulfilling prophecy and teacher expectations. Michigan State University, East Lansing. Institute for Research on Teaching, pp. 15–16. July, 1982. http://files.eric.ed.gov/fulltext/ED221530.pdf.

54. Brophy, J. Research on the self-fulfilling prophecy and teacher expectations. ERIC. July 1982. http://files.eric.ed.gov/fulltext/ED221530.pdf. Accessed March 17, 2014.

55. Silverman, J. Through a data set, darkly. *Pacific Standard*. January 8, 2014. http://www.psmag.com/navigation/books-and-culture/data-set-darkly-quantitative-analysis-secret-understanding-culture-72410/. Accessed March 17, 2014.

56. Cernak, E. Why data theft poses a big risk to small businesses. *USA Today*. May 6, 2013. http://www.usatoday.com/story/cybertruth/2013/05/06/data-breach-small-business-cybersecurity-online-privacy/2138713/. Accessed February 16, 2014.

57. Satter, R. Report: Spies use smartphone apps to track people. Associated Press. January 27, 2014. http://bigstory.ap.org/article/report-spies-use-smartphone-apps-track-people. Accessed February 16, 2014.

58. Angwin, J. and Valentino-DeVries, J. Google's iPhone tracking: Web giant, others bypassed apple browser settings for guarding privacy. *The Wall Street Journal*. February 27, 2012. http://online.wsj.com/news/articles/SB10001424052970204880404577225380456599176. Accessed February 16, 2014.

59. Glenny, M. *DarkMarket: How Hackers Became the New Mafia*, pp. 119–120. New York: Vintage, 2011.

60. Finley, K. The Google clones that power NSA surveillance. *Wired*. December 12, 2013. http://www.wired.com/wiredenterprise/2013/12/opensource_nsa/. Accessed December 31, 2013.

13

Epilogue

Thus far, we have taken the reader through what is big data, some of its history, the tools used, the statistical methods, an overview of data, as well as some of the advantages and disadvantages of big data. The intent was to provide a reasonably specific overview to understand where to be skeptical of breathless reporting on big data while demonstrating how big data may be a valuable contribution to an organization. Furthermore, we hope, by drawing in examples from many disciplines, we helped illustrate the way in which business, science, medicine, and other fields are facing related problems in data interpretation and analysis. Ideas created to resolve the problems of one discipline very often prove practical in other disciplines. In data analysis, as is the case with any complex phenomenon, the nuances matter. But, how does this specifically affect you?

In his classic 1984 business novel, *The Goal*, Eliyahu Goldratt describes a businessman whose automation did not function as intended. The reason is that he did not use the technology where it mattered most, to alleviate bottlenecks. While *The Goal* is a work of fiction, its popularity arises in large part because it applies abstract concepts to very specific situations. A reader of the novel can see very clearly through fiction why essential business and logistic truths exist as they do. It is obvious that technology needs to be applied to a specific problem.

Unlike assembly line automation, big data systems are inherently flexible. We can repurpose a server and software package by analyzing new data sets. Unlike many other technologies, the same data analytical techniques can help you better understand your customers enable you to enhance the overall quality of your workforce, respond more quickly to market movements, squeeze inefficiencies from your supply chain, and anticipate equipment breakdowns before they occur. Big data is a uniquely flexible and powerful technology but still cannot be applied willy-nilly. It must answer questions that are useful to the user and whose answers are in the data. These questions depend on the facts of the case and the framework used to understand them. The frameworks outlined below are two that have gained fame within their respective circles and proven their usefulness.

A word of caution is in order. Depending on how mature your market is, big data may or may not help you steal a march on your competition. If you are a relatively successful online retailer and want to begin to move against Amazon, big data will not provide you a competitive advantage that Amazon and other heavy hitters do not already have, unless you think of a novel yet practical use of big data that they have not yet thought of and are unlikely to think of soon. The odds of finding such a use are slim. Once one company in an industry adopts a new competitive approach, there is little stopping others from trying the same thing (with the caveat that some will clearly fail in their attempts).

Should this stop you from considering a big data approach? No. In your industry, big data may simply be a cost of doing business. Just as many small restaurants get by just fine without a website while a website is a necessity for a mid-sized bank, you will need to make a realistic assessment of your industry and your firm. This will involve a thoughtful analysis of your competitive situation, that of others in your industry, and what exactly you can realistically accomplish with big data. Big data is not a panacea. If you read industry publications and see where big data can make your organization stronger, then by all means consider taking your first steps toward implementing it. If you cannot see how to apply big data, then you are better off waiting until you know what concrete steps you can take. This is no time for wishful thinking, as wishful thinking will just cost you money.

If your organization already collects data but does a poor job storing and analyzing it, your first step is to store and use that data. Look at where its inaccuracies and incompleteness lie and do what you can to fix it. Only when you understand and can use the data that you have with the tools readily available should you consider jumping to big data. Remember that big data is complex and reasonably expensive and will deliver poor results if you feed bad data into it.

A good theory will not survive a clash with data that contradict it. Big data is here to stay because, for any dangers that may lurk within your analyses and your data, there is simply no better guide to business decisions out there. Significant caution is in order in making large, expensive decisions based on a single analytical result from a big data system, but in many cases the cost of a mistaken assumption is low enough that even a modest increase in decision-making capability can very much increase your organization's effectiveness. Think of the cost-benefit balance on misjudging potential credit card fraud.

However, even if you decide not to incorporate big data into your own firm as an in-house ability, you may very well be contracting third-party service providers who use big data. Firms that assist in the hiring process, such as our previous example of Evolv, and firms that provide analysis as an add-on service to other items they sell you, such as the services that Monsanto is providing to seed buyers, are good examples. If you understand big data and how it is applied by suppliers, then understand that you are still using big data in some capacity. By gaining this understanding, you will avoid spending resources and sharing information where it is unnecessary. In addition, as the discussion below includes the use of big data to increase your organization's bargaining power with suppliers, your understanding of how big data works (including the nature of data sets and statistical tests) will increase your bargaining power with these firms.

One way to diagram how big data can be applied is the five forces analysis, as developed by the respected business strategy author, Michael Porter. The strength of this model is that it permits a view of a business from multiple perspectives, such as suppliers, customers, substitutes, new entrants, and the rivalry between existing firms. A key weakness should likewise be obvious; this model does not address nonprofits, political campaigns, government agencies, and other organizations that have benefited from big data. The needs of these organizations will be addressed through the lens of the observe, orient, decide, act (OODA) loop afterwards. The OODA loop differs from the five forces model in that it is a dynamic model that is agnostic to the type of competition it addresses. Despite being the creation of an eccentric and brilliant pilot in the US Air Force, we will later see how the OODA loop is highly flexible across disciplines. It works in sports, politics, war, business, and almost any other field in which there is a competition to decisively defeat an opponent or enemy. Its emphasis on rapid adjustment makes it ideally suited to the strengths of big data.

MICHAEL PORTER'S FIVE FORCES MODEL

Although the five forces model was never intended to address big data, and it is a descriptive rather than prescriptive model, its open nature makes it directly applicable to the issues we are examining. Where the five forces are most powerful is in examining a business at a high level and gaining a feel for the "lay of the land." Such an analysis is not sufficient in and of itself. We will in fact see in our discussion of the five forces how it can be summarized in Figure 13.1.[1]

How could big data specifically address a strategy as defined by Porter's model?

Bargaining Power of Customers

Earlier in the book, we discussed the use of big data by Monsanto to provide a value-added service to those farmers to whom it sells seeds. Whereas farmers benefit from the analysis that Monsanto can provide, these same services raise the switching costs for the farmers if they consider another seed supplier. In essence, the firm is using big data to package a service along with the goods it sells.

Firms such as Amazon use a buyer's history to anticipate the needs of those buyers and market complementary products, or products that may be a suitable replacement for the product on the screen, to secure a purchase early before the buyer changes his or her mind, or to prevent the customer from looking elsewhere if a suitable product does not immediately appear on the screen.

Target's efforts to identify customers who are pregnant provide a more long-term attempt to secure its place in the customer's shopping routine. Rather than trying to nail down particular sales, Target is trying to use a natural transition point in a family's life to become the retailer of choice.

The purchase of data sets from third-party firms enables firms to reach customers of which they may not otherwise have been aware. Such data sets may provide low success rates, but they enable firms to identify consumers who may want a product they never even knew they wanted. This

FIGURE 13.1
Diagram of Michael Porter's five forces.

method is not new—one of the authors first discovered *The Economist* a decade and a half ago through a random envelope in the mail that was triggered by purchased data—but big data is facilitating it.

Big data also facilitates price discrimination. Airlines and hotel chains have long known that business customers will generally pay more than customers traveling for personal reasons. One way such price discrimination was conducted was by pricing fares and rooms that included weekends differently from those that only involved weeknights. A business customer will usually not want to spend weekends away from home, so including a weekend night in one's itinerary could lower the price. What was not possible was price discrimination on a customer-by-customer basis. That is changing.

A 2013 investigation covered by *The Wall Street Journal* found

> the Staples Inc. website displays different prices to people after estimating their locations. More than that, Staples appeared to consider the person's distance from a rival brick-and-mortar store, either OfficeMax Inc. or Office Depot Inc. If rival stores were within 20 miles or so, Staples.com usually showed a discounted price... the Journal's testing also showed that areas that tended to see the discounted prices had a higher average income than areas that tended to see higher prices.

The *Journal* states

> the idea of an unbiased, impersonal Internet is fast giving way to an online world that, in reality, is increasingly tailored and targeted. Websites are adopting techniques to glean information about visitors to their sites, in real time, and then deliver different versions of the Web to different people. Prices change, products get swapped out, wording is modified, and there is little way for the typical website user to spot it when it happens.[2]

Other companies that the journal discussed that use customer data for price discrimination include Rosetta Stone, Orbitz, Home Depot, Office Depot, and Discover Financial Services. Also mentioned was Amazon's abortive attempt at price discrimination that ended in 2000 with Amazon refunding money to customers who paid the higher price.

As the above examples illustrate, there are many ways to gain and secure customers using big data. The examples above include business-to-business sales as well as business-to-customer. They include the use of big data to create a service for the customer that is difficult for competitors to replicate as well as the use of big data in the background to learn more about those customers and anticipate their needs.

As well as finding and gaining loyalty from customers, we have seen how big data can be used to increase margins through price discrimination. Regardless of the ethical questions surrounding the charging of different prices to different customers for the same products, the temptation to secure a higher margin from those willing to pay more will not disappear and will likely become more common as big data spreads. Along with purchased data, geography, and web-browsing history, we can expect data about customers to come from general data, such as weather or economic trends in the areas where the customers live, as well as specific information such as the example of solar panels gleaned from Google Earth images mentioned earlier in the book.

Bargaining Power of Suppliers

An article on SpendMatters.com by IBM procurement product marketing leader Doug Macdonald examines some of the ways firms have used big data to improve their situation with their suppliers. These include examples such as:

- A mining firm that used big data to combine 18 different enterprise resource planning (ERP) systems to gain control over previously unreliable spend and supplier data to use economies of scale to gain somewhere in the vicinity of $1 billion in savings.
- A packaged goods company that used big data to consolidate its different systems acquired through mergers to gain improved visibility and increase its cost savings between 20% and 50% in key categories.
- A manufacturer of auto parts that used big data to gain greater transparency into its suppliers' financial health and weed out those at risk of becoming insolvent, thereby threatening the reliability of important sectors of the supply chain in the event of another economic downturn.[3]

By their nature, the relationships with suppliers will be more opaque than will those with retail customers. As consumers or small businesses, the techniques used by those we buy from may require some thought to understand, but we can see them. A contract negotiated with a supplier may involve nondisclosure agreements or other steps to conceal the relationships involved. One of the authors once spoke with a businessman in a business-to-business firm who described very deliberately refraining from discussing any relationships that he enjoyed with his suppliers or those customers to whom he was a key supplier. This is typical.

Big data, with the proper data set, can provide you insights into the raw materials prices paid by your suppliers. It can help you suggest inefficiencies that can be wrung out of a supply chain. It can provide an internal picture of what you have historically paid to different suppliers and the results of using those suppliers. There are price indices, transport data, and public data sources that will fill in some of these gaps and enable educated inferences.

Threat of New Entrants

In many ways, the way to control the threat of new entrants is through the same techniques that are used to improve a bargaining position with customers. By tying customers to products and services, you are increasing their cost of switching suppliers. A new Amazon is unlikely to replace the Amazon that most of us have used. The convenience of customer recommendations builds path-dependent behavior. Very many consumers have developed a path dependency with Amazon or Apple that is not easy to break.

Netflix is a firm that understands this well. Netflix unseated and then struck a fatal blow to Blockbuster. It is a firm that uses customer data and machine learning to become very convenient and difficult to give up for movie fans. Those with exotic tastes in movies will find Netflix's recommendations to be hit or miss, but those who love more mainstream movies will find that Netflix has an uncanny ability to recommend the perfect film. If you switch, you lose that and you start from zero. A new competitor in the market would find it difficult to compete with Netflix's convenience.

Big data is also used to identify and eliminate inefficiencies that render an organization more vulnerable. It does this both by making data transparent within an organization and by analyzing everything from spend to call center performance. Inefficiencies provide opportunities for competitors. Wal-Mart's relentless use of data to drive efficiency means that few brick-and-mortar stores can match it. Its niche is a hard-won position of strength. Data allowed Wal-Mart to elbow aside firms that could not manage their inventory so precisely. Yes, Wal-Mart has tremendous bargaining power, but its price advantage also comes from the firm's relentless drive to eliminate waste.

Big data is also driving improvements in product development. Online firms commonly run multiple versions of their websites to assess how design affects click-through rates and product purchases. This includes the A-B testing that we discussed earlier in this book, but it can extend beyond that. Zynga gleans 25 TB of customer data a day from its Farmville game, using the insights of how players interact with animals to design more appealing animals to keep players engaged. Ford Motor Company used text analytics to scour websites about how drivers perceived its three-blinker system. This is where moving the blinker lever all the way up or down turns on the blinker until the car completes a turn, whereas moving the lever slightly blinks the light three times to indicate a lane change. Using big data to search the web, Ford then had customer perceptions about this blinker clustered to see whether this European feature should make it to American cars. If you have owned or rented a Ford recently, you should be familiar with this feature.[4]

Customer sentiment analysis is another area where firms try to keep their clients happy and their reputation intact. If being a customer becomes a habit, then fewer customers will leave. Have you ever heard of an angry burst on Twitter causing embarrassment to a firm? Do you know of anyone who has raved over a new product on Facebook? If so, you are looking at one tiny chunk of information that in aggregate is extremely valuable.

Firms can and do mine this information to find positive sentiment to build toward and get ahead of negative sentiment before it causes too much damage. Negative sentiment that spreads is called reputational risk. In fact, there are firms dedicated to helping other companies manage reputational risk that may or may not be of a company's own making. Shell learned this the hard way in 2012 when Greenpeace and the Yes Men created a fake website giving the appearance of being a Shell website displaying a callous disregard on the part of Shell toward the environment in the Arctic. One of those involved in the hoax, Travis Nichols, a Greenpeace "polar and oceans media officer" wrote on CNN.com:

> The response has been staggering—nearly 4 million page views, 12,000 user-generated ads and a cascade of tweets. This reaction from the public shows Shell has serious problems in the court of public opinion, and that it ignores Arctic defenders at its peril. By using the most popular form of contemporary communication—social media—to bypass Shell's billions, our supporters undermined the company's social license to operate and brought global attention to its greed and willful ignorance of science.[5]

Unfortunately, this case is not isolated and will not be the last of its type. It comes in a long line of attacks that predate the ridiculous and long-discredited rumors of Satanism promoted by a popular packaged goods manufacturer. Rumors that spread, no matter how ridiculous, will grip paranoid imaginations and lead to both formal and informal boycotts. Your firm may need to respond forcefully and proactively to such rumors in the future, and big data will be an ally in getting out in front of them to protect the reputation of your organization and prevent the loss of customers.

Others

The other two of Michael Porter's five forces are existing rivalries among market participants and the threat of substitute products or services. Several of the examples from the three forces outlined above also fit these two. There is no need to go through these final two in detail here, but now that you have seen a broad sample of how big data is being used in the real world, you will have a better understanding of how big data can help your firm's competitive position.

Again, there are the caveats, and you need to know which questions to ask, to know how you will react to different answers, and to have access to quality data that answer those questions. You can address these strategic issues by enhancing your marketing, engineering, finance, speed to market, customer retention, cost control, and so on through the skillful use of big data. Quality analysis trumps pretty PowerPoint slides when it comes to deciding a strategy.

THE OODA LOOP

The OODA loop was the brainchild of the eccentric genius fighter pilot of the US Air Force, Colonel John Boyd. Standing for observe, orient, decide, act, the OODA loop is not actually a loop *per se*. It is a strategy of acting and reacting before your enemy or opponent has a chance to react. Unlike in chess, in real life a competitor can execute multiple moves at once without leaving time for a countermove. However, to effectively move and act, it is necessary to understand the situation of one's opponent without the opponent having a comparable insight into one's motives and actions.

There is less structure to the OODA loop than there is to the five forces model, but it is every bit as powerful. Strategy is not an ideological practice in which one method is right and therefore another is wrong. More than one strategic framework can be applied simultaneously. However, unlike the five forces model, the OODA loop can be (and is) applied to military, sports, and police settings. In our earlier discussions of police applications of big data, we saw how it can enable police to get out ahead of criminals and to act proactively to apprehend them before they can cause too much damage and even to prevent crime by addressing and eliminating situations that enable it to flourish. Better credit card fraud detection likewise enables credit card companies and customers to lower the profitability for fraudsters by stopping their activities before they make too many purchases.

In any situation in which time is of the essence, and where data is available to guide action, it is possible to use big data to "get inside the OODA loop" of the adversary. When a credit card company detects fraud and shuts off the card before any sizeable profit is made, then the company has taken an action that increases the cost to the fraudster while minimizing the gain. When police use big data to anticipate either an individual crime (an ability that really does exist in analyzing gang hits) or the likelihood of many crimes in a particular area, they can often intervene and prevent the crime from ever taking place. Unsurprisingly, big data is also becoming embedded into sports far beyond what Billy Beane of the Oakland A's could have ever dreamt when he began using a data-driven recruitment model. Competition is simultaneously driving and adopting big data.

IMPLEMENTING BIG DATA

Once you understand the questions that you wish to answer or the issues that you wish to explore, you need to understand your data. What data will you buy from others? What is the cost of the data? Is it good data? Does it address the phenomena that you are trying to understand? How much does the data cost and how is the cost structured? What are you allowed to do with the data? Will you use proprietary data? Do you understand what your sensors really measure or what your computer system is really pulling? What formulae are used? How do you define different measurements? Must you manually input data, and if so, do you know the degree to which those who enter it use it in a uniform manner? If it is customer data, do you know what you are permitted to collect and use based on laws such as the Health Insurance Portability and Accountability Act for customer medical data or privacy laws within the European Union? Have there been any changeovers in software, systems, or sensors?

If you are trying to track long-term trends, and you are not collecting or storing that data, then you will want to start. If you generate abundant data and want to analyze it quickly, then you may be able to incorporate big data into your organization relatively quickly.

A common issue that occurs within a business is the problem of data silos. Big data can alleviate many problems arising from data silos. It is common to hear of a business replicating efforts, reinventing the same items more than once, sending multiple representatives to the same client with different messages, and stepping into a legal or strategic pit more than once when the lesson should have been learned the first time. It is common to find the information that could have prevented this stored across computers, servers, portable hard drives, thumb drives, DVDs, and the occasional old floppy disk in offices across the organization. As big data is designed to pull in information across storage media and file type, and to work with jagged data (data that lacks consistent format and columns, not fitting into a neat table) and unstructured data (reports, websites, the results of web crawling), it is often helpful in bringing together knowledge from across the company. Because of the messiness of this data, though, you will need to understand that a big data project is not an IT project handled in isolation. As a manager, you understand the importance of buy-in, but a big data project may need more buy-in than anticipated.

There are several reasons for this. First of all, a big data project will very likely be unlike previous IT projects that your staff has worked on. Even high-tech savvy staff in your firm will tie your new project to what they know. They understand the Internet and search engines, and they understand business intelligence. It is the act of uniting these technologies that may be a challenge. When those charged with implementing your new system ask subject matter experts what they want, the answers are likely to be framed in terms of previous systems. Big data is a new and disruptive technology and for this reason, an iterative approach (known in software development as "agile") will likely be needed. You may very well need to support a project that is developed and then presented to users for their feedback. If you are accustomed to the traditional "waterfall" method of project management, this will require some adjustment.

The flipside of this promise is that big data also has its limitations. You will need to set expectations or understand where those who are setting expectations are coming from and support them. Your Hadoop implementation will not replace your ERP software, and it is not meant to replace it.

A second reason big data may be a challenge arises because so many well-designed systems are effective at depersonalizing knowledge. In many companies, certain staff members gain security and prestige by becoming domain experts and helping colleagues locate and interpret key information. If you were the gatekeeper of knowledge about a particular business practice and the data reported from it, you might not like to see supporting documentation and your reports being searched with the same ease that one searches the Internet. In fact, that documentation may be searched with technology very similar to that which the Internet itself uses.

A similar feeling of insecurity may arise because of the time that can be saved by a system that pulls together a broad array of diverse data. The convenience of saving time in searching is nice. Knowing that a large amount of time is being saved by yourself and 50 colleagues is not as nice. Your staff may be worried about becoming redundant. The people side of a big data implementation is easy to dismiss, but you should not dismiss it. People's jobs and livelihoods are on the line. If they feel threatened, they may very well undermine the project. This is not hatefulness, spite, or Luddism; it is a natural human reaction when one's livelihood and identity are threatened.

Just as you need a strategic vision to make the most of your big data implementation, you will need a need a more detailed view to frame it for yourself and your staff. Time saved by automating information searches or by using predictive analytics to better target your staff's efforts can be used to trim back staff, or it can be used to empower staff to contribute more to the firm.

This in and of itself may create resistance. An article on the *Harvard Business Review* blog by Jeff Bladt and Bob Filbin, two individuals who apply data science to organizations that help at-risk youth, points out how a data-driven approach may be entangled in organizational politics. It breaks employees into four groups:

- Highly regarded, high performing
- Highly regarded, low performing
- Lowly regarded, low performing
- Lowly regarded, high performing

The article argues that highly regarded, high-performing employees are counterintuitively likely to be data skeptics because, "They are already perceived as doing quality work; adding hard numbers can, at best, affirm this narrative, and at worst submarine the good thing they have going. There is a reasonable fear that the outputs used to measure their performance will not fully capture the true value of their contributions."[6]

The authors go on to argue that lowly regarded, low-performing workers are unlikely to get too worked up about data-driven management. Those who are lowly regarded yet high performing will see data-driven management as a welcome development and embrace it. However, those who are highly regarded but do not perform well are likely to oppose a data culture: "There's not a lot that can be done for this group. The malleable ones will eventually come around, but those stuck in their heuristical ways will undermine and cavil the creeping in of a data-informed culture."

There are a multitude of ways data will affect your organization. As is the case with any project, a big data implementation is not merely an implementation, but it is a people project. As big data will illuminate the results of decisions made by knowledge workers and management, you will need to address the needs of these individuals to keep them from becoming opponents. This means listening.

As big data is applying technology to do the jobs of knowledge workers, it will still require those workers to understand and clarify the results. To illustrate this point, write down several metrics that your organization uses. What different units are used and what are the different conventions and conversions? Are there different formulae used? Do your European, Asian, and Western Hemisphere offices use different measures? Do you use government statistics? Do different governments use different calculations? You are looking at the nuances involved. Your knowledge workers will remain important because they understand those metrics that are part of their jobs. One of the authors of this book has on multiple occasions been involved in determining exactly what the numbers mean and has on many occasions been left befuddled without the intervention of an outside expert. These experts will be absolutely vital to the act of implementation, and they will remain vital once the system is in place. Workers will retain their importance to your organization by eliminating the time they spent trying to find something, as your big data system is freeing them up to become more productive.

By pulling in your employees and involving them in solving problems, finding new opportunities in the data, and advocating for your business, you are boosting productivity. You need to know what questions you want answered and what issues you wish to explore with your big data system to get the most of it. That does not mean you should limit it to just that job. If your employees play in the data, discuss it, and have the opportunity to act on it, you may find ways that they can leverage that data to boost your bottom line. There is likely no reason your firm cannot use what it learns from its data to offer new services, trim waste, and solidify its market position. You already have the people that understand your business, and now you are freeing their time to help you boost your business.

NONLINEAR, QUALITATIVE THINKING

At the end of all of our commentary and all your patience as a reader, we want to throw some perspective on problem solving. Big data is perhaps the greatest leap forward in quantitative reasoning in the last century. We can only expect our tools to become even more powerful as we encounter new processing problems, make forays into quantum computing, and find other clever ways to manage our processing and data.

Alternatively, we might realize that all problems are quantitative or that, in fact, the quantitative approach may not be the best method for solving certain problems, especially that class of problems often called "wicked." We have other alternatives, even when they occasionally sound like hand waving, that we can use to help us move forward:

- Intuition, that alogical, often overused concept that is really based on the Latin word for "looking directly into"
- Improvisation, or moving with the problem in a sort of cognitive dance
- Play
- Phenomenological approaches: the phenomenological approach may be the most interesting. When using a phenomenological approach, we will often apply certain techniques called "reductions":
  - The phenomenological reduction, where we deliberately "bracket" or isolate our object of concern as the thing itself, shorn of assumptions and other cultural barnacles

- The transcendental reduction, where we examine the object of consideration as immanent (in our minds) rather than as transcendental (out there)
- The eidetic reduction, where we examine the object cognitively to see which parts of this thing must be there, and which parts are actually nonmandatory accretions

If the phenomenological approach sounds difficult, that is because it is difficult. A true phenomenologist works diligently at self-examination in order to shear off as many biases as possible with rigorous thought. Some have gone as far as calling the reduction a form of meditation, and in the sense of reflection, perhaps this approach is correct.[7] With a phenomenological approach, we will reflect on the problem, we will consider it under various degrees of cognitive freedom, and we will allow the object, in essence, to speak to us on its own terms. The goal is to free our minds from the so-called common sense which is really a variety of cultural indoctrination.

For example, if we are looking at customer sensations, perceptions, and feelings when purchasing a product, we might examine this situation from a phenomenological point of view to see what this object is to the customer. We may even participate in what is generally called qualitative research, which is an entirely different domain to what we see with big data. Our point here is that we do not want to become so imbued with the idea of quantitative domination that we lose sight of the fact that other modalities have value as well. One need only review the history of the logical positivist movement to see the quandaries that arise when the world becomes a mere object.

CLOSING

Thank you for time and your interest in our book on big data. We hope that you have learned something from a practical, hands-on point of view. And, as we have emphasized time and again in our book, you should never stop verifying and replicating your results. Big data will never be the "be all, end all" solution, as its more enthusiastic proponents market it . However, it just may be the most powerful tool you have used to guide you in making human decisions based on human values and human goals.

REFERENCES

1. Porter, M. *On Competition: Updated and Expanded Edition*, pp. 3–36. Harvard Business Press, Boston, 2008.
2. Valentino-DeVries, J., Singer-Vine, J. and Soltani, A. Websites vary prices, deals based on users' information. *The Wall Street Journal*. December 24, 2012. http://online.wsj.com/news/articles/SB10001424127887323777204578189391813881534. Accessed February 15, 2014.
3. Macdonald, D. Big data: The big opportunity in spend and supplier management. *Spend Matters*. November 21, 2013. http://spendmatters.com/2013/11/21/big-data-big-opportunity-spend-supplier-management/. Accessed February 17, 2014.
4. Rosenbush, S. and Totty, M. How big data is changing the whole equation for business. *The Wall Street Journal*. March 10, 2013. http://online.wsj.com/news/articles/SB10001424127887324178904578340071261396666. Accessed February 24, 2014.
5. Nichols, T. Shell Oil's multibillion dollar Arctic hoax. CNN.com. August 1, 2012. http://www.cnn.com/2012/08/01/opinion/nichols-greenpeace-shell-oil-spoof/index.html. Accessed February 24, 2014.
6. Bladt, J. and Filbin, B. Who's afraid of data-driven management? *Harvard Business Review Blog*. May 16, 2014. http://blogs.hbr.org/2014/05/whos-afraid-of-data-driven-management/. Accessed June 8, 2014.
7. Cogan, J. The phenomenological reduction. *The Internet Encyclopedia of Philosophy*. 2006. http://www.iep.utm.edu/phen-red/. Accessed March 11, 2014.

Index